Deep Learning for Medical Image Analysis

THE ELSEVIER AND MICCAI SOCIETY BOOK SERIES

Chairman of the Series Board: Alejandro F. Frangi

Advisory Board

Titles

MICCAI

Deep Learning for Medical Image Analysis

Second Edition

Edited by

S. Kevin Zhou
School of Biomedical Engineering
University of Science and Technology of China (USTC)
Hefei, China

Hayit Greenspan
Medical Image Processing and Analysis Lab
Biomedical Engineering Department
Tel-Aviv University
Tel Aviv, Israel

Dinggang Shen
School of Biomedical Engineering
ShanghaiTech University &
United Imaging Intelligence
Shanghai, China

ACADEMIC PRESS
An imprint of Elsevier

Academic Press is an imprint of Elsevier
125 London Wall, London EC2Y 5AS, United Kingdom
525 B Street, Suite 1650, San Diego, CA 92101, United States
50 Hampshire Street, 5th Floor, Cambridge, MA 02139, United States
The Boulevard, Langford Lane, Kidlington, Oxford OX5 1GB, United Kingdom

ISBN: 978-0-323-85124-4

For information on all Academic Press publications
visit our website at https://www.elsevier.com/books-and-journals

Publisher: Mara Conner
Acquisitions Editor: Tim Pitts
Editorial Project Manager: Emily Thomson
Production Project Manager: Kamesh R
Cover Designer: Christian Bilbow

Typeset by VTeX

Working together
to grow libraries in
developing countries

www.elsevier.com • www.bookaid.org

Contents

PART 1 Deep learning theories and architectures

CHAPTER 3   CapsNet for medical image segmentation   75

Minh Tran, Viet-Khoa Vo-Ho, Kyle Quinn, Hien Nguyen, Khoa Luu, and Ngan Le

CHAPTER 4   Transformer for medical image analysis   99

Fahad Shamshad, Salman Khan, Syed Waqas Zamir, Muhammad Haris Khan, Munawar Hayat, Fahad Shahbaz Khan, and Huazhu Fu

PART 4 Medical image segmentation, registration, and applications

PART 5 Others

Contributors

Cheng Bian

Tencent Jarvis Lab, Shenzhen, China

Alastair D. Burt

Faculty of Health and Medical Sciences, University of Adelaide, Adelaide, SA, Australia

Translational and Clinical Research Institute, Newcastle University, Newcastle upon Tyne, United Kingdom

Xiaohuan Cao

Shanghai United Imaging Intelligence, Co., Ltd., Shanghai, China

Aaron Carass

Department of Electrical and Computer Engineering, Johns Hopkins University, Baltimore, MD, United States

Gustavo Carneiro

Australian Institute for Machine Learning, University of Adelaide, Adelaide, SA, Australia

Centre for Vision, Speech and Signal Processing, University of Surrey, Guildford, United Kingdom

Kenny H. Cha

Division of Imaging, Diagnostics, and Software Reliability, CDRH, U.S Food and Drug Administration, Silver Spring, MD, United States

Yang Chen

Southeast University, Nanjing, China

Qinglin Dong

Cortical Architecture Imaging and Discovery Lab, School of Computing, The University of Georgia, Athens, GA, United States

James Duncan

Department of Biomedical Engineering, New Haven, CT, United States

Division of Bioimaging Sciences, Department of Radiology & Biomedical Imaging, New Haven, CT, United States

Nicha Dvornek

Department of Biomedical Engineering, New Haven, CT, United States

Division of Bioimaging Sciences, Department of Radiology & Biomedical Imaging, New Haven, CT, United States

Jingfan Fan
School of Optics and Photonic, Beijing Institute of Technology, Beijing, China

Huazhu Fu
Institute of High Performance Computing, Agency for Science, Technology and Research, Singapore, Singapore

Yue Gao
School of Software, Tsinghua University, Beijing, China

Bao Ge
School of Physics and Information Technology, Shaanxi Normal University, Xi'an, China

Alexej Gossmann
Division of Imaging, Diagnostics, and Software Reliability, CDRH, U.S Food and Drug Administration, Silver Spring, MD, United States

Shuo Han
Department of Biomedical Engineering, The Johns Hopkins School of Medicine, Baltimore, MD, United States

Munawar Hayat
Monash University, Melbourne, VIC, Australia

Mengshen He
School of Physics and Information Technology, Shaanxi Normal University, Xi'an, China

Yufan He
Department of Electrical and Computer Engineering, Johns Hopkins University, Baltimore, MD, United States

Xintao Hu
School of Automation, Northwestern Polytechnical University, Xi'an, China

Heng Huang
College of Mathematical Medicine, Zhejiang Normal University, Jinhua, China

Qiu Huang
Shanghai Jiao Tong University, Shanghai, China

Eunjin Jeon
Korea University, Department of Brain and Cognitive Engineering, Seongbuk-Gu, Seoul, Korea

Shuyi Ji
School of Software, Tsinghua University, Beijing, China

Xi Jiang

MOE Key Lab for Neuroinformation, School of Life Science and Technology, University of Electronic Science and Technology of China, Chengdu, China

Fahad Shahbaz Khan

Mohamed bin Zayed University of Artificial Intelligence, Abu Dhabi, United Arab Emirates

Muhammad Haris Khan

Mohamed bin Zayed University of Artificial Intelligence, Abu Dhabi, United Arab Emirates

Salman Khan

Mohamed bin Zayed University of Artificial Intelligence, Abu Dhabi, United Arab Emirates

Wonjun Ko

Korea University, Department of Brain and Cognitive Engineering, Seongbuk-Gu, Seoul, Korea

Ngan Le

Department of Computer Science & Computer Engineering, University of Arkansas, Fayetteville, NC, United States

Jianqin Lei

Department of Ophthalmology, First Affiliated Hospital of Xi'an Jiaotong University, Xi'an, PR China

Lei Li

School of Data Science, Fudan University, Shanghai, China

Qing Li

State Key Laboratory of Cognitive Neuroscience and Learning, Beijing Normal University, Beijing, China

Xiaoxiao Li

Department of Electrical & Computer Engineering, University of British Columbia, Vancouver, BC, Canada

Yuexiang Li

Tencent Jarvis Lab, Shenzhen, China

Dong Liang

Shenzhen Institute of Advanced Technology, Chinese Academy of Sciences, Shenzhen, China

Dingkun Liu

School of Optics and Photonic, Beijing Institute of Technology, Beijing, China

Luyan Liu
Tencent Jarvis Lab, Shenzhen, China

Tianming Liu
Cortical Architecture Imaging and Discovery Lab, School of Computing, The University of Georgia, Athens, GA, United States

Yihao Liu
Department of Electrical and Computer Engineering, Johns Hopkins University, Baltimore, MD, United States

Yiheng Liu
School of Physics and Information Technology, Shaanxi Normal University, Xi'an, China

Yuyuan Liu
Australian Institute for Machine Learning, University of Adelaide, Adelaide, SA, Australia

Khoa Luu
Department of Computer Science & Computer Engineering, University of Arkansas, Fayetteville, NC, United States

Kai Ma
Tencent Jarvis Lab, Shenzhen, China

Gabriel Maicas
Australian Institute for Machine Learning, University of Adelaide, Adelaide, SA, Australia

Ahmad Wisnu Mulyadi
Korea University, Department of Brain and Cognitive Engineering, Seongbuk-Gu, Seoul, Korea

Hien Nguyen
Department of Electrical & Computer Engineering, Houston, TX, United States

Gyutaek Oh
Department of Bio and Brain Engineering, KAIST, Daejeon, Korea

Nicholas Petrick
Division of Imaging, Diagnostics, and Software Reliability, CDRH, U.S Food and Drug Administration, Silver Spring, MD, United States

Jerry L. Prince
Department of Electrical and Computer Engineering, Johns Hopkins University, Baltimore, MD, United States

Ning Qiang

School of Physics and Information Technology, Shaanxi Normal University, Xi'an, China

Kyle Quinn

Department of Biomedical Engineering, University of Arkansas, Fayetteville, NC, United States

Holger R. Roth

NVIDIA, Santa Clara, CA, United States

Berkman Sahiner

Division of Imaging, Diagnostics, and Software Reliability, CDRH, U.S Food and Drug Administration, Silver Spring, MD, United States

Ravi K. Samala

Division of Imaging, Diagnostics, and Software Reliability, CDRH, U.S Food and Drug Administration, Silver Spring, MD, United States

Fahad Shamshad

Mohamed bin Zayed University of Artificial Intelligence, Abu Dhabi, United Arab Emirates

Dinggang Shen

Shanghai United Imaging Intelligence, Co., Ltd., Shanghai, China

School of Biomedical Engineering, ShanghaiTech University, Shanghai, China

Seon Ho Shin

Lyell McEwin Hospital, University of Adelaide, Adelaide, SA, Australia

Rajvinder Singh

Lyell McEwin Hospital, University of Adelaide, Adelaide, SA, Australia

Lawrence H. Staib

Department of Biomedical Engineering, New Haven, CT, United States

Division of Bioimaging Sciences, Department of Radiology & Biomedical Imaging, New Haven, CT, United States

Heung-Il Suk

Korea University, Department of Artificial Intelligence, Seongbuk-Gu, Seoul, Korea

Korea University, Department of Brain and Cognitive Engineering, Seongbuk-Gu, Seoul, Korea

Kaicong Sun

School of Biomedical Engineering, ShanghaiTech University, Shanghai, China

Yu Tian

Australian Institute for Machine Learning, University of Adelaide, Adelaide, SA, Australia

Harvard Medical School, Harvard University, Cambridge, MA, United States

South Australian Health and Medical Research Institute, Adelaide, SA, Australia

Minh Tran

Department of Computer Science & Computer Engineering, University of Arkansas, Fayetteville, NC, United States

Pamela Ventola

Child Study Center, Yale University, New Haven, CT, United States

Johan W. Verjans

South Australian Health and Medical Research Institute, Adelaide, SA, Australia

Viet-Khoa Vo-Ho

Department of Computer Science & Computer Engineering, University of Arkansas, Fayetteville, NC, United States

Ge Wang

Rensselaer Polytechnic Institute, Troy, NY, United States

Han Wang

College of Biomedical Engineering and Instrument Science, Zhejiang University, Hangzhou, China

Jiyao Wang

Department of Biomedical Engineering, New Haven, CT, United States

Qiyuan Wang

University of Science and Technology of China (USTC), Hefei, China

Sihang Wang

School of Data Science, Fudan University, Shanghai, China

Xiaosong Wang

NVIDIA, Santa Clara, CA, United States

Si Wen

Division of Imaging, Diagnostics, and Software Reliability, CDRH, U.S Food and Drug Administration, Silver Spring, MD, United States

Fuping Wu

School of Data Science, Fudan University, Shanghai, China

Zihao Wu

Cortical Architecture Imaging and Discovery Lab, School of Computing, The University of Georgia, Athens, GA, United States

Daguang Xu

NVIDIA, Santa Clara, CA, United States

Steven Xu

Cortical Architecture Imaging and Discovery Lab, School of Computing, The University of Georgia, Athens, GA, United States

Ziyue Xu

NVIDIA, Santa Clara, CA, United States

Peng Xue

School of Biomedical Engineering, ShanghaiTech University, Shanghai, China

Zhong Xue

Shanghai United Imaging Intelligence, Co., Ltd., Shanghai, China

Dong Yang

NVIDIA, Santa Clara, CA, United States

Jong Chul Ye

Graduate School of AI, KAIST, Daejeon, Korea

Jee Seok Yoon

Korea University, Department of Brain and Cognitive Engineering, Seongbuk-Gu, Seoul, Korea

Syed Waqas Zamir

Inception Institute of Artificial Intelligence, Abu Dhabi, United Arab Emirates

Lu Zhang

Computer Science and Engineering, University of Texas at Arlington, Arlington, TX, United States

Wei Zhang

School of Computer and Cyber Sciences, Augusta University, Augusta, GA, United States

Jun Zhao

Shanghai Jiao Tong University, Shanghai, China

Lin Zhao

Cortical Architecture Imaging and Discovery Lab, School of Computing, The University of Georgia, Athens, GA, United States

Shijie Zhao
School of Automation, Northwestern Polytechnical University, Xi'an, China

Yefeng Zheng
Tencent Jarvis Lab, Shenzhen, China

S. Kevin Zhou
University of Science and Technology of China (USTC), Hefei, China

Dajiang Zhu
Computer Science and Engineering, University of Texas at Arlington, Arlington, TX, United States

Juntang Zhuang
Department of Biomedical Engineering, New Haven, CT, United States

Xiahai Zhuang
School of Data Science, Fudan University, Shanghai, China

Leonardo Zorron Cheng Tao Pu
Department of Gastroenterology at Austin Health, Heidelberg, VIC, Australia

Lianrui Zuo
Department of Electrical and Computer Engineering, Johns Hopkins University, Baltimore, MD, United States
Laboratory of Behavioral Neuroscience, National Institute on Aging, National Institutes of Health, Baltimore, MD, United States

Foreword

Computational medical image analysis has become a leading research field at the intersection of informatics, computational sciences, and medicine, supported by a vibrant community of researchers working in universities, industry, and clinical centers.

Over the past decade, deep learning methods have revolutionized the computer vision community, providing effective new solutions to many long-standing image analysis problems. For this revolution to enter the field of medical image analysis, dedicated methods need to be designed that take into account the specificity of medical images.

Medical images capture the anatomy and physiology of patients by measuring the geometric, biophysical, and biochemical properties of living tissue. These images are acquired using algorithms that exploit complex medical imaging processes, the principles of which must be well understood, as well as those governing the complex structures and functions of the human body.

The book "Deep learning for medical image analysis (1st edition)," edited by S. Kevin Zhou, Hayit Greenspan, and Dinggang Shen, leading researchers in academia and industry, who have developed machine learning methods for medical image analysis, has been a great success. This second edition builds on its success and expands its exposition of deep learning approaches for medical image analysis, including medical image reconstruction and synthesis, medical image segmentation, medical image registration, to name just a few of the most important problems addressed. The book, which begins with an introduction to neural networks, deep learning, and deep reinforcement learning, as well as the latest CapsNet and transformer network architectures, presents a set of new deep learning methods applied to a variety of clinical problems and imaging modalities operating at different scales, including X-rays, magnetic resonance imaging (anatomical and functional), computed tomography, colonoscopy, optical coherence tomography angiography, etc.

This impressive collection of excellent contributions will surely continue to serve and inspire all the researchers interested in the development of new machine learning methods in the rapidly evolving field of medical image analysis.

Nicholas Ayache, Ph.D.
Inria, Sophia Antipolis, France
June 14, 2023

Deep learning theories and architectures

An introduction to neural networks and deep learning

Ahmad Wisnu Mulyadi[b], Jee Seok Yoon[b], Eunjin Jeon[b], Wonjun Ko[b], and Heung-Il Suk[a,b]
[a]*Korea University, Department of Artificial Intelligence, Seongbuk-Gu, Seoul, Korea*
[b]*Korea University, Department of Brain and Cognitive Engineering, Seongbuk-Gu, Seoul, Korea*

1.1 Introduction

A brain or biological neural network is considered as the most well-organized system that processes information from different senses such as sight, hearing, touch, taste and smell in an efficient and intelligent manner. One of the key mechanisms for information processing in a human brain is that the complicated high-level information is processed by means of the collaboration, i.e., connections (called synapses), of a large number of the structurally simple elements (called neurons). In machine learning, artificial neural networks are a family of models that mimic the structural elegance of the neural system and learn patterns inherent in observations.

1.2 Feed-forward neural networks

This section introduces neural networks that process information in a feed-forward manner. Throughout the chapter, matrices and vectors are denoted as boldface uppercase letters and boldface lowercase letters, respectively, and scalars are denoted as normal italic letters. For a transpose operator, a superscript $^\top$ is used.

1.2.1 Perceptron

The simplest learnable artificial neural model, known as *perceptron* [1], is structured with input visible units $\{v_i\}_{i=1}^{D}$, trainable connection weights $\{w_i\}_{i=1}^{D}$ and a bias w_0, and an output unit y as shown in Fig. 1.1(a). Since the perceptron model has a single layer of an output unit, not counting the input visible layer, it is also called a single-

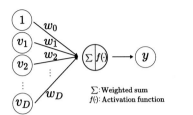
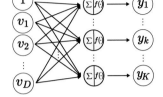

(a) Single output (a.k.a. perceptron)   (b) Multiple outputs

FIGURE 1.1

An architecture of a single-layer neural network.

layer neural network. Given an observation[1] or datum $\mathbf{v} \in \mathbb{R}^D$, the value of the output unit y is obtained from an activation function $f(\cdot)$ by taking the weighted sum of the inputs as follows:

$$y(\mathbf{v}; \Theta) = f\left(\sum_{i=1}^{D} v_i w_i + w_0\right) = f\left(\mathbf{w}^\top \mathbf{v} + w_0\right), \tag{1.1}$$

where $\Theta = \{\mathbf{w}, w_0\}$ denotes a parameter set, $\mathbf{w} = \{w_i\}_{i=1}^{D} \in \mathbb{R}^D$ is a connection weight vector and w_0 is a bias. Let us introduce a pre-activation variable z that is determined by the weighted sum of the inputs, i.e., $z = \mathbf{w}^\top \mathbf{v} + w_0$. As for the activation function $f(\cdot)$, a *"logistic sigmoid"* function, i.e., $\sigma(z) = \frac{1}{1+\exp(-z)}$, is commonly used for a binary classification task.

Regarding a multi-output task, e.g., multi-class classification or multi-output regression, it is straightforward to extend the perceptron model by adding multiple output units $\{y_k\}_{k=1}^{K}$ (Fig. 1.1(b)), one for each class, with their respective connection weights $\{w_{ki}\}_{i=1,\dots,D;k=1,\dots,K}$ as follows:

$$y_k(\mathbf{v}; \Theta) = f\left(\sum_{i=1}^{D} v_i w_{ki} + w_{ko}\right) = f\left(\mathbf{w}_k^\top \mathbf{v} + w_{k0}\right), \tag{1.2}$$

where $\Theta = \{\mathbf{W} \in \mathbb{R}^{K \times D}\}$, w_{ki} denotes a connection weight from v_i to y_k. As for the activation function, it is common to use a *"softmax"* function $s(z_k) = \frac{\exp(z_k)}{\sum_{l=1}^{K} \exp(z_l)}$ for multi-class classification, where the output values can be interpreted as probability.

---

[1] Each unit in the visible layer takes a scalar value as input. Thus the observation should be represented in a vector form with elements of raw voxel intensities or features, for instance.

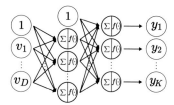

FIGURE 1.2

An architecture of a two-layer neural network.

1.2.2 Multi-layer perceptron

One of the main limitations of the single-layer neural network comes from its linear separation for a classification task, despite the use of nonlinear activation function. This limitation can be circumvented by introducing a so-called "*hidden*" layer between the input layer and the output layer as shown in Fig. 1.2. For a two-layer neural network, which is also known as *multi-layer perceptron* (MLP), we can write its composition function as follows:

$$y_k\,(\mathbf{v}; \Theta) = f^{(2)} \left(\sum_{j=1}^{M} w_{kj}^{(2)}\, f^{(1)} \left(\sum_{i=1}^{D} w_{ji}^{(1)} v_i \right) \right), \tag{1.3}$$

where the superscript denotes a layer index, M denotes the number of hidden units and $\Theta = \{\mathbf{W}^{(1)} \in \mathbb{R}^{M \times D}, \mathbf{W}^{(2)} \in \mathbb{R}^{K \times M}\}$. Hereafter, the bias term is omitted for simplicity. It is possible to add a number of hidden layers $(L - 1)$ and the corresponding estimation function is defined as

$$y_k = f^{(L)} \left(\sum_{l} w_{kl}^{(L)}\, f^{(L-1)} \left(\sum_{m} w_{lm} f^{(L-2)} \left(\cdots f^{(1)} \left(\sum_{i} w_{ji}^{(1)} x_i \right) \right) \right) \right). \tag{1.4}$$

Although different types of activation functions can be applied to different layers or even different units, in theory, it is common to apply the same type of activation function for the hidden layers in the literature. Here, it should be a nonlinear function; otherwise, the function will be represented by a single-layer neural network with a weight matrix equal to the resulting matrix of multiplying weight matrices of hidden layers. Regarding the activation function, a sigmoidal function such as a *logistic sigmoid* function and a *hyperbolic tangent* function $\tanh(z) = \frac{\exp(z) - \exp(-z)}{\exp(z) + \exp(-z)}$ is commonly used in earlier models thanks to their nonlinear and differential characteristics. However, the two activation functions make it difficult to train the neural network when stacking layers deeply. In this respect, recent works [2–5] proposed other nonlinear functions, and their details are provided in Section 1.6.2.

1.2.3 Learning in feed-forward neural networks

In terms of network learning, there are two fundamental problems, namely, network architecture learning and network parameters learning. While the network architecture learning still remains an open question,[2] there exists an efficient algorithm for network parameters learning as circumstantiated below.

The problem of learning parameters of an L-layer neural network can be formulated as error function minimization. Given a training data set $\{\mathbf{x}_n, \mathbf{t}_n\}_{n=1}^{N}$, where $\mathbf{x}_n \in \mathbb{R}^D$ denotes an observation and $\mathbf{t}_n \in \{0, 1\}^K$ denotes a class indicator vector with one-of-K encoding, i.e., for a class k, only the kth element in a vector $\mathbf{t}_n$ is 1 and all the other elements are 0. For a K-class classification, it is common to use a cross-entropy cost function defined as follows:

$$E(\mathbf{W}) = -\sum_{n=1}^{N}\sum_{k=1}^{K} t_{nk} \ln y_{nk}, \qquad (1.5)$$

where t_{kn} denotes the kth element of the target vector $\mathbf{t}_n$. y_{kn} is the kth element of the prediction vector $\mathbf{y}_n$ for $\mathbf{x}_n$, which is obtained by Eq. (1.4) with the parameter set $\mathbf{W} = [\mathbf{W}^{(1)}, \mathbf{W}^{(2)}, \cdots, \mathbf{W}^{(L)}]$.

The error function in Eq. (1.5) is highly nonlinear and nonconvex. Thus there is no analytic solution of the parameter set $\mathbf{W}$ that minimizes Eq. (1.5). Instead, we resort to a gradient descent algorithm by updating the parameters iteratively. Specifically, the parameters of L-layers, $\mathbf{W}$, are updated as follows:

$$\mathbf{W}_{(\tau+1)} = \mathbf{W}_{(\tau)} - \eta \nabla E(\mathbf{W}_{(\tau)}), \qquad (1.6)$$

where τ denotes an iteration index, η is a learning rate, while denoting $\nabla E(\mathbf{W}) = \left[\frac{\partial E}{\partial \mathbf{W}^{(1)}}, \frac{\partial E}{\partial \mathbf{W}^{(2)}}, \cdots, \frac{\partial E}{\partial \mathbf{W}^{(L)}}\right]$ as the gradient set of $\mathbf{W}$ that are obtained by means of error backpropagation [6]. To compute the derivative of an error function E with respect to the parameters of lth layer, i.e., $\mathbf{W}^{(l)}$, we propagate errors from the output layer back to the input layer by a chain rule:

$$\frac{\partial E}{\partial \mathbf{W}^{(l)}} = \frac{\partial E}{\partial \mathbf{a}^{(L)}}\frac{\partial \mathbf{a}^{(L)}}{\partial \mathbf{a}^{(L-1)}} \cdots \frac{\partial \mathbf{a}^{(l+2)}}{\partial \mathbf{a}^{(l+1)}}\frac{\partial \mathbf{a}^{(l+1)}}{\partial \mathbf{a}^{(l)}}\frac{\partial \mathbf{a}^{(l)}}{\partial \mathbf{z}^{(l)}}\frac{\partial \mathbf{z}^{(l)}}{\partial \mathbf{W}^{(l)}}, \qquad (1.7)$$

where $\mathbf{z}^{(l)}$ and $\mathbf{a}^{(l)}$ denote, respectively, the pre-activation vector and the activation vector of the layer l and $\mathbf{a}^{(L)} = \mathbf{y}$. Note that $\frac{\partial E}{\partial \mathbf{a}^{(L)}}$, or equally $\frac{\partial E}{\partial \mathbf{y}}$, corresponds to the error computed at the output layer. For the estimation of the gradient of an error function E with respect to the parameter $\mathbf{W}^{(l)}$, it utilizes the error propagated from the output layer through the chains in the form of $\frac{\partial \mathbf{a}^{(k+1)}}{\partial \mathbf{a}^{(k)}}$, $k = l, l + 1, \ldots, L - 1$, along with $\frac{\partial \mathbf{a}^{(l)}}{\partial \mathbf{z}^{(l)}}\frac{\partial \mathbf{z}^{(l)}}{\partial \mathbf{W}^{(l)}}$. The fraction $\frac{\partial \mathbf{a}^{(k+1)}}{\partial \mathbf{a}^{(k)}}$ can also be computed in a similar way as

---

[2] It is mostly designed empirically.

follows:

$$\frac{\partial \mathbf{a}^{(l+1)}}{\partial \mathbf{a}^{(l)}} = \frac{\partial \mathbf{a}^{(l+1)}}{\partial \mathbf{z}^{(l+1)}} \frac{\partial \mathbf{z}^{(l+1)}}{\partial \mathbf{a}^{(l)}}, \tag{1.8}$$

$$= f'\left(\mathbf{z}^{(l)}\right)\left(\mathbf{W}^{(l+1)}\right)^{\top}, \tag{1.9}$$

where $f'\left(\mathbf{z}^{(l)}\right)$ denotes a gradient of an activation function $f^{(l)}$ with respect to the pre-activation vector $\mathbf{z}^{(l)}$.

As for the parameter update in Eq. (1.6), there are two different approaches depending on the timing of parameter update, namely, batch gradient descent and stochastic gradient descent. The batch gradient descent updates the parameters based on the gradients ∇E evaluated over the whole training samples. Meanwhile, the stochastic gradient descent sequentially updates weight parameters by computing gradient on the basis of one sample at a time. When it comes to large-scale learning such as deep learning, it is advocated to apply stochastic gradient descent [7]. As a trade-off between batch gradient and stochastic gradient, a mini-batch gradient descent method, which computes and updates the parameters on the basis of a small set of samples, is commonly used in the literature [8].

1.3 Convolutional neural networks

In conventional multi-layer neural networks, the inputs are always in vector form. However, for (medical) images, the structural or configural information among neighboring pixels or voxels is another source of information. Hence, vectorization inevitably destroys such structural and configural information in images. A convolutional neural network (CNN) that typically has convolutional layers interspersed with pooling (or sub-sampling) layers and then followed by fully connected layers as in a standard multi-layer neural network (Fig. 1.3) is designed to better utilize such spatial and configuration information by taking 2D or 3D images as input. Unlike the conventional multi-layer neural networks, a CNN exploits extensive weight-sharing to reduce the degrees of freedom of models. A pooling layer helps reduce computation time and gradually builds up spatial and configural invariance.

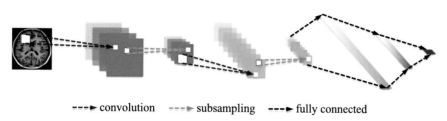

$--\blacktriangleright$ convolution $---\blacktriangleright$ subsampling $---\blacktriangleright$ fully connected

FIGURE 1.3

An architecture of a convolutional neural network.

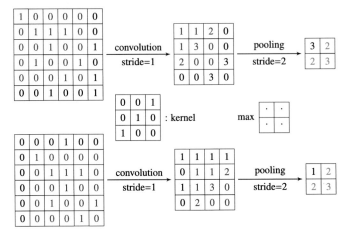

FIGURE 1.4

Illustration of translation invariance in convolution neural network. The bottom leftmost input is a translated version of the upper leftmost input image by one-pixel right and one-pixel down.

1.3.1 Convolution and pooling layer

The role of a convolution layer is to detect local features at different positions in the input feature maps with learnable kernels $k_{ij}^{(l)}$, i.e., connection weights between the feature map i at the layer $l-1$ and the feature map j at the layer l. Specifically, the units of the convolution layer l compute their activations $\mathbf{A}_j^{(l)}$ based only on a spatially contiguous subset of units in the feature maps $\mathbf{A}_i^{(l-1)}$ of the preceding layer $l-1$ by convolving the kernels $k_{ij}^{(l)}$ as follows:

$$\mathbf{A}_j^{(l)} = f\left(\sum_{i=1}^{M^{(l-1)}} \mathbf{A}_i^{(l-1)} * k_{ij}^{(l)} + b_j^{(l)}\right), \qquad (1.10)$$

where $M^{(l-1)}$ denotes the number of feature maps in the layer $l-1$, $*$ denotes a convolution operator, $b_j^{(l)}$ is a bias parameter and $f(\cdot)$ is a nonlinear activation function. Due to the local connectivity and weight sharing, we can greatly reduce the number of parameters compared to a fully connected neural network, and it is possible to avoid overfitting. Further, when the input image is shifted, the activation of the units in the feature maps are also shifted by the same amount, which allows a CNN to be equivariant to small shifts, as illustrated in Fig. 1.4. In the figure, when the pixel values in the input image are shifted by one-pixel right and one-pixel down, the outputs after convolution are also shifted by one-pixel right and one-pixel down.

A pooling layer follows a convolution layer by downsampling the feature maps of the preceding convolution layer. Specifically, each feature map in a pooling layer is linked with a feature map in the convolution layer, and each unit in a feature map of the pooling layer is computed based on a subset of units in a receptive field. Similar to the convolution layer, the receptive field that finds a maximal value among the units in its field is convolved with the convolution map but with a stride of the size of the receptive field so that the contiguous receptive fields are not overlapped. The role of the pooling layer is to progressively reduce the spatial size of the feature maps and to reduce the number of parameters and computation involved in the network. Another important function of the pooling layer is for translation invariance over small spatial shifts in the input. In Fig. 1.4, while the bottom leftmost image is a translated version of the top leftmost image by one-pixel right and one-pixel down, their outputs after convolution and pooling operations are the same, especially for the units in green.

1.3.2 Computing gradients

Assume that a convolution layer is followed by a pooling layer. In such a case, units in a feature map of a convolution layer l are connected to a single unit of the corresponding feature map in the pooling layer $l + 1$. By up-sampling the feature maps of the pooling layer to recover the reduced size of maps, all we need to do is to multiply with the derivative of the activation function evaluated at the convolution layer's pre-activations $\mathbf{Z}_j^{(l)}$ as follows:

$$\Delta_j^{(l)} = f' \left(\mathbf{Z}_j^{(l)} \right) \odot \text{up} \left(\Delta_j^{(l+1)} \right), \qquad (1.11)$$

where $\odot$ and up$(\cdot)$ denote an element-wise multiplication and up-sampling operation, respectively.

For the case when a current layer, whether it is a pooling layer or a convolution layer, is followed by a convolution layer, we must figure out which patch in the current layer's feature map corresponds to a unit in the next layer's feature map. The kernel weights multiplying the connections between the input patch and the output unit are exactly the weights of the convolutional kernel. The gradients for the kernel weights are computed by the chain rule similar to backpropagation. However, since the same weights are now shared across many connections, we need to sum the gradients for a given weight over all the connections using the kernel weights as follows:

$$\frac{\partial E}{\partial k_{ij}^{(l)}} = \sum_{u,v} \Delta_{j;(u,v)}^{(l)} \mathbf{P}_{i;(u,v)}^{(l-1)}, \qquad (1.12)$$

where $\mathbf{P}_{i;(u,v)}^{(l-1)}$ denotes the patch in the ith feature map of the layer $l - 1$, i.e., $\mathbf{A}_i^{(l-1)}$, which was multiplied by $k_{ij}^{(l)}$ during convolution to compute the element at (u, v) in the output feature map $\mathbf{A}_j^{(l)}$.

1.3.3 Deep convolutional neural networks

With the advances in computing hardware, recent works utilizing neural networks have grown in depth (i.e., convolution and pooling layers) and width (i.e., channel size). However, as CNNs get deeper and wider, the difficulties (e.g., computational cost, vanishing gradients and degradation) in training them also grow. Thus various methods for improving the computational efficiency of deep models are described in the following sections.

1.3.3.1 Skip connection

Skip connection, or shortcut connection, constructs an alternative path for gradients to flow from one layer to layers in the deeper part of the neural network. Specifically, skip connection constructs a path that jumps over one or more layers via addition or concatenation. For example, residual connections [9] constructs the skip connections via addition as follows:

$$\mathbf{A}^{(l)} = f\left(\mathbf{A}^{(l-1)} * \mathbf{k}^{(l)} + \mathbf{b}^{(l)}\right) + \mathbf{A}^{(l-1)}, \tag{1.13}$$

where $\mathbf{k}^{(l)}$ and $\mathbf{b}^{(l)}$ is the kernel and bias parameter, respectively. Similarly, dense connection [10] constructs the skip connection via channel-wise concatenation. This construction via concatenation allows connections to receive from all previously connected feature maps, introducing $\frac{l(l+1)}{2}$ connections in the lth skip connection instead of l connections in residual connection.

1.3.3.2 Inception module

Inception module [11] was introduced to significantly reduce the computational cost of deep neural networks via sparse multi-scale processing. Specifically, it reduces the number of arithmetic operations of convolution functions by reducing the filter size, i.e., introducing sparsity, via 1×1 convolution layers followed by convolution layers in different kernel sizes. In practice, the inception module achieved state-of-the-art performance in image classification tasks while reducing the number of arithmetic operations by 100 times compared to its counterparts. Several improvements to the inception module were made throughout the past decade. For example, Inception-v2 and -v3 [12] utilize even sparser, i.e., smaller kernel sizes, convolution operations to improve the computational efficiency. Inception-v4, or Inception-ResNet-v1 and -v2 [13], include the skip connection construction in addition to the multi-scale convolution operations.

1.3.3.3 Attention

Attention mechanism in deep learning allows neural networks to attend to salient information from noisy data but also can act as a memory function. These attention methods can be broadly categorized by the form of the attention function: soft *vs.* hard attention, global *vs.* local attention, and multi-head attention. Soft attention [14], also commonly known as global attention [15], places attention over all patches of an image, while hard attention [16] selects a single patch at a time. To this end, soft attention is generally more favorable in terms of computational efficiency due to the fact that hard attention models are nondifferentiable and require special techniques such as reinforcement learning. As such, local attention [14] is a differential model

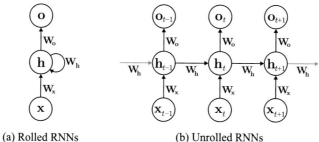

(a) Rolled RNNs   (b) Unrolled RNNs

FIGURE 1.5

Graphical illustration of RNNs with the (a) rolled and (b) unrolled computational graph over the timesteps.

that combines the advantages of soft and hard attention. Meanwhile, multi-head attention [17] attends to different information in a parallel manner.

In practice, attention mechanisms for medical image analysis typically utilize channel-wise and spatial-wise attention [18] as well as global attention [19] to improve the model performance. Note that such attention techniques have been used as a tool for visual interpretation methods [20] as well, where most attended regions can localize the features that support the decision made by a neural network.

1.4 Recurrent neural networks

The (medical) images are commonly embodied with corresponding attributes at the time of measurement. In the case of the medical domain, it could be the subject's clinical measurements (i.e., vital measurements, lab results, clinical notes, etc.). Then the (multi-modal) sequential data emerge as these data were measured periodically, which require distinguished deep models for effectively incorporating the entire timespan of such data. Thus we dispense this section to concisely cover the recurrent neural networks (RNNs) as it is reputably robust in handling variable-length sequential data over diverse (clinical) downstream tasks.

1.4.1 Recurrent cell

RNNs process the sequential data through the so-called recurrent cell, as illustrated in Fig. 1.5. Suppose that the T-length sequential data $\mathbf{X} = [\mathbf{x}_1, \ldots, \mathbf{x}_t, \ldots, \mathbf{x}_T]$ with $\mathbf{x}_t \in \mathbb{R}^D$ comes with the corresponding labels $\mathbf{Y} \in \mathbb{R}^{T \times K}$, where $\mathbf{y}_t \in \{0, 1\}^K$. For each timestep, a typical recurrent cell integrates the input with the previous hidden state as

$$\mathbf{h}_t = \tanh(\mathbf{W_x}\mathbf{x}_t + \mathbf{W_h}\mathbf{h}_{t-1} + \mathbf{b}), \tag{1.14}$$

where $\mathbf{W_x}$, $\mathbf{W_h}$ and $\mathbf{b}$ denote the input and hidden state transformation weights as well as the bias, respectively. Here, the hyperbolic tangent served as the activation function to transform the outcomes into $[-1, 1]$. Meanwhile, the initial hidden state $\mathbf{h}_0$ could be either initialized with zeros or inferred from auxiliary networks. Thus, as $\mathbf{h}_t$ holds the summarization of the underlying information in the sequences so far, the prediction $\hat{\mathbf{y}}_t$ could be inferred as

$$\mathbf{o}_t = \mathbf{W_o}\mathbf{h}_t + \mathbf{c}, \tag{1.15}$$

$$\hat{\mathbf{y}}_t = \text{softmax}(\mathbf{o}_t), \tag{1.16}$$

with $\mathbf{W_o}$ and $\mathbf{c}$ denote the weights and bias, correspondingly. Note that other circumstances may employ only the last hidden state $\mathbf{h}_T$ for predicting the single label $\mathbf{y}$. For now, let us assume that sequence of data and its label has an equal length so that we require the model to predict it for each tth timestep. Thus we train the RNNs by devising the following loss function over entire T-length sequences as

$$E(\Theta) = -\sum_{t=1}^{T}\sum_{k=1}^{K} y_{tk} \ln \hat{y}_{tk}. \tag{1.17}$$

As RNNs incorporate the forward propagation over the whole timestep of sequences, the gradient should be evaluated via a backpropagation through time [21]. Furthermore, as the weights of the recurrent cell are shared across the sequences, starting from the output, we can calculate each gradient with respect to $\mathbf{W_o}$ and $\mathbf{c}$, respectively, as follows:

$$\frac{\partial E}{\partial \mathbf{W_o}} = \sum_{t=1}^{T} \frac{\partial E_t}{\partial \mathbf{W_o}} = \sum_{t=1}^{T} \frac{\partial E_t}{\partial \hat{\mathbf{y}}_t} \frac{\partial \hat{\mathbf{y}}_t}{\partial \mathbf{o}_t} \frac{\partial \mathbf{o}_t}{\partial \mathbf{W_o}} = \sum_{t=1}^{T} (\hat{\mathbf{y}}_t - \mathbf{y}_t)\mathbf{h}_t^{\top} \tag{1.18}$$

$$\frac{\partial E}{\partial \mathbf{c}} = \sum_{t=1}^{T} \frac{\partial E_t}{\partial \mathbf{c}} = \sum_{t=1}^{T} \frac{\partial E_t}{\partial \hat{\mathbf{y}}_t} \frac{\partial \hat{\mathbf{y}}_t}{\partial \mathbf{o}_t} \frac{\partial \mathbf{o}_t}{\partial \mathbf{c}} = \sum_{t=1}^{T} (\hat{\mathbf{y}}_t - \mathbf{y}_t) \tag{1.19}$$

Subsequently, we could aggregate the gradients with respect to weights $\mathbf{W_x}$, $\mathbf{W_h}$ and bias $\mathbf{b}$ across the entire timesteps as

$$\frac{\partial E}{\partial \mathbf{W_x}} = \sum_{t=1}^{T}\sum_{\tau=1}^{t+1} \frac{\partial E_{t+1}}{\partial \hat{\mathbf{y}}_{t+1}} \frac{\partial \hat{\mathbf{y}}_{t+1}}{\partial \mathbf{h}_{t+1}} \frac{\partial \mathbf{h}_{t+1}}{\partial \mathbf{h}_\tau} \frac{\partial \mathbf{h}_\tau}{\partial \mathbf{W_x}}, \tag{1.20}$$

$$\frac{\partial E}{\partial \mathbf{W_h}} = \sum_{t=1}^{T}\sum_{\tau=1}^{t+1} \frac{\partial E_{t+1}}{\partial \hat{\mathbf{y}}_{t+1}} \frac{\partial \hat{\mathbf{y}}_{t+1}}{\partial \mathbf{h}_{t+1}} \frac{\partial \mathbf{h}_{t+1}}{\partial \mathbf{h}_\tau} \frac{\partial \mathbf{h}_\tau}{\partial \mathbf{W_h}}, \tag{1.21}$$

$$\frac{\partial E}{\partial \mathbf{b}} = \sum_{t=1}^{T}\sum_{\tau=1}^{t+1} \frac{\partial E_{t+1}}{\partial \hat{\mathbf{y}}_{t+1}} \frac{\partial \hat{\mathbf{y}}_{t+1}}{\partial \mathbf{h}_{t+1}} \frac{\partial \mathbf{h}_{t+1}}{\partial \mathbf{h}_\tau} \frac{\partial \mathbf{h}_\tau}{\partial \mathbf{b}}. \tag{1.22}$$

1.4.2 **Vanishing gradient problem**

As the RNNs deal with the T-length sequential data, the more it has longer T, it involves the higher risk of getting either gradient vanishing or exploding issues due to the repetitive matrix multiplications in inferring the gradients across the timesteps [22]. To this end, an improvement upon the vanilla recurrent cell was proposed to address such issue and was pioneered by the long-short term memory (LSTM) [23], as it incorporates a dedicated memory cell and gating mechanism to adequately govern the information flow over the sequences, allowing for long-term dependencies learning.

Such an LSTM cell is comprised of several following gating operations:

$$\mathbf{f}_t = \sigma(\mathbf{W}_f[\mathbf{h}_{t-1} \oplus \mathbf{x}_t] + \mathbf{b}_f), \tag{1.23}$$

$$\mathbf{i}_t = \sigma(\mathbf{W}_i[\mathbf{h}_{t-1} \oplus \mathbf{x}_t] + \mathbf{b}_i), \tag{1.24}$$

$$\tilde{\mathbf{c}}_t = \tanh(\mathbf{W}_c[\mathbf{h}_{t-1} \oplus \mathbf{x}_t] + \mathbf{b}_c), \tag{1.25}$$

$$\mathbf{c}_t = \mathbf{f}_t \mathbf{c}_{t-1} + \mathbf{i}_t \tilde{\mathbf{c}}_t, \tag{1.26}$$

$$\mathbf{o}_t = \sigma(\mathbf{W}_o[\mathbf{h}_{t-1} \oplus \mathbf{x}_t] + \mathbf{b}_o), \tag{1.27}$$

$$\mathbf{h}_t = \mathbf{o}_t \tanh(\mathbf{c}_t), \tag{1.28}$$

with $\oplus$ denotes the concatenation operator. In a nutshell, given the input $\mathbf{x}_t$ and $\mathbf{h}_{t-1}$, an LSTM cell introduces the $\mathbf{f}_t$ and $\mathbf{i}_t$, which served as the forget and input gate, respectively. These factors then regulate which information shall be pruned or retained to be stored in the new cell state $\mathbf{c}_t$. It further incorporates the cell state to obtain the current hidden state $\mathbf{h}_t$ by considering the output gate $\mathbf{o}_t$. Therefore due to incorporating these gating mechanisms and the novel memory cell, the meaningful information can then be conveyed over by the recurrence cell to the (distant) future timesteps, mitigating the issue of vanishing (or exploding) gradient, and also promising an improvement over the downstream task. Finally, similar to vanilla RNNs, we could further employ such hidden state $\mathbf{h}_t$ for obtaining the predicted label for each timestep $\hat{\mathbf{y}}_t$ as follows:

$$\hat{\mathbf{y}}_t = \text{softmax}(\mathbf{W}_y \mathbf{h}_t + \mathbf{b}_y). \tag{1.29}$$

In addition to the LSTM, these days numerous alternatives to the vanilla recurrent cell were proposed, with peephole LSTM [24] and gated recurrent unit (GRU) [25] being the two most popular among them.

1.5 **Deep generative models**

1.5.1 **Restricted Boltzmann machine**

A restricted Boltzmann machine (RBM) is a two-layer undirected graphical model with visible and hidden units in each layer. Note that the visible units $\mathbf{v} \in \mathbb{R}^D$ are related to observations, and the hidden units $\mathbf{h} \in \mathbb{R}^F$ represent the structures or dependencies over the visible units. It assumes symmetric connectivity $\mathbf{W} \in \mathbb{R}^{D \times F}$ between the visible layer and the hidden layer but no connections within the layers, and each layer has a bias term, $\mathbf{a} \in \mathbb{R}^D$ and $\mathbf{b} \in \mathbb{R}^F$, respectively. Due to the symmetry of the weight matrix $\mathbf{W}$, it is possible to reconstruct the input observations from the hidden representations. Hence, an RBM is naturally regarded as an autoencoder [26] and these favorable characteristics are used in RBM parameters learning [26]. In RBM, a joint probability of $(\mathbf{v}, \mathbf{h})$ is given by

$$P(\mathbf{v}, \mathbf{h}; \Theta) = \frac{1}{Z(\Theta)} \exp[-E(\mathbf{v}, \mathbf{h}; \Theta)], \qquad (1.30)$$

where $\Theta = \{\mathbf{W}, \mathbf{a}, \mathbf{b}\}$, $E(\mathbf{v}, \mathbf{h}; \Theta)$ is an energy function, and $Z(\Theta)$ is a partition function that can be obtained by summing over all possible pairs of $\mathbf{v}$ and $\mathbf{h}$. For the sake of simplicity, by assuming binary visible and hidden units, which are the commonly studied case, the energy function $E(\mathbf{v}, \mathbf{h}; \Theta)$ is defined as

$$E(\mathbf{v}, \mathbf{h}; \Theta) = -\mathbf{h}^\top \mathbf{W} \mathbf{v} - \mathbf{a}^\top \mathbf{v} - \mathbf{b}^\top \mathbf{h} = -\sum_{i=1}^{D} \sum_{j=1}^{F} v_i w_{ij} h_j - \sum_{i=1}^{D} a_i v_i - \sum_{j=1}^{F} b_j h_j.$$
$$(1.31)$$

The conditional distribution of the hidden units given the visible units and also the conditional distribution of the visible units given the hidden units are respectively computed as

$$P(h_j = 1 | \mathbf{v}; \Theta) = \sigma \left(b_j + \sum_{i=1}^{D} w_{ij} v_i \right) \qquad (1.32)$$

$$P(v_i = 1 | \mathbf{h}; \Theta) = \sigma \left(a_i + \sum_{j=1}^{F} w_{ij} h_j \right) \qquad (1.33)$$

where $\sigma(\cdot)$ is a logistic sigmoid function. Due to the unobservable hidden units, the objective function is defined as the marginal distribution of the visible units as

$$P(\mathbf{v}; \Theta) = \frac{1}{Z(\Theta)} \sum_{\mathbf{h}} \exp(-E(\mathbf{v}, \mathbf{h}; \Theta)). \qquad (1.34)$$

The RBM parameters are usually trained using a contrastive divergence algorithm [27] that maximizes the log-likelihood of observations.

1.5.2 Deep belief network

Since an RBM is a kind of an autoencoder, it is straightforward to stack multiple RBMs for deep architecture construction, similar to stacked autoencoder (SAE) (will be covered later in Section 1.6.1), which results in a single probabilistic model called a Deep Belief Network (DBN). That is, a DBN has one visible layer $\mathbf{v}$ and a series of hidden layers $\mathbf{h}^{(1)}, \cdots, \mathbf{h}^{(L)}$. Between any two consecutive layers, let $\{\Theta^{(l)}\}_{l=1}^{L}$ denote the corresponding RBM parameters. Note that while the top two layers still form an undirected generative model, i.e., RBM, the lower layers form directed generative models. Hence, the joint distribution of the observed units $\mathbf{v}$ and the L hidden layers $\mathbf{h}^{(l)}$ ($l = 1, \ldots, L$) in DBN is given as follows:

$$P\left(\mathbf{v}, \mathbf{h}^{(1)}, \cdots, \mathbf{h}^{(L)}\right) = \left(\prod_{l=0}^{L-2} P(\mathbf{h}^{(l)}|\mathbf{h}^{(l+1)})\right) P\left(\mathbf{h}^{(L-1)}, \mathbf{h}^{(L)}\right) \qquad (1.35)$$

where $\mathbf{h}^{(0)} = \mathbf{v}$, $P(\mathbf{h}^{(l)}|\mathbf{h}^{(l+1)})$ corresponds to a conditional distribution for the units of the layer l given the units of the layer $l+1$, and $P\left(\mathbf{h}^{(L-1)}, \mathbf{h}^{(L)}\right)$ denotes the joint distribution of the units in the layers $L-1$ and L.

As for the parameter learning, the pretraining scheme described in Section 1.6.1 can also be applied as follows:

 (i) Train the first layer as an RBM with $\mathbf{v} = \mathbf{h}^{(0)}$.
 (ii) Use the first layer to obtain a representation of the input that will be used as observation for the second layer, i.e., either the mean activations of $P(\mathbf{h}^{(1)} = 1|\mathbf{h}^{(0)})$ or samples of $P(\mathbf{h}^{(1)}|\mathbf{h}^{(0)})$.
(iii) Train the second layer as an RBM, taking the transformed data (samples or mean activations) as training examples (for the visible layer of the RBM).
 (iv) Iterate (ii) and (iii) for the desired number of layers, each time propagating upward either samples or mean activations.

This greedy layerwise training of the DBN can be justified as increasing a variational lower bound on the log-likelihood of the data [26]. After the greedy layerwise procedure is completed, it is possible to perform generative fine-tuning using the wake-sleep algorithm [28]. However, in practice, no further procedure is made to train the whole DBN jointly. In order for the use of a DBN in classification, a trained DBN can also be directly used to initialize a deep neural network with the trained weights and biases. Then the deep neural network can be fine-tuned by means of backpropagation and (stochastic) gradient descent.

1.5.3 Deep Boltzmann machine

A deep Boltzmann machine (DBM) is also structured by stacking multiple RBMs in a hierarchical manner. However, unlike DBN, all the layers in DBM still form an undirected generative model after stacking RBMs. For a classification task, DBM replaces its RBM at the top hidden layer with a discriminative RBM [29]. That is, the top hidden layer is now connected to both the lower hidden layer and an additional label layer (the label of the input). In order to learn the parameters, including the connectivities among hidden layers and another connectivity between the top hidden layer and the label layer, we maximize the log-likelihood of the observed data (i.e., the visible data and a class-label) with a gradient-based optimization strategy.

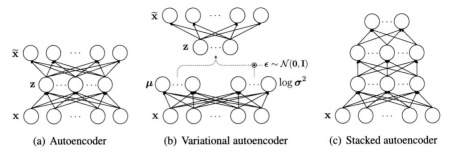

(a) Autoencoder   (b) Variational autoencoder   (c) Stacked autoencoder

FIGURE 1.6

A graphical illustration of (a) an autoencoder, (b) variational autoencoder, and (c) stacked autoencoder. Note that the dashed red arrows indicate the reparameterization trick.

In this way, a DBM can be trained to discover hierarchical and discriminative feature representations [29]. Similar to DBN, it can be applied for a greedy layerwise pre-training strategy to provide a good initial configuration of the parameters, which helps the learning procedure converge much faster than random initialization. However, since the DBM integrates both bottom-up and top-down information, the first and last RBMs in the network need modification by using weights twice as big as in one direction. Then it is performed for iterative alternation of variational mean-field approximation to estimate the posterior probabilities of hidden units and stochastic approximation to update model parameters.

1.5.4 Variational autoencoder

1.5.4.1 Autoencoder

An autoencoder, also called as auto-associator, is a special type of a two-layer neural network composed of an input layer, a hidden layer and an output layer. The input layer is fully connected to the hidden layer (i.e., an encoder), which is further fully connected to the output layer (i.e., a decoder) as illustrated in Fig. 1.6(a). Depending on the nature of the input data, the choices upon the type of such neural network are quite broad, ranging from straightforward MLP, CNNs to graph neural networks (GNNs). In general, the aim of an autoencoder is to learn a latent or compressed representation of the input by minimizing the reconstruction error between the input and the reconstructed values from the learned representation.

Let D_H and D_I denote the number of hidden units and the number of input units in a neural network, respectively. An autoencoder maps an input $\mathbf{x} \in \mathbb{R}^{D_I}$ to a latent representation $\mathbf{z} \in \mathbb{R}^{D_H}$ through a linear mapping and then a nonlinear transformation with a nonlinear activation function f as follows:

$$\mathbf{z} = f(\mathbf{W}\mathbf{x} + \mathbf{b}), \tag{1.36}$$

where $\mathbf{W} \in \mathbb{R}^{D_H \times D_I}$ is an encoding weight matrix, and $\mathbf{b} \in \mathbb{R}^{D_H}$ is a bias vector. The representation $\mathbf{z}$ of the hidden layer is then mapped back to a vector $\widetilde{\mathbf{x}} \in \mathbb{R}^{D_I}$, which approximately reconstructs the input vector $\mathbf{x}$ by another mapping as follows:

$$\tilde{\mathbf{x}} = \mathbf{W}'\mathbf{z} + \mathbf{b}' \approx \mathbf{x}, \tag{1.37}$$

where $\mathbf{W}' \in \mathbb{R}^{D_I \times D_H}$ and $\mathbf{b}' \in \mathbb{R}^{D_I}$ are a decoding weight matrix and a bias vector, respectively. Structurally, the number of input units and the number of output units is determined by the dimension of an input vector. Meanwhile, the number of hidden units can be determined based on the nature of the data. If the number of hidden units is less than the dimension of the input data, then the autoencoder can be used for dimensionality reduction. However, it is worth noting that to obtain complicated nonlinear relations among input features, it is possible to allow the number of hidden units to be even larger than the input dimension, from which we can still find an interesting structure by imposing a sparsity constraint [30,31].

From a learning perspective, the goal of an autoencoder is to minimize the reconstruction error between the input $\mathbf{x}$ and the output $\tilde{\mathbf{x}}$ with respect to the parameters. Given a training set $\{\mathbf{X}, \tilde{\mathbf{X}}\} = \{\mathbf{x}_i, \tilde{\mathbf{x}}_i\}_{i=1}^{N}$, let $E(\mathbf{X}, \tilde{\mathbf{X}}) = \frac{1}{2}\sum_{i=1}^{N}\|\mathbf{x}_i - \tilde{\mathbf{x}}_i\|_2^2$ denote a reconstruction error over training samples. To encourage sparseness of the hidden units, it is common to use Kullback–Leibler (KL) divergence to measure the difference between the average activation $\hat{\rho}_j$ of the jth hidden unit over the training samples and the target average activation ρ defined as [32],

$$\text{KL}(\rho||\hat{\rho}_j) = \rho \log \frac{\rho}{\hat{\rho}_j} + (1 - \rho) \log \frac{1 - \rho}{1 - \hat{\rho}_j}. \tag{1.38}$$

Then our objective function can be written as

$$E(\mathbf{X}, \tilde{\mathbf{X}}) + \gamma \sum_{j}^{D_H} \text{KL}(\rho||\hat{\rho}_j), \tag{1.39}$$

where γ denotes a sparsity control parameter. With the introduction of the KL divergence, the error function is penalized by a large average activation of a hidden unit over the training samples by setting ρ to be small. This penalization drives the activation of many hidden units to be equal or close to zero by making sparse connections between layers.

1.5.4.2 Variational autoencoder

We could further extend the concept of the autoencoder as the deep generative model by means of variational autoencoder (VAE), as illustrated in Fig. 1.6(b). In contrast with vanilla autoencoder, a VAE takes into account the prior distributions of the latent representation $\mathbf{z}$ via $p(\mathbf{z})$, in which we assume that such latent vector governing the generation the data $\mathbf{x}$ through a conditional distribution $p(\mathbf{x}|\mathbf{z})$. Furthermore, a typical VAE approximate the intractable true posterior $p(\mathbf{z}|\mathbf{x})$ by introducing an approximate posterior $q(\mathbf{z}|\mathbf{x})$ using a Gaussian distribution $\mathcal{N}(\mu, \sigma^2\mathbf{I})$. Such mean and variance are inferred from the respective encoding neural networks (i.e., encoder $\mathcal{E}$) as

$$\mu = \mathcal{E}_\mu(\mathbf{x}; \phi), \quad \log \sigma^2 = \mathcal{E}_\sigma(\mathbf{x}; \phi), \tag{1.40}$$

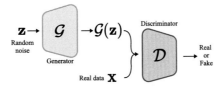

FIGURE 1.7

Illustration of a generative adversarial network.

with ϕ denoting the parameters of such networks. To obtain the latent representation $\mathbf{z}$, we draw $\epsilon \sim \mathcal{N}(\mathbf{0}, \mathbf{I})$ and further apply the reparameterization trick [33] such that

$$\mathbf{z} = \boldsymbol{\mu} + \boldsymbol{\sigma} \odot \epsilon. \tag{1.41}$$

Such a trick is necessary for enabling the optimization of the network's parameters via gradient-based approaches. Furthermore, we could generate the $\mathbf{x}$ by utilizing the latent representation $\mathbf{z}$ through a decoding neural network $\mathcal{D}$ with parameters θ as

$$\mathbf{x} = \mathcal{D}(\mathbf{z}; \theta). \tag{1.42}$$

Finally, VAE is trained to optimize the variational evidence lower bound (ELBO) through the objective function in Eq. (1.43), consisting of an expected reconstruction error as well as KL divergence to impose the approximate posterior $q(\mathbf{z}|\mathbf{x})$ as being close as possible to the prior $p(\mathbf{z})$:

$$\mathbb{E}_{q(\mathbf{z}|\mathbf{x})}[\log p(\mathbf{x}|\mathbf{z})] - \mathrm{KL}(q(\mathbf{z}|\mathbf{x})||p(\mathbf{z})) \tag{1.43}$$

1.5.5 Generative adversarial network

Recently, generative adversarial network (GAN), a deep learning-based implicit density estimation model, has demonstrated its characteristic caliber of generation by learning deep representations of data distribution without labels [34]. As conceptualized in Fig. 1.7, GAN is composed of two neural networks: (i) a *generator* $\mathcal{G}$, which tries to synthesize *realistic samples*, $\mathcal{G}(\mathbf{z})$, using a latent code vector $\mathbf{z}$; and (ii) a *discriminator* $\mathcal{D}$ that learns to discriminate the real sample $\mathbf{x}$ from the generated one, i.e., $\mathcal{G}(\mathbf{z})$, by estimating a probability of whether the input is real. GAN, to simultaneously optimize those two neural networks $\mathcal{G}$ and $\mathcal{D}$, uses a *game theory*-based min-max objective function:

$$\min_{\mathcal{G}} \max_{\mathcal{D}} \mathbb{E}_{p_{\mathbf{x}}}[\log \mathcal{D}(\mathbf{x})] + \mathbb{E}_{p_{\mathbf{z}}}[\log(1 - \mathcal{D}(\mathcal{G}(\mathbf{z})))], \tag{1.44}$$

where $p_{\mathbf{x}}$ and $p_{\mathbf{z}}$ denote the real data distribution and the latent code distribution, respectively. Mathematically, in Eq. (1.44), the Jensen–Shannon distance (JSD) estimates the distance between those two distributions, the real and the generated data distributions. Note that $\mathcal{G}$ is minimized when $\mathcal{D}(\mathcal{G}(\mathbf{z}))$ is coming close to 1, i.e., the generator makes realistic samples, and $\mathcal{D}$ is maximized when $\mathcal{D}(\mathbf{x})$ is going to 1 as well as $\mathcal{D}(\mathcal{G}(\mathbf{z}))$ reaches 0; therefore $\mathcal{D}$ tries to correctly decide the real and fake samples. Since GAN has shown promising generation performance, there is still room for improvement with a modification of the loss function [35,36]. In this regard, attempts to exploit other distances for the GAN loss function instead of the JSD have gained widespread attention from deep learning researchers.

Mao et al. [35] slightly modified the GAN loss function and named their method least-square GAN (LSGAN). More specifically, they minimized the Pearson-χ^2 distance between the real and the synthesized data distributions. To do so, they modified the loss to

$$\min_{\mathcal{D}} \frac{1}{2}\mathbb{E}_{p_{\mathbf{x}}}[\log(\mathcal{D}(\mathbf{x}) - a)^2] + \frac{1}{2}\mathbb{E}_{p_{\mathbf{z}}}[\log(\mathcal{D}(\mathcal{G}(\mathbf{z})) - b)^2] \qquad (1.45)$$

$$\text{and } \min_{\mathcal{G}} \frac{1}{2}\mathbb{E}_{p_{\mathbf{z}}}[\log(\mathcal{D}(\mathcal{G}(\mathbf{z})) - c)^2], \qquad (1.46)$$

and set $a = c = 1$ while $b = 0$. This modified objective function gives a greater gradient value to fake samples, which are farther from the decision boundary of real samples, thereby suppressing the gradient vanishing problem.

Similar to LSGAN [35], Arjovsky et al. [36] also focused on replacing the JSD to the other distance. They showed that the Wasserstein distance can be applied to the GAN objective function in a mathematically rigorous manner and proposed a modified loss function:

$$\min_{\mathcal{G}} \max_{\mathcal{F}} \mathbb{E}_{p_{\mathbf{x}}}[\mathcal{F}(\mathbf{x})] - \mathbb{E}_{p_{\mathbf{z}}}[\mathcal{F}(\mathcal{G}(\mathbf{z}))], \qquad (1.47)$$

where $\mathcal{F}$, a *critic*, is the 1-Lipschitz function, which is used instead of the discriminator. In this objective, the critic scores the realness or fakeness of the input, whereas the discriminator estimates the probability of whether the input is real. To make the critic satisfy the Lipschitz constraint, Arjovsky et al. used weight clipping on the critic $\mathcal{F}$ and this method is widely known as Wasserstein GAN (WGAN). On the other hand, Gulrajani et al. [37] removed the weight clipping by adding a regularization term, the so-called gradient penalty (GP). The objective function of WGAN with GP is

$$\min_{\mathcal{G}} \max_{\mathcal{F}} \mathbb{E}_{p_{\mathbf{x}}}[\mathcal{F}(\mathbf{x})] - \mathbb{E}_{p_{\mathbf{z}}}[\mathcal{F}(\mathcal{G}(\mathbf{z}))] + \lambda \cdot \mathbb{E}_{p_{\hat{\mathbf{x}}}}[(\|\nabla_{\hat{\mathbf{x}}}\mathcal{F}(\hat{\mathbf{x}})\|_2 - 1)^2], \qquad (1.48)$$

where $\| \cdot \|_2$ is the ℓ^2-norm and $\hat{\mathbf{x}}$ is defined as

$$\hat{\mathbf{x}} = \epsilon \cdot \mathbf{x} + (1 - \epsilon) \cdot \mathcal{G}(\mathbf{z}), \epsilon \sim U[0, 1]. \qquad (1.49)$$

Here, Gulrajani et al. give penalization to weights of the critic network. By doing so, WGAN with GP also could gratify the Lipschitz condition.

1.6 Tricks for better learning

Earlier, LeCun et al. presented that by transforming data to have an identity covariance and a zero mean, i.e., data whitening, the network training could converge faster [38,39]. Besides such a simple trick, recent studies have devised other nice tricks to better train deep models.

1.6.1 Parameter initialization in autoencoder

In regards to the autoencoder, note that the outputs of units in the hidden layer of the encoding networks become the latent representation of the input vector. However, due to its simple shallow structural characteristic, the representational power of a single-layer autoencoder is known to be very limited. However, when stacked with multiple autoencoders by taking the activation values of hidden units of an autoencoder as the input to the following upper autoencoder and building a SAE (Fig. 1.6(c)), it is possible to improve the representational power greatly [40]. Thanks to the hierarchical structure, one of the most important characteristics of the SAE is to learn or discover highly nonlinear and complicated patterns such as the relations among input features. When an input vector is presented to a SAE, the different layers of the network represent different levels of information. That is, the lower the layer in the network, the simpler the patterns that are learned; the higher the layer, the more complicated or abstract patterns inherent in the input feature vector. With regard to training parameters of the weight matrices and the biases in an SAE, a straightforward way is to apply backpropagation with the gradient-based optimization technique starting from random initialization by regarding the SAE as a conventional multi-layer neural network. Unfortunately, it is generally known that deep networks trained in that manner perform worse than networks with a shallow architecture, suffering from falling into a poor local optimum [31]. A greedy layerwise learning [26] could be used to circumvent this problem. The key idea in a greedy layerwise learning is to train one layer at a time by maximizing the variational lower bound. That is, we first train the 1st hidden layer with the training data as input, and then train the 2nd hidden layer with the outputs from the 1st hidden layer as input, and so on. That is, the representation of the lth hidden layer is used as input for the $(l + 1)$-th hidden layer. This greedy layerwise learning is performed as "*pretraining*" (Figs. 1.8(a)–1.8(c)). The important feature of pre-training is that it is conducted in an unsupervised manner with a standard backpropagation algorithm [41]. When it comes to a classification problem, we stack another output layer on top of the SAE (Fig. 1.8(d)) with an appropriate activation function. This top output layer is used to represent the class-label of an input sample. Then by taking the pretrained connection weights as the initial parameters for the hidden units and randomly initializing the connection weights between the top hidden layer and the output layer, it is possible to train the whole parameters jointly in a supervised manner by gradient descent with a backpropagation algorithm. Note that the initialization of the parameters via pretraining helps the supervised optimization, called "*fine-tuning*," reduce the risk of falling into poor local optima [26,31].

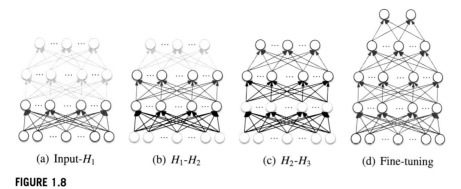

(a) Input-H_1 (b) H_1-H_2 (c) H_2-H_3 (d) Fine-tuning

FIGURE 1.8

Greedy layerwise pretraining (highlighted with the blue connections in (a–c)) and fine-tuning of the whole network. (H_i denotes the ith hidden layer in the network.)

1.6.2 Activation functions

In a deep learning framework, the main purpose of the activation function is to introduce nonlinearity into deep neural networks. The nonlinearity means that the output of the neural network cannot be reproduced from *affine transformations*, i.e., the output must be different from a linear combination of the input values.

There are many old-fashioned nonlinear activations such as the *logistic sigmoid*, and the *hyperbolic tangent*. But the gradient of those functions vanishes as the values of the respective inputs increases or decreases, which is known as one of the sources to cause the vanishing gradient problem. In this regard, Nair and Hinton suggested using a *rectified linear unit* (ReLU) function [2]. The ReLU function only takes positive input values:

$$\text{ReLU}(x) = \max(0, x), \qquad (1.50)$$

thereby validating its usefulness to improve training time by resolving the vanishing gradient problem. However, the ReLU has two mathematical problems: (i) it is nondifferentiable at $x = 0$, and thus not valid to be used along with a gradient-based method; (ii) it is unbounded on the positive side and can be a potential problem to cause overfitting. Nonetheless, as for the first problem, since it is highly unlikely that the input to any hidden unit will be at exactly $x = 0$ at any time, in practice, the gradient of the ReLU at $x = 0$ is set either 0 or 1. Regarding the unboundedness, the application of a regularization technique is helpful to limit the magnitude of weights, thus circumventing the overfitting issue. The curve for the ReLU function is depicted in Fig. 1.9(a).

Since the ReLU activation showed its power, many variations are proposed for more robust and sound learning. A *leaky ReLU* (lReLU) is one of the improved versions of the ReLU function [3]. For the ReLU function, the gradient is 0 for $x < 0$, which would deactivate the outputs in the negative region. The leaky ReLU function

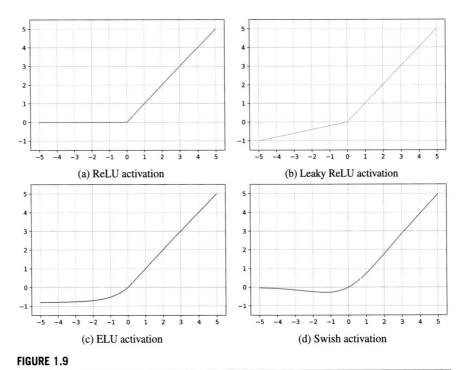

FIGURE 1.9

Plots of (a) rectified linear unit (ReLU), (b) leaky ReLU, (c) exponential linear unit (ELU) and (d) Swish activation functions.

slightly activates negative outputs to address this problem and is defined as

$$lReLU(x, a) = \max(a \cdot x, x), \tag{1.51}$$

where $0 < a < 1$ is a constant. The leaky ReLU has a small positive slope a in the negative area. Therefore it allows backpropagation for negative outputs. The curve for the leaky ReLU function is shown in Fig. 1.9(b).

Furthermore, a *parameterized ReLU* (pReLU) is another variant of the ReLU [3]. It is proposed to tackle the issue of the negative slope to be learned. On the one hand, the parameterized ReLU also gives a small positive slope to the negative values. On the other hand, the slope can be learned, whereas the other slope of the leaky ReLU is a constant. Thus the parameterized ReLU is defined as

$$pReLU(x) = \max(\alpha \cdot x, x), \tag{1.52}$$

and, the most appropriate value of α is also learned by performing backpropagation.

Meanwhile, an *exponential linear unit* (ELU) modifies the slope of the negative part of the leaky ReLU function [4]. Unlike the leaky ReLU or parameterized ReLU functions, the ELU exploits a log curve for activating the negative values instead of a straight line. The ELU is simply defined as

$$\text{ELU}(a, x) = \begin{cases} x & \text{if } x > 0 \\ a \cdot (e^x - 1) & \text{otherwise,} \end{cases} \tag{1.53}$$

where $0 < a < 1$ is a constant. The curve for the ELU is plotted in Fig. 1.9(c).

Finally, *Swish* function is a lesser-known function, which is proposed by [5]. Swish is more computationally efficient than variants of the ReLU and improves the performance of many deep neural networks. This function is defined as

$$\text{Swish}(x) = \sigma(x) \cdot x. \tag{1.54}$$

Fig. 1.9(d) depicts the curve of Swish function.

1.6.3 Optimizers

As aforementioned, the backward propagation of error is used for a deep neural network training. In this regard, gradient descent is a fundamental and genetic algorithm to optimize parameters by iteratively backpropagating loss values. Let us denote that sets of training data samples and labels as $\{\mathbf{X}, \mathbf{Y}\} = \{\mathbf{x}_i, \mathbf{y}_i\}_{i=1}^{N}$, where $\mathbf{x}_i$ and $\mathbf{y}_i$ are the ith sample and its corresponding label, and N is the number of total training samples. Then gradient descent updates parameters of the deep neural network Θ as follows:

$$\Theta \leftarrow \Theta - \eta \frac{\partial}{\partial \Theta} \mathcal{L}(\Theta, \mathbf{X}, \mathbf{Y}), \tag{1.55}$$

where η and $\mathcal{L}$ denote predefined learning rate and loss function, respectively.

The main problem with gradient descent is that it uses the whole training data set to compute the gradient values at every step, which is very impractical for a deep neural network with big data. On the other hand, stochastic gradient descent samples a random instance from the training data and estimates the gradient value based on that instance. Simply, stochastic gradient descent can be defined as

$$\Theta \leftarrow \Theta - \eta \frac{\partial}{\partial \Theta} \mathcal{L}(\Theta, \mathbf{X}_B, \mathbf{Y}_B), \tag{1.56}$$

where $\mathbf{X}_B = \{\mathbf{x}_i | \mathbf{x}_i \in \mathbf{X}, |\mathbf{X}_B| = B\}$ and $\mathbf{Y}_B = \{\mathbf{y}_i | \mathbf{y}_i \in \mathbf{Y}, |\mathbf{Y}_B| = B\}$ are subsets of training samples and labels, respectively, which contain B numbers of instances. Furthermore, by introducing randomness to the instance sampling, stochastic gradient descent can effectively escape from local optima. However, it also has a drawback since the algorithm can never settle at the global minimum point. Thus, to tackle this dilemma, a gradually reduced learning rate is widely used.

Since gradient descent or stochastic gradient descent can be a good optimizer, training a very deep neural network can be a painfully slow work. In order to speed up the network optimization procedure, many optimizers are proposed. *Momentum optimizer* is one of the most successful training algorithms. It is inspired by momentum optimization [42]. The momentum optimizer simply sets a momentum vector $\mathbf{m}$, which accelerates the direction of the network training:

$$\mathbf{m} \leftarrow \beta\mathbf{m} - \eta\frac{\partial}{\partial\Theta}\mathcal{L}(\Theta, \mathbf{X}_B, \mathbf{Y}_B), \tag{1.57}$$

$$\Theta \leftarrow \Theta + \mathbf{m}, \tag{1.58}$$

where $\beta \in [0, 1]$ is another hyperparameter to decide the level of momentum.

Meanwhile, let us imagine that if a training algorithm can correct the direction of network optimization earlier toward the global optimum point. The *AdaGrad* algorithm successfully achieves this correction by estimating a scale vector $\mathbf{s}$ and applying it to the gradient value [43]. In other words, AdaGrad decreases the learning rate for parameters with large changes during optimization and increases the learning rate for parameters that do not by introducing the scale:

$$\mathbf{s} \leftarrow \mathbf{s} + \frac{\partial\mathcal{L}(\Theta, \mathbf{X}_B, \mathbf{Y}_B)}{\partial\Theta} \otimes \frac{\partial\mathcal{L}(\Theta, \mathbf{X}_B, \mathbf{Y}_B)}{\partial\Theta}, \tag{1.59}$$

$$\Theta \leftarrow \Theta - \eta\frac{\partial\mathcal{L}(\Theta, \mathbf{X}_B, \mathbf{Y}_B)}{\partial\Theta} \oslash \sqrt{\mathbf{s} + \varepsilon}, \tag{1.60}$$

where $\otimes$ and $\oslash$ is the element-wise multiplication and the element-wise division, while ε is a smoothing term to avoid zero-division. AdaGrad performs well for simple convex problems, but it often stops too early when parameters change dramatically for a complex and high-dimensional curved surface.

Therefore to tackle the AdaGrad early stop risk, *RMSProp* optimizer accumulates only the gradient values from the recent iterations whereas AdaGrad exploits all the gradients [44]:

$$\mathbf{s} \leftarrow \beta\mathbf{s} + (1 - \beta)\frac{\partial\mathcal{L}(\Theta, \mathbf{X}_B, \mathbf{Y}_B)}{\partial\Theta} \otimes \frac{\partial\mathcal{L}(\Theta, \mathbf{X}_B, \mathbf{Y}_B)}{\partial\Theta}, \tag{1.61}$$

$$\Theta \leftarrow \Theta - \eta\frac{\partial\mathcal{L}(\Theta, \mathbf{X}_B, \mathbf{Y}_B)}{\partial\Theta} \oslash \sqrt{\mathbf{s} + \varepsilon}. \tag{1.62}$$

Meanwhile, there also exists the *Adam* optimizer, which is based on adaptive momentum estimation [45]. It combines the main ideas of momentum optimizer and RMSProp algorithm. Adam keeps an exponentially decaying average of gradient values at past iterations such as momentum optimizer and also exploits an exponentially decaying average of squared gradient values at past iterations similar to RMSProp:

$$\mathbf{m} \leftarrow \beta_1\mathbf{m} - (1 - \beta_1)\frac{\partial\mathcal{L}(\Theta, \mathbf{X}_B, \mathbf{Y}_B)}{\partial\Theta}, \tag{1.63}$$

$$\mathbf{s} \leftarrow \beta_2\mathbf{s} + (1 - \beta_2)\frac{\partial\mathcal{L}(\Theta, \mathbf{X}_B, \mathbf{Y}_B)}{\partial\Theta} \otimes \frac{\partial\mathcal{L}(\Theta, \mathbf{X}_B, \mathbf{Y}_B)}{\partial\Theta}, \tag{1.64}$$

$$\hat{\mathbf{m}} \leftarrow \frac{\mathbf{m}}{1 - \beta_1^t}, \tag{1.65}$$

$$\hat{\mathbf{s}} \leftarrow \frac{\mathbf{s}}{1 - \beta_2^t}, \tag{1.66}$$

$$\boldsymbol{\Theta} \leftarrow \boldsymbol{\Theta} + \eta \hat{\mathbf{m}} \oslash \sqrt{\hat{\mathbf{s}} + \varepsilon}, \tag{1.67}$$

where $t = 1, ..., T$ is the iteration number and T is the predefined total iteration number and $\beta_1, \beta_2 \in [0, 1]$ are decaying hyperparameters.

1.6.4 Regularizations

In an effort to reduce the overfitting problem in deep models, various regularization techniques have been proposed to this day. As large variance in model weights lead to poor generalization error, typical regularization techniques add a penalty term to the error function to put a constrain on the value of the model weights $\mathbf{w}$ as follows:

$$E(\mathbf{w}) = E_D(\mathbf{w}) + E_R(\mathbf{w}), \tag{1.68}$$

where $E_D(\mathbf{w})$ is the data-dependent error, and $E_R(\mathbf{w})$ is the regularization term. To this end, one of the most frequently used regularizers is the ℓ_p norm regularizer, such that $E_R(\mathbf{w}) = \lambda \sum_i |w_i|^p$. Here, λ is the regularization coefficient that controls the sparsity of the model weights and the relative importance of the regularization term. In the case of ℓ_2 norm regularizer, also known as ridge regularizer [46], the values of model weights are closer to zero, which lead to sparse model weights (i.e., less model complexity). In comparison, ℓ_1 norm regularizer, also known as LASSO [47], reduces the value of model weights closer or equal to zero at the cost of steeper gradient descent. Thus, LASSO may be more suitable for cases where variable selection is desirable, and ridge regularizer may be more suitable for data sets with severe local minima. To combine the advantages of LASSO and ridge regularizer, ElasticNet [48] uses both ℓ_1 and ℓ_2 norm, i.e., $E_R(\mathbf{w}) = \sum_i \lambda_1 |w_i|^1 + \lambda_2 |w_i|^2$, with λ_1 and λ_2 served as the respective regularization coefficient.

Another approach for reducing overfitting is to fit fixed-sized models with every possible setting and average their predictions given the same data set, i.e., a technique called ensemble. As this is not computationally possible in the real world, a dropout [49] approximates this ensemble by dropping randomly selected neurons in a model in each training iteration. Thus, the calculated posterior probability is the outcome of models with neuronal connections different in every training iteration. In addition, by randomly dropping neurons, the model is less likely to suffer from co-adaptation of neurons by preventing neurons from having the same information across the model. For instance, for each sample in a mini-batch during training of convolutional layer, dropout redefines the feature map in Eq. (1.10):

$$\mathbf{A}_j^{(l)} := f \left(\sum_{i=1}^{M^{(l-1)}} (\mathbf{r}^{(l-1)} \odot \mathbf{A}_i^{(l-1)}) * k_{ij}^{(l)} + b_j^{(l)} \right), \tag{1.69}$$

where $\mathbf{r}^{(l-1)} \sim \text{Bernoulli}(\pi^{(l)})$ denotes a masking matrix that masks dropped neurons, and $\pi^{(l)}$ is the dropout rate that determines the amount of dropped neurons.

During the testing times, the dropout rate is set as an identity matrix so that no neurons are dropped, and the model can perform with its full potential.

1.6.5 Normalizations

With the recent growth of deep learning, normalization methods of the intermediate features [50–53] have attracted significant attention for better learning. First, Ioffe and Szegedy [50] observed that the distribution of network activations varies among each mini-batch during training, which they defined as *internal covariate shift*. It causes a longer time and an unstable training process. To tackle this issue, Ioffe and Szegedy introduced a batch normalization (BN) technique that ensures the zero-mean and unit-variance properties for each mini-batch statistic and the optimal scale and shift parameters for each layer. Specifically, let $\mathbf{X} \in \mathbb{R}^{N \times C \times H \times W}$ denote an input feature where N is the batch size and C, H, W indicate the number of channels, height and width, respectively. According to [50], BN is formulated as follows:

$$\mathbf{X}' = \gamma \frac{\mathbf{X} - \boldsymbol{\mu}_{\text{BN}}}{\sqrt{\sigma_{\text{BN}}^2 + \epsilon}} + \boldsymbol{\beta}. \tag{1.70}$$

Here, the mean $\boldsymbol{\mu}_{\text{BN}} \in \mathbb{R}^C$ and variance $\sigma_{\text{BN}}^2 \in \mathbb{R}^C$ of the mini-batch is calculated as follows:

$$\boldsymbol{\mu}_{\text{BN}} = \frac{1}{NHW} \sum_{n=1}^{N} \sum_{h=1}^{H} \sum_{w=1}^{W} \mathbf{X}_{n,c,h,w}, \tag{1.71}$$

$$\sigma_{\text{BN}}^2 = \frac{1}{NHW} \sum_{n=1}^{N} \sum_{h=1}^{H} \sum_{w=1}^{W} (\mathbf{X}_{n,c,h,w} - \boldsymbol{\mu}_{\text{BN}})^2. \tag{1.72}$$

Also, ϵ is a small constant that helps to avoid dividing by zero. $\gamma \in \mathbb{R}^C$ and $\beta \in \mathbb{R}^C$ are the scale and shift parameters for the corresponding layer, trained through backpropagations. The mini-batch statistics, i.e., $\boldsymbol{\mu}_{\text{BN}}$ and σ_{BN}^2, of the whole training data set are accumulated with momentum, and then the running mean and variance are used for a test. Their experiments showed that the BN could considerably shorten the training time and stabilize training [50].

Despite these benefits of BN, it requires a large computational cost to calculate different statistics per timestep and a layer, which makes it challenging to be applied for a sequential model (e.g., RNN, LSTM, etc.). In order to address these limitations, Ba et al. proposed a layer normalization (LN) [51], where the input feature is normalized along the feature dimension by computing $\boldsymbol{\mu}_{\text{LN}} \in \mathbb{R}^N$ and $\sigma_{\text{LN}}^2 \in \mathbb{R}^N$:

$$\boldsymbol{\mu}_{\text{LN}} = \frac{1}{CHW} \sum_{c=1}^{C} \sum_{h=1}^{H} \sum_{w=1}^{W} \mathbf{X}_{n,c,h,w}, \tag{1.73}$$

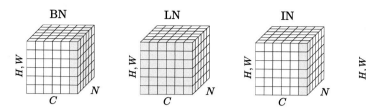

FIGURE 1.10

Illustrative comparison of normalization methods. Each tensor denotes a feature map with a shape of [$N \times C \times (H, W)$] where N is the batch size, C is the number of channels and (H, W) indicate the spatial axes. The patches in purple are normalized by the same mean and variance.

$$\sigma_{\text{LN}}^2 = \frac{1}{CHW} \sum_{c=1}^{C} \sum_{h=1}^{H} \sum_{w=1}^{W} (\mathbf{X}_{n,c,h,w} - \mu_{\text{LN}})^2. \qquad (1.74)$$

Since LN is independent of the batch, for a test, LN conducts the feature normalization with the test set's statistics. By following [51], LN performs well on the sequential models rather than BN.

Unlike BN and LN, instance normalization (IN) [52] computes the mean $\mu_{\text{IN}} \in \mathbb{R}^{N \times C}$ and variance $\sigma_{\text{IN}}^2 \in \mathbb{R}^{N \times C}$ across each channel for each sample as follows:

$$\mu_{\text{IN}} = \frac{1}{HW} \sum_{h=1}^{H} \sum_{w=1}^{W} \mathbf{X}_{n,c,h,w}, \qquad (1.75)$$

$$\sigma_{\text{IN}}^2 = \frac{1}{HW} \sum_{h=1}^{H} \sum_{w=1}^{W} (\mathbf{X}_{n,c,h,w} - \mu_{\text{IN}})^2. \qquad (1.76)$$

IN normalizes the intermediate features with each mean and variance, Eqs. (1.75) and (1.76), at training and testing time, respectively. By doing so, the instance-specific style properties are removed; therefore it is suitable for a style transfer task.

Similar to LN and IN, Wu and He [53] devised a group normalization (GN) method independent of the batch size. They assumed that the channels in an image are not completely independent. For this reason, GN computes the mean and variance over groups (hyperparameters) of channels for each training sample and normalizes the features with the calculated statistics. Here, GN also has the scale and shift parameters per channel. According to the number of groups (G), GN becomes LN ($G = 1$) or IN ($G = C$). In [53], GN is less sensitive to the batch size with respect to the performance compared to BN. The differences among BN, LN, IN and GN are illustrated in Fig. 1.10.

In addition to [50–53], there have been efforts to enhance performance and efficiency for more specific tasks by normalizing features, e.g., the variants of BN [54–56], the variants of IN [57–59], the combinations of different normalization methods [60,61], a neural network-based normalization method [62], etc.

1.7 Open-source tools for deep learning

With the great successes of deep learning methods in different fields, the leading groups in deep learning have publicized their source codes, tools or even their deep models trained for some applications. Thanks to their great efforts, it is easy for those who are not familiar with deep models to build their own systems or methods. Here, we listed the most widely used tools for deep learning along with their features.

- Tensorflow[3] is an end-to-end open-source library for developing deep learning architectures. It provides many *built-in,* state-of-the-art, deep neural network architectures and recent optimization algorithms. GPU acceleration is further adaptable without any code modification. In addition, it also offers the Tensorboard as an auxiliary tool that enables the user to visualize the graphical models of the networks and track the numerous metrics (i.e., losses, accuracies, etc.), which are beneficial for monitoring the training of the network.
- Keras[4] is another notably high-level open-source library for developing deep learning networks built upon several popular libraries, including the Tensorflow. As such, it brought over the capability and scalability of its lower libraries while providing user-friendly deep learning experimentations.
- PyTorch[5] is a computing framework with wide support for machine learning algorithms. It allows to use of GPUs and to build neural networks and train it with efficient optimization techniques.
- MXNet[6] is an open-source deep learning framework that supports a distributed system among multiple GPUs, sponsored by Apache Incubator. It can be integrated into various programming languages, e.g., Python, C++, Java, Matlab®, R, etc.

References

[1] F. Rosenblatt, The perceptron: a probabilistic model for information storage and organization in the brain, Psychological Review (1958) 65–386.
[2] V. Nair, G.E. Hinton, Rectified linear units improve restricted Boltzmann machines, in: International Conference on Machine Learning, 2010, pp. 807–814.
[3] B. Xu, N. Wang, T. Chen, M. Li, Empirical evaluation of rectified activations in convolutional network, arXiv preprint, arXiv:1505.00853, 2015.
[4] D. Clevert, T. Unterthiner, S. Hochreiter, Fast and accurate deep network learning by exponential linear units (elus), in: International Conference on Learning Representations, 2016, pp. 1–14.
[5] P. Ramachandran, B. Zoph, Q.V. Le, Searching for activation functions, in: International Conference on Learning Representations, 2018, pp. 1–13.

---

[3] https://www.tensorflow.org/.
[4] https://keras.io/.
[5] https://pytorch.org/.
[6] https://mxnet.apache.org/.

[6] D.E. Rumelhart, G.E. Hinton, R.J. Williams, Learning representations by back-propagating errors, Nature 323 (6088) (1986) 533–536.

[7] G. Montavon, G. Orr, K.-R. Müller, Neural Networks: Tricks of the Trade, vol. 7700, Springer, 2012.

[8] M. Li, T. Zhang, Y. Chen, A.J. Smola, Efficient mini-batch training for stochastic optimization, in: International Conference on Knowledge Discovery and Data Mining, 2014, pp. 661–670.

[9] K. He, X. Zhang, S. Ren, J. Sun, Deep residual learning for image recognition, in: IEEE Conference on Computer Vision and Pattern Recognition, 2016, pp. 770–778.

[10] G. Huang, Z. Liu, L. Van Der Maaten, K.Q. Weinberger, Denscly connected convolutional networks, in: IEEE Conference on Computer Vision and Pattern Recognition, 2017, pp. 4700–4708.

[11] C. Szegedy, W. Liu, Y. Jia, P. Sermanet, S. Reed, D. Anguelov, D. Erhan, V. Vanhoucke, A. Rabinovich, Going deeper with convolutions, in: IEEE Conference on Computer Vision and Pattern Recognition, 2015, pp. 1–9.

[12] C. Szegedy, V. Vanhoucke, S. Ioffe, J. Shlens, Z. Wojna, Rethinking the inception architecture for computer vision, in: IEEE Conference on Computer Vision and Pattern Recognition, 2016, pp. 2818–2826.

[13] C. Szegedy, S. Ioffe, V. Vanhoucke, A.A. Alemi, Inception-v4, inception-resnet and the impact of residual connections on learning, in: S.P. Singh, S. Markovitch (Eds.), AAAI Conference on Artificial Intelligence, 2017, pp. 4278–4284.

[14] K. Xu, J. Ba, R. Kiros, K. Cho, A. Courville, R. Salakhudinov, R. Zemel, Y. Bengio, Show, attend and tell: neural image caption generation with visual attention, in: International Conference on Machine Learning, 2015, pp. 2048–2057.

[15] T. Luong, H. Pham, C.D. Manning, Effective approaches to attention-based neural machine translation, in: Conference on Empirical Methods in Natural Language Processing, 2015, pp. 1412–1421.

[16] J. Serra, D. Suris, M. Miron, A. Karatzoglou, Overcoming catastrophic forgetting with hard attention to the task, in: International Conference on Machine Learning, 2018, pp. 4548–4557.

[17] A. Vaswani, N. Shazeer, N. Parmar, J. Uszkoreit, L. Jones, A.N. Gomez, Ł. Kaiser, I. Polosukhin, Attention is all you need, in: Advances in Neural Information Processing Systems, 2017, pp. 5998–6008.

[18] D. Linsley, D. Shiebler, S. Eberhardt, T. Serre, Learning what and where to attend, in: International Conference on Learning Representations, 2018, pp. 1–21.

[19] J. Hu, L. Shen, G. Sun, Squeeze-and-excitation networks, in: IEEE Conference on Computer Vision and Pattern Recognition, 2018, pp. 7132–7141.

[20] S. Wiegreffe, Y. Pinter, Attention is not not explanation, in: Conference on Empirical Methods in Natural Language Processing and the International Joint Conference on Natural Language Processing, 2019, pp. 11–20.

[21] P. Werbos, Backpropagation through time: what it does and how to do it, Proceedings of the IEEE 78 (10) (1990) 1550–1560.

[22] S. Hochreiter, The vanishing gradient problem during learning recurrent neural nets and problem solutions, International Journal of Uncertainty, Fuzziness and Knowledge-Based Systems 06 (02) (1998) 107–116.

[23] S. Hochreiter, J. Schmidhuber, Long short-term memory, Neural Computation 9 (8) (1997) 1735–1780.

[24] F. Gers, J. Schmidhuber, Recurrent nets that time and count, in: IEEE-INNS-ENNS International Joint Conference on Neural Networks, 2000, pp. 189–194.

[25] K. Cho, B. van Merrienboer, Ç. Gülçehre, D. Bahdanau, F. Bougares, H. Schwenk, Y. Bengio, Learning phrase representations using RNN encoder-decoder for statistical machine translation, in: Conference on Empirical Methods in Natural Language Processing, 2014, pp. 1724–1734.

[26] G.E. Hinton, R.R. Salakhutdinov, Reducing the dimensionality of data with neural networks, Science 313 (5786) (2006) 504–507.

[27] G.E. Hinton, Training products of experts by minimizing contrastive divergence, Neural Computation 14 (8) (2002) 1771–1800.

[28] G. Hinton, P. Dayan, B. Frey, R. Neal, The wake-sleep algorithm for unsupervised neural networks, Science 268 (5214) (1995) 1158–1161.

[29] H. Larochelle, Y. Bengio, Classification using discriminative restricted Boltzmann machines, in: International Conference on Machine Learning, 2008, pp. 536–543.

[30] H. Lee, C. Ekanadham, A. Ng, Sparse deep belief net model for visual area v2, in: Advances in Neural Information Processing Systems, 2008, pp. 873–880.

[31] H. Larochelle, Y. Bengio, J. Louradour, P. Lamblin, Exploring strategies for training deep neural networks, Journal of Machine Learning Research 10 (2009) 1–40.

[32] H.-C. Shin, M.R. Orton, D.J. Collins, S.J. Doran, M.O. Leach, Stacked autoencoders for unsupervised feature learning and multiple organ detection in a pilot study using 4D patient data, IEEE Transactions on Pattern Analysis and Machine Intelligence 35 (8) (2013) 1930–1943.

[33] D.P. Kingma, M. Welling, Auto-encoding variational Bayes, in: International Conference on Learning Representations, 2014, pp. 1–14.

[34] I. Goodfellow, J. Pouget-Abadie, M. Mirza, B. Xu, D. Warde-Farley, S. Ozair, A. Courville, Y. Bengio, Generative adversarial nets, in: Advances in Neural Information Processing Systems, 2014, pp. 2672–2680.

[35] X. Mao, Q. Li, H. Xie, R.Y. Lau, Z. Wang, S. Paul Smolley, Least squares generative adversarial networks, in: IEEE International Conference on Computer Vision, 2017, pp. 2794–2802.

[36] M. Arjovsky, S. Chintala, L. Bottou, Wasserstein generative adversarial networks, in: International Conference on Machine Learning, 2017, pp. 214–223.

[37] I. Gulrajani, F. Ahmed, M. Arjovsky, V. Dumoulin, A.C. Courville, Improved training of Wasserstein gans, in: Advances in Neural Information Processing Systems, 2017, pp. 5767–5777.

[38] Y. LeCun, L. Bottou, G.B. Orr, K.R. Müller, Efficient BackProp, in: Neural Networks: Tricks of the Trade, Springer Berlin Heidelberg, Berlin, Heidelberg, 1998, pp. 9–50.

[39] S. Wiesler, H. Ney, A convergence analysis of log-linear training, in: J. Shawe-taylor, R. Zemel, P. Bartlett, F. Pereira, K. Weinberger (Eds.), Advances in Neural Information Processing Systems, 2011, pp. 657–665.

[40] Y. Bengio, P. Lamblin, D. Popovici, H. Larochelle, Greedy layer-wise training of deep networks, in: Advances in Neural Information Processing Systems, 2007, pp. 153–160.

[41] C.M. Bishop, Neural Networks for Pattern Recognition, Oxford University Press, 1995.

[42] I. Sutskever, J. Martens, G. Dahl, G. Hinton, On the importance of initialization and momentum in deep learning, in: International Conference on Machine Learning, 2013, pp. 1139–1147.

[43] J. Duchi, E. Hazan, Y. Singer, Adaptive subgradient methods for online learning and stochastic optimization, Journal of Machine Learning Research 12 (7) (2011).

[44] S. Ruder, An overview of gradient descent optimization algorithms, arXiv preprint, arXiv:1609.04747, 2016.

[45] D.P. Kingma, J. Ba, Adam: a method for stochastic optimization, in: International Conference on Learning Representations, 2015, pp. 1–15.

[46] A.E. Hoerl, R.W. Kennard, Ridge regression: biased estimation for nonorthogonal problems, Technometrics 12 (1) (1970) 55–67.

[47] R. Tibshirani, Regression shrinkage and selection via the lasso, Journal of the Royal Statistical Society 58 (1) (1996) 267–288.

[48] H. Zou, T. Hastie, Regularization and variable selection via the elastic net, Journal of the Royal Statistical Society 67 (2) (2005) 301–320.

[49] N. Srivastava, G. Hinton, A. Krizhevsky, I. Sutskever, R. Salakhutdinov, Dropout: a simple way to prevent neural networks from overfitting, Journal of Machine Learning Research 15 (1) (2014) 1929–1958.

[50] S. Ioffe, C. Szegedy, Batch normalization: accelerating deep network training by reducing internal covariate shift, in: International Conference on Machine Learning, 2015, pp. 448–456.

[51] J.L. Ba, J.R. Kiros, G.E. Hinton, Layer normalization, arXiv preprint, arXiv:1607.06450, 2016.

[52] D. Ulyanov, A. Vedaldi, V. Lempitsky, Instance normalization: the missing ingredient for fast stylization, arXiv preprint, arXiv:1607.08022, 2016.

[53] Y. Wu, K. He, Group normalization, in: European Conference on Computer Vision, 2018, pp. 3–19.

[54] H. de Vries, F. Strub, J. Mary, H. Larochelle, O. Pietquin, A.C. Courville, Modulating early visual processing by language, in: Advances in Neural Information Processing Systems, 2017, pp. 6594–6604.

[55] S. Ioffe, Batch renormalization: towards reducing minibatch dependence in batch-normalized models, in: Advances in Neural Information Processing Systems, 2017, pp. 1945–1953.

[56] S.-H. Gao, Q. Han, D. Li, M.-M. Cheng, P. Peng, Representative batch normalization with feature calibration, in: IEEE Conference on Computer Vision and Pattern Recognition, 2021, pp. 8669–8679.

[57] V. Dumoulin, J. Shlens, M. Kudlur, A learned representation for artistic style, in: International Conference on Learning Representations, 2017, pp. 1–26.

[58] X. Huang, S. Belongie, Arbitrary style transfer in real-time with adaptive instance normalization, in: IEEE International Conference on Computer Vision, 2017, pp. 1501–1510.

[59] Y. Jing, X. Liu, Y. Ding, X. Wang, E. Ding, M. Song, S. Wen, Dynamic instance normalization for arbitrary style transfer, in: AAAI Conference on Artificial Intelligence, vol. 34, 2020, pp. 4369–4376.

[60] H. Nam, H.-E. Kim, Batch-instance normalization for adaptively style-invariant neural networks, in: Advances in Neural Information Processing Systems, 2018, pp. 2563–2572.

[61] P. Luo, R. Zhang, J. Ren, Z. Peng, J. Li, Switchable normalization for learning-to-normalize deep representation, IEEE Transactions on Pattern Analysis and Machine Intelligence 43 (2) (2019) 712–728.

[62] R. Zhang, Z. Peng, L. Wu, Z. Li, P. Luo, Exemplar normalization for learning deep representation, in: IEEE Conference on Computer Vision and Pattern Recognition, 2020, pp. 12726–12735.

Deep reinforcement learning in medical imaging

S. Kevin Zhou and Qiyuan Wang

University of Science and Technology of China (USTC), Hefei, China

2.1 Introduction

Reinforcement learning (RL) is a framework for learning a sequence of actions that maximizes the expected reward [50,88]. Deep reinforcement learning (DRL) is the result of marrying deep learning with reinforcement learning [66]. DRL allows reinforcement learning to scale up to previously intractable problems. Deep learning and reinforcement learning were selected by MIT Technology Review as one of the 10 Breakthrough Technologies[1] in 2013 and 2017, respectively. The combination of these two powerful technologies currently constitutes one of the state-of-the-art frameworks in artificial intelligence.

Recent years have witnessed rapid progress in DRL, resulting in significant performance improvement in many areas, including games [66], robotics [19], natural language processing [60] and computer vision [9]. Unlike supervised learning, DRL framework can deal with sequential decisions, and learn with highly delayed supervised information (e.g., the success or failure of a decision is available only after multiple timesteps). Since the DRL agent's decisions affect the world state, one cannot propagate the gradient from the reward to past actions without explicitly modeling the joint distribution between decisions and the world state. Traditional supervised learning lacks this explicit modeling, thus is not effective in learning with sequential actions and delayed rewards. DRL can also deal with *nondifferentiable metrics*. For example, one can use DRL to search for an optimal deep network architecture [117] or parameter settings to maximize the classification accuracy, which is clearly nondifferentiable with respect to the number of layers or the choice of nonlinear rectifier functions. However, DRL is not the only viable approach for network architecture search (NAS); in [56], network architecture is sought using supervised learning. Another use of DRL is in finding efficient search sequence for speeding up detection [25] or optimal transformation sequence for improving registration accuracy. DRL can also mitigate the issue of high memory consumption in processing high-dimensional

---

[1] https://www.technologyreview.com/10-breakthrough-technologies/.

medical images. For example, a DRL-based object detection can focus on a small image region at a time, which incurs a lower memory footprint, then decide next regions to process.

Despite its successes, application of this DRL technology to medical imaging remains to be fully explored [115]. This is partly due to the lack of a systematic understanding of the DRL's strengths or weaknesses when it is applied to medical data. Our goal here is to provide our readers good knowledge about of the principle of DRL and a thorough coverage of the latest examples of how DRL is used for solving medical imaging tasks. We structure the rest of paper as follows: (i) introduction to deep reinforcement learning with its generation framework and latest learning strategies; (ii) how to use DRL for solving medical image analysis tasks, which is the main part that covers the literature review; (iii) fundamental challenges and future potential of DRL in medical domains and (iv) conclusions.

There are a few DRL survey papers such as [5,20,50]. However, they cover basic principles and various applications of DRL. Our survey centers around the essential topic of DRL in medical imaging and marginally in healthcare applications.

2.2 Basics of reinforcement learning

Here, we focus on how the RL problem can be formalized as an agent that is able to make decisions in an environment to optimize some objectives. Key aspects of RL include: (i) Addressing the sequential decision making; (ii) There is no supervisor, and only a reward presented as a scalar number; and (iii) Feedback is highly delayed. The interaction between agent and environment is illustrated in Fig. 2.1. The standard theory of RL is defined by a Markov Decision Process (MDP), in which rewards depend on the last state and action only. However, most of real-world decision-making is based on a non-Markovian model, in which the next state depends on more than the current state and action. This work only focuses on MDP; the readers can learn more of the recent research on non-MDP in [14], [22], [63] with different aspects discussed, e.g., non-MDP using Spiking Neural Networks (SNNs), Non-Markovian Rewards and Q-learning convergence for non-MDP.

2.2.1 Markov decision process

An MDP is typically defined by five elements $\{S, A, T, R, \gamma\}$, where S is a set of *state/observation* space of an environment and s_0 is a starting state; A is a set of *actions* the agent can choose from; T is a *transition probability* function $T(s_{t+1}|s_t, a_t)$, specifying the probability that the environment transitions to state $s_{t+1} \in S$ if the agent takes action $a \in \mathcal{A}$ in state $s_t \in S$; R is a *reward* function where $r_{t+1} = R(s_t, s_{t+1})$ is a reward received for taking action a_t at state s_t and transfer to the next state s_{t+1}; $\gamma \in [0, 1]$ is a discount factor that determines how much an agent cares about rewards in the future. A full sequence $(s_0, a_0, r_1, s_1, a_1, r_2, ...)$ is called a *trajectory* $\mathcal{T}$. Theoretically, a trajectory goes to infinity, but the episodic

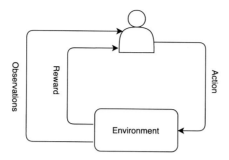

FIGURE 2.1

An schematic illustration of the interaction between agent and environment in RL.

property holds in most practical cases. One trajectory of some finite length τ is called an *episode*.

In order to estimate how good it is for an agent to utilize a policy π to visit a state s, a value function is introduced. The value is the mathematical expectation of return and value approximation is obtained by Bellman expectation equation as follows:

$$V^{\pi}(s_t) = \mathbb{E}[r_{t+1} + \gamma V^{\pi}(s_{t+1})]. \tag{2.1}$$

$V^{\pi}(s_t)$ is also known as the *state-value function* as it evaluates the value of a state s at time step t, and the expectation term can be expanded as a product of policy, transition probability and return as follows:

$$V^{\pi}(s_t) = \sum_{a_t \in A} \pi(a_t | s_t) \sum_{s_{t+1} \in S} T(s_{t+1} | s_t, a_t)[R(s_t, s_{t+1}) + \gamma V^{\pi}(s_{t+1})]. \tag{2.2}$$

This Eq. (2.2) is called a Bellman equation [23,44,50]. The goal of an MDP problem is to compute an optimal policy π^* such that $V^{\pi^*}(s) > V^{\pi}(s)$ for every policy π and every state $s \in S$. To represent the optimal value of each state-action, Q-value is defined as

$$Q^{\pi^*}(s_t, a_t) = \sum_{s_{t+1}} T(s_{t+1} | s_t, a_t)[R(s_t, s_{t+1}) + \gamma V^{\pi^*}(s_{t+1})]. \tag{2.3}$$

Many solution techniques are available to compute an optimal policy for a given MDP. Recently, DRL merging RL with Deep Learning (DL) has been proposed and developed rapidly. Thanks to the rich context representation of DL, DRL that expresses value and policy by a neural network can deal with high-dimensional continuous data [45,64]. In general, these techniques can be divided into model-free and model-based methods, depending on whether an explicit model is constructed or not. Here, "model" refers to the environment itself that is defined by the two quantities: transition probability function $T(s_{t+1} | s_t, a_t)$ and reward function $R(s_t, s_{t+1})$. The comparison between model-based RL and model-free RL is given in Table 2.1. In this table, we compare different factors that invoke the effectiveness of an RL method where it is model-based or model-free.

Table 2.1 Comparison between model-based RL and model-free RL.

Factors	Model-based RL	Model-free RL
# of iterations between agent & environment	Small	Big
Convergence	Fast	Slow
Prior knowledge of transitions	Yes	No
Flexibility	Strongly depends on a learned model	Adjusts based on trials and errors

2.2.2 Model-free methods

A model-free method tries to estimate the transition probability function and the reward function from the experiences to exploit them in acquisition of policy. There are three approaches, namely, value-based methods, policy gradient methods and actor-critic methods to implement model-free algorithms.

2.2.2.1 Policy gradient methods

In this approach, RL task is considered as optimization with stochastic first-order optimization. Policy gradient methods directly optimize the discounted expected reward to obtain the optimal policy π^* without any additional information about MDP. In general, this approach optimizes the following objective function, which is defined as a function of θ:

$$G(\theta) = \mathbb{E}_{\mathcal{T} \sim \pi_\theta} \sum_{t=1} \gamma^{t-1} R(s_{t-1}, s_t) \to \max_\theta . \tag{2.4}$$

For any MDP and differentiable policy π_θ, the gradient of objective Eq. (2.4) is defined by policy gradient theorem [89] as follows:

$$\nabla_\theta G(\theta) = \mathbb{E}_{\mathcal{T} \sim \pi_\theta} \sum_{t=0} \gamma^t Q^\pi(s_t, a_t) \nabla_\theta \log \pi_\theta(a_t | s_t). \tag{2.5}$$

2.2.2.2 Value-based methods

In this approach, the optimal policy π^* is implicitly conducted by gaining an approximation of optimal Q-function $Q^*(s, a)$. In value-based methods, the agent updates the value function to learn a suitable policy while the policy-based RL agent learns the policy directly. Q-learning is a typical value-based method. The updating rule of Q-learning with a learning rate λ is defined as

$$Q(s_t, a_t) = Q(s_t, a_t) + \lambda \delta_t, \tag{2.6}$$

where $\delta_t = R(s_t, s_{t+1}) + \gamma [\max_a Q(s_{t+1}, a)] - Q(s_t, a)$ is the temporal difference (TD) error.

DQN [67] extends deep neural networks to Q-learning and is the most famous DRL model, which learns policies directly from high-dimensional inputs as given in Fig. 2.2(a). In general, DQN stabilizes the learning of Q-function by experience replay and the frozen target network. In experience replay, the agent's experiences at each time step are stored in a replay buffer (a fixed-size data set) and the Q-network is updated by SGD with samples from a mini-batch. Compared to standard online Q-learning, experience replay aims to avoid divergence, remove sample correlations, and improve data efficiency. However, replay buffer does not differentiate important transitions. Target network addresses this limitation by proposing another network during Q-learning update process.

Taking the regression problem as an instance and letting y denote the target of our regression task, the regression with input (s, a), target $y(s, a)$ and the MSE loss function. The output y and MSE loss are defined as in Eq. (2.7):

$$y(s_t, a_t) = R(s_t, s_{t+1}) + \gamma \max_{a_{t+1}} Q^*(s_{t_1}, a_{t+1}, \theta_t);$$
$$\mathcal{L}^{DQN} = \mathcal{L}(y(s_t, a_t), Q^*(s_t, a_t, \theta_t)) = ||y(s_t, a_t) - Q^*(s_t, a_t, \theta_t)||^2; \tag{2.7}$$

where $\theta \in \mathbb{R}^{|S||R|}$ is vector of parameters and s_{t+1} is a sample from $T(s_{t+1}|s_t, a_t)$ with input of (s_t, a_t). Q^* is Q-value under the optimal policy π^*.

Minimizing the loss function yields a gradient descent step formula to update θ as follows:

$$\theta_{t+1} = \theta_t - \alpha_t \frac{\partial \mathcal{L}^{DQN}}{\partial \theta}, \tag{2.8}$$

where α_t is a learning rate.

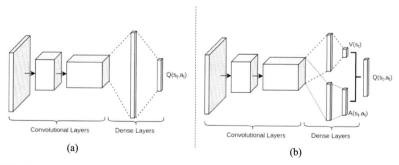

(a)   (b)

FIGURE 2.2

(a): Network structure of Deep Q-Network (DQN), where Q-values Q(s,a) are generated for all actions for a given state. (b): Network structure of dueling DQN, where value function $V(s)$ and advantage function $A(s, a)$ are combined to predict Q-values $Q(s, a)$ for all actions for a given state.

Recently, different variants have been proposed to deal with the limitations of DQN. Double DQN is an improvement of DQN by combining double Q-learning [28] with DQN to reduce observed overestimations with better performance. To address the incorrect updating of Q^* for unfavorable state, Wang et al. [99] incorporate the approximation of V^* explicitly in computational graph by introducing an advantage function. Deep Recurrent Q-Network (DRQN) [27] employs RNN into DQN by replacing the first fully-connected layer with an RNN to address the limitation of memory and imperfect information at each decision point. Multi-step DQN [17] is one of the most popular improvements of DQN by substituting one-step approximation with N-steps. See Fig. 2.3.

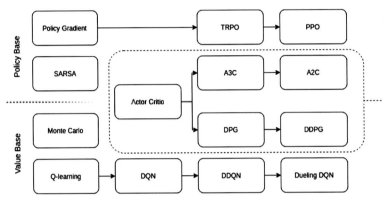

FIGURE 2.3

A roadmap of model-free reinforcement learning algorithms.

2.2.2.3 Actor-critic methods

Compared with value-based methods, policy gradient methods are better for continuous and stochastic environments and have a faster convergence [45,71]. However, value-based methods are more sample efficient and steady [58,68]. Lately, actor-critics [41] [65] is invented to address the aforementioned limitations. Actor-critic architecture computes the policy gradient using a value-based critic function to estimate expected future reward. The principal idea of actor-critics is to divide the model into two parts: (i) computing an action based on a state and (ii) producing the Q value of the action. As given in Fig. 2.4, the actor takes as input the state s_t and outputs the best action a_t. It essentially controls how the agent behaves by learning the optimal policy (policy-based). The critic, on the other hand, evaluates the action by computing the value function (value-based). The most basic actor-critic method (beyond the tabular case) is naive policy gradients (REINFORCE). Actor-critic is an improvement of policy gradient with a value-based critic Γ and is rewritten as

$$\mathcal{G}^\theta(\pi) = \mathbb{E}_{\mathcal{T}_\tau} \sum_{t=0} log(\pi_\theta(a_t|s_t))\gamma^t \Gamma_t. \tag{2.9}$$

The critic function Γ can be defined as $Q^{\pi}(s_t, a_t)$ or $Q^{\pi}(s_t, a_t) - V_t^{\pi}$ or $R[s_{t-1}, s_t] + V_{t+1}^{\pi} - V_t^{\pi}$.

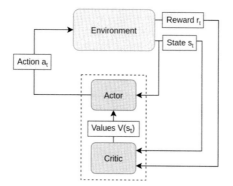

FIGURE 2.4

The flow chart shows the structure of actor critic algorithm with action a, state s and reward r.

Advantage actor-critic (A2C) [65], one of the most famous Actor-critic methods, consists of two neural networks, i.e., an actor network $\pi_\theta(a_t|s_t)$ representing for policy and a critic network V_θ^{π} with parameters θ approximately estimating actor's performance. At time t, the A2C algorithm can be implemented as the following steps:

- Step 1: Compute advantage function:

$$A^{\pi}(s_t, a_t) = R(s_t, s_{t+1}) + \gamma V_\theta^{\pi}(s_{t+1}) - V_\theta^{\pi}(s_t) \qquad (2.10)$$

- Step 2: Compute target value:

$$y = R(s_t, s_{t+1}) + \gamma V_\theta^{\pi}(s_{t+1}) \qquad (2.11)$$

- Step 3: Compute critic loss with MSE loss:

$$\mathcal{L} = \frac{1}{B} \sum_T ||y - V^{\pi}(s_t))||^2, \qquad (2.12)$$

where B is batch size and $V^{\pi}(s_t)$ is defined by

$$V^{\pi}(s_t) = \mathbb{E}_{a_t \sim \pi(a_t|s_t)} \mathbb{E}_{s_{t+1} \sim T(s_{t+1}|a_t, s_t)}(R(s_t, s_{t+1}) + \gamma V^{\pi}(s_{t+1})) \qquad (2.13)$$

- Step 4: Compute critic gradient:

$$\nabla^{critic} = \frac{\partial \mathcal{L}}{\partial \theta} \qquad (2.14)$$

- Step 5: Compute actor gradient:

$$\nabla^{actor} = \frac{1}{B}\sum_T \nabla_\theta \log \pi\, (a_t|s_t) A^\pi\,(s_t, a_t) \qquad (2.15)$$

Besides A2C, asynchronous advantage actor critic (A3C) [65] is another strategy to implement an actor critic agent. Compared with A2C, A3C that asynchronously executes different agents in parallel on multiple instances of the environment shows more memory efficiency. In order to overcome the limitation of speed, Babaeizadeh et al. [6] propose GA3C that achieves a significant speed up compared to the original CPU implementation.

2.2.3 Model-based methods

2.2.3.1 Value function

The objective of value function methods is to obtain the best policy by maximizing the value functions in each state. DQN [67] that has been successfully applied to classic Atari and illustrated in Fig. 2.2 uses CNNs to deal with high-dimensional state space to approximate the Q-value function.

Monte Carlo Tree Search (MCTS) [16] is one of the most popular methods with look-ahead search and is combined with the DNN-based transition model to build a model-based DRL [3]. In this work, the learned transition model predicts the next frame and rewards one step ahead using the input of the last four frames of the agent's first-person-view image and the current action. This model is then used by the MCTS algorithm to plan the best sequence of actions for the agent to perform.

Jia et al. [37] propose model-based DRL, Value-Targeted Regression (VTR), for regret minimization. In their work, a set of models that are "consistent" with the data collected is constructed at each episode. The consistency is defined as the total squared error, whereas the value function is determined by solving the optimistic planning problem with the constructed set of models.

2.2.3.2 Policy search

Policy search methods aim to directly find policies by means of gradient-free or gradient-based methods. Model-ensemble trust-region policy optimization (ME-TRPO) [43] is mainly based on trust region policy optimization (TRPO) [82], which imposes a trust region constraint on the policy to further stabilize learning.

Model-based meta-policy optimization (MB-MPO) [15] addresses the performance limitation of model-based DRL compared against model-free DRL when learning dynamics models. MB-MPO learns an ensemble of dynamics models and forms a policy that can quickly adapt to any model in the ensemble with one policy gradient step. As a result, the learned policy exhibits less model-bias without the need to behave conservatively.

A summary of both model-based and model-free DRL algorithms is given in Table 2.2. In this table, we also categorize DRL techniques into either on-policy or

Table 2.2 Summary of model-based and model-free DRL algorithms consisting of value-based and policy gradient methods.

DRL Algorithms	Description	Category
DQN [67]	Deep Q Network	Value-based, Off-policy
Double DQN [93]	Double Deep Q Network	Value-based, Off-policy
Dueling DQN [99]	Dueling Deep Q Network	Value-based, Off-policy
MCTS [3]	Monte Carlo tree search	Valued-based, On-Policy
UCRL-VTR [37]	optimistic planning problem	Valued-based, On-Policy
DDPG [55]	DQN with Deterministic Policy Gradient	Policy gradient, Off-policy
TRPO [82]	Trust Region Policy Optimization	Policy gradient, On-policy
PPO [83]	Proximal Policy Optimization	Policy gradient, On-policy
ME-TRPO [43]	Model-Ensemble Trust-Region Policy Optimization	Policy gradient, On-policy
MB-MPO [15]	Model-Based Meta-Policy Optimization	Policy gradient, On-policy
A3C [65]	Asynchronous Advantage Actor Critic	Actor Critic, On-Policy
A2C [65]	Advantage Actor Critic	Actor Critic, On-Policy

off-policy. In on-policy RL, the policy π^k is updated with data collected by π^k itself. In off-policy RL, each policy has its own data collection; then the data collected from π^0, π^1, ..., π^k is used to trained π^{k+1}.

2.3 **DRL in medical imaging**

We find that DRL finds its use in at least three scenarios. (i) DRL is commonly used for parametric medical image analysis tasks such as landmark detection, image registration and view plane localization. Compared with traditional supervised learning, formulating these tasks under the DRL framework offers several compelling benefits. First, DRL methods process only a small number of image locations instead of performing an exhaustive search over the hypothesis space, making them computationally efficient. Second, sequential processing of small image regions drastically reduces the memory footprint. Third, the DRL formulation can optimally balance time efficiency and accuracy in a principled manner. Finally, DRL's sequential visual search is consistent with the cascade and fixation mechanisms in biological systems, potentially giving rise to more robust features. (ii) DRL also finds its use in other optimization tasks such as hyper-parameter tuning, image augmentation selection, neural architecture search, etc., most of which share a common theme of nondifferential optimization. Exhaustive grid search for these tasks is time consuming and DRL is used to learn an efficient search policy. (iii) Finally, DRL is used in several miscellaneous topics such as surgical gesture categorization. Figs. 2.5, 2.7 and 2.8 contain a list of selected papers. The selection is made among publications in top journals and conferences up to mid-2022. The list is by no means exhaustive. For each reference, we also provide the task with its concerned image modality and anatomy and offer some

FIGURE 2.5

The literature of parametric medical image analysis.

remarks when appropriate. Fig. 2.6 shows the number of DRL papers published every year, which clearly indicates a growing trend. In most of the listed papers, model-free learning algorithms are used.

Below, we provide a thorough survey of DRL approaches in the first and second scenarios.

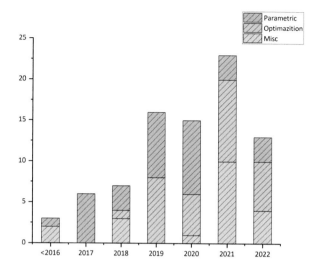

FIGURE 2.6

The number of DRL papers in medical imaging published. The papers are organized into three categories: parametric medical image analysis ("Parametric"), solving optimization in medical imaging ("Optimization") and miscellaneous topics ("Misc").

2.3.1 DRL for parametric medical image analysis

In many medical image analysis tasks, there are model parameters $\xi = [\xi_1, \xi_2, \ldots, \xi_n]$ to be estimated, given an image I. Table 2.3 exhibits a collection of common tasks and their associated model parameters. Currently, most model parameters are low-dimensional.

Table 2.3 Common medical image analysis tasks and their associated model parameters. x, y, z are for translation, α, β, γ for rotation, s for scaling and $[a, b, c, d]$ for depicting a plane.

Task	Parameters
2D landmark detection	$\xi = [x, y]$
3D landmark detection	$\xi = [x, y, z]$
Rigid 2D object detection	$\xi = [x, y, \alpha, s]$
Rigid 3D object detection	$\xi = [x, y, z, \alpha, \beta, \gamma, s]$
Rigid 2D/3D registration	$\xi = [x, y, z, \alpha, \beta, \gamma]$
View plane localization in 3D	$\xi = [a, b, c, d]$
Others	ξ depends on the task

Below we first present a general DRL formulation for parametric medical image analysis and then proceed to cover each analysis task in a separate subsection.

FIGURE 2.7

The literature of solving optimization using DRL.

2.3.1.1 Formulation

To formulate a problem into the DRL framework, we have to define three key elements of DRL.

Action. An action $a \in A$, where A is the action space, is what the agent takes to interact with the environment, which is the image I.

One way of defining an action is to move each parameter, say the ith parameter, independently by $\pm \delta \xi_i$ while keeping the other parameters the same. The action space A is given by

$$A = \{\pm \delta \xi_1, \pm \delta \xi_2, \ldots, \pm \delta \xi_n\}. \tag{2.16}$$

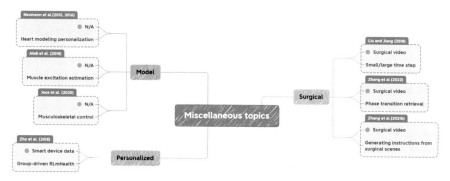

FIGURE 2.8

The literature of miscellaneous topics.

With this definition, the cardinality of the action space is $|A| = 2n$.

The action space should be specified to guarantee the reachability, that is, starting an initial guess ξ^0, it is possible to reach an arbitrarily-valued parameter, say $\hat{\xi} = [\hat{\xi}_1, \hat{\xi}_2, \ldots, \hat{\xi}_n]$. With the above definition, the reachability is trivially guaranteed, up to quantization error, by taking a series of actions: simply accumulating multiple steps of $\pm\delta\xi_i$ to move the ith parameter by an amount of $\hat{\xi}_i - \xi_i^0$, and repeating this for each of the dimensions.

State. The state is in regard to both the environment and the agent after all actions are taken so far.

Using the action space defined in (2.16), the agent is at its state ξ_t after taking an action a_t:

$$\xi_t = \xi_{t-1} + a_t = \xi_0 + \sum_{i=1}^{t} a_i. \tag{2.17}$$

Note that the state of the environment is often chosen as an image (or image patch) "centered" at ξ_t denoted by $I[\xi_t]$. Other noncentered design choices are possible, too.

Reward. In general, the reward function should provide incentive signals when the target is hit or closer and penalize signals otherwise. Designing reward functions for reinforcement learning models is not easy. One design method is called inverse RL [1] or "apprenticeship learning," which learns a reward function that reproduces observed behaviors.

A commonly used reward function is given as below:

$$R(s_t, s_{t-1}, a_t) = D(\xi_{t-1}, \hat{\xi}) - D(\xi_t, \hat{\xi}), \tag{2.18}$$

where $D(\xi_1, \xi_2)$ is a distance function that measures the difference between ξ_1 and ξ_2. If certain action reduces the difference, then a positive reward is obtained; otherwise, a negative reward is obtained.

To further intensify the effect of reward especially when the change in the difference is small, one can use

$$R'(s_t, s_{t-1}, a_t) = sgn(R(s_t, s_{t-1}, a_t)), \tag{2.19}$$

where $sgn(x)$ takes the sign of the value x. So, if certain action reduces the difference, then a positive reward $+1$ is obtained; otherwise, a negative reward -1 is obtained.

Once we have these three elements, we can invoke the DQL algorithm to trigger the learning process. Once the Q-function is learned, we can choose the action that maximizes the Q-function at each iteration.

It is clear that the search trajectory (or path) is implicitly related to the three elements. An alternative is to make the path explicit, that is, path supervision [53,102]. One path supervision approach is to guide the selection of the action that maximizes the reward in a greedy fashion for every iteration.

2.3.1.2 Landmark detection

Medical landmarks are commonly used to represent distinct points in an image that likely coincide with anatomical structures. In clinical practices, landmarks play important roles in interpreting and navigating the image. Also, landmarks are used to derive measurements (e.g., width, length and size) of organs [102], and to trigger subsequent, computationally intensive medical image analysis applications.

Artificial agent. In a series of papers, Ghesu et al. [24–26] present a multi-scale approach for detecting anatomical landmarks in a 3D volume using an artificial agent. The landmark is represented as a 3D point and the actions include moving one-voxel step to the left, right, up, down, forward and back. The reward function is given by (2.18).

At each scale, a scale-specific Q-function is learned to enable the agent to effectively search for objects in the image. The search starts at the coarsest scale level, where the search model is trained for convergence from any starting point in the image. Upon convergence, the scale level is changed to the next level and the search continues. The process is repeated on the following scales until convergence on the finest scale. The convergence criterion is met when trajectories converge on small, oscillatory-like cycles.

In addition, the constrained spatial distribution of anatomical landmarks using statistical shape modeling and robust estimation theory [90] is used to offer a probabilistic guarantee on the spatial coherence of the identified landmarks and to recognize if there are landmarks missing from the field-of-view. This shape fitting further makes the detection of landmarks more robust.

The proposed method is tested on detecting a cohort of 49 landmarks in a complete data set of 5043 3D-CT scans over 2000 patients. When evaluating the detection performance, the landmarks 3 cm within the image border are ignored. This value is selected in agreement with our expert annotators. Perfect detection results with no false positives or negatives are reported.

Vlontzos et al. [94] consider the interdependence between multiple landmarks as they are associated with the human anatomy. It is likely that localizing one landmark helps detect the other landmarks. They propose to train a set of multiple collaborative agents using reinforcement learning in order to detect multiple landmarks, instead of a naive approach that learns many separate agents, one agent for each landmark. It is shown that the multi-agent RL achieves significantly better accuracy by reducing the detection error by 50% on detecting 7–14 landmarks for three tasks, consumes fewer computational resources, and reduces the training time, when compared with the naive approach.

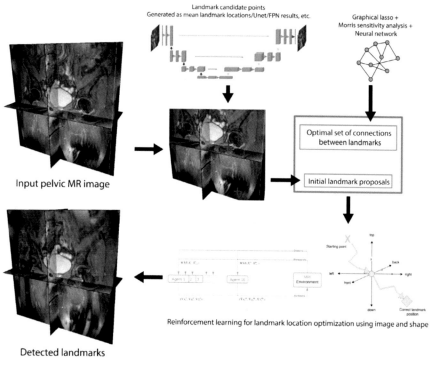

FIGURE 2.9

The summary of the proposed framework in [8].

Similarly, Bekkouch et al. [8] propose a novel framework based on multi-landmark environment analysis with reinforcement learning for automated hip abnormality detection from MR images. They merge the concepts of the graphical lasso and Morris sensitivity analysis with deep neural networks to quantitatively estimate the contribution of individual landmark and landmark subgroup locations to the other landmark locations. Fig. 2.9 illustrate the proposed framework of this paper, which is mainly composed of three main components. Specifically, it includes a segmentation neural network for detection of landmark proposals, a combination of graphical lasso, Morris sensitivity analysis and neural networks for identification of optimal connections between landmark and reinforcement learning for landmark position optimization using both landmark candidate points and connection-based shape model.

The framework was validated on a total of 337 T1-, T2- and proton density-weighted MR images of 260 patients with the aim to measure the lateral center-edge angle (LCEA), femoral neck-shaft angle (NSA), and the anterior and posterior acetabular sector angles (AASA and PASA) of the hip and derive the quantitative abnormality metrics from these angles. The resulting overall landmark detection error of 1.5 mm and angle measurement error of 1.4° indicates a superior performance in comparison to existing methods. Some visualization of landmarks detected by the proposed framework are displayed in Fig. 2.10.

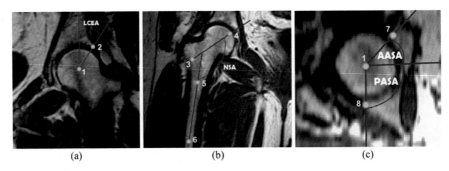

(a) (b) (c)

FIGURE 2.10

Illustration of all landmarks (green dots) automatically detected by [8]. The landmarks include (a, c) femoral head center, (a) lateral acetabular rim, (b) femoral shaft orientation (2 landmarks), (b) femoral neck orientation (2 landmarks), (c) anterior acetabular rim, (c) posterior acetabular rim. These eight landmarks are defined for each femur resulting in 16 landmarks in total. The landmarks are numbered to see correspondences. Illustrations of lateral center-edge (LCEA), femoral neck-shaft (NSA) and anterior and posterior acetabular sector angles (AASA, PASA) automatically detected and quantified by the framework.

Zhang et al. [111] incorporate priors on physical structure of the fetal body to optimize multi-agent for detection of fetal landmarks. In this work, they use graph communication layers to improve the communication among agents based on a graph where each node represents a fetal body landmark. The proposed network architecture contains two parts corresponding to shared CNNs for feature extraction and graph communication networks to merge the information of correlated landmarks. Furthermore, the distance between agents and physical structures such as the fetal limbs is used as a reward. The evaluation is conducted on 19,816 3D BOLD MRI volumes acquired on a 3T Skyra scanner. The proposed method achieves an average detection accuracy of 87.3% under a 10-mm threshold and 6.9 mm as the mean error. In [48], a communicative multi-agent reinforcement learning method is proposed for detecting landmarks in an adult MRI and fetal ultrasound brain image. The experiments demonstrate the use of multiple cooperating agents by learning their communication with each other outperforms previous approaches that are based on single agents.

Browning et al. [11] propose a novel method derived from the full-width-half-maxima of q-value probability distributions for estimating the uncertainty of a distributional deep q-learning (distDQN) landmark detection agent. They train two dist-DQN models targeting the locations of knee fibular styloid and intercondylar eminence of the tibia. The framework is validated on 1552 MR sequences (Sagittal PD, PDFS and T2FS) with an approximate 75%, 5%, 20% training, validation and test split. Errors for the two landmarks was 3.25 ± 0.12 mm and 3.06 ± 0.10 mm, respectively (mean $\pm$ standard error). Mean errors for the two landmarks are 28% lower than a nondistributional DQN baseline (3.16 ± 0.11 mm vs. 4.36 ± 0.27 mm). Besides, the dist-DQN derived uncertainty metric has an AUC of 0.91 for predicting out-of-distribution images. The methods illustrate the double benefit of improved error rate and the ability to defer reviews to experts.

Supervised action classification. Xu et al. [102] propose to approach landmark detection as image partitioning. This nontrivial approach is derived from path supervision. Consider an agent that seeks an optimal action path from any location at (x, y) toward a landmark $l = (\hat{x}, \hat{y})$, which is composed of optimal action steps at pixels along the path on an image grid Ω including a unit movement $d_x^{(a)} \in \{-1, 0, 1\}$ and $d_y^{(a)} \in \{-1, 0, 1\}$. The optimal action step $\hat{a}$ is selected as the one with minimal Euclidean distance to the landmark l after its associated movement. The selection of $\hat{a}$ falls into four regions (one for each action type). This generates a discrete action map $a(x, y)$ that represents the pixelwise optimal action step moving toward the target landmark location.

During training, a fully convolutional neural network, called a deep image-to-image network (DI2IN), can be employed to estimate the action map for a given image. During testing, an aggregate approach is proposed to derive the landmark location from the estimated action map. In experiments on detecting landmarks from a cardiac or obstetric ultrasound image in two data sets with 1353 and 1642 patients, respectively, it is demonstrated that the proposed approach achieves the best results when compared with then state-of-the-art approaches that include the artificial agent.

2.3.1.3 Image registration

Robust image registration in medical imaging is essential for the comparison or fusion of images, acquired from various perspectives, in different modalities or at different times. In terms of modeling the registration, there are two ways: rigid and nonrigid.

Rigid registration. Rigid registration is fully specified by a few number of transformation parameters. Traditionally, image registration is solved by optimizing an image matching metric such as normalized correlation coefficient or mutual information as a cost function, which is difficult due to the nonconvex nature of the matching problem.

Liao et al. [53] propose an artificial agent to perform image registration. It casts the image registration problem as a process of finding the best sequence of motion actions (e.g., up, down, left, right, etc.) that yields the desired image registration parameter. The input to the agent is the 3D raw image data and the current estimate

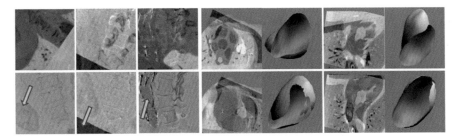

FIGURE 2.11

Registration examples shown as the difference between the reference and floating images, before (upper row) and after (lower row) registration. The mesh overlay before and after registration is shown for cardiac use case for improved visualization. Picture courtesy of [53].

of image registration parameter, and the output of the agent, which is modeled using a deep convolutional neural network, is the next optimal action. Further, it utilizes the path supervision approach to supervise the end-to-end training. Since the agent is learned, it avoids the issue of current approaches that are often customized to a specific problem and sensitive to image quality and artifacts. In experiments, the proposed approach is evaluated on two data sets: spine (87 pairs of CT & CBCT images) and heart (97 pairs of CT & CBCT images). On both data sets, the artificial agent outperforms several state-of-the-art registration methods by a large margin in terms of both accuracy and robustness. See Fig. 2.11.

Similarly, Ma et al. [61] use the artificial agent to register a 2.5D depth image and a 3D CT. Different from [53], it uses dueling DQN to learn the Q function instead of path supervision. Further, although it involves a six degree-of-freedom transformation, the search space is simplified into two translations and one rotation as the rest of the transformation can be determined/inferred through the sensor calibration process together with the depth sensor readings. It also invokes orthographic projection to generate 2D images that are fed into the Q function. Quantitative evaluations are conducted on 1788 pairs of CT and depth images from real clinical setting, with 800 as training. The proposed method achieves state-of-the-art performance, when compared with several approaches including [26].

To deal with the high diversity of tissue appearance across modalities for multi-modality image registration, Hu et al. [31] reformulate the 2D image registration as a decision-making and spatio-temporal problem. They propose an asynchronous reinforcement learning framework, where convolutional long-short-term-memory is incorporated to extract spatial-temporal image features and landmark-error-driven reward function is advocated to guide the agent to the correct registration direction. Besides, a Monte Carlo roll-out strategy is performed as look-ahead guidance to overcome the unknown terminal state problem in a testing phase.

As the problem formulated, given a fixed image I_f and a moving image I_m, each with a different modality, the goal of 2D multimodal image registration is to estimate

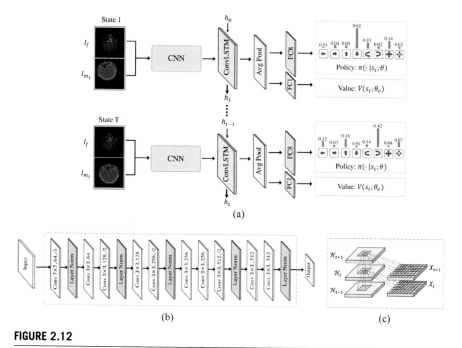

FIGURE 2.12

The model of spatiotemporal agent. (a) An overview of our network. (b) Details of the CNN part. (c) The inner structure of convLSTM unit. Picture courtesy of [31].

the best spatial transformation T_t that establishes pixelwise spatial correspondence between these two images. T_t is parameterized by two translations $[t_x, t_y]$, one rotation α and one scaling s. The action space is discretized and it allows the agent to move the entire image and explore the entire registration parameter space freely.

They integrate the cascaded convLSTM after the initial convolution layer. The model of spatiotemporal agent is presented in Fig. 2.12. This mechanism not only implicitly discovers frame variations over time but also gets long-term spatial features from the extracted short-term spatial features. The spatial-temporal redundancies can be fully exploited.

To avoid a parameter unit discrepancy problem, they leverage salient points that are detected by Difference of Gaussian (DoG) maxima to define the reward function. Landmark reference set P_G, composed of DoG keypoints, is generated from the ground truth of moving image. For each training episode, the landmarks $\tilde{P}_G$ are warped using the inverse of the transformation matrix. The reward function for a_t is defined as follows:

$$r_t = -D = -\frac{1}{|P_G|}\sum_i \|p_i - \tilde{p}_i \circ T_{t+1}\|_2 \, , \, p_i \in P_G, \tilde{p}_i \in \tilde{P}_G. \tag{2.20}$$

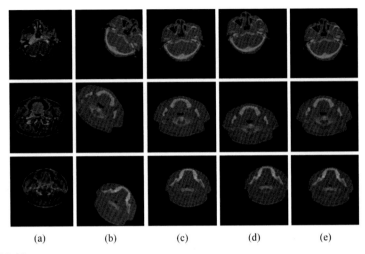

(a)   (b)   (c)   (d)   (e)

FIGURE 2.13

Visual comparison between [31] and [53] method on $\widetilde{E}_2$. (a) The fixed image, (b) the moving image, (c) the ground truth, (d) Liao's method, (e) the proposed method. Picture courtesy of [31].

For testing phase, a Monte Carlo (MC) sampling-based method is proposed, where N different searching paths are simulated at a particular state whose state value is greater than tr or a maximum searching depth D has achieved. The final prediction for the transformation matrix is a weighted averaging of the transformation matrix results for all trajectories. The data sets used in their experiments are composed of MR and CT images, obtained from 99 patients. Their proposed method achieves the best performance for all registration tasks with significant improvements. The visualizations of comparisons between [53] and their methods are illustrated in Fig. 2.13.

Nonrigid registration. When a rigid transformation is insufficient to describe the transformation between two images, a nonrigid registration comes into play, which has more than 6 parameters in 3D to optimize, depending on the class of nonrigid registration.

Krebs et al. [42] extend the artificial agent approach to handle nonrigid registration. In particular, the parametric space of a statistical deformation model for an organ-centered registration of MR prostate images is explored. There are $m = 15$ PCA modes in 2D and $m = 25$ modes in 3D kept to model the prostate deformation, with $2 \times m$ actions are defined.

To tackle the difficulty of obtaining trustworthy ground-truth deformation fields, Krebs et al. [42] proceed with a large number of synthetically deformed image pairs derived from only a small number of inter-subject pairs. Note that the extracted ground truth reaches a median DICE coefficients of 0.96 in 2D and 0.88 in 3D. The Q function is then learned.

| Initial | Shrink (x2) | Translate (x2) | Shrink (x2) | Translate and Trigger |

FIGURE 2.14

The illustration of the detection process, with the learned DRL agent outputting a series of allowable actions to realize final detection of a 3D lesion. Picture courtesy of [62].

The algorithm is tested on inter-subject registration of prostate MR data (41 3D volume in total with 8 for testing, resulting in 56 inter-subject pairs). For the 2D experiment, the middle slice of each volume is utilized. Before the nonrigid registration, the initial translation registration is performed using the Elastix approach [40] by registering each of the test images to an arbitrarily chosen template from the training database. The final registration result reaches a median DICE score of 0.88 in 2D and 0.76 in 3D, both better than competing state-of-the-art registration algorithms.

2.3.1.4 Object/lesion localization and detection

DRL is also leveraged to detect objects [38], [62] presented such an approach for detecting breast lesions from dynamic contrast-enhanced magnetic resonance imaging (DCE-MRI). The bounding box for a 3D lesion is defined as $\mathbf{b} = [b_x, b_y, b_z, b_w, b_h, b_d]$, where b_x, b_y, b_z denote the top-left-front corner and b_w, b_h, b_d define the lower-right-back corner of the bounding box. The actions are defined as $\{l_x^+, l_x^-, l_y^+, l_y^-, l_z^+, l_z^-, s^+, s^-, w\}$, where l, s, w are translation, scale and trigger actions, with the subscripts x, y, z denoting the horizontal, vertical or depth translation and superscripts $+, -$ meaning positive or negative translation and up or down scaling. The signed reward function is used. DQN is learned based on the ResNet architecture. See Fig. 2.14.

Experiments are conducted on DCE-MRI volumes from 117 patients. The training set contains 58 patients annotated with 72 lesions, and the testing set has 59 patients and 69 lesions. Results show a similar accuracy to state-of-the-art approaches, but with significantly reduced detection time.

In [75], a sequential learning task is formulated to estimate from a giga-pixel whole slide image (WSI) the immunohistochemical (IHC) scoring of human epidermal growth factor receptor 2 (HER2) on invasive breast cancer (BC), which is a significant predictive and prognostic marker. To solve this task, DRL is employed to learn a parameterized policy to identify diagnostically relevant regions of interest (ROIs) based on current inputs, which are comprised of two image patches cropped at 40× and 20× magnification levels. The selected ROIs are processed by a CNN for HER2 scores. This avoids the need to process all the sub-image patches of a given tile and saves a large of amount of computations. Refer to Fig. 2.15 for some illustrative results of HER2 scoring.

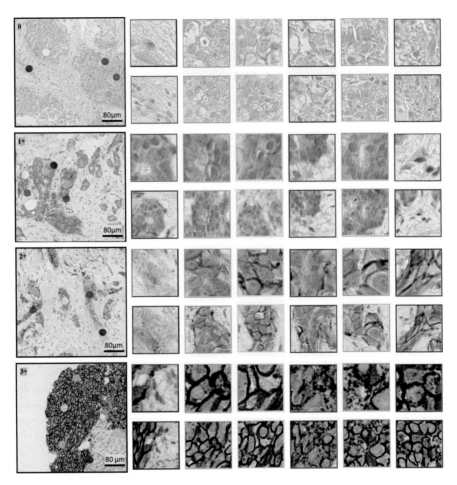

FIGURE 2.15

Example of four image tiles with selected regions-of-interest (ROIs) predicted by [75], for each HER2 score (0-3+), respectively. The first column shows the input images and colored disks show the predicted locations. The remaining columns show the selected regions at 40× and 20× around the selected locations. The first selected region is shown with blue bounding boxes and the last selected region is shown with red bounding boxes. Picture courtesy of [75].

Xu et al. [101] take the computational challenge of breast cancer classification from a histopathological image. Due to the large size of a histopathological image, pathologists in clinical diagnosis first find an abnormal region and then investigate the detail within the region. Such a human attention mechanism inspires an attention-based deep learning approach. It consists of two networks for selection and classification tasks separately. The selection network is trained using DRL, which outputs a

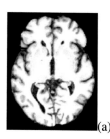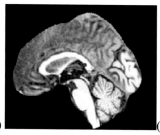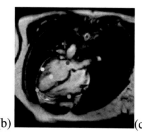

(a)   (b)   (c)

FIGURE 2.16

The viewing planes for detection: (a) Brain axial ACPC plane, (b) Brain mid sagittal plane (c) Cardiac apical four chamber plane. The landmarks are visualized for better definition of the plane and used for error calculation. Picture courtesy of [4].

soft decision about whether the cropped patch is necessary for classification. These selected patches are used to train the classification network, which in turn provides feedback to the selection network to update its selection policy. Such a co-evolution training strategy enables fast convergence and high classification accuracy. Evaluation based on a public breast cancer histopathological image database of 7909 images and eight subclasses of breast cancers from 82 patients (58 malignant and 24 benign) demonstrates about 98% classification accuracy while only taking 50% of the training time of the previous hard-attention approach.

2.3.1.5 View plane localization

Alansary et al. [4] propose to use DRL to detect canonical view planes in MR brain and cardiac volumes. A plane in 3D $ax + by + cz + d = 0$ is parameterized by a 4D vector $[a, b, c, d]$. The eight actions are defined as $\{\pm\delta_{\xi_x}, \pm\delta_{\xi_y}, \pm\delta_{\xi_z}, \delta_d, \}$, which update the plane parameters as $a = cos(\xi_x + \delta_{\xi_x}), b = cos(\xi_y + \delta_{\xi_y}), c = cos(\xi_z + \delta_{\xi_z})$ and $d = d + \delta_d$. The signed reward function is used. Further a multi-scale strategy is utilized, with the action steps are refined in a coarse-to-fine fashion.

The experiments are based on 382 brain MR volumes (isotropic 1 mm) and 455 short-axis cardiac MR volumes ($1.25 \times 1.25 \times 2$ mm^3). Fig. 2.16 visualize the viewing planes to be detected. The specific Q-learning strategies include DQN, DDQN (Double DQN), Duel DQN and Duel DDQN. The detection of the anterior–posterior commissure (ACPC) and mid-sagittal planes reach an error less than 2 mm and the detection of the apical four chamber plane reaches an error around 5 mm, where the error is measured as the distance between anatomical landmarks and the detected planes and the landmarks are accordingly specified for the ACPC and mid-sagittal planes.

Dou et al. [18] study how to use a DRL agent to localize two standard planes of transthalamic (TT) and transcerebellar (TC) positions in a 3D ultrasound volume of the fetal head. The plane parameterization, action space and reward function are defined in a similar manner to [4]. To ease the localization, they propose to augment the agent with a warm start module for better initialization and an active termination module for drift prevention. Based on their extensive validation on in-house data sets of 430 prenatal US volumes, the proposed approach improves both the accuracy and efficiency of the localization system. Recently, Yang et al. [105] update the active termination strategy into the adaptive dynamic termination to improve inference efficiency of the reinforcement framework. Specifically, RNN model performs one inference every two iterations based on the current zero-padding Q-value sequence, enabling an early stop at the iteration step having the first three repeated predictions.

Huang et al. [33] localize multiple uterine standard planes in 3D ultrasound simultaneously by a multi-agent DRL, which is equipped by one-shot neural architecture search (NAS) module. In this work, gradient-based search using a differentiable architecture sampler (GDAS) is employed to accelerate and stabilize the training process. Furthermore, to improve the system robustness against the noisy environment, a landmark-aware alignment model is utilized. The spatial relationship among standard planes is learned by a recurrent neural network (RNN). They conduct the experiment on an in-house data set of 683 volumes which show that multiple agents with recurrent network obtain the best performance.

2.3.1.6 Plaque tracking

Analysis of atherosclerotic plaque in clinical application relies on the use of Intravascular Optical Coherence Tomography (IVOCT), in which a continuous and accurate plaque tracking algorithm is necessary. However, it is challenging to do so due to speckle noise, complex and various intravascular morphology, and a large number of IVOCT images in a pullback. The detected plaque section is represented as a sector with unified radius and the sector is represented as two-tuples $d = (\Theta_S, \Theta)$, where Θ denotes the scale (included angle) of the detected sector, $\Theta_S \in [0, 2\pi]$ denotes the localization (starting angle on the polar coordinate space) of the detected sector. The eight transform actions are Bidirectional Expansion (BE), Bidirectional Contraction (BC), Contra Rotation (COR), Clockwise Rotation (CLR), Contra Unilateral Expansion (COUE), Clockwise Unilateral Expansion (CLUE), Clockwise Unilateral Contraction (CLUC) and Contra Unilateral Contraction (COUC). The reward function is defined as

$$R = \begin{cases} 1 & if\ IOU(d^a, g) - IOU(d, g) > 0; \\ -1 & if\ IOU(d^a, g) - IOU(d, g) < 0; \\ 1 & if\ IOU(d^a, g) - IOU(d, g) = 0 \\ & \&\ IOU(d^a, g) > 0.95; \\ -1 & if\ IOU(d^a, g) - IOU(d, g) = 0 \\ & \&\ IOU(d^a, g) < 0.95, \end{cases} \tag{2.21}$$

where g is the ground truth sector region, d is the current detected sector and d^a is the next detected sector based on current selected action. $IOU(d^a, g)) = IOU(d, g)$ only happens when stop action is selected.

2.3.1.7 *Vessel centerline extraction*

Zhang et al. [112] propose to use deep reinforcement learning for vessel centerline tracing in multi-modality 3D volumes. The ground truth vessel center points are given as $\mathbf{G} = [\mathbf{g_0}, \mathbf{g_1}, \ldots, \mathbf{g_n}]$. The key idea is to learn a navigation model for an agent to trace the vessel centerline through an optimal trajectory $\mathbf{P} = [\mathbf{p_0}, \mathbf{p_1}, \ldots, \mathbf{p_m}]$. The action space is defined as $\mathcal{A} = \{left, right, top, bottom, front, back\}$, that is, moving to one of six neighboring voxels.

For the current point $\mathbf{p_t}$, a corresponding point $\mathbf{g_d}$ on the centerline that has the minimum distance to the point $\mathbf{p_t}$ is first found. A point-to-curve measure is then defined as

$$D(\mathbf{p_t}, \mathbf{G}) = \|\lambda(\mathbf{p_t} - \mathbf{g_{d+1}}) + (1 - \lambda)(\mathbf{g_{d+2}} - \mathbf{g_d})\|. \qquad (2.22)$$

It consists of two terms. The first term pulls the agent position toward the ground truth centerline and the second term enforces the agent toward the direction of the curve. With the aid of $D(\mathbf{p_t}, \mathbf{G})$, the reward function is given as

$$r_t = \begin{cases} D(\mathbf{p_t}, \mathbf{G}) - D(\mathbf{p_{t+1}}, \mathbf{G}), & if \ \|\mathbf{p_t} - \mathbf{g_d}\| \leq l \\ \|\mathbf{p_t} - \mathbf{g_d}\| - \|\mathbf{p_{t+1}} - \mathbf{g_d}\|, & otherwise \end{cases} \qquad (2.23)$$

For evaluation, the authors collect 531 contrasted CT, 887 noncontrasted CT, 737 C-arm CT and 232 MR volumes from multiple sites over the world. For the original 12-bit images, the voxel intensity is clipped and normalized within [500,2000]. The intensity distribution of MR is mapped to that of CT. All these volumes are then mixed for training and testing. The proposed algorithm achieves better performance when compared with a supervised 3D CNN approach.

Zhang et al. [113] make use of DDQN and 3D dilated CNN to address the problem of accurate coronary artery centerline. Their network consists of two parts: a DDQN-based tracker to predict the next action and a branch-aware detector to detect the branch points and radius of coronary artery. With such network architecture, it requires only one seed as input to extract an entire coronary tree. The two-branch network has been evaluated on CAT08 challenge and obtains state-of-the-art performance while it costs only 7 s for inference. Fig. 2.17 shows an example of traced aorta centerlines in the curved planar reformatting (CPR) view.

Recently, inspired by the sequential nature of both DRL and tree-traversal process, Li et al. [52] present a Deep Reinforced Tree-traversal (DRT) agent that infers tree-structure centerlines from a given initial point. The framework takes raw local patches and generates tree-structured centerlines sequentially. They introduce road mark and dynamic reward mechanisms to make tree-structure vessels learnable and impart the agent how to learn correspondingly. Also, a multi-task discriminator is raised to simultaneously detect bifurcations and decide terminations. For Coronary Artery Centerline Extraction, this method surpasses other existing methods by a large margin in terms of the time and memory efficiency on a cardiac CTA data set that contains 280 patients from 4 clinical institutions.

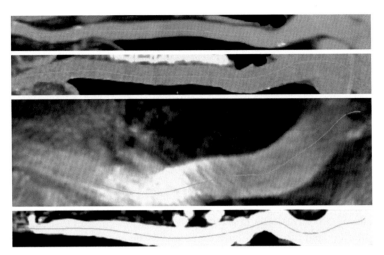

FIGURE 2.17

Example of traced aorta centerlines in the curved planar reformatting (CPR) view. Picture courtesy of [112].

2.3.2 Solving optimization using DRL

Because DRL can handle the nondifferential metrics, it is widely used to solve optimization problems where conventional methods fall apart. Fig. 2.7 is an array of such applications including tuning hyper-parameters for radiotherapy planning, selecting the right image augmentation selection for image classification, searching best neural architecture for segmentation and avoiding poor images via a learned acquisition strategy.

2.3.2.1 Image classification

Akrout et al. [2] propose to integrate a CNN classification model with a RL-based Question Answering (QA) agent for skin disease classification. To better identify the underlying condition, the DNN-based agent learns how to ask the patient about the presence of symptoms, using the visual information provided by CNN and the answers to the asked questions. It is demonstrated that the integrated approach increases the classification accuracy over 20% when compared to the CNN-only approach that uses only the visual information. It narrows down the diagnosis faster in terms of the average number of asked questions, when compared with a conventional decision-tree-based QA agent.

Cheng et al. [13] study how to use semantic segmentation that produces a hard attention map for improved classification performance. In particular, a segmentation agent and a classification model are jointly learned. The segmentation agent, which produces a segmentation mask, is trained via a reinforcement learning framework, with reward being the classification accuracy. The classification model is learned using both original and masked data as inputs. Promising results are obtained on Stanford MURA data set, consisting of 14,863 musculoskeletal studies of elbows, finger, forearm, hand, humerus, shoulder and wrist with 9045 normal and 5818 abnormal labeled cases and on a hip fracture data set, consisting of 1118 pelvic radiographs with 6 classes: no fracture, intertrochanteric fracture, displaced femoral neck fracture, nondisplaced femoral neck fracture, arthroplasty and ORIF (previous internal fixation). Fig. 2.18 shows some sample X-Ray images and their corresponding attention maps.

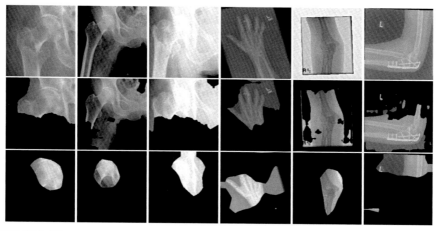

FIGURE 2.18

X-Ray examples (top) and the masks created by [13] (middle) and DenseNet+GradCam (bottom) for hip, hand and elbow. Picture courtesy of [13].

To combat the issue of data shortage in medical image classification, synthesizing realistic medical images offers a viable solution. Ye et al. [106] investigate the issue of synthetic sample selection for improved image classification in order to assure the quality of synthetic images for data augmentation purposes because some of the generated images are not realistic and pollute the data distribution. The authors train a DRL agent via proximal policy optimization (PPO) to choose synthetic images containing reliable and informative features, using the classification accuracy as the reward. Extensive experiments are conducted on two image data sets of cervical and lymph node histopathology images and the performances are improved by 8.1% and 2.3%, respectively.

Wang et al. [95] combines four different types of ultrasonography to discriminate between benign and malignant breast nodules by proposing a multi-modal network. In their network, the modalities interact through a RL framework under weight-sharing, i.e., automatically find the optimal weighting across modalities to increase accuracy. Corresponding to four modalities, there are four streams (ResNet18 is used as backbone) and each stream provides one loss. Together with four losses from four streams, there is another fusion loss. All of the five losses are weighted by coefficients, which are automatically learned through an RL framework. The auto-weighting network is evaluated on 1616 sets of multi-modal ultrasound images of breast nodules and it shows that multi-modal methods outperform single-modal methods.

Promoting the prediction confidence and preserving modality-specific properties after fusion are common challenges of multi-modality 3D medical image analysis. To deal with the two difficulties, Zhu et al. [116] present a novel Reinforcement Learning (RL) driven approach, where Two RL-based agents are learned for dynamical intra-modal and inter-modal features enhancement to learn latent modality representation and underlying correlations among different modalities. Specially, they took two key techniques based on the characteristics of multi-modality medical images. First, they propose an iterative hybrid-enhancement network to integrate intra-features and inter-features, where the enhanced intra-features in each iteration are regarded as the state of two designed agents in the next training iteration. Second, they take the prediction confidence increment as the supervision of the agents to promote the prediction confidence.

For the RL-Based Intra-modality Learning, in every training iteration, individual 3D convolution layers first embed every volume to modality-specific features and implement enhancement with intra-modality enhancement weights determined by the intra-agent. The proposed intra-enhancement action can facilitate sharing of intra-modality spatial relationships among different modalities. For RL-Based Inter-modality Learning, features fused by different high-level modality-specific representations are forwarded to two independent RNN termed intra-agent and inter-agent. Different modalities own different enhancement weights. Following fully-connected layer embeds the enhanced fusion features to primary fusion representation, which includes comprehensive features of all modalities. The splitting output of fusion features preserves respective modality-specific properties. The enhanced fusion features are then utilized for final decision making. Besides, they define the reward as increments of the soft-max prediction probability on the ground truth labels for the optimization of two agents. Experiments validated on T1, T1ce, T2 and FLAIR volumes of 165 subjects from the BraTS 2018 demonstrate the effectiveness of their approach.

2.3.2.2 Image segmentation

Medical image segmentation aims at finding the exact boundary of an anatomical or pathological structure in a medical image. In the most general form, an image segmentation approach assigns semantic labels to pixels. By grouping the pixels with the same label, object segmentation is realized. From image segmentation, clinical measurements such as organ volume can be computed and diseases such as enlarged liver can be diagnosed.

There are early approaches that use RL for image segmentation [81,87,98], based on a limited number of parameters to derive image segmentation results. This severely limits the segmentation performances. Yang et al. [103] present a RL searching approach to optimize the training strategy for 3D medical image segmentation, which boosts the performance of the baseline models.

Bae et al. [7] make an attempt to apply Neural architecture search (NAS) [117] to medical image segmentation, aiming to modify a U-Net base architecture so that the image segmentation performance is improved. The search space constitutes multiple factors, including input size, pooling type, filter size and stride size, activation type, skip connection point and dilation rate. Using the searched U-Net, the segmentation performances on the medical segmentation decathlon (MSD) challenges are better than those of the nnU-Net approach [35], which is considered as state-of-the-art approach. In order to learn an optimal augmentation under an end-to-end segmentation framework, Qin et al. [76] propose to train both augmentation and segmentation modules simultaneously and use the errors in segmentation procedure as feedback to adjust the augmentation module. In addition to scarce annotation, class-imbalance issue is also addressed in Dual-Unet [104], which proposes a semi-supervised approach that leverages RL as a pre-localization step for catheter segmentation. Dual-Unet is trained on both limited labeled and abundant unlabeled images with a two-stage procedure. By iteratively incorporating user hints, Liao et al. [54] propose IteR-MRL with multi-agent reinforcement learning to capture the dependency among voxels for segmentation task as well as to reduce the exploration space to a tractable size.

With a novel auto-weighted supervision framework, Wang et al. [97] tackle the scar and edema segmentation from multi-sequence cardiac magnetic resonance (CMR). They explore the interactions among different supervised layers under a task-specific objective using reinforcement learning. This RL-based method effectively learns the optimal weighting of different supervision layers, thereby achieving better performance than traditional deep supervision methods.

Recently, Huang et al. [34] extend reinforcement learning to weakly supervised nodule segmentation from breast ultrasound images. They propose a novel and general box-only WSS framework called Flip Learning, which is based on DRL. The target in the label box will be erased gradually to flip the classification tag with a Multi-agent Reinforcement Learning framework, and the erased region will be considered as the segmentation result finally. This mechanism exploit the prior boundary knowledge and accelerate the learning process. The workflow of the method is illustrated in Fig. 2.19. Some cases of flip learning are presented in Fig. 2.20.

Besides, two rewards named classification score and intensity distribution reward are designed to avoid under- and over-segmentation respectively. Specifically, the classification score reward (CSR) is used for pushing the agents' erasing for label flipping, while the intensity distribution reward (IDR) is employed to limit the over-segmentation. They also employ a coarse-to-fine (C2F) strategy to simplify agents' learning for residuals decreasing and segmentation performance improvement. They apply the proposed framework to nodule segmentation task on a total of 1723 2D US images collected from 1129 patients and achieve high accuracy. The significant results also demonstrate the great potential to narrow the gap between fully-supervised and weakly-supervised learning.

Zhang et al. [110] propose a Weakly-Supervised Teacher-Student network (WSTS) to address the liver tumor segmentation in nonenhanced images by leveraging additional box-level-labeled data. A Teacher Module learns to detect and segment

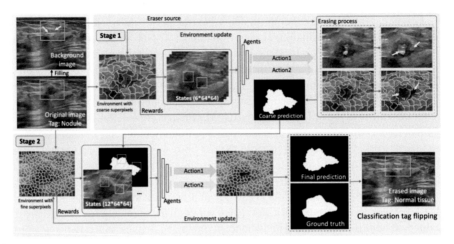

FIGURE 2.19

The workflow of the proposed framework. Picture courtesy of [34].

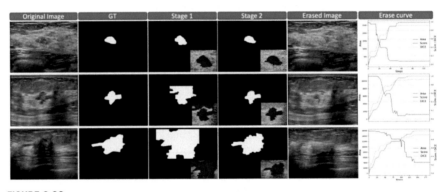

FIGURE 2.20

Typical cases of Flip Learning. Mask predictions have been post-processed. Note that the classification tags of original images are "nodule," and after two-stage erasing, their tags will flip to "normal tissue." The erase curves show the variation of classification scores during erasing. Picture courtesy of [34].

the tumor in enhanced images during training, which facilitates the Student Module to detect and segment the tumor in nonenhanced images independently during testing. To determine the tumor location and size correctly, WSTS proposes Dual-strategy DRL (DDRL). The DDRL develops two tumor detection strategies to jointly determine the tumor location in enhanced images by creatively introducing a relative-entropy bias in the DRL. To accurately predict a tumor mask for the box-level-labeled enhanced image, and thus improve tumor segmentation in nonenhanced images, the WSTS proposes an Uncertainty-Sifting Self-Ensembling (USSE). The USSE exploits the weakly-labeled data with self-ensembling and evaluates the prediction reliability with a newly-designed multi-scale uncertainty-estimation. They validate the method on liver axial MRI images collected from 250 patients, where the experiment achieves 83.11% of Dice and 85.12% of Recall in 50 patient testing data after training by 200 patient data (half amount data is box-level-labeled).

2.3.2.3 Image acquisition and reconstruction

CT metal artifacts, whose presence affects clinical decision-making, are produced because of there is an inconsistency between the imaging physics and idealized assumption used in the CT reconstruction algorithm. While there are many metal artifact reduction (MAR) algorithms in the literature that post-process the already acquired data say from a pre-determined cone beam CT imaging trajectory or reconstructed images, Zaech et al. [108] propose to design a task-aware, patient-specific imaging trajectory in order to avoid acquiring "poor" images that give rise to beam hardening, photon starvation and noise. Such a design strategy is learned offline via a DRL agent that predicts the next acquisition angle that maximizes a final detectability score. Fig. 2.21 compares the reconstructed images from a straightforward short-scan and a task-aware trajectory recommended by the agent. It is clear that the metal artifacts are reduced.

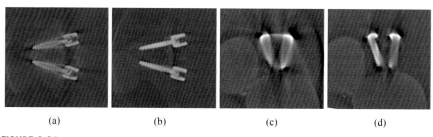

(a)   (b)   (c)   (d)

FIGURE 2.21

Two examples of axial slices from a volume reconstructed from (a,c) a straightforward short-scan and (b,d) a task-aware trajectory recommended by the agent. It is evident that the visual quality of the images reconstructed by using the agent is better. Picture courtesy of [108].

CT iterative reconstruction solves an optimization problem that uses a total variation (TV) regularization [79]:

$$f^* = \arg\min_f \frac{1}{2}|Pf - g|^2 + |\lambda \cdot \nabla f|, \qquad (2.24)$$

where f^* is the image to be reconstructed, P is the x-ray projection operator, g is the measured projection signals, ∇f computes the gradient of the image and λ is a vector of regularization coefficient, which is spatially varying for better modeling. The choice of λ is crucial for final image quality, but tuning such parameters is nontrivial. Shen et al. [85] propose to use a DRL agent that learns a parameter-tuning policy network (PTPN) for such a tuning task. It is demonstrated that, with the aid of the agent, the final image quality reaches a level similar to that with human expert tuning.

Shen et al. [86] propose to use DRL to learn a personalized CT scan so that the final reconstructed image quality is maximized, given a fixed-dose budget. The key idea is to learn a sequential strategy that selects the acquisition angle and the needed dose for this chosen angle. The reward function is computed as

$$R(s_t, s_{t-}, a_t) = PSNR(I_t, I) - PSNR(I_{t-1}, I), \tag{2.25}$$

where I is the ground-truth image, I_t is the reconstructed image at time step t and $PSNR(I', I)$ represents the Peak Signal-to-Noise Ratio (PSNR) value of the reconstructed image I'. Experiments are conducted using the data sets from 2016 NIH-AAPM-Mayo Clinic Low Dose CT Grand Challenge, demonstrating that the learned scanning policy yields better overall reconstruction results with the acquisition angles and dose are adaptively adjusted.

Pineda et al. [72] propose to optimize the sequence of k-space measurements, aiming to reduce the number of measurements taken, and thus accelerate the acquisition. By formulating it as a partially observable Markov decision process, a policy that maps history of k-space measurements to an index of k-space measurement to acquire next is then learned using DDQN. Similar to (2.25), the reward is defined as the decrease in reconstruction metric with respect to the previous reconstruction. Experiments on the fastMRI data set of knees [109] demonstrate that the learned policy outperforms other competing policies in terms of final reconstruction quality, over a large range of acceleration factors. Recently, Li et al. [49] extend pixelRL [21] by assigning each pixel of the input image an agent that changes the pixel value. In their work, both reinforcement learning techniques and classical image filters are taken into to reconstruct MRI.

2.3.2.4 Radiotherapy planning

Radiotherapy planning often involves optimizing an objective function with constraints, which consists of multiple terms that are weighted. Weigh adjusting requires expertise from a human expert in order to yield a high quality plan. Shen et al. [85] leverage DRL to learn a weight-tuning policy network (WTPN) that takes the current dose volume histogram of a plan as input and outputs an action that adjusts weights, with a reward function that promotes the sparing of organs at risk. The agent is then applied for planning the high-dose-rate brachy therapy for five patients, yielding the quality score 10.7% higher than human planners.

2.3.2.5 Video summarization

Recently, Liu et al. [57] introduce a fully automatic video summarization method using DRL. Their network contains an encoder–decoder CNN to first extract visual representation and then feed the feature into a Bi-LSTM to model time dependency. Finally, the RL network interprets the summarization task as a decision-making process and takes actions on whether a frame should be selected for the summary set or not. In their framework, the reward is defined as the quality of the selected frames in terms of their representation, diversity, as well as the likelihood of being a standard diagnostic view plane. The proposed network can be implemented as either supervised or unsupervised manner and it obtains state-of-the-art summarization performance with highest F_1 score. The experiments are conducted based on ultrasound videos.

Recording several keyframes during the dynamic ultrasound scanning is important to recognize diagnostic features and perform the diagnosis. Inspired by observing the sonographer's behavior, Huang et al. [32] propose a reinforcement learning-based framework that can automatically extract keyframes from US videos. It is equipped with a customized reward function that integrates guidance from expert annotation, nodule presence and diagnostic attributes. In general, a raw video is first processed by a detection-based nodule filtering module to remove redundant information and focus on the lesion region. The filtered video is then passed to the agent to make suitable action based on aforementioned reward signal for every frame.

Experiments validated on 2606 videos of breast lesions demonstrate the effectiveness of their method.

2.4 Future perspectives

DRL is a powerful framework for medical image analysis tasks. It has been successfully applied to various tasks, including image-based parameter inference in landmark localization, object detection and registration. DRL has also been demonstrated to be an effective alternative for solving difficult optimization problems, including tuning parameters, selecting augmentation strategies and neural architecture search. However, realizing the full potential of DRL for medical imaging requires solving several challenges ahead of us and relying on the adoptions of latest DRL advances.

2.4.1 Challenges ahead

We foresee that successful application of DRL to medical image analysis needs to address the following challenges:

- Defining a reward function. It is usually hard to define or curate a learnable reward function for the task at hand because it requires the knowledge from different domains that may not always be available. A reward function with too long delay makes training difficult because there is no feedback on how to improve the performance during the episode.
- Q-learning when high-dimensional. Training a Q-function on a high-dimensional and continuous action space is challenging. For this reason, existing works using low-dimensional parameterization, typically less than 10 with an exception [42] that uses 15D and 25D to model 2D and 3D registration, respectively.
- Data availability. DRL requires a large amount of training data or expert demonstrations, which are expensive and hard to come by especially in medical domains. It is therefore challenging to collect enough data for training. Developing more

data-efficient DRL algorithms is desirable to make this technology more widely applicable to the medical imaging community.

- Dynamic environment. Currently, the approaches we have reviewed assume a stationary environment, from which observations are made. However, the reinforcement learning framework naturally accommodates a dynamic environment, that is, the environment itself evolves with the state and action. It is difficult to deal with the changing state and action.

- User interaction. Another aspect worth more attention is user interaction. In the context of parametric medical image analysis, the user input essentially is an external force to escape from the local minimum trap, which gives rise to the current result. However, the subsequent behavior after escaping is largely unexplored.

- Reproducibility. Reproducibility is another issue. According to [29], reproducing existing DRL work is not a straightforward task because there are nondeterministic factors even in standard benchmark environments and intrinsic variations with respect to specific methods. This statement also holds for DRL in medical imaging.

2.4.2 The latest DRL advances

The following latest DRL advances are worth attention and may promote new insights for many medical image analysis tasks:

- Inverse DRL. Different from DRL, inverse DRL [69] [1], a specific form of imitation learning [70], infers the reward function of an agent, given its policy or observed behavior, thereby avoiding a manual specification of its reward function. Inverse RL has been successfully applied to many domains [1] such as high-dimensional robot systems [59] and autonomous driving [114].

- Multi-Agent DRL. Most of the successful DRL applications involve multiple players and require a model with multiple agents. Learning in a multi-agent scenario is more difficult than a single-agent scenario because of non-stationarity [30], multi-dimensionality [12], credit assignment [100], etc. Depending on whether the multi-agent DRL approach is either fully cooperative or fully competitive, agents can either collaborate to optimize a long-term utility or compete so that the utility is summed to zero. It is a relatively easy task if the agents interacts with the same environment. However, multi-agent DRL could become more challenging if the agents interact with very different environments. Recent works on multi-agent RL extend to many applications such as game [10], [47], robotics [74], autonomous driving [51], stock trading [78] and social science [46].

- Meta RL. As aforementioned, DRL algorithms consume large amounts of experience in order to learn an individual task and are unable to generalize the learned policy to newer problems. To alleviate the data challenge, meta-RL algorithms [84], [96] are studied to enable agents to learn new skills from small amounts of experience. Recently, there is a research interest in meta RL such as [73], [107], [77], [80], each using a different approach.

- Imitation learning. Imitation learning is close to learning from demonstrations, which aims at training a policy to mimic an expert's behavior given the samples collected from that expert. Imitation learning is also considered as an alternative to RL/DRL to solve sequential decision-making problems. Besides inverse DRL, an imitation learning approach aforementioned, behavior cloning is another imitation learning approach to train policy under supervised learning. Recently, imitation learning have been applied to various domains and derives some variants such as [92], [91], [39], [36].

2.5 Conclusions

In this paper, we present a survey of literature on the use of deep reinforcement learning in medical imaging, which demonstrates the great potential of DRL in medicine and healthcare. RL framework offers several compelling advantages compared to the traditional supervised learning approach, including (i) more computationally efficient inference, (ii) a smaller memory footprint or better scaling up to large image resolutions and (iii) optimal balancing between time efficiency and accuracy. The existing DRL applications for medical imaging are roughly divided into parametric medical image analysis tasks, solving optimization tasks in medical imaging and miscellaneous applications. The remaining challenges that need to be addressed and the latest DRL advances that might promote new insights are finally discussed.

References

[1] P. Abbeel, A.Y. Ng, Apprenticeship learning via inverse reinforcement learning, in: Proceedings of the International Conference on Machine Learning, Association for Computing Machinery, 2004, pp. 1–8.

[2] M. Akrout, A.m. Farahmand, T. Jarmain, L. Abid, Improving skin condition classification with a visual symptom checker trained using reinforcement learning, in: International Conference on Medical Image Computing and Computer-Assisted Intervention (MICCAI), Springer, 2019, pp. 549–557.

[3] S. Alaniz, Deep reinforcement learning with model learning and Monte Carlo tree search in Minecraft, in: Conference on Reinforcement Learning and Decision Making, 2018.

[4] A. Alansary, L.L. Folgoc, G. Vaillant, O. Oktay, Y. Li, W. Bai, J. Passerat-Palmbach, R. Guerrero, K. Kamnitsas, B. Hou, et al., Automatic view planning with multi-scale deep reinforcement learning agents, arXiv:1806.03228, 2018.

[5] K. Arulkumaran, M.P. Deisenroth, M. Brundage, A.A. Bharath, Deep reinforcement learning: a brief survey, IEEE Signal Processing Magazine 34 (2017) 26–38.

[6] M. Babaeizadeh, I. Frosio, S. Tyree, J. Clemons, J. Kautz, GA3C: GPU-based A3C for deep reinforcement learning, arXiv:1611.06256, 2016.

[7] W. Bae, S. Lee, Y. Lee, B. Park, M. Chung, K.H. Jung, Resource optimized neural architecture search for 3D medical image segmentation, in: International Conference on

Medical Image Computing and Computer-Assisted Intervention (MICCAI), Springer, 2019, pp. 228–236.

[8] I.E.I. Bekkouch, B. Maksudov, S. Kiselev, T. Mustafaev, T. Vrtovec, B. Ibragimov, Multi-landmark environment analysis with reinforcement learning for pelvic abnormality detection and quantification, Medical Image Analysis 78 (2022) 102417.

[9] A. Bernstein, E. Burnaev, Reinforcement learning in computer vision, in: Tenth International Conference on Machine Vision, International Society for Optics and Photonics, 2018, p. 106961S.

[10] N. Brown, T. Sandholm, Superhuman AI for multiplayer poker, Science 365 (2019) 885–890.

[11] J. Browning, M. Kornreich, A. Chow, J. Pawar, L. Zhang, R. Herzog, B.L. Odry, Uncertainty aware deep reinforcement learning for anatomical landmark detection in medical images, in: International Conference on Medical Image Computing and Computer-Assisted Intervention, Springer, 2021, pp. 636–644.

[12] L. Busoniu, R. Babuska, B. De Schutter, A comprehensive survey of multiagent reinforcement learning, IEEE Transactions on Systems, Man and Cybernetics. Part C, Applications and Reviews 38 (2008) 156–172.

[13] K. Cheng, C. Iriondo, F. Calivá, J. Krogue, S. Majumdar, V. Pedoia, Adversarial policy gradient for deep learning image augmentation, in: International Conference on Medical Image Computing and Computer-Assisted Intervention (MICCAI), Springer, 2019, pp. 450–458.

[14] A.M. Clarke, J. Friedrich, E.M. Tartaglia, S. Marchesotti, W. Senn, M.H. Herzog, Human and machine learning in non-Markovian decision making, PLoS ONE 10 (2015) e0123105.

[15] I. Clavera, J. Rothfuss, J. Schulman, Y. Fujita, T. Asfour, P. Abbeel, Model-based reinforcement learning via meta-policy optimization, arXiv:1809.05214, 2018.

[16] R. Coulom, Efficient selectivity and backup operators in Monte-Carlo tree search, in: Proceedings of the 5th International Conference on Computers and Games, 2006, pp. 72–83.

[17] K. De Asis, J.F. Hernandez-Garcia, G.Z. Holland, R.S. Sutton, Multi-step reinforcement learning: a unifying algorithm, in: Proceedings of the AAAI Conference on Artificial Intelligence, 2018.

[18] H. Dou, X. Yang, J. Qian, W. Xue, H. Qin, X. Wang, L. Yu, S. Wang, Y. Xiong, P.A. Heng, et al., Agent with warm start and active termination for plane localization in 3D ultrasound, in: International Conference on Medical Image Computing and Computer-Assisted Intervention (MICCAI), Springer, 2019, pp. 290–298.

[19] C. Finn, S. Levine, P. Abbeel, Guided cost learning: deep inverse optimal control via policy optimization, in: Proceedings of the International Conference on Machine Learning, 2016, pp. 49–58.

[20] V. François-Lavet, P. Henderson, R. Islam, M.G. Bellemare, J. Pineau, An introduction to deep reinforcement learning, arXiv:1811.12560, 2018.

[21] R. Furuta, N. Inoue, T. Yamasaki, Pixelrl: fully convolutional network with reinforcement learning for image processing, IEEE Transactions on Multimedia 22 (2020) 1704–1719.

[22] M. Gaon, R. Brafman, Reinforcement learning with non-Markovian rewards, in: Proceedings of the AAAI Conference on Artificial Intelligence, 2020, pp. 3980–3987.

[23] M. Geist, O. Pietquin, A brief survey of parametric value function approximation, Rapport interne, Supélec, 2010.

[24] F.C. Ghesu, B. Georgescu, S. Grbic, A. Maier, J. Hornegger, D. Comaniciu, Towards intelligent robust detection of anatomical structures in incomplete volumetric data, Medical Image Analysis 48 (2018) 203–213.

[25] F.C. Ghesu, B. Georgescu, S. Grbic, A.K. Maier, J. Hornegger, D. Comaniciu, Robust multi-scale anatomical landmark detection in incomplete 3D-CT data, in: International Conference on Medical Image Computing and Computer-Assisted Intervention (MIC-CAI), Springer, 2017, pp. 194–202.

[26] F.C. Ghesu, B. Georgescu, T. Mansi, D. Neumann, J. Hornegger, D. Comaniciu, An artificial agent for anatomical landmark detection in medical images, in: International Conference on Medical Image Computing and Computer-Assisted Intervention (MIC-CAI), Springer, 2016, pp. 229–237.

[27] A. Graves, A. Mohamed, G.E. Hinton, Speech recognition with deep recurrent neural networks, arXiv:1303.5778, 2013.

[28] H.V. Hasselt, Double q-learning, in: Advances in Neural Information Processing Systems, 2010, pp. 2613–2621.

[29] P. Henderson, R. Islam, P. Bachman, J. Pineau, D. Precup, D. Meger, Deep reinforcement learning that matters, arXiv:1709.06560, 2017.

[30] P. Hernandez-Leal, M. Kaisers, T. Baarslag, E.M. de Cote, A survey of learning in multiagent environments: dealing with non-stationarity, arXiv:1707.09183, 2017.

[31] J. Hu, Z. Luo, X. Wang, S. Sun, Y. Yin, K. Cao, Q. Song, S. Lyu, X. Wu, End-to-end multimodal image registration via reinforcement learning, Medical Image Analysis 68 (2021) 101878.

[32] R. Huang, Q. Ying, Z. Lin, Z. Zheng, L. Tan, G. Tang, Q. Zhang, M. Luo, X. Yi, P. Liu, et al., Extracting keyframes of breast ultrasound video using deep reinforcement learning, Medical Image Analysis 102490 (2022).

[33] Y. Huang, X. Yang, R. Li, J. Qian, X. Huang, W. Shi, H. Dou, C. Chen, Y. Zhang, H. Luo, A. Frangi, Y. Xiong, D. Ni, Searching collaborative agents for multi-plane localization in 3D ultrasound, in: International Conference on Medical Image Computing and Computer-Assisted Intervention (MICCAI), 2020.

[34] Y. Huang, X. Yang, Y. Zou, C. Chen, J. Wang, H. Dou, N. Ravikumar, A.F. Frangi, J. Zhou, D. Ni, Flip learning: erase to segment, in: International Conference on Medical Image Computing and Computer-Assisted Intervention, Springer, 2021, pp. 493–502.

[35] F. Isensee, J. Petersen, A. Klein, D. Zimmerer, P.F. Jaeger, S. Kohl, J. Wasserthal, G. Koehler, T. Norajitra, S. Wirkert, et al., nnU-Net: self-adapting framework for u-net-based medical image segmentation, arXiv:1809.10486, 2018.

[36] E. Jang, A. Irpan, M. Khansari, D. Kappler, F. Ebert, C. Lynch, S. Levine, C. Finn, Bc-z: zero-shot task generalization with robotic imitation learning, in: Conference on Robot Learning, PMLR, 2022, pp. 991–1002.

[37] Z. Jia, L. Yang, C. Szepesvari, M. Wang, Model-based reinforcement learning with value-targeted regression, in: Proceedings of the 2nd Conference on Learning for Dynamics and Control, The Cloud, 2020, pp. 666–686.

[38] Z. Jie, X. Liang, J. Feng, X. Jin, W. Lu, S. Yan, Tree-structured reinforcement learning for sequential object localization, in: Advances in Neural Information Processing Systems, 2016, pp. 127–135.

[39] H. Karnan, G. Warnell, X. Xiao, P. Stone, Voila: visual-observation-only imitation learning for autonomous navigation, in: 2022 International Conference on Robotics and Automation (ICRA), IEEE, 2022, pp. 2497–2503.

[40] S. Klein, M. Staring, K. Murphy, M.A. Viergever, J.P. Pluim, Elastix: a toolbox for intensity-based medical image registration, IEEE Transactions on Medical Imaging 29 (2010) 196–205.

[41] V.R. Konda, J.N. Tsitsiklis, Actor-critic algorithms, in: Advances in Neural Information Processing Systems, 2000, pp. 1008–1014.

[42] J. Krebs, T. Mansi, H. Delingette, L. Zhang, F.C. Ghesu, S. Miao, A.K. Maier, N. Ayache, R. Liao, A. Kamen, Robust non-rigid registration through agent-based action learning, in: International Conference on Medical Image Computing and Computer-Assisted Intervention (MICCAI), Springer, 2017, pp. 344–352.

[43] T. Kurutach, I. Clavera, Y. Duan, A. Tamar, P. Abbeel, Model-ensemble trust-region policy optimization, 2018.

[44] M.G. Lagoudakis, Value Function Approximation, Springer US, Boston, MA, 2017, pp. 1311–1323.

[45] K. Lee, S.A. Kim, J. Choi, S.W. Lee, Deep reinforcement learning in continuous action spaces: a case study in the game of simulated curling, in: J. Dy, A. Krause (Eds.), Proceedings of the International Conference on Machine Learning, PMLR, 2018, pp. 2937–2946.

[46] J.Z. Leibo, V.F. Zambaldi, M. Lanctot, J. Marecki, T. Graepel, Multi-agent reinforcement learning in sequential social dilemmas, arXiv:1702.03037, 2017.

[47] S. Leonardos, G. Piliouras, Exploration-exploitation in multi-agent learning: catastrophe theory meets game theory, Artificial Intelligence 304 (2022) 103653.

[48] G. Leroy, D. Rueckert, A. Alansary, Communicative reinforcement learning agents for landmark detection in brain images, in: Machine Learning in Clinical Neuroimaging and Radiogenomics in Neuro-Oncology, Springer, 2020, pp. 177–186.

[49] W. Li, X. Feng, H. An, X.Y. Ng, Y.J. Zhang, MRI reconstruction with interpretable pixel-wise operations using reinforcement learning, in: Proceedings of the AAAI Conference on Artificial Intelligence, 2020, pp. 792–799.

[50] Y. Li, Deep reinforcement learning: an overview, arXiv:1701.07274, 2017.

[51] Y. Li, D. Ma, Z. An, Z. Wang, Y. Zhong, S. Chen, C. Feng, V2x-sim: multi-agent collaborative perception dataset and benchmark for autonomous driving, IEEE Robotics and Automation Letters 7 (2022) 10914–10921.

[52] Z. Li, Q. Xia, Z. Hu, W. Wang, L. Xu, S. Zhang, A deep reinforced tree-traversal agent for coronary artery centerline extraction, in: International Conference on Medical Image Computing and Computer-Assisted Intervention, Springer, 2021, pp. 418–428.

[53] R. Liao, S. Miao, P. de Tournemire, S. Grbic, A. Kamen, T. Mansi, D. Comaniciu, An artificial agent for robust image registration, in: Proceedings of the AAAI Conference on Artificial Intelligence, 2017, pp. 4168–4175.

[54] X. Liao, W. Li, Q. Xu, X. Wang, B. Jin, X. Zhang, Y. Wang, Y. Zhang, Iteratively-refined interactive 3D medical image segmentation with multi-agent reinforcement learning, in: Proceedings of the IEEE Conference on Computer Vision and Pattern Recognition (CVPR), 2020, pp. 9394–9402.

[55] T.P. Lillicrap, J.J. Hunt, A.e. Pritzel, N. Heess, T. Erez, Y. Tassa, D. Silver, D. Wierstra, Continuous control with deep reinforcement learning, arXiv:1509.02971, 2015.

[56] H. Liu, K. Simonyan, Y. Yang, Darts: differentiable architecture search, arXiv:1806.09055, 2018.

[57] T. Liu, Q. Meng, A. Vlontzos, J. Tan, D. Rueckert, B. Kainz, Ultrasound video summarization using deep reinforcement learning, in: International Conference on Medical Image Computing and Computer-Assisted Intervention (MICCAI), 2020, pp. 483–492.

[58] W. Liu, F. Liu, R. Tang, B. Liao, G. Chen, P.A. Heng, Balancing between accuracy and fairness for interactive recommendation with reinforcement learning, in: H.W. Lauw, R.C.W. Wong, A. Ntoulas, E.P. Lim, S.K. Ng, S.J. Pan (Eds.), Advances in Knowledge Discovery and Data Mining, Springer International Publishing, Cham, 2020, pp. 155–167.

[59] W. Liu, J. Zhong, R. Wu, B.L. Fylstra, J. Si, H.H. Huang, Inferring human-robot performance objectives during locomotion using inverse reinforcement learning and inverse optimal control, IEEE Robotics and Automation Letters 7 (2022) 2549–2556.

[60] J. Luketina, N. Nardelli, G. Farquhar, J. Foerster, J. Andreas, E. Grefenstette, S. Whiteson, T. Rocktäschel, A survey of reinforcement learning informed by natural language, arXiv:1906.03926, 2019.

[61] K. Ma, J. Wang, V. Singh, B. Tamersoy, Y.J. Chang, A. Wimmer, T. Chen, Multimodal image registration with deep context reinforcement learning, in: International Conference on Medical Image Computing and Computer-Assisted Intervention (MICCAI), Springer, 2017, pp. 240–248.

[62] G. Maicas, G. Carneiro, A.P. Bradley, J.C. Nascimento, I. Reid, Deep reinforcement learning for active breast lesion detection from DCE-MRI, in: International Conference on Medical Image Computing and Computer-Assisted Intervention (MICCAI), Springer, 2017, pp. 665–673.

[63] S.J. Majeed, M. Hutter, On q-learning convergence for non-Markov decision processes, in: IJCAI, 2018, pp. 2546–2552.

[64] W. Masson, P. Ranchod, G. Konidaris, Reinforcement learning with parameterized actions, in: Proceedings of the AAAI Conference on Artificial Intelligence, AAAI Press, 2016, pp. 1934–1940.

[65] V. Mnih, A.P. Badia, M. Mirza, A. Graves, T. Lillicrap, T. Harley, D. Silver, K. Kavukcuoglu, Asynchronous methods for deep reinforcement learning, in: Proceedings of the International Conference on Machine Learning, 2016, pp. 1928–1937.

[66] V. Mnih, K. Kavukcuoglu, D. Silver, A. Graves, I. Antonoglou, D. Wierstra, M. Riedmiller, Playing Atari with deep reinforcement learning, arXiv:1312.5602, 2013.

[67] V. Mnih, K. Kavukcuoglu, D. Silver, A.A. Rusu, J. Veness, M.G. Bellemare, A. Graves, M. Riedmiller, A.K. Fidjeland, G. Ostrovski, et al., Human-level control through deep reinforcement learning, Nature 518 (2015) 529.

[68] O. Nachum, M. Norouzi, K. Xu, D. Schuurmans, Bridging the gap between value and policy based reinforcement learning, in: I. Guyon, U.V. Luxburg, S. Bengio, H. Wallach, R. Fergus, S. Vishwanathan, R. Garnett (Eds.), Advances in Neural Information Processing Systems, Curran Associates, Inc., 2017.

[69] A.Y. Ng, S.J. Russell, Algorithms for inverse reinforcement learning, in: Proceedings of the International Conference on Machine Learning, Morgan Kaufmann Publishers Inc., San Francisco, CA, USA, 2000, pp. 663–670.

[70] T. Osa, J. Pajarinen, G. Neumann, J.A. Bagnell, P. Abbeel, J. Peters, An algorithmic perspective on imitation learning, https://doi.org/10.1561/2300000053, 2018.

[71] J. Peters, J.A. Bagnell, Policy Gradient Methods, Springer US, Boston, MA, 2010, pp. 774–776.

[72] L. Pineda, S. Basu, A. Romero, R. Calandra, M. Drozdzal, Active mr k-space sampling with reinforcement learning, in: International Conference on Medical Image Computing and Computer-Assisted Intervention (MICCAI), Springer, 2020, pp. 23–33.

[73] V.H. Pong, A.V. Nair, L.M. Smith, C. Huang, S. Levine, Offline meta-reinforcement learning with online self-supervision, in: International Conference on Machine Learning, PMLR, 2022, pp. 17811–17829.

[74] E. Potokar, S. Ashford, M. Kaess, J.G. Mangelson, Holoocean: an underwater robotics simulator, in: 2022 International Conference on Robotics and Automation (ICRA), IEEE, 2022, pp. 3040–3046.

[75] T. Qaiser, N.M. Rajpoot, Learning where to see: a novel attention model for automated immunohistochemical scoring, IEEE Transactions on Medical Imaging 38 (2019) 2620–2631.

[76] T. Qin, Z. Wang, K. He, Y. Shi, Y. Gao, D. Shen, Automatic data augmentation via deep reinforcement learning for effective kidney tumor segmentation, in: IEEE International Conference on Acoustics, Speech and Signal Processing (ICASSP), 2020, pp. 1419–1423.

[77] K. Rakelly, A. Zhou, C. Finn, S. Levine, D. Quillen, Efficient off-policy meta-reinforcement learning via probabilistic context variables, in: Proceedings of the International Conference on Machine Learning, 2019, pp. 5331–5340.

[78] A. Ranjan, A.K. Mahadani, T.A. Rashid, Multi-agent reinforcement learning for stock market strategy analysis, in: Multi Agent Systems, Springer, 2022, pp. 197–219.

[79] L.I. Rudin, S. Osher, E. Fatemi, Nonlinear total variation based noise removal algorithms, Physica D. Nonlinear Phenomena 60 (1992) 259–268.

[80] S.U. Saeed, Y. Fu, V. Stavrinides, Z.M. Baum, Q. Yang, M. Rusu, R.E. Fan, G.A. Sonn, J.A. Noble, D.C. Barratt, et al., Image quality assessment for machine learning tasks using meta-reinforcement learning, Medical Image Analysis 78 (2022) 102427.

[81] F. Sahba, H.R. Tizhoosh, M.M. Salama, A reinforcement learning framework for medical image segmentation, in: IJCNN, 2006, pp. 511–517.

[82] J. Schulman, S. Levine, P. Moritz, M.I. Jordan, P. Abbeel, Trust region policy optimization, arXiv:1502.05477, 2015.

[83] J. Schulman, F. Wolski, P. Dhariwal, A. Radford, O. Klimov, Proximal policy optimization algorithms, arXiv:1707.06347, 2017.

[84] N. Schweighofer, K. Doya, Meta-learning in reinforcement learning, Neural Networks 16 (2003) 5–9.

[85] C. Shen, Y. Gonzalez, L. Chen, S.B. Jiang, X. Jia, Intelligent parameter tuning in optimization-based iterative ct reconstruction via deep reinforcement learning, IEEE Transactions on Medical Imaging 37 (2018) 1430–1439.

[86] Z. Shen, Y. Wang, D. Wu, X. Yang, B. Dong, Learning to scan: a deep reinforcement learning approach for personalized scanning in ct imaging, arXiv:2006.02420, 2020.

[87] M. Shokri, H.R. Tizhoosh, Using reinforcement learning for image thresholding, in: Electrical and Computer Engineering, 2003. IEEE CCECE 2003. Canadian Conference on, IEEE, 2003, pp. 1231–1234.

[88] R.S. Sutton, A.G. Barto, Reinforcement Learning: An Introduction, MIT Press, 2018.

[89] R.S. Sutton, D.A. McAllester, S.P. Singh, Y. Mansour, Policy gradient methods for reinforcement learning with function approximation, in: Advances in Neural Information Processing Systems 12, 2000, pp. 1057–1063.

[90] P.H. Torr, A. Zisserman, Mlesac: a new robust estimator with application to estimating image geometry, Computer Vision and Image Understanding 78 (2000) 138–156.

[91] Y. Tsurumine, Y. Cui, E. Uchibe, T. Matsubara, Deep reinforcement learning with smooth policy update: application to robotic cloth manipulation, Robotics and Autonomous Systems 112 (2019) 72–83.

[92] Y. Tsurumine, Y. Cui, K. Yamazaki, T. Matsubara, Generative adversarial imitation learning with deep p-network for robotic cloth manipulation, in: 2019 IEEE-RAS 19th International Conference on Humanoid Robots (Humanoids), 2019, pp. 274–280.

[93] H. van Hasselt, A. Guez, D. Silver, Deep reinforcement learning with double q-learning, arXiv:1509.06461, 2015.

[94] A. Vlontzos, A. Alansary, K. Kamnitsas, D. Rueckert, B. Kainz, Multiple landmark detection using multi-agent reinforcement learning, in: International Conference on Medical Image Computing and Computer-Assisted Intervention (MICCAI), Springer, 2019, pp. 262–270.

[95] J. Wang, J. Miao, X. Yang, R. Li, G. Zhou, Y. Huang, Z. Lin, W. Xue, X. Jia, J. Zhou, et al., Auto-weighting for breast cancer classification in multimodal ultrasound, in: International Conference on Medical Image Computing and Computer-Assisted Intervention (MICCAI), Springer, 2020, pp. 190–199.

[96] J.X. Wang, Z. Kurth-Nelson, D. Tirumala, H. Soyer, J.Z. Leibo, R. Munos, C. Blundell, D. Kumaran, M. Botvinick, Learning to reinforcement learn, arXiv:1611.05763, 2016.

[97] K.N. Wang, X. Yang, J. Miao, L. Li, J. Yao, P. Zhou, W. Xue, G.Q. Zhou, X. Zhuang, D. Ni, Awsnet: an auto-weighted supervision attention network for myocardial scar and edema segmentation in multi-sequence cardiac magnetic resonance images, Medical Image Analysis 77 (2022) 102362.

[98] L. Wang, K. Lekadir, S.L. Lee, R. Merrifield, G.Z. Yang, A general framework for context-specific image segmentation using reinforcement learning, IEEE Transactions on Medical Imaging 32 (2013) 943–956.

[99] Z. Wang, T. Schaul, M. Hessel, H. Van Hasselt, M. Lanctot, N. De Freitas, Dueling network architectures for deep reinforcement learning, arXiv:1511.06581, 2015.

[100] D.H. Wolpert, K. Tumer, Optimal payoff functions for members of collectives, in: Modeling Complexity in Economic and Social Systems, World Scientific, 2002, pp. 355–369.

[101] B. Xu, J. Liu, X. Hou, B. Liu, J. Garibaldi, I.O. Ellis, A. Green, L. Shen, G. Qiu, Attention by selection: a deep selective attention approach to breast cancer classification, IEEE Transactions on Medical Imaging 39 (2019) 1930–1941.

[102] Z. Xu, Q. Huang, J. Park, M. Chen, D. Xu, D. Yang, D. Liu, S.K. Zhou, Supervised action classifier: approaching landmark detection as image partitioning, in: International Conference on Medical Image Computing and Computer-Assisted Intervention (MICCAI), Springer, 2017, pp. 338–346.

[103] D. Yang, H. Roth, Z. Xu, F. Milletari, L. Zhang, D. Xu, Searching learning strategy with reinforcement learning for 3D medical image segmentation, in: International Conference on Medical Image Computing and Computer-Assisted Intervention (MICCAI), Springer, 2019, pp. 3–11.

[104] H. Yang, C. Shan, A.F. Kolen, P.H.N. de With, Deep q-network-driven catheter segmentation in 3D US by hybrid constrained semi-supervised learning and dual-unet, in: International Conference on Medical Image Computing and Computer-Assisted Intervention (MICCAI), 2020, pp. 646–655.

[105] X. Yang, H. Dou, R. Huang, W. Xue, Y. Huang, J. Qian, Y. Zhang, H. Luo, H. Guo, T. Wang, et al., Agent with warm start and adaptive dynamic termination for plane localization in 3d ultrasound, IEEE Transactions on Medical Imaging 40 (2021) 1950–1961.

[106] J. Ye, Y. Xue, L.R. Long, S. Antani, Z. Xue, K.C. Cheng, X. Huang, Synthetic sample selection via reinforcement learning, in: International Conference on Medical Image Computing and Computer-Assisted Intervention (MICCAI), Springer, 2020, pp. 53–63.

[107] T. Yu, D. Quillen, Z. He, R. Julian, K. Hausman, C. Finn, S. Levine, Meta-world: a benchmark and evaluation for multi-task and meta reinforcement learning, in: Conference on Robot Learning, 2020, pp. 1094–1100.

[108] J.N. Zaech, C. Gao, B. Bier, R. Taylor, A. Maier, N. Navab, M. Unberath, Learning to avoid poor images: towards task-aware c-arm cone-beam ct trajectories, in: International Conference on Medical Image Computing and Computer-Assisted Intervention (MICCAI), Springer, 2019, pp. 11–19.

[109] J. Zbontar, F. Knoll, A. Sriram, M.J. Muckley, M. Bruno, A. Defazio, M. Parente, K.J. Geras, J. Katsnelson, H. Chandarana, et al., fastMRI: an open dataset and benchmarks for accelerated MRI, arXiv:1811.08839, 2018.

[110] D. Zhang, B. Chen, J. Chong, S. Li, Weakly-supervised teacher-student network for liver tumor segmentation from non-enhanced images, Medical Image Analysis 70 (2021) 102005.

[111] M. Zhang, J. Xu, E. Abaci Turk, P.E. Grant, P. Golland, E. Adalsteinsson, Enhanced detection of fetal pose in 3D MRI by deep reinforcement learning with physical structure priors on anatomy, in: International Conference on Medical Image Computing and Computer-Assisted Intervention (MICCAI), 2020, pp. 396–405.

[112] P. Zhang, F. Wang, Y. Zheng, Deep reinforcement learning for vessel centerline tracing in multi-modality 3D volumes, in: International Conference on Medical Image Computing and Computer-Assisted Intervention (MICCAI), Springer, 2018, pp. 755–763.

[113] Y. Zhang, G. Luo, W. Wang, K. Wang, Branch-aware double dqn for centerline extraction in coronary ct angiography, in: International Conference on Medical Image Computing and Computer-Assisted Intervention (MICCAI), 2020, pp. 35–44.

[114] Z. Zhao, Z. Wang, K. Han, R. Gupta, P. Tiwari, G. Wu, M.J. Barth, Personalized car following for autonomous driving with inverse reinforcement learning, in: 2022 International Conference on Robotics and Automation (ICRA), IEEE, 2022, pp. 2891–2897.

[115] S.K. Zhou, H. Greenspan, C. Davatzikos, J.S. Duncan, B. van Ginneken, A. Madabhushi, J.L. Prince, D. Rueckert, R.M. Summers, A review of deep learning in medical imaging: image traits, technology trends, case studies with progress highlights, and future promises, arXiv:2008.09104, 2020.

[116] Z. Zhu, L. Wang, B. Magnier, L. Zhu, D. Zhang, L. Yu, Reinforcement learning driven intra-modal and inter-modal representation learning for 3d medical image classification, in: International Conference on Medical Image Computing and Computer-Assisted Intervention, Springer, 2022, pp. 604–613.

[117] B. Zoph, Q.V. Le, Neural architecture search with reinforcement learning, arXiv:1611.01578, 2016.

CapsNet for medical image segmentation

3

Minh Tran[a], **Viet-Khoa Vo-Ho**[a], **Kyle Quinn**[b], **Hien Nguyen**[c], **Khoa Luu**[a], **and Ngan Le**[a]

[a]*Department of Computer Science & Computer Engineering, University of Arkansas, Fayetteville, NC, United States*
[b]*Department of Biomedical Engineering, University of Arkansas, Fayetteville, NC, United States*
[c]*Department of Electrical & Computer Engineering, Houston, TX, United States*

3.1 Convolutional neural networks: limitations

Despite outperforming in various computer vision tasks, CNNs ignore the geometrical relationships of objects. As a result, CNNs are sensitive to image rotation and affine transformation, which are not present in the training data. Recent works have shown that small translations or rescalings of the input image can drastically change the network's performance. To address such limitations in CNNs, their generalization relies on a large-scale training data, which captures various input variations such as rotations and viewpoint changes. In this section, we first report some quantified analyses of this phenomenon. We then analyze how the CNNs architectures do not produce invariance.

The lack of invariance of modern CNNs to small image deformation was reported in [8,2,33,3]. Take [3] as an instance. Azulay and Weiss selected three different CNN architectures—VGG16, ResNet50, InceptionRes- NetV2— from the Keras package and three other different CNN architectures—VGG16, ResNet50, DenseNet121—from the Pytorch package. They tested 1000 images with four different protocols including crop, Translation - Embedding - Black, Translation - Embedding - Inpainting, Scale - Embedding - Black to systematically quantify the effect of invariance to CNNs. In the first protocol, a random square is randomly chosen within the original image and the square is resized to be 224x224. In the second protocol, the image is down-sampled so that its minimal dimension is of size 100 while maintaining the aspect ratio, and embedding it in a random location within the 224x224 image, while filling in the rest of the image with black pixels. They then shift the embedding location by a single pixel, again creating two images that are identical up to a shift by a single pixel. In the third protocol, they repeat the embedding experiment but rather than filling in the rest of the image with black pixels we use a simple inpainting algorithm (each black pixel is replaced by a weighted average of the nonblack pixels in its neighborhood). The fourth protocol is similar to the second protocol, but rather than shifting the embedding location, they keep the embedding location fixed and change the size of the embedded image by a single pixel. They used "P(Top-1 change)" and "mean absolute change" (MAC) to measure the network sensitivity. The first metric "P(Top-1 change)" is invariant to any monotonic transformation of the output of the final layer of the network, while the second one tells us the possibility that changes in the top-1 prediction are due to very small differences between the most likely class and the second most likely class. The quantitative analysis on three Keras networks was discussed in [3], which indicates that CNNs are not fully translation-invariant.

Furthermore, in a CNN, a pooling layer works as a messenger between two layers and transfers the activation information from one layer to the next layer. By doing that, a pooling layer can indicate the presence of a part, but is unable to capture the spatial relation among the parts. Clearly, a pooling operation (e.g., max-pooling) does not make the model invariant to viewpoint changes. Moreover, each filter of convolutional layers works like a feature detector in a small region of the input features. When going deeper into a network, the detected low-level features are aggregated and become high-level features that can be used to distinguish between different objects. The higher-level features in a CNN are built as a weighted sum of lower-level features. Thus geometric relationships among features are not taken into account.

Over the years, different techniques have been developed to tackle the aforementioned limitations in CNNs. Most common solutions including data augmentation techniques, increase the data size to include transformations.

3.2 Capsule network: fundamental

Inspired by how a visual image was constructed from geometrical objects and matrices that represent relative positions and orientation, Hinton [11] proved that preserving hierarchical pose relationships among object parts is important to correctly classify and recognize an object. This is also known as inverse graphics, similar to how the brain recognizes the object. To address the limitations in CNNs, Hinton [11] proposed to replace neuron's scalar output, which only represents the activation of replicated feature detectors with vector output (a.k.a. capsule). Each capsule will learn a visual entity (e.g., a part of an object). The output of each capsule is presented by a vector that contains both the probability that this entity is present and a set of "instantiation parameters" that capture different properties of the entity.

CapsNet [27] was proposed to address the above intrinsic limitations of CNNs. CapsNet strengthens feature learning by retaining more information at the aggregation layer for pose reasoning and learning the part-whole relationship. Different from CNNs that contain a backbone network to extract features, several fully connected layers and N-way Soft-Max produce the classification logits; a CapsNet contains more complex with five components as follows:

- Nonshared transformation module: the primary capsules are transformed to execute votes by nonshared transformation matrices.

- Dynamic routing layer: to group input capsules to produce output capsules with high agreements in each output capsule.
- Squashing function: to squash the capsule vectors' lengths to the range of [0, 1).
- Marginal classification loss: to work together with the squashed capsule representation.
- Reconstruction loss: to recover the original image from the capsule representations.

The network architecture comparison between CNNs and CapsNet is shown in Fig. 3.1 whereas the operators, input and output comparison are given in Fig. 3.2. In CNNs, each filter takes in charge of feature detector in a small region of the input features and as we go deeper. The detected low-level features are aggregated and become high-level features that can be used to distinguish between different objects. However, by doing so, each feature map only contains information about the presence of the feature, and the network relies on fix learned weight matrix to link features between layers. It leads to the problem that the model cannot generalize well to unseen changes in the input [1]. In CapsNet, each layer aims to learn a part of an object together with its properties and represents them in a vector. The entity of previous layer represents simple objects whereas the next layers represent complex objects through the voting process.

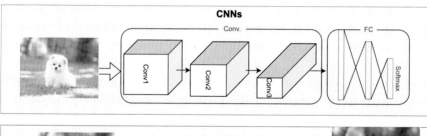

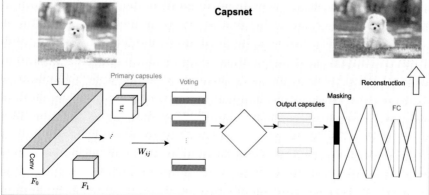

FIGURE 3.1

Network architecture comparison between CNNs and CapsNet.

		Capsule	Neuron
Input from lower-level capsules/neurons		vector(u_i)	scalar(x_i)
Operations	**Linear/Affine transformation**	$\hat{v}_{j\|i} = W_{ij}u_i + B_j$	$a_{j\|i} = w_{ij}x_i + b_j$
	Coupling coefficients	$c_{ij} = softmax(b_{ij})$	–
	Sum	$s_j = \sum_i c_{ij}\hat{v}_{j\|i}$	$z_j = \sum_i 1.a_{j\|i}$
	Nonlinearity activation	$v_j = \frac{\|\|s_j\|\|^2}{1+\|\|s_j\|\|^2}\frac{s_j}{\|\|s_j\|\|}$	$h_{w,b}(x) = f(z_j)$
	Update couplings by agreement	$b_{ij} = b_{ij} + \hat{v}_{j\|i}.v_j$	–
Output		vector(v_j)	scalar(h)

FIGURE 3.2

Operators comparison between CNNs and CapsNet.

Let denote $F_0 \in \mathbb{R}^{C \times W \times H}$ the visual feature map, which is extracted by a few convolutional layers. It then is reshaped as primary capsules $F_1 \in \mathbb{R}^{\frac{C}{D_i} \times W \times H \times D_i}$, where D_i is the dimensions of the primary capsules. In such design, there is $\frac{C}{D_i} \times W \times H$ number of capsules, each of capsule is in $\mathbb{R}^{D_i}$. Let $W_{ij} \in \mathbb{R}^{D_i \times [N \times R_o]}$ be a transformer matrix, each primary capsule u_i is transformed to make a vote as $\hat{v}_{j|i} = W_{ij}u_i + B_j$, where N is output classes and D_o is the dimension of output capsules. In CapsNet, a dynamic routing process at the tth iteration takes all votes into consideration to compute weight c_{ij} for each vote $\tilde{u}_{j|i}$ as follows:

$$s_j^t = \sum_{i=1}^{N} c_{ij}^t \hat{v}_{j|i}$$
$$v_j^t = f^{squash}(s_j^t)$$
$$c_{ij}^{t+1} = \frac{exp(b_{ij} + \sum_{m=1}^{t} v_j^m \hat{v}_{j|i})}{\sum_{k=1} exp(b_{ik} + \sum_{m=1}^{t} v_k^m \hat{v}_{k|i})} \qquad (3.1)$$
$$b_{ij} = b_{ij} + \hat{v}_{j|i} v_j^t$$

b_{ij} is log prior probability, c_{ij} is coupling coefficient that models the degree with which $\hat{v}_{j|i}$ is able to predict s_j. It is initialized as $c_{ij} = \frac{exp(b_{ij})}{\sum_k exp(b_{ik})}$. f^{squash} is a squashing function that maps the length of a vector to $[0, 1)$, i.e.,

$$v_j = f^{squash}(s) = \frac{|s|^2}{1 + |s|^2}\frac{s}{|s|} \qquad (3.2)$$

The classification loss is defined as a margin loss as follows:

$$\mathcal{L}_m = I_k max(0, m^+ - |v_k|)^2 + \lambda(1 - I_k)max(0, |v_k|) - m^-)^2 \qquad (3.3)$$

As suggested by [27], m^+, m^-, λ are set 0.9, 0.1 0.5; $I_k = 1$ if the object of the kth class is present in the input.

Algorithm 3.1 The pseudo-code of the dynamic routing algorithm.

Data: Capsule v_i at layer (l).

Result: Capsule v_j at layer (l+1).

  1: Initial: for all capsule i in layer (l) and capsule j in layer (l + 1), $b_{ij} \leftarrow 0$

  2: **for** each iteration **do**

  3:      **for** all capsule i at layer (l) **do** $c_{ij} \leftarrow \text{softmax}(b_{ij})$

  4:      **end for**

  5:      **for** all capsule j at layer (l+1) **do**

  6:          $s_j = \sum_{i=1}^{N} c_{ij}^t \hat{v}_{j|i}$

  7:          $v_j = f^{squash}(s_j)$

  8:      **end for**

  9:      **for** all capsule i in layer (l) and capsule j in layer (l + 1) **do**

 10:          $b_{ij} = b_{ij} + \hat{v}_{j|i} v_j$

 11:      **end for**

 12: **end for**

The reconstruction loss is computed as a regularization term in the loss function. The pseudo-code of the dynamic routing algorithm is presented in Algorithm 3.1.

Now, let consider the back-propagation through routing iterations. Assuming that there are K iterations and M capsules at output $v_1^k, v_2^K, ...v_M^K$, gradients through the routing procedure are

$$\frac{\partial \mathcal{L}}{\partial \hat{v}_{j|i}} = \frac{\partial \mathcal{L}}{\partial v_j^K} \frac{\partial v_j^K}{\partial s_j^K} c_{ij}^K + \sum_{m=1}^{M} \frac{\partial \mathcal{L}}{\partial v_m^K} \frac{\partial v_m^K}{\partial s_m^K} \hat{v}_{m|i} \frac{\partial c_{im}^K}{\partial \hat{v}_{j|i}} \tag{3.4}$$

The second term in Eq. (3.4) is actually the main computational burden of the expensive routing.

We further investigate the robustness CapsNet when comparing it with CNNs as follows:

- Translation invariant: While CNNs are able to identify if the object exists in a certain region, they are unable to identify the position of one object relative to another. Thus CNNs cannot model spatial relationships between objects/features. As shown in Fig. 3.3, CNNs can tell if it is a dog image or face image but it cannot tell the spatial relationship between the dog and the picture or position relation between facial components.
- Require less data to generalize: CNNs require together massive amounts of data that represents each object in various positions and poses. Then we train the CNNs on this huge data set with a hope that the network is able to see enough examples of the object to generalize. Thus, to better generalize over variations of the same object, CNNs are trained on multiple copies of every sample, each being slightly different. Data augmentation is one of the most common techniques to make the CNNs model more robust. With CapsNet, it encodes invariant part-whole spatial

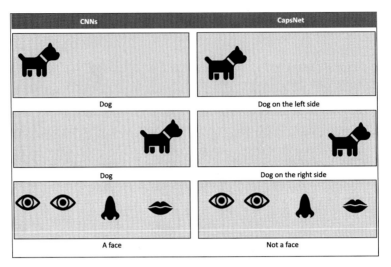

FIGURE 3.3

Translation invariant comparison between CNNs and CapsNet.

relationships into learned weights. Thus, CapsNet is able to encode various positions and poses information of parts and the invariant part-whole relationships to generalize to unseen variations of the objects.

- Interpretability: There have been a large number of interpretation methods proposed to understand individual classifications of CNNs; model interpretability is still a significant challenge for CNNs. By taking part-whole relation into consideration, the higher capsule in CapsNet is interpretable and explainable. Thus CapsNet is inherently more interpretable networks than traditional neural networks as capsules tend to encode specific semantic concepts. Especially, the disentangled representations captured by CapsNet often correspond to human understandable visual properties of input objects, e.g., rotations and translations.

3.3 Capsule network: related work

There have been different mechanisms proposed to improve the performance of CapsNet. In general, we categorize them into two groups. The first one aims to propose various effective dynamic routing mechanisms to improve dynamic routing [27]. Dynamic routing identifies the weights of predictions made by the lower-level capsules, called coupling coefficients by an iterative routing-by-agreement mechanism. EM Routing [12] updates coupling coefficients iteratively using Expectation-Maximization. By utilizing attention modules augmented by differentiable binary routers, [6] proposes a straight-through attentive routing to reduce the high-computational complexity of dynamic routing iterations in [27]. To increase the computational efficiency, Mobiny et al. [17] proposes a consistent dynamic routing mechanism that results in $3\times$ speedup of CapsNet. Recently, [26] proposes a new capsule routing algorithm derived from Variational Bayes for fitting a mixture of transforming Gaussians to show that it is possible to transform a capsule network into a Capsule-VAE. To reduce the parameters of CapsNet, [12,25] propose to use a matrix or a tensor to represent an entity instead of a vectors. The second category focuses on network architecture such as combining both Convolutional layers and Capsule layers [24], unsupervised capsule auto-encoder [14], Aff-CapsNets and Memory-augmented CapsNet [19]. While [9] removes the dynamic routing by sharing the transformation matrix, [10] replaces the dynamic routing with a multi-head attention-based graph pooling approach to achieve better interpretability. Recently, Mobiny et al. [18] proposed DECAPS, which utilize Inverted Dynamic Routing (IDR) mechanism to group lower-level capsules before sending them to higher-level capsules as well as employ a Peekaboo training procedure to encourage the network to focus on fine-grained information through a second-level attention scheme. DECAPS has outperformed experienced, well-trained thoracic radiologists [20].

3.4 CapsNets in medical image segmentation

This section introduces various recent CapsNets that have been proposed in medical image segmentation.

3.4.1 2D-SegCaps

CapsNet has been mainly applied to image classification and image recognition; its performance is still limited compared to the state-of-the-art by CNNs-based approaches. 2D-SegCaps [15,16] was the first CapsNet proposed for semantic image segmentation and illustrated as in Fig. 3.4. As stated by [15,16], performing semantic image segmentation with a CapsNet is extremely challenging because of high-computational complexity during the routing process, which takes place between every parent and every possible child. The 2D-SegCaps is an UNet-based architecture with Capsule blocks are at both encoder and decoder paths. It contains four components corresponding to (i) visual feature extraction, which produces 16 feature maps of the same spatial dimensions, (ii) convolutional capsule at the encoder path, (iii) de-convolutional capsule at the decoder path and (iv) reconstruction regularization at decoder path. Details of the four components are as follows:

- **Feature extraction:** 2D-SegCaps network takes a large 2D image 512×512 (e.g., a slice of a MRI scan) as its input. The image is passed through a 2D Conv layer, which produces 16 feature maps of the same spatial dimensions, $512 \times 512 \times 16$. This becomes input of the following convolutional capsule layers.
- **Convolutional capsule encoder:** The process of convolutional capsules and routing to any given layer l in the network are given as follows:

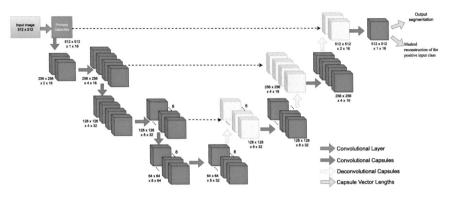

FIGURE 3.4

Network architecture of 2D-SegCaps [15,16] for biomedical image segmentation. The network is an UNet-based architecture with Capsule blocks that are at both encoder and decoder paths.

- At layer l: There exists a set of capsule types

$$T^l = t_1^l, t_2^l, ..., t_n^l, n \in \mathbb{N} \tag{3.5}$$

For every t_i^l, there exists an $h^l \times w^l$ grid of d^l-dimensional child capsules

$$C = c_{1,1}, c_{1,2}, ...c_{1,w^l}, c_{2,1}, ..., c_{h^l,w^l}, \tag{3.6}$$

where $h^l \times w^l$ is the spatial dimensions of the output of layer $l - 1$.

- At layer $l + 1$, there exists a set of capsule types

$$T^{l+1} = t_1^{l+1}, t_2^{l+1}, ..., t_m^{l+1}, m \in \mathbb{N} \tag{3.7}$$

For every t_i^{l+1}, there exists an $h^{l+1} \times w^{l+1}$ grid of d^{l+1}-dimensional parent capsules

$$P = p_{1,1}, p_{1,2}, ...p_{1,w^{l+1}}, p_{2,1}, ..., c_{h^{l+1},w^{l+1}}, \tag{3.8}$$

where $h^{l+1} \times w^{l+1}$ is the spatial dimensions of the output of layer l.

- For every parent capsule type $t_i^{l+1} \in T^{l+1}$, every parent capsule p_{xy} receives a set of "prediction vectors," each value is for each capsule type in T^l, i.e., $[\hat{v}_{xy|t_1^l}, \hat{v}_{xy|t_2^l}, ...\hat{v}_{xy|t_n^l}]$. This set of prediction vectors is defined as the matrix multiplication between a learned transformation matrix for the given parent capsule type, $M_{t_j^{l+1}}$, and the sub-grid of child capsules outputs, $V_{xy|t_i^l}$. The sub-grid of child capsules outputs $V_{xy|t_i^l} \in \mathcal{R}^{h^k \times w^k \times d^l}$, where h^k, w^k, d^l are the dimensions of the user-defined kernel, for all capsule types $t_i^l \in T^l$. Each parents capsules has dimension $M_{t_j^{l+1}} \in \mathcal{R}^{h^k \times w^k \times d^l \times d^{l+1}}$. The $\hat{v}_{xy|t_i^l} \in \mathcal{R}^{d^{l+1}}$ is computed as

$$\hat{v}_{xy|t_i^l} = M_{t_j^{l+1}} V_{xy|t_i^l} \qquad (3.9)$$

To reduce total number of learned parameters, 2D-SegCaps shares transformation matrices across members of the grid, i.e., $M_{t_j^{l+1}}$ does not depend on the spatial location. This transformation matrix is shared across all spatial locations within a given capsule type. Such mechanism is similar to how convolutional kernels scan an input feature map and this is the main difference between 2D-SegCaps and CapsNet. The parent capsule $p_{xy} \in P$ for parent capsule type $t_j^{l+1} \in T^{l+1}$ is then computed as follows:

$$p_{xy} \sum_n c_{t_i^l|xy} \hat{v}_{xy|t_i^l} \qquad (3.10)$$

where $c_{t_i^l|xy}$ is coupling coefficient defined in Eq. (3.1), i.e., $c_{t_i^l|xy} = \dfrac{exp(b_{t_i^l|xy})}{\sum_{t_j^{l+1}} exp(b_{t_i^l|t_j^{l+1}})}$. The output capsule is then computed using a nonlinear squashing function as defined in Eq. (3.1) as follows:

$$v_{xy} = f^{squash}(p_{xy}) \qquad (3.11)$$

Lastly, the agreement is measured as the scalar product

$$b_{xy} = v_{xy} \hat{v}_{xy|t_i^l} \qquad (3.12)$$

Unlike dynamic routing in CapsNet [27], 2D-SegCaps locally constrains the creation of the prediction vectors. Furthermore, 2D-SegCaps only routes the child capsules within the user-defined kernel $h^k \times w^k$ to the parent, rather than routing every single child capsule to every single parent.

- **De-convolutional capsule decoder:** De-convolutional capsules are as similar as the convolutional capsules; however, the prediction vectors are now formed using the transpose of the operation previously described. In the de-convolutional capsules, the set of prediction vectors are defined as the matrix multiplication between a learned transformation matrix, $M_{t_j^{l+1}}$ for a parent capsule type $t_j^{l+1} \in T^{l+1}$ and the sub-grid of child capsules outputs, $U_{xy|t_i^l}$ for each capsule type in $t_i^l \in T^l$. For each member of the grid, we can then form our prediction vectors again by the following equation:

$$\hat{u}_{xy|t_j^l} = M_{t_j^{l+1}} U_{xy|t_i^l} \qquad (3.13)$$

Similar to the convolutional capsule encoder, $\hat{u}_{xy|t_j^l}$ is the input to the dynamic routing algorithm to form our parent capsules and $\hat{u}_{xy|t_j^l} \in \mathcal{R}^{d^{l+1}}$.

- **Reconstruction regularization:** This component aims to model the distribution of the positive input class and treat all other pixels as background, the segmentation capsules which do not belong to the positive class is masked out. The reconstruction is performed via a three 1×1 Conv. layers. Then it is computed by a mean-squared error (MSE) loss between only the positive input pixels and this reconstruction. The supervised loss for the reconstruction regularization is computed as follows:

$$R = I \times S | S \in \{0, 1\}$$
$$\mathcal{L}_{Reco} = \frac{\gamma}{H \times W} ||R - O||, \tag{3.14}$$

where I is the input image, R is the reconstruction target, S is the ground-truth segmentation mask and O is the output of the reconstruction network. γ is weighting coefficient for the reconstruction loss and set to $1 - 0.001$.

2D-SegCaps [15,16] is trained with a supervised loss function. There are three loss functions included in the algorithm as follows:

- **Margin loss:** The margin loss is adopted from [27] and it is defined between the predicted label y and the ground truth label y^* as follows:

$$\mathcal{L}_{margin} = y^* \times (\max(0, 0.9 - y))^2 + \tag{3.15}$$
$$0.5 \times (1 - y^*) \times (\max(0, y - 0.1))^2.$$

Particularly, we compute the margin loss ($\mathcal{L}_{margin}$) on the capsule encoder output with down-sampled ground truth segmentation.
- **Weighted cross entropy loss:** We compute the weighted cross-entropy loss ($\mathcal{L}_{CE}$) on the convolutional decoder.
- **Reconstruction regularization:** We also regularize the training with a network branch that aims at reconstructing the original input with masked mean-squared errors ($\mathcal{L}_{Reco}$) as in Eq. (3.14).

The total loss is the weighted sum of the three losses as follows:

$$\mathcal{L} = \mathcal{L}_{margin} + \mathcal{L}_{CE} + \mathcal{L}_{Reco} \tag{3.16}$$

2D-SegCaps has obtained promising performance on LUNA16 data set [28]; however, Survarachakan et al. [30] has shown that 2D-SegCaps performance is significantly decreased on the MSD data set [29] compared with Unet-based architectures. Furthermore, Survarachakan et al. [30] extend 2D-SegCaps to Multi-SegCaps to support multiple class segmentation. Unlike 2D-SegCaps, the output capsule layer in Multi-SegCaps is modified to output $N16D$ output capsules, where N is the number of classes in the data set, including background, and the predicted class is the one represented by the capsule with the longest Euclidean length. Thus, Multi-SegCaps attempts to reconstruct the pixels belonging to all classes, except for the background class instead of a single target class as in 2D-SegCaps.

Like other CapsNet, 2D-SegCaps and Multi-SegCaps have the limitation of high-computational complexity, which is caused by dynamic routing. To address such concern, Survarachakan et al. [30] makes use of EM-routing [12] and proposes EM-routing SegCaps. The EM-routing SegCaps architecture uses matrix capsules with EM-routing and is shown in Fig. 3.5. The main difference between EM-routing SegCaps and 2D-SegCaps is that convolutional capsule layers accept the poses and activations from capsules in the previous layer and output new poses and activations for the capsules in the next via the Expectation-Maximization routing algorithm (EM-routing). In EM-routing SegCaps, all child capsules cast an initial vote of the output for every capsule in the next layer, using its own pose matrices before performance EM-routing. To cast this vote, a transformation matrix going into the parent capsule is trained and shared by all child capsules. In EM-routing SegCaps, predictions are first computed and then forwarded to the EM-routing algorithm, along with the activations from the previous layer. The EM-routing algorithm is run for three iterations before it returns to the final pose and activations for all capsules in the current layer. By replacing dynamic routing in 2D-SegCaps by EM-routing, the performance of EM-routing SegCaps is not much improved compared to 2D-SegCaps.

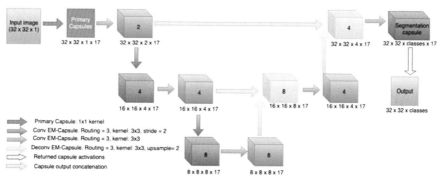

FIGURE 3.5

EM-routing SegCaps architecture.

3.4.2 3D-SegCaps

2D-SegCaps has shown promising performance on 2D medical image segmentation, however, it ignores the temporal relationship when performing on 3D images, e.g., MRIs and CT scans. Nguyen et al. [22] extends 2D-SegCaps to 3D-SegCaps by incorporating temporal information into capsules. Similar to 2D-SegCaps, 3D-SegCaps contains four components corresponding to visual feature extraction, convolutional capsule layers, de-convolutional capsule layers and reconstruction regularization. Details of four components are as follows:

- **Feature extraction:** 3D-SegCaps network takes a volumetric data as its input. The volumetric data is passed through a 3D Conv layer, which produces 16 feature maps of the same spatial dimensions, $64 \times 64 \times 64 \times 16$. This becomes the input for the following convolutional capsule layers.

- **Convolutional capsule encoder:** The process of convolutional capsules and routing to any given layer l in the network are given as follows:
  - At layer l: There exists a set of capsule types

$$T^l = t_1^l, t_2^l, ..., t_n^l, n \in \mathbb{N} \tag{3.17}$$

For every t_i^l, there exists an $h^l \times w^l \times r^l$ grid of d^l-dimensional child capsules

$$C = \{c_{1,1,1}, c_{1,1,2}, ...c_{1,1,r^l}, c_{1,2,1}, ..., c_{1,w^l,1}, c_{2,1,1}, ..., c_{h^l,1,1}, \\ ...c_{1,w^l,r^l}, ..., c_{h^l,w^l,1}, ...c_{h^l,1,r^l}, ...c_{h^l,w^l,r^l}\} \tag{3.18}$$

where $h^l \times w^l \times r^l$ is the spatial dimensions of the output of layer $l - 1$.
  - At layer $l + 1$, there exists a set of capsule types

$$T^{l+1} = t_1^{l+1}, t_2^{l+1}, ..., t_m^{l+1}, m \in \mathbb{N} \tag{3.19}$$

For every t_i^{l+1}, there exists an $h^{l+1} \times w^{l+1} \times r^{l+1}$ grid of d^{l+1}-dimensional parent capsules

$$P = \{p_{1,1,1}, p_{1,1,2}, ...p_{1,1,r^l}, p_{1,2,1}, ..., p_{1,w^l,1}, p_{2,1,1}, ..., p_{h^l,1,1}, \\ ...p_{1,w^l,r^l}, ..., p_{h^l,w^l,1}, ...p_{h^l,1,r^l}, ...p_{h^l,w^l,r^l}\} \tag{3.20}$$

where $h^{l+1} \times w^{l+1} \times r^{l+1}$ is the spatial dimension of the output of layer l.
  - For every parent capsule type $t_i^{l+1} \in T^{l+1}$, every parent capsule p_{xyz} receives a set of "prediction vectors," each value is for each capsule type in T^l, i.e., $[\hat{v}_{xyz|t_1^l}, \hat{v}_{xyz|t_2^l}, ...\hat{v}_{xyz|t_n^l}]$. This set of prediction vectors is defined as the matrix multiplication between a learned transformation matrix for the given parent capsule type, $M_{t_j^{l+1}}$, and the sub-grid of child capsules outputs, $V_{xyz|t_i^l}$. The sub-grid of child capsules outputs $V_{xyz|t_i^l} \in \mathcal{R}^{h^k \times w^k \times r^k \times d^l}$, where h^k, w^k, r^k, d^l are the dimensions of the user-defined kernel, for all capsule types $t_i^l \in T^l$. Each parents capsules has dimension $M_{t_j^{l+1}} \in \mathcal{R}^{h^k \times w^k \times r^k \times d^l \times d^{l+1}}$. The $\hat{v}_{xyz|t_i^l} \in \mathcal{R}^{d^{l+1}}$ is computed as

$$\hat{v}_{xyz|t_i^l} = M_{t_j^{l+1}} V_{xyz|t_i^l} \tag{3.21}$$

To reduce a total number of learned parameters, 3D-SegCaps shares transformation matrices across members of the grid, i.e., $M_{t_j^{l+1}}$ does not depend on the spatial location. This transformation matrix is shared across all spatial locations within a given capsule type. Such a mechanism is similar to how convolutional kernels scan an input feature map and this is the main difference between 3D-SegCaps and CapsNet. The parent capsule $p_{xyz} \in P$ for the parent capsule type $t_j^{l+1} \in T^{l+1}$ is then computed as follows:

$$p_{xyz} \sum_n c_{t_i^l|xyz} \hat{v}_{xyz|t_i^l} \tag{3.22}$$

where $c_{t_i^l|xyz}$ is coupling coefficient defined in Eq. (3.1), i.e., $c_{t_i^l|xyz} = \frac{exp(b_{t_i^l|xyz})}{\sum_{t_j^{l+1}} exp(b_{t_i^l|t_j^{l+1}})}$. Similar to 2D-SegCaps, the output capsule is then computed using a nonlinear squashing function as defined in Eq. (3.1) as follows:

$$v_{xyz} = f^{squash}(p_{xyz}) \qquad (3.23)$$

Finally, the agreement is measured as the scalar product

$$b_{xyz} = v_{xyz}\hat{v}_{xyz|t_i^l} \qquad (3.24)$$

- **De-convolutional capsule decoder:** De-convolutional capsules are similar to the one in 2D-SegCaps, in which the set of prediction vectors are defined again as the matrix multiplication between a learned transformation matrix, $M_{t_j^{l+1}}$ for a parent capsule type $t_j^{l+1} \in T^{l+1}$ and the sub-grid of child capsules outputs, $U_{xyz|t_i^l}$ for each capsule type in $t_i^l \in T^l$. For each member of the grid, we can then form our prediction vectors again by the following equation:

$$\hat{u}_{xyz|t_j^l} = M_{t_j^{l+1}} U_{xyz|t_i^l} \qquad (3.25)$$

where $\hat{u}_{xyz|t_j^l}$ is the input to the dynamic routing algorithm to form our parent capsules and $\hat{u}_{xyz|t_j^l} \in \mathcal{R}^{d^{l+1}}$.
- **Reconstruction regularization**: This component is implemented as in the same manner as it is in 2D-SegCaps.

3.4.3 3D-UCaps

By taking temporal information into consideration, segmentation performance by 3D-SegCaps has been improved compared to 2D-SegCaps. However, the achievement by 3D-SegCaps is still lower than the SOTA performance by 3D-UNets. The observation by [22] has shown that capsule design is capable of extracting richer representation comparing to traditional neural network design. Thus, the convolutional capsule layer is utilized to encode visual representation in 3D-UCaps. Furthermore, under an encoder–decoder network architecture, the decoder path aims to produce a high-detailed segmentation task, which has been highly accurately performed by de-convolutional layers. Thus, de-convolutional layers are used at the decoder path in 3D-UCaps, which is the main difference between 3D-UCaps and 3D-SegCaps. This replacement does not only improve segmentation performance but also reduce computational cost caused by the dynamic routing. The entire network of 3D-UCaps is shown in Fig. 3.6. In CapsNet and CNNs, it follows Unet-like architecture [7] and contains four main components as follows:

- **Visual feature extractor:** A set of dilated convolutional layers is used to convert the input to high-dimensional features that can be further processed by capsules.

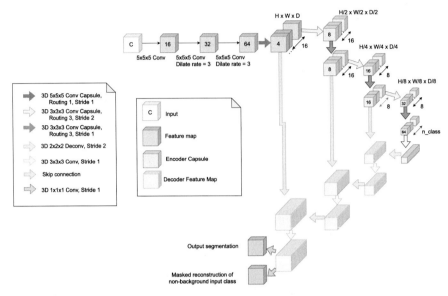

FIGURE 3.6

3D-UCaps architecture with four components: visual feature extraction; convolutional capsule encoder, de-convolutional decoder and reconstruction regularization. The number on the blocks indicates the number of channels in the convolution layer and the dimension of capsules in capsule layers.

It contains three convolution layers with the number of channels increased from 16 to 32 then 64, kernel size $5 \times 5 \times 5$ and dilate rate set to 1, 3 and 3, respectively. The output of this part is a feature map of size $H \times W \times D \times 64$.

- **Convolutional capsule encoder:** This component is designed as a similar mechanism as the one designed in 3D-SegCaps. The implemented details of this component is as follows: The visual feature from the previous component can be cast (reshaped) into a grid of $H \times W \times D$ capsules, each represented as a single 64-dimensional vector. In the convolutional capsule encoder, it is suggested to be designed with more capsule types in low-level layers and less capsule types in high-level layers. This is due to the fact that low-level layers represent a simple object while high-level layers represent complex objects and the clustering nature of routing algorithm [12]. The number of capsule types in the encoder path of our network are set to (16, 16, 16, 8, 8, 8), respectively. This is in contrast to the design in 2D-SegCaps and 3D-SegCaps where the numbers of capsules are increasing (1, 2, 4, 4, 8, 8) along the encoder path. The number of capsule types in the last convolutional capsule layer is equal to the number of categories in the segmentation, which can be further supervised by a margin loss [27]. The output from a convolution capsule layer has the shape $H \times W \times D \times C \times A$, where C is the number of capsule types and A is the dimension of each capsule.

- **De-convolutional decoder:** The decoder of 3D Unet [7] is used in the expanding path. This contains de-convolution, skip connection, convolution and BatchNorm layers [13] to generate the segmentation from features learned by capsule layers. The features are reshaped to $H \times W \times D \times (C \star A)$ before passing them to the next convolution layer or concatenating with skip connections.
- **Reconstruction regularization:** This component is implemented as in the same manner as it is in 3D-SegCaps.

3.4.4 SS-3DCapsNet

Despite the recent success of CapsNet-based approaches in medical image segmentation, there remains a wide range of challenges: (1) Most methods are based on supervised learning, which is prone to many data problems like small-scale data, low-quality annotation, small objects, ambiguous boundaries, to name a few. These problems are not straightforward to overcome: labeling medical data is laborious and expensive, requiring an expert's domain knowledge. (2) Capsule networks for medical segmentation do not outperform CNNs yet, even though the performance gap gets significantly closer [22].

To address the aforementioned limitations, Tran et al. [31] improve 3D-UCaps and propose SS-3DCapsNet, a self-supervised capsule network. Self-supervised learning (SSL) is a technique for a learning feature representation in a network without requiring a labeled data set. A common workflow to apply SSL is to train the network in an unsupervised manner by learning with a pretext task in the pre-training stage, and then fine-tuning the pre-trained network on a target downstream task. In the case of MIS, the suitable pretext tasks can be considered in four categories: context-based, generation-based, free semantic label-based and cross-modal-based. In SS-3DCapsNet [31], the pretext task is based on image reconstruction. See Fig. 3.7.

The pretext task and downstream task in SS-3DCapsNet are detailed as follows:

- **Pretext task:** In computer vision, it is common to use pseudo-labels defined by different image transformations, e.g., rotation, random crop, adding noise, blurring, scaling, flipping, jigsaw puzzle, etc. to supervise the pretext task. While such transformations work well for classification as a downstream task, they cannot be applied directly into image segmentation. In SS-3DCapsNet [31], image reconstruction from various transformations, i.e., noisy, blurring, zero-channels (R,G,B), swapping as shown in Fig. 3.8 is utilized to perform the pretext task. Let $\mathcal{F}$ is the visual representation network. The transformation is defined as $\{T_i\}_{i=1}^{i=N}$, where T_0 is an identity transformation and N is set as 6 corresponding to six transformations (Fig. 3.8). Let V denote as the original input volumetric data. The pretext task is performed by applying two random transformations $T_i, T_j (i, j \in [0, 6))$ into V. The transformed data is then $T_i(V)$ and $T_j(V)$, respectively. The visual feature of transformed data after applying the network $\mathcal{F}$ is V_j and V_j, where $V_i = \mathcal{F}(T_i(V))$ and $V_j = \mathcal{F}(T_j(V))$. The network $\mathcal{F}$ is trained with a reconstruction loss defined by

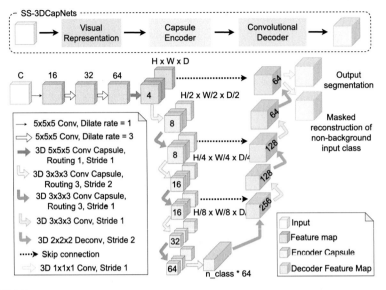

FIGURE 3.7

SS-3DCapsNet architecture with three components: visual representation; convolutional capsule encoder, and de-convolutional decoder. Number of the blocks indicates the number of channels in a convolution layer and dimension of capsules in capsule layers.

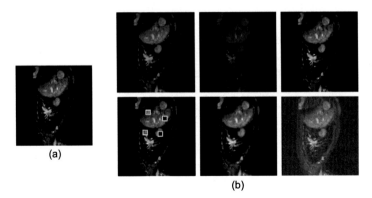

FIGURE 3.8

Examples of six transformations for self-supervised learning. (a): original image. (b) from left to right, top to bottom: zeros-green-channel, zeros-red-channel, zeros-blue-channel, swapping (4 swapped patches are shown in yellow boxes), blurring, noisy.

$$\mathcal{L}_{pretext}(V_i, V_j) = ||V_i - V_j||_2. \qquad (3.26)$$

The pretext task procedure is illustrated in Fig. 3.9.

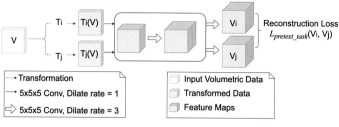

FIGURE 3.9

Our pretext task with reconstruction loss.

- **Downstream task:** After pre-training, the SS-3DCapsNet network is trained with annotated data on the medical segmentation task. The total loss function to train this downstream task is a sum of three losses, i.e., margin loss, weighted cross-entropy loss and reconstruction regularization loss as defined in Eq. (3.16).

3.4.5 Comparison

In this section, the comparison will be conducted regarding both network architecture and performance accuracy.

The network architecture comparison between various CapsNet-based approaches for medical image segmentation is shown in Table 3.1.

Table 3.1 Network architecture comparison between various CapsNet-based image segmentation.

	Input	Initialization	Encoder	Decoder
2D-SegCaps [15,16]	2D still image	Random	Capsule	Capsule
3D-SegCaps [22]	3D volumetric	Random	Capsule	Capsule
3D-UCaps [22]	3D volumetric	Random	Capsule	De-convolution
SS-3DCapsNet [31]	3D volumetric	SSL	Capsule	De-convolution

To compare the performance of various CapNets-based approaches, small-size data sets such as iSeg [32], Cardiac and Hippocampus [29] are selected to conduct experimental results. Samples from three data sets are visualized in Fig. 3.10.

- **iSeg data set:** [32] is an infant brain data set consisting of 10 subjects with ground-truth labels for training and 13 subjects without ground-truth labels for testing. Subjects were selected from the Baby Connectome Project [4] and have an average age between [5.5–6.5] months at the time of scanning. Each subject includes T1-weighted and T2-weighted images with a size of $144 \times 92 \times 256$ and image resolution of $1 \times 1 \times 1$ mm. The difficulty of this data set lies in the low contrast between tissues in the infant brain MRI that can reduce the accuracy of the automatic segmentation algorithms.

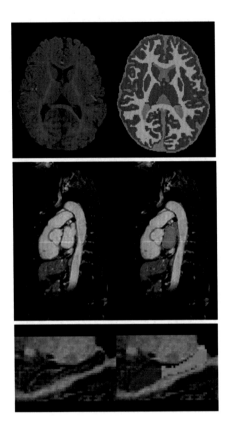

FIGURE 3.10

Visualization of samples from iSeg (first row), Cardiac (second row), and Hippocampus (third row).

- **Cardiac:** [29] is a mono-modal MRI data set containing 20 training images and 10 testing images covering the entire heart acquired during a single cardiac phase. This data set was provided by King's College London and obtained with voxel resolution $1.2 \times 1.25 \times 2.75$ mm^3.
- **Hipposcampus:** [29] is a larger-scale mono-modal MRI data set taken from the Psychiatric Genotype/Phenotype Project data repository at Vanderbilt University Medical Center (Nashville, TN, USA). It consists of 260 training and 130 testing samples acquired with a 3D T1-weighted MPRAGE sequence (TI/TR/TE, 860/8.0/3.7 ms; 170 sagittal slices; voxel size, $1 \times 1 \times 1$ mm^3). The task of this data set is segmenting two neighboring small structures (posterior and anterior hippocampus) with high precision.

For iSeg, the experimental results is followed by [5] in which 9 subjects are used to train and subject #9 is used to test. On Cardiac and Hippocampus [29], the experiments are conducted by 4-fold cross-validation.

The comparison is conducted by Pytorch. Patch size is selected as follows: $64 \times 64 \times 64$ for iSeg and Hippocampus, $128 \times 128 \times 128$ for Cardiac. All the networks were trained without any data augmentation. Adam optimizer with an initial learning rate of 0.0001 is chosen. The learning rate is decayed by 0.05 if the Dice score on the validation set does not increase for 50,000 iterations. Early stopping is set at 250,000 iterations as in [15].

Table 3.2 Performance comparison on iSeg-2017.

Method	Depth	Dice Score			
		WM	GM	CSF	Average
2D-SegCaps [15]	16	82.80	84.19	90.19	85.73
3D-SegCaps [22]	16	86.49	88.53	93.62	89.55
3D-UCaps [22]	17	90.21	91.12	94.93	92.08
Our SS-3DCapsNet [31]	17	90.78	91.48	94.92	92.39

Table 3.3 Comparison on Cardiac with 4-fold cross-validation.

SegCaps (2D) [15]	66.96
Multi-SegCaps (2D) [30]	66.96
3D-UCaps [22]	89.69
SS-3DCapsNet [31]	89.77

Table 3.4 Comparison on Hippocampus with 4-fold.

Method	Anterior			Posterior		
	Recall	Precision	Dice	Recall	Precision	Dice
Multi-SegCaps (2D) [30]	80.76	65.65	72.42	84.46	60.49	70.49
EM-SegCaps (2D) [30]	17.51	20.01	18.67	19.00	34.55	24.52
3D-UCaps [22]	81.70	80.19	80.99	80.2	79.25	79.48
SS-3DCapsNet [31]	81.84	81.49	81.59	80.71	80.21	79.97

The performance comparison on various CapsNet-based medical image segmentation approaches is shown in Table 3.2, Table 3.3 and Table 3.4 corresponding to iSeg, Cardiac and Hippocampus data sets.

3.5 Discussion

Although CNNs have achieved outstanding performance on various tasks including medical image segmentation, they suffer from the loss of part-whole relationships and geometric information. CapsNet was proposed to address such limitations. 3D-UCaps [22] conducted an analysis with two experiments on small-size data sets iSeg with rotation equivariance and invariance properties to various artifacts as follows:

- **Rotation equivariance**: In the first experiment, the testing subject is rotated from 0 to 90 degrees (15, 30, 45, 60, 75, 90) on the x-axis, y-axis, z-axis and all-axes. The performance comparison on rotation equivariance between 3D-SegCaps and 3D-UNet is shown in Fig. 3.11. Furthermore, the performance comparison between various networks, i.e., 3D-UCaps, 3D-SegCaps, 2D-SegCaps and 3D-UNet on a particular axis, i.e., z-axis is shown in Fig. 3.12.

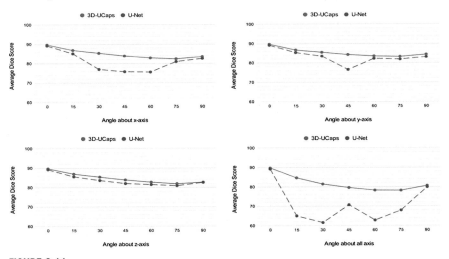

FIGURE 3.11

Performance comparison on iSeg of 3D-UCaps and 3D-UNet with rotation equivariance on x, y, z, and all axes.

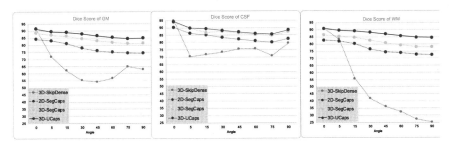

FIGURE 3.12

Performance comparison on iSeg with various networks on a particular axis rotation equivariance.

- **Various artifact**: In the second experiment, MonAI [21] and TorchIO [23] are utilized to create artifacts. The performance comparison on iSeg between 3D-UCaps and 3D-UNet is shown in Table 3.5.

CapsNets, along with their capability of modeling, the part-whole relationships have obtained remarkable results in various tasks including medical image seg-

Table 3.5 Performance comparison between 3D-UCaps and 3D-UNet on iSeg with various artifacts.

Artifact	3D-UCaps			3D-UNet		
	WM	GM	CSF	WM	GM	CSF
Without artifact	87.47	88.91	92.75	86.83	88.06	92.70
Gibbs artifact	87.33	88.81	92.38	86.68	88.02	88.82
Motion artifact	82.32	84.24	83.04	79.55	81.35	73.56
Ghosting artifact	82.04	88.10	70.42	78.54	81.29	79.88
Spike artifact	86.73	88.65	92.73	83.6	85.42	87.34
Shading artifact	85.75	86.12	87.95	79.91	81.54	86.77

mentation. The aforementioned discussion has proved that CapsNets significantly outperform CNNs for small-size data sets, which is a common case in medical image segmentation applications due to the lack of annotated data. The experimental results also show that CapsNets obtain higher robustness to affine transformations than CNNs; however, their performances are still limited on unseen transformed inputs and their computational complexity is still high. Exploring hybrid architecture between CapsNet-based and traditional neural network is therefore a promising approach to medical image analysis while keeping model complexity and computation cost plausible.

Acknowledgments

This material is based upon work supported by the National Science Foundation under Award No. OIA-1946391, NSF 1920920 RII Track 2 FEC, NSF 2223793 EFRI BRAID, NSF 2119691 AI SUSTEIN, NSF 2236302.

References

[1] Michael A. Alcorn, et al., Strike (with) a pose: neural networks are easily fooled by strange poses of familiar objects, in: Proceedings of the IEEE/CVF Conference on Computer Vision and Pattern Recognition, 2019, pp. 4845–4854.

[2] Aharon Azulay, Yair Weiss, Why do deep convolutional networks generalize so poorly to small image transformations?, arXiv preprint, arXiv:1805.12177, 2018.

[3] Aharon Azulay, Yair Weiss, Why do deep convolutional networks generalize so poorly to small image transformations?, Journal of Machine Learning Research (2020).

[4] Baby Connectome Project, http://babyconnectomeproject.org. (Accessed 1 February 2022).

[5] Toan Duc Bui, Jitae Shin, Taesup Moon, Skip-connected 3D DenseNet for volumetric infant brain MRI segmentation, Biomedical Signal Processing and Control 54 (2019) 101613.

[6] Zhenhua Chen, David Crandall, Generalized capsule networks with trainable routing procedure, arXiv preprint, arXiv:1808.08692, 2018.

[7] Özgün Çiçek, et al., 3D U-Net: learning dense volumetric segmentation from sparse annotation, in: International Conference on Medical Image Computing and Computer-Assisted Intervention, Springer, 2016, pp. 424–432.

[8] Logan Engstrom, et al., A rotation and a translation suffice: Fooling cnns with simple transformations, 2018.

[9] Jindong Gu, Volker Tresp, Improving the robustness of capsule networks to image affine transformations, in: Proceedings of the IEEE/CVF Conference on Computer Vision and Pattern Recognition, 2020, pp. 7285–7293.

[10] Jindong Gu, Volker Tresp, Interpretable graph capsule networks for object recognition, in: Proceedings of the AAAI Conference on Artificial Intelligence (AAAI), 2020.

[11] Geoffrey E. Hinton, Alex Krizhevsky, Sida D. Wang, Transforming auto-encoders, in: International Conference on Artificial Neural Networks, Springer, 2011, pp. 44–51.

[12] Geoffrey E. Hinton, Sara Sabour, Nicholas Frosst, Matrix capsules with EM routing, in: International Conference on Learning Representations, 2018.

[13] Sergey Ioffe, Christian Szegedy, Batch normalization: accelerating deep network training by reducing internal covariate shift, in: International Conference on Machine Learning, PMLR, 2015, pp. 448–456.

[14] Adam Kosiorek, et al., Stacked capsule autoencoders, Advances in Neural Information Processing Systems 32 (2019).

[15] Rodney LaLonde, Ulas Bagci, Capsules for object segmentation, arXiv preprint, arXiv:1804.04241, 2018.

[16] Rodney LaLonde, et al., Capsules for biomedical image segmentation, Medical Image Analysis 68 (2021) 101889.

[17] Aryan Mobiny, Hien Van Nguyen, Fast capsnet for lung cancer screening, in: International Conference on Medical Image Computing and Computer-Assisted Intervention, Springer, 2018, pp. 741–749.

[18] Aryan Mobiny, et al., Decaps: detail-oriented capsule networks, in: International Conference on Medical Image Computing and Computer-Assisted Intervention, Springer, 2020, pp. 148–158.

[19] Aryan Mobiny, et al., Memory-augmented capsule network for adaptable lung nodule classification, IEEE Transactions on Medical Imaging 40 (10) (2021) 2869–2879.

[20] Aryan Mobiny, et al., Radiologist-level COVID-19 detection using CT scans with detail-oriented capsule networks, arXiv preprint, arXiv:2004.07407, 2020.

[21] MONAI: Medical Open Network for AI, https://monai.io. (Accessed 15 October 2021).

[22] Tan Nguyen, Binh-Son Hua, Ngan Le, 3D-UCaps: 3D capsules unet for volumetric image segmentation, in: International Conference on Medical Image Computing and Computer-Assisted Intervention, Springer, 2021, pp. 548–558.

[23] Fernando Pérez-García, Rachel Sparks, Sebastien Ourselin, TorchIO: a Python library for efficient loading, preprocessing, augmentation and patch-based sampling of medical images in deep learning, Computer Methods and Programs in Biomedicine 208 (2021) 106236.

[24] Sai Samarth, R. Phaye, et al., Multi-level dense capsule networks, in: Asian Conference on Computer Vision, Springer, 2018, pp. 577–592.

[25] Jathushan Rajasegaran, et al., Deepcaps: going deeper with capsule networks, in: Proceedings of the IEEE/CVF Conference on Computer Vision and Pattern Recognition, 2019, pp. 10725–10733.

[26] Fabio De Sousa Ribeiro, Georgios Leontidis, Stefanos Kollias, Capsule routing via variational Bayes, in: Proceedings of the AAAI Conference on Artificial Intelligence, vol. 34, 04 2020, pp. 3749–3756.

[27] Sara Sabour, Nicholas Frosst, Geoffrey E. Hinton, Dynamic routing between capsules, in: Conference on Neural Information Processing Systems, 2017.

[28] Arnaud Arindra Adiyoso Setio, et al., Validation, comparison, and combination of algorithms for automatic detection of pulmonary nodules in computed tomography images: the LUNA16 challenge, Medical Image Analysis 42 (2017) 1–13.

[29] Amber L. Simpson, et al., A large annotated medical image dataset for the development and evaluation of segmentation algorithms, arXiv preprint, arXiv:1902.09063, 2019.

[30] Shanmugapriya Survarachakan, et al., Capsule nets for complex medical image segmentation tasks, in: CVCS, 2020.

[31] Minh Tran, et al., SS-3DCapsNet: self-supervised 3D capsule networks for medical segmentation on less labeled data, arXiv preprint, arXiv:2201.05905, 2022.

[32] Li Wang, et al., Benchmark on automatic six-month-old infant brain segmentation algorithms: the iSeg-2017 challenge, IEEE Transactions on Medical Imaging 38 (9) (2019) 2219–2230.

[33] Richard Zhang, Making convolutional networks shift-invariant again, in: International Conference on Machine Learning, PMLR, 2019, pp. 7324–7334.

Transformer for medical image analysis

4

Fahad Shamshad[a], Salman Khan[a], Syed Waqas Zamir[b], Muhammad Haris Khan[a],
Munawar Hayat[c], Fahad Shahbaz Khan[a], and Huazhu Fu[d]

[a]*Mohamed bin Zayed University of Artificial Intelligence, Abu Dhabi, United Arab Emirates*
[b]*Inception Institute of Artificial Intelligence, Abu Dhabi, United Arab Emirates*
[c]*Monash University, Melbourne, VIC, Australia*
[d]*Institute of High Performance Computing, Agency for Science, Technology and Research,*
Singapore, Singapore

4.1 Introduction

Recent advancements in convolutional neural networks (CNNs) [1–4] have made leaping improvements on numerous medical imaging modalities, including radiography [5], endoscopy [6], Computed Tomography (CT) [7,8], Mammography Images (MG) [9], ultrasound images [10], Magnetic Resonance Imaging (MRI) [11,12] and Positron Emission Tomography (PET) [13], to name a few. Despite the progress, the long-term dependencies within the image are ignored by the CNNs due to the local receptive field in the convolution operation.

To effectively capture the long-term dependencies, the attention-based transformer models have become an attractive solution and have been recently shown to fully replace the standard convolutions in deep neural networks by operating on a sequence of image patches, giving rise to Vision Transformers (ViTs) [14]. Furthermore, recent research indicates that the prediction errors of ViTs are more consistent with those of humans than CNNs [15–18], sparking great interest in the medical imaging community to adopt these models to medical image analysis tasks.

Inspired from the success of transformers in medical imaging, in this chapter, we aim to provide a holistic overview of the applications of transformer models in medical imaging. Specifically, we present a comprehensive overview of more than 125 relevant papers by categorizing them based on their applications in the medical imaging. These applications include medical image segmentation, detection, classification, reconstruction and synthesis.

4.2 Medical image segmentation

Accurate medical image segmentation is a crucial step in computer-aided diagnosis, image-guided surgery and treatment planning. The global context modeling capabil-

Deep Learning for Medical Image Analysis. https://doi.org/10.1016/B978-0-32-385124-4.00012-X
Copyright © 2024 Elsevier Inc. All rights reserved.

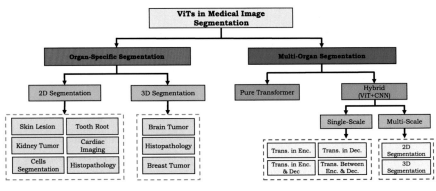

FIGURE 4.1

Taxonomy of ViT-based medical image segmentation approaches.

ity of transformers is crucial for accurate medical image segmentation because the organs spread over a large receptive field can be effectively encoded by modeling the relationships between spatially distant pixels (e.g., lungs segmentation). Furthermore, the background in medical scans is generally scattered (e.g., in ultrasound scan [19]); therefore learning global context between the pixels corresponding to the background can help the model in preventing misclassification.

Below, we highlight various attempts to integrate ViT-based models for medical image segmentation. We broadly classify the ViT-based segmentation approaches into *organ-specific* and *multi-organ* categories, as depicted in Fig. 4.1, due to the varying levels of context modeling required in both sets of methods.

4.2.1 Organ-specific segmentation

ViT-based organ-specific approaches generally consider a specific aspect of the underlying organ to design architectural components or loss functions. We mention specific examples of such design choices in this section. We have further categorized organ-specific categories into 2D and 3D-based approaches depending on the input type.

4.2.1.1 2D segmentation

Here, we describe the organ-specific ViT-based segmentation approaches for 2D medical scans.

Skin lesion segmentation. Accurate skin lesion segmentation for identifying melanoma (cancer cells) is crucial for cancer diagnosis and subsequent treatment planning. However, it remains a challenging task due to significant variations in color, size, occlusions and contrast of skin lesion areas, resulting in ambiguous boundaries [20], and consequently deterioration in segmentation performance. To address the issue of ambiguous boundaries, Wang et al. [21] propose a novel Boundary-Aware Transformer (BAT). Specifically, they design a boundarywise attention gate in transformer architecture to exploit the prior knowledge about boundaries. The auxiliary supervision of the boundarywise attention gate provides feedback to train BAT effectively. Extensive experiments on ISIC 2016+PH2 [22,23] and ISIC 2018 [24] validate the efficacy of their boundary-wise prior. Similarly, Wu et al. [25] propose a dual encoder-based feature adaptive transformer network (FAT-Net) that consists of CNN and transformer branches in the encoder. To effectively fuse the features from these two branches, a memory-efficient decoder and feature adaptation module have been designed. Experiments on ISIC 2016-2018 [22,26,24], and PH2 [23] data sets demonstrate the effectiveness of FAT-Net fusion modules.

Tooth root segmentation. Tooth root segmentation is one of the critical steps in root canal therapy to treat periodontitis (gum infection) [27]. However, it is challenging due to blurry boundaries and overexposed and underexposed images. To address these challenges, Li et al. [28] propose Group Transformer UNet (GT UNet) that consists of transformer and convolutional layers to encode global and local context, respectively. A shape-sensitive Fourier descriptor loss function [29] has been proposed to deal with the fuzzy tooth boundaries. Furthermore, grouping and bottleneck structure has been introduced in the GT UNet to significantly reduce the computational cost. Experiments on their in-house tooth root segmentation data set with six evaluation metrics demonstrate the effectiveness of GT UNet architectural components and Fourier-based loss function. In another work, Li et al. [30] propose anatomy-guided multibranch Transformer (AGMB-Transformer) to incorporate the strengths of group convolutions [31] and progressive transformer network. Experiments on their self-collected data set of 245 tooth root X-ray images show the effectiveness of the AGMB-Transformer.

Cardiac image segmentation. Despite their impressive performance in medical image segmentation, transformers are computationally demanding to train and come with a high parameter budget. To handle these challenges for cardiac image segmentation task, Deng et al. [32] propose TransBridge, a lightweight parameter-efficient hybrid model. TransBridge consists of transformers and CNNs based encoder-decoder structure for left ventricle segmentation in echocardiography. Specifically, the patch embedding layer of the transformer has been re-designed using the shuffling layer [33] and group convolutions to significantly reduce the number of parameters. Extensive experiments on the large-scale left ventricle segmentation data set, echo-cardiographs [34] demonstrate the benefit of TransBridge over CNNs and transformer-based baseline approaches [35].

Kidney tumor segmentation. Accurate segmentation of kidney tumors via computer diagnosis systems can reduce the effort of radiologists and is a critical step in related surgical procedures. However, it is challenging due to varying kidney tumor sizes and the contrast between tumors and their anatomical surroundings. To address these challenges, Shen et al. [36] propose a hybrid encoder–decoder architecture, COTR-Net, that consists of convolution and transformer layers for end-to-end kidney, kidney cyst and kidney tumor segmentation. Specifically, the encoder of COTR-Net consists of several convolution-transformer blocks, and the decoder comprises several up-sampling layers with skip connections from the encoder. The encoder weights have been initialized using a pre-trained ResNet [37] architecture to accelerate convergence, and deep supervision has been exploited in the decoder layers to boost segmentation performance. Furthermore, the segmentation masks are refined using morphological operations as a post-processing step. Extensive experiments on the Kidney Tumor Segmentation data set (KiTS21) [38] demonstrate the effectiveness COTR-Net.

Cell segmentation. Inspired from the Detection Transformers (DETR) [39], Prange-meier et al. [40] propose Cell-DETR, a transformer-based framework, for instance, segmentation of biological cells. Specifically, they integrate a dedicated attention branch to the DETR framework to obtain instancewise segmentation masks in addition to box predictions. During training, focal loss [41] and Sorenson dice loss [39] are used for the segmentation branch. To enhance performance, they integrate three residual decoder blocks [37] in Cell-DETR to generate accurate instance masks. Experiments on their in-house yeast cells data set demonstrate the effectiveness of Cell-DETR relative to UNet based baselines [42]. Similarly, existing medical imaging segmentation approaches generally struggle for Corneal endothelial cells due to blurry edges caused by the subject's movement [43]. This demands preserving more local details and making full use of the global context. Considering these attributes, Zhang et al. [44] propose a Multi-Branch hybrid Transformer Network (MBT-Net) consisting of convolutional and transformer layers. Specifically, they propose a body-edge branch that provides precise edge location information and promotes local consistency. Extensive ablation studies on their self-collected TM-EM3000 and public Alisarine data set [45] of corneal endothelial cells show the effectiveness of MBT-Net architectural components.

4.2.1.2 3D medical segmentation

Here, we describe ViT-based segmentation approaches for volumetric medical data.

Brain tumor segmentation. An automatic and accurate brain tumor segmentation approach can lead to the timely diagnosis of neurological disorders such as Alzheimer's disease. Recently, ViT-based models have been proposed to segment brain tumors effectively. Wang et al. [46] have made the first attempt to leverage transformers for 3D multimodal brain tumor segmentation by effectively modeling local and global features in both spatial and depth dimensions. Specifically, their encoder–decoder architecture, TransBTS, employs a 3D CNN to extract local 3D volumetric spatial features and transformers to encode global features. Progressive up-sampling in the 3D CNN-based decoder has been used to predict the final segmentation map. To further boost the performance, they make use of test-time augmentation. Extensive experimentation on BraTS 2019[1] and BraTS 2020[2] data sets show the effectiveness

---

[1] https://www.med.upenn.edu/cbica/brats2019.
[2] https://www.med.upenn.edu/cbica/brats2020.

of their proposed approach compared to CNN-based methods. Unlike most of the ViT-based image segmentation approaches, TransBTS does not require pre-training on large data sets and has been trained from scratch. In another work, inspired from the architectural design of TransBTS [46], Jia and Shu [47] propose Bi-Transformer UNet (BiTr-UNet) that performs relatively better on BraTS 2021 [48] segmentation challenge. Different from TransBTS [46], BiTr-UNet consists of an attention module to refine encoder and decoder features and has two ViT layers (instead of one as in TransBTS). Furthermore, BiTr-UNet adopts a post-processing strategy to eliminate a volume of predicted segmentation if the volume is smaller than a threshold [49] followed by model ensemble via majority voting [50]. Similarly, Peiris et al. [51] propose a light-weight UNet shaped volumetric transformer, VT-UNet, to segment 3D medical image modalities in a hierarchical manner. Specifically, two self-attention layers have been introduced in the encoder of VT-UNet to capture both global and local contexts. Furthermore, the introduction of window-based self-attention and cross-attention modules and Fourier positional encoding in the decoder significantly improve the accuracy and efficiency of VT-UNet. Experiments on BraTs 2021 [48] show that VT-UNet is robust to data artifacts and exhibits strong generalization ability. In another similar work, Hatamizadeh et al. [52] propose Swin UNet based architecture, Swin UNETR, that consists of Swin transformer as the encoder and a CNN-based decoder. Specifically, Swin UNETR computes self-attention in an efficient shifted window partitioning scheme and is a top-performing model on BraTs 2021 [48] validation set.

Breast tumor segmentation. Detection of breast cancer in the early stages can reduce the fatality rate by more than 40% [53]. Therefore, automatic breast tumor detection is of immense importance to doctors. Recently, Zhu et al. [54] propose a region aware transformer network (RAT-Net) to effectively fuse the Breast tumor region information into multiple scales to obtain precise segmentation. Extensive experiments on a large ultrasound breast tumor segmentation data set show that RAT-Net outperforms CNN and transformer-based baselines. Similarly, Liu et al. [55] also propose a hybrid architecture consisting of transformer layers in the decoder part of 3D UNet [56] to effectively segment tumors from volumetric breast data.

4.2.2 Multi-organ segmentation

Multi-organ segmentation aims to segment several organs simultaneously and is challenging due to inter-class imbalance and varying sizes, shapes and contrast of different organs. ViT models are particularly suitable for the multi-organ segmentation due to their ability to effectively model global relations and differentiate multiple organs. We have categorized multi-organ segmentation approaches based on the architectural design, as these approaches do not consider any organ-specific aspect and generally focus on boosting performance by designing effective and efficient architectural modules [57]. We categorize multi-organ segmentation approaches into *pure transformer* (only ViT layers) and *hybrid architectures* (both CNNs and ViTs layers).

4.2.2.1 Pure transformers

Pure transformer-based architectures consist of only ViT layers and have seen fewer applications in medical image segmentation compared to hybrid architectures as both global and local information is crucial for dense prediction tasks like segmentation [58]. Recently, Karimi et al. [59] propose a pure transformer-based model for 3D medical image segmentation by leveraging self-attention [60] between neighboring linear embedding of 3D medical image patches. They also propose a method to effectively pre-train their model when only a few labeled images are available. Extensive experiments show the effectiveness of their convolution-free network on three benchmark 3D medical imaging data sets related to brain cortical plate [61], pancreas and hippocampus. One of the drawbacks of using pure transformer-based models in segmentation is the quadratic complexity of self-attention with respect to the input image dimensions. This can hinder the ViTs applicability in the segmentation of high-resolution medical images. To mitigate this issue, Cao et al. [62] propose Swin-UNet that, like the Swin transformer [63], computes self-attention within a local window and has linear computational complexity with respect to the input image. Swin-UNet also contains a patch expanding layer for upsampling decoder's feature maps and shows superior performance in recovering fine details compared to bilinear upsampling. Experiments on Synapse and ACDC [64] data set demonstrate the effectiveness of the Swin-UNet architectural design.

4.2.2.2 Hybrid architectures

Hybrid architecture-based approaches combine the complementary strengths of transformers and CNNs to effectively model global context and capture local features for accurate segmentation. We have further categorized these hybrid models into single and multi-scale approaches.

4.2.2.2.1 Single-scale architectures

These methods process the input image information at one scale only and have seen widespread applications in medical image segmentation due to their low computational complexity compared to multi-scale architectures. We can sub-categorized single-scale architectures based on the position of the transformer layers in the model. These sub-categories include *Transformer in Encoder, Transformer between Encoder and Decoder, Transformer in Encoder and Decoder* and *Transformer in Decoder.*

Transformer in encoder. Most initially developed transformer-based medical image segmentation approaches have transformer layers in the model's encoder. The first work in this category is TransUNet [58] that consists of 12 transformer layers in the encoder. These transformer layers encode the tokenized image patches from the CNN layers. The resulting encoded features are up-sampled via up-sampling layers in the decoder to output the final segmentation map. With skip-connection incorporated, TransUNet sets new records (at the time of publication) on synapse multi-organ segmentation data set [65] and automated cardiac diagnosis challenge (ACDC) [64]. In other work, Zhang et al. [66] propose TransFuse to effectively fuse features from the transformer and CNN layers via the BiFusion module. The BiFusion module leverages the self-attention and the multi-modal fusion mechanism to selectively fuse the features. Extensive evaluation of TransFuse on multiple modalities (2D and 3D), including Polyp segmentation, skin lesion segmentation, Hip segmentation and prostate segmentation, demonstrate its efficacy. Both TransUNet [58] and TransFuse [66] require pre-training on the ImageNet data set [67] to effectively learn the positional encoding of the images. To learn this positional bias without any pre-training, Valanarasu et al. [68] propose a modified gated axial attention layer [69] that works well on small medical image segmentation data sets. Furthermore, to boost segmentation performance, they propose a Local-Global training scheme to focus on the fine details of input images. Extensive experimentation on brain anatomy segmentation [70], gland segmentation [71] and MoNuSeg (microscopy) [72] demonstrate the effectiveness of their proposed gated axial attention module.

In another work, Tang et al. [73] introduce Swin UNETR, a novel self-supervised learning framework with proxy tasks to pre-train the transformer encoder on 5050 images of the CT data set. They validate the effectiveness of pre-training by fine-tuning the transformer encoder with a CNN-based decoder on the downstream task of MSD and BTCV segmentation data sets. Similarly, Sobirov et al. [74] show that transformer-based models can achieve comparable results to state-of-the-art CNN-based approaches on the task of head and neck tumor segmentation. Few works have also investigated the effectiveness of transformer layers by integrating them into the encoder of UNet-based architectures in a plug-and-play manner. For instance, Chang et al. [75] propose TransClaw UNet by integrating transformer layers in the encoding part of the Claw UNet [76] to exploit multi-scale information. TransClaw-UNet achieves an absolute gain of 0.6 in dice score compared to Claw-UNet on Synapse multi-organ segmentation data set and shows excellent generalization. Similarly, inspired from the LeViT [77], Xu et al. [78] propose LeViT-UNet, which aims to optimize the trade-off between accuracy and efficiency. LeViT-UNet is a multi-stage architecture that demonstrates good performance and generalization ability on synapse and ACDC benchmarks.

Transformer between encoder and decoder. In this category, transformer layers are between the encoder and decoder of a U-Shape architecture. These architectures are more suitable to avoid the loss of details during down-sampling in the encoder layers. The first work in this category is TransAttUNet [79] that leverages guided attention and multi-scale skip connection to enhance the flexibility of traditional UNet. Specifically, a robust self-aware attention module has been embedded between the encoder and decoder of UNet to concurrently exploit the expressive abilities of global spatial attention and transformer self-attention. Extensive experiments on five benchmark medical imaging segmentation data sets demonstrate the effectiveness of TransAttUNet architecture. Similarly, Yan et al. [80] propose Axial Fusion Transformer UNet (AFTer-UNet) that contains a computationally efficient axial fusion layer between encoder and decoder to effectively fuse inter- and intra-slice information for 3D medical image segmentation. Experimentation on BCV [81], Thorax-85 [82] and SegTHOR [83] data sets demonstrate the effectiveness of their proposed fusion layer.

Transformer in encoder and decoder. Few works integrate transformer layers in both encoder and decoder of a U-shape architecture to better exploit the global context for medical image segmentation. The first work in this category is UTNet [84] that efficiently reduces the complexity of the self-attention mechanism from quadratic to linear [85]. Furthermore, to model the image content effectively, UTNet exploits the two-dimensional relative position encoding [86]. Experiments show strong generalization ability of UTNet on multi-label and multi-vendor cardiac MRI challenge data set cohort [87]. Similarly, to optimally combine convolution and transformer layers for medical image segmentation, Zhou et al. [88] propose nnFormer, an interleave encoder–decoder-based architecture, where convolution layer encodes precise spatial information and transformer layer encodes global context. Like Swin transformers [63], the self-attention in nnFormer has been computed within a local window to reduce the computational complexity. Moreover, deep supervision in the decoder layers has been employed to enhance performance. Experiments on ACDC and synapse data sets show that nnFormer surpass Swin-UNet [62] (transformer-based medical segmentation approach) by over 7% (dice score) on the Synapse data set. In other work, Lin et al. [89] propose Dual Swin Transformer UNet (DS-TransUNet) to incorporate the advantages of the Swin transformer in U-shaped architecture for medical image segmentation. They split the input image into nonoverlapping patches at two scales and feed them into the two Swin transformer-based branches of the encoder. A novel transformer interactive fusion module has been proposed to build long-range dependencies between different scale features in encoder. DS-TransUNet outperforms CNN-based methods on four standard data sets related to Polyp segmentation, ISIC 2018, GLAS and Datascience bowl 2018.

Transformer in decoder. Li et al. [90] investigate the use of transformer as an upsampling block in the decoder of the UNet for medical image segmentation. Specifically, they adopt a window-based self-attention mechanism to better complement the up-sampled feature maps while maintaining efficiency. Experiments on MSD Brain and synapse data sets demonstrate the superiority of their architecture compared to bilinear up-sampling. In another work, Li et al. [91] propose SegTran, a squeeze-and-expansion transformer for 2D and 3D medical image segmentation. Specifically, the squeeze block regularizes the attention matrix, and the expansion block learns diversified representations. Furthermore, a learnable sinusoidal positional encoding has been proposed that helps the model to encode spatial relationships. Extensive experiments on Polyp, BraTS19 and REFUGE20 (fundus images) segmentation challenges demonstrate the strong generalization ability of SegTran.

4.2.2.2.2 Multi-scale architectures

These architectures process input at multiple scales to effectively segment organs having irregular shapes and different sizes. Here, we highlight various attempts to integrate the multi-scale architectures for medical image segmentation. We further group these approaches into 2D and 3D segmentation categories based on the input image type.

2D segmentation. Most ViT-based multi-organ segmentation approaches struggle to capture information at multiple scales as they partition the input image into fixed-size patches, thereby losing useful information. To address this issue, Zhang et al. [92] propose a pyramid medical transformer, PMTrans, which leverage multi-resolution attention to capture correlation at different image scales using a pyramidal architecture [93]. PMTrans works on multi-resolution images via an adaptive partitioning scheme of patches to access different receptive fields without changing the overall complexity of self-attention computation. Extensive experiments on three medical imaging data sets of GLAS [71], MoNuSeg [94] and HECKTOR [95] show the effectiveness of exploiting multi-scale information. In other work, Ji et al. [96] propose a Multi-Compound transformer (MCTrans) that learns not only feature consistency of the same semantic categories but also capture correlation among different semantic categories for accurate segmentation [97]. Specifically, MCTrans captures cross-scale contextual dependencies via the transformer self-attention module and learned semantic correspondence among different categories via transformer cross-attention module. An auxiliary loss has also been introduced to improve feature correlation of the same semantic category. Extensive experiments on six benchmark segmentation data sets demonstrate the effectiveness of the architectural components of MCTrans.

3D segmentation. The majority of multi-scale architectures have been proposed for 2D medical image segmentation. To directly handle volumetric data, Hatamizadeh et al. [98] propose a ViT-based architecture (UNETR) for 3D medical image segmentation. UNETR consists of a pure transformer as the encoder to learn sequence representations of the input volume. The encoder is connected to a CNN-based decoder via skip connections to compute the final segmentation output. UNETR achieves impressive performance on BTCV [99] and MSD [81] segmentation data sets. One of the drawbacks of UNETR is its large computational complexity in processing large 3D input volumes. To mitigate this issue, Xie et al. [35] propose a computationally efficient deformable self-attention module [100] that casts attention only to a small set using multi-scale features, to reduce the computational and spatial complexities. Experiments on BTCV [99] demonstrate the effectiveness of their deformable self-attention module for 3D multi-organ segmentation.

4.3 Medical image classification

Accurate classification of medical images plays an essential role in aiding clinical care and treatment. In this section, we comprehensively cover applications of ViTs in medical image classification. We have broadly categorized these approaches into COVID-19, tumor and retinal disease classification-based methods due to a different set of challenges associated with these categories as shown in Fig. 4.2.

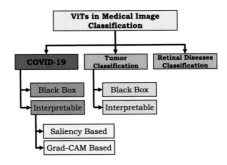

FIGURE 4.2

Taxonomy of ViT-based medical image classification approaches. The influx of ViT-based COVID-19 classification approaches makes it a dominating category in the taxonomy.

4.3.1 COVID-19 diagnosis

Studies suggest that COVID-19 can potentially be better diagnosed with radiological imaging as compared to tedious real-time polymerase chain reaction (RT-PCR) test [101–103]. Recently, ViTs have been successfully employed for diagnosis and severity prediction of COVID-19, showing SOTA performance. In this section, we briefly describe the impact of ViTs in advancing recent efforts on automated image analysis for the COVID-19 diagnosis process. Most of these works use three modalities, including Computerized tomography (CT), Ultrasound scans (US) and X-ray. We have further categorized ViT-based COVID-19 classification approaches into *Black-box models* and *interpretable models* according to the level of explainability offered.

4.3.1.1 Black-box models

ViT-based Black-box models for COVID-19 imaging classification generally focus on improving accuracy by designing novel and efficient ViT architectures. However, these models are not easily interpretable, making it challenging to gain user-trust. We have further sub-categorized black-box models into 2D and 3D categories, depending on the input image type. Below, we briefly describe these approaches:

2D: The high-computational cost of ViTs hinders their deployment on portable devices, thereby limiting their applicability in real-time COVID-19 diagnosis. Perera et al. [104] propose a lightweight **Point-of-Care Transformer (POCFormer)** to diagnose COVID-19 from lungs images captured via portable devices. Specifically, POCFormer leverages Linformer [85] to reduce the space and time complexity of self-attention from quadratic to linear. POCFormer has two million parameters that are about half of MobileNetv2 [105], thus making it suitable for real-time diagnosis. Experiments on COVID-19 lungs POCUS data set [106,107] demonstrate the effectiveness of their proposed architecture with above 90% classification accuracy. In other work, [108] proposed ViT-based model for COVID-19 diagnosis by exploiting a new attention mechanism named Vision Outlooker (VOLO) [109]. VOLO is effective for **encoding fine-level features** into ViT token representation, thereby improving classification performance. Further, they leverage the transfer learning approach to handle the issue of insufficient and generally unbalanced COVID-19 data sets. Experiments on two publicly available COVID-19 CXR data sets [110,107] demonstrate the effectiveness of their architecture. Similarly, Jiang and Lin [111] leverage **Swin transformer** [63] and **transformer-in-transformer** [112] to classify COVID-19 images from pneumonia and normal images. To further boost the accuracy, they employ model ensembling using a weighted average. Research progress in ViT-based COVID-19 diagnosis approaches is heavily impeded due to the requirement of a large amount of labeled COVID-19 data, thereby demanding collaborations among hospitals. This collaboration is difficult due to limited consent by patients, privacy concerns and ethical data usage [113]. To mitigate this issue, Park et al. [114] proposed a **Federated Split Task-Agnostic (FESTA) framework that leveraged the merits of Federated and Split Learning** [115,116] in utilizing ViT to simultaneously process multiple chest X-ray tasks, including the diagnosis in COVID-19 chest X-ray images on a massive decentralized data set. Specifically, they split ViT into the shared transformer body and task-specific heads and demonstrate the suitability of ViT body to be shared across relevant tasks by leveraging multi-task learning (MTL) [117] strategy. They affirm the suitability of ViTs for collaborative learning in medical imaging applications via extensive experiments on the CXR data set.

3D: Most of the ViT-based approaches for COVID-19 classification operate on 2D information only. However, as suggested by [118], the symptoms of COVID-19 might be present at different depths (slices) for different patients. To exploit both 2D and 3D information, Hsu et al. [119] propose a hybrid network consisting of transformers and CNNs. Specifically, they determine the importance of slices based on significant symptoms in the CT scan via Wilcoxon signed-rank test [120] with Swin transformer [63] as the backbone network. To further exploit the intrinsic features in the spatial and temporal dimensions, they propose a convolutional CT scan aware transformer module to fully capture the context of the 3D scans. Extensive experiments on the COVID-19-CT data set show the effectiveness of their proposed architectural components. Similarly, Zhang and Wen [121] also proposed the Swin transformer-based two-stage framework for the diagnosis of COVID-19 in the 3D CT scan data set [122]. Specifically, their framework consists of UNet-based lung segmentation model followed by the image classification with Swin transformer [63] backbone.

4.3.1.2 Interpretable models

Interpretable models aim to show the features that influence the decision of a model the most, generally via visualization techniques like saliency-based methods, Grad-CAM, etc. Due to their interpretable nature, these models are well suited to gain the trust of physicians and patients and, therefore, have paved their way for clinical deployment. We have further divided interpretable models into saliency-based [123] and Grad-CAM [124]-based visualization approaches.

Saliency based visualization. Park et al. [126] propose a ViT-based method for COVID-19 diagnosis by exploiting the low-level CXR features extracted from the

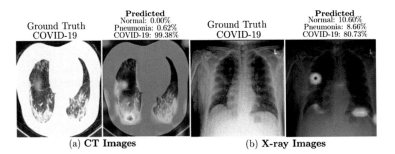

(a) **CT Images**   (b) **X-ray Images**

FIGURE 4.3

CT scans (a) and X-ray (b) images along with their ground truth labels (left) and saliency maps (right). For Figure (a), xViTCOS-CT localized suspicious lesion regions exhibiting ground glass opacities, consolidation, reticulations in bilateral postero basal lung. xViTCOS-CT [125] is able predict these regions correctly. For Figure (b), the radiologist's interpretation is: *thick walled cavity in right middle zone with surrounding consolidation.* As shown in the last column, xViTCOS-CXR [125] is able predict it correctly. Figure courtesy of [125].

pre-trained backbone network. The backbone network has been trained in a self-supervised manner (using contrastive-learning based SimCLR [127] method) to extract abnormal CXR features embeddings from large and well-curated CXR data set of CheXpert [128]. These feature embeddings have been leveraged by the ViT model for high-level diagnosis of COVID-19 images. Extensive experiments on three CXR test data sets acquired from different hospitals demonstrate the superiority of their approach compared to CNN-based models. They also validated the generalization ability of their proposed approach and adopted saliency map visualizations [129] to provide interpretable results. Similarly, Gao et al. [130] propose COVID-ViT to classify COVID from non-COVID images as part of the MIA-COVID19 challenge [122]. Their experiments on 3D CT lungs images demonstrated the superiority of ViT-based approach over DenseNet [131] baseline in terms of the F1 score. In another work, Mondal et al. [125] introduce xViTCOS for COVID-19 screening from the lung CT and X-ray images. Specifically, they pre-train xViTCOS on ImageNet to learn generic image representations and fine-tune the pre-trained model on a large chest radiographic data set. Further, xViTCOS leverage the explainability-driven saliency-based approach [129] with clinically interpretable visualizations to highlight the role of critical factors in the resulting predictions, as shown in Fig. 4.3. Experiments on COVID CT-2A [132] and their privately collected chest X-ray data set demonstrate the effectiveness of xViTCOS.

Grad-CAM based visualization. Shome et al. [133] propose a ViT-based model to diagnose COVID-19 infection at scale. They combine several open-source COVID-19 CXR data sets to form a large-scale multi-class and binary classification data set. For better visual representation and model interpretability, they further create Grad-CAM based visualization [124].

4.3.2 **Tumor classification**

A tumor is an abnormal growth of body tissues and can be cancerous (malignant) or noncancerous (benign). Early-stage malignant tumor diagnosis is crucial for subsequent treatment planning and can greatly improve the patient's survival rate. In this section, we review ViT-based models for tumor classification. These models can be mainly categorized into *Black-box models* and *interpretable models*. We highlight the relevant anatomies in bold.

Black-box models. TransMed [134] is the first work that leverages ViTs for medical image classification. It is a hybrid CNN and transformer-based architecture that is capable of classifying **parotid** tumors in the multi-modal MRI medical images. TransMed also employs a novel image fusion strategy to effectively capture mutual information from images of different modalities, thereby achieving competitive results on their privately collected parotid tumor classification data set. Later, Lu et al. [135] propose a two-stage framework that first performs contrastive pre-training on glioma sub-type classification in the **brain** followed by the feature aggregation via proposed transformer-based sparse attention module. Ablation studies on the TCGA-NSCLC [136] data set show the effectiveness of their two-stage framework. For the task of **breast** cancer classification, Gheflati and Rivaz [137] systematically evaluate the performance of pure and hybrid pre-trained ViT models. Experiments on two breast ultrasound data sets provided by Al-Dhabyani et al. [138] and Yap et al. [139] show that Vit-based models provide better results than those of the CNNs for classifying images into benign, malignant and normal categories. Similarly, other works employ hybrid transformer-CNN architectures to solve medical classification problem for different organs. For instance, Khan and Lee [140] propose gene-transformer to predict the **lung** cancer subtypes. Experiments on the TCGA-NSCLC [136] data set demonstrates the superiority of the gene transformer over CNN baselines. Chen et al. [141] present a multi-scale GasHis-transformer to diagnose gastric cancer in the **stomach**. Jiang et al. [142] propose a hybrid model to diagnose acute lymphocytic leukemia by using symmetric cross-entropy loss function.

Interpretable models. Since the annotation procedure is expensive and laborious, one label is assigned to a set of instances (bag) in whole slide imaging (WSI) based pathology diagnosis. This type of weakly supervised learning is known as Multiple Instance Learning (MIL) [143], where a bag is labeled positive if at least one instance is positive or labeled negative when all instances in a bag are negative. Most of the current MIL methods assume that the instances in each bag are independent and identically distributed, thereby neglecting the correlation among different instances. Shao et al. [144] present TransMIL to explore both morphological and spatial information in weakly supervised WSI classification. Specifically, TransMIL aggregates morphological information with two transformer-based modules and a position encoding layer. To encode spatial information, a pyramid position encoding generator is proposed. Further, the attention scores from the TransMIL have been visualized to demonstrate interpretability. TransMIL shows state-of-the-art performance on three different computational pathology data sets CAMELYON16 **(breast)** [145], TCGA-NSCLC **(lung)** [136] and TCGA-R **(kidney)** [146]. To diagnose **lung** tumors, Zheng et al. [147] propose the graph transformer network (GTN) to leverage the graph-based representation of WSI. GTN consists of a graph convolutional layer [148], a transformer layer and a pooling layer. GTN further employs GraphCAM [129] to identify regions that are highly associated with the class label. Extensive evaluations on the TCGA data set [136] show the effectiveness of GTN.

4.3.3 Retinal disease classification

Yu et al. [149] propose the MIL-ViT model, which is first pre-trained on a large fundus image data set and later fine-tuned on the downstream task of the retinal disease classification. MIL-ViT architecture uses a MIL-based head that can be used with ViT in a plug-and-play manner. Evaluation performed on APTOS2019 [150] and RFMiD2020 [151] data sets shows that MIL-ViT is achieving a more favorable performance than CNN-based baselines. Most data-driven approaches treat diabetic retinopathy (DR) grading and lesion discovery as two separate tasks, which may be sub-optimal as the error may propagate from one stage to the other. To jointly handle both these tasks, Sun et al. [152] propose a lesion aware transformer (LAT) that consists of a pixel relation-based encoder and a lesion-aware transformer decoder. In particular, they leverage transformer decoder to formulate lesion discovery as a weakly supervised lesion localization problem. LAT model sets state-of-the-art on Messidor-1 [153], Messidor-2 [153] and EyePACS [154] data sets. Yang et al. [155] propose a hybrid architecture consisting of convolutional and transformer layers for fundus disease classification on the OIA data set [156]. Similarly, Wu et al. [157] and AlDahoul et al. [158] also verify that ViT models are more accurate in DR grading than their CNNs counterparts.

4.4 Medical image detection

In medical image analysis, object detection refers to localization and identification of a region of interest (ROIs) such as lung nodules from X-ray images and is typically an essential aspect of diagnosis. However, it is one of the most time-consuming tasks for clinicians, thereby demanding the accurate computer-aided diagnosis (CAD) system to act as a second observer that may accelerate the process. Following the success of CNNs in medical image detection [159,160], recently few attempts have been made to improve performance further using transformer models. These approaches are mainly based on the detection transformer (DETR) framework [161].

Shen et al. [162] propose the first hybrid framework COTR, consisting of convolutional and transformer layers for end-to-end polyp detection. Specifically, the encoder of COTR contains six hybrid convolution-in-transformer layers to encode features, whereas the decoder consists of six transformer layers for object querying followed by a feed-forward network for object detection. COTR performs better than DETR on

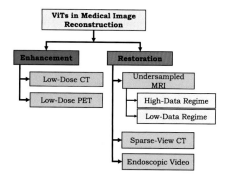

FIGURE 4.4

Taxonomy of ViT-based medical image reconstruction approaches.

two different data sets, ETIS-LARIB and CVC-ColonDB. The DETR model [161] is also adapted in other works [163,164] for the end-to-end polyp detection [163], and detecting lymph nodes in T2 MRI scans for the assessment of lymphoproliferative diseases [164].

4.5 Medical image reconstruction

The goal of medical image reconstruction is to obtain a clean image from a degraded input. For example, recovering a high-resolution MRI image from its under-sampled version. It is a challenging task due to its ill-posed nature. Moreover, exact analytic inverse transforms in many practical medical imaging scenarios are unknown. Recently, ViTs have been shown to address these challenges effectively. We categorize the relevant works into *medical image enhancement* and *medical image restoration* areas, as depicted in Fig. 4.4.

4.5.1 Medical image enhancement

ViTs have achieved impressive success in the enhancement of medical images, mostly in the application of Low-Dose Computed Tomography (LDCT) [165,166]. In LDCT, the X-ray dose is reduced to prevent patients from being exposed to high radiation. However, this reduction comes at the expense of CT image quality degradation and requires effective enhancement algorithms to improve the image quality and, subsequently, diagnostic accuracy.

4.5.1.1 LDCT enhancement

Zhang et al. [167] propose an hybrid architecture TransCT that leverages the internal similarity of the LDCT images to effectively enhance them. TransCT first decomposes the LDCT image into high-frequency (HF) (containing noise) and low-frequency (LF) parts. Next, it removes the noise from the HF part with the assistance of latent textures. To reconstruct the final high-quality LDCT images, TransCT further integrates features from the LF part to the output of the transformer decoder. Experiments on the Mayo LDCT data set [168] demonstrate the effectiveness of TransCT over CNN-based approaches. To perform LDCT image enhancement, Wang et al. [169] propose a convolution-free ViT-based encoder–decoder architecture TED-Net. It employs a token-to-token block [170] to enrich the image tokenization via a cascaded process. To refine contextual information, TED-Net introduces dilation and cyclic-shift blocks [62] in tokenization. TED-Net shows favorable performance on the Mayo Clinic LDCT data set [168]. In another work, Luthra et al. [171] propose Eformer, which is transformer-based residual learning architecture for LDCT images denoising. To focus on edges, Eformer uses the power of the Sobel–Feldman operator [172,173] in the proposed edge enhancement block to boost denoising performance. Moreover, to handle the over-smoothness issue, the multi-scale perceptual loss [172] is used. Eformer achieves impressive image quality gains in terms PSNR, SSIM and RMSE on the AAPM-Mayo Clinic data set [168].

4.5.1.2 LDPET enhancement

Like LDCT, Low-dose positron emission tomography (LDPET) images reduce the harmful radiation exposure of standard-dose PET (SDPET) at the expense of sacrificing diagnosis accuracy. To address this challenge, Luo et al. [174] propose an end-to-end generative adversarial network (GAN)-based method integrated with transformers, namely, Transformer-GAN, to effectively reconstruct SDPET images from the corresponding LDPET images. Specifically, the generator of transformer-GAN consists of a CNN-based encoder to learn compact feature representation, a transformer network to encode global context and a CNN-based decoder to restore feature representation. They also introduce adversarial loss to obtain reliable and clinically acceptable images. Extensive experiments on their in-house collected clinical human brain PET data set show the effectiveness of transformer-GAN quantitatively and qualitatively.

4.5.2 Medical image restoration

Medical image restoration entails transforming signals collected by acquisition hardware (like MRI scanners) into interpretable images that can be used for diagnosis and treatment planning. Recently, ViT-based models have been proposed for multiple medical image restoration tasks, including under-sampled MRI restoration, Sparse-View CT image reconstruction, and endoscopic video reconstruction. These models have pushed the boundaries of existing learning-based systems in terms of reconstruction accuracy. Next, we briefly highlight these approaches.

4.5.2.1 Under-sampled MRI reconstruction

Reducing the number of MRI measurements can result in faster scan times and a reduction in artifacts due to patients movement at the expense of aliasing artifacts in the image [175].

High-data regime approaches. Approaches in this category assume the availability of large MRI training data sets to train the ViT model. Feng et al. [176] propose transformer-based architecture, MTrans, for accelerated multi-modal MR imaging. The main component of MTrans is the cross-attention module that extracts and fuses complementary features from the auxiliary modality to the target modality. Experiments on fastMRI and uiMRI data sets for reconstruction and super-resolution tasks show that MTrans achieve good performance gains over previous methods. However, MTrans requires separate training for MR reconstruction and super-resolution tasks. To jointly reconstruct and super-resolve MRI images, Feng et al. [177] propose the task-transformer that leverages the power of multi-task learning to fuse complementary information between the reconstruction branch and the super-resolution branch. Experiments are performed on the public IXI and private MRI brain data sets. Similarly, Mahapatra and Ge [178] propose a hybrid architecture to super-resolve MRI images by exploiting the complementary advantages of both CNNs and ViTs. They also propose novel loss functions [179] to preserve semantic and structural information in the super-resolved images.

Low-data regime approaches. One drawback of the aforementioned approaches is the requirement of a massive paired data set of under-sampled and corresponding fully sampled MRI acquisitions to train ViT models. To alleviate the data requirement issue, Korkmaz et al. [180,181] propose a zero-shot framework, SLATER, that leverages prior induced by randomly initialized neural networks [182,183] for unsupervised MR image reconstruction. Specifically, during inference, SLATER inverts its transformer-based generative model via iterative optimization over-network weights to minimize the error between the network output and the under-sampled multi-coil MRI acquisitions while satisfying the MRI forward model constraints. SLATER yields quality improvements on single and multi-coil MRI brain data sets over other unsupervised learning-based approaches. Similarly, Lin and Heckel [184] show that a ViT model pre-trained on ImageNet, when fine-tuned on only 100 fastMRI images, not only yields sharp reconstructions but is also more robust toward anatomy shifts compared to CNNs.

4.5.2.2 Sparse-view CT reconstruction

Sparse-view CT [185] can effectively reduce the effective radiation dose by acquiring fewer projections. However, a decrease in the number of projections demands sophisticated image processing algorithms to achieve high-quality image reconstruction [186]. Wang et al. [187] present a hybrid CNN-transformer, named Dual-Domain Transformer (DuDoTrans), by considering the global nature of sinogram's sampling process to better restore high-quality images. In the first step, DuDoTrans reconstructs low-quality reconstructions of sinogram via filtered back projection step and learnable DuDo consistency layer. In the second step, a residual image reconstruction module performs enhancement to yield high-quality images. Experiments are performed on the NIH-AAPM data set [168] to show generalizability and robustness (against noise and artifacts) of DuDoTrans.

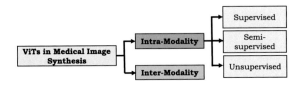

FIGURE 4.5

Taxonomy of ViT-based medical image synthesis approaches.

4.5.2.3 Endoscopic video reconstruction

Reconstructing surgical scenes from a stereoscopic video is challenging due to surgical tool occlusion and camera viewpoint changes. Long et al. [188] propose E-DSSR to reconstruct surgical scenes from stereo endoscopic videos. Specifically, E-DSSR contains a lightweight stereo transformer module to estimate depth images with high confidence and a segmentor network to accurately predict the surgical tool's mask. Extensive experiments on the Hamlyn Centre Endoscopic Video data set [189] and privately collected DaVinci robotic surgery data set demonstrate the robustness of E-DSSR against abrupt camera movements and tissue deformations in real time.

4.6 Medical image synthesis

In this section, we provide an overview of the applications of ViTs in medical image synthesis. Most of these approaches incorporate adversarial loss to synthesize realistic and high-quality medical images, albeit at the expense of training instability [190]. We have further classified these approaches into *intra-modality synthesis* and *inter-modality synthesis* due to a different set of challenges in both categories, as shown in Fig. 4.5.

4.6.1 Intra-modality approaches

The goal of intra-modality synthesis is to generate higher-quality images from the relatively lower quality input images of the same modality. Next, we describe the details of ViT-based intra-modality medical image synthesis approaches.

4.6.1.1 Supervised methods

Supervised image synthesis methods require paired source and target images to train ViT-based models. Paired data is difficult to obtain due to annotation cost and time constraints, thereby generally hindering the applicability of these models in medical imaging applications. Zhang et al. [191] focus on synthesizing infant brain structural MRIs (T1w and T2w scans) using both transformer and performer (simplified self-attention) layers [192]. Specifically, they design a novel multi-resolution pyramid-like UNet framework, PTNet, utilizing performer encoder, performer decoder and transformer bottleneck to synthesize high-quality infant MRI. They demonstrate the superiority of PTNet both qualitatively and quantitatively compared to pix2pix [193] and pix2pixHD [194] on a large-scale infant MRI data set [195]. Furthermore, in addition to better synthesis quality, PTNet has a reasonable execution time of around 30 slices per second.

4.6.1.2 Semi-supervised methods

Semi-supervised approaches typically require small amounts of labeled data along with large unlabeled data to train models effectively. Kamran et al. [196] propose a multi-scale conditional generative adversarial network (GAN) [193] using ViT as a discriminator. They train their proposed model in a semi-supervised way to simultaneously synthesize Fluorescein Angiography (FA) images from fundus photographs and predict retinal degeneration. They use softmax activation after MLP head output and a categorical CE loss for classification. Besides adversarial loss, they also use MSE and perceptual losses to train their network. For the ViT discriminator, they use an embedding feature loss, calculated using positional and patch features from the transformer encoder layers, by utilizing both real and synthesized FA images. Their quantitative results in terms of Frechet inception distance [197] and kernel inception distance [198] demonstrate the superiority of their approach over baseline methods on diabetic retinopathy data set provided by Hajeb et al. [199].

4.6.1.3 Unsupervised methods

These approaches are particularly suitable for medical image synthesis tasks as they do not require paired training data sets. Recently, Ristea et al. [200] propose a cycle-consistent generative adversarial transformer (CyTran) to translate unpaired contrast CT scans to noncontrast CT scans and volumetric image registration of contrast CT scans to noncontrast CT scans. To handle high-resolution CT images, they propose hybrid convolution and multi-head attention-based architecture. CyTran is unsupervised due to the integration of cyclic loss. Moreover, they introduce the Coltea-Lung-CT100W data set formed of 100 3D anonymized triphasic lung CT scans of female patients.

4.6.2 Inter-modality approaches

The inter-modality approaches aim to synthesize targets to capture the useful structural information in the source images of different modalities. Examples include CT to MRI translation or vice versa. Due to challenges associated with inter-modal translation, only supervised approaches have been explored.

Dalmaz et al. [201] introduce a novel synthesis approach, ResViT, for the multi-modal imaging based on a conditional deep adversarial network with ViT-based generator. Specifically, ResViT employs convolutional and transformer branches within a residual bottleneck to preserve both local precision and contextual sensitivity along with the realism of adversarial learning. The bottleneck comprises novel aggregated residual transformer blocks to synergistically preserve local and global context, with a weight-sharing strategy to minimize model complexity. The effectiveness of

ResViT model is demonstrated on two multi-contrast brain MRI data sets, BraTS [202] and a multi-modal pelvic MRI-CT data set [203].

4.7 Discussion and conclusion

From the papers reviewed in this chapter, it is evident that ViTs have pervaded every area of medical imaging. To keep pace with this rapid development, we recommend organizing the relevant workshops in top computer vision and medical imaging conferences and arranging special issues in prestigious journals to quickly disseminate the relevant research to the medical imaging community. Concluding, in this chapter, we briefly cover the core concepts behind the success of transformer models and then provide a comprehensive literature review of transformers in a broad range of medical imaging tasks including segmentation, detection, classification, reconstruction and synthesis. Despite their impressive performance, we anticipate there is still much exploration left to be done with transformers in medical imaging, and we hope this chapter provides a roadmap to researchers to progress this field further.

References

[1] Ian Goodfellow, Yoshua Bengio, Aaron Courville, Deep Learning, MIT Press, 2016.

[2] Yann LeCun, Bernhard Boser, John S. Denker, Donnie Henderson, Richard E. Howard, Wayne Hubbard, Lawrence D. Jackel, Backpropagation applied to handwritten zip code recognition, Neural Computation 1 (4) (1989) 541–551.

[3] Alex Krizhevsky, Ilya Sutskever, Geoffrey E. Hinton, Imagenet classification with deep convolutional neural networks, Advances in Neural Information Processing Systems 25 (2012) 1097–1105.

[4] Zhuang Liu, Hanzi Mao, Chao-Yuan Wu, Christoph Feichtenhofer, Trevor Darrell, Saining Xie, A convnet for the 2020s, arXiv preprint, arXiv:2201.03545, 2022.

[5] Paras Lakhani, Baskaran Sundaram, Deep learning at chest radiography: automated classification of pulmonary tuberculosis by using convolutional neural networks, Radiology 284 (2) (2017) 574–582.

[6] Jun Ki Min, Min Seob Kwak, Jae Myung Cha, Overview of deep learning in gastrointestinal endoscopy, Gut and Liver 13 (4) (2019) 388.

[7] Tobias Würfl, Florin C. Ghesu, Vincent Christlein, Andreas Maier, Deep learning computed tomography, in: International Conference on Medical Image Computing and Computer-Assisted Intervention, Springer, 2016, pp. 432–440.

[8] Michael M. Lell, Marc Kachelrieß, Recent and upcoming technological developments in computed tomography: high speed, low dose, deep learning, multienergy, Investigative Radiology 55 (1) (2020) 8–19.

[9] Azam Hamidinekoo, Erika Denton, Andrik Rampun, Kate Honnor, Reyer Zwiggelaar, Deep learning in mammography and breast histology, an overview and future trends, Medical Image Analysis 47 (2018) 45–67.

[10] Shengfeng Liu, Yi Wang, Xin Yang, Baiying Lei, Li Liu, Shawn Xiang Li, Dong Ni, Tianfu Wang, Deep learning in medical ultrasound analysis: a review, Engineering 5 (2) (2019) 261–275.

[11] Alexander Selvikvåg Lundervold, Arvid Lundervold, An overview of deep learning in medical imaging focusing on mri, Zeitschrift für Medizinische Physik 29 (2) (2019) 102–127.

[12] Zeynettin Akkus, Alfiia Galimzianova, Assaf Hoogi, Daniel L. Rubin, Bradley J. Erickson, Deep learning for brain mri segmentation: state of the art and future directions, Journal of Digital Imaging 30 (4) (2017) 449–459.

[13] Andrew J. Reader, Guillaume Corda, Abolfazl Mehranian, Casper da Costa-Luis, Sam Ellis, Julia A. Schnabel, Deep learning for pet image reconstruction, IEEE Transactions on Radiation and Plasma Medical Sciences 5 (1) (2020) 1–25.

[14] Alexey Dosovitskiy, Lucas Beyer, Alexander Kolesnikov, Dirk Weissenborn, Xiaohua Zhai, Thomas Unterthiner, Mostafa Dehghani, Matthias Minderer, Georg Heigold, Sylvain Gelly, et al., An image is worth 16x16 words: transformers for image recognition at scale, arXiv preprint, arXiv:2010.11929, 2020.

[15] Muzammal Naseer, Kanchana Ranasinghe, Salman Khan, Munawar Hayat, Fahad Shahbaz Khan, Ming-Hsuan Yang, Intriguing properties of vision transformers, arXiv preprint, arXiv:2105.10497, 2021.

[16] Eva Portelance, Michael C. Frank, Dan Jurafsky, Alessandro Sordoni, Romain Laroche, The emergence of the shape bias results from communicative efficiency, arXiv preprint, arXiv:2109.06232, 2021.

[17] Robert Geirhos, Kantharaju Narayanappa, Benjamin Mitzkus, Tizian Thieringer, Matthias Bethge, Felix A. Wichmann, Wieland Brendel, Partial success in closing the gap between human and machine vision, arXiv preprint, arXiv:2106.07411, 2021.

[18] Shikhar Tuli, Ishita Dasgupta, Erin Grant, Thomas L. Griffiths, Are convolutional neural networks or transformers more like human vision?, arXiv preprint, arXiv:2105.07197, 2021.

[19] Danilo Avola, Luigi Cinque, Alessio Fagioli, Gianluca Foresti, Alessio Mecca, Ultrasound medical imaging techniques: a survey, ACM Computing Surveys 54 (3) (2021) 1–38.

[20] Yading Yuan, Automatic skin lesion segmentation with fully convolutional-deconvolutional networks, arXiv preprint, arXiv:1703.05165, 2017.

[21] Jiacheng Wang, Lan Wei, Liansheng Wang, Qichao Zhou, Lei Zhu, Jing Qin, Boundary-aware transformers for skin lesion segmentation, in: International Conference on Medical Image Computing and Computer-Assisted Intervention, Springer, 2021, pp. 206–216.

[22] David Gutman, Noel C.F. Codella, Emre Celebi, Brian Helba, Michael Marchetti, Nabin Mishra, Allan Halpern, Skin lesion analysis toward melanoma detection: a challenge at the international symposium on biomedical imaging (isbi) 2016, hosted by the international skin imaging collaboration (isic), arXiv preprint, arXiv:1605.01397, 2016.

[23] Teresa Mendonça, Pedro M. Ferreira, Jorge S. Marques, André R.S. Marcal, Jorge Rozeira, Ph 2-a dermoscopic image database for research and benchmarking, in: 2013 35th Annual International Conference of the IEEE Engineering in Medicine and Biology Society (EMBC), IEEE, 2013, pp. 5437–5440.

[24] Noel Codella, Veronica Rotemberg, Philipp Tschandl, M. Emre Celebi, Stephen Dusza, David Gutman, Brian Helba, Aadi Kalloo, Konstantinos Liopyris, Michael Marchetti, et al., Skin lesion analysis toward melanoma detection 2018: a challenge hosted by the international skin imaging collaboration (isic), arXiv preprint, arXiv:1902.03368, 2019.

[25] Huisi Wu, Shihuai Chen, Guilian Chen, Wei Wang, Baiying Lei, Zhenkun Wen, Fat-net: feature adaptive transformers for automated skin lesion segmentation, Medical Image Analysis (2021) 102327.

[26] Matt Berseth, Isic 2017-skin lesion analysis towards melanoma detection, arXiv preprint, arXiv:1703.00523, 2017.

[27] Hui Gao, Oksam Chae, Individual tooth segmentation from ct images using level set method with shape and intensity prior, Pattern Recognition 43 (7) (2010) 2406–2417.

[28] Yunxiang Li, Shuai Wang, Jun Wang, Guodong Zeng, Wenjun Liu, Qianni Zhang, Qun Jin, Yaqi Wang, Gt u-net: a u-net like group transformer network for tooth root segmentation, in: International Workshop on Machine Learning in Medical Imaging, Springer, 2021, pp. 386–395.

[29] Charles T. Zahn, Ralph Z. Roskies, Fourier descriptors for plane closed curves, IEEE Transactions on Computers 100 (3) (1972) 269–281.

[30] Yunxiang Li, Guodong Zeng, Yifan Zhang, Jun Wang, Qun Jin, Lingling Sun, Qianni Zhang, Qisi Lian, Guiping Qian, Neng Xia, et al., Agmb-transformer: anatomy-guided multi-branch transformer network for automated evaluation of root canal therapy, IEEE Journal of Biomedical and Health Informatics (2021).

[31] François Chollet, Xception: deep learning with depthwise separable convolutions, in: Proceedings of the IEEE Conference on Computer Vision and Pattern Recognition, 2017, pp. 1251–1258.

[32] Kaizhong Deng, Yanda Meng, Dongxu Gao, Joshua Bridge, Yaochun Shen, Gregory Lip, Yitian Zhao, Yalin Zheng, Transbridge: a lightweight transformer for left ventricle segmentation in echocardiography, in: International Workshop on Advances in Simplifying Medical Ultrasound, Springer, 2021, pp. 63–72.

[33] Qing-Long Zhang, Yu-Bin Yang, Sa-net: shuffle attention for deep convolutional neural networks, in: ICASSP 2021-2021 IEEE International Conference on Acoustics, Speech and Signal Processing (ICASSP), IEEE, 2021, pp. 2235–2239.

[34] David Ouyang, Bryan He, Amirata Ghorbani, Neal Yuan, Joseph Ebinger, Curtis P. Langlotz, Paul A. Heidenreich, Robert A. Harrington, David H. Liang, Euan A. Ashley, et al., Video-based ai for beat-to-beat assessment of cardiac function, Nature 580 (7802) (2020) 252–256.

[35] Yutong Xie, Jianpeng Zhang, Chunhua Shen, Yong Xia Cotr, Efficiently bridging cnn and transformer for 3d medical image segmentation, arXiv preprint, arXiv:2103.03024, 2021.

[36] Zhiqiang Shen, Hua Yang, Zhen Zhang, Shaohua Zheng, Automated kidney tumor segmentation with convolution and transformer network, 2021.

[37] Kaiming He, Xiangyu Zhang, Shaoqing Ren, Jian Sun, Deep residual learning for image recognition, in: Proceedings of the IEEE Conference on Computer Vision and Pattern Recognition, 2016, pp. 770–778.

[38] The 2021 kidney and kidney tumor segmentation challenge, https://kits21.kits-challenge.org/. (Accessed 20 January 2022).

[39] Nicolas Carion, Francisco Massa, Gabriel Synnaeve, Nicolas Usunier, Alexander Kirillov, Sergey Zagoruyko, End-to-end object detection with transformers, in: European Conference on Computer Vision, Springer, 2020, pp. 213–229.

[40] Tim Prangemeier, Christoph Reich, Heinz Koeppl, Attention-based transformers for instance segmentation of cells in microstructures, in: 2020 IEEE International Conference on Bioinformatics and Biomedicine (BIBM), IEEE, 2020, pp. 700–707.

[41] Tsung-Yi Lin, Priya Goyal, Ross Girshick, Kaiming He, Piotr Dollár, Focal loss for dense object detection, in: Proceedings of the IEEE International Conference on Computer Vision, 2017, pp. 2980–2988.

[42] Olaf Ronneberger, Philipp Fischer, Thomas Brox, U-net: convolutional networks for biomedical image segmentation, in: International Conference on Medical Image Computing and Computer-Assisted Intervention, Springer, 2015, pp. 234–241.

[43] Bert Van den Bogerd, Nadia Zakaria, Bianca Adam, Steffi Matthyssen, Carina Koppen, Sorcha Ní Dhubhghaill, Corneal endothelial cells over the past decade: are we missing the mark (er)?, Translational Vision Science & Technology 8 (6) (2019) 13.

[44] Yinglin Zhang, Risa Higashita, Huazhu Fu, Yanwu Xu, Yang Zhang, Haofeng Liu, Jian Zhang, Jiang Liu, A multi-branch hybrid transformer network for corneal endothelial cell segmentation, arXiv preprint, arXiv:2106.07557, 2021.

[45] Alfredo Ruggeri, Fabio Scarpa, Massimo De Luca, Christian Meltendorf, Jan Schroeter, A system for the automatic estimation of morphometric parameters of corneal endothelium in alizarine red-stained images, British Journal of Ophthalmology 94 (5) (2010) 643–647.

[46] Wenxuan Wang, Chen Chen, Meng Ding, Hong Yu, Sen Zha, Jiangyun Li, Transbts: multimodal brain tumor segmentation using transformer, in: International Conference on Medical Image Computing and Computer-Assisted Intervention, Springer, 2021, pp. 109–119.

[47] Qiran Jia, Hai Shu, Bitr-unet: a cnn-transformer combined network for mri brain tumor segmentation, arXiv preprint, arXiv:2109.12271, 2021.

[48] Ujjwal Baid, Satyam Ghodasara, Suyash Mohan, Michel Bilello, Evan Calabrese, Errol Colak, Keyvan Farahani, Jayashree Kalpathy-Cramer, Felipe C. Kitamura, Sarthak Pati, et al., The rsna-asnr-miccai brats 2021 benchmark on brain tumor segmentation and radiogenomic classification, arXiv preprint, arXiv:2107.02314, 2021.

[49] Fabian Isensee, Jens Petersen, Andre Klein, David Zimmerer, Paul F. Jaeger, Simon Kohl, Jakob Wasserthal, Gregor Koehler, Tobias Norajitra, Sebastian Wirkert, et al., nnu-net: self-adapting framework for u-net-based medical image segmentation, arXiv preprint, arXiv:1809.10486, 2018.

[50] Louisa Lam, S.Y. Suen, Application of majority voting to pattern recognition: an analysis of its behavior and performance, IEEE Transactions on Systems, Man and Cybernetics. Part A. Systems and Humans 27 (5) (1997) 553–568.

[51] Himashi Peiris, Munawar Hayat, Zhaolin Chen, Gary Egan, Mehrtash Harandi, A volumetric transformer for accurate 3d tumor segmentation, arXiv preprint, arXiv:2111.13300, 2021.

[52] Ali Hatamizadeh, Vishwesh Nath, Yucheng Tang, Dong Yang, Holger Roth, Daguang Xu, Swin unetr: swin transformers for semantic segmentation of brain tumors in mri images, arXiv preprint, arXiv:2201.01266, 2022.

[53] Qinghua Huang, Yaozhong Luo, Qiangzhi Zhang, Breast ultrasound image segmentation: a survey, International Journal of Computer Assisted Radiology and Surgery 12 (3) (2017) 493–507.

[54] Xiner Zhu, Haoji Hu, Hualiang Wang, Jincao Yao, Di Ou, Dong Xu, et al., Region aware transformer for automatic breast ultrasound tumor segmentation, 2021.

[55] Yiyao Liu, Yi Yang, Wei Jiang, Tianfu Wang, Baiying Lei, 3d deep attentive u-net with transformer for breast tumor segmentation from automated breast volume scanner, in: 2021 43rd Annual International Conference of the IEEE Engineering in Medicine & Biology Society (EMBC), IEEE, 2021, pp. 4011–4014.

[56] Özgün Çiçek, Ahmed Abdulkadir, Soeren S. Lienkamp, Thomas Brox, Olaf Ronneberger, 3d u-net: learning dense volumetric segmentation from sparse annotation, in: International Conference on Medical Image Computing and Computer-Assisted Intervention, Springer, 2016, pp. 424–432.

[57] Yang Lei, Yabo Fu, Tonghe Wang, Richard L.J. Qiu, Walter J. Curran, Tian Liu, Xiaofeng Yang, Deep learning in multi-organ segmentation, arXiv preprint, arXiv: 2001.10619, 2020.

[58] Jieneng Chen, Yongyi Lu, Qihang Yu, Xiangde Luo, Ehsan Adeli, Yan Wang, Le Lu, Alan L. Yuille, Yuyin Zhou, Transunet: transformers make strong encoders for medical image segmentation, arXiv preprint, arXiv:2102.04306, 2021.

[59] Davood Karimi, Serge Vasylechko, Ali Gholipour, Convolution-free medical image segmentation using transformers, arXiv preprint, arXiv:2102.13645, 2021.

[60] Xiaolong Wang, Ross Girshick, Abhinav Gupta, Kaiming He, Non-local neural networks, in: Proceedings of the IEEE Conference on Computer Vision and Pattern Recognition, 2018, pp. 7794–7803.

[61] Haoran Dou, Davood Karimi, Caitlin K. Rollins, Cynthia M. Ortinau, Lana Vasung, Clemente Velasco-Annis, Abdelhakim Ouaalam, Xin Yang, Dong Ni, Ali Gholipour, A deep attentive convolutional neural network for automatic cortical plate segmentation in fetal mri, IEEE Transactions on Medical Imaging 40 (4) (2020) 1123–1133.

[62] Hu Cao, Yueyue Wang, Joy Chen, Dongsheng Jiang, Xiaopeng Zhang, Qi Tian, Manning Wang, Swin-unet: Unet-like pure transformer for medical image segmentation, arXiv preprint, arXiv:2105.05537, 2021.

[63] Ze Liu, Yutong Lin, Yue Cao, Han Hu, Yixuan Wei, Zheng Zhang, Stephen Lin, Baining Guo, Swin transformer: hierarchical vision transformer using shifted windows, in: ICCV, 2021.

[64] Olivier Bernard, Alain Lalande, Clement Zotti, Frederick Cervenansky, Xin Yang, Pheng-Ann Heng, Irem Cetin, Karim Lekadir, Oscar Camara, Miguel Angel Gonzalez Ballester, et al., Deep learning techniques for automatic mri cardiac multi-structures segmentation and diagnosis: is the problem solved?, IEEE Transactions on Medical Imaging 37 (11) (2018) 2514–2525.

[65] Synapse multi-organ segmentation dataset, https://www.synapse.org/#!Synapse: syn3193805/wiki/217789. (Accessed 20 January 2022).

[66] Yundong Zhang, Huiye Liu, Qiang Hu, Transfuse: fusing transformers and cnns for medical image segmentation, arXiv preprint, arXiv:2102.08005, 2021.

[67] Jia Deng, Wei Dong, Richard Socher, Li-Jia Li, Kai Li, Li Fei-Fei, Imagenet: a large-scale hierarchical image database, in: 2009 IEEE Conference on Computer Vision and Pattern Recognition, IEEE, 2009, pp. 248–255.

[68] Jeya Maria Jose Valanarasu, Poojan Oza, Ilker Hacihaliloglu, Vishal M. Patel, Medical transformer: gated axial-attention for medical image segmentation, arXiv preprint, arXiv:2102.10662, 2021.

[69] Huiyu Wang, Yukun Zhu, Bradley Green, Hartwig Adam, Alan Yuille, Liang-Chieh Chen, Axial-deeplab: stand-alone axial-attention for panoptic segmentation, in: European Conference on Computer Vision, Springer, 2020, pp. 108–126.

[70] Puyang Wang, Nick G. Cuccolo, Rachana Tyagi, Ilker Hacihaliloglu, Vishal M. Patel, Automatic real-time cnn-based neonatal brain ventricles segmentation, in: 2018 IEEE 15th International Symposium on Biomedical Imaging (ISBI 2018), IEEE, 2018, pp. 716–719.

[71] Korsuk Sirinukunwattana, Josien P.W. Pluim, Hao Chen, Xiaojuan Qi, Pheng-Ann Heng, Yun Bo Guo, Li Yang Wang, Bogdan J. Matuszewski, Elia Bruni, Urko Sanchez, et al., Gland segmentation in colon histology images: the glas challenge contest, Medical Image Analysis 35 (2017) 489–502.

[72] Neeraj Kumar, Ruchika Verma, Deepak Anand, Yanning Zhou, Omer Fahri Onder, Efstratios Tsougenis, Hao Chen, Pheng-Ann Heng, Jiahui Li, Zhiqiang Hu, et al., A multi-organ nucleus segmentation challenge, IEEE Transactions on Medical Imaging 39 (5) (2019) 1380–1391.

[73] Yucheng Tang, Dong Yang, Wenqi Li, Holger Roth, Bennett Landman, Daguang Xu, Vishwesh Nath, Ali Hatamizadeh, Self-supervised pre-training of swin transformers for 3d medical image analysis, arXiv preprint, arXiv:2111.14791, 2021.

[74] Ikboljon Sobirov, Otabek Nazarov, Hussain Alasmawi, Mohammad Yaqub, Automatic segmentation of head and neck tumor: how powerful transformers are?, arXiv preprint, arXiv:2201.06251, 2022.

[75] Yao Chang, Hu Menghan, Zhai Guangtao, Zhang Xiao-Ping, Transclaw u-net: claw u-net with transformers for medical image segmentation, arXiv preprint, arXiv:2107.05188, 2021.

[76] Chang Yao, Jingyu Tang, Menghan Hu, Yue Wu, Wenyi Guo, Qingli Li, Xiao-Ping Zhang, Claw u-net: a unet-based network with deep feature concatenation for scleral blood vessel segmentation, arXiv preprint, arXiv:2010.10163, 2020.

[77] Ben Graham, Alaaeldin El-Nouby, Hugo Touvron, Pierre Stock, Armand Joulin, Hervé Jégou, Matthijs Douze, Levit: a vision transformer in convnet's clothing for faster inference, arXiv preprint, arXiv:2104.01136, 2021.

[78] Guoping Xu, Xingrong Wu, Xuan Zhang, Xinwei He, LeViT-UNet: make faster encoders with transformer for medical image segmentation, arXiv preprint, arXiv:2107.08623, 2021.

[79] Bingzhi Chen, Yishu Liu, Zheng Zhang, Guangming Lu, David Zhang, Transattunet: multi-level attention-guided u-net with transformer for medical image segmentation, arXiv preprint, arXiv:2107.05274, 2021.

[80] Xiangyi Yan, Hao Tang, Shanlin Sun, Haoyu Ma, Deying Kong, Xiaohui Xie, After-unet: axial fusion transformer unet for medical image segmentation, arXiv preprint, arXiv:2110.10403, 2021.

[81] Amber L. Simpson, Michela Antonelli, Spyridon Bakas, Michel Bilello, Keyvan Farahani, Bram Van Ginneken, Annette Kopp-Schneider, Bennett A. Landman, Geert Litjens, Bjoern Menze, et al., A large annotated medical image dataset for the development and evaluation of segmentation algorithms, arXiv preprint, arXiv:1902.09063, 2019.

[82] Xuming Chen, Shanlin Sun, Narisu Bai, Kun Han, Qianqian Liu, Shengyu Yao, Hao Tang, Chupeng Zhang, Zhipeng Lu, Qian Huang, et al., A deep learning-based auto-segmentation system for organs-at-risk on whole-body computed tomography images for radiation therapy, Radiotherapy and Oncology 160 (2021) 175–184.

[83] Zoé Lambert, Caroline Petitjean, Bernard Dubray, Su Kuan, Segthor: segmentation of thoracic organs at risk in ct images, in: 2020 Tenth International Conference on Image Processing Theory, Tools and Applications (IPTA), IEEE, 2020, pp. 1–6.

[84] Yunhe Gao, Mu Zhou, Dimitris N. Metaxas, Utnet: a hybrid transformer architecture for medical image segmentation, in: International Conference on Medical Image Computing and Computer-Assisted Intervention, Springer, 2021, pp. 61–71.

[85] Sinong Wang, Belinda Z. Li, Madian Khabsa, Han Fang, Hao Ma, Linformer: self-attention with linear complexity, arXiv preprint, arXiv:2006.04768, 2020.

[86] Irwan Bello, Barret Zoph, Ashish Vaswani, Jonathon Shlens, Quoc V. Le, Attention augmented convolutional networks, in: Proceedings of the IEEE/CVF International Conference on Computer Vision, 2019, pp. 3286–3295.

[87] Víctor M. Campello, Polyxeni Gkontra, Cristian Izquierdo, Carlos Martín-Isla, Alireza Sojoudi, Peter M. Full, Klaus Maier-Hein, Yao Zhang, Zhiqiang He, Jun Ma, et al., Multi-centre, multi-vendor and multi-disease cardiac segmentation: the m&ms challenge, IEEE Transactions on Medical Imaging 40 (12) (2021) 3543–3554.

[88] Hong-Yu Zhou, Jiansen Guo, Yinghao Zhang, Lequan Yu, Liansheng Wang, Yizhou Yu, nnformer: interleaved transformer for volumetric segmentation, arXiv preprint, arXiv: 2109.03201, 2021.

[89] Ailiang Lin, Bingzhi Chen, Jiayu Xu, Zheng Zhang, Guangming Lu, Ds-transunet: dual swin transformer u-net for medical image segmentation, arXiv preprint, arXiv:2106. 06716, 2021.

[90] Yijiang Li, Wentian Cai, Ying Gao, Xiping Hu, More than encoder: introducing transformer decoder to upsample, arXiv preprint, arXiv:2106.10637, 2021.

[91] Shaohua Li, Xiuchao Sui, Xiangde Luo, Xinxing Xu, Yong Liu, Rick Siow Mong Goh, Medical image segmentation using squeeze-and-expansion transformers, arXiv preprint, arXiv:2105.09511, 2021.

[92] Zhuangzhuang Zhang, Baozhou Sun, Weixiong Zhang, Pyramid medical transformer for medical image segmentation, arXiv preprint, arXiv:2104.14702, 2021.

[93] Golnaz Ghiasi, Charless C. Fowlkes, Laplacian pyramid reconstruction and refinement for semantic segmentation, in: European Conference on Computer Vision, Springer, 2016, pp. 519–534.

[94] Neeraj Kumar, Ruchika Verma, Sanuj Sharma, Surabhi Bhargava, Abhishek Vahadane, Amit Sethi, A dataset and a technique for generalized nuclear segmentation for computational pathology, IEEE Transactions on Medical Imaging 36 (7) (2017) 1550–1560.

[95] Vincent Andrearczyk, Valentin Oreiller, Mario Jreige, Martin Vallières, Joel Castelli, Hesham Elhalawani, Sarah Boughdad, John O. Prior, Adrien Depeursinge, Overview of the hecktor challenge at miccai 2020: automatic head and neck tumor segmentation in pet/ct, in: 3D Head and Neck Tumor Segmentation in PET/CT Challenge, Springer, 2020, pp. 1–21.

[96] Yuanfeng Ji, Ruimao Zhang, Huijie Wang, Zhen Li, Lingyun Wu, Shaoting Zhang, Ping Luo, Multi-compound transformer for accurate biomedical image segmentation, in: International Conference on Medical Image Computing and Computer-Assisted Intervention, Springer, 2021, pp. 326–336.

[97] Changqian Yu, Jingbo Wang, Changxin Gao, Gang Yu, Chunhua Shen, Nong Sang, Context prior for scene segmentation, in: Proceedings of the IEEE/CVF Conference on Computer Vision and Pattern Recognition, 2020, pp. 12416–12425.

[98] Ali Hatamizadeh, Dong Yang, Holger Roth, Daguang Xu, Unetr: transformers for 3d medical image segmentation, arXiv preprint, arXiv:2103.10504, 2021.

[99] B. Landman, Z. Xu, J. Eugenio Igelsias, M. Styner, T. Langerak, A. Klein, Miccai multi-atlas labeling beyond the cranial vault–workshop and challenge, in: Proc. MICCAI: Multi-Atlas Labeling Beyond Cranial Vault-Workshop Challenge, 2015.

[100] Jifeng Dai, Haozhi Qi, Yuwen Xiong, Yi Li, Guodong Zhang, Han Hu, Yichen Wei, Deformable convolutional networks, in: Proceedings of the IEEE International Conference on Computer Vision, 2017, pp. 764–773.

[101] Tao Ai, Zhenlu Yang, Hongyan Hou, Chenao Zhan, Chong Chen, Wenzhi Lv, Qian Tao, Ziyong Sun, Liming Xia, Correlation of chest ct and rt-pcr testing for coronavirus

disease 2019 (Covid-19) in China: a report of 1014 cases, Radiology 296 (2) (2020) E32–E40.

[102] Yicheng Fang, Huangqi Zhang, Jicheng Xie, Minjie Lin, Lingjun Ying, Peipei Pang, Wenbin Ji, Sensitivity of chest ct for Covid-19: comparison to rt-pcr, Radiology 296 (2) (2020) E115–E117.

[103] Dandan Chen, Xinqing Jiang, Yong Hong, Zhihui Wen, Shuquan Wei, Guangming Peng, Xinhua Wei, Can chest ct features distinguish patients with negative from those with positive initial rt-pcr results for coronavirus disease (Covid-19)?, American Journal of Roentgenology 216 (1) (2021) 66–70.

[104] Shehan Perera, Srikar Adhikari, Alper Yilmaz, Pocformer: a lightweight transformer architecture for detection of Covid-19 using point of care ultrasound, arXiv preprint, arXiv:2105.09913, 2021.

[105] Mark Sandler, Andrew Howard, Menglong Zhu, Andrey Zhmoginov, Liang-Chieh Chen, Mobilenetv2: inverted residuals and linear bottlenecks, in: Proceedings of the IEEE Conference on Computer Vision and Pattern Recognition, 2018, pp. 4510–4520.

[106] Jannis Born, Gabriel Brändle, Manuel Cossio, Marion Disdier, Julie Goulet, Jérémie Roulin, Nina Wiedemann, Pocovid-net: automatic detection of Covid-19 from a new lung ultrasound imaging dataset (pocus), arXiv preprint, arXiv:2004.12084, 2020.

[107] Joseph Paul Cohen, Paul Morrison, Lan Dao, Karsten Roth, Tim Q. Duong, Marzyeh Ghassemi, Covid-19 image data collection: prospective predictions are the future, arXiv preprint, arXiv:2006.11988, 2020.

[108] Chengeng Liu, Qingshan Yin, Automatic diagnosis of Covid-19 using a tailored transformer-like network, Journal of Physics. Conference Series 2010 (2021) 012175.

[109] Li Yuan, Qibin Hou, Zihang Jiang, Jiashi Feng, Shuicheng Yan, Volo: vision outlooker for visual recognition, arXiv preprint, arXiv:2106.13112, 2021.

[110] Muhammad E.H. Chowdhury, Tawsifur Rahman, Amith Khandakar, Rashid Mazhar, Muhammad Abdul Kadir, Zaid Bin Mahbub, Khandakar Reajul Islam, Muhammad Salman Khan, Atif Iqbal, Nasser Al Emadi, et al., Can ai help in screening viral and Covid-19 pneumonia?, IEEE Access 8 (2020) 132665–132676.

[111] Juntao Jiang, Shuyi Lin, Covid-19 detection in chest x-ray images using swin-transformer and transformer in transformer, arXiv preprint, arXiv:2110.08427, 2021.

[112] Kai Han, An Xiao, Enhua Wu, Jianyuan Guo, Chunjing Xu, Yunhe Wang, Transformer in transformer, arXiv preprint, arXiv:2103.00112, 2021.

[113] Qi Dou, Tiffany Y. So, Meirui Jiang, Quande Liu, Varut Vardhanabhuti, Georgios Kaissis, Zeju Li, Weixin Si, Heather H.C. Lee, Kevin Yu, et al., Federated deep learning for detecting Covid-19 lung abnormalities in ct: a privacy-preserving multinational validation study, npj Digital Medicine 4 (1) (2021) 1–11.

[114] Sangjoon Park, Gwanghyun Kim, Jeongsol Kim, Boah Kim, Jong Chul Ye, Federated split vision transformer for Covid-19cxr diagnosis using task-agnostic training, arXiv preprint, arXiv:2111.01338, 2021.

[115] Qiang Yang, Yang Liu, Tianjian Chen, Yongxin Tong, Federated machine learning: concept and applications, ACM Transactions on Intelligent Systems and Technology 10 (2) (2019) 1–19.

[116] Praneeth Vepakomma, Otkrist Gupta, Tristan Swedish, Ramesh Raskar, Split learning for health: distributed deep learning without sharing raw patient data, arXiv preprint, arXiv:1812.00564, 2018.

[117] Rich Caruana, Multitask learning, Machine Learning 28 (1) (1997) 41–75.

[118] Thomas C. Kwee, Robert M. Kwee, Chest ct in Covid-19: what the radiologist needs to know, Radiographics 40 (7) (2020) 1848–1865.

[119] Chih-Chung Hsu, Guan-Lin Chen, Mei-Hsuan Wu, Visual transformer with statistical test for Covid-19 classification, arXiv preprint, arXiv:2107.05334, 2021.

[120] Robert F. Woolson, Wilcoxon signed-rank test, in: Wiley Encyclopedia of Clinical Trials, 2007, pp. 1–3.

[121] Lei Zhang, Yan Wen, A transformer-based framework for automatic Covid19 diagnosis in chest cts, in: Proceedings of the IEEE/CVF International Conference on Computer Vision, 2021, pp. 513–518.

[122] Dimitrios Kollias, Anastasios Arsenos, Levon Soukissian, Stefanos Kollias, Miacov19d: Covid-19 detection through 3-d chest ct image analysis, arXiv preprint, arXiv:2106.07524, 2021.

[123] Runmin Cong, Jianjun Lei, Huazhu Fu, Ming-Ming Cheng, Weisi Lin, Qingming Huang, Review of visual saliency detection with comprehensive information, IEEE Transactions on Circuits and Systems for Video Technology 29 (10) (2018) 2941–2959.

[124] Ramprasaath R. Selvaraju, Michael Cogswell, Abhishek Das, Ramakrishna Vedantam, Devi Parikh, Dhruv Batra, Grad-cam: visual explanations from deep networks via gradient-based localization, in: Proceedings of the IEEE International Conference on Computer Vision, 2017, pp. 618–626.

[125] Arnab Kumar Mondal, Arnab Bhattacharjee, Parag Singla, A.P. Prathosh, xvitcos: Explainable vision transformer based Covid-19 screening using radiography, 2021.

[126] Sangjoon Park, Gwanghyun Kim, Yujin Oh, Joon Beom Seo, Sang Min Lee, Jin Hwan Kim, Sungjun Moon, Jae-Kwang Lim, Jong Chul Ye, Vision transformer for Covid-19 cxr diagnosis using chest x-ray feature corpus, arXiv preprint, arXiv:2103.07055, 2021.

[127] Ting Chen, Simon Kornblith, Mohammad Norouzi, Geoffrey Hinton, A simple framework for contrastive learning of visual representations, in: International Conference on Machine Learning, PMLR, 2020, pp. 1597–1607.

[128] Jeremy Irvin, Pranav Rajpurkar, Michael Ko, Yifan Yu, Silviana Ciurea-Ilcus, Chris Chute, Henrik Marklund, Behzad Haghgoo, Robyn Ball, Katie Shpanskaya, et al., Chexpert: a large chest radiograph dataset with uncertainty labels and expert comparison, in: Proceedings of the AAAI Conference on Artificial Intelligence, vol. 33, 2019, pp. 590–597.

[129] Hila Chefer, Shir Gur, Lior Wolf, Transformer interpretability beyond attention visualization, in: Proceedings of the IEEE/CVF Conference on Computer Vision and Pattern Recognition, 2021, pp. 782–791.

[130] Xiaohong Gao, Yu Qian, Alice Gao, Covid-vit: classification of Covid-19 from ct chest images based on vision transformer models, arXiv preprint, arXiv:2107.01682, 2021.

[131] Gao Huang, Zhuang Liu, Laurens Van Der Maaten, Kilian Q. Weinberger, Densely connected convolutional networks, in: Proceedings of the IEEE Conference on Computer Vision and Pattern Recognition, 2017, pp. 4700–4708.

[132] Hayden Gunraj, Ali Sabri, David Koff, Alexander Wong, Covid-net ct-2: enhanced deep neural networks for detection of Covid-19 from chest ct images through bigger, more diverse learning, arXiv preprint, arXiv:2101.07433, 2021.

[133] Debaditya Shome, T. Kar, Sachi Nandan Mohanty, Prayag Tiwari, Khan Muhammad, Abdullah AlTameem, Yazhou Zhang, Abdul Khader Jilani Saudagar, Covidtransformer: interpretable Covid-19 detection using vision transformer for healthcare, International Journal of Environmental Research and Public Health 18 (21) (2021) 11086.

[134] Yin Dai, Yifan Gao, Fayu Liu, Transmed: transformers advance multi-modal medical image classification, Diagnostics 11 (8) (2021) 1384.

[135] Mengkang Lu, Yongsheng Pan, Dong Nie, Feihong Liu, Feng Shi, Yong Xia, Dinggang Shen, Smile: sparse-attention based multiple instance contrastive learning for glioma sub-type classification using pathological images, in: MICCAI Workshop on Computational Pathology, PMLR, 2021, pp. 159–169.

[136] Sandy Napel, Sylvia K. Plevritis, Nsclc radiogenomics: initial Stanford study of 26 cases, Cancer Imaging Arch (2014).

[137] Behnaz Gheflati, Hassan Rivaz, Vision transformers for classification of breast ultrasound images, arXiv preprint, arXiv:2110.14731, 2021.

[138] Walid Al-Dhabyani, Mohammed Gomaa, Hussien Khaled, Aly Fahmy, Dataset of breast ultrasound images, Data in Brief 28 (2020) 104863.

[139] Moi Hoon Yap, Gerard Pons, Joan Martí, Sergi Ganau, Melcior Sentís, Reyer Zwiggelaar, Adrian K. Davison, Robert Marti, Automated breast ultrasound lesions detection using convolutional neural networks, IEEE Journal of Biomedical and Health Informatics 22 (4) (2017) 1218–1226.

[140] Anwar Khan, Boreom Lee, Gene transformer: transformers for the gene expression-based classification of lung cancer subtypes, arXiv preprint, arXiv:2108.11833, 2021.

[141] Haoyuan Chen, Chen Li, Xiaoyan Li, Ge Wang, Weiming Hu, Yixin Li, Wanli Liu, Changhao Sun, Yudong Yao, Yueyang Teng, et al., Gashis-transformer: a multi-scale visual transformer approach for gastric histopathology image classification, arXiv preprint, arXiv:2104.14528, 2021.

[142] Zhencun Jiang, Zhengxin Dong, Lingyang Wang, Wenping Jiang, Method for diagnosis of acute lymphoblastic leukemia based on vit-cnn ensemble model, Computational Intelligence and Neuroscience (2021) 2021.

[143] Glenn Fung, Murat Dundar, Balaji Krishnapuram, R. Bharat Rao, Multiple instance learning for computer aided diagnosis, Advances in Neural Information Processing Systems 19 (2007) 425.

[144] Zhuchen Shao, Hao Bian, Yang Chen, Yifeng Wang, Jian Zhang, Xiangyang Ji, Yongbing Zhang, Transmil: transformer based correlated multiple instance learning for whole slide image classification, arXiv preprint, arXiv:2106.00908, 2021.

[145] Babak Ehteshami Bejnordi, Mitko Veta, Paul Johannes Van Diest, Bram Van Ginneken, Nico Karssemeijer, Geert Litjens, Jeroen A.W.M. Van Der Laak, Meyke Hermsen, Quirine F. Manson, Maschenka Balkenhol, et al., Diagnostic assessment of deep learning algorithms for detection of lymph node metastases in women with breast cancer, JAMA 318 (22) (2017) 2199–2210.

[146] The cancer genome atlas program, https://www.cancer.gov/about-nci/organization/ccg/research/structural-genomics/tcga. (Accessed 20 January 2022).

[147] Yi Zheng, Rushin Gindra, Margrit Betke, Jennifer Beane, Vijaya B. Kolachalama, A deep learning based graph-transformer for whole slide image classification, medRxiv, 2021.

[148] Thomas N. Kipf, Max Welling, Semi-supervised classification with graph convolutional networks, arXiv preprint, arXiv:1609.02907, 2016.

[149] Shuang Yu, Kai Ma, Qi Bi, Cheng Bian, Munan Ning, Nanjun He, Yuexiang Li, Hanruo Liu, Yefeng Zheng, Mil-vt: multiple instance learning enhanced vision transformer for fundus image classification, in: International Conference on Medical Image Computing and Computer-Assisted Intervention, Springer, 2021, pp. 45–54.

[150] Aptos 2019 blindness detection: detect diabetic retinopathy to stop blindness before it's too late, https://www.kaggle.com/c/aptos2019-blindness-detection. (Accessed 20 January 2022).

[151] Gwenolé Quellec, Mathieu Lamard, Pierre-Henri Conze, Pascale Massin, Béatrice Cochener, Automatic detection of rare pathologies in fundus photographs using few-shot learning, Medical Image Analysis 61 (2020) 101660.

[152] Rui Sun, Yihao Li, Tianzhu Zhang, Zhendong Mao, Feng Wu, Yongdong Zhang, Lesion-aware transformers for diabetic retinopathy grading, in: Proceedings of the IEEE/CVF Conference on Computer Vision and Pattern Recognition, 2021, pp. 10938–10947.

[153] Etienne Decencière, Xiwei Zhang, Guy Cazuguel, Bruno Lay, Béatrice Cochener, Caroline Trone, Philippe Gain, Richard Ordonez, Pascale Massin, Ali Erginay, et al., Feedback on a publicly distributed image database: the messidor database, Image Analysis & Stereology 33 (3) (2014) 231–234.

[154] Jorge Cuadros, George Bresnick, Eyepacs: an adaptable telemedicine system for diabetic retinopathy screening, Journal of Diabetes Science and Technology 3 (3) (2009) 509–516.

[155] Honggang Yang, Jiejie Chen, Mengfei Xu, Fundus disease image classification based on improved transformer, in: 2021 International Conference on Neuromorphic Computing (ICNC), IEEE, 2021, pp. 207–214.

[156] Ophthalmic image analysis dataset, https://github.com/nkicsl/OIA. (Accessed 20 January 2022).

[157] Jianfang Wu, Ruo Hu, Zhenghong Xiao, Jiaxu Chen, Jingwei Liu, Vision transformer-based recognition of diabetic retinopathy grade, Medical Physics (2021).

[158] Nouar AlDahoul, Hezerul Abdul Karim, Myles Joshua Toledo Tan, Mhd Adel Momo, Jamie Ledesma Fermin, Encoding retina image to words using ensemble of vision transformers for diabetic retinopathy grading, F1000Research 10 (2021) 948.

[159] Fangzhou Liao, Ming Liang, Zhe Li, Xiaolin Hu, Sen Song, Evaluate the malignancy of pulmonary nodules using the 3-d deep leaky noisy-or network, IEEE Transactions on Neural Networks and Learning Systems 30 (11) (2019) 3484–3495.

[160] Nilay Ganatra, A comprehensive study of applying object detection methods for medical image analysis, in: 2021 8th International Conference on Computing for Sustainable Global Development (INDIACom), IEEE, 2021, pp. 821–826.

[161] Xizhou Zhu, Weijie Su, Lewei Lu, Bin Li, Xiaogang Wang, Jifeng Dai, Deformable detr: deformable transformers for end-to-end object detection, arXiv preprint, arXiv:2010.04159, 2020.

[162] Zhiqiang Shen, Chaonan Lin, Shaohua Zheng, Cotr: convolution in transformer network for end to end polyp detection, arXiv preprint, arXiv:2105.10925, 2021.

[163] Shijie Liu, Hongyu Zhou, Xiaozhou Shi, Junwen Pan, Transformer for polyp detection, arXiv preprint, arXiv:2111.07918, 2021.

[164] Tejas Sudharshan Mathai, Sungwon Lee, Daniel C. Elton, Thomas C. Shen, Yifan Peng, Zhiyong Lu, Ronald M. Summers, Lymph node detection in t2 mri with transformers, arXiv preprint, arXiv:2111.04885, 2021.

[165] Muralikrishna Gopal, Shaad E. Abdullah, James J. Grady, James S. Goodwin, Screening for lung cancer with low-dose computed tomography: a systematic review and meta-analysis of the baseline findings of randomized controlled trials, Journal of Thoracic Oncology 5 (8) (2010) 1233–1239.

[166] Alexandre Sadate, Bob V. Occean, Jean-Paul Beregi, Aymeric Hamard, Takieddine Addala, Hélène de Forges, Pascale Fabbro-Peray, Julien Frandon, Systematic review and meta-analysis on the impact of lung cancer screening by low-dose computed tomography, European Journal of Cancer 134 (2020) 107–114.

[167] Zhicheng Zhang, Lequan Yu, Xiaokun Liang, Wei Zhao, Lei Xing, Transct: dual-path transformer for low dose computed tomography, arXiv preprint, arXiv:2103.00634, 2021.

[168] Cynthia H. McCollough, Adam C. Bartley, Rickey E. Carter, Baiyu Chen, Tammy A. Drees, Phillip Edwards, David R. Holmes III, Alice E. Huang, Farhana Khan, Shuai Leng, et al., Low-dose ct for the detection and classification of metastatic liver lesions: results of the 2016 low dose ct grand challenge, Medical Physics 44 (10) (2017) e339–e352.

[169] Dayang Wang, Zhan Wu, Hengyong Yu, Ted-net: convolution-free t2t vision transformer-based encoder-decoder dilation network for low-dose ct denoising, arXiv preprint, arXiv:2106.04650, 2021.

[170] Li Yuan, Yunpeng Chen, Tao Wang, Weihao Yu, Yujun Shi, Zihang Jiang, Francis E.H. Tay, Jiashi Feng, Shuicheng Yan, Tokens-to-token vit: training vision transformers from scratch on imagenet, arXiv preprint, arXiv:2101.11986, 2021.

[171] Achleshwar Luthra, Harsh Sulakhe, Tanish Mittal, Abhishek Iyer, Santosh Yadav, Eformer: edge enhancement based transformer for medical image denoising, arXiv preprint, arXiv:2109.08044, 2021.

[172] Tengfei Liang, Yi Jin, Yidong Li, Tao Wang, Edcnn: edge enhancement-based densely connected network with compound loss for low-dose ct denoising, in: 2020 15th IEEE International Conference on Signal Processing (ICSP), vol. 1, IEEE, 2020, pp. 193–198.

[173] F.G. Irwin, et al., An isotropic 3x3 image gradient operator, Presentation at Stanford AI Project 2014 (02) (1968).

[174] Yanmei Luo, Yan Wang, Chen Zu, Bo Zhan, Xi Wu, Jiliu Zhou, Dinggang Shen, Luping Zhou, 3d transformer-gan for high-quality pet reconstruction, in: International Conference on Medical Image Computing and Computer-Assisted Intervention, Springer, 2021, pp. 276–285.

[175] Chang Min Hyun, Hwa Pyung Kim, Sung Min Lee, Sungchul Lee, Jin Keun Seo, Deep learning for undersampled mri reconstruction, Physics in Medicine and Biology 63 (13) (2018) 135007.

[176] Chun-Mei Feng, Yunlu Yan, Geng Chen, Huazhu Fu, Yong Xu, Ling Shao, Accelerated multi-modal mr imaging with transformers, arXiv preprint, arXiv:2106.14248, 2021.

[177] Chun-Mei Feng, Yunlu Yan, Huazhu Fu, Li Chen, Yong Xu, Task transformer network for joint mri reconstruction and super-resolution, arXiv preprint, arXiv:2106.06742, 2021.

[178] Dwarikanath Mahapatra, Zongyuan Ge, Mr image super resolution by combining feature disentanglement cnns and vision transformers, 2021.

[179] Taesung Park, Jun-Yan Zhu, Oliver Wang, Jingwan Lu, Eli Shechtman, Alexei A. Efros, Richard Zhang, Swapping autoencoder for deep image manipulation, arXiv preprint, arXiv:2007.00653, 2020.

[180] Yilmaz Korkmaz, Salman U.H. Dar, Mahmut Yurt, Muzaffer Özbey, Tolga Çukur, Unsupervised mri reconstruction via zero-shot learned adversarial transformers, arXiv preprint, arXiv:2105.08059, 2021.

[181] Yilmaz Korkmaz, Mahmut Yurt, Salman Ul Hassan Dar, Muzaffer Özbey, Tolga Cukur, Deep mri reconstruction with generative vision transformers, in: International Workshop on Machine Learning for Medical Image Reconstruction, Springer, 2021, pp. 54–64.

[182] Dmitry Ulyanov, Andrea Vedaldi, Victor Lempitsky, Deep image prior, in: Proceedings of the IEEE Conference on Computer Vision and Pattern Recognition, 2018, pp. 9446–9454.

[183] Adnan Qayyum, Inaam Ilahi, Fahad Shamshad, Farid Boussaid, Mohammed Bennamoun, Junaid Qadir, Untrained neural network priors for inverse imaging problems: a survey, 2021.

[184] Kang Lin, Reinhard Heckel, Vision transformers enable fast and robust accelerated mri, 2021.

[185] Yoseob Han, Jong Chul Ye, Framing u-net via deep convolutional framelets: application to sparse-view ct, IEEE Transactions on Medical Imaging 37 (6) (2018) 1418–1429.

[186] Hiroyuki Kudo, Taizo Suzuki, Essam A. Rashed, Image reconstruction for sparse-view ct and interior ct—introduction to compressed sensing and differentiated backprojection, Quantitative Imaging in Medicine and Surgery 3 (3) (2013) 147.

[187] Ce Wang, Kun Shang, Haimiao Zhang, Qian Li, Yuan Hui, S. Kevin Zhou, Dudotrans: dual-domain transformer provides more attention for sinogram restoration in sparse-view ct reconstruction, arXiv preprint, arXiv:2111.10790, 2021.

[188] Yonghao Long, Zhaoshuo Li, Chi Hang Yee, Chi Fai Ng, Russell H. Taylor, Mathias Unberath, Qi Dou, E-dssr: efficient dynamic surgical scene reconstruction with transformer-based stereoscopic depth perception, in: International Conference on Medical Image Computing and Computer-Assisted Intervention, Springer, 2021, pp. 415–425.

[189] Menglong Ye, Edward Johns, Ankur Handa, Lin Zhang, Philip Pratt, Guang-Zhong Yang, Self-supervised Siamese learning on stereo image pairs for depth estimation in robotic surgery, arXiv preprint, arXiv:1705.08260, 2017.

[190] Chen Liu, Mathieu Salzmann, Tao Lin, Ryota Tomioka, Sabine Süsstrunk, On the loss landscape of adversarial training: identifying challenges and how to overcome them, arXiv preprint, arXiv:2006.08403, 2020.

[191] Xuzhe Zhang, Xinzi He, Jia Guo, Nabil Ettehadi, Natalie Aw, David Semanek, Jonathan Posner, Andrew Laine, Yun Wang, Ptnet: a high-resolution infant mri synthesizer based on transformer, arXiv preprint, arXiv:2105.13993, 2021.

[192] Krzysztof Choromanski, Valerii Likhosherstov, David Dohan, Xingyou Song, Andreea Gane, Tamas Sarlos, Peter Hawkins, Jared Davis, Afroz Mohiuddin, Lukasz Kaiser, et al., Rethinking attention with performers, arXiv preprint, arXiv:2009.14794, 2020.

[193] Phillip Isola, Jun-Yan Zhu, Tinghui Zhou, Alexei A. Efros, Image-to-image translation with conditional adversarial networks, in: Proceedings of the IEEE Conference on Computer Vision and Pattern Recognition, 2017, pp. 1125–1134.

[194] Ting-Chun Wang, Ming-Yu Liu, Jun-Yan Zhu, Andrew Tao, Jan Kautz, Bryan Catanzaro, High-resolution image synthesis and semantic manipulation with conditional gans, in: Proceedings of the IEEE Conference on Computer Vision and Pattern Recognition, 2018, pp. 8798–8807.

[195] Antonios Makropoulos, Emma C. Robinson, Andreas Schuh, Robert Wright, Sean Fitzgibbon, Jelena Bozek, Serena J. Counsell, Johannes Steinweg, Katy Vecchiato, Jonathan Passerat-Palmbach, et al., The developing human connectome project: a minimal processing pipeline for neonatal cortical surface reconstruction, NeuroImage 173 (2018) 88–112.

[196] Sharif Amit Kamran, Khondker Fariha Hossain, Alireza Tavakkoli, Stewart Lee Zuckerbrod, Kenton M. Sanders, Salah A. Baker, Vtgan: semi-supervised retinal image synthesis and disease prediction using vision transformers, arXiv preprint, arXiv:2104.06757, 2021.

[197] Martin Heusel, Hubert Ramsauer, Thomas Unterthiner, Bernhard Nessler, Sepp Hochreiter, Gans trained by a two time-scale update rule converge to a local Nash equilibrium, Advances in Neural Information Processing Systems 30 (2017).

[198] Mikołaj Bińkowski, Danica J. Sutherland, Michael Arbel, Arthur Gretton, Demystifying mmd gans, arXiv preprint, arXiv:1801.01401, 2018.

[199] Shirin Hajeb Mohammad Alipour, Hossein Rabbani, Mohammad Reza Akhlaghi, Diabetic retinopathy grading by digital curvelet transform, in: Computational and Mathematical Methods in Medicine, 2012, 2012.

[200] Nicolae-Catalin Ristea, Andreea-Iuliana Miron, Olivian Savencu, Mariana-Iuliana Georgescu, Nicolae Verga, Fahad Shahbaz Khan, Radu Tudor Ionescu, Cytran: cycle-consistent transformers for non-contrast to contrast ct translation, arXiv preprint, arXiv:2110.06400, 2021.

[201] Onat Dalmaz, Mahmut Yurt, Tolga Çukur, Resvit: residual vision transformers for multi-modal medical image synthesis, arXiv preprint, arXiv:2106.16031, 2021.

[202] Bjoern H. Menze, Andras Jakab, Stefan Bauer, Jayashree Kalpathy-Cramer, Keyvan Farahani, Justin Kirby, Yuliya Burren, Nicole Porz, Johannes Slotboom, Roland Wiest, et al., The multimodal brain tumor image segmentation benchmark (brats), IEEE Transactions on Medical Imaging 34 (10) (2014) 1993–2024.

[203] Tufve Nyholm, Stina Svensson, Sebastian Andersson, Joakim Jonsson, Maja Sohlin, Christian Gustafsson, Elisabeth Kjellén, Karin Söderström, Per Albertsson, Lennart Blomqvist, et al., Mr and ct data with multiobserver delineations of organs in the pelvic area—part of the gold atlas project, Medical Physics 45 (3) (2018) 1295–1300.

Deep learning methods

2

An overview of disentangled representation learning for MR image harmonization

5

Lianrui Zuo[a,b], Yihao Liu[a], Jerry L. Prince[a], and Aaron Carass[a]

[a]*Department of Electrical and Computer Engineering, Johns Hopkins University, Baltimore, MD, United States*

[b]*Laboratory of Behavioral Neuroscience, National Institute on Aging, National Institutes of Health, Baltimore, MD, United States*

5.1 Introduction

Magnetic resonance (MR) imaging has become one of the most popular imaging modalities due to its soft tissue contrast and imaging flexibility. The flexibility in acquisition enables multiple contrast images to be acquired in a single imaging session by changing pulse sequences or acquisition parameters. For example, T_1-weighted (T_1-w) and T_2-weighted (T_2-w) images are two of the most commonly acquired contrasts in MR imaging, where T_1-w images often show balanced gray matter (GM) and white matter (WM) contrast, whereas fluid-tissue contrast can be better visualized in T_2-w images [1]. However, this imaging flexibility also makes it hard to standardize MR acquisitions, which is detrimental to reproducibility [2]. The lack of standardization in acquisition is commonly reflected in undesired variations in the image contrast. This is particularly problematic in multi-site imaging, as the image contrast often varies with pulse sequence, acquisition parameters and scanner manufacturers [3,4]. Even for the same scanner, software updates and scanner calibration can cause substantial variations in image contrast. As shown in Fig. 5.1, the two T_1-w images of the same subject were both acquired using the magnetic-prepared rapid gradient echo (MPRAGE) sequence, but they show different image contrast.

5.1.1 Domain shift

The undesired contrast variation of MR images is a long-standing challenge to modern medical image analyses. Consider image segmentation for instance, which is increasingly built upon machine learning (ML) and deep learning (DL) methods. It

135

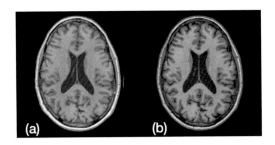

FIGURE 5.1

(a) and (b) are T_1-w MPRAGE images of the same subject acquired from two different sites.

is not hard to imagine that a segmentation model designed for computational tomography (CT) images is likely to fail on MR images, since the two imaging modalities are based on different physical properties of the human anatomy and the appearance of the images are drastically different. Unfortunately, the same problem is present when considering just MR images [5]. For example, we might expect a performance drop for a segmentation model trained on the MPRAGE image of Fig. 5.1(a) when applied to Fig. 5.1(b), which has different contrast. This effect can be formalized as a *domain shift* problem [6]. The segmentation model only *generalizes* to data that have a similar distribution as that used during training. When the distribution between the training and testing data differ, domain shift occurs. In this chapter, we focus on T_1-w and T_2-w MR images, and we define *domain* to be a set of MR images from the same scanner with the same scanning protocol and parameters. This means that T_1-w and T_2-w images from Sites A and B should be treated as four distinct domains, X_{A_1}, X_{A_2}, X_{B_1} and X_{B_2}, where we use an alphabetical index to represent site and a numerical index to represent different MR contrasts. Fig. 5.2 shows an example of the four domains.

Roughly speaking, there are three research directions to alleviate domain shift in MR imaging: 1) statistical harmonization, 2) adjusting the segmentation model to achieve greater generalizability and 3) mapping data from the testing domain to the training domain. With statistical harmonization, the segmentation model is applied to data from various sites and then the output segmentation metrics are passed through statistical models in which site, scanner and protocol are included as model covariates. The goal is to use statistical modeling to factor out the covariates, and thus directly harmonize the segmentation metrics without changing the images. A detailed analysis of these approaches is beyond the scope of this chapter; we note, however, that such methods usually require a large number of subjects to perform an accurate correction [7].

To improve the generalizability of a segmentation model that was previously trained on domain X_{A_1} but with desired application on both X_{A_1} and X_{B_1}, the most straightforward solution is to retrain the model with data from both domains. However, such retraining has several serious limitations. First, the novel testing domain

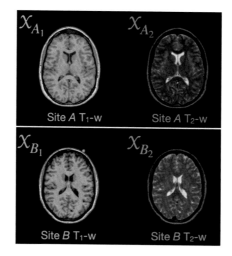

FIGURE 5.2

Four different image domains constructed by T_1-w and T_2-w images from two sites. Multi-contrast images are routinely acquired within each imaging session.

$\mathcal{X}_{B_1}$ may not have labels (i.e., manual delineations) to support a retraining of the segmentation model in a supervised manner. Second, in MR imaging, such retraining on both domains means pooling data across sites, which is restricted due to patient privacy. To overcome the first challenge, researchers have proposed methods to take advantage of the unlabeled testing domain data as a regularization. In [8,9], domain-invariant features are learned using image data from both the training and testing domains, and those features are then used to aid the segmentation. To overcome the data sharing challenge in medical imaging, Zhang et al. [10] use data augmentation to enrich the training domain, so that a better generalized segmentation model can be learned with a more variable data set. Alternatively, federated learning [11] can circumvent the data sharing problem. Improving generalizability is an important consideration when designing and training segmentation models. However, for pretrained models and non-DL models, modifying model design to improve generalizability is usually not applicable.

Mapping image data across domains, on the other hand, alleviates domain shift without changing the existing segmentation model. Image harmonization falls into this category. Based on image-to-image translation (IIT), MR image harmonization learns an intensity translation function $f(\cdot; w)$ to map images from a source domain $\mathcal{X}_s = \{x_s\}$ to a target domain $\mathcal{X}_t = \{x_t\}$, where w are parameters of $f(\cdot)$. The source domain is the novel testing domain, where the domain shift occurs (e.g., $\mathcal{X}_{B_1}$) and the target domain represents the original domain where the segmentation model was previously trained (e.g., $\mathcal{X}_{A_1}$). After harmonization, images from the testing domain are no longer novel to the segmentation model, and domain shift is alleviated. He et al. [12,13] proposed an auto-encoder-based unsupervised domain adaptation approach, where a domain adaptor is fine-tuned at test time to map images between testing and training domains. Dewey et al. [14], Zuo et al. [3,15] used disentangled representations to harmonize MR images across sites. As image harmonization does not have any requirements for the segmentation model, IIT-based harmonization has clear advantages over model generalization methods when updating the segmentation model is undesired or not allowed. Although image harmonization uses IIT to translate images across domains, IIT and harmonization have some differences, due to the nature of MR imaging, which we discuss in the next section.

5.1.2 Image-to-image translation and harmonization

IIT methods in general can be categorized into supervised and unsupervised, depending on the data required in training. For example, a CT-MR synthesis method is supervised if it requires paired CT and MR images of the same anatomy as training data [16]. Whether paired training data are present makes a difference in designing IIT models. Specifically, if paired data are available, pixel-to-pixel error (e.g., $||f(x_s; w) - x_t||_2$) are typically used as a cost function during training. For IIT-based harmonization, the image translation function $f(\cdot; w)$ learns two major things: preserving the anatomical information (*geometry accuracy*) and adjusting the image contrast to match the target domain (*domain accuracy*). For DL-based harmonization, the learned knowledge of $f(\cdot; w)$ is embedded in neural network weights w. This means that $f(\cdot; w)$ can only be used to translate images in the same domain and direction it was trained with. For example, if a T_1-w to T_2-w synthesis model was trained to translate images from $\mathcal{X}_{A_1}$ to $\mathcal{X}_{A_2}$, it usually cannot directly be applied to translate images from $\mathcal{X}_{A_2}$ to $\mathcal{X}_{A_1}$ or from $\mathcal{X}_{B_1}$ to $\mathcal{X}_{B_2}$.

Unsupervised IIT methods do not have paired data for training, thus pixel-to-pixel error cannot be directly calculated. To achieve domain accuracy, domain discriminators are usually used [17–20]. For example, CycleGAN [17] translates images from domains $\mathcal{X}_s$ to $\mathcal{X}_t$ by learning an image translation function $f(\cdot; w_s): \mathcal{X}_s \to \mathcal{X}_t$ and a domain discriminator $D_t(\cdot): \mathcal{X}_t \to \mathbb{R}$, which guides $f(\cdot; w_s)$ to generate images matching the target domain. Meanwhile, an inverse translation function $f(\cdot; w_t): \mathcal{X}_t \to \mathcal{X}_s$ and a counter domain discriminator $D_s(\cdot): \mathcal{X}_s \to \mathbb{R}$ are learned jointly. An advantage of CycleGAN is that bi-directional image translation can be achieved using $f(\cdot; w_t)$ and $f(\cdot; w_s)$. However, this also means CycleGAN generally requires a large number of model parameters, which is a downside when there are many domains involved in the IIT. Encouraging geometry accuracy is more challenging due to the absence of pixel-to-pixel correspondence in training. Several works [17,18,20,21] use cycle consistency—assuming an identity transformation after a forward and an inverse translation (i.e., $I = f(f(\cdot; w_s); w_t) = f(f(\cdot; w_t); w_s)$)—to regularize the model to preserve geometry during IIT. However, cycle consistency is an implicit regularization of geometry accuracy, thus geometry shift can still occur [22]. Yang et al. [23] uses feature-level consistency as an extra constraint to regularize the geometry in unsupervised CT-MR synthesis. Despite these research efforts, geometry shift remains challenging for unsupervised IIT.

Table 5.1 Summary of IIT methods that are designed to solve or can be applied to solve supervised and unsupervised harmonization problems.

	Supervised IIT	Unsupervised IIT
Supervised Harmonization	• DeepHarmony [2,24]	–
Unsupervised Harmonization	• Dewey et al. [14] • CALAMITI [3,15]	• CycleGAN [17] • UNIT [18] • MUNIT [20] • StarGAN [19] • DCMIT [21]

MR image harmonization uses IIT to translate MR images across domains (in most cases across sites or scanners). Because IIT in harmonization is usually conducted across sites, acquiring paired data in harmonization usually means recruiting subjects that travel across different imaging sites. Obviously, such traveling subjects or *inter-site* paired data can be burdensome and hard to maintain in large-scale multisite studies. This is a drawback in supervised harmonization [2,24], which relies on traveling subjects for domain accuracy and geometry accuracy. On the other hand, unsupervised harmonization does not need traveling subjects for training. Ideally, all unsupervised IIT methods can be used in unsupervised harmonization, but geometry shift is a concern. Fortunately, there is a unique aspect of MR imaging that enables us to overcome the geometry shift problem. As we discussed in Section 5.1, multi-contrast MR images of the same anatomy are routinely acquired within a single imaging session thanks to the flexibility of MR imaging. We call these images *intra-site* paired data. Although these data cannot be used as traveling subjects in harmonization, they could potentially be used to train a better IIT model, as they provide pixel-to-pixel correspondence. The intra-site paired data motivate a third type of image harmonization method, namely unsupervised harmonization with supervised IIT. The harmonization is unsupervised because no traveling subjects are required, whereas the supervised part comes from the intra-site paired images. In Table 5.1, we provide a summary of general IIT and image harmonization methods, which we discuss in detail in the following sections.

5.2 IIT and disentangled representation learning

Without a special design, intra-site paired data (i.e., paired T$_1$-w and T$_2$-w) alone do not permit unsupervised harmonization. The key reason is that the knowledge the supervised IIT model learned during training is embedded in network weights w, and $f(\cdot; w)$ only allows for translating images within each site. To harmonize MR images across sites, we first need an "indicator" variable to inform $f(\cdot; w)$ about the target site of IIT during testing. Second, $f(\cdot; w)$ needs to be generalizable in a way that the knowledge learned from supervised IIT with intra-site paired data is applicable to inter-site unsupervised IIT. Disentangled representation learning sat-

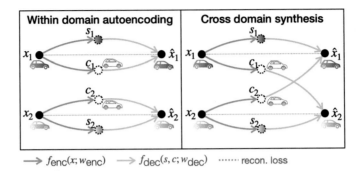

FIGURE 5.3

Using paired data x_1 and x_2, training supervised disentangled IIT includes two steps: within domain auto-encoding and cross-domain synthesis. Both domain accuracy and geometry accuracy are achieved using pixel-to-pixel reconstruction loss.

isfies these two requirements. The objective of disentangled representation learning is to learn two or more latent representations from a given input image, such that the latent representations are independent or conditionally independent. In disentangled representation based-IIT (disentangled IIT), the two latent representations are usually domain-specific and domain-invariant. At this point, we use c to denote the domain-invariant variable (c stands for "common") and s to denote domain-specific variable (s stands for "specific"). For MR image harmonization, we expect c to represent anatomical information, which does not and should not vary from domain to domain; while we expect s to capture contrast or acquisition related information, which we want to standardize in MR imaging.

With latent representations, IIT now includes encoding and decoding. The encoding step generates representations s and c from an input image with an encoding function $f_{enc}(x; w_{enc})$: $\mathcal{X} \rightarrow \mathcal{S} \times \mathcal{C}$. During decoding, the decoding function with different parameters generates a synthetic image based on s and c, i.e., $f_{dec}(s, c; w_{dec})$: $\mathcal{S} \times \mathcal{C} \rightarrow \mathcal{X}$. Before explaining how disentangled IIT permits harmonization, we first show how disentangled IIT is achieved with deep neural networks.

5.2.1 Supervised IIT and disentangling

Supervised IIT has paired data, for example, paired T_1-w and T_2-w images, which we denote as x_1 and x_2. As shown in Fig. 5.3, training supervised disentangled IIT has two major steps: within domain auto-encoding and cross-domain synthesis. The goal is to learn two disentangled variables s and c, where s represents domain-specific information (e.g., contrast or style) and c captures domain-invariant information (e.g., anatomy or content). Both domain accuracy and geometry accuracy are achieved with pixel-to-pixel reconstruction loss (e.g., $||\hat{x}_1 - x_1||_2$). During the within domain auto-encoding step, x_1 and x_2 are sent to an encoder to extract latent representations (s_1, c_1) and (s_2, c_2), respectively. Then a decoder is applied to (s_1, c_1) and (s_2, c_2)

to reconstruct the two MR images. The goal of this auto-encoding step is to learn representations s and c, such that the two variables *together* capture essential information about x. Until now the latent representations s and c are not disentangled at all and the within domain auto-encoding step is no different than partitioning the latent variables of a traditional auto-encoder [25]. It is the cross-domain synthesis step that encourages s and c to be disentangled. In this step, latent variables c_1 and c_2 are swapped before decoding. Since c is supposed to capture domain-invariant features, swapping c_1 and c_2 should not affect the final reconstruction results; we are expecting

$$x_1 \approx \hat{x}_1 = f_{dec}(s_1, c_1; w_{dec}) = f_{dec}(s_1, c_2; w_{dec}) \qquad (5.1)$$

$$x_2 \approx \hat{x}_2 = f_{dec}(s_2, c_2; w_{dec}) = f_{dec}(s_2, c_1; w_{dec}). \qquad (5.2)$$

The key here is to enforce c to capture domain-invariant (common) information, thus the decoder has to rely on s for domain-specific information. To further encourage c_1 and c_2 to be similar, a similarity loss between the two variables is commonly used [9,14,15,18,26]. However, there is a trivial solution to the current supervised disentangled IIT training framework: c could learn no information about input variable x (e.g., blank or totally random), and s captures all the essential information to reconstruct the original image. To avoid a trivial solution, s is usually constrained to be a low dimensional variable (e.g., $s \in \mathbb{R}^2$) to encourage c to be utilized, as described in [9,14,26].

A clear advantage of disentangled IIT is the improved interpretability, which DL-based methods usually lack. For example, the original generative adversarial networks (GANs) [27] generate images from random noise; the variability in generated images is usually explained by the entire latent noise variable, which has poor interpretability. In contrast, Kulkarni et al. [28] partitioned the latent representations into several parts and forced each part to explain certain properties of the images (e.g., azimuth angle, elevation angle, etc.). Therefore, images with desired properties can be generated using $f_{dec}(\cdot; w_{dec})$ by manipulating the corresponding dimensions of the latent variable. Based on the early work by Kulkarni et al. [28], several supervised disentangled IIT methods were proposed in recent years [9,14,15,26,29–32]. The core disentangling frameworks are similar to Fig. 5.3; Chartsias et al. [9] introduced a segmentation network further regularizing c to capture the common anatomical information of different modalities; Ouyang et al. [26] introduced the margin hinge loss to encourage a better disentanglement between s and c.

It is worth mentioning that there are other areas of research that are closely related to supervised disentangled IIT. For example, invariant representation learning or fair representation learning are approaches with latent representations that are agnostic to certain variations. These invariant features are typically used to train another model with improved generalizability. In [33], the authors extracted scanner invariant features from diffusion-weighted MR images. These scanner invariant features were then used to achieve more consistent multi-site image analyses. Adeli et al. [34] proposed a method to extract features invariant to certain selected variables (e.g., age, disease) using adversarial training. The authors reported improved classification performance

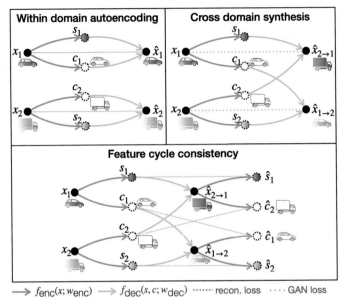

FIGURE 5.4

Unsupervised disentangled IIT does not have cross-domain paired data for training. Therefore the cross-domain synthetic images are denoted as $\hat{x}_{source\rightarrow target}$. GAN loss is used to achieve domain accuracy, and geometry accuracy is implicitly encouraged by feature cycle consistency loss.

with reduced biases using the learned features. Invariant representation learning is related to supervised disentangled IIT, as both methods learn domain-invariant representations. The difference between the two is also obvious—disentangled IIT also learns domain-specific features that represent the variability across domains. As we show in Section 5.3, domain-specific features play an important role in MR image harmonization.

5.2.2 Unsupervised IIT and disentangling

Unsupervised disentangled IIT does not have cross-domain paired data for training. As shown in Fig. 5.4, x_1 and x_2 are no longer paired (e.g., T_1-w images of different anatomies imaged at different sites). The first step of unsupervised disentangled IIT is identical to the supervised case, where latent features s and c are learned by doing self-reconstruction. The cross-domain synthesis step in unsupervised disentangled IIT also swaps the domain-invariant variables c_1 and c_2 to generate two cross-domain synthetic images. However, c_1 and c_2 are representing different anatomies this time and, therefore, the two cross-domain synthetic images $\hat{x}_{1\rightarrow 2}$ and $\hat{x}_{2\rightarrow 1}$ differ in both contrast and anatomy. Due to the lack of pixel-to-pixel correspondence, domain accuracy is achieved by GAN loss, where two domain discriminators $D_1(\cdot)\colon \mathcal{X}_1 \rightarrow \mathbb{R}$

and $D_2(\cdot): \mathcal{X}_2 \rightarrow \mathbb{R}$ are trained to distinguish between real images and cross-domain synthetic images. The encoder and decoder try to "fool" the discriminators by producing images that fall in the correct domain. To encourage geometry accuracy, feature cycle consistency is typically used as a third step in unsupervised disentangled IIT [18,20,21]. The synthetic images cycle back to the encoder. The underlying assumption is that the synthetic images will produce the same disentangled representations from which those images are generated, i.e.,

$$(s_1, c_2) \approx (\hat{s}_1, \hat{c}_2) = f_{\text{enc}} \left(f_{\text{dec}} \left(s_1, c_2; w_{\text{dec}} \right); w_{\text{enc}} \right) \tag{5.3}$$

$$(s_2, c_1) \approx (\hat{s}_2, \hat{c}_1) = f_{\text{enc}} \left(f_{\text{dec}} \left(s_2, c_1; w_{\text{dec}} \right); w_{\text{enc}} \right). \tag{5.4}$$

Similar to CycleGAN [17], cycle consistency is an implicit regularization of the geometry accuracy, thus geometry shift is a drawback of unsupervised disentangled IIT. The same training framework as Fig. 5.4 was applied in [20,35,36] to learn disentangled representations for segmentation and image generation. Note that domain discriminators and feature cycle consistency could also be applied in supervised disentangled IIT to further regularize domain and geometry accuracy.

There are other research areas that learn disentangled representations without paired training data. For example, Higgins et al. [37], Burgess et al. [38], X. Chen et al. [39], R.T. Chen et al. [40] learn disentangled representations from a single input image. Here, we highlight that these methods differ from unsupervised disentangled IIT in how disentangled representations are learned. Higgins et al. [37], Burgess et al. [38], Chen et al. [40] use an implicit loss on each dimension of the latent space to either encourage independence or penalize the total correlations between dimensions. As mentioned in [9], these methods should be categorized as factorized representation learning. Since the representations are learned from a single image, these methods usually do not perform as well as unsupervised disentangled IIT [41], which includes cross-domain unpaired data in training.

5.3 Unsupervised harmonization with supervised IIT

In this section, we focus on a recently proposed unsupervised harmonization approach CALAMITI (contrast anatomy learning and analysis for MR image translation and integration) [3,15] and show how the intra-site paired data in MR imaging permit unsupervised harmonization with supervised IIT. CALAMITI bears merits from both supervised and unsupervised IIT: better geometry and domain accuracy without traveling subjects.

5.3.1 The disentangling framework of CALAMITI

CALAMITI uses intra-site paired T_1-w and T_2-w images to achieve inter-site unsupervised harmonization. As shown in Fig. 5.2, T_1-w and T_2-w images from Sites A and B are denoted as x_{A_1}, x_{A_2}, x_{B_1} and x_{B_2}. The basic assumption of CALAMITI

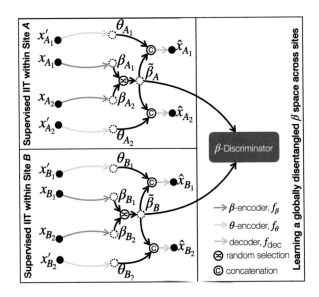

FIGURE 5.5

The disentangling framework of the CALAMITI. T_1-w and T_2-w images from Sites A and B are denoted as x_{A_1}, x_{A_2}, x_{B_1} and x_{B_2}, respectively. x' has the same contrast but different anatomies as x.

is that an MR image x is a function of the underlying anatomy and the associated imaging parameters. CALAMITI first uses a β-encoder $f_\beta(\cdot; w_\beta)$ and a θ-encoder $f_\theta(\cdot; w_\theta)$ to extract disentangled anatomical and contrast representations β and θ from MR images, where β is domain-invariant and θ captures most domain-specific variations. For intra-site paired images, the learned domain-invariant and domain-specific representations are usually anatomy and contrast, respectively. The disentangled representations β and θ are then combined using a decoder network $f_{dec}(\beta, \theta; w_{dec})$ to generate a synthetic MR image. For simplicity, we omit the model parameters w for the remainder of the chapter.

Fig. 5.5 shows the framework of CALAMITI trained on Sites A and B. Supervised disentangled IIT is conducted on each site. First, β and θ are extracted from images x and x', respectively, where x' has the same contrast but different anatomy as x—this is achieved by selecting different 2D slices from the same volume. The reason why θ is calculated from x' instead of x is to prevent θ from capturing unnecessary anatomical information. Since T_1-w and T_2-w images of each site (e.g., x_{A_1} and x_{A_2}) have the same anatomy, we would expect β_{A_1} to be similar (if not identical) to β_{A_2}. A similarity loss (i.e., $||\beta_{A_1} - \beta_{A_2}||_1$) and a random shuffling have been installed between β_{A_1} and β_{A_2} to encourage β similarity. The random shuffling step randomly picks a β before decoding. The randomly selected β, denoted as $\tilde{\beta}$, is then combined with a θ to produce a synthetic image using $f_{dec}(\cdot)$. We note that the framework in Fig. 5.5 is a hybrid model of the supervised disentangled IIT framework we introduced in Fig. 5.3. Specifically, when reconstructing $\hat{x}_{A_1}$, if $\tilde{\beta}_A = \beta_{A_1}$, which means the random selection operator happened to choose β_{A_1} to combine with θ_{A_1} before decoding, the whole model is trained to perform within domain auto-encoding. Similarly, if $\tilde{\beta}_A = \beta_{A_2}$ when generating $\hat{x}_{A_1}$, the model is trained to perform cross-domain synthesis. The same $f_\beta(\cdot)$, $f_\theta(\cdot)$, and $f_{\text{dec}}(\cdot)$ are applied to Site B (and potentially other sites) for training supervised disentangled IIT.

Ideally, after training supervised disentangled IIT on each site, inter-site harmonization can be achieved by combining β from a source site with a θ from the target site. For example, T_1-w harmonization from Site A to Site B is achieved by $f_{\text{dec}}(\beta_{A_1}, \theta_{B_1})$. However, such inter-site harmonization may not succeed if β_{A_1} and β_{B_1} are encoded differently. Since training only involves supervised disentangled IIT within each site, it is possible that $f_\beta(\cdot)$ learns a specific β space for each site. In that case, β is site-variant and combining β and θ across sites would be nonideal. We refer to this scenario as *locally* disentangled β and θ, which we would like to avoid in harmonization.

In a locally disentangled β space, we would be able to identify the site class from a given β. Therefore, the key to avoid a locally disentangled β space is to force β's from each site to be similarly distributed, which we regard as a *globally* disentangled β space across sites. In CALAMITI, a β discriminator $D_\beta(\cdot)$ was introduced to guide the β-encoder to learn a globally disentangled β space, as shown in Fig. 5.5. $D_\beta(\cdot)$ and $f_\beta(\cdot)$ together forms an adversarial training scheme, where $D_\beta(\cdot)$ tries to classify if an input β variable is from the first training site (Site A) or not, and $f_\beta(\cdot)$ tries to "fool" $D_\beta(\cdot)$ by generating more consistently distributed β's across sites. The implication that $D_\beta(\cdot)$ is a binary classifier instead of a more intuitive multi-class classifier that directly predicts the site label is described in Section 5.3.3.

5.3.2 Network architecture

The network architecture of CALAMITI is shown in Fig. 5.6. $f_\beta(\cdot)$ and $f_{\text{dec}}(\cdot)$ have a four-level (four down-sampling layers) U-Net [42] structure, where $f_{\text{dec}}(\cdot)$ has twice as many channels at each convolutional block. $D_\beta(\cdot)$ has four convolutional layers followed by two fully connected layers. $f_\theta(\cdot)$ has a similar architecture as $D_\beta(\cdot)$, but has two output branches that produce the mean and log variance of θ, i.e., μ_θ and $\log \sigma_\theta$. $f_\beta(\cdot)$, $f_\theta(\cdot)$ and $f_{\text{dec}}(\cdot)$ make the CALAMITI model a conditional variational auto-encoder (CVAE), where β is the condition. Before decoding, a θ value is sampled from $\mathcal{N}(\theta; \mu_\theta, \sigma_\theta)$. This allows CALAMITI to generate new contrast images by sampling θ space. The dimension of input image x is 288×288. β is a multichannel one-hot encoded image that has the same spatial dimension as input image x. The one-hot encoding restricts the capacity of β, thus preventing β from capturing contrast information. θ is a low dimension random variable.

5.3.3 Domain adaptation

MR image harmonization is designed to solve the domain shift problem in downstream analyses. However, IIT-based harmonization methods usually need to be

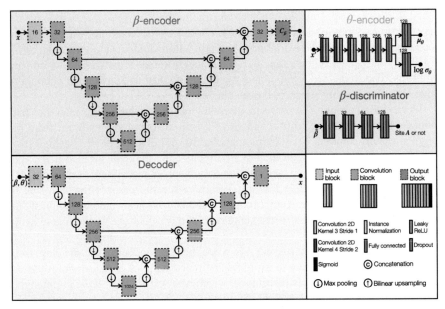

FIGURE 5.6

The network architecture of CALAMITI.

trained on a pool of images from multiple sites ahead of downstream analyses. When gathering data from multiple sites is not allowed, or there is a novel site on board, domain shift could also occur in image harmonization. To solve this problem, CALAMITI has a domain adaptation process that allows the harmonization model to be fine-tuned on a subset of data only from the novel site. The fine-tuned harmonization model can then be used to harmonize MR images between previously trained sites and the novel fine-tuning site. Specifically, a CALAMITI model was pre-trained on Sites A and B, and now there is a novel site, Site C, on board, the most straightforward way to harmonize images from Sites C to A is to retrain the CALAMITI model involving Sites A, B and C. However, this retraining is usually time consuming and could be impossible when gathering data from the three sites are prohibited. Fortunately, CALAMITI can be fine-tuned solely on Site C and fulfill the harmonization task from Site C to A. During CALAMITI fine-tuning, supervised disentangled IIT is conducted on T_1-w and T_2-w images of Site C, i.e., x_{C_1} and x_{C_2}. In general, such fine-tuning could result in a Site C specific β space, which hinders harmonization. To avoid a Site C specific β space during fine-tuning, CALAMITI uses the following strategies. First, the weights of $D_\beta(\cdot)$ are frozen during fine-tuning. Therefore, $D_\beta(\cdot)$ will produce a high adversarial loss for $f_\beta(\cdot)$ if the newly learned β_C mismatches the previously learned β's. The only way to reduce this high adversarial loss is for $f_\beta(\cdot)$ to generate β_C's that are indistinguishable from β's of Site A. Second, only the output block of $f_\beta(\cdot)$ and the fully connected layers of $f_\theta(\cdot)$ are allowed to be updated during fine-tuning (see Fig. 5.6 for network architectures). This is routinely

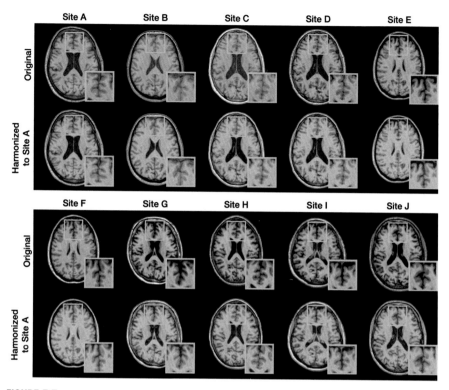

FIGURE 5.7

T_1-w images from Sites A to J were harmonized to Site A. Contrast change after harmonization can be better seen on GM regions.

used in unsupervised domain adaptation methods [12,13] to prevent the network from changing drastically during fine-tuning. After fine-tuning on Site C, harmonization from Site C to Site A can be performed by first calculating θ_{A_1} with the original $f_\theta(\cdot)$ and β_{C_1} with the fine-tuned $f_\beta(\cdot)$, then combining the two latent representations using $f_{\text{dec}}(\beta_{C_1}, \theta_{A_1})$. As a consequence, Site C can also be harmonized to Site B, by computing θ_{B_1} and combining with β_{C_1}.

5.3.4 Experiments and results

We evaluate CALAMITI and other unsupervised IIT methods using MR images from 10 sites—labeled A to J—including 1.5T and 3T Philips and Siemens scanners. MR images were pre-processed using N4 inhomogeneity correction, registration to a MNI 1 mm^3 isotropic resolution template and followed by white matter peak normalization [43]. Super-resolution was conducted on 2D acquired T_2-w images. Fig. 5.7 shows the T_1-w images from Sites A to J harmonized to Site A using CALAMITI.

Table 5.2 Numerical evaluations of different unsupervised harmonization methods based on held-out traveling subjects. Both SSIM and PSNR are reported as "mean"±"standard deviation." In each column, the bold numbers denote the best mean performance for that inter-site harmonization. Where "No Har" corresponds to no harmonization and "Hist" is histogram matching based harmonization.

		Site $C \to D$	Site $D \to C$	Site $E \to F$	Site $F \to E$
No Har	SSIM	0.7647 ± 0.0151	0.7647 ± 0.0151	0.8517 ± 0.0343	0.8517 ± 0.0343
	PSNR	25.62 ± 0.85	25.62 ± 0.85	27.86 ± 1.24	27.86 ± 1.24
Hist	SSIM	0.7293 ± 0.0368	0.8090 ± 0.0374	0.8248 ± 0.0529	0.8014 ± 0.0786
	PSNR	25.99 ± 0.47	27.86 ± 0.53	26.40 ± 1.89	27.20 ± 2.41
CycleGAN [17]	SSIM	0.7975 ± 0.0208	0.8286 ± 0.0100	0.8257 ± 0.0202	0.8320 ± 0.0204
	PSNR	26.87 ± 0.42	28.05 ± 0.45	27.84 ± 1.41	28.27 ± 1.37
Dewey et al. [14]	SSIM	0.7817 ± 0.0160	0.8145 ± 0.0101	0.8320 ± 0.0158	0.8346 ± 0.0311
	PSNR	26.51 ± 0.48	27.43 ± 0.39	27.57 ± 0.92	28.10 ± 0.89
CALAMITI [3]	SSIM	$\mathbf{0.8096 \pm 0.222}$	$\mathbf{0.8590 \pm 0.0213}$	$\mathbf{0.8599 \pm 0.0269}$	$\mathbf{0.8556 \pm 0.0376}$
	PSNR	$\mathbf{27.48 \pm 0.49}$	$\mathbf{28.48 \pm 0.55}$	$\mathbf{28.19 \pm 1.22}$	$\mathbf{28.38 \pm 1.12}$

Contrast changes can be better visualized on GM regions, and it is clear that the contrast of the 10 sites becomes more similar after harmonization.

In Table 5.2, we provide quantitative comparisons between CALAMITI and other unsupervised harmonization methods. The harmonization models were all trained on 2D images, and then combined into 3D following [2,3] before evaluation. Longitudinal scans from different scanners with a short period of time between visits were used as inter-site traveling subjects for quantitative evaluations. Both structural similarity index measurement (SSIM) and peak signal-to-noise ratio (PSNR) were calculated between harmonized images and the true target site images. Paired signed rank Wilcoxon tests were conducted between CALAMITI and other comparison methods with the null hypothesis that the difference of SSIM or PSNR between two comparison methods have zero median.

The learned disentangled θ space embeds rich information for research beyond harmonization. Fig. 5.8(b) shows a two-dimensional θ space ($\theta \in \mathbb{R}^2$) of T_1-w and T_2-w images from Sites A to J. It is prominent that T_1-w images (circles) and T_2-w images (diamonds) are separated in θ space. Furthermore, MR images acquired from different sites are also separated; visually, we note that the greater the difference in contrast the further apart in θ space sites are (e.g., Sites B and G). We then use the data-driven θ space to quantitatively monitor the contrast change during harmonization. As shown in Fig. 5.8(a), T_1-w images from the 10 sites are harmonized to Site A, and the arrows in Fig. 5.8(c) show the changes of θ value of these images before and after harmonization. Not only do the image contrasts become similar after harmonization, the closely clustered θ values after harmonization also reassures us that the harmonized images are now carrying similar contrast information.

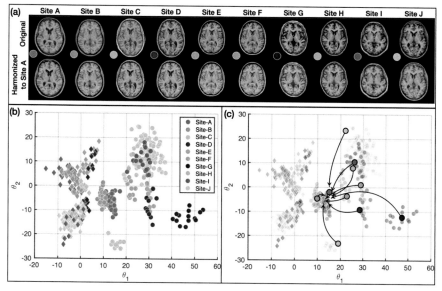

FIGURE 5.8

(a) MR images from Sites A to J are harmonized to Site A. **(b)** θ values of T_1-w (circles) and T_2-w (diamonds) images from 10 sites. **(c)** Change of θ of the 10 images in (a) during harmonization.

5.4 Conclusions

In this chapter, we provided an overview of current disentangled representation learning methods for MR image harmonization. We show how disentangled representations can be learned by supervised and unsupervised IIT. Importantly, we demonstrated that the unique intra-site paired images in MR imaging enable unsupervised harmonization via supervised disentangled IIT, which has the merits of both supervised and unsupervised IIT. In Section 5.3, we showcase a recently proposed unsupervised MR image harmonization method, CALAMITI, that is built upon supervised disentangled IIT. CALAMITI has shown superior performance than other unsupervised MR harmonization methods with broad applicability to large scale multi-site studies.

Acknowledgments

The authors thank BLSA participants. This work was supported in part by the Intramural Research Program of the NIH, National Institute on Aging.

References

[1] R.W. Brown, et al., Magnetic Resonance Imaging: Physical Principles and Sequence Design, second edition, Wiley, 2014.

[2] B.E. Dewey, C. Zhao, J.C. Reinhold, A. Carass, K.C. Fitzgerald, E.S. Sotirchos, S. Saidha, J. Oh, D.L. Pham, P.A. Calabresi, DeepHarmony: a deep learning approach to contrast harmonization across scanner changes, Magnetic Resonance Imaging 64 (2019) 160–170.

[3] L. Zuo, B.E. Dewey, Y. Liu, Y. He, S.D. Newsome, E.M. Mowry, S.M. Resnick, J.L. Prince, A. Carass, Unsupervised mr harmonization by learning disentangled representations using information bottleneck theory, NeuroImage (2021) 118569.

[4] American College of Radiology, Phantom test guidance for use of the large MRI phantom for the ACR MRI accreditation program, released: 4/17/18, https://www.acraccreditation.org/-/media/ACRAccreditation/Documents/MRI/LargePhantomGuidance.pdf, 2018.

[5] M. Shao, S. Han, A. Carass, X. Li, B.E. Dewey, A.M. Blitz, J.L. Prince, L.M. Ellingsen, Shortcomings of ventricle segmentation using deep convolutional networks, in: Understanding and Interpreting Machine Learning in Medical Image Computing Applications. MLCN 2018, DLF 2018, IMIMIC 2018, in: Lecture Notes in Computer Science, vol. 11038, Springer Berlin Heidelberg, 2018, pp. 79–86.

[6] W. Yan, Y. Wang, S. Gu, L. Huang, F. Yan, L. Xia, Q. Tao, The domain shift problem of medical image segmentation and vendor-adaptation by unet-gan, in: International Conference on Medical Image Computing and Computer-Assisted Intervention, Springer, 2019, pp. 623–631.

[7] W.E. Johnson, C. Li, A. Rabinovic, Adjusting batch effects in microarray expression data using empirical Bayes methods, Biostatistics 8 (1) (2007) 118–127.

[8] M. Long, Y. Cao, J. Wang, M. Jordan, Learning transferable features with deep adaptation networks, in: International Conference on Machine Learning, PMLR, 2015, pp. 97–105.

[9] A. Chartsias, T. Joyce, G. Papanastasiou, S. Semple, M. Williams, D.E. Newby, R. Dharmakumar, S.A. Tsaftaris, Disentangled representation learning in cardiac image analysis, Medical Image Analysis 58 (2019) 101535.

[10] L. Zhang, X. Wang, D. Yang, T. Sanford, S. Harmon, B. Turkbey, B.J. Wood, H. Roth, A. Myronenko, D. Xu, et al., Generalizing deep learning for medical image segmentation to unseen domains via deep stacked transformation, IEEE Transactions on Medical Imaging 39 (7) (2020) 2531–2540.

[11] J. Konečný, B. McMahan, D. Ramage, Federated optimization: distributed optimization beyond the datacenter, arXiv:1511.03575, 2015.

[12] Y. He, A. Carass, L. Zuo, B.E. Dewey, J.L. Prince, Self domain adapted network, in: 23rd International Conference on Medical Image Computing and Computer Assisted Intervention (MICCAI 2020), Springer, 2020, pp. 437–446.

[13] Y. He, A. Carass, L. Zuo, B.E. Dewey, J.L. Prince, Autoencoder based self-supervised test-time adaptation for medical image analysis, Medical Image Analysis (2021) 102136.

[14] B.E. Dewey, L. Zuo, A. Carass, Y. He, Y. Liu, E.M. Mowry, S. Newsome, J. Oh, P.A. Calabresi, J.L. Prince, A disentangled latent space for cross-site MRI harmonization, in: 23rd International Conference on Medical Image Computing and Computer Assisted Intervention (MICCAI 2020), Springer, 2020, pp. 720–729.

[15] L. Zuo, B.E. Dewey, A. Carass, Y. Liu, Y. He, P.A. Calabresi, J.L. Prince, Information-based disentangled representation learning for unsupervised MR harmonization, in: International Conference on Information Processing in Medical Imaging, Springer, 2021, pp. 346–359.

[16] M. Singh, E. Pahl, S. Wang, A. Carass, J. Lee, J.L. Prince, Accurate estimation of total intracranial volume in mri using a multi-tasked image-to-image translation network, in: Medical Imaging 2021: Image Processing, vol. 11596, International Society for Optics and Photonics, 2021, p. 115960I.

[17] J.-Y. Zhu, T. Park, P. Isola, A.A. Efros, Unpaired image-to-image translation using cycle-consistent adversarial networks, in: Proceedings of the IEEE International Conference on Computer Vision, 2017, pp. 2223–2232.

[18] M.-Y. Liu, T. Breuel, J. Kautz, Unsupervised image-to-image translation networks, in: Advances in Neural Information Processing Systems, 2017, pp. 700–708.

[19] Y. Choi, M. Choi, M. Kim, J.-W. Ha, S. Kim, J. Choo, Stargan: unified generative adversarial networks for multi-domain image-to-image translation, in: Proceedings of the IEEE Conference on Computer Vision and Pattern Recognition, 2018, pp. 8789–8797.

[20] X. Huang, M.-Y. Liu, S. Belongie, J. Kautz, Multimodal unsupervised image-to-image translation, in: Proceedings of the European Conference on Computer Vision, 2018, pp. 172–189.

[21] X. Liu, F. Xing, G. El Fakhri, J. Woo, A unified conditional disentanglement framework for multimodal brain mr image translation, in: 2021 IEEE 18th International Symposium on Biomedical Imaging (ISBI), IEEE, 2021, pp. 10–14.

[22] J.P. Cohen, M. Luck, S. Honari, Distribution matching losses can hallucinate features in medical image translation, in: International Conference on Medical Image Computing and Computer-Assisted Intervention, Springer, 2018, pp. 529–536.

[23] H. Yang, J. Sun, A. Carass, C. Zhao, J. Lee, Z. Xu, J. Prince, Unpaired brain mr-to-ct synthesis using a structure-constrained cyclegan, in: Deep Learning in Medical Image Analysis and Multimodal Learning for Clinical Decision Support, Springer, 2018, pp. 174–182.

[24] B.E. Dewey, C. Zhao, A. Carass, J. Oh, P.A. Calabresi, P.C.M. van Zijl, J.L. Prince, Deep harmonization of inconsistent MR data for consistent volume segmentation, in: Workshop on Simulation and Synthesis in Medical Imaging (SASHIMI) Held in Conjunction with the 21st International Conference on Medical Image Computing and Computer Assisted Intervention (MICCAI 2018), in: Lecture Notes in Computer Science, vol. 11037, Springer Berlin Heidelberg, 2018, pp. 22–30.

[25] D.P. Kingma, M. Welling, Auto-encoding variational Bayes, arXiv preprint, arXiv:1312.6114, 2013.

[26] J. Ouyang, E. Adeli, K.M. Pohl, Q. Zhao, G. Zaharchuk, Representation disentanglement for multi-modal MR analysis, in: 27th Inf. Proc. in Med. Imaging (IPMI 2021), in: Lecture Notes in Computer Science, Springer Berlin Heidelberg, 2021, pp. 321–333.

[27] I. Goodfellow, J. Pouget-Abadie, M. Mirza, B. Xu, D. Warde-Farley, S. Ozair, A. Courville, Y. Bengio, Generative adversarial networks, Communications of the ACM 63 (11) (2020) 139–144.

[28] T.D. Kulkarni, W.F. Whitney, P. Kohli, J. Tenenbaum, Deep convolutional inverse graphics network, Advances in Neural Information Processing Systems 28 (2015) 2539–2547.

[29] Y. Liu, L. Zuo, A. Carass, Y. He, A. Filippatou, S.D. Solomonand, S. Saidha, P.A. Calabresi, J.L. Prince, Variational intensity cross channel encoder for unsupervised vessel segmentation on OCT angiography, in: Medical Imaging 2020: Image Processing, vol. 11313, International Society for Optics and Photonics, 2020, p. 113130Y.

[30] Y. Liu, A. Carass, L. Zuo, Y. He, S. Han, L. Gregori, S. Murray, R. Mishra, J. Lei, P.A. Calabresi, et al., Disentangled representation learning for OCTA vessel segmentation with limited training data, IEEE Transactions on Medical Imaging 41 (12) (2022) 3686–3698.

[31] R. Hamaguchi, K. Sakurada, R. Nakamura, Rare event detection using disentangled representation learning, in: Proceedings of the IEEE/CVF Conference on Computer Vision and Pattern Recognition, 2019, pp. 9327–9335.

[32] L. Zuo, Y. Liu, Y. Xue, S. Han, M. Bilgel, S.M. Resnick, J.L. Prince, A. Carass, Disentangling a single MR modality, in: Data Augmentation, Labelling, and Imperfections, Springer Nature, Switzerland, Cham, 2022, pp. 54–63.

[33] D. Moyer, G. Ver Steeg, C.M. Tax, P.M. Thompson, Scanner invariant representations for diffusion MRI harmonization, Magnetic Resonance in Medicine 84 (4) (2020) 2174–2189.

[34] E. Adeli, Q. Zhao, A. Pfefferbaum, E.V. Sullivan, L. Fei-Fei, J.C. Niebles, K.M. Pohl, Representation learning with statistical independence to mitigate bias, in: Proceedings of the IEEE/CVF Winter Conference on Applications of Computer Vision, 2021, pp. 2513–2523.

[35] M. Ning, C. Bian, D. Wei, S. Yu, C. Yuan, Y. Wang, Y. Guo, K. Ma, Y. Zheng, A new bidirectional unsupervised domain adaptation segmentation framework, in: International Conference on Information Processing in Medical Imaging, Springer, 2021, pp. 492–503.

[36] A.H. Jha, S. Anand, M. Singh, V. Veeravasarapu, Disentangling factors of variation with cycle-consistent variational auto-encoders, in: Proceedings of the European Conference on Computer Vision (ECCV), 2018, pp. 805–820.

[37] I. Higgins, L. Matthey, A. Pal, C. Burgess, X. Glorot, M. Botvinick, S. Mohamed, A. Lerchner, beta-vae: Learning basic visual concepts with a constrained variational framework, 2016.

[38] C.P. Burgess, I. Higgins, A. Pal, L. Matthey, N. Watters, G. Desjardins, A. Lerchner, Understanding disentangling in beta-vae, arXiv preprint, arXiv:1804.03599, 2018.

[39] X. Chen, Y. Duan, R. Houthooft, J. Schulman, I. Sutskever, P. Abbeel, Infogan: interpretable representation learning by information maximizing generative adversarial nets, in: Proceedings of the 30th International Conference on Neural Information Processing Systems, 2016, pp. 2180–2188.

[40] R.T. Chen, X. Li, R. Grosse, D. Duvenaud, Isolating sources of disentanglement in variational autoencoders, arXiv preprint, arXiv:1802.04942, 2018.

[41] F. Locatello, S. Bauer, M. Lucic, G. Raetsch, S. Gelly, B. Schölkopf, O. Bachem, Challenging common assumptions in the unsupervised learning of disentangled representations, in: International Conference on Machine Learning, PMLR, 2019, pp. 4114–4124.

[42] O. Ronneberger, P. Fischer, T. Brox, U-net: convolutional networks for biomedical image segmentation, in: International Conference on Medical Image Computing and Computer-Assisted Intervention, Springer, 2015, pp. 234–241.

[43] J.C. Reinhold, B.E. Dewey, A. Carass, J.L. Prince, Evaluating the impact of intensity normalization on mr image synthesis, in: Medical Imaging 2019: Image Processing, vol. 10949, International Society for Optics and Photonics, 2019, p. 109493H.

Hyper-graph learning and its applications for medical image analysis

Yue Gao and Shuyi Ji
School of Software, Tsinghua University, Beijing, China

6.1 Introduction

The hyper-graph is a flexible structure that contains two fundamental components: the vertex and the hyper-edge. The unlimited number of vertices that are connected by a hyper-edge makes it degree-free. As a result, the hyper-graph is much more expandable than a simple graph and can naturally model complex and high-order interactions among data.

In fact, complex data correlations are not rare but ubiquitous, especially in medical image analysis. For example, when making diagnoses, data in different modalities are often required to provide comprehensive information about the human body. How to utilize the complementary information from different modalities and model the complex correlations among them is a challenging issue. Besides, patches are often treated as the smallest unit in medical image analysis and similar patches may share similar patterns. Modeling and exploring the high-order correlations between the patches is also helpful for specific tasks such as cancer tissue classification. Due to its superiority in complex relationships modeling, hyper-graph is widely applied in medical image analysis, in which the data correlations are quite complex.

The typical paradigm of hyper-graph learning being applied in medical image analysis can be formulated as that: first, construct a hyper-graph, in which the subject or patch is modeled as a vertex and each vertex and its neighbors are connected by a hyper-edge; then hyper-graph learning is conducted to investigate the complex associations in data and improve vertex representations, which can be further employed for downstream applications such as medical image retrieval, mild cognitive impairment (MCI) identification, cancer tissue classification, medical image segmentation and childhood autism diagnosis.

The remainder of this chapter is organized as follows. The hyper-graph is first introduced with some fundamental knowledge in Section 6.2. The hyper-graph neural network (HGNN) framework, which consists of general and dynamic HGNNs, is presented in Section 6.3. In Section 6.4, we review some typical applications of hyper-graph learning in medical image analysis and elaborate on two applications in Section 6.5 and Section 6.6, i.e., COVID-19 identification using CT images and

Deep Learning for Medical Image Analysis. https://doi.org/10.1016/B978-0-32-385124-4.00015-5

153

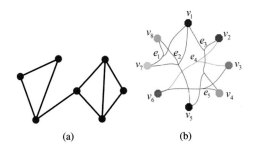

FIGURE 6.1

The comparison between a simple graph and a hyper-graph. The left part is the simple graph and the right part is the hyper-graph, in which v denotes vertice and e indicates edge. This figure is from [18].

survival prediction on whole slides histopathological images. We finally make a summary in Section 6.7.

6.2 Preliminary of hyper-graph

Mathematically, a hyper-graph can be viewed as a generalization of a graph. For instance, Fig. 6.1 exemplifies a graph and a hyper-graph. As shown in Fig. 6.1, a hyper-graph differs from a simple graph in that the number of vertices that each hyper-edge can connect is unlimited, as opposed to a simple graph in which fixedly two vertices are connected by a single edge. In modeling the complex correlations (beyond pairwise) with flexible hyper-edges, the hyper-graph shows significant advantages over the simple graph, whose edge degree is necessary 2. Due to its advantages in complex correlation modeling, the hyper-graph has been widely applied in a variety of applications like object classification [46,37].

A hyper-graph is usually indicated as $\mathcal{G} = (\mathcal{V}, \mathcal{E}, \mathbf{W})$. The $\mathcal{V}$ and $\mathcal{E}$ are sets of node and hyper-edge, respectively. $\mathbf{W}$ is the weight matrix for hyper-edge. As discussed above, the hyper-edge is a subset of all vertices. Specifically, each hyper-edge $e \in \mathcal{E}$ is given a weight $w(e)$, indicating the importance of the connection in the hyper-graph. That is, we have $\mathrm{diag}(\mathbf{W}) = [w(e_1), w(e_2), \ldots, w(e_{|\mathcal{E}|})]$. Given a hyper-graph $\mathcal{G}$, its structure is often expressed by an incidence matrix $\mathbf{H} \in \{0, 1\}^{|\mathcal{V}| \times |\mathcal{E}|}$. The value of the entry in $\mathbf{H}$ denotes if the node v belongs to the hyper-edge e:

$$\mathbf{H}(v, e) = \begin{cases} 1 & \text{if } v \in e \\ 0 & \text{if } v \notin e \end{cases} . \tag{6.1}$$

Sometimes the value of the entry is not simply 0 or 1, but a continuous value in $[0, 1]$. In this case, the entry $\mathbf{H}(v, e)$ can be defined as either the likelihood that $v \in e$ or the significance of v for e. The following are definitions for degrees of v and e:

$$\delta(e) = \sum_{v \in \mathcal{V}} \mathbf{H}(v, e) \tag{6.2}$$

and

$$d(v) = \sum_{e \in \mathcal{E}} w(e) * \mathbf{H}v, e), \tag{6.3}$$

respectively.

The Laplacian matrix is crucial for graph/hyper-graph theory. The Laplacian matrix of the simple graph and hyper-graph usually takes the form as

$$\mathbf{\Delta} = \mathbf{D} - \mathbf{A} \tag{6.4}$$

and

$$\mathbf{\Delta} = \mathbf{D}_v - \mathbf{HWD}_e^{-1}\mathbf{H}^\top. \tag{6.5}$$

Here, $\mathbf{D}_e$ and $\mathbf{D}_v$ are hyper-edge and vertex degree diagonal matrices, respectively. $\mathbf{A}$ indicates the adjacency matrix and $\mathbf{D}$ is the node degree matrix. The normalization form of Eq. (6.5) is further defined as

$$\mathbf{\Delta} = \mathbf{I} - \mathbf{D}_v^{-1/2}\mathbf{HWD}_e^{-1}\mathbf{H}^\top\mathbf{D}_v^{-1/2}. \tag{6.6}$$

6.3 Hyper-graph neural networks

Many computer vision tasks, including 3D object recognition and detection have extensively used the hyper-graph. In these applications, a set of objects are first embedded into the hyper-graph structure, and then the hyper-graph learning method is utilized to capture high-order relationships among data. Hyper-graph learning (also called hyper-graph computing) is first introduced in [47], as a propagation inference procedure on the hyper-graph. Usually, it can be divided into transductive and inductive inference. In this chapter, we mainly discuss the transductive inference paradigm.

The aim of hyper-graph learning is to make vertices with strong connections closer in some spaces. Conventional hyper-graph learning techniques, however, have a limited range of applications due to their expensive time-space complexity, particularly when used with large-scale data.

Recent years have seen a rise in interest in effective hyper-graph learning that makes use of deep learning's strengths, as in [14,24]. In the following of this section, we first present the common ways for hyper-graph structure generation. Then the general hyper-graph neural network (HGNN) framework [14] is introduced. Finally, the dynamic hyper-graph neural network (DHGNN) [24] framework is presented for efficient and effective hyper-graph learning. In these methods, to mine the complex correlations among objects, a hyper-edge convolution is developed after modeling the objects into a hyper-graph structure.

6.3.1 Hyper-graph structure generation

Given the visual data, first and foremost, generating a hyper-graph structure is essential in formulating the correlations. There are generally two categories of hyper-graph generation approaches for visual data: distance-based approaches and attribute-based approaches.

Distance-based approaches. Each visual object can be modeled as a vertex, and the core of this kind of method is to connect the vertices that are close in the feature space. To fulfill this, nearest neighbor searching-based (NNS) approaches and clustering-based approaches are usually used to generate the hyper-graph. In NNS, we connect each node's K nearest neighbors with a hyper-edge. By contrast, the goal of clustering-based methods is to connect vertices within a hyper-edge by clustering them with widely-used methods like K-means. The "distance" discussed above is measured in feature space. Besides, the distance can also be location (spatial) distance. Specifically, each vertex will be linked with its K nearest spatial neighbors.

Attribute-based approaches. This kind of method uses attribute information to construct the hyper-graph. Specifically, each visual object can be modeled as a vertex and has its attributes. The objects that share the same attribute will be linked by a hyper-edge.

Example. Take the visual object classification task as an example. Given the features of N visual object data $\mathbf{X} = [\mathbf{x_1}, \ldots, \mathbf{x_n}]^\top$, we can construct the hyper-graph structure based on their distances. Specifically, we first model each visual object as a vertex. Then K nearest neighbors are found for each centroid using Euclidean distance (other metrics are also plausible). These neighbors are finally connected with a hyper-edge. By this, we can obtain the incidence matrix $\mathbf{H} \in \mathbb{R}^{N \times N}$, in which $N \times (K+1)$ entries are equal to 1 and others are equal to 0. Such a generated hyper-graph structure is then fed into the HGNNs to learn the high-order correlations among data.

6.3.2 General hyper-graph neural networks

A brief introduction to the hyper-graph Laplacian is provided in this subsection, followed by a discussion of the spectral convolution operator on hyper-graph. Then some details pertaining to the overall framework will be given.

Spectral convolution on hyper-graph. We consider the vertex classification task on hyper-graph as an example. It is first described as a regularization problem [47]:

$$\arg \min_{f} \{\mathcal{R}_{emp}(f) + \Omega(f)\}. \tag{6.7}$$

In this case, $\mathcal{R}_{emp}(f)$ represents the supervised loss, while $f(\cdot)$ denotes the classification function. $\Omega(f)$ is denoted as the regularization term, which can be defined as

$$\Omega(f) = \frac{1}{2} \sum_{e \in \mathcal{E}} \sum_{\{u,v\} \in \mathcal{V}} \frac{w(e)h(u,e)h(v,e)}{\delta(e)} \left(\frac{f(u)}{\sqrt{d(u)}} - \frac{f(v)}{\sqrt{d(v)}} \right)^2. \tag{6.8}$$

Let $\theta = \mathbf{D}_v^{-1/2}\mathbf{H}\mathbf{W}\mathbf{D}_e^{-1}\mathbf{H}^\top\mathbf{D}_v^{-1/2}$ and $\boldsymbol{\Delta} = \mathbf{I} - \boldsymbol{\Theta}$, the normalized $\Omega(f)$ is defined as

$$\Omega(f) = f^\top \boldsymbol{\Delta}, \tag{6.9}$$

where $\boldsymbol{\Delta}$ is the hyper-graph Laplacian as introduced in Eq. (6.6).

Given a hyper-graph $\mathcal{G} = (\mathcal{V}, \mathcal{E}, \boldsymbol{\Delta})$, the eigen decomposition $\boldsymbol{\Delta} = \boldsymbol{\Phi}\boldsymbol{\Lambda}\boldsymbol{\Phi}^\top$ is conducted to obtain the orthonormal eigenvectors $\boldsymbol{\Phi} = \mathrm{diag}(\phi_1, \dots, \phi_n)$ and $\boldsymbol{\Lambda} = \mathrm{diag}(\lambda_1, \dots, \lambda_n)$ (n is the number of vertices and diag indicates diagonal matrix). In $\boldsymbol{\Lambda}$, the diagonal elements correspond to nonnegative eigenvalues. Consider the Fourier transform of the signal on hyper-graph $\mathbf{x} = (\mathbf{x_1}, \dots, \mathbf{x_n})$:

$$\hat{\mathbf{x}} = \boldsymbol{\Phi}^\top \mathbf{x}. \tag{6.10}$$

Here, eigenvectors correspond to Fourier bases and eigenvalues correspond to the frequencies. By this, we can give the spectral convolution operator of a signal $\mathbf{x}$ as follows:

$$\mathbf{g} \star \mathbf{x} = \boldsymbol{\Phi}((\boldsymbol{\Phi}^\top\mathbf{g}) \odot (\boldsymbol{\Phi}^\top\mathbf{x})) = \boldsymbol{\Phi}g(\boldsymbol{\Lambda})\boldsymbol{\Phi}^\top\mathbf{x}, \tag{6.11}$$

in which $\mathbf{g}$ is a filter, $g(\boldsymbol{\Lambda}) = \mathrm{diag}(g(\lambda_1), \dots, \mathbf{g}(\lambda_n))$ is a Fourier coefficients function and $\odot$ indicates the elementwise Hadamard product. However, the computation cost of Eq. (6.11) is high since the forward and inverse Fourier transform operations are computed in $O(n^2)$ complexity. Therefore, we parametrize $g(\boldsymbol{\Lambda})$ with K-order polynomials and further choose the truncated Chebyshev expansion $T_k(x)$ following [6]. $T_k(x)$ (order k) is obtained by $T_k(x) = 2xT_{k-1}(x) - T_{k-2}(x)$, where $T_0(x) = 1$ and $T_1(x) = x$. The $g(\boldsymbol{\Lambda})$ then gives the following form:

$$\mathbf{g} \star \mathbf{x} \approx \sum_{k=0}^{K} \theta_k T_k(\tilde{\boldsymbol{\Delta}})\mathbf{x}, \tag{6.12}$$

where $T_k(\tilde{\boldsymbol{\Delta}})$ is the Chebyshev polynomial of order k. $\tilde{\boldsymbol{\Delta}} = \frac{2}{\lambda_{max}}\boldsymbol{\Delta} - \mathbf{I}$ is the scaled Laplacian. In this way, the expensive computational cost of Laplacian eigenvectors can be eliminated and only simple matrix operations such as additions and multiplications are included. Furthermore, considering the scale adaptability issue of neural networks [28], $\lambda_{max} \approx 2$ is suggested. K is set as 1 to control the order of convolution operation. In fact, with $K = 1$, hyper-graph Laplacian is already capable of modeling complex correlations among vertices. Further simplifications can be made to the spectral convolution operation by

$$\mathbf{g} \star \mathbf{x} \approx \theta_0 \mathbf{x} - \theta_1 \mathbf{D}^{-1/2}\mathbf{H}\mathbf{W}\mathbf{D}_e^{-1}\mathbf{H}^\top\mathbf{D}_v^{-1/2}x, \tag{6.13}$$

where θ_0 and θ_1 are parameters of filters. To prevent the overfitting issue, we simplify it using one parameter θ:

$$\begin{cases} \theta_1 = -\frac{1}{2}\theta \\ \theta_0 = \frac{1}{2}\theta\mathbf{D}_v^{-1/2}\mathbf{H}\mathbf{D}_e^{-1}\mathbf{H}^\top\mathbf{D}_v^{-1/2} \end{cases}. \tag{6.14}$$

Substituting Eq. (6.14) into Eq. (6.12), the following simplified spectral convolution can be reached:

$$\mathbf{g} \star \mathbf{x} \approx \frac{1}{2}\theta \mathbf{D}_v^{-1/2}\mathbf{H}(\mathbf{W}+\mathbf{I})\mathbf{D}_e^{-1}\mathbf{H}^\top \mathbf{D}_v^{-1/2}\mathbf{x}$$
$$\approx \theta \mathbf{D}_v^{-1/2}\mathbf{H}\mathbf{W}\mathbf{D}_e^{-1}\mathbf{H}^\top \mathbf{D}_v^{-1/2}\mathbf{x}. \tag{6.15}$$

Usually, $\mathbf{W}$ is set as an identity matrix initially, indicating that all hyper-edges share the same weights. Given a hyper-graph signal $\mathbf{X} \in \mathbb{R}^{n \times C_1}$ with n nodes (C_1 is the dimension of features), the overall hyper-graph convolution is formulated by

$$\mathbf{Z} = \mathbf{D}_v^{-1/2}\mathbf{H}\mathbf{W}\mathbf{D}_e^{-1}\mathbf{H}^\top \mathbf{D}_v^{-1/2}\mathbf{X}\Theta, \tag{6.16}$$

where $\Theta \in \mathbb{R}^{C_1 \times C_2}$ is the learnable parameter. In the hyper-graph, features are extracted through the application of the filter Θ. $\mathbf{Z} \in \mathbb{R}^{n \times C_2}$ is the output of the hyper-graph neural networks and can be used for downstream applications.

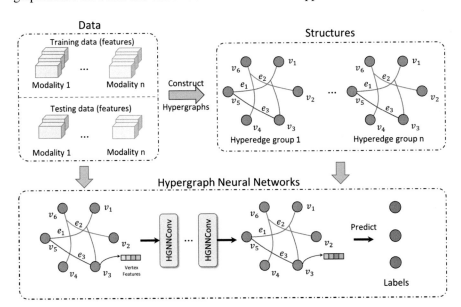

FIGURE 6.2

The general HGNN framework.

Framework. Fig. 6.2 illustrates the overall framework of the general HGNN. The multi-modality data set contains several vertices linked with features, which is divided into training data and testing data. Then we can construct the hyper-graph structure from the multi-modality data set and generate the hyper-graph incidence matrix $\mathbf{H}$ based on methods introduced in Section 6.3.1. The hyper-graph structure $\mathbf{H}$ as well as the node representations are both input into the HGNN.

Fig. 6.3 shows the details of the hyper-graph convolution layer (HGNN layer). As introduced before, we can build a HGNN layer $f(\mathbf{X}, \mathbf{W}, \boldsymbol{\Theta})$ by

$$\mathbf{X}^{(l+1)} = \sigma(\mathbf{D}_v^{-1/2}\mathbf{H}\mathbf{W}\mathbf{D}_e^{-1}\mathbf{H}^{\top}\mathbf{D}_v^{-1/2}\mathbf{X}^{(l)}\boldsymbol{\Theta}^{(l)}), \qquad (6.17)$$

where $\mathbf{X}^{(1)} \in \mathbb{R}^{N \times C}$ is the representations at layer l. $\mathbf{X}^{(0)}$ is the initial vertex features and $\sigma(\cdot)$ indicates any nonlinear activation functions. Each HGNN layer performs node-edge-node feature transform upon hyper-graph structure, which may be thought of as a two-stage refinement. The message passing pathways from the hyper-edges (column) to the nodes (row) are determined by the $\mathbf{H}$. In order to extract the C_2-dimensional features, the l-layer vertex representations $\mathbf{X}^{(l)}$ is first processed by the learnable parameters $\boldsymbol{\Theta}^{(l)}$. In the second stage, the hyper-edge feature, is obtained by aggregating the representations of vertices belongs to the hyper-edge. This process is achieved by multiplying matrix $\mathbf{H}^{\top} \in \mathbb{R}^{E \times N}$. Then enhanced node representations are obtained by gathering corresponding hyper-edge representations, which is achieved by multiplying matrix $\mathbf{H}$. Finally, the nonlinear activation function $\sigma(\cdot)$ is applied. It is noted that the role of $\mathbf{D}_v$ and $\mathbf{D}_e$ in Eq. (6.17) is normalization. By using a node-edge-node transformation, the HGNN layer is able to effectively distill high-order information on hyper-graphs.

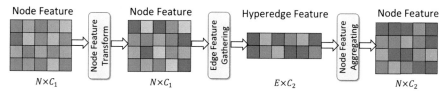

FIGURE 6.3

The hyper-graph convolution layer.

6.3.3 Dynamic hyper-graph neural networks

In data modeling, hyper-graph structure directly affects effectiveness. However, the initially constructed hyper-graph is probably not a suitable description for data. To tackle this, the dynamic hyper-graph neural networks (DHGNN) framework is presented in detail. As shown in Fig. 6.4, DHGNN is composed of two parts: dynamic hyper-graph construction (DHC) and hyper-graph convolution (HConv). We will elaborate on these two modules as well as the multi-hyper-graph fusion techniques. The implementation of DHGNN will also be discussed in the following.

Dynamic hyper-graph construction. In this part, we introduce how to generate and dynamically update the hyper-graph structure. Given n samples with features $\mathbf{X} = [\mathbf{x}_1, \mathbf{x}_2, ..., \mathbf{x}_n]$ in which $\mathbf{x}_i$ $(i = 1, 2, ..., n)$ indicates the embedding of the ith sample, a hyper-graph $\mathcal{G} = \{\mathcal{V}, \mathcal{E}\}$ can be generated. Here, the notation are the same as that introduced in Section 6.2. Let $Con(e)$ denote the set of vertices contained in hyper-edge e, and $Adj(u)$ is the set of hyper-edges, which contain the vertex u. The $Con(e)$

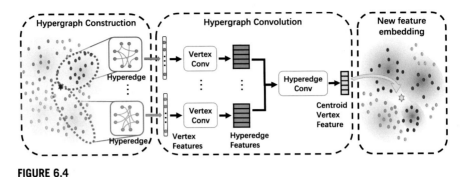

FIGURE 6.4

The illustration of DHGNN framework. This figure is from [24].

and $Adj(u)$ can then be formulated as

$$\begin{cases} Con(e) = \{u_1, u_2, ..., u_{k_e}\} \\ Adj(u) = \{e_1, e_2, ..., e_{k_u}\} \end{cases}, \qquad (6.18)$$

where k_e is the number of nodes belongs to hyper-edge e. k_u is the number of hyper-edges that node u belongs to. To utilize the local and global structure information, we combine k-NN and k-means methods for dynamic hyper-graph construction. Specifically, for each vertex u (the centroid vertex), we find its $k - 1$ nearest neighbors and connect them along with u using a hyper-edge. Besides, in each layer, the k-means approach is conducted on the overall embedding matrix. Specifically, each node will have adjacent hyper-edges assigned based on its nearest clusters.

The DHC is performed on the overall feature embeddings of each layer. The initial hyper-graph structure is initialized as the input representations. As the network going deeper, the hyper-edge set is dynamically updated and can better reflect the intrinsic correlations of data. By doing this, better hyper-graph structures for complex data association modeling can be created.

Hyper-graph convolution. The constructed hyper-graph structure along with the vertex features are then fed into the hyper-graph convolution module, which includes two stages: vertex convolution $VertexConv$ and hyper-edge convolution $EdgeConv$. In the first stage the embeddings of nodes, which belongs to a hyper-edge, are gathered to form the corresponding hyper-edge feature. Then the feature of the centroid vertex is updated by aggregating the adjacent hyper-edges' features.

In our method, vertex convolution is achieved by multiplying a transform matrix by the vertex feature matrix. The transform matrix $\mathbf{T}$ is learned through a multi-layer perception, weighting and permuting vertices in the corresponding hyper-edges. Compared with a fixed, pre-determined transform matrix, the learned transform matrix can better adapt to the vertex features. For hyper-edge convolution, a 1-dimensional convolution is adopted to compute the weighted sum of the adjacent hyper-edge features to update the feature of the centroid vertex. Fig. 6.5 illustrates the overall process of hyper-graph convolution.

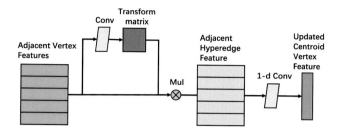

FIGURE 6.5

Hyper-graph convolution module. For k adjacent vertices of centroid vertex, a $k \times k$ transform matrix is calculated by convolution, which is multiplied with the input node feature map to obtain adjacent hyper-edge features. Then a 1-dimension convolution is used to weight and aggregate adjacent hyper-edge features to update the centroid vertex feature. This figure is from [24].

With the vertex convolution and hyper-edge convolution submodules, we now present a dynamic hyper-graph convolution layer. For each hyper-edge e in $Adj(u)$, we first sample k vertices in e and obtain $\mathbf{X}_u \in \mathbb{R}^{k \times d}$, where d is the dimension of embeddings. The $VertexConv$ aggregates node embeddings $\mathbf{X}_u$ to the hyper-edge feature $\mathbf{x}_e \in \mathbb{R}^d$. Then for the central node u, $EdgeConv$ gathers adjacent hyper-edge embeddings to update its feature $\mathbf{x}_u$. Finally, $\mathbf{x}_u$ is activated by σ to $\mathbf{y}_u$. Multiple dynamic hyper-graph convolution layers are stacked to form a DHGNN model. Additionally, for multi-hyper-graph, we add a multi-hyper-graph fusion block after the convolution procedure as mentioned above for feature fusion.

Multi-hyper-graph fusion. When applied to the data assigned with different aspects of attributes (*e.g.*, multi-modal data), multiple hyper-graphs are needed to capture the high-order correlations from different perspectives. Therefore, a multi-hyper-graph fusion block is devised to fuse information flow from multiple hyper-graphs after hyper-graph convolution. Considering that different aspects of properties should contribute distinctively to feature fusion, an attention mechanism is adopted to automatically capture such differences, which is formulated as Eq. (6.19).

$$\begin{cases} w = softmax(\mathbf{xW} + \mathbf{b}) \\ \mathbf{x}_f = \sum_{i=0}^{M} w^i \mathbf{x}^i \end{cases} , \qquad (6.19)$$

in which M denotes the number of aspects, $\mathbf{x}^i$ denotes feature of the ith aspect and $\mathbf{x}_f$ denotes the fused feature. $\mathbf{W}$ and $\mathbf{b}$ are learnable parameters. The overall procedure is visualized in Fig. 6.6.

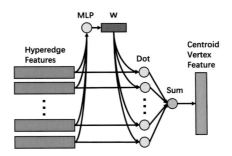

FIGURE 6.6

The multi-hyper-edge fusion block. This figure is from [24].

6.3.4 Hyper-graph learning toolbox

Here, we introduce two practical hyper-graph learning toolboxes to help better understand and utilize hyper-graph learning for different applications. The first one is THU-HyperG, an open-source library for classical hyper-graph learning written in Python.[1] It implements several classical hyper-graph learning algorithms for classification and clustering tasks. THU-HyperG includes two crucial components: hyper-graph generation and hyper-graph learning. THU-HyperG offers a number of hyper-graph generation techniques from network-based to distance-based methods. Transductive and inductive hyper-graph learning, as well as the dynamic hyper-graph structure updating approaches, have all been implemented in THU-HyperG.

The other useful toolbox is *THU-DeepHypergraph* (THU-DH).[2] Similar to THU-HyperG, THU-DH is also an open-source toolbox written in Python. It is a general HGNN framework built upon PyTorch. Hyper-graph modeling (hyper-graph construction) and hyper-graph convolution are two major components of THU-DH. THU-DH offers common APIs for hyper-graph modeling, providing methods based on attributes and features. For hyper-graph convolution, the spectral and spatial convolution operators have been implemented in THU-DH. By combining several submodules, researchers may easily use THU-DH to handle a variety of applications, such as node classification and graph regression. Data pre-processing modules are also given for some specific tasks like pathological image sampling. In order to assist users in getting started quickly and evaluating intuitively, example codes and visualization tools are provided.

For both THU-HyperG and THU-DH, sparse matrix techniques are utilized to reduce the computational cost.

---

[1] https://github.com/iMoonLab/THU-HyperG.
[2] https://github.com/iMoonLab/THU-DeepHypergraph.

6.4 **Hyper-graph learning for medical image analysis**

Hyper-graph learning is a flexible and powerful tool for data representation learning because of its ability in modeling and exploring complex correlations among objects. Recently, much effort has been devoted to applying hyper-graph computing in medical image analysis, such as medical image retrieval [16], MCI identification [19,32], cancer tissue classification, medical image segmentation [11] and childhood autism diagnosis [45].

In medical image retrieval, a multi-graph learning-based approach is introduced to assist MCI diagnosis [16]. It mainly includes two parts, i.e., the query class prediction for candidate selection as well as ranking. First, the relationships between the query subject and a group of training subjects are modeled into a multi-graph structure. Then, multi-graph learning is conducted to alternately predict the relevance of the query to known classes. Besides, multiple graphs should have different importance and the optimal weight distribution is also learned in this procedure. In the stage of ranking, a new multi-graph is generated for the query and the candidates to learn the relationships.

In MCI identification, the centralized hyper-graph learning algorithm is devised to incorporate four magnetic resonance imaging (MRI) sequences to identity MCI [19]. Four hyper-graphs are first constructed for each MRI sequence to capture the high-order correlations among subjects. The MCI identification task can then be modeled as a binary classification problem and centralized hyper-graph learning is conducted to solve this problem. To utilize the underlying coherence among multiple modalities, Liu et al. [32] introduce a view-aligned hyper-graph learning (VAHL) framework, which directly captures the consistency of views under the modality-incomplete case. Specifically, a hyper-graph is constructed for each modality based upon their sparse representation. Then the VAHL method is devised to model the coherence and finally make the classification decision for MCI diagnosis. Bakht et al. also apply hyper-graph learning in colorectal cancer tissue classification. They first extract the patch-level deep features, based on which the hyper-graph structure is constructed to capture complex correlations among patches. In the hyper-graph, the patches are formulated as vertices and the hyper-edges are assigned according to the Euclidean distance. The generated hyper-graph and the corresponding vertex feature are fed into the hyper-graph neural networks to conduct tissue classification.

For the medical image segmentation task, Dong et al. [11] devise a hierarchical hyper-graph learning-based method for multi-atlas segmentation. A hyper-graph is first generated to connect the similar voxels (having a similar patchwise appearance) in the target image. The hyper-edge in the hyper-graph also connects the target voxel and related voxels from atlas images. The core idea of the proposed methods is to propagate a set of known voxels labels from atlas images to unknown target voxels through hyper-graph learning.

In childhood autism diagnosis, Zhang et al. [45] devise the multi-modal dynamic hyper-graph learning framework utilizing two kinds of functional connectivities. Based upon the extracted features of functional connectivities, two hyper-graphs are constructed for each modality respectively to capture the high-order correlations among several subjects.

6.5 Application 1: hyper-graph learning for COVID-19 identification using CT images

Hyper-graph learning could be adopted for the classification task. It could build a hyper-graph topology to express the data relationship among several examples. This technique could be applied to the medical area such as the identification of COVID-19 using CT. Here, we introduce the work in [8]. It leverages an uncertainty-based hyper-graph learning method for precise pulmonary identification.

There has been considerable concern regarding the Coronavirus disease COVID-19 since late 2019. It is caused by a highly contagious virus that causes severe respiratory difficulty as well as numerous organ failure [29,4,30,40,23].

The Chinese government's guideline [34], issued in early 2020, states that for respiratory or blood samples, COVID-19 requires complex diagnostic methods, including genetic testing. Identifying features such as diffusion in CT as a feature of the disease is a reliable and effective technique, according to recent studies on lung CT scans [12,21,41]. Particularly, COVID-19 symptoms are identified on CT by symmetrical and regional ground-class with consolidative lung opacities, and the greater the severity of the illness, the more the lung involvement and the more linear opacities [41,1].

Many machine learning-based experiments have been undertaken to lessen the effort for diagnosing COVID-19 [21,29,33,44,36]. However, there are two major challenges: **(1)** Confusion cases. The radiological appearance of COVID-19 could be easily confused with other pneumonia, especially in the early stage. That proposes a serious challenge for diagnosis. **(2)** Noisy data. Another challenge is that the collected clinical data in this emergent situation include large variances, such as CT manufactures and patient movements. Therefore how to handle such noisy data with uncertain quality to determine it from normal is an essential, urgent but challenging task.

The Uncertainty Vertex-weighted Hyper-graph Learning (UVHL) introduced here could be used to classify COVID-19 and normal using hyper-graph learning using CT images. To indicate if the testing case is a disease or normal, we must use the latent association between these diseases and normal cases. Using a vertex-weighted hyper-graph structure, the framework formulates the correlation between different cases, as illustrated in Fig. 6.7. Two metrics are created with the "uncertainty measurement" module: noisy data aleatoric uncertainty and incapacity of the model. Then the UVHL can learn from the hyper-graph in order to forecast the next case, which is able to incorporate the measured data uncertainty values to identify misleading patterns in noisy data and eliminate them as well as give more attention to nodes that are distributed circling the classification boundary in latent representation space, simultaneously. Additionally, the proposed framework can use multi-modal data/features

CAP   COVID-19

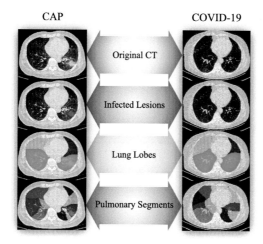

FIGURE 6.7

Lung scans, preprocessed results of infected tumors and lung fields are displayed on CAP (left) and COVID-19 (right) patients. This figure is from [7].

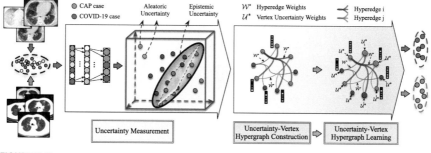

FIGURE 6.8

Illustration of the UVHL framework. This figure is from [7].

if they are available. A total of 1495 COVID-19 cases and 1027 CAP cases have been collected. CAP and COVID-19 can be identified with a good accuracy of 90% using the suggested approach, as demonstrated by experimental results.

6.5.1 Method

Here, to identify illness, we introduce the UVHL method. The framework is shown in Fig. 6.8. The suggested method consists of three steps, namely, data uncertainty measurement, hyper-graph modeling and uncertainty-vertex hyper-graph learning.

Uncertainty measurement. For the model to avoid being adversely affected by low-quality noise data and to learn more high-order representations for critical distinctive-

tough samples, the first stage of this framework is designed as uncertainty mea-surement. This module can generate uncertainty scores to initialize the weights of samples. Basically, the uncertainty factors can be divided into two branches:

a. *Aleatoric uncertainty.* A high level of noise is present in the data or the data is gathered in error and is of poor quality.
b. *Epistemic uncertainty.* A significant amount of scrutiny is placed on distinguish-ing models near the decision boundary due to the clustering of case features.

Next, the method for the uncertainty calculation will be detailed.

Aleatoric uncertainty. The aleatoric uncertainty is a metric for determining the qual-ity of noisy data. In order to capture aleatoric uncertainty, Θ must be calculated in a way that minimizes the difference between true and predicted distributions $P_D(x)$, $P_\Theta(x)$ over training samples:

$$\hat{\Theta} = \arg\min_\Theta \frac{1}{N} \sum_{i=1}^{N} D_{KL}\left(P_D(x) \| P_\Theta(x)\right). \tag{6.20}$$

Hence, KL-divergence can be used to define the loss function: $L(\Theta) = L_{KL}(\Theta)$, which will be minimized during training. The loss of a single sample is formulated as Eq. (6.21):

$$
\begin{aligned}
L(\Theta) &= D_{KL}\left(P_D(\mathbf{x}) \| P_\Theta(\mathbf{x})\right) \\
&= \int P_D(\mathbf{x}) \log P_D(\mathbf{x}) d\mathbf{x} - \int P_D(\mathbf{x}) \log P_\Theta(\mathbf{x}) d\mathbf{x} \\
&= \frac{\mathbb{CE}(\mathbf{y}, f_\Theta(\mathbf{x}))}{2\sigma_\Theta^2(\mathbf{x})} + \frac{\log\left(\sigma_\Theta^2(\mathbf{x})\right)}{2} + \frac{\log(2\pi)}{2} - H(P_D(\mathbf{x})),
\end{aligned}
\tag{6.21}
$$

where $\mathbb{CE}$ represents the *cross-entropy* function, $f_\Theta : \mathbb{R}^{191} \mapsto \mathbb{R}^2$ is the network using *softmax* to convert features for binary predictions, $\mathbf{x} \in \mathbb{R}^{191}$ represents each patient's feature vector, and $\mathbf{y} \in \mathbb{R}^2$ stands for the label. $H(P_D(\mathbf{x}))$ represents the en-tropy of $P_D(\mathbf{x})$. σ_Θ^2 represents the predicted variance. In order to prevent a division by 0, we substitute $\log\sigma_\Theta^2(\mathbf{x})$ with $\alpha_\Theta(\mathbf{x})$. Thus $\alpha_\Theta : \mathbb{R}^{191} \mapsto \mathbb{R}^1$ is a useful tool for estimating uncertainty.

When optimizing, the last two terms in the formulation (6.21) are redundant. So, we have the formulation (6.22) of N samples:

$$L(\Theta) = \frac{1}{N} \sum_i^N \left(\frac{1}{2} exp(-\alpha_\Theta(\mathbf{x}_i))\mathbb{CE}(\mathbf{y}_i, f_\Theta(\mathbf{x}_i)) + \frac{1}{2}\alpha_\Theta(\mathbf{x}_i) \right). \tag{6.22}$$

Models tend to forecast a larger $\alpha_\Theta(\mathbf{x_i})$ when there is a high *cross-entropy* of the $y_\Theta(\mathbf{x}_i)$ and $\mathbf{y}_i$ in order to reduce loss caused by inputs with high uncertainty. This method allows the network to become more resilient to noisy input as a result of correct labeling. In the task, as the aleatoric uncertainty, to detect low-quality information, $\mathcal{A}_\Theta(\mathbf{x}_i)$ is designated as aleatoric uncertainty.

$$\mathcal{A}_\Theta(\mathbf{x}_i) = \sigma_\Theta^2(\mathbf{x}_i) = exp(\alpha_\Theta(\mathbf{x_i})). \tag{6.23}$$

Epistemic uncertainty. Basically, it refers to the model's ability to estimate appropriately. Dropout variational inference is one popular practical approach for approximate inference [15]. MC dropout is an estimation method that uses the Monte Carlo method. The approximate predictive distribution is derived from formulation (6.24):

$$q\left(\mathbf{y}^*|\mathbf{x}^*\right) = \int p\left(\mathbf{y}^*|\mathbf{x}^*, \omega\right) q(\omega)\mathrm{d}\omega, \tag{6.24}$$

where $\omega = \{\mathbf{W}_i\}_{i=1}^L$ is the random variables set for a L-layered model. $\mathbf{x}^*$ and $\mathbf{y}^*$ represent the MC dropout model's inputs and outputs, respectively. However, tests are conducted with open dropout layers, contrary to traditional settings. By predicting the same sample for repeated K times, we can obtain epistemic uncertainty through the variance of these K values.

The anticipated outcome for a single sample can be expressed as formulation (6.25):

$$\mathbf{E}_{q(\mathbf{y}^*|\mathbf{x}^*)}\left(\mathbf{y}^*\right) \approx \frac{1}{K}\sum_{k=1}^K \widehat{\mathbf{y}}^*\left(\mathbf{x}^*, \omega^k\right), \tag{6.25}$$

or more specifically, in this task:

$$\mathbf{E}(f_{\widehat{\Theta}}(\mathbf{x}_i)) \approx \frac{1}{K}\sum_{k=1}^K f_{\widehat{\Theta}(\omega^k)}(\mathbf{x}_i). \tag{6.26}$$

By combining aleatoric uncertainty with epistemic uncertainty, we can approximate epistemic uncertainty as [27] in formulation (6.27):

$$\begin{aligned}\mathcal{E}(f_{\widehat{\Theta}}(\mathbf{x}_i)) \approx{} & \mathcal{A}_{\widehat{\Theta}}(\mathbf{x}_i) + \frac{1}{K}\sum_{k=1}^K f_{\widehat{\Theta}(\omega^k)}(\mathbf{x}_i)^\top f_{\widehat{\Theta}(\omega^k)}(\mathbf{x}_i) \\ & - \mathbf{E}(f_{\widehat{\Theta}(\omega^k)}(\mathbf{x}_i))^\top \mathbf{E}(f_{\widehat{\Theta}(\omega^k)}(\mathbf{x}_i)),\end{aligned} \tag{6.27}$$

where i represents the i_{th} sample and k represents the k_{th} test using dropout.

Note that $\mathcal{E}(f_{\widehat{\Theta}}(\mathbf{x}_i)) \approx \mathcal{A}_{\widehat{\Theta}}(\mathbf{x}_i)$ (epistemic uncertainty) is mainly composed of aleatoric uncertainty. Therefore when $\mathcal{E}(f_{\widehat{\Theta}}(\mathbf{x}_i))$ reaches higher, it mostly indicates poor data quality rather than a constraint in the model's categorization capacity. Thus the quality of the data and weight vertices based on it can be captured by utilizing epistemic uncertainty.

Uncertainty-vertex hyper-graph construction. The second stage constructs a hyper-graph with the information on uncertainty. Over the entire data set, we compute

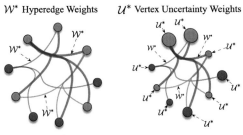

$\mathcal{W}^*$ Hyperedge Weights $\mathcal{U}^*$ Vertex Uncertainty Weights

Hypergraph   Vertex-weighted Hypergraph

FIGURE 6.9

A vertex-weighted hyper-graph also includes hyper-edge weights, as well as a weight for each vertex, which indicates significance or uncertainty. This figure is from [7].

mean and standard deviation as μ_e, s_e to normalize epistemic uncertainty $\mathscr{E}(f_{\hat{\Theta}}(\mathbf{x}_i))$. Afterwards, *sigmoid* function $\sigma(\cdot)$ is used to verify that the weights vary between 0 and 1. λ represents the adjustable parameter. Weights of all data are shown in formulation (6.28):

$$\mathcal{U}_i = \sigma\left(\lambda \frac{\mathscr{E}(f_{\hat{\Theta}}(\mathbf{x}_i)) - \mu_e}{s_e}\right). \tag{6.28}$$

All of the samples in the data set are constructed as vertices, formulated as $\mathcal{P} = \langle \mathcal{F}, L, \mathcal{U} \rangle$. Unlike traditional hyper-graphs, which are merely concerned with features $\mathcal{F}$ and labels L, the uncertainty-vertex hyper-graph (UVHL) beyond takes into consideration the weight of each vertex $\mathcal{U}$ representing the importance of data. All of n samples can be denoted as $\mathbf{P} = \{\mathcal{P}_1, \mathcal{P}_2, ..., \mathcal{P}_n\}$. For the traditional method, the structure of hyper-graph is $G = \langle V, \mathcal{E}, \mathbf{W} \rangle$. V represents the set of vertex, where vertices indicate objects. $\mathcal{E}$ represents the set of hyper-edge and weights for hyper-edges are pre-defined in the matrix $\mathbf{W}$. The structure of the UVHL contains an additional U, which is vertex weights represented as a diagonal matrix. Vertex weights U are then used to build an incidence matrix $\mathbf{H}$ indicating the connection between vertices:

$$\mathbf{H}(v_i, e_p) = \begin{cases} \mathcal{U}_i, & v_i \in e_p \\ 0, & v_i \notin e_p \end{cases}. \tag{6.29}$$

This stage results in the hyper-graph structure.

Uncertainty-vertex hyper-graph learning. In Fig. 6.9, when convolutional layers act equally among vertices, the suggested UVHL examines every vertex weight independently, as opposed to the traditional hyper-graph learning approach. More important vertices can have more attention in the learning process.

The optimize task involves learning a relevance matrix $\mathbf{F}$ that needs to be estimated, with the corresponding cost function defined as

$$Q_{\mathbf{U}}(\mathbf{F}) = \arg\min_{\mathbf{F}} \left\{ \Omega(\mathbf{F}) + \lambda \mathcal{R}_{emp}(\mathbf{F}) \right\}. \tag{6.30}$$

Following is a rewrite of the regularizer $\Omega(\cdot)$ and empirical loss $\mathcal{R}_{emp}(\cdot)$:

$$\Omega(\mathbf{F}, \mathcal{V}, \mathbf{U}, \mathcal{E}, \mathbf{W}) = tr(\mathbf{F}^\top(\mathbf{U}^\top - \mathbf{U}^\top\Theta_\mathbf{U}\mathbf{U})\mathbf{F})$$

$$\mathcal{R}_{emp}(\mathbf{F}, \mathbf{U}) = \sum_{k=1}^{K}\left\|\mathbf{F}(:,k) - \mathbf{Y}(:,k)\right\|^2, \tag{6.31}$$

where $\Theta_\mathbf{U} = \mathbf{D}_v^{-\frac{1}{2}}\mathbf{H}\mathbf{W}\mathbf{D}_e^{-1}\mathbf{H}^\top\mathbf{D}_v^{-\frac{1}{2}}$. The vertex-weighted loss function $\mathcal{R}_{emp}(\cdot)$ for uncertainty is shown below:

$$\mathcal{R}_{emp}(\mathbf{F}, \mathbf{U}) = tr(\mathbf{F}^\top\mathbf{U}^\top\mathbf{U}\mathbf{F} + \mathbf{Y}^\top\mathbf{U}^\top\mathbf{U}\mathbf{Y}$$
$$- 2\mathbf{F}^\top\mathbf{U}^\top\mathbf{U}\mathbf{Y}). \tag{6.32}$$

This leads to the following target label matrix $\mathbf{F}$:

$$\mathbf{F} = \lambda(\mathbf{U}^\top - \mathbf{U}^\top\Theta_\mathbf{U}\mathbf{U} + \lambda\mathbf{U}^\top\mathbf{U})^{-1}\mathbf{U}^\top\mathbf{U}\mathbf{Y}. \tag{6.33}$$

As described above, using the label matrix $\mathbf{F} \in \mathbb{R}^{n \times K}$ ($K = 2$ in this task), the representations for data in case b (illustrated in Section 6.5.1) is optimized by the higher relevance value, named "high-order representations."

The extracted and optimized high-order representations for patients (denoted as the vertex in UVHL) are transferred into rows of $\mathbf{F} \in \mathbb{R}^{n \times 2}$. As a result, the model's output is a binary vector for each patient. After comparing the values of the two elements in the vector, we can predict the pneumonia type (COVID-19 and CAP).

6.5.2 Experiments

Data set. The pneumonia multi-modal data, including CT images and statistic data, are provided first, followed by the pre-processing of these data. After pre-processing, multi-modal features, i.e., image visualization features, hand-crafted features and personal general information, can be extracted. Then these data can be used in the UVHL for the identification of COVID-19.

Among the 2522 CT images in this study, 1495 come from COVID-19 patients and 1027 from CAP patients. All COVID-19 cases were verified positive by RT-PCR and were obtained between January 2020 and February 2020. From July 2018 through February 2020, CAP images were acquired. Before being forwarded for examination, all images were de-identified. The Institutional Review Boards of the involved institutes authorized this study. Due to the study's retrospective character, written informed consent was waived.

Preprocessing. For each patient, both CT scan image features and statistical hand-crafted features are extracted. The lungs, 5 lung lobes, 18 pulmonary segments and infected lesions are first segmented by a deep learning-based network [36] in a portal program.

There are $\mathbb{R}^{96}$ statistics handcrafted features required, including histogram distribution, lesion surface area, extra density and mass and so on [39]. For image features, radiomics is conducted on infected lesions, inducing $\mathbb{R}^{93}$ dimensions for each patient, including gray-level co-occurrence matrices and first-order intensity statistics. With age and gender information given, concatenation of the representations for each patient results in $\mathbf{x} \in \mathbb{R}^{191}$.

Evaluation metrics. Here, a classification result is positive if it is COVID-19 and negative if it is normal. And if the result is correct, it is described as true and as false and vice versa. Six evaluation criteria are used in the experiments to evaluate the effectiveness of each method:

1. Accuracy (*ACC*): *ACC* calculates the fraction of properly categorized samples. $ACC = \frac{TP+TN}{TP+TN+FP+FN}$.
2. Sensitivity (*SEN*): *SEN* calculates the percentage by measuring true positives accurately because it reflects the ratio of patients that were misdiagnosed. This evaluation metric is more important in genuine medical diagnostic application settings. $SEN = \frac{TP}{TP+FN}$.
3. Specificity (*SPEC*): By *SPEC*, the ratio of true negatives can be accurately quantified. This is an indicator of omissions in diagnosis. $SPEC = \frac{TN}{TN+FP}$.
4. Balance (*BAC*): *BAC* is calculated by dividing *SEN* and *SPEC* by the mean value. $BAC = \frac{SEN+SPEC}{2}$.
5. Positive Predictive Value (*PPV*): *PPV* calculates the percentage of true positives among identified positives. $PPV = \frac{TP}{TP+FP}$.
6. Negative Predictive Value (*NPV*): *NPV* calculates the percentage of true negatives among identified negatives. $NPV = \frac{TN}{TN+FN}$.

Implementation. There are 1495 instances of disease and 1027 instances of normal in the entire data set for the experiment, with all features normalized to [0, 1]. We split them into ten subsets at random and do 10-fold cross-validation. We report the mean and standard deviation of 10 experiments.

For the UVHL model, hyper-edges are constructed by using K-nearest neighbor (KNN) clustering. For representation learning, it is critical to build a sufficient hyper-graph structure. However, it is difficult to determine how to choose the K value in the hyper-edge creation process. A big K number would link too many vertices and generate noise, whereas its capacity would be limited if K were too small as it would connect only a few vertices. The approach described below is used to establish a fitting K. Choosing a pool of K that can be modified depending on the type of data is the first step. It is set to [2, 3, ..., 20] as the pool of K. In the training data, 5-fold cross-validation is performed with different K values. Once several K have been trained, the K is selected according to performance for testing. This allows for an entirely automated and optimum selection of K.

Results and discussions. A comparison of UVHL and other approaches is illustrated in Fig. 6.10 along with a detailed mean value and t-test significance report in Table 6.1. The following could be attracted from these findings.

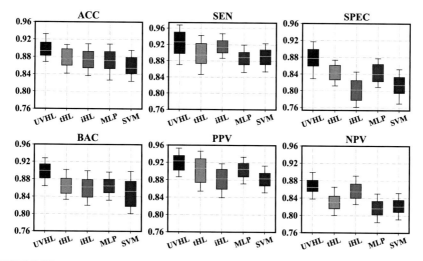

FIGURE 6.10

UVHL performance compared to other methods. Based on the results, UVHL out-performs all other methods. This figure is from [7].

1. UVHL provides the most consistent performance across the board. The method outperforms SVM and MLP, i.e., obtains 4.813% and 3.602% relative improvement in *ACC*), suggesting that the hyper-graph-based strategy is capable of tackling the pneumonia classification task.
2. In comparison to other hyper-graph-based methodologies, for example, inductive hyper-graph learning (iHL) [46] and transductive hyper-graph learning (tHL) [20], this approach can outperform furthermore when importing the uncertainty scores, about 3.115% and 2.958% relative improvement, respectively.
3. More specifically, regarding each detail criterion, UVHL can improve the accuracy, sensitivity and specificity, showing that we are capable of enhancing the recalling of COVID-19 patients (higher *SEN*) and reducing the workload of doctors (higher *SPEC*), simultaneously.

Analysis on few labeled data. Since it is expensive to collect large-scale training data for COVID-19, difficult and private-sensitive to collect, it is meaningful to investigate how this framework performs in the low-resource data situation. The experiments are conducted as follows. The scale of data is kept unchanged but the training data is shrunk, i.e., the annotated COVID-19, and CAP cases. In detail, instead of choosing full-scale training data, we randomly choose 10, 20, 30, ... and 100 labeled samples as training data, and randomly choose 100 labeled samples as validation data. The rest of the data is used for testing. For example, when the training data scale is 10, the validation data scale is 100 and the rest 2412 is used for testing correspondingly. Despite the fact that the training set is decreased, each method's effectiveness is mea-

Table 6.1 Analysis of pneumonia data of different compared methods ("†" indicates the significance testing, $p-value < 0.001$).

Methods		ACC		SEN		SPEC		BAC		PPV		NPV	
SVM	(p-value)	0.85884	8.3824e-4	0.88902	5.7014e-3	0.80999	9.8357e-6	0.84950	6.3223e-6	0.88219	8.2747e-4	0.82148	4.1927e-4
MLP	(p-value)	0.86888	1.3914e-4	0.88503	8.1923e-4	0.84245	7.3121e-6	0.86374	9.2958e-6	0.90191	1.5186e-3	0.81741	7.0136e-4
iHL [46]	(p-value)	0.87299	9.1836e-4	0.91682	0.0538	0.80193	8.8322e-7	0.85938	2.6611e-6	0.88114	1.9356e-7	0.85934	0.0546
tHL [20]	(p-value)	0.87448	4.4017e-3	0.89397	0.0037	0.84280	1.9258e-5	0.86838	2.0182e-4	0.90114	2.0127e-3	0.83262	3.3156e-3
UVHL	(std)	**0.90018**†	±0.0223	**0.91909**†	±0.0291	**0.87259**†	±0.0274	**0.89584**†	±0.0210	**0.91958**†	±0.0222	**0.86851**†	±0.0483

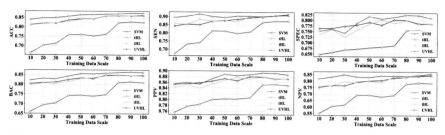

FIGURE 6.11

Performance evaluation of training data of various sizes. This figure is from [7].

sured using a 10-fold cross-validation strategy. The results of six metrics are shown in Fig. 6.11. The conclusions of the analysis are as follows:

1. For *ACC*, *SEN* and *SPEC*, UVHL stays ahead of other methods from beginning to end. This result demonstrates that with the advantages of hyper-graph structure as well as uncertainty modules, the model is capable of mining the distinctive representations of COVID-19 reducing the missing diagnosis cases. Therefore it is relatively reliable to serve as a diagnosing and analysis COVID-19 tool under low-resource data situations.

2. Across all of the boards, the proposed method delivers the best performance at the start. This result attributes to the advantages of semi-supervised learning, (i.e., hyper-graph learning), having the ability to perform better when the scale of training data is low.

3. In comparison to other hyper-graph-based methodologies, for example, inductive hyper-graph learning, and transductive hyper-graph learning, UVHL performs quite outstanding under the shrunk training data. This situation shows that we can achieve better performance when plugging the uncertainty module.

4. The SVM performs poorly when the scale of training data is low. Although it fits the classification task rapidly when the resource raising, it still cannot perform reliably. This is because the method requires abundant high-quality data, which is a frustrating issue in the task of COVID-19 as the data is difficult to collect.

Overall, the results demonstrate that in this specific task, screening patients with COVID-19 from CAP, the framework UVHL is suitable, performing rapidly and accurately.

6.6 Application 2: hyper-graph learning for survival prediction on whole slides histopathological images

It is extremely challenging to model the representation in gigapixel histopathological whole-slide images (WSIs). This brings a problem to related applications, such as survival prediction based on WSIs. A hyper-graph could explore high-order correlation among large-scale data, which is crucial for WSI modeling. Thus, the hyper-graph-based method could improve the performance in these tasks. Recent work such as [10,9] established hyper-graphs in WSI modeling and achieved excellent performance.

6.6.1 Ranking-based survival prediction on histopathological whole-slide images

In [10], a ranking-based method has been proposed to model WSI representation for survival prediction. Hyper-graph neural networks are applied in this method, aiming at effectively fusing large-scale information in WSI.

Predicting the survival using WSIs [49] is a popular medical imaging task [31,43, 48,42]. Based on histopathological WSIs, this task attempts to directly simulate the time elapsed between when follow-up began and the conclusion of the study (e.g., biological death).

For each patient, previous studies have run regression models on their WSI to attempt to predict survival [43,42,31], while disregarding the patients' relative ranking order. The ranking order is much more important when comparing data points than the prediction of each individual data item [2]. When compared to single values for each person, the ranking order information within the group is more important for differentiating the objectives.

There are two crucial problems that need to be solved. First, explore how a single WSI can better be used to predict danger. Second, how should the survival prediction procedure incorporate ranking order information.

Ranking information is taken into consideration during the learning process by RankSurv, a ranking-based survival prediction approach using whole-slide images. For hazard prediction, a hyper-graph representation of WSI patches is developed first. Then, utilizing pairwise survival data, a ranking-based prediction method is carried out.

A total of three medical data sets have been used in the experiments. According to the results, the method improves significantly and consistently when in comparison to existing state-of-the-art methods.

6.6.1.1 Method

As shown in Fig. 6.12, there are three stages in Ranking-based Survival Prediction Network (RankSurv): "preprocessing," "hazard prediction" and "survival rank prediction" in order to estimate both survival hazard scores and pairwise ranking outcomes. A raw patch-level feature set is collected from the original WSI input data in the first step. The patch-level features are then passed into the hazard prediction step for fine-tuning and calculation of the hazard score. In addition, the pairwise ranking loss provides supervision to a ranking-specific back-propagation method.

Preprocessing. When WSIs are provided from M patients and the corresponding labels. The following is a representation of the input data: $\mathbb{D}_{in} = \{C_1, C_2, ..., C_M\}$,

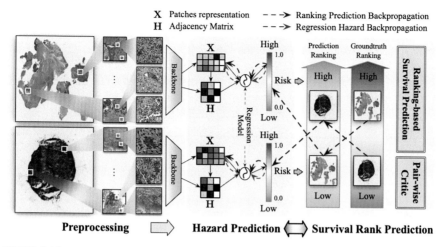

X Patches representation   – – –▷ Ranking Prediction Backpropagation
H Adjacency Matrix   – – –▷ Regression Hazard Backpropagation

Preprocessing ⟹ **Hazard Prediction** ⟺ **Survival Rank Prediction**

FIGURE 6.12

The pipeline of RankSurv. To begin with, raw patch-level features are taken from raw images using a backbone model. Next, the signal matrix **X** for the hyper-graph and the incident matrix **H** or the hyper-edges are computed. A regression module exploits the representation of hyper-graph spectral convolutional layers and masters the ability to forecast the risk of provided WSIs after being trained by multiple hyper-graph spectral convolutional layers. A third stage enhances performance and representation by fine-tuning pairwise ranking as well as hazard prediction back-propagation. This figure is from [10].

$M \geq 2$, $C_i = \langle I_i, t_i, \delta_i \rangle$, $i \in [1, M]$, where I_i represents the ith image, t_i and δ_i are the observation period and whether is death or not, respectively. For each case, either a censored time (T_{censor}) or survival time (T_{event}) is observed. As indicated by the δ_i value, the survival status of the patient is represented by a binary value, where 1 represents a case that has not been censored and 0 represents one that has.

With the OTSU method [35], we scale down, mask and separate instructive tissues or cells to prevent noises like blood, blank and erosion from appearing in the image, and choose K (e.g., 2000) patches in it. Model pre-trained by ImageNet as a backbone [38] then generates the principal patch-level visual features $X = \{x_1, x_2, ..., x_M\}$, $x_i \in \mathbb{R}^{K \times F}$, where x_i represents the ith case's feature matrix, and the F represents the patch feature's vector dimension. This preliminary processing method is prompted by [49], and a previously validated pre-trained model is used to stratify complicated tissue patterns based on raw features collected from it [3].

Hazard prediction using hyper-graph representation. In Fig. 6.12, in order to anticipate survival risks, we provide X raw patch features from the previous pre-processing. Many options are available for learning survival-specific representations, including CNN-based models [49], GCN-based models and FCN-based models [42]. Additionally, RankSurv represents hierarchy information using a hyper-graph structure [17,14,24] in addition to the baselines above. It is crucial that the hyper-graph spectral convolution is used for survival prediction. On the hyper-graph, translation does not have a unique mathematical concept from an *spatial* perspective, an *spectral* hyper-graph convolution based on the [14] is presented. The hyper-graph is made up of N hyper-edges, and K entries from the K-nearest neighbor method are assigned to each hyper-edge based on Euclidean distance, and for the incidence matrix $\mathbf{H} \in \mathbb{R}^{N \times k}$, linked nodes have a value of 1 and others have a value of 0. The hyper-edge offers the option for integrating and mixing the most comparable K patches, providing a way of learning the hierarchical grouping pattern beyond a pairwise graph structure. The formulation briefly depicts the hyper-graph convolutional layer (6.34):

$$\mathbf{X}^{(l+1)} = \sigma \left(\mathbf{D}_v^{-1/2} \mathbf{H} \mathbf{W} \mathbf{D}_e^{-1} \mathbf{H}^\top \mathbf{D}_v^{-1/2} \mathbf{X}^{(l)} \mathbf{\Theta}^{(l)} \right), \qquad (6.34)$$

where $\mathbf{X}^{(l)} \in \mathbb{R}^{N \times C}$ stands for a signal with N vertices in the lth layer, $\mathbf{X}^{(l+1)}$ represents layer l's output, σ represents the nonlinear activation function such as $ReLU(\cdot)$ and $\mathbf{\Theta}^{(l)}$ represents the layer l's learnable parameter. The N hyper-edges could represent the N patterns of pathogenic factors after several layers of spectral convolution. Prediction of survival is based on patch-level features that are finally learned. Through the use of a fully connected layer, survival hazards can be predicted temporally after compressing $\mathbf{X_n}$ into $X \in \mathbb{R}^{1 \times C_n}$. The observation time t_i supervises the regression hazard scale back-propagation procedure.

Survival rank prediction. It is the final but crucial module of the framework that provides the most insight, i.e., which supervises the back-propagation in a higher-level ranking prediction. The most likely cause of the comparison error is that the model cannot discriminate between two similar situations. A Bayesian-based method known as Bayesian Concordance Readjust (BCR) might improve the ranking prediction even further. Let $\mathcal{H}_i$ and $\mathcal{H}_j$ represent the scores based on hazards of ith and jth samples from $\mathbb{D}_{in}$, and $\widehat{\mathcal{H}}_i, \widehat{\mathcal{H}}_j$ stand for their corresponding predicted hazard scores, respectively. A second step in the hazard prediction process produces fine-tuned feature maps $\mathcal{F}_i$ and $\mathcal{F}_j$. Concordance index (C-indices) [22] are commonly used to measure the goodness-of-fit of logistic regression models for binary outcomes. The definition is as follows:

$$C_{index}(\mathbb{D}_{in}) = \frac{1}{M} \sum_{i:\delta_i=1} \sum_{j:T_i<T_j} I[(T_i, X_i) < (T_j, X_j)], \qquad (6.35)$$

where M represents the sum of pairs of patients for comparison, $I[\cdot]$ represents the indicator function and T represents the truth. In the C-index value range, 0 is the lowest and 1 is the highest. It is also true that a model with a higher C-index value is better able to predict, and vice versa. The worst scenario is represented by 0, the best by 1, and the random estimation by 0.5. It should be noted that the C-index indicator matrix has a distinct feature, as indicated following:

$$I(X_i, X_j) + I(X_j, X_i) = 1, \qquad (6.36)$$

which indicates that this task's goal function needs to satisfy this characteristic, i.e., $F(X_i, X_j) = 1 - F(X_j, X_i)$.

By using the Bayesian optimization criteria, it is possible to learn and monitor the concordance index in an alternative way to the usual calculation process. Optimum pairwise ranking is the goal of formulation, i.e., increasing $P(\Theta|\mathbb{D}_{in})$ as much as possible in the formulation (6.37):

$$P(\Theta|\widetilde{\mathbb{D}_{in}}) = \frac{P(\Theta)P(\widetilde{\mathbb{D}_{in}}|\Theta)}{P(\widetilde{\mathbb{D}_{in}})} \propto P(\Theta)P(\widetilde{\mathbb{D}_{in}}|\Theta) := \widetilde{\mathcal{I}(\mathbb{D}_{in})}, \quad (6.37)$$

where Θ stands for the parameter vector, and $\widetilde{\mathbb{D}_{in}}$ represents input data $\mathbb{D}_{in}$ latent representations. In each set of data, predictions and rankings are independent. As a result, the model's purpose is revised to maximize the following formulation (6.38):

$$C_{index}(\mathbb{D}_{in}) = \mathcal{I}(\mathbb{D}_{in}) \odot \widetilde{\mathcal{I}(\mathbb{D}_{in})}. \quad (6.38)$$

In the formulation above, the likelihood function $P(\widetilde{\mathbb{D}_{in}}|\Theta)$ is computed as follows:

$$P(\widetilde{\mathbb{D}_{in}}|\Theta) := \sum_{i,j \in \mathbb{D}_{in}} F(i, j). \quad (6.39)$$

As for the target function F, the formula is as follows:

$$F(i, j) = \delta(\widehat{X_{ij}}(\Theta)), \delta(x) := \frac{1}{1 + e^{-x}}, \quad (6.40)$$

where $\widehat{X_{ij}}(\Theta)$ the operation fulfilling $\widehat{X_{ij}}(\Theta) = -\widehat{X_{ji}}(\Theta)$. In the model, $\widehat{X_{ij}}(\Theta) := \mathbb{W} \cdot (X_i(\Theta) - X_j(\Theta))^\top$, where $\mathbb{W}^{1 \times C_n}$ stands for a vector of linear weights and $X_i(\Theta) \in \mathbb{R}^{1 \times C_n}$ is the last layer's output with squeezing. Furthermore, a variance-covariance matrix Σ_Θ is used to determine a broad prior density $P(\Theta)$ based on a zero-mean normal distribution:

$$P(\Theta) \sim N(0, \Sigma_\Theta). \quad (6.41)$$

As a result, the BCR loss is developed as follows:

$$Loss = -\log\left(\delta(\mathbb{W} \cdot (X_i - X_j)^\top)\right). \quad (6.42)$$

Using the target function F, the final predictions are generated.

6.6.1.2 Experiments

Evaluation metric. Each model's ability to predict survival is measured by its C-index [22]. Furthermore, evaluation measures such as Receiver Operating Characteristic (ROC) [13] are also used. The data is divided into two groups based on real-time survival time: high and low, signifying a favorable prognosis and a bad prognosis,

Table 6.2 Data set Statistics.

Datasets	Cancer Type	Subset		Whole		Quality	Avg. Size
		No. Patient	No. WSI	No. Patient	No. WSI		
TCGA	LUSC	463	535	504	1612	Medium	0.72GB
TCGA	GBM	365	491	617	2053	Low	0.50GB
NLST	ADC & SCC	263	425	452	1225	High	0.74GB

respectively. Based on ranking prediction, the hazard of each sample is used as a classification criterion. Based on different thresholds, the area under the curve (AUC) is illustrated in Fig. 6.13.

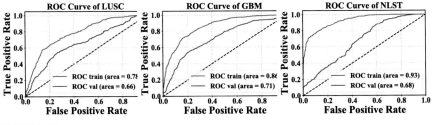

FIGURE 6.13

The proposed RankSurv method's ROC curves on three data sets. This figure is from [10].

Compared methods. Among the state-of-the-art methods compared in the experiments are: Several state-of-the-art methods are selected for comparison:

- DeepConvSurv [48] is a survival prediction model using CNN first. In this method, WSI samples are directly used for CNN training.
- WSISA [49] introduces another estimation model using CNN, which comprises multiple discrete steps for separately training numerous DeepConvSurv models.
- GCN [28] is a model built on a general graph convolutional network. The sampled patches provide an additional baseline for the survival prediction job, with the graph structure formed from the sampled patches.
- DeepGraphSurv [31] takes into account topological connections using spectral GCN. The Cox regression model [5] is used in its regression model.
- Multi-instance Learning for Survival Prediction (MILSurv) [42] presents a model that takes into account several slides from a single patient and predicts based on global representations.

Data sets. The suggested method here is evaluated using 3 data sets, 1 brain carcinoma data and 2 lung cancer data from the TCGA database [25]. The statistics of these data sets are shown in Table 6.2. There are two ways to use these three data sets. On the one hand, for the training and evaluation, RankSurv follows the experimental settings of earlier approaches [31,49,43], i.e., randomly using the same experimental settings as earlier approaches. These data sets are known as "Subset" data sets

Table 6.3 Experimental results of different methods on subset data set and whole data set ("†" stands for the significance testing, $p\text{-}value < 0.001$).

Methods	Datasets					
	Subset Data set			Whole Data set		
	LUSC	GBM	NLST	LUSC	GBM	NLST
DeepConvSurv [48]	0.5784	0.5231	0.5144	0.4962	0.5008	0.4933
GCN [28]	0.6280	0.5901	0.6687	0.5923	0.6044	0.5910
DeepGraphSurv [31]	0.6606	0.6215	0.7066	0.5964	0.5877	0.6212
WSISA [49]	0.6380	0.5760	0.6539	0.6076	0.5789	0.5836
MILSurv [42]	–	0.6570	0.6780	0.6235	0.6165	0.6354
RankSurv	**0.6791**†	**0.6722**†	**0.7183**†	**0.6608**†	**0.6627**†	**0.6820**†

since they are utilized in this way. On the other hand, on the entire data set derived from these three data sets, we train and compare the suggested approach with its competitors. The data sets utilized in this way are referred to as "Whole" data sets. Parameter are determined using five-fold cross-validation within randomly selected training data sets. A comparison of the mean performance is performed for each set of parameter values.

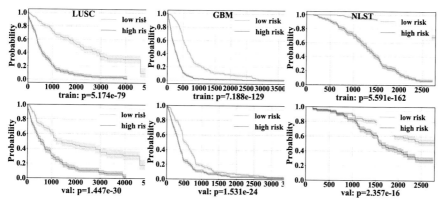

FIGURE 6.14

The proposed RankSurv method's KM-estimation curves on three data sets. This figure is from [10].

Results and discussions. Table 6.3 outlines the comparing results of all approaches. Table 6.3 indicates the following observations based on quantitative data. In the actual world, patients may just be concerned with whether their present ailment is significant or not. Therefore, logistic regression could be used to classify prognosis into two groups: high and low. RankSurv performs admirably in this assignment. Therefore, we obtain the AUC curve given in Fig. 6.13 on three data sets. Furthermore, the univariate KM-estimation [26], according to Fig. 6.14, might be used to determine the overall difference between groups with high and low prognosis. As a result of

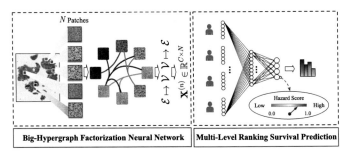

FIGURE 6.15

The illustration of the two-stage pipeline. This figure is from [9].

RankSurv's hazard prediction, all samples are classified as high or low. P-values with log rank and substantial variations in probability curves of the high and low categories demonstrate the validity of the conclusion.

6.6.2 Big hyper-graph factorization neural network for survival prediction from whole slide image

In this subsection, we further briefly introduce the designed big hyper-graph neural network [9] for tackling large-scale data.

Histopathological whole-slide imaging (WSI) has become increasingly popular as a tool for predicting patient survival in recent years. Because of the large amount of pixel data included in a gigapixel WSI, it is difficult to effectively use cell-level structural data. In recent research, graph-based models are usually constructed from a small set of image patches. On the other hand, the sampling scale is one of the major bottlenecks since it prevents transductive learning from expanding.

To circumvent the sample size barrier while building a large hyper-graph, we suggest the factorization neural network, which separately integrates the connection between sizable vertices as well as hyper-edges to semantic spaces with 2 low dimensions, allowing for dense sampling. Fig. 6.15 and Fig. 6.16 show the framework and the factorization module of the proposed model. After compressing low-dimensional relationship representations for each WSI, the hyper-graph convolutional layers provide global representations. As well as multi-level ranking supervision, metric-driven learning is accomplished by learning from patients on the global horizon. Multiple tests are performed on 3 publicly available cancer data sets and compared to baselines, the suggested approaches consistently outperforms them.

When sampling 8000 patches per WSI, the b-HGFN beats all other methods, as seen in Fig. 6.17. For example, achieves relative improvements of 1.91%, 1.71% and 1.50% on three data sets, respectively, when compared to RankSurv. Besides that, the proposed method significantly outperforms RankSurv.

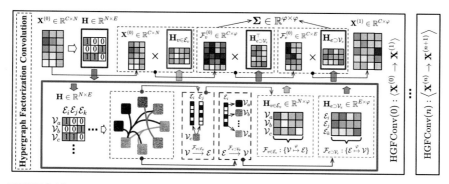

FIGURE 6.16

The illustration of how the Big-Hyper-graph Factorization Neural Network (b-HGFN) extract a high-order representation from patches. There are two matrices, **H** and **X**, which represent the incidence matrices and feature, respectively. Factorization is represented by the green frame. An input frame is shown in red. Vertices and hyper-edges output incidence matrices are represented by orange and blue frames, respectively. Above are three dot frames that illustrate the entire convolution process. This figure is from [9].

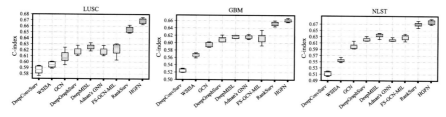

FIGURE 6.17

Comparison of the C-index for b-HGFN and other methods. This figure is from [9].

6.7 Conclusions

In this chapter, we have begun with the preliminary of hyper-graph and have presented the flexible and effective hyper-graph learning methods. Furthermore, we have reviewed some typical applications of hyper-graph learning in medical image analysis and elaborated on two applications, i.e., identification of diseases with CT imaging and survival prediction on whole slide images.

References

[1] Adam Bernheim, et al., Chest CT findings in coronavirus disease-19 (COVID-19): relationship to duration of infection, Radiology (2020) 200463.
[2] Christopher J.C. Burges, From ranknet to lambdarank to lambdamart: an overview, Learning 11 (23-581) (2010) 81.

[3] Dmitrii Bychkov, et al., Deep learning based tissue analysis predicts outcome in colorectal cancer, Scientific Reports 8 (1) (2018) 1–11.

[4] Nanshan Chen, et al., Epidemiological and clinical characteristics of 99 cases of 2019 novel coronavirus pneumonia in Wuhan, China: a descriptive study, The Lancet 395 (10223) (2020) 507–513.

[5] David R. Cox, Regression models and life-tables, Journal of the Royal Statistical Society, Series B, Methodological 34 (2) (1972) 187–202.

[6] Michaël Defferrard, et al., Convolutional neural networks on graphs with fast localized spectral filtering, in: NeurIPS, 2016, pp. 3844–3852.

[7] Donglin Di, et al., Hypergraph learning for identification of COVID-19 with CT imaging, arXiv preprint, arXiv:2005.04043, 2020.

[8] Donglin Di, et al., Hypergraph learning for identification of COVID-19 with CT imaging, Medical Image Analysis 68 (2021) 101910.

[9] Donglin Di, et al., Big-hypergraph factorization neural network for survival prediction from whole slide image, IEEE Transactions on Image Processing (2022).

[10] Donglin Di, et al., Ranking-based survival prediction on histopathological whole-slide images, in: MICCAI, Springer, 2020, pp. 428–438.

[11] Pei Dong, et al., Multi-atlas segmentation of anatomical brain structures using hierarchical hypergraph learning, IEEE Transactions on Neural Networks and Learning Systems 31 (8) (2019) 3061–3072.

[12] Yicheng Fang, et al., Sensitivity of chest CT for COVID-19: comparison to RT-PCR, Radiology (2020) 200432.

[13] Tom Fawcett, An introduction to ROC analysis, Pattern Recognition Letters 27 (8) (2006) 861–874.

[14] Yifan Feng, et al., Hypergraph neural networks, in: AAAI, vol. 33, 2019, pp. 3558–3565.

[15] Yarin Gal, et al., Dropout as a Bayesian approximation: representing model uncertainty in deep learning, in: ICML, 2016, pp. 1050–1059.

[16] Yue Gao, et al., Medical image retrieval using multi-graph learning for MCI diagnostic assistance, in: MICCAI, Springer, 2015, pp. 86–93.

[17] Yue Gao, et al., 3-D object retrieval and recognition with hypergraph analysis, IEEE Transactions on Image Processing 21 (9) (2012) 4290–4303.

[18] Yue Gao, et al., Hypergraph learning: methods and practices, IEEE Transactions on Pattern Analysis and Machine Intelligence (2020).

[19] Yue Gao, et al., MCI identification by joint learning on multiple MRI data, in: MICCAI, Springer, 2015, pp. 78–85.

[20] Yue Gao, et al., Visual-textual joint relevance learning for tag-based social image search, IEEE Transactions on Image Processing 22 (1) (2012) 363–376.

[21] Ophir Gozes, et al., Rapid AI development cycle for the coronavirus (COVID-19) pandemic: initial results for automated detection & patient monitoring using deep learning ct image analysis, arXiv preprint, arXiv:2003.05037, 2020.

[22] Patrick J. Heagerty, et al., Survival model predictive accuracy and ROC curves, Biometrics 61 (1) (2005) 92–105.

[23] Michelle L. Holshue, et al., First case of 2019 novel coronavirus in the United States, The New England Journal of Medicine (2020).

[24] Jianwen Jiang, et al., Dynamic hypergraph neural networks, in: IJCAI, AAAI Press, 2019, pp. 2635–2641.

[25] Cyriac Kandoth, et al., Mutational landscape and significance across 12 major cancer types, Nature 502 (7471) (2013) 333.

[26] Edward L. Kaplan, et al., Nonparametric estimation from incomplete observations, Journal of the American Statistical Association 53 (282) (1958) 457–481.

[27] Alex Kendall, et al., What uncertainties do we need in Bayesian deep learning for computer vision?, in: NeurIPS, 2017, pp. 5574–5584.

[28] Thomas N. Kipf, et al., Semi-supervised classification with graph convolutional networks, in: ICLR, 2016.

[29] Lin Li, et al., Artificial intelligence distinguishes COVID-19 from community acquired pneumonia on chest CT, Radiology (2020) 200905.

[30] Qun Li, et al., Early transmission dynamics in Wuhan, China, of novel coronavirus–infected pneumonia, The New England Journal of Medicine (2020).

[31] Ruoyu Li, et al., Graph CNN for survival analysis on whole slide pathological images, in: MICCAI, Springer, 2018, pp. 174–182.

[32] Mingxia Liu, et al., View-aligned hypergraph learning for Alzheimer's disease diagnosis with incomplete multi-modality data, Medical Image Analysis 36 (2017) 123–134.

[33] Ali Narin, Ceren Kaya, Ziynet Pamuk, Automatic detection of coronavirus disease (Covid-19) using x-ray images and deep convolutional neural networks, Pattern Analysis & Applications 24 (3) (2021) 1207–1220.

[34] General Office of National Health Committee, et al., Office of state administration of traditional Chinese medicine, in: Notice on the Issuance of a Programme for the Diagnosis and Treatment of Novel Coronavirus (2019-nCoV) Infected Pneumonia (Trial Version 5), 2020.

[35] Nobuyuki Otsu, A threshold selection method from gray-level histograms, IEEE Transactions on Systems, Man and Cybernetics 9 (1) (1979) 62–66.

[36] Fei Shan, et al., Lung infection quantification of COVID-19 in CT images with deep learning, arXiv preprint, arXiv:2003.04655, 2020.

[37] Heyuan Shi, et al., Hypergraph-induced convolutional networks for visual classification, IEEE Transactions on Neural Networks and Learning Systems 30 (10) (2018) 2963–2972.

[38] Karen Simonyan, et al., Very deep convolutional networks for large-scale image recognition, arXiv:1409.1556, 2014.

[39] Yong Sub Song, et al., Volume and mass doubling times of persistent pulmonary subsolid nodules detected in patients without known malignancy, Radiology 273 (1) (2014) 276–284.

[40] Dawei Wang, et al., Clinical characteristics of 138 hospitalized patients with 2019 novel coronavirus–infected pneumonia in Wuhan, China, JAMA (2020).

[41] Xingzhi Xie, et al., Chest CT for typical 2019-nCoV pneumonia: relationship to negative RT-PCR testing, Radiology (2020) 200343.

[42] Jiawen Yao, et al., Deep multi-instance learning for survival prediction from whole slide images, in: MICCAI, Springer, 2019, pp. 496–504.

[43] Jiawen Yao, et al., Deep correlational learning for survival prediction from multi-modality data, in: MICCAI, Springer, 2017, pp. 406–414.

[44] Jianpeng Zhang, et al., Covid-19 screening on chest x-ray images using deep learning based anomaly detection, arXiv preprint, arXiv:2003.12338, 2020.

[45] Zizhao Zhang, et al., Diagnosis of childhood autism using multi-modal functional connectivity via dynamic hypergraph learning, in: CAAI International Conference on Artificial Intelligence, Springer, 2021, pp. 123–135.

[46] Zizhao Zhang, et al., Inductive multi-hypergraph learning and its application on view-based 3D object classification, IEEE Transactions on Image Processing 27 (12) (2018) 5957–5968.

[47] Denny Zhou, et al., Learning with hypergraphs: clustering, classification, and embedding, in: NeurIPS, 2007, pp. 1601–1608.

[48] Xinliang Zhu, et al., Deep convolutional neural network for survival analysis with pathological images, in: BIBM, IEEE, 2016, pp. 544–547.

[49] Xinliang Zhu, et al., Wsisa: making survival prediction from whole slide histopathological images, in: CVPR, 2017, pp. 7234–7242.

Unsupervised domain adaptation for medical image analysis

7

Yuexiang Li, Luyan Liu, Cheng Bian, Kai Ma, and Yefeng Zheng

Tencent Jarvis Lab, Shenzhen, China

7.1 Introduction

With the recent development of deep learning, an increasing number of studies tried to develop computer aided diagnosis (CAD) system for medical images. Although the existing studies significantly improved the diagnosis performance of CAD systems, the generality of the established models was merely investigated as data from single source domain was often used. Such a single-domain-trained model usually fails to generalize well to the test set collected from another domain. As illustrated in Fig. 7.1, the colonoscopic video frames collected by CVC-Clinic [1] is warm-toned (higher red intensity) compared to the ones from the ETIS-Larib center [2]; the fundus images captured by different instruments (Zeiss Visucam 500 vs. Canon) have different illuminations and the intensity distribution is totally different between magnetic resonance imaging (MRI) and computed tomography (CT) images. Such data distribution variation between model's training and test data sets is referred to as the domain shift problem. Domain adaptation (DA) is one of the effective methods to alleviate the problem of domain shift between multi-centers and accordingly improve the generalization capability of models, i.e., transferring the trained models to novel data sets and tasks (target domain) that have obvious data distribution difference to their training data (source domain) [3,4]. Most of existing DA methods align the feature distributions of source and target domains in a shared space by optimizing deep models to minimize some measure of domain shift such as maximum mean discrepancy (MMD) or correlation distances. For example, the deep domain confusion method [5] used MMD to learn a representation that was both discriminative and domain-invariant. The deep adaptation network [6] applied MMD to embedding layers to match higher-order statistics of the source and target distributions. In contrast, Yang et al. [7] proposed to learn a shared semantic space with correlation alignment for multi-modal data representations. However, those works require the prior knowledge of data annotation in the target domain, which limits their applications for general tasks.

Loosening the requirement of labeled samples in the target domain, unsupervised domain adaptation (UDA) methods have received more and more attention in the

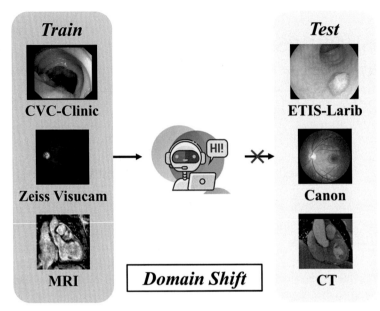

FIGURE 7.1

Illustration of the domain shift problem encountered in medical image processing. There are gaps between centers (CVC-Clinic vs. ETIS-Larib), instruments (Zeiss Visucam vs. Canon) and modalities (MRI vs. CT). The models trained on one domain usually fail to generalize well to another.

community. These methods are closely related to generative adversarial learning [8] in that they minimize the distribution discrepancy by attempting to deceive a co-trained discriminator to ensure the distribution of source and target domain samples indistinguishable. Ajakan et al. [9] proposed a domain-adversarial neural network to transfer domain knowledge, which introduces an adversarial training objective to learn a representation that cannot discriminate between the source and target domains. Benjdira et al. [10] proposed a UDA method for the context of semantic segmentation, which transfers an RGB (i.e., red, green and blue) image to a near infrared red-green image based on CycleGAN [11]. Cycle-consistent adversarial DA (CyCADA) [12] trained CycleGAN and the segmentation network simultaneously to deal with the source and target domains with similar styles but different patterns. The CoGAN method [13] adopted two GANs to generate the source and target images, respectively, and enforced the high-level layer parameters of the two GANs to learn a domain-invariant feature space. Aside from having similar hard weight-sharing constraints, UNIT [14], as an extension of CoGAN, assumed that there existed a shared-latent space in which a pair of corresponding images from different domains could be mapped to the same latent representation. Through such latent representation, the domain adaptation can be accomplished. To further increase the output diversity, Lee et al. [15] proposed a disentangled representation framework, namely, DRIT, with

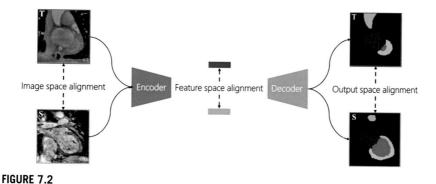

FIGURE 7.2

Different types of UDA approaches align the information of source and target domains at different stages of network training.

unpaired training data. DRIT embedded images into two spaces—a domain-invariant content space capturing shared information across domains, and a domain-specific attribute space to achieve diversity of the translated results. For the application on a medical image, Rau et al. [16] implemented a pix2pix [17] framework to synthesize endoscopic images. This method required pairwise data (i.e., endoscopic and depth images) for network training, which is difficult to fulfill in practical applications. In contrast, Mahmood et al. [18] proposed an unsupervised approach for medical image synthesis, which loosened the requirement of paired training data, i.e., producing synthetic data only using the endoscopic images. Chen et al. [19] transferred the X-ray images from a new data set to the domain of training images before testing using a GAN model. Such an adaptation increases the test accuracy. Similarly, Zhang et al. [20] also proposed a task driven generative adversarial network to translate X-ray images between different domains. More recently, various domain adaptation approaches [21–25] have been proposed, which introduced novel ideas, such as self-supervised learning [24] and active learning [25], into the area of unsupervised domain adaptation.

According to the alignment spaces between source and target domains, current UDA approaches can be grouped to three categories: image space alignment, feature space alignment and output space alignment. As shown in Fig. 7.2, different kinds of unsupervised domain adaptation approaches align the data from two domains in different stages of the training of segmentation network (i.e., the encoder and decoder in Fig. 7.2). Concretely, the image space alignment based methods aim to perform image-to-image (I2I) translation to narrow down the gap of image style between source and target images before the training of segmentation network. For the feature space alignment based approaches, they align the features of source and target images extracted by the segmentation network in the shared latent space during the network training. The output space alignment based methods usually add modules at the end of segmentation network to align the predictions of source and target images.

It is worthwhile to mention that image space alignment based methods are task-agnostic, compared to the task-specific feature/output space alignment-based domain adaptation. Concretely, the image space alignment-based UDA approaches translate images from source domain to the target domain without manual annotations. The translated images can be used to train a network with any kind of labels, e.g., image-level label for classification or pixelwise annotations for segmentation. In contrast, the target task for feature/output space alignment based approaches needs to be pre-defined (e.g., classification or segmentation), since they require the labels of source images for domain alignment. In other words, for the task-agnostic image space alignment-based UDA approaches, the manual annotations are used after the step of domain adaptation, i.e., separated training steps, while the task-specific feature/output space alignment based approaches jointly optimize the domain adaptation and the specific application-oriented task.

Following, we will introduce each kind of UDA approaches in detail. The introduction of image space alignment based UDA approaches is presented in Section 7.2. Then we present the mechanism underlying feature space alignment in Section 7.3. The detailed information of output space alignment is provided in Section 7.5. In Section 7.6, we give a conclusion to this chapter.

7.2 Image space alignment

Witnessing the success of cycle-consistency-based approaches (e.g., CycleGAN [11], DiscoGAN [26] and DualGAN [27]), an increasing number of researchers [28–31] made their efforts to the area of unpaired I2I translation. However, recent studies [32,33] proved that cycle-consistency-based frameworks easily suffer from the problem of content distortion during image translation. Let T be a bijective geometric transformation (e.g., translation, rotation, scaling or even nonrigid transformation) with inverse transformation T^{-1}, the following generators G'_{AB} and G'_{BA} are also cycle consistent:

$$G'_{AB} = G_{AB}T, \ G'_{BA} = G_{BA}T^{-1}, \tag{7.1}$$

where the G_{AB} and G_{BA} are the original cycle-consistent generators establishing two mappings between domains A and B. Consequently, due to lack of penalty in content disparity between source and translated images, the content of a translated image by cycle-consistency-based frameworks may be distorted by T, which is unacceptable in medical image processing.

To tackle the problem, we introduce a novel **GAN** (MI^{2}GAN) [34] to maintain the contents of **Medical Image** during I2I domain adaptation by maximizing the **Mutual Information** between the source and translated images. Our idea relies on two observations: 1) the content features containing the information of image-objects can be fully disentangled from the domain information; and 2) the mutual information, measuring the information that two variables share, can be used as a metric for image-object preservation. Mutual information constraint has been widely used for various

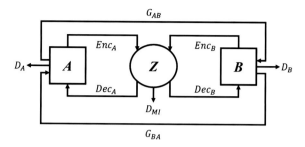

FIGURE 7.3

The framework of our MI²GAN. Similar to CycleGAN [11], our MI²GAN adopts paired generators (G_{AB} and G_{BA}) and discriminators (D_B and D_A) to achieve cross-domain image translation. To preserve image-contents, X-shape dual auto-encoders ($\{Enc_A, Dec_A\}$ and $\{Enc_B, Dec_B\}$) and a mutual information discriminator (D_{MI}) are implemented.

medical image processing tasks, such as image registration [35]. Given two variables X and Y, the mutual information I shared by X and Y can be formulated as

$$I(X; Y) = KL(\mathbb{J}||\mathbb{M}), \tag{7.2}$$

where $\mathbb{J}$ and $\mathbb{M}$ are joint distribution and the product of marginals of X and Y, respectively; KL is the Kullback–Leibler divergence. Specifically, $\mathbb{J} = p(y|x)p(x)$ and $\mathbb{M} = p(y)p(x)$, where $x \in X$ and $y \in Y$; $p(x)$ and $p(y)$ are the distributions of X and Y, respectively; and $p(y|x)$ is the conditional probability of y given x.

Since the posterior probability $p(y|x)$ is difficult to be directly estimated [36], we measure and maximize the MI between source and translated images based on the approach similar to [37]. Specifically, the content features of source and translated images are first extracted by the paired adversarial auto-encoders, which are then fed to a discriminator for the estimation of mutual information. Extensive experiments are conducted to validate the effectiveness of our MI²GAN. The experimental results demonstrate that the proposed MI²GAN can not only produce plausible translated images, but also significantly reduce the performance degradation caused by the domain shift.

7.2.1 MI²GAN

The pipeline of our MI²GAN is presented in Fig. 7.3. Similar to current cycle-consistency-based GAN [11], our MI²GAN adopts paired generators (G_{AB} and G_{BA}) and discriminators (D_B and D_A) to achieve cross-domain image translation without paired training samples. To distill the content features from domain information, X-shape dual auto-encoders (i.e., Enc_A, Dec_A, Enc_B and Dec_B) are implemented. The encoders (i.e., Enc_A and Enc_B) are responsible to embed the content information of source and translated images into the same latent space Z, while the decoders (i.e., Dec_A and Dec_B) aim to transform the embedded content features to their own do-

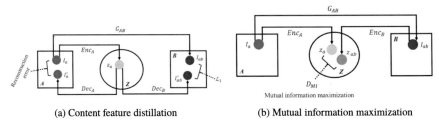

(a) Content feature distillation   (b) Mutual information maximization

FIGURE 7.4

The pipelines of the main components contained in our framework. (a) X-shape dual auto-encoders for content feature distillation and (b) mutual information maximization via a discriminator.

mains using domain-related information. Therefore, to alleviate the content distortion problem during image translation, we only need to maximize the mutual information between the content features of source and translated images, which is achieved by our mutual information discriminator. In the following, we present the modules for content feature disentanglement and mutual information maximization in detail.

7.2.1.1 X-shape dual auto-encoders

We propose the X-shape dual auto-encoders (AEs), consisting of Enc_A, Dec_A, Enc_B and Dec_B, to disentangle the features containing content information. As the mappings between domains A and B are symmetrical, we take the content feature distillation of images from domain A as an example. The pipeline is shown in Fig. 7.4(a). Given an input image (I_a), the auto-encoder (Enc_A and Dec_A) embeds it into a latent space z_a and then reconstructs it back as I'_a, which can be formulated as

$$z_a = Enc_A(I_a), \quad I'_a = Dec_A(z_a). \tag{7.3}$$

The embedded feature z_a contains the information of content and domain A. To disentangle them, z_a is mapped to domain B via Dec_B:

$$I'_{ab} = Dec_B(z_a), \tag{7.4}$$

where I'_{ab} is the mapping result of z_a.

As shown in Fig. 7.4, apart from the X-shape dual AEs, there is another translation path between domains A and B: $I_{ab} = G_{AB}(I_a)$, where I_{ab} is the translated image yielded by G_{AB}. Through simultaneously minimizing the pixel-wise L1 norm between I_{ab} and I'_{ab}, and reconstruction error between I_a and $I_{a'}$, Dec_A and Dec_B are encouraged to recover domain-related information from the latent space (in short, the encoders remove domain information and the decoders recover it), which enable them to map the z_a to two different domains. Therefore the information contained in z_a is highly related to the image-objects without domain bias. The content feature distillation loss ($\mathcal{L}_{dis}$), combining aforementioned two terms, can be formulated as

$$\mathcal{L}_{dis} = ||I_{ab} - I'_{ab}||_1 + ||I_a - I_{a'}||_1. \tag{7.5}$$

7.2.1.2 Mutual information discriminator

Using our X-shape dual AEs, the content features of source I_a and translated I_{ab} images can be disentangled to z_a and z_{ab}, respectively. The content feature of translated image preserving image-objects should contain similar information to that of source image. To this end, the encoder (Enc_B) needs to implicitly impose statistical constraints onto learned representations, which thereby pushes the translated distribution of Z_{ab} to match the source Z_a (i.e., mutual information maximization between Z_a and Z_{ab}, as shown in Fig. 7.4), where Z_{ab} and Z_a are two sub-spaces of Z.

Exploiting adversarial training, which matches the distribution of synthesized images to that of real ones, this can be achieved by training a mutual information discriminator (D_{MI}) to distinguish between samples coming from the joint distribution, $\mathbb{J}$, and the product of marginals, $\mathbb{M}$, of the two sub-spaces Z_a and Z_{ab} [37]. We use a lower bound to the mutual information ($\mathcal{I}$ defined in Eq. (7.2)) based on the Donsker–Varadhan representation of the KL-divergence, which can be formulated as

$$\mathcal{I}(Z_a; Z_{ab}) \geq \widehat{\mathcal{I}}^{(DV)}(Z_a; Z_{ab}) = \mathbb{E}_{\mathbb{J}}\left[D_{MI}(z_a, z_{ab})\right] - \log \mathbb{E}_{\mathbb{M}}\left[e^{D_{MI}(z_a, z_{ab})}\right] \quad (7.6)$$

where $D_{MI} : z_a \times z_{ab} \to \mathbb{R}$ is a discriminator function modeled by a neural network.

To constitute the real ($\mathbb{J}$) and fake ($\mathbb{M}$) samples for the D_{MI}, an image is randomly selected from domain B and encoded to z_b. The z_a is then concatenated to z_{ab} and z_b, respectively, which forms the samples from the joint distribution ($\mathbb{J}$) and the product of marginals ($\mathbb{M}$) for the mutual information discriminator.

7.2.1.3 Objective

With the previously defined feature distillation loss ($\mathcal{L}_{dis}$) and mutual information discriminator, the full objective $\mathcal{L}$ for the proposed MI^{2}GAN is summarized as

$$\begin{aligned}
\mathcal{L} = &\mathcal{L}_{adv}(G_{BA}, D_A) + \mathcal{L}_{adv}(G_{AB}, D_B) + \alpha \mathcal{L}_{cyc}(G_{AB}, G_{BA}) \\
&+ \beta \mathcal{L}_{dis}(G_{AB}, Enc_A, Dec_A, Dec_B) + \beta \mathcal{L}_{dis}(G_{BA}, Enc_B, Dec_B, Dec_A) \quad (7.7) \\
&+ \widehat{\mathcal{I}}(G_{AB}, Enc_A, Enc_B, D_{MI}) + \widehat{\mathcal{I}}(G_{BA}, Enc_A, Enc_B, D_{MI})
\end{aligned}$$

where $\mathcal{L}_{adv}$ and $\mathcal{L}_{cyc}$ are adversarial and cycle-consistency losses, respectively, the same as those proposed in [11]. The weights α and β to balance $\mathcal{L}_{cyc}$ and $\mathcal{L}_{dis}$, respectively, are both set to 10.

7.2.2 Implementation details

In this section, the implementation details are provided. The proposed MI^{2}GAN is implemented using PyTorch. The whole framework is trained for 100 epochs with the Adam solver [38]. The initial learning rate is set to 0.0001 and the images are resized to 512×512 pixels.

7.2.2.1 Network architecture

Consistent to the standard CycleGAN [11], the proposed MI^{2}GAN has pair-wise generators (G_{AB}, G_{BA}) and discriminators (D_B, D_A). Furthermore, the generators

Table 7.1 The architecture of encoder. The Conv and IN denote the convolutional and instance normalization layers, respectively. The "Layer Info" contains the parameters of convolutional layers (number of channels, kernel size, stride and padding). The input size is 512×512 pixels.

Layers	Encoder	Layer Info	Output size
1	Conv, IN, ReLU	(64, 3, 1, 1)	512×512
2	Conv, IN, ReLU	(128, 4, 2, 1)	256×256
3	Conv, IN, ReLU	(192, 4, 2, 1)	128×128
4	Conv, IN, ReLU	(256, 4, 2, 1)	64×64
5	Conv	(256, 1, 1, 0)	64×64

Table 7.2 The architecture of mutual information discriminator. The Conv, IN and L-ReLU denote the convolutional, instance normalization and leaky ReLU layers, respectively. The "Layer Info" contains the parameters of convolutional layers (number of channels, kernel size, stride and padding). The input feature size is 64×64 pixels.

Layers	Discriminator	Layer Info	Output size
1	Conv, L-ReLU	(64, 4, 2, 1)	32×32
2	Conv, IN, L-ReLU	(128, 4, 2, 1)	16×16
3	Conv, IN, L-ReLU	(256, 4, 2, 1)	8×8
4	Conv, IN, L-R LU	(512, 4, 2, 1)	4×4
4	Conv, IN, L-ReLU	(512, 4, 1, 1)	2×2
4	Conv	(1, 4, 1, 1)	2×2

employ instance normalization [39] to produce plausible translated images, while the discriminators adopt the PatchGAN architecture [17,40] to yield patchwise predictions. The architectures of encoders (Enc_A and Enc_B) and mutual information discriminator are presented in Table 7.1 and Table 7.2, respectively.

7.2.2.2 Optimization process

The optimization of $\mathcal{L}_{dis}$ and $\widehat{I}$ is performed in the same manner of $\mathcal{L}_{adv}$—fixing X-shape dual AEs, D_{MI} and D_A/D_B to optimize G_{BA}/G_{AB} first, and then optimize AEs, D_{MI} and D_A/D_B, respectively, with fixed G_{BA}/G_{AB}. Therefore, similar to discriminators, our X-shape dual AEs and mutual information discriminator can directly pass the knowledge of image-objects to the generators, which helps them to improve the quality of translated results in terms of object preservation.

7.2.3 Experiments

Deep neural networks often suffer from performance degradation when applied to a new test data set with domain shift (e.g., color and illumination difference) caused by different imaging conditions. Our MI^{2}GAN tries to address the problem by translating the test images to the same domain of the training set. In this section, to validate the effectiveness of the proposed MI^{2}GAN, we evaluate it on several publicly available data sets.

7.2.3.1 Data sets

Colonoscopic data sets. The publicly available colonoscopic video data sets, i.e., CVC-Clinic (CVC for short) [1] and ETIS-Larib (ETIS for short) [2], are selected for multi-center adaptation. The CVC data set is composed of 29 sequences with a total of 612 images. The ETIS consists of 196 images, which can be manually separated to 29 sequences as well. These short videos were extracted from the colonoscopy videos captured by different centers using different endoscopic devices. All the frames of the short videos contain polyps. In this experiment, the extremely small ETIS data set (196 frames) is used as the test set, while the relatively larger CVC data set (612 frames) is used for network optimization (80:20 for training and validation).

REFUGE. The REFUGE challenge data set [41] consists of 1200 fundus images for optic disc (OD) and optic cup (OC) segmentation, which were partitioned to training (400), validation (400) and test (400) sets by the challenge organizer. The images available in this challenge were acquired with two different fundus cameras—Zeiss Visucam 500 for the training set and Canon CR-2 for the validation and test sets, resulting in visual gap between training and validation/test samples. Since the test set is unavailable, we conduct experiment on I2I adaptation between the training and validation sets. The public training set is separated to new training and validation sets according to the ratio of 80:20, and the public validation set is used as the test set.

Baselines overview and evaluation criterion. Several unpaired image-to-image domain adaptation frameworks, including CycleGAN [11], UNIT [14] and DRIT [15], are taken as baselines for the performance evaluation. The direct transfer approach, which directly takes the source domain data for testing without any adaptation, is also involved for comparison. The Dice score (DSC), which measures the spatial overlap index between the segmentation results and ground truth, is adopted as the metric to evaluate the segmentation accuracy.

7.2.3.2 Ablation study

Content feature distillation. We invite three experienced experts to manually tune two CVC images to the domain of ETIS (as shown in the first row of Fig. 7.5), i.e., tuning the image conditions such as color and saturation based on the statistical histogram of the ETIS domain, denoted as "CVC→ETIS" in Fig. 7.5. The two paired images contain the same content information but totally different domain-related styles. To ensure our X-shape dual auto-encoders really learn to disentangle the content features from domain information, we sent the paired images to X-shape dual AEs and visualize the content features produced by Enc_A and Enc_B using class activation map (CAM) [42] (as illustrated in the second row of Fig. 7.5). For comparison, the CVC images are also sent to Enc_B for content feature distillation. It can

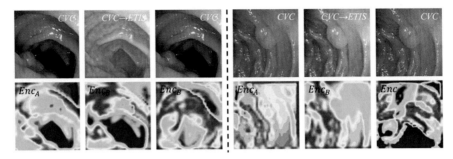

FIGURE 7.5

Content features (the second row) produced by the encoders of our X-shape dual AEs for the input images (the first row) from different domains. The "CVC→ETIS" (middle) denotes the CVC images (left) manually tuned to the ETIS domain by experienced experts.

Table 7.3 DSC (%) of the polyp segmentation on colonoscopy and the segmentation of optical cup (OC) and optical disk (OD) on REFUGE fundus images, respectively.

	Colonoscopy		Fundus			
	CVC (val.)	ETIS (test)	$OC_{val.}$	$OD_{val.}$	OC_{test}	OD_{test}
Direct transfer		64.33			81.66	93.49
DRIT [15]		28.32			64.79	69.03
UNIT [14]	80.79	23.46	85.83	95.42	71.63	74.58
CycleGAN [11]		52.41			71.53	85.83
MI²GAN (Ours)		**72.86**			**83.49**	**94.87**
MI²GAN w/o D_{MI}		65.96			77.27	92.17

be observed that the CVC and "CVC→ETIS" images, respectively, going through Enc_A and Enc_B result in the similar activation patterns, while the encoders yield different patterns for the CVC images. The experimental results demonstrate that the encoders of our X-shape dual AEs are domain-specific, which are able to remove their own domain-related information from the embedding space.

Mutual information discriminator. To validate the contribution made by the mutual information discriminator, we evaluate the performance of MI²GAN without D_{MI}. The evaluation results are presented in Table 7.3. The segmentation accuracy on the test set significantly drops to 65.96%, 77.27% and 92.17% for polyp, OC and OD, respectively, with the removal of D_{MI}, which demonstrates the importance of D_{MI} for image-content preserving domain adaptation.

7.2.3.3 Comparison to state of the art

Different I2I domain adaptation approaches are applied to the colonoscopic and fundus image data sets, respectively, which translate the test images to the domain of the training set to narrow the gap between them and improve the model generalization.

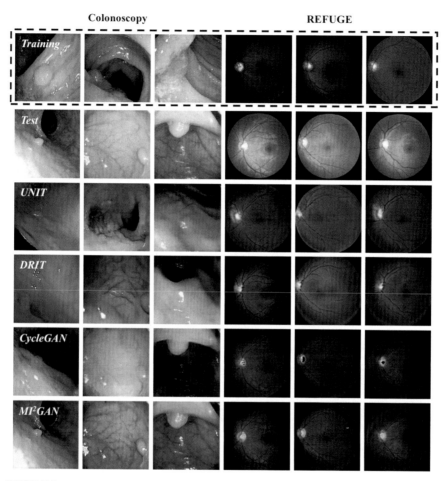

FIGURE 7.6

Comparison of images produced by different I2I adaptation approaches. Here, the test images (the second row) are transferred toward the training domain (with exemplars shown in the first row).

The adaptation results generated by different I2I domain adaptation approaches are presented in Fig. 7.6. The first row of Fig. 7.6 shows the exemplars from the training sets of colonoscopy and REFUGE data sets. Content distortions are observed in the adaptation results produced by most of the existing I2I translation approaches. In contrast, our MI^{2}GAN yields plausible adaptation results while excellently preserving the image contents.

For quantitative analysis, we present the segmentation accuracy of deep learning networks with different adaptation approaches in Table 7.3. To comprehensively assess the adaptation performance of our MI^{2}GAN, we adopt two widely-used deep learning networks, i.e., ResUNet-50 [43,44] and DeepLab-V3 [45], for the polyp segmentation and OC/OD segmentation, respectively. As shown in Table 7.3, due to the lack of capacity of image-content preservation, most of existing I2I domain adaptation approaches degrade the segmentation accuracy for both tasks, compared to the direct transfer. The DRIT [15] yields the highest degradation of DSC, -40.87%, -16.87% and -24.46% for polyp, OC and OD, respectively. Conversely, the proposed MI^{2}GAN remarkably boosts the segmentation accuracy of polyp ($+8.53\%$), OC ($+1.83\%$) and OD ($+1.38\%$) to the direct transfer, which are close to the accuracy on the validation set.

7.3 Feature space alignment

Feature space alignment based UDA methods try to align the information of source and target data in the latent space. One of the simplest way to achieve such an information alignment is using a discriminator to distinguish the origin of embedded features (from source/target images). Here, we introduce an advanced feature space alignment UDA framework [46], which utilizes the uncertainty information to improve the model performance. As shown in Fig. 7.7, the uncertainty information cannot only measure the model confidence but also directly and quantitatively reflect the inaccurate segmentation regions in the UDA task.

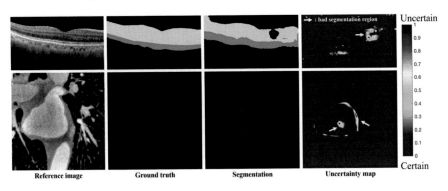

FIGURE 7.7

Examples of uncertainty maps and corresponding predictions on target domain images from the cross-domain data set. As we can see, the high energy regions of the uncertainty maps are highly related to the inaccurately segmented regions.

The proposed uncertainty-aware feature space alignment framework, as shown in Fig. 7.8, includes a transfer branch and an adaptation branch. In general, the transfer branch intends to learn meaningful features from source domain data to get accurate segmentation results, while the adaptation branch aims at adapting the target domain features to the source domain for mitigating the domain shift problem, similar to other UDA approaches [47]. Nevertheless, the proposed uncertainty estimation

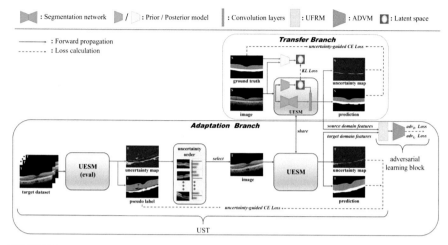

FIGURE 7.8

The workflow of the uncertainty-aware domain alignment framework. To extract the cross-domain transferable features, the ground truth, uncertainty map and prediction of the input image are used to update the uncertainty estimation and segmentation module (UESM) by uncertainty-aware cross-entropy (UCE) loss. Particularly, the Kullback–Leibler (KL) loss leverages source image and its ground truth forcing the prior model to learn the approximate distribution from the posterior model. The uncertainty-aware self-training (UST) process and adversarial learning block align the target domain and source domain features iteratively. Specifically, we implement the adversarial learning block with an uncertainty-aware feature recalibration module (UFRM) following the adversarial training module (ADVM) to finely rectify the alignment between the source and target domain features.

and segmentation module (UESM) utilizes the simultaneously estimated uncertainty information to constrain the segmentation network to focus on the low confidence regions. To update the weights of UESM in the training stage, a novel uncertainty-aware cross-entropy (UCE) loss is proposed to back propagate the conjoint uncertainty gradients. In the adaptation branch, we also propose to use an uncertainty-aware self-training (UST) process to guide the network training, starting from easy cases to hard ones to boost the domain adaptation performance progressively. Meanwhile, an adversarial learning block, including an uncertainty feature recalibration module (UFRM) that is inspired by [48] and an adversarial training module (ADVM), is introduced to finely align the feature distributions extracted by UESM from both domains.

7.3.1 Uncertainty-aware feature space domain adaptation

The core concept of the proposed method is to train a deep neural network model that accurately estimates the segmentation masks for images from different domains. To achieve the satisfactory DA performance, an adversarial learning block is applied to

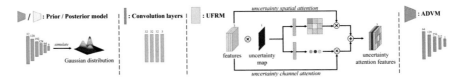

FIGURE 7.9

The detailed structures of the proposed modules corresponding to Fig. 7.8.

align the features extracted from different domains. Furthermore, in order to improve the network's performance by suppressing the low confidence regions, we propose an uncertainty estimation and segmentation module (UESM) that generates uncertainty information to guide the training process of the segmentation model. The uncertainty information is also used in a self-training scheme to help enforce the easy-to-hard sample selection strategy.

7.3.1.1 Adversarial learning block for feature space alignment

Due to the deficiency of annotations in the target domain, we adopt the adversarial learning framework to minimize the discrepancy of the feature space between source and target domains. The proposed adversarial learning block is composed of an uncertainty-based feature recalibration module (UFRM) and an adversarial training module (ADVM). Details of the modules are illustrated as in Fig. 7.9. Different from [49,50,47] that only used high-level extracted features for UDA, the proposed UFRM utilizes uncertainty information to recalibrate the extracted features for better adaptation performance in the following steps: First, it utilizes the uncertainty map to re-weight the output feature maps generated by UESM. Then it utilizes the updated feature maps to generate the channel and spatial attention weights by convolution operations. Next, it multiplies these attention weights with the original feature maps and sum them to get the uncertainty attention feature maps. Lastly, the uncertainty attention feature maps are fed to ADVM for the adversarial learning, where the adversarial losses of UESM G and domain discriminator D are defined as

$$\mathcal{L}_{adv_D} = - \mathbb{E}_{X_S \sim \mathbb{S}} \log D(R(G(X_S; \Theta_g); \Theta_r); \Theta_d)$$
$$- \mathbb{E}_{X_\mathscr{T} \sim \mathscr{T}} (1 - \log D(R(G(X_\mathscr{T}; \Theta_g); \Theta_r); \Theta_d)), \tag{7.8}$$

$$\mathcal{L}_{adv_G} = -\mathbb{E}_{X_\mathscr{T} \sim \mathscr{T}} \log D(R(G(X_\mathscr{T}; \Theta_g); \Theta_r); \Theta_d), \tag{7.9}$$

where R is the UFRM; Θ_r is the parameter of R; D is the discriminator and Θ_d is the parameter of D.

7.3.1.2 Uncertainty estimation and segmentation module

Fig. 7.9 shows the architecture details of our uncertainty estimation and segmentation module. Different from the existing methods using dropout over spatial features to estimate the uncertainty [51–53], we adopt a lightweight solution from [54] that combines a segmentation network with a conditional variational auto-encoder (CVAE) for the uncertainty estimation, where the uncertainty is measured as the variance of the network's output. To generate diverse predictions for a given image, UESM utilizes a prior network to model the distribution of the segmentation variants of the given input as an N-dimensional latent space $\mathbb{R}^N$, in which a random sampling process could be repeated infinite times to produce a unlimited number of hypotheses. The sampling process of the prior distribution is mathematically formulated as

$$\mathbf{z} \sim D_{prior}(\cdot|X) = \mathcal{N}(\mu_{prior}(X; \Theta_{prior}), diag(\sigma_{prior}(X; \Theta_{prior}))), \quad (7.10)$$

where X is a set of given images; $\mathbf{z}$ is the variant vector randomly sampled from the prior distribution $D_{prior}(\cdot|X)$, which is modeled as a multivariate Gaussian distribution (MGD); $\mu_{prior} \in \mathbb{R}^N$ and $\sigma_{prior} \in \mathbb{R}^N$ are the mean and variance of $D_{prior}(\cdot|X)$, respectively; $\mathcal{N}(\cdot)$ represents Gaussian distribution and $diag(\cdot)$ represents a diagonal matrix.

Given an input image X, we randomly draw a sample vector $\mathbf{z} \in \mathbb{R}^N$ from the prior latent space according to Eq. (7.10) and broadcast it to an N-channel latent space variable with the same size of the segmentation mask. The latent space variable is then concatenated with the feature maps of the segmentation network to generate the final segmentation mask. Such sampling process is then repeated M times (i.e., $M = 4$ in the experiments for a reasonable balance between efficiency and accuracy) to generate a series of segmentation masks $\hat{P}_1, ..., \hat{P}_M$ and the uncertainty map is estimated by calculating the variance of the segmentation masks [53]. The average prediction P_i and uncertainty U_i for the input image X_i are mathematically defined as

$$P_i = \frac{1}{M} \sum_{m=1}^{M} \hat{P}_m, \quad (7.11)$$

$$U_i = \frac{1}{M} \sum_{m=1}^{M} (\hat{P}_m - P_i)^2. \quad (7.12)$$

To train such prior network that represents the informatic latent space $\mathbb{R}^N$ with a prior distribution $D_{prior}(\cdot|X)$, a posterior network is introduced, which is utilized to model a posterior distribution by the given segmentation ground truth Y and image X. $\mu_{posterior} \in \mathbb{R}^N$ and $\sigma_{posterior} \in \mathbb{R}^N$ are learned from the posterior network to determine the posterior distribution $D_{posterior}(\cdot|X, Y)$ modeled as an MGD. The segmentation ground truth is therefore embedded into the posterior distribution. The sampling process of the posterior distribution can be formulated as

$$\mathbf{z} \sim D_{posterior}(\cdot|X, Y) = \mathcal{N}(\mu_{posterior}(X, Y; \Theta_{posterior}), \\ diag(\sigma_{posterior}(X, Y; \Theta_{posterior}))). \quad (7.13)$$

Given X_S as source images and Y_S as the corresponding segmentation ground truth, the Kullback–Leibler divergence loss is applied to pull the two distributions

---

Algorithm 7.1 The training procedure of the proposed method.

Require:

    Images from source domain $\mathbb{S}$, X_S

    Images from target domain $\mathbb{T}$, X_T

    Segmentation annotations from $\mathbb{S}$, Y_S

Ensure:

1:   Train the transfer branch without the adaptation branch until it converges (more than 2000 iterations)

2:   Initialize UESM G of the adaptation branch with the weights from step 1

3:   **while** *epoch* ≤ 50 **do**

4:       Adopt self-training scheme to select top K samples with the lowest uncertainty values from $\mathbb{T}$ to form the target subset $\mathscr{T}$

5:       **for** each sample i in $\mathscr{T}$ **do**

6:          Fix the weights of G and get pseudo mask $\hat{Y}_T^i$ from the adaptation branch

7:          Extract the features $\mathcal{F}_S^i$ of X_S^i and the features $\mathcal{F}_{\mathscr{T}}^i$ of $X_{\mathscr{T}}^i$ from G to update the discriminator network D by $\mathcal{L}_{adv_D}$

8:          Obtain prediction P_S^i of X_S^i and $P_{\mathscr{T}}^i$ of $X_{\mathscr{T}}^i$ from two branches

9:          Unlock G and fix D, then use $\mathcal{F}_S^i$ and $\mathcal{F}_{\mathscr{T}}^i$ to compute $\mathcal{L}_{adv_G}$

10:        Compute $\mathcal{L}_{KL}$ with the prior MGD G_{prior} and the posterior MGD $G_{posterior}$ from the transfer branch

11:        Compute $\mathcal{L}_S$ with P_S^i and Y_S^i from the transfer branch, then calculate $\mathcal{L}_T$ with $P_{\mathscr{T}}^i$ and $\hat{Y}_T^i$ from the adaptation branch

12:        Update G

13:      **end for**

14:     Update $K \rightarrow K + k'$

15: **end while**

---

into each other in the source domain as in the following:

$$L_{KL} = \mathbb{E}_{\mathbf{z} \sim D_{post}} \left(\log D_{post}(\mathbf{z}|Y_S, X_S) - \log D_{prior}(\mathbf{z}|X_S) \right). \qquad (7.14)$$

As illustrated in Fig. 7.8, UESM is involved in both the transfer and the adaptation branches. The prior network and the segmentation network in UESM of the transfer branch are trained from scratch with the source domain data. Once the training process finishes, the weight parameters of the prior network are frozen and only the segmentation network gets updated during the adaptation phase. A detailed workflow of the training process is shown in Algorithm 7.1.

7.3.1.3 Uncertainty-aware cross-entropy loss

Different from the vanilla weighted cross-entropy loss, which is designed to handle the unbalanced data, the proposed uncertainty-aware cross-entropy loss forces the framework to minimize the error from high uncertainty regions of prediction maps to obtain accurate segmentation. In order to obtain the uncertainty guided cross-entropy loss, the calculated uncertainty map is normalized and processed at first, and then applied to the original cross-entropy loss map with elementwise multiplication, functioned similarly as spatial attention. The designed loss function is formulated as

$$\mathcal{L}_S = -\mathbb{E}_{x_S \sim \mathbb{S}} \left(\sum_{i=1}^{M_s} Y_S^i \log G(X_S^i; \Theta_g) \odot (1 + Normalize(U_S^i)) \right), \quad (7.15)$$

where X_S denotes the source image from the source data set $\mathbb{S}$, which contains M_s samples; Y_S is the corresponding segmentation ground truth; G is UESM; Θ_g denotes the parameters of G; symbol $\odot$ represents the elementwise multiplication; U_S represents the uncertainty map of X_S and $\mathbf{1}$ represents a unit matrix with the same size as U_S. Since the absolute uncertainty values U_S can be small, the uncertainty map is rescaled to the range of [0, 1].

7.3.1.4 Uncertainty-aware self-training

An uncertainty-aware self-training (UST) scheme is proposed to further alleviate the domain shift problem. Different from other methods that assess task difficulties with a softmax probability, we propose to use a novel easy-to-hard learning strategy based on the uncertainty. The proposed UST consists of two steps for the sample selection in the target domain. In the first step, the uncertainty value U is obtained for every X_T from the target data set $\mathbb{T}$, which are then sorted in an ascending order according to the U value. Next, top K most confident images are picked from $\mathbb{T}$ to form the target subset $\mathcal{T}$ as the target adaptation training set. In the second step, the prediction of the subset $\mathcal{T}$ from the first step is processed to obtain the pseudo mask, by suppressing the probabilities that are lower than a pre-defined threshold. Afterwards, the prediction, the pseudo mask and the uncertainty map from the current iteration are used to calculate the UCE loss as following:

$$\mathcal{L}_T = -\mathbb{E}_{X_{\mathcal{T}} \sim \mathcal{T}} \left(\sum_{i=1}^{K} \hat{Y}_{\mathcal{T}}^i \log G(X_{\mathcal{T}}^i; \Theta_g) \odot (1 + Normalize(U_{\mathcal{T}}^i)) \right), \quad (7.16)$$

where $X_{\mathcal{T}}$ denotes target image; $\hat{Y}_{\mathcal{T}}$ is a pseudo mask of $X_{\mathcal{T}}$ and $U_{\mathcal{T}}$ represents the uncertainty map of $X_{\mathcal{T}}$. Specifically, $\hat{Y}_{\mathcal{T}}$ can be formulated as

$$\hat{Y}_{\mathcal{T}}^i = \begin{cases} 0 & P_{\mathcal{T}}^i < \tau, \\ P_{\mathcal{T}}^i & P_{\mathcal{T}}^i \geq \tau, \end{cases} \quad (7.17)$$

where $P_{\mathcal{T}}^i$ denotes the prediction of $X_{\mathcal{T}}$ from the first step of G and τ is the pre-defined threshold value. Specifically, for every epoch, the first step performs once to form $\mathcal{T}$, whereas the second step will traverse the entire $\mathcal{T}$ to train the UESM and the adversarial learning block. Finally, we update K with the fixed step k'. Noted that K should be smaller than the size of $\mathcal{T}$, if not, we replace it with length of $\mathcal{T}$. More details about the training procedure are listed in Algorithm 7.1.

7.3.1.5 Overall objective

Finally, combined with the aforementioned losses, the full objective function $\mathcal{L}_{FULL}$ is formulated as

$$\mathcal{L}_{FULL} = \lambda_S \mathcal{L}_S + \lambda_T \mathcal{L}_T + \lambda_D \mathcal{L}_{adv_D} + \lambda_G \mathcal{L}_{adv_G} + \lambda_{KL} L_{KL}, \qquad (7.18)$$

where λ_S, λ_T, λ_D, λ_G, λ_{KL} are the weights for $\mathcal{L}_S$, $\mathcal{L}_T$, $\mathcal{L}_{adv_D}$, $\mathcal{L}_{adv_G}$ and L_{KL}, respectively.

7.4 Experiments

Data sets. Two cross-domain data sets are used to evaluate the proposed framework, including a cross-device data set and a cross-modality data set. The cross-device data set contains retinal OCT images collected from two different devices, including 537 images from the Heidelberg Spectralis OCT instrument (Heidelberg Engineering, Inc., Heidelberg, Germany) and 623 images from the AngioVue OCT instrument (Optovue, Inc., Freemont, CA). The retinal and choroidal layers of the OCT images were manually annotated by experienced retina specialists as the ground-truth segmentation. For the cross-modality data set, the cardiac data set provided by *MMWHS* is used, which contains 20 MRI volumes and 20 CT volumes [55]. Manual annotations of the ascending aorta (AA), the left atrium blood cavity (LA-Blood), the left ventricle blood cavity (LV-Blood) and the myocardium of the left ventricle (LV-Myo) for both MRI and CT volumes are provided. Representative images from the cross-device and cross-modality databases are shown in Fig. 7.10 and more details about the two data sets are listed in Table 7.4.

Training protocol. The source domain and target domain images are randomly split into two parts, 80% for training and the rest 20% as the test set. For the source domain, both images and the corresponding ground-truth labels are used during the training procedure. In contrast, for the target domain, only images are used for the training procedure and no ground-truth labels are required. The performance of the framework is evaluated on the test set of the target domain.

Implementation details. The proposed framework is implemented with PyTorch and all experiments are conducted with an NVIDIA Tesla P40 GPU with 24 GB of memory. For the convenience of description, the symbol $S2T$ denotes the configuration of using source domain $\mathbb{S}$ for training and target domain $\mathbb{T}$ for testing. Similarly, symbol $T2T$ refers to the configuration that both training and test data are from the target domain $\mathbb{T}$. In addition, PatchGAN [17] is adopted as the discriminator D and the proposed UESM module as the generator G.

During the training procedure, the Adam optimizer is adopted with the initial learning rate set as 1×10^{-4} for both G and D. Hyper-parameters in Eq. (7.18) (λ_s, λ_t, λ_D, λ_G and λ_{KL}) are empirically set to 1.0, 0.1, 1.0, 0.003 and 0.1, respectively. In the UESM module, four samples are randomly drawn from the latent space, so as

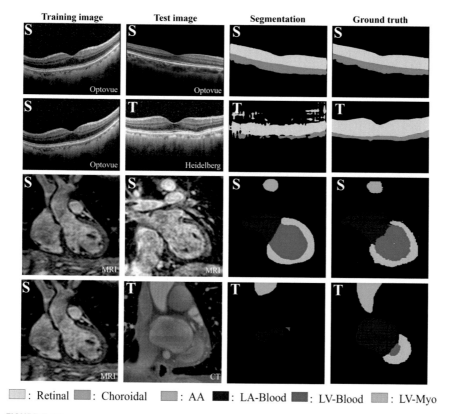

| : Retinal   : Choroidal   : AA ■ : LA-Blood ■ : LV-Blood   : LV-Myo

FIGURE 7.10

Model degradation happens on distinct domains called domain shift. The capital characters "S" or "T" on the top-left stand for the images captured from the source or target domain, respectively. We present the corresponding manufacturer or modality of the image on the bottom-right. The first two rows give the examples of domain shift when we train and test on different devices (Optovue and Heidelberg). The yellow and blue colors denote retinal and choroidal layers, respectively. In addition, last two rows show that the model performance degrades severely when the model is tested on different cardiac modality data (MRI and CT). The blue, red, orange and green colors denote the left ventricle blood cavity (LV-Blood), the left atrium blood cavity (LA-Blood), the myocardium of the left ventricle (LV-MYO) and the ascending aorta (AA), respectively.

Table 7.4 Statistics of the OCT cross-device data set and the MMWHS [55] cross-modality cardiac data set.

Data set	Device/Modality	Domain	Patients	Image size
OCT	Optovue	Source	537	630×496
	Heidelberg	Target	623	630×496
Cardiac	MRI	Source	20	256×256×(47~127)
	CT	Target	20	256×256×(142~251)

Table 7.5 Comparison results of UESM with DropNet [57], a dropout-based method. Dice: Dice score is represented in percentage; ADB: average distance of boundaries is represented in millimeters; Time: the inference time of per image.

Method	Retinal		Choroidal		Mean		Time
	Dice	**ADB**	**Dice**	**ADB**	**Dice**	**ADB**	
Vanilla DropNet	87.60	9.19	73.08	13.21	80.34	11.20	54.97 ms
DropNet + UCE loss	90.35	6.59	75.97	6.96	83.16	6.78	55.72 ms
UESM + UCE loss	**92.84**	**5.23**	**80.53**	**6.79**	**86.69**	**6.01**	**21.13 ms**

to balance the efficiency and accuracy of the uncertainty map estimation. Meanwhile, in the UST training scheme, the initially selected number of top K confident samples and the incremental step size k' are set as 200 and 50, respectively. For a fair comparison with a unified framework, volume data from the cross-modality data set is sliced to train the model.

Evaluation criteria. Dice coefficient (DSC) and the average symmetric surface distance (ASSD) are utilized to evaluate the segmentation performance of the proposed framework on the MMWHS cross-modality data set, so as to compare with other methods in the literature under the same evaluation metrics. For the cross-device OCT data set, DSC and average distance of boundaries (ADB) [56] are used to evaluate the performance of the proposed framework.

7.4.1 Exploration on uncertainty estimation

To investigate the efficiency and effectiveness of the proposed uncertainty estimation module (denoted as the UESM), the model performance is compared with the traditional uncertainty estimation method using dropout as introduced in [57] (denoted as the DropNet). Since the uncertainty estimation module plays the same role in both transfer branch and adaptation branch, for the simplicity of comparison, the transfer branch is isolated for direct training and evaluation of the segmentation network with the source domain data. Three sets of experiments are conducted to evaluate the performance, including the vanilla DropNet with DeepLab V2 backbone as baseline, DropNet with the proposed UCE loss and the proposed UESM module. As listed in Table 7.5, by introducing UCE loss to the vanilla DropNet, the mean Dice is improved by 2.8%. By replacing DropNet with the proposed UESM module, the performance is further improved by 3.5%, indicating the effectiveness of the UESM module. In addition, the inference time of different methods is listed in Table 7.5 as well. Under the same experiment setup of drawing four samples, the proposed method is 2.6 times faster than the vanilla DropNet. Therefore the proposed UESM module outperforms traditional DropNet for uncertainty estimation in both efficiency and effectiveness.

In addition, to further demonstrate the efficacy of the UESM module, uncertainty induced precision-recall (PR) curve is plotted, as shown in Fig. 7.11. The segmentation map and the corresponding uncertainty map of the holdout test set from both

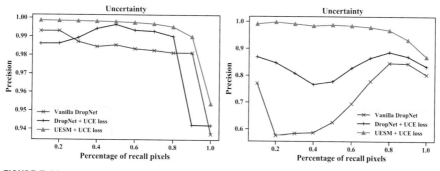

FIGURE 7.11

The uncertainty precision-recall curve on S2S (left) and S2T (right) tasks by three uncertainty estimation methods on the cross-device data set.

the source domain and the target domain are obtained at first. Then the segmentation result of individual pixels are sorted in the ascending order according to the uncertainty value. Under different ratios of the selected uncertainty values, the precision of the corresponding segmentation result is recorded and plotted, i.e., the PR curve. Theoretically, the lower the uncertainty score is, the higher the possibility that the model is able to make the correct prediction, and vice versa. Thus the ideal uncertainty induced PR curve should drop monotonically. When training the module with the source domain data and testing on the same domain (S2S scheme), both DropNet and the proposed UESM module (left chart of Fig. 7.8) follow the same pattern. However, when training with the source domain data and testing on the target domain (S2T scheme), the PR curve of DropNet decreases in the beginning and then increases in the region of 40%–80% recall region, violating the ideal PR curve change tendency. This indicates that the DropNet is not able to capture and estimate the uncertainty distribution of the target domain accurately, thus may not be the ideal choice for estimating the uncertainty information on the target domain. On the contrary, the precision of the UESM module drops monotonically on both tasks, indicating that the degree of uncertainty is monotonically correlated to the model's performance. Therefore, the proposed UESM module is reliable for the uncertainty estimation in both S2S and S2T tasks.

Moreover, to explore the potential of the uncertainty estimation module, the transition trend of uncertainty along with the training iteration is visualized. As shown in Fig. 7.12, the uncertainty map generated by UESM is able to capture the substantial cross-domain difference with high uncertainty scores at the beginning of the training. As the number of training iterations increases, the value of uncertainty decreases progressively and inclines to converge to the structure boundaries, i.e., the most challenging regions for segmentation. Therefore the uncertainty map generated by the proposed module is capable of evaluating the confidence of prediction at individual pixels, especially for the UDA task.

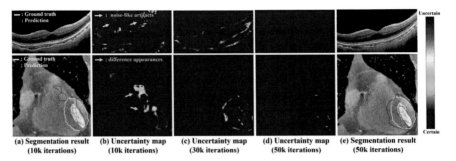

(a) Segmentation result   (b) Uncertainty map   (c) Uncertainty map   (d) Uncertainty map   (e) Segmentation result
(10k iterations)   (10k iterations)   (30k iterations)   (50k iterations)   (50k iterations)

FIGURE 7.12

Visualization of the uncertainty maps during the framework training: (a) The input image overlapping with predictions after 10k iterations. (b–d) uncertainty maps after 10k, 30k, 50k iterations. (e) The input image overlapping with predictions after 50k iterations. The green arrows denote that the uncertainty maps are able to capture the imaging deficiency cross-devices. Whereas, orange arrows imply that the high uncertainty values come from different modality appearances.

7.4.2 Comparison with existing UDA frameworks

To evaluate the performance of the proposed framework compared with other existing UDA frameworks, extensive experiments are carried out on the two cross-domain data sets, including the *MMWHS* cross-modality data set and the OCT cross-device data set. It is worth noting that SIFA [62] is the state-of-the-art UDA method on the *MMWHS* data set, meanwhile AdaptSegNet [58], BDL [59], CLAN [60] and DISE [61] are the state-of-the-art UDA methods for natural images. Therefore we choose them as baselines for comparison.

Table 7.6 summarizes the experimental results of the proposed method and the above-mentioned UDA frameworks. The proposed method outperforms the listed state-of-the-art UDA frameworks for both cross-device data set and cross-modality data set. In particular, for the cross-device data set, the performance of the proposed method is close to that of the T2T, which is the theoretical upper limit of the UDA tasks. For the cross-modality data set, the proposed method achieves a performance improvement of 45.9% compared with the S2T baseline in mean Dice score and surpasses the existing UDA frameworks, among which only the SIFA framework [62] is originally tested on the *MMWHS* data set. However, it is worth noting that since the specific training details of the SIFA framework is not provided in the original paper, we are not able to reproduce the optimal model performance as reported in the paper. Thus, two results for the SIFA framework are listed in Table 7.6, including the re-implemented model performance and the original model performance reported in [62]. As the comparison experiments indicate, the proposed framework achieves the best overall performance among the listed frameworks for both cross-device and cross-modality data sets, with representative results as shown in Fig. 7.13.

Table 7.6 Comparisons of the proposed methods and the state-of-the-art UDA algorithms. Dice: Dice score is represented in percentage; ADB: average distance of boundaries is represented in millimeters; ASSD: average symmetric surface distance is represented in millimeters.

Method	Cross-device						Cross-modality									
	Retinal		Choroidal		Mean		AA		LA-Blood		LV-Blood		LV-Myo		Mean	
	Dice	ADB	Dice	ADB	Dice	ADB	Dice	ADB	Dice	ASSD	Dice	ASSD	Dice	ASSD	Dice	ASSD
S2T (lower bound)	87.80	7.68	74.85	7.41	81.33	7.55	27.51	20.56	43.29	27.06	46.51	10.39	25.15	11.73	35.62	17.44
T2T (upper bound)	97.63	1.52	91.31	2.48	94.47	2.00	92.66	1.98	94.26	1.76	90.98	2.72	84.81	2.88	90.68	2.34
AdaptSegNet [58]	88.02	6.22	75.06	6.97	81.54	6.60	65.35	8.11	80.63	5.28	81.43	3.99	69.34	3.58	74.18	5.24
BDL [59]	87.37	6.50	73.31	6.69	80.34	6.60	67.10	10.84	80.55	7.04	82.68	3.53	61.06	4.16	72.85	6.39
CLAN [60]	88.66	6.41	78.15	6.85	83.41	6.63	63.81	9.07	79.93	5.29	84.40	3.36	66.76	**3.50**	73.73	5.31
DISE [61]	90.23	7.30	81.05	6.04	85.64	6.67	71.75	6.73	82.20	4.72	83.69	3.75	60.75	7.72	74.60	5.73
SIFA [62]	88.52	9.10	72.02	10.60	80.27	9.85	67.20	17.47	69.33	23.75	69.68	10.93	60.23	7.63	66.61	14.95
SIFA [62]*	–	–	–	–	–	–	81.10	10.60	76.40	7.40	75.70	6.70	58.70	7.80	72.98	8.13
Proposed Method	**95.78**	**2.78**	**87.64**	**3.82**	**91.71**	**3.30**	**82.00**	**4.45**	**87.21**	**3.92**	**85.38**	**3.43**	**71.50**	4.33	**81.52**	**4.03**

* The asterisk symbol denotes the experiment results from the original paper.

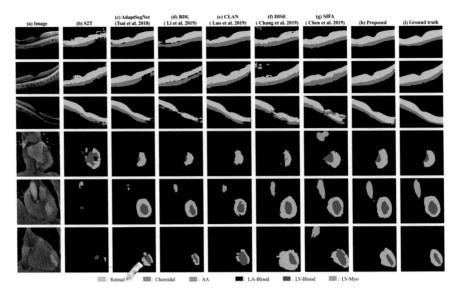

FIGURE 7.13

Comparison of different methods for target domain data segmentation. Top three rows present images from a Heidelberg equipment. Bottom three rows present CT images. From left to right: (a) the original target domain data; (b) results of the source domain segmentor; (c–e) results of different unsupervised domain adaptation methods; (f) results of the proposed framework; (e) ground truth.

7.5 Output space alignment

The output space alignment UDA approaches tried to align the information of data from two domains in the output space of segmentation network. For example, Adapt-SegNet [58] added a domain discriminator to the output space of the segmentation network to align the feature distribution across the source and target domains. Various output space alignment based UDA approaches have been proposed for medical image applications. For example, Dou et al. [47] proposed a domain critic module and a domain adaptation module for the unsupervised cross-modality adaptation problem. The output space alignment based UDA methods require the pixelwise manual annotations of source data for information alignment, which are indeed inefficient and error-prone. The wrong-labelled samples, behaving as "noise," can potentially degrade the performance of domain adaptation (i.e., we do not know whether the discrepancy of the output between the source and target domains comes from the domain shift or the label noise); thus it is challenging to simultaneously deal with the problems of domain shift and noisy label.

Aiming to alleviate the above mentioned problems, we introduce a robust cross-denoising framework [63], which is resilient to noisy annotations and domain shift. Concretely, two different networks are implemented to play roles as peer reviewers

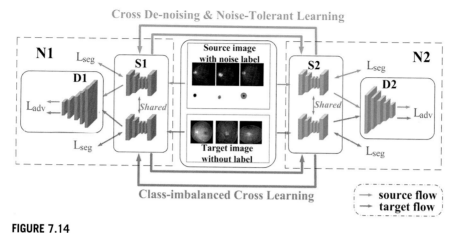

FIGURE 7.14

Pipeline of our proposed unsupervised domain adaptation framework.

to selectively learn from the data with reliable clean labels. Furthermore, a class-imbalanced self-learning strategy is introduced to estimate the most reliable labels for the target domain. Here, we first briefly review the existing studies on noisy label learning, and then introduce the robust cross-denoising feature space alignment UDA framework in details.

Training CNNs with the presence of corrupted labels is a challenging task, which has attracted numerous researchers working toward solutions. Among those works, one of the representative methods is [64], which proposed a MentorNet to supervise the training of a StudentNet and select samples that were probably correct. Another work, [65], introduced a co-teaching strategy to robustly train the deep neural networks under noisy supervision. For medical imaging, Xue et al. [66] proposed an iterative learning strategy for imperfectly labeled skin lesion image classification, combating the lack of clean annotated medical data. Existing approaches on robust learning from noisy labels are mostly focused on the image classification task, which leaves segmentation with corrupted labels an unsolved problem. Hence, we propose a novel solution to address the medical image segmentation task with both domain shift and contaminated label problems at the same time.

7.5.1 Robust cross-denoising network

In this section, we introduce the robust cross-denoising UDA framework in details. As shown in Fig. 7.14, our proposed cross-denoising network (CD-Net) consists of two different networks (i.e., N1, N2), both of which include a segmentation network (resp., S1, S2) and a discriminator (resp., D1, D2). N1 and N2, playing roles as two experts, can generate different decision boundaries, thus there should be differences in their learning abilities and opinions. For network N1, we follow the spirit of DeepLabv2 [67] architecture with ResNet101 [43] as backbone to achieve initial

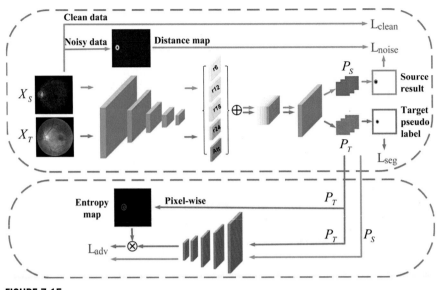

FIGURE 7.15

Architecture of the sub-network N1.

segmentation results. For network N2, in order to learn discriminative features different from N1, we adopt DeepLabv3+ architecture with MobileNetv2 as backbone [68]. To boost the segmentation ability of N1 to the same level of N2, we design a novel atrous spatial pyramid pooling (ASPP) structure [68] with multi-attention mechanism [69] for N1, which is shown in Fig. 7.15, so as to enhance the feature expression ability and enrich the multi-scale information of the network. As regard to D1 and D2, we adopt the same architecture, which is a 5-layer fully convolutional network. D1 and D2 are trained to distinguish between the source prediction and the target prediction by adversarial learning, and guide the segmentation network to focus on the local structure similarity. In the testing stage, we only use N1 to generate the final segmentation results.

7.5.1.1 Robust cross-denoising learning

Our proposed robust cross-denoising algorithm is shown in Algorithm 7.2. With a subset of data C_k (step 3), we train two different networks N_1 and N_2 to select a proportion of samples with small training loss (steps 6 and 7). As previously observed for deep networks [70], easy cases can be learned first, and then the networks gradually fit to the hard cases with the number of epochs increased. Therefore, in a noisy data set, the network learns clean and easy parts of data in the early stage, and thus has the abilities to filter out noisy pattern using loss values. The number of filtered samples is controlled by preservation rate γ, which increases (step 13) until it filters out all the potential noisy data. Since the learning and filtering ability of networks is not strong enough in early epochs, the preservation rate is initialized with a small

---

Algorithm 7.2 Cross-denoising Algorithm.

Input: The source domain training set X_S, model parameters Ω^1 and Ω^2, noise ratio β, preservation rate γ, learning rate δ, epoch number T, iteration numbers K and M.

1: **for** $t = 1$ to T **do**
2:     Initialize $\gamma = \gamma_0$
3:     Randomly sample a subset C_k from X_S
        // Sample γ of small-loss instances from each
        // peer network as high-quality data:
4:     **for** $k = 1$ to K **do**
5:         Compute the overall loss function by Eq. (7.21)
6:         $C_k^1 = argmin_{\hat{C}_k:|\hat{C}_k| \geq \gamma |C_k|} \mathcal{L}_{our}(\hat{C}_k | \omega = 0)$ and
7:         $C_k^2 = argmin_{\hat{C}_k:|\hat{C}_k| \geq \gamma |C_k|} \mathcal{L}_{our}(\hat{C}_k | \omega = 0)$
            // Exchange the high-quality data C_k^1 and C_k^2 to
            // update the peer network N_2 and N_1
8:         **for** $i = 1$ to M **do**
9:             Update $\Omega^1 = \Omega^1 - \delta \nabla \mathcal{L}_{our}(\hat{C}_k^2)$
10:            Update $\Omega^2 = \Omega^2 - \delta \nabla \mathcal{L}_{our}(\hat{C}_k^1)$
11:        **end for**
12:    **end for**
13:    Update $\gamma = min\left\{\frac{t \times (1-\beta)}{T}, 1 - \beta\right\}$
14: **end for**
15: Output model parameters Ω^1 and Ω^2.

---

value and becomes larger when epochs increase. After that, the selected high-quality data from one network is fed into its peer network as reliable knowledge to update parameters (steps 9 and 10). Since two networks have different structure and learning abilities, they can filter different types of error introduced by noisy labels. Although the error caused by noisy labels is propagated back from one network itself, the other network can adaptively correct the training error with a prediction disagreement between two networks. Based on such peer-review strategy, each network selects its small-loss samples as the high-quality data, and updates its peer network by such clean samples to further reduce the training error.

7.5.1.2 Overall training objective

The proposed cross-denoising domain adaptation network includes two loss functions: noise-tolerant segmentation loss and noise-robust adversarial loss. Among the high-quality data selected by the network, not all of them are clean data, some of them may be mixed with noisy data. In order to learn from clean labels and corrupted labels, respectively, we separate the data into two groups, i.e., data with reliable label (clean data) and noisy label (noisy data) based on the prediction confidence. For the noise-tolerant segmentation loss $\mathcal{L}_{seg}$, it consists of segmentation loss for clean data and corrupted data, which is shown in Eq. (7.19). When the instance is grouped in clean data, the noise-filtering segmentation loss is equal to $\mathcal{L}_{clean}$ ($\omega = 0$); otherwise, it is formulated as $\mathcal{L}_{noise}$ ($\omega = 1$),

$$\mathcal{L}_{seg}(p, y) = (1 - \omega)\mathcal{L}_{clean} + \omega\mathcal{L}_{noise}. \tag{7.19}$$

Since the unlabeled data in the target domain can be regarded as the extreme case of data with noisy labels, the direct prediction in the target domain is usually inaccurate and noisy, which affects the convergence and generalization of adversarial learning. To maximize prediction certainty, an "entropy map" is multiplied by the predictions for the target domain image, which increases the loss weight for the pixels with inaccurate and noisy estimated labels, and reduces the loss weight for accurate and clean estimated labels. The entropy map of the predicted result in the target domain is defined as $\mathcal{F}(X_i) = -\sum_{i=1}^{h \times w \times c} p_i \log(p_i)$. We adopt the entropy map as an indicator to weight the noise-robust adversarial loss L_{adv}, which is defined as

$$\mathcal{L}_{adv}(X_S, X_T) = - E[log(D(G(X_S)))] \\ - E[(\lambda_{entr}\mathcal{F}(X_T) + \epsilon) + log(1 - D(G(X_T)))], \tag{7.20}$$

where G is the segmentation network; λ_{entr} is the balancing hyper-parameter corresponding to information entropy map; and ϵ is to ensure the stability of the training process in the case of a small $\mathcal{F}(X_T)$.

The training objective function for our proposed noise-robust segmentation method can be formulated as the following min-max criterion:

$$\mathcal{L}_{our} = \min_{G} \max_{D} \mathcal{L}_{seg}(p, y) + \lambda_{adv}\mathcal{L}_{adv}, \tag{7.21}$$

where λ_{adv} denotes the hyper-parameter controlling the weights of the adversarial loss, which is empirically set as 0.001. Furthermore, we propose a class-imbalanced cross-learning algorithm for the model to learn with the corrupted labels. Please refer to our paper [63] for the details.

7.5.2 Experiments

Data sets. In this study, we verify our approach on two public optic disc (OD) and optic cup (OC) segmentation data sets, including the REFUGE challenge data set [41] and the Drishti-GS data set [71] (Table 7.7). We refer the REFUGE training set as the source domain, the REFUGE validation set and Drishti-GS data set as the target domains 1 and 2, respectively. The source domain contains some ground truth labels and imperfect labels, while the target domain contains no labels. Each target domain is further split into a training set for unsupervised DA (ignoring the labels) and a test set. The source and target domain images are acquired by different scanners resulting in different color and texture characteristics of the images. Extensive experiments on these two public databases with different noise levels and noise ratios are conducted to verify the effectiveness of our proposed approach.

Table 7.7 Summary of data sets used in the experiments.

Domain	Data set	Training	Test	Size
Source	REFUGE training set	400	None	2124 × 2056
Target 1	REFUGE validation set	300	100	1634 × 1634
Target 2	Drishti-GS	50	51	2047 × 1759

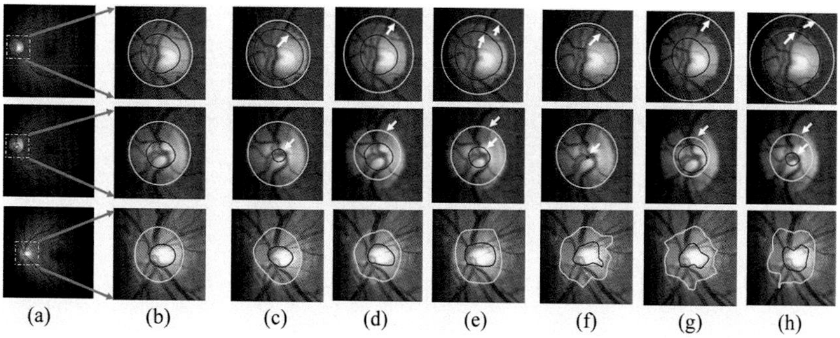

(a)   (b)   (c)   (d)   (e)   (f)   (g)   (h)

FIGURE 7.16

Examples of generated noisy labels. Each row shows a different example and columns from (c) to (h) represents dilated, eroded and nonrigidly transformed labels, respectively. (a) Original images, (b) ground-truth, (c)(d)(e) labels with low noise level, (f)(g)(h) labels with high-noise level.

We generate three types of noisy labels as shown in Fig. 7.16: (i) enlarging the label mask by dilation, (ii) shrinking the labels by erosion and (iii) deforming the labels by elastic deformation. Varying the amount of dilation, erosion and deformation, we generate corrupted noisy data sets with different noise levels, which are measured as function $\alpha = \sum_{i=1}^{c} (1 - DI_i)$, where DI_i is the Dice coefficient between generated noisy labels and ground-truth of class i. Specifically, we empirically set low noise level as $0.1 \le \alpha \le 0.4$ and high-noise level as $0.4 \le \alpha \le 0.7$. We also set different noise ratio β that represents portion of corrupted samples randomly selected from the training set, where $\beta \in (0.1, 0.5, 0.9)$.

Implementation details. The proposed method is implemented using PyTorch on four Tesla P40 GPUs with 96 GB memory in total. We use the stochastic gradient descent optimizer with a momentum of 0.9 to train the segmentation network, and the Adam optimizer to train the discriminator. The initial learning rates are 2.5×10^{-4} and 1×10^{-4} for the segmentation network and the discriminator, respectively.

7.5.2.1 Comparative study

We compare our proposed method with the state-of-the-art unsupervised DA methods including BDL [59], pOSAL [72] and BEAL [73] for the OD and OC segmentation on different noise levels and noise ratios. The Dice coefficients (DI) of OD and OC are used as evaluation criteria.

Table 7.8 Test accuracy of different methods from the REFUGE training set to the REFUGE validation set (REF) and the Drishti-GS test set (DGS), respectively. (*, *) represents (DI_{disc}, DI_{cup}).

Noise Level	Pretrain	Noise Ratio	BDL [59] REF	BDL [59] DGS	pOSAL [72] REF	pOSAL [72] DGS	BEAL [73] REF	BEAL [73] DGS	Proposed REF	Proposed DGS
Low	With	0	(94.6, 87.4)	(94.6, 82.8)	(94.9, 88.7)	(95.5, 84.5)	(93.3, 83.1)	(93.8, 85.0)	(**95.3, 89.4**)	(**96.1, 85.9**)
		0.1	(94.8, 88.7)	(94.6, 83.1)	(**95.4**, 88.0)	(**95.3**, 83.6)	(93.1, 82.0)	(93.4, 83.1)	(**95.1, 89.3**)	(95.1, **83.8**)
		0.5	(94.9, 89.0)	(94.3, 80.8)	(94.9, 85.9)	(94.9, 80.9)	(90.2, 80.5)	(93.1, 82.1)	(**95.4, 89.6**)	(**95.8, 84.2**)
		0.9	(94.2, 86.8)	(94.0, 82.6)	(94.5, 85.8)	(94.8, 80.6)	(87.7, 80.5)	(93.2, 78.0)	(**95.3, 89.4**)	(**95.1, 82.9**)
	W/O	0.1	(94.2, 86.7)	(92.6, 82.5)	(94.1, 87.9)	(94.8, 81.4)	(92.7, 77.1)	(92.4, 78.2)	(**94.7, 88.4**)	(**95.1, 83.8**)
		0.5	(93.2, 86.0)	(87.6, 81.1)	(94.0, 85.0)	(92.6, 78.4)	(87.8, 75.8)	(87.3, 78.0)	(**94.8, 86.7**)	(**94.4, 83.7**)
		0.9	(90.6, 76.5)	(85.6, 80.3)	(92.5, 83.6)	(88.6, 77.7)	(82.8, 69.1)	(83.5, 74.7)	(**94.1, 84.6**)	(**92.7, 83.4**)
High	With	0.1	(94.7, 83.3)	(94.1, 81.1)	(94.7, 86.5)	(92.6, 81.3)	(92.4, 81.8)	(92.6, 80.1)	(**95.1, 89.0**)	(**94.6, 83.0**)
		0.5	(91.6, 79.6)	(87.9, 68.5)	(85.8, 75.6)	(91.3, 78.7)	(89.1, 77.2)	(92.4, 74.9)	(**93.9, 85.6**)	(**93.4, 81.3**)
		0.9	(90.2, 74.3)	(85.9, 65.1)	(84.5, 76.0)	(91.6, 76.3)	(75.9, 66.9)	(90.4, 73.5)	(**93.0, 83.6**)	(**92.4, 82.7**)
	W/O	0.1	(89.5, 75.9)	(89.2, 72.3)	(88.2, 78.7)	(87.5, 59.0)	(91.2, 73.8)	(68.2, 56.5)	(**94.5, 88.8**)	(**92.7, 83.0**)
		0.5	(85.8, 75.6)	(85.6, 66.9)	(83.9, 74.5)	(85.0, 54.4)	(86.9, 69.1)	(73.4, 59.6)	(**93.8, 84.7**)	(**93.0, 81.8**)
		0.9	(84.7, 66.0)	(81.6, 68.7)	(79.0, 72.0)	(81.6, 56.3)	(77.8, 53.2)	(70.5, 50.7)	(**92.9, 81.1**)	(**91.8, 80.4**)

Table 7.8 presents the performance comparison of all the methods transferring from the REFUGE training to the REFUGE validation and Drishti-GS test data sets with different noise levels and noise ratios. As for the REFUGE data set (REF), we notice that the impact of label noise is not identical for all neural networks. On the clean-annotated/"no noise" data set, all methods work well and our proposed method achieves the best performance, with DI_{disc} of 95.3% and DI_{cup} of 89.4%. But as the noise ratio increases, the competitor methods have different degrees of degradation while our method can still maintain a stable and robust result. It is because we not only identify high-quality data effectively, but also avoid the error accumulation issue and assimilate the gains of clean data. Therefore, our method can reach higher performance and properly handle the harder cases. Furthermore, we observe that when using a pre-trained model at low noise level, the performance shows no sign of declining at some cases. This indicates that the pre-trained model can improve model robustness [74] and take the mild noise as a form of "data augmentation," which relaxes the learning criterion and boosts the performance of competitors and our method. When training at high-noise level, the performances of the competitor methods are declining sharply with the increase of noise ratio. In contrast, our method can detect the most reliable data and learn from samples prone to be corrupted, thus we can learn more discriminative features and achieve better performance. More specifically, in the hardest case of 0.9 noisy ratio, our method beats the best competitor pOSAL with 17.6% DI_{disc} and 12.6% DI_{cup} improvement when training from scratch.

The results on the Drishti-GS data set (DGS) have the similar trends as REF. Because the distributions of RFUGE and Drishti-GS data sets are quite different, the performance of competitors is in steep decline for the larger domain shift, while our method can alleviate such domain shift and learn from pseudo labels with high confidence. Concretely, at 0.9 noisy ratio (i.e., 90% of samples with corrupted labels), our method beats the best competitor BDL with 12.5% DI_{disc} and 13.5% DI_{cup} improvement when training from scratch. The qualitative testing results on the REFUGE and Drishti-GS data sets are visualized in Fig. 7.17. In the case of no noise, the competitor methods can locate the approximate location but fail to generate accurate boundaries of OD and OC. In contrast, our method successfully localizes the OD and OC and generates more accurate boundaries. With noise added, the differences between the segmentation results of competitors and ground-truth become prominent, while our model can still achieve promising results and show its superiority over other methods.

7.6 Conclusion

Automatic and accurate segmentation of anatomical structures on medical images is crucial for detecting various potential diseases. However, the performance of deep neural networks may significantly degrade on different modalities or devices, due to the difference across domains, i.e., domain shift problem. As a potential solution, unsupervised domain adaptation (UDA) causes the increasing attention from

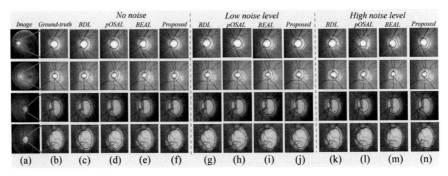

FIGURE 7.17

Results of different methods for OD and OC segmentation with different noise levels at noise ratio of 0.5. Each row presents one typical example. (a) Original image, (b) ground-truth, (c)(g)(k) BDL method [59], (d)(h)(l) pOAL method [72], (e)(i)(m) BEAL method [73] and (f)(j)(n) our proposed method. Segmentation boundaries for OD and OC are shown in red and black, respectively.

the community. In this chapter, we categorized current UDA approaches into three classes (i.e., image space alignment, feature space alignment and output space alignment), and introduced one typical approach in each category in detail. Briefly, the image space alignment based methods aim to perform image-to-image (I2I) translation to narrow down the gap of image style between source and target images before the training of segmentation network. For the feature space alignment based approaches, they align the features of source and target images extracted by the segmentation network in the shared latent space during the network training. The output space alignment based methods usually add modules at the end of segmentation network to align the predictions of source and target images. Experimental results on various public medical image data sets demonstrated that UDA can remarkably alleviate the domain shift problem, i.e., narrowing down the gap between cross-domain and in-domain performance of the models.

References

[1] D. Vazquez, J. Bernal, F.J. Sanchez, G. Fernandez-Esparrach, A.M. Lopez, A. Romero, M. Drozdzal, A. Courville, A benchmark for endoluminal scene segmentation of colonoscopy images, Journal of Healthcare Engineering (2017).

[2] J. Silva, A. Histace, O. Romain, X. Dray, B. Granado, Toward embedded detection of polyps in WCE images for early diagnosis of colorectal cancer, International Journal of Computer Assisted Radiology and Surgery 9 (2) (2014) 283–293.

[3] A. Torralba, A.A. Efros, Unbiased look at dataset bias, in: IEEE Conference on Computer Vision and Pattern Recognition, 2011, pp. 1521–1528.

[4] J. Donahue, Y. Jia, O. Vinyals, J. Hoffman, N. Zhang, E. Tzeng, T. Darrell, DeCAF: a deep convolutional activation feature for generic visual recognition, in: International Conference on Machine Learning, 2014, pp. 647–655.

[5] E. Tzeng, J. Hoffman, N. Zhang, K. Saenko, T. Darrell, Deep domain confusion: maximizing for domain invariance, arXiv preprint, arXiv:1412.3474, 2014.

[6] M. Long, Y. Cao, J. Wang, M.I. Jordan, Learning transferable features with deep adaptation networks, in: International Conference on Machine Learning, 2015, pp. 97–105.

[7] Z. Yang, Z. Lin, P. Kang, J. Lv, Q. Li, W. Liu, Learning shared semantic space with correlation alignment for cross-modal event retrieval, ACM Transactions on Multimedia Computing Communications and Applications 16 (1) (2020) 1–22.

[8] I. Goodfellow, J. Pouget-Abadie, M. Mirza, B. Xu, D. Warde-Farley, S. Ozair, A. Courville, Y. Bengio, Generative adversarial nets, in: Advances in Neural Information Processing Systems, 2014, pp. 2672–2680.

[9] H. Ajakan, P. Germain, H. Larochelle, F. Laviolette, M. Marchand, Domain-adversarial neural networks, arXiv preprint, arXiv:1412.4446, 2014.

[10] B. Benjdira, Y. Bazi, A. Koubaa, K. Ouni, Unsupervised domain adaptation using generative adversarial networks for semantic segmentation of aerial images, Remote Sensing 11 (11) (2019) 1369.

[11] J. Zhu, T. Park, P. Isola, A.A. Efros, Unpaired image-to-image translation using cycle-consistent adversarial networks, in: IEEE International Conference on Computer Vision, 2017.

[12] J. Hoffman, E. Tzeng, T. Park, J.-Y. Zhu, P. Isola, K. Saenko, A.A. Efros, T. Darrell, CyCADA: cycle-consistent adversarial domain adaptation, arXiv preprint, arXiv:1711.03213.

[13] M.-Y. Liu, O. Tuzel, Coupled generative adversarial networks, in: Advances in Neural Information Processing Systems, 2016, pp. 469–477.

[14] M.-Y. Liu, T. Breuel, J. Kautz, Unsupervised image-to-image translation networks, in: Advances in Neural Information Processing Systems, 2017.

[15] H.Y. Lee, H.Y. Tseng, J.B. Huang, M.K. Singh, M.H. Yang, Diverse image-to-image translation via disentangled representations, in: European Conference on Computer Vision, 2018.

[16] A. Rau, P. Edwards, O. Ahmad, et al., Implicit domain adaptation with conditional generative adversarial networks for depth prediction in endoscopy, International Journal of Computer Assisted Radiology and Surgery 14 (2019) 1167–1176.

[17] P. Isola, J.-Y. Zhu, T. Zhou, A.A. Efros, Image-to-image translation with conditional adversarial networks, in: IEEE Conference on Computer Vision and Pattern Recognition, 2017, pp. 1125–1134.

[18] F. Mahmood, R. Chen, N.J. Durr, Unsupervised reverse domain adaptation for synthetic medical images via adversarial training, IEEE Transactions on Medical Imaging 37 (12) (2018) 2572–2581.

[19] C. Chen, Q. Dou, H. Chen, P.A. Heng, Semantic-aware generative adversarial nets for unsupervised domain adaptation in chest X-ray segmentation, in: International Workshop on Machine Learning in Medical Imaging, 2018.

[20] Y. Zhang, S. Miao, T. Mansi, R. Liao, Task driven generative modeling for unsupervised domain adaptation: application to X-ray image segmentation, in: International Conference on Medical Image Computing and Computer Assisted Intervention, 2018.

[21] L. Liu, Z. Zhang, S. Li, K. Ma, Y. Zheng, S-CUDA: self-cleansing unsupervised domain adaptation for medical image segmentation, Medical Image Analysis 74 (2021) 102214.

[22] M. Ning, D. Wei, D. Lu, S. Yu, K. Ma, C. Yuan, C. Bian, Y. Zheng, Multi-anchor active domain adaptation for semantic segmentation, in: International Conference on Computer Vision, 2021.

[23] M. Ning, C. Bian, D. Wei, S. Yu, C. Yuan, Y. Wang, Y. Guo, K. Ma, Y. Zheng, A new bidirectional unsupervised domain adaptation segmentation framework, in: International Conference on Information Processing in Medical Imaging, 2021.

[24] X. Xie, J. Chen, Y. Li, L. Shen, K. Ma, Y. Zheng, Self-supervised CycleGAN for object-preserving image-to-image domain adaptation, in: European Conference on Computer Vision, 2020.

[25] J. Chen, Y. Li, K. Ma, Y. Zheng, Generative adversarial networks for video-to-video domain adaptation, in: AAAI Conference on Artificial Intelligence, 2020.

[26] T. Kim, M. Cha, H. Kim, J. Lee, J. Kim, Learning to discover cross-domain relations with generative adversarial networks, in: International Conference on Machine Learning, 2017.

[27] Z. Yi, H. Zhang, P. Tan, M. Gong, DualGAN: unsupervised dual learning for image-to-image translation, in: IEEE International Conference on Computer Vision, 2017, pp. 2849–2857.

[28] A. Shrivastava, T. Pfister, O. Tuzel, J. Susskind, W. Wang, R. Webb, Learning from simulated and unsupervised images through adversarial training, in: IEEE Conference on Computer Vision and Pattern Recognition, 2017.

[29] Y. Chen, Y.-K. Lai, Y.-J. Liu, CartoonGAN: generative adversarial networks for photo cartoonization, in: IEEE Conference on Computer Vision and Pattern Recognition, 2018.

[30] S. Ma, J. Fu, C. Wen Chen, T. Mei, DA-GAN: instance-level image translation by deep attention generative adversarial networks, in: IEEE Conference on Computer Vision and Pattern Recognition, 2018.

[31] H. Fu, M. Gong, C. Wang, K. Batmanghelich, K. Zhang, D. Tao, Geometry-consistent generative adversarial networks for one-sided unsupervised domain mapping, in: IEEE Conference on Computer Vision and Pattern Recognition, 2019.

[32] S. Huang, C. Lin, S. Chen, Y. Wu, P. Hsu, S. Lai, AugGAN: cross domain adaptation with GAN-based data augmentation, in: European Conference on Computer Vision, 2018.

[33] Z. Zhang, L. Yang, Y. Zheng, Translating and segmenting multimodal medical volumes with cycle- and shape-consistency generative adversarial network, in: IEEE Conference on Computer Vision and Pattern Recognition, 2018.

[34] X. Xie, J. Chen, Y. Li, L. Shen, K. Ma, Y. Zheng, MI^{2}GAN: generative adversarial network for medical image domain adaptation using mutual information constraint, in: International Conference on Medical Image Computing and Computer Assisted Intervention, 2020.

[35] J.P.W. Pluim, J.B.A. Maintz, M.A. Viergever, Mutual-information-based registration of medical images: a survey, IEEE Transactions on Medical Imaging 22 (8) (2003) 986–1004.

[36] X. Chen, Y. Duan, R. Houthooft, J. Schulman, I. Sutskever, P. Abbeel, InfoGAN: interpretable representation learning by information maximizing generative adversarial nets, in: Advances in Neural Information Processing Systems, 2016.

[37] R.D. Hjelm, A. Fedorov, S. Lavoie-Marchildon, K. Grewal, P. Bachman, A. Trischler, Y. Bengio, Learning deep representations by mutual information estimation and maximization, in: International Conference on Learning Representations, 2019.

[38] D.P. Kingma, J. Ba, Adam: a method for stochastic optimization, arXiv preprint, arXiv:1412.6980, 2014.

[39] D. Ulyanov, A. Vedaldi, V. Lempitsky, Instance normalization: the missing ingredient for fast stylization, arXiv preprint, arXiv:1607.08022, 2016.

[40] C. Li, M. Wand, Precomputed real-time texture synthesis with Markovian generative adversarial networks, in: European Conference on Computer Vision, 2016.

[41] J.I. Orlando, H. Fu, J.B. Breda, K. van Keer, D.R. Bathula, A. Diaz-Pinto, R. Fang, P.-A. Heng, J. Kim, J. Lee, et al., REFUGE challenge: a unified framework for evaluating automated methods for glaucoma assessment from fundus photographs, Medical Image Analysis 59 (2020) 101570.

[42] B. Zhou, A. Khosla, A. Lapedriza, A. Oliva, A. Torralba, Learning deep features for discriminative localization, in: IEEE Conference on Computer Vision and Pattern Recognition, 2016.

[43] K. He, X. Zhang, S. Ren, J. Sun, Deep residual learning for image recognition, in: IEEE Conference on Computer Vision and Pattern Recognition, 2016, pp. 770–778.

[44] O. Ronneberger, P. Fischer, T. Brox, U-Net: convolutional networks for biomedical image segmentation, in: International Conference on Medical Image Computing and Computer Assisted Intervention, 2015.

[45] L.-C. Chen, G. Papandreou, F. Schroff, H. Adam, Rethinking atrous convolution for semantic image segmentation, arXiv preprint, arXiv:1706.05587, 2017.

[46] C. Bian, C. Yuan, J. Wang, M. Li, X. Yang, S. Yu, K. Ma, J. Yuan, Y. Zheng, Uncertainty-aware domain alignment for anatomical structure segmentation, Medical Image Analysis 64 (2020) 101732.

[47] Q. Dou, C. Ouyang, C. Chen, H. Chen, P.-A. Heng, Unsupervised cross-modality domain adaptation of ConvNets for biomedical image segmentations with adversarial loss, in: International Joint Conference on Artificial Intelligence, 2018, pp. 691–697.

[48] A.G. Roy, N. Navab, C. Wachinger, Concurrent spatial and channel 'squeeze & excitation' in fully convolutional networks, in: International Conference on Medical Image Computing and Computer Assisted Intervention, 2018, pp. 421–429.

[49] N. Dong, M. Kampffmeyer, X. Liang, Z. Wang, W. Dai, E. Xing, Unsupervised domain adaptation for automatic estimation of cardiothoracic ratio, in: International Conference on Medical Image Computing and Computer Assisted Intervention, 2018, pp. 544–552.

[50] J. Ren, I. Hacihaliloglu, E.A. Singer, D.J. Foran, X. Qi, Adversarial domain adaptation for classification of prostate histopathology whole-slide images, in: International Conference on Medical Image Computing and Computer Assisted Intervention, 2018, pp. 201–209.

[51] A. Kendall, V. Badrinarayanan, R. Cipolla, Bayesian SegNet: model uncertainty in deep convolutional encoder-decoder architectures for scene understanding, arXiv preprint, arXiv:1511.02680, 2015.

[52] S. Sedai, B. Antony, D. Mahapatra, R. Garnavi, Joint segmentation and uncertainty visualization of retinal layers in optical coherence tomography images using Bayesian deep learning, in: Computational Pathology and Ophthalmic Medical Image Analysis, 2018, pp. 219–227.

[53] T. Nair, D. Precup, D.L. Arnold, T. Arbel, Exploring uncertainty measures in deep networks for multiple sclerosis lesion detection and segmentation, in: International Conference on Medical Image Computing and Computer Assisted Intervention, 2018, pp. 655–663.

[54] S. Kohl, B. Romera-Paredes, C. Meyer, J. De Fauw, J.R. Ledsam, K. Maier-Hein, S.A. Eslami, D.J. Rezende, O. Ronneberger, A probabilistic U-Net for segmentation of ambiguous images, in: Advances in Neural Information Processing Systems, 2018, pp. 6965–6975.

[55] X. Zhuang, J. Shen, Multi-scale patch and multi-modality atlases for whole heart segmentation of MRI, Medical Image Analysis 31 (2016) 77–87.

[56] X. Yang, H. Dou, R. Li, X. Wang, C. Bian, S. Li, D. Ni, P.-A. Heng, Generalizing deep models for ultrasound image segmentation, in: International Conference on Medical Image Computing and Computer Assisted Intervention, 2018, pp. 497–505.

[57] Y. Gal, Z. Ghahramani, Dropout as a Bayesian approximation: representing model uncertainty in deep learning, in: International Conference on Machine Learning, 2016, pp. 1050–1059.

[58] Y.-H. Tsai, W.-C. Hung, S. Schulter, K. Sohn, M.-H. Yang, M. Chandraker, Learning to adapt structured output space for semantic segmentation, in: IEEE Conference on Computer Vision and Pattern Recognition, 2018, pp. 7472–7481.

[59] Y. Li, L. Yuan, N. Vasconcelos, Bidirectional learning for domain adaptation of semantic segmentation, in: IEEE Conference on Computer Vision and Pattern Recognition, 2019.

[60] Y. Luo, L. Zheng, T. Guan, J. Yu, Y. Yang, Taking a closer look at domain shift: category-level adversaries for semantics consistent domain adaptation, in: Proceedings of the IEEE Conference on Computer Vision and Pattern Recognition, 2019, pp. 2507–2516.

[61] W.-L. Chang, H.-P. Wang, W.-H. Peng, W.-C. Chiu, All about structure: adapting structural information across domains for boosting semantic segmentation, in: Proceedings of the IEEE Conference on Computer Vision and Pattern Recognition, 2019, pp. 1900–1909.

[62] C. Chen, Q. Dou, H. Chen, J. Qin, P.-A. Heng, Synergistic image and feature adaptation: towards cross-modality domain adaptation for medical image segmentation, arXiv preprint, arXiv:1901.08211, 2019.

[63] Q. Zhang, L. Liu, K. Ma, C. Zhuo, Y. Zheng, Cross-denoising network against corrupted labels in medical image segmentation with domain shift, in: International Joint Conference on Artificial Intelligence, 2020, pp. 1047–1053.

[64] L. Jiang, Z. Zhou, T. Leung, L.-J. Li, L. Fei-Fei, MentorNet: learning data-driven curriculum for very deep neural networks on corrupted labels, in: International Conference on Machine Learning, 2017.

[65] B. Han, Q. Yao, X. Yu, G. Niu, M. Xu, W. Hu, I. Tsang, M. Sugiyama, Co-teaching: robust training of deep neural networks with extremely noisy labels, in: Advances in Neural Information Processing Systems, 2018.

[66] C. Xue, Q. Dou, X. Shi, H. Chen, P.-A. Heng, Robust learning at noisy labeled medical images: applied to skin lesion classification, in: IEEE International Symposium on Biomedical Imaging, 2019.

[67] L.-C. Chen, G. Papandreou, I. Kokkinos, K. Murphy, A.L. Yuille, DeepLab: semantic image segmentation with deep convolutional nets, atrous convolution, and fully connected CRFs, IEEE Transactions on Pattern Analysis and Machine Intelligence 40 (4) (2016) 834–848.

[68] L.-C. Chen, Y. Zhu, G. Papandreou, F. Schroff, H. Adam, Encoder-decoder with atrous separable convolution for semantic image segmentation, in: European Conference on Computer Vision, 2018.

[69] J. Fu, J. Liu, H. Tian, Y. Li, Y. Bao, Z. Fang, H. Lu, Dual attention network for scene segmentation, in: IEEE Conference on Computer Vision and Pattern Recognition, 2018.

[70] X. Yu, B. Han, J. Yao, G. Niu, I. Tsang, M. Sugiyama, How does disagreement help generalization against label corruption?, in: International Conference on Machine Learning, 2019.

[71] J. Sivaswamy, S.R. Krishnadas, G.D. Joshi, M. Jain, A.U.S. Tabish, Drishti-GS: retinal image dataset for optic nerve head (ONH) segmentation, in: IEEE International Symposium on Biomedical Imaging, 2014.

[72] S. Wang, L. Yu, X. Yang, C.-W. Fu, P.-A. Heng, Patch-based output space adversarial learning for joint optic disc and cup segmentation, IEEE Transactions on Medical Imaging 38 (11) (2019) 2485–2495.

[73] S. Wang, L. Yu, K. Li, X. Yang, C.-W. Fu, P.-A. Heng, Boundary and entropy-driven adversarial learning for fundus image segmentation, in: International Conference on Medical Image Computing and Computer Assisted Intervention, 2019.

[74] D. Hendrycks, K. Lee, M. Mazeika, Using pre-training can improve model robustness and uncertainty, in: International Conference on Machine Learning, 2019.

Medical image reconstruction and synthesis

Medical image synthesis and reconstruction using generative adversarial networks

Gyutaek Oh[a] **and Jong Chul Ye**[b]

[a]*Department of Bio and Brain Engineering, KAIST, Daejeon, Korea*
[b]*Graduate School of AI, KAIST, Daejeon, Korea*

8.1 Introduction

Inspired by the success of deep learning in computer vision tasks, deep learning approaches have been extensively investigated to solve the problems in the medical imaging field. The deep learning approaches have shown outstanding results in spite of the reduced run-time computational complexity compared to conventional methods.

Most of early studies were based on the supervised learning that requires the input data and matched label data. Unfortunately, it is difficult to obtain the matched pairs of input and label data in the medical imaging field because the acquisition of label data demands additional risk or time (e.g., excessive radiation exposure in CT, long acquisition time in MRI).

When the matched label data are not available, the generative adversarial network (GAN) [1] can be a practical approach. Due to the ability to learn target distribution, GANs enable unpaired image generations from a random distribution. Furthermore, variations of GANs can translate images from the original distribution to other distributions, so many researchers have focused on the application of this type of GANs for unsupervised learning in medical imaging.

This chapter is organized as follows. Various types of GANs that can be applied to the medical image synthesis or reconstruction will be introduced in Section 8.2. Then, in Section 8.3, applications of GAN to solve the problems in the medical imaging field will be presented. Last, the summary of this chapter will be provided in Section 8.4.

Deep Learning for Medical Image Analysis. https://doi.org/10.1016/B978-0-32-385124-4.00018-0

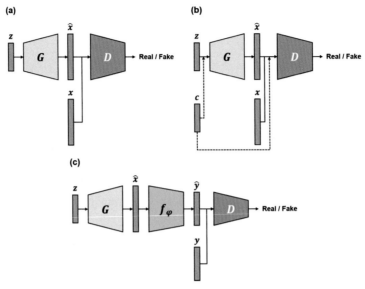

FIGURE 8.1

Training procedure of GANs for image generation. (a) GAN, (b) cGAN and (c) Ambient-GAN.

8.2 Types of GAN

8.2.1 GAN

The generative adversarial network (GAN) [1] was proposed to generate images in the target distribution from input random noises. In the training phase of GAN, the generator G and the discriminator D play a minmax game as follows:

$$\min_{G} \max_{D} \mathcal{L}_{GAN}(D, G) = \min_{G} \max_{D} \mathbb{E}_x[\log D(x)] + \mathbb{E}_z[\log(1 - D(G(z)))] \quad (8.1)$$

where x and z denote the real images in the target distribution and random noises, respectively. Also, the discriminator D outputs a scalar value in the range [0, 1], and this value represents the probability that the input image of the discriminator is a real image. By playing the minmax game, the discriminator tried to distinguish the real and generated fake images, and the generator tries to generate more realistic images that can fool the discriminator.

Fig. 8.1(a) depicts detailed training procedure of GAN. First, the random noise z is sampled from the prior noise distribution p_z. Then the generator receives sampled noise as an input and produces a fake image $\hat{x}$. Meanwhile, the discriminator takes images as inputs, and classifies them as real or fake images. If the optimization process in (8.1) is stable, the discriminator can no longer distinguish between real and fake images, and the generator produces a realistic image at the end of the training.

8.2.2 **Conditional GAN**

Although the GAN succeeded to generate images from random noise, the original GAN was not designed to control image generation using a specific condition. The conditional GAN (cGAN) [2] solved this problem by providing the condition as additional information to the generator and discriminator. Specifically, the optimization process of cGAN is formulated as follows:

$$\min_{G}\max_{D}\mathcal{L}_{cGAN}(D,G)=$$
$$\min_{G}\max_{D}\mathbb{E}_{x,c}[\log D(x,c)]+\mathbb{E}_{z,c}[\log(1-D(G(z,c),c))] \quad (8.2)$$

where c is the additional information or condition. As shown in Fig. 8.1(b), the condition c is fed to the generator or discriminator. By feeding the information c, the generator and discriminator can be conditioned. For example, if the c is class label, the generator can produces images belonging to that class, and the discriminator distinguishes between real and fake images by considering the condition.

Furthermore, the cGAN can be applied to the image-to-image translation. Pix2Pix [3] is one of the methods for image-to-image translation using cGAN. In Pix2Pix, the condition c and y becomes images of the input domain and target domain, respectively. Therefore, the generator learns how to generate the target domain images conditioned on the input domain image. In addition, Pix2Pix employs the $L1$ loss between the input domain image and matched target domain image:

$$\mathcal{L}_{L1}(G)=\min_{G}\mathbb{E}_{x,z,c}[\|y-G(z,c)\|_1]. \quad (8.3)$$

Thus the final objective function of Pix2Pix can be formulated as

$$\min_{G}\max_{D}\mathcal{L}_{Pix2Pix}(D,G)=\min_{G}\max_{D}\mathcal{L}_{cGAN}(D,G)+\lambda\mathcal{L}_{L1}(G) \quad (8.4)$$

where λ is an appropriate hyper-parameter that controls the weight of $L1$ loss.

8.2.3 **AmbientGAN**

The training of GAN requires a large number of high quality samples in the target distribution. However, it is difficult to obtain these samples in many applications. For example, to generate high resolution images, a large number of high-resolution images are required for the training of GAN. This can be a particularly big problem in the medical imaging fields because the medical images require more risk and time than natural images (e.g., radiation exposure of CT, long acquisition time of MRI).

Specifically, let x and y be the real images in the target domain and measurement domain, respectively. Also, $\hat{x}$ denotes the fake image from the generator. The discriminator of the original GAN distinguishes x and $\hat{x}$ as real or fake images. However, if x does not exist or the number of samples is not sufficient, it is difficult to train the original GAN.

To reduce the need for a large number of high-quality sample, the AmbientGAN [4] was proposed. In AmbientGAN, the networks train with incomplete or noisy measurements y by integrating the forward measurement model. Let f_φ is the forward measurement model, which is parameterized by φ. Also, assume the distribution of φ is known so that φ can be sampled from the distribution. So, if the number of measurements y is enough, it is possible to discriminate the samples on the measurement space, not on the target space. Specifically, Fig. 8.1(c) illustrates the training procedure of the AmbientGAN. Similar to the original GAN, the generator of the AmbientGAN generates the fake image from the random noise. Then the generated image is passed through the forward operator f_φ, and the fake measurement $y = f_\varphi(x)$ is generated. Finally, the discriminator of AmbientGAN classifies real and fake measurements, so it does not require fully observed samples:

$$\min_G \max_D \mathcal{L}_{AmbientGAN}(D, G) =$$
$$\min_G \max_D \mathbb{E}_y[\log D(y)] + \mathbb{E}_{z,\varphi}[\log(1 - D(f_\varphi(G(z))))]. \tag{8.5}$$

8.2.4 Least squares GAN and Wasserstein GAN

Although the GAN shows the potential of unsupervised learning, it has limitations such as the vanishing gradients or mode collapse. To address these issues, some variants of GAN that modifies the objective function in (8.1) have been proposed.

The least squares GAN (LSGAN) [5] was proposed to overcome the vanishing gradients problem of the original GAN. In LSGAN, the Pearson χ^2 divergence is minimized, and it yields the optimization process as follows:

$$\min_D L_{LSGAN}(D) = \frac{1}{2}\mathbb{E}_x[(D(x) - 1)^2] + \frac{1}{2}\mathbb{E}_z[(D(G(z)))^2],$$
$$\min_G L_{LSGAN}(G) = \frac{1}{2}\mathbb{E}_z[(D(G(z)) - 1)^2]. \tag{8.6}$$

The optimization process in (8.6) produces more gradients when updating the generator, so the training of LSGAN is more stable than that of the original GAN.

The Wasserstein GAN (WGAN) [6,7] is another variant of GAN to address the limitations of the original GAN. By minimizing Earth-Mover distance or Wasserstein distance, WGAN solves the vanishing gradients problem and mode collapse problem of the original GAN. Its optimization process can be represented by the following formulation:

$$\min_G \max_{D \in Lip_1} L_{WGAN}(D, G) = \min_G \max_{D \in Lip_1} \mathbb{E}_x[D(x)] - \mathbb{E}_z[D(G(z))] \tag{8.7}$$

where Lip_1 denotes the 1-Lipschitz function space. This constraint can be achieved through weight clipping of the discriminator [6] or additional gradient penalty loss [7].

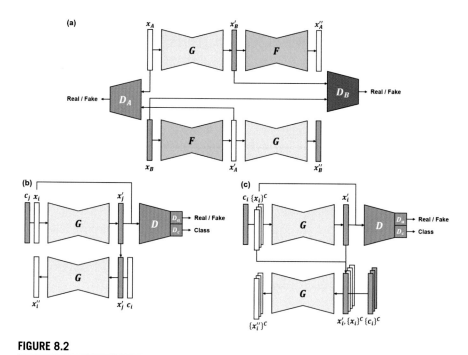

FIGURE 8.2

Training procedure of GANs for image-to-image translation. (a) CycleGAN, (b) StarGAN and (c) CollaGAN.

8.2.5 Cycle-consistent GAN

Image-to-image translation is another important topic in unsupervised learning. As introduced in Section 8.2.2, the studies such as Pix2Pix tries to solve the image-to-image translation problem using the paired data set which contains the input data and matched ground truth data. Unfortunately, in many cases, the paired data set for image-to-image translation is not available. For example, the zebra image that matches with a specific horse image is not exist. Therefore, image-to-image translation methods that can be trained with unpaired data set are required. The cycle-consistent GAN (CycleGAN) [8] alleviates the need of paired data by employing the adversarial loss and cycle-consistency loss.

Specifically, assume that there are two domains, A and B, and x_A and x_B are the samples of the domain A and B, respectively. To translate an image from one domain to another domain, the CycleGAN contains two generators as shown in Fig. 8.2(a). The generator G learns the mapping from A to B, while another generator F learns the mapping from B to A. Also, there are two discriminators D_A and D_B, so each discriminator distinguishes real and fake images in each domain. The adversarial training of generators and discriminators can be done by following the objective function:

$$L_{GAN}(G, D_B) = \mathbb{E}_{x_B}[\log D_B(x_B)] + \mathbb{E}_{x_A}[\log(1 - D_B(G(x_A)))],$$
$$L_{GAN}(F, D_A) = \mathbb{E}_{x_A}[\log D_A(x_A)] + \mathbb{E}_{x_B}[\log(1 - D_A(G(x_B)))]. \tag{8.8}$$

Here, L_{GAN} can be changed to other type of loss such as LSGAN loss for stable training.

However, with only the adversarial losses in (8.8), the generators can map the input to arbitrary random images in the target domain. Therefore, the additional constraint that makes the generators map an input image to an appropriate target domain image is required. CycleGAN solves this problem by making the two generators inverse of each other. To ensure that each generator is the inverse of each other, the cycle consistency loss is added:

$$L_{cyc}(G, F) = \mathbb{E}_{x_A}[\|F(G(x_A)) - x_A\|_1] + \mathbb{E}_{x_B}[\|G(F(x_B)) - x_B\|_1]. \tag{8.9}$$

Therefore, the CycleGAN can be trained with the following full objective function:

$$\min_{G,F} \max_{D_A, D_B} L_{CycleGAN}(G, F, D_A, D_B)$$
$$= \min_{G,F} \max_{D_A, D_B} L_{GAN}(G, D_B) + L_{GAN}(F, D_A) + \lambda L_{cyc}(G, F) \tag{8.10}$$

where λ is a hyper-parameter that controls the weight of cycle consistency loss.

8.2.6 Optimal transport driven CycleGAN

After the success of CycleGAN, many follow-up studies related to CycleGAN have been conducted. Some of studies [9,10] tries to reveal the mathematical meaning of the structure of CycleGAN, and find that a family of CycleGAN architecture can be derived from a dual formulation of the optimal transport by using a specially designed penalized least squares (PLS) cost as a transportation cost. The theory provides a systematic approach to design a novel optimal transport driven CycleGAN (OT-CycleGAN) architecture for various inverse problems.

In inverse problems, a noisy measurement $y \in \mathcal{Y}$ from an unobserved image $x \in \mathcal{X}$ is modeled by

$$y = \mathcal{H}x + w \tag{8.11}$$

where w is the measurement noise and $\mathcal{H} : \mathcal{X} \mapsto \mathcal{Y}$ is the measurement operator. In [9], a PLS cost function with a novel deep learning was proposed:

$$c(x, y; G_\Theta, \mathcal{H}) = \|y - \mathcal{H}x\| + \|G_\Theta(y) - x\| \tag{8.12}$$

where G_Θ is a neural network with the parameter Θ and the input y. For unsupervised learning using optimal transport, it is assumed that (8.12) is a transport cost between the two domains $\mathcal{X}$ and $\mathcal{Y}$ with probability distributions with measures μ and ν, respectively. Then Kantorovich dual optimal transport formulation [11], which minimizes the average transport cost for between two measures $\mathcal{X}$ and $\mathcal{Y}$, is given by

$$\min_{G_\Theta, \mathcal{H}} \mathbb{K}(\Theta, \mathcal{H}) = \min_{G_\Theta, \mathcal{H}} \max_{\varphi_\Phi, \psi_\Xi} L(G_\Theta, \mathcal{H}; \varphi_\Phi, \psi_\Xi), \tag{8.13}$$

where

$$L(G_\Theta, \mathcal{H}; \varphi_\Phi, \psi_\Xi) = \gamma L_{cyc}(G_\Theta, \mathcal{H}) + L_{WGAN}(G_\Theta, \mathcal{H}; \varphi_\Phi, \psi_\Xi). \quad (8.14)$$

In (8.14), L_{cyc} denotes the cycle consistency loss in (8.9), L_{WGAN} is the WGAN loss in (8.7) and γ is an appropriate hyper-parameter. Also, Kantorovich 1-Lipschitz potentials φ_Φ and ψ_Ξ correspond to the Wasserstein GAN discriminators. Specifically, L_{cyc} and L_{WGAN} are given by

$$L_{cyc}(G_\Theta, \mathcal{H}) = \mathbb{E}_x[\|G_\Theta(\mathcal{H}x) - x\|_1] + \mathbb{E}_y[\|\mathcal{H}G_\Theta(y) - y\|_1], \quad (8.15)$$

$$L_{WGAN}(\Theta, \mathcal{H}; \Phi, \Xi) = \left(\mathbb{E}_x[\varphi_\Phi(x)] - \mathbb{E}_y[\varphi_\Phi(G_\Theta(y))]\right)$$
$$+ \left(\mathbb{E}_y[\psi_\Xi(y)] - \mathbb{E}_x[\psi_\Xi(\mathcal{H}x)]\right). \quad (8.16)$$

In the OT-CycleGAN, various options for $\mathcal{H}$ are possible. If the forward physics $\mathcal{H}$ is unknown, it can be replaced with the neural network H_Υ similar to the conventional CycleGAN. In case of the forward operator is unknown linear convolution, then $\mathcal{H}$ can be set to a simple linear convolutional layer instead of the complex neural network. Last, if $\mathcal{H}$ is known, the maximization of the discriminator ψ_Ξ with respect to Ξ does not affect the generator G_Θ. Therefore, the discriminator ψ_Ξ can be neglected, and this consideration leads to a novel OT-CycleGAN architecture with only one generator and one discriminator. Specifically, L_{cyc} and L_{WGAN} for OT-CycleGAN when $\mathcal{H}$ is known can be reformulated as

$$L_{cyc}(G_\Theta) = \mathbb{E}_x[\|G_\Theta(\mathcal{H}x) - x\|_1] + \mathbb{E}_y[\|\mathcal{H}G_\Theta(y) - y\|_1], \quad (8.17)$$

$$L_{WGAN}(G_\Theta; \varphi_\Phi) = \mathbb{E}_x[\varphi_\Phi(x)] - \mathbb{E}_y[\varphi_\Phi(G_\Theta(y))]. \quad (8.18)$$

8.2.7 StarGAN

Although CycleGAN shows successful results in image-to-image translation between two domains, the limited scalability is one of the limitations of CycleGAN. For example, if image-to-image translation between four domains is required, then total of 6 CycleGANs (12 generators and 12 discriminators) should be trained. To overcome the limited scalability, StarGAN [12] was proposed for multi-domain image-to-image translation.

In Fig. 8.2(b), the training scheme of the StarGAN is shown. Here, x_i is an image in ith domain, where $i = 1, \cdots, N$ and N denotes the total number of domains. There are two main differences between CycleGAN and StarGAN where StarGAN enables multi-domain translation. First, the generator of StarGAN takes an image x_i and a target domain information c_j together as inputs, where the target domain information is given by binary or one-hot vector. By providing target domain information, the generator of StarGAN translates ith domain image to jth domain image where $i \neq j$. Therefore, it is possible to translate the image to an image of arbitrary domain by changing the target domain information. The second difference is that the discriminator of StarGAN has two tails, D_{GAN} and D_{cls}, and the outputs of two tails have different meaning. D_{GAN} outputs the probability that the input image of the discriminator is a real image like other GANs:

$$L_{GAN}(G, D_{GAN}) = \mathbb{E}_{x_i}[\log D_{GAN}(x_i)] \\ + \mathbb{E}_{x_i, c_j, i \neq j}[\log(1 - D_{GAN}(G(x_i, c_j)))]. \tag{8.19}$$

On the other hand, D_{cls} outputs the probability distribution of domains for a given input image. In other words, the discriminator learns how to classify input images to corresponding class during the training. Therefore the generator not only have to fool the discriminator, but also generates the fake images that can be classified to the target domain by the discriminator. This can be done by following the classification loss:

$$L_{cls}(D_{cls}) = \mathbb{E}_{x_i, c_i}[\log(D_{cls}(c_i|x_i))], \\ L_{cls}(G) = \mathbb{E}_{x_i, c_j, i \neq j}[-\log(D_{cls}(c_j|G(x_i, c_j)))]. \tag{8.20}$$

Furthermore, the reconstruction loss which is analogous to the cycle consistency loss in CycleGAN is employed:

$$L_{rec}(G) = \mathbb{E}_{x_i, c_i, c_j, i \neq j}[\|G(G(x_i, c_j), c_i) - x_i\|_1]. \tag{8.21}$$

Finally, the training of StarGAN can be done by following the optimization process:

$$\min_{G} \max_{D_{GAN}, D_{cls}} L_{StarGAN}(G, D_{GAN}, D_{cls}) \\ = \min_{G} \max_{D_{GAN}, D_{cls}} L_{GAN}(G, D_{GAN}) \\ + \lambda_{cls} L_{cls}(D_{cls}) + \lambda_{cls} L_{cls}(G) + \lambda_{rec} L_{rec}(G) \tag{8.22}$$

where λ_{cls} and λ_{rec} are appropriate hyper-parameters.

8.2.8 Collaborative GAN

In the medical imaging field, it is important to estimate the missing data from other data. For example, MRI can provide several types of contrast images (e.g., T_1, T_2, FLAIR) and each of them provides unique anatomical or diagnostic information. However, it is difficult to acquire all contrasts in practice because the acquisition time of MRI is too long. Therefore the method for estimating missing elements from other observed data is required, and this task is called missing data imputation.

CycleGAN or StarGAN can be used for missing data imputation. However, each of them have some limitations. As mentioned in the previous section, the scalability of CycleGAN is limited, so as the number of domains increases, the number of generators should also increase. In the case of StarGAN, it requires only one generator for multi-domain translation. However, the generator of StarGAN uses only single domain input to estimate the missing element. In most cases in a missing data imputation task, the data of different domains are associated with each other. Therefore it is possible to estimate missing data more accurate if the multiple data from different domains are used synergistically.

The Collaborative GAN (CollaGAN) [13] was proposed for missing data imputation by utilizing multiple domains' data together. Fig. 8.2(c) depicts the flow of CollaGAN training. For the simple explanation, assume that there are four domains ($N = 4$), a, b, c and d. If the target domain is a, then the generator of CollaGAN tries to estimate x_a from multiple images from other domains $\{x_a\}^C = \{x_b, x_c, x_d\}$, where the subscript C denotes the complementary set. It can be formulated as

$$x_i' = G(\{x_i\}^C, c_i) \qquad (8.23)$$

where $i \in \{a, b, c, d\}$ is the target domain index, and c_i denotes the condition for the target domain.

Because the CollaGAN employs the multiple inputs, the cycle consistency loss or reconstruction loss should be modified for CollaGAN. After generating the target domain image x_a', the input domain images $\{x_b, x_c, x_d\}$ are reconstructed by using x_a':

$$
\begin{aligned}
x_{b|a}'' &= G(\{x_a', x_c, x_d\}, c_b) \\
x_{c|a}'' &= G(\{x_a', x_b, x_d\}, c_c) \\
x_{d|a}'' &= G(\{x_a', x_b, x_c\}, c_d).
\end{aligned}
\qquad (8.24)
$$

Then the multiple cycle consistency loss when the target domain is a can be defined as follows:

$$L_{mcc,a}(G) = \|x_{b|a}'' - x_b\|_1 + \|x_{c|a}'' - x_c\|_1 + \|x_{d|a}'' - x_d\|_1. \qquad (8.25)$$

The multiple cycle consistency can be formulated by the following equation in general:

$$L_{mcc,i}(G) = \sum_{i \neq j} \|x_{j|i}'' - x_j\|_1. \qquad (8.26)$$

The remaining loss functions for CollaGAN are similar with those of StarGAN. First, the discriminator tries to distinguish real or fake images, and the generator tries to fool the discriminator by the following GAN loss:

$$
\begin{aligned}
&L_{GAN}(G, D_{GAN}) = \\
&\mathbb{E}_{x_i}[\log D_{GAN}(x_i)] + \mathbb{E}_{\{x_i\}^C, c_i}[\log(1 - D_{GAN}(G(\{x_i\}^C, c_i)))].
\end{aligned}
\qquad (8.27)
$$

Also, the classification loss is employed for the CollaGAN:

$$
\begin{aligned}
L_{cls}(D_{cls}) &= \mathbb{E}_{x_i, c_i}[\log(D_{cls}(c_i|x_i))], \\
L_{cls}(G) &= \mathbb{E}_{\{x_i\}^C, c_i}[-\log(D_{cls}(c_i|G(\{x_i\}^C, c_i)))].
\end{aligned}
\qquad (8.28)
$$

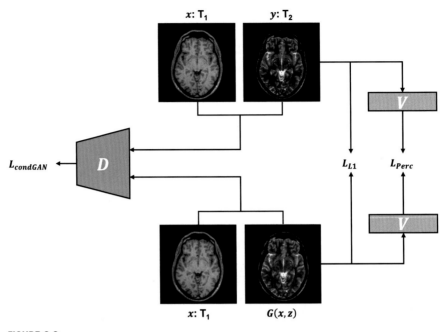

FIGURE 8.3

pGAN: conditional GAN for MR contrast image synthesis with paired data.

Finally, the objective function of CollaGAN can be written as follows:

$$\min_{G} \max_{D_{GAN}, D_{cls}} L_{CollaGAN}(G, D_{GAN}, D_{cls})$$

$$= \min_{G} \max_{D_{GAN}, D_{cls}} L_{GAN}(G, D_{GAN}) \tag{8.29}$$

$$+ \lambda_{cls} L_{cls}(D_{cls}) + \lambda_{cls} L_{cls}(G) + \lambda_{mcc} L_{mcc}(G)$$

8.3 Applications of GAN for medical imaging

8.3.1 Multi-contrast MR image synthesis using cGAN

As mentioned in Section 8.2.2, cGAN can be applied to synthesize images in the target domain from source domain images.

First, pGAN [14] is a conditional GAN for paired MRI data set, which is similar with Pix2Pix. Fig. 8.3 shows the architecture and flow of the pGAN. Assume that x and y are images of the source and target domain, respectively, and z is a random noise. For example, x and y can be a T_1-weighted image and a T_2-weighted image in multi-contrast MR image synthesis. In pGAN, LSGAN loss with the condition x

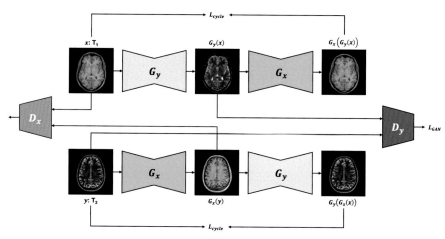

FIGURE 8.4

cGAN: conditional GAN for MR contrast image synthesis with unpaired data.

is employed for the adversarial loss to stabilize the training process:

$$L_{condGAN}(D, G) = -\mathbb{E}_{x,y}[(D(x, y) - 1)^2] - \mathbb{E}_{x,z}[D(x, G(x, z))^2]. \quad (8.30)$$

Furthermore, because the paired data is available, it is possible to incorporate pixelwise loss between the network output and target domain image, and it can be formulated by

$$L_{L1}(G) = \mathbb{E}_{x,y,z}[\|y - G(x, z)\|_1] \quad (8.31)$$

where L_{L1} is the $L1$ loss. In addition, the perceptual loss is adopted for more realistic image synthesis as follows:

$$L_{Perc}(G) = \mathbb{E}_{x,y}[\|V(y) - V(G(x, z))\|_1] \quad (8.32)$$

where V is a pre-trained network for extracting features from images. Therefore, the final objective function of pGAN can be written as follows:

$$L_{pGAN} = L_{condGAN}(D, G) + \lambda L_{L1}(G) + \lambda_{Perc} L_{Perc}(G). \quad (8.33)$$

In many cases, the paired or registered data set is not available. In this case, cGAN [14] can be trained with unregistered images by exploiting cycle consistency loss. As similar with the CycleGAN, cGAN contains two generators G_x, G_y and two discriminators D_x, D_y as shown in Fig. 8.4. The cycle consistency loss for cGAN

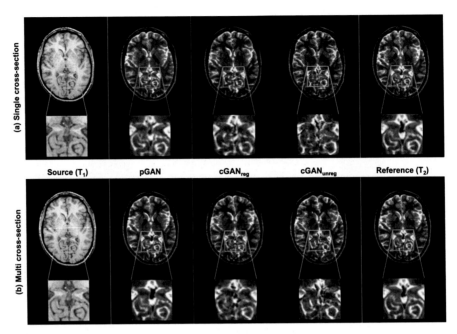

FIGURE 8.5

MR contrast image synthesis results using pGAN and cGAN. cGAN_reg and cGAN_unreg denote cGAN trained on registered and unregistered images, respectively. The source image is T_1-weighted image and the reference image is T_2-weighted image. The results were synthesized using (a) single cross-section and (b) multi-cross-section.

can be expressed by

$$L_{cycle}(G_x, G_y) = \mathbb{E}_x[\|x - G_x(G_y(x))\|_1] + \mathbb{E}_y[\|y - G_y(G_x(y))\|_1]. \quad (8.34)$$

By integrating the above cycle consistency loss with the adversarial loss, the cGAN can be trained with the following final loss function:

$$L_{cGAN}(D_x, D_y, G_x, G_y) = L_{GAN}(D_x, G_z) + L_{GAN}(D_y, G_y) \\ + \lambda_{cycle} L_{cycle}(G_x, G_y). \quad (8.35)$$

Fig. 8.5 shows the synthesized results using pGAN or cGAN. Because the objective function of pGAN includes the $L1$ loss between the output and ground truth, it shows higher quality results when compared to cGAN_reg. On the other hand, cGAN_unreg restores detailed structures in the synthetic contrast image even though it was trained with unregistered data set. Furthermore, pGAN and cGAN show results with improved quality when they were trained using multi-cross-section because the neighboring voxels have structural correlations and the networks can utilize this information.

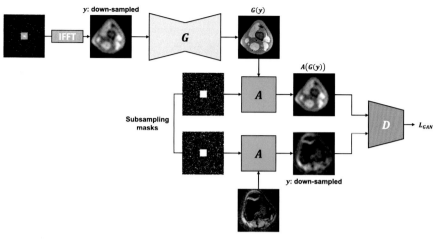

FIGURE 8.6

AmbientGAN for MRI reconstruction without fully-sampled MR images.

8.3.2 MRI reconstruction without fully-sampled data using AmbientGAN

MRI provides high resolution anatomical and functional images without radiation exposure. However, it requires long acquisition time due to the acquisition physics of MRI. To reduce the acquisition time, only the subset of k-space samples are acquired, and then fully-sampled images are reconstructed from acquired down-sampled images.

For the reconstruction of fully-sampled MR images, many deep learning methods have been investigated and they have shown prominent performance and fast reconstruction time. However, most of deep learning methods are based on the supervised learning which requires down-sampled input and matched fully-sampled label. Unfortunately, it is difficult to obtain fully-sampled label MR images due to the long scan time. Therefore, the reconstruction method that can be trained without paired data set is required.

In many cases, the information about the sub-sampling mask is known (e.g., acceleration factor, auto calibration region). Because the forward operator from fully-sampled data to down-sampled data can be drawn from the known distribution, the AmbientGAN can be a solution for the MRI reconstruction without paired data. The unsupervised training procedure using AmbientGAN for MRI reconstruction is depicted in Fig. 8.6 [15]. Because the purpose of this AmbientGAN is to reconstruct fully-sampled data from down-sampled data, the input of the generator becomes the down-sampled data y. After generating fully-sampled data, this image is downsampled in the k-space domain by sub-sampling mask which is randomly sampled from a set of sub-sampling masks. Then the discriminator distinguishes the real measurement and fake measurement. The objective function for training this Am-

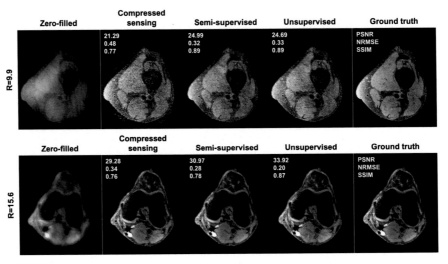

FIGURE 8.7

MRI reconstruction results using compressed sensing, unsupervised and semi-supervised learning. R denotes the acceleration factor of zero-filled images.

bientGAN can be written as

$$\min_{G} \max_{D} \mathbb{E}_y[\log D(y)] + \mathbb{E}_{y,A}[\log(1 - D(A(G(y))))] \qquad (8.36)$$

where A denotes the forward operator, which consists of the Fourier transform and sub-sampling operation.

Fig. 8.7 shows the MRI reconstruction results using conventional compressed sensing (CS), unsupervised and semi-supervised learning. Here, unsupervised denotes the method using the AmbientGAN in Fig. 8.6. Also, the vanilla GAN was employed for the semi-supervised learning. As shown in Fig. 8.7, the unsupervised learning provides reconstruction results with less noise compared to the CS method. Furthermore, the quantitative metric values of the unsupervised learning are higher than those of CS method. In addition, the result of unsupervised learning is comparable with that of semi-supervised learning even though the unsupervised learning was trained without fully-sampled data.

8.3.3 Low dose CT denoising using CycleGAN

Multi-phase coronary CT angiography is usually used for the diagnosis of heart diseases. Because the multi-phase coronary CT requires multiple acquisition, some of phase images usually taken at low dose to reduce the radiation exposure of patients. Unfortunately, low dose CT images have noise that makes it difficult to diagnose the diseases.

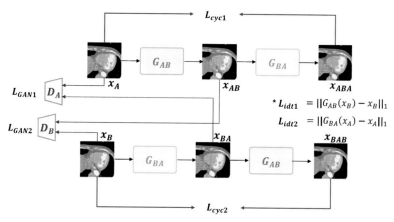

FIGURE 8.8

CycleGAN for low dose CT de-noising.

Many of deep learning studies have succeeded in reducing the noise of low dose CT images, but they are implemented based on the supervised learning that requires matched pairs of low dose and full dose CT images. However, the acquisition of matched pairs of low dose and full dose CT images requires the additional radiation exposure to patients. To address this issue, the method for low dose CT de-noising using CycleGAN was developed [16].

Fig. 8.8 shows the architecture of CycleGAN for low dose CT de-noising. Here, $x_A \in A$ and $x_B \in B$ are low dose and full dose CT images, respectively. To train the CycleGAN for CT de-noising, the adversarial loss in (8.8) and the cycle consistency loss in (8.9) are necessary. In addition, in multi-phase coronary CT, the phase of heart and the dose modulation are often misaligned. If the misalignment is occurred, the input of the generator G_{AB}, which originally takes a low dose image as an input, can be a full dose image. Therefore, an additional loss is required so that generators do not change the detail of the input images when the input domain is reversed. Following identity loss can enforce the generators to satisfy the condition:

$$L_{idt}(G_{AB}, G_{BA}) = \mathbb{E}_{x_B}[\|G_{AB}(x_B) - x_B\|_1] + \mathbb{E}_{x_A}[\|G_{BA}(x_A) - x_A\|_1]. \quad (8.37)$$

The final objective function of CycleGAN for low dose CT de-noising can be written as follows:

$$
\begin{aligned}
L_{cycleGAN}(G_{AB}, G_{BA}, D_A, D_B) = & L_{GAN}(G_{AB}, D_B) + L_{GAN}(G_{BA}, D_A) \\
& + \lambda_{cyc} L_{cyc}(G_{AB}, G_{BA}) \\
& + \lambda_{idt} L_{idt}(G_{AB}, G_{BA}).
\end{aligned} \quad (8.38)
$$

The low dose CT de-noising results are shown in Fig. 8.9. As shown in the third column of Fig. 8.9, the supervised learning provides clean CT images, but some de-

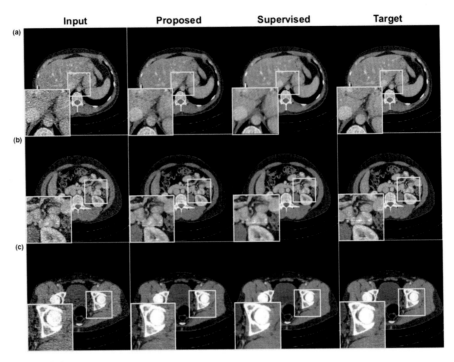

FIGURE 8.9

Low dose CT de-noising results using CycleGAN and supervised learning. Intensity range of images is $(-300, 300)$ [HU].

tails of images are blurry. On the other hand, the CycleGAN reduces the noises of the input images, so the results are similar with the target images.

8.3.4 MRI reconstruction without paired data using OT-CycleGAN

As introduced in previous section, the CycleGAN architecture can be derived from the optimal transport theory with a novel PLS cost. Also, if the forward operator is known, the architecture of OT-CycleGAN can be simplified. Therefore, OT-CycleGAN can be applied for MRI reconstruction [17] when the paired data set is not available.

In accelerated MRI with multi-coil acquisition, the forward measurement model can be described as

$$Y = \mathcal{F}^{-1} \mathcal{P}_\Omega \mathcal{F} X \tag{8.39}$$

where

$$\begin{aligned} X &= [x^{(1)}, \cdots, x^{(C)}], \\ Y &= [y^{(1)}, \cdots, y^{(C)}]. \end{aligned} \tag{8.40}$$

Here, the subscript $^{(i)}$ denotes the ith coil and C is the number of coils, and $x^{(i)}$ is the fully-sampled image, $y^{(i)}$ is the down-sampled image, $\mathcal{F}$ is the 2D Fourier transform, $\mathcal{F}^{-1}$ is the inverse 2D Fourier transform and $\mathcal{P}_\Omega$ is the projection to Ω that denotes k-space sampling indices. Consequently, the PLS cost in (8.12) can be extended to the multi-coil MRI reconstruction problem as follows:

$$c(X, Y; \Theta) = \sum_{i=1}^{C} \|y^{(i)} - \mathcal{H}x^{(i)}\| + \|G_\Theta(y^{(i)}) - x^{(i)}\| \qquad (8.41)$$

where

$$\mathcal{H} = \mathcal{F}^{-1}\mathcal{P}_\Omega\mathcal{F}. \qquad (8.42)$$

However, the main problem of using (8.41) is that a discriminator should compare all coil images channel by channel. To address this issue, the element-wise square-root of sum-of-the-squares (SSoS) operation, $\mathcal{M}$, that combine coil images to a single image can be applied:

$$z = \mathcal{M}X \qquad (8.43)$$

where

$$z_n = \left(\sum_{i=1}^{C} |x_n^{(i)}|^2 \right)^{\frac{1}{2}}, \qquad (8.44)$$

where $x_n^{(i)}$ is the nth element of the ith coil image. Therefore, the following cost function can be derived:

$$c(X, Y; \Theta) = \sum_{i=1}^{C} \|\mathcal{M}y^{(i)} - \mathcal{M}\mathcal{H}x^{(i)}\| + \|\mathcal{M}G_\Theta(y^{(i)}) - \mathcal{M}x^{(i)}\|. \qquad (8.45)$$

By applying (8.45), the coil sensitivity dependency can be removed, and the discriminator compares real and fake SSoS images.

Fig. 8.10 depicts the OT-CycleGAN architecture for accelerated MRI reconstruction. Since the forward operator $\mathcal{H}$ is known, OT-cycleGAN for accelerated MRI has only one generator and discriminator. Accordingly, the training procedure can be more stable, and the training time is reduced compared to the conventional Cycle-GAN. Furthermore, the loss functions are calculated for the SSoS images to remove the coil sensitivity dependency. OT-CycleGAN loss functions can be reformulated for MRI reconstruction as follows:

$$L_{cyc}(G_\Theta) = \mathbb{E}_X[\|\mathcal{M}G_\Theta(\mathcal{F}^{-1}\mathcal{P}_\Omega\mathcal{F}X) - \mathcal{M}X\|_1]$$
$$+ \mathbb{E}_Y[\|\mathcal{M}\mathcal{F}^{-1}\mathcal{P}_\Omega\mathcal{F}G_\Theta(Y) - \mathcal{M}Y\|_1], \qquad (8.46)$$

$$L_{WGAN}(G_\Theta; \varphi_\Phi) = \mathbb{E}_X[\varphi_\Phi(\mathcal{M}X)] - \mathbb{E}_Y[\varphi_\Phi(\mathcal{M}G_\Theta(Y))]. \qquad (8.47)$$

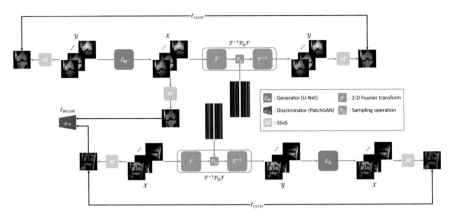

FIGURE 8.10

OT-CycleGAN for MRI reconstruction.

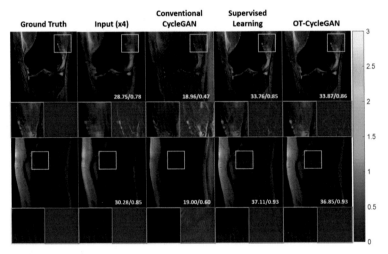

FIGURE 8.11

Multi-coil MRI reconstruction results using the conventional CycleGAN, supervised learning, and OT-CycleGAN. PSNR and SSIM values are denoted in the corner of each image.

MRI reconstruction results using conventional CycleGAN, supervised learning, and OT-CycleGAN are shown in Fig. 8.11. Because the training of conventional CycleGAN is unstable, the reconstructed images are unnatural and the aliasing pattern due to the subsampling still remains in the reconstructed images. The supervised learning that is trained with matched pair of fully-sampled and down-sampled images successfully reconstructs high quality MR images. On the other hand, OT-CycleGAN shows competitive results compared to the supervised learning even though it was trained with an unpaired MRI data set.

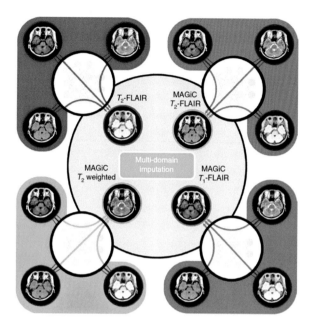

FIGURE 8.12

Schematic diagram of CollaGAN for MR contrast image imputation. There are four domains: conventional T_2-FLAIR (red circle) and T_2-FLAIR (green circle), T_2 weighted (yellow circle) and T_1-FLAIR (orange circle) from synthetic MRI.

8.3.5 MR contrast imputation using CollaGAN

The CollaGAN was developed for missing data imputation by using multiple images from different domains. Accordingly, missing MR contrast image synthesis is one of the problems that can be solved by CollaGAN [13,18]. The schematic diagram of CollaGAN for MR contrast image imputation is illustrated in Fig. 8.12. As shown in the figure, if the T_2-FLAIR image was not acquired, then it can be synthesized by the generator of CollaGAN. Here, the generator takes contrast images from other domains to utilize the information from various domains synergistically. This property makes the CollaGAN specialized for missing data imputation compared to other image-to-image translation methods.

Fig. 8.13 shows the input of CollaGAN and the imputation results using various methods. Because the CollaGAN exploits the information from various domains, it shows accurate results, which are similar with the target images. On the other hand, the results from CycleGAN or StarGAN show different aspect or pixel intensity compared to target images because they only use a single input image to generate missing element.

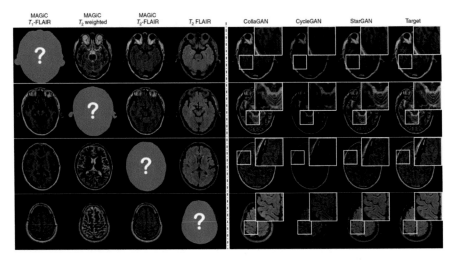

FIGURE 8.13

Input images of the network (left) and MR contrast image imputation results using Cycle-GAN, StarGAN and CollaGAN (right).

8.4 Summary

In this chapter, we covered the types of GAN that can be applied to medical image synthesis and reconstruction. Thanks to GAN's ability to learn the probability distribution, unconditional or conditional image generation and image-to-image translation are possible without any pairs of input data and corresponding label data. In addition, we confirmed that these GANs have an important role for unsupervised learning in medical imaging field, and shows prominent results in various applications. Although the surprising results have been shown, research on medical image reconstruction or synthesis using GAN is still in progress, and there is plenty of room for further development.

References

[1] I. Goodfellow, J. Pouget-Abadie, M. Mirza, B. Xu, D. Warde-Farley, S. Ozair, et al., Generative adversarial nets, Advances in Neural Information Processing Systems (2014) 27.
[2] M. Mirza, S. Osindero, Conditional generative adversarial nets, arXiv preprint, arXiv: 1411.1784, 2014.
[3] P. Isola, J.Y. Zhu, T. Zhou, A.A. Efros, Image-to-image translation with conditional adversarial networks, in: Proceedings of the IEEE Conference on Computer Vision and Pattern Recognition, 2017, pp. 1125–1134.
[4] A. Bora, E. Price, A.G. Dimakis, AmbientGAN: generative models from lossy measurements, in: International Conference on Learning Representations, 2018.

[5] X. Mao, Q. Li, H. Xie, R.Y. Lau, Z. Wang, S. Paul Smolley, Least squares generative adversarial networks, in: Proceedings of the IEEE International Conference on Computer Vision, 2017, pp. 2794–2802.

[6] M. Arjovsky, S. Chintala, L. Bottou, Wasserstein generative adversarial networks, in: International Conference on Machine Learning, PMLR, 2017, pp. 214–223.

[7] I. Gulrajani, F. Ahmed, M. Arjovsky, V. Dumoulin, A.C. Courville, Improved training of Wasserstein gans, Advances in Neural Information Processing Systems (2017) 30.

[8] J.Y. Zhu, T. Park, P. Isola, A.A. Efros, Unpaired image-to-image translation using cycle-consistent adversarial networks, in: Proceedings of the IEEE International Conference on Computer Vision, 2017, pp. 2223–2232.

[9] B. Sim, G. Oh, J. Kim, C. Jung, J.C. Ye, Optimal transport driven CycleGAN for unsupervised learning in inverse problems, SIAM Journal on Imaging Sciences 13 (4) (2020) 2281–2306.

[10] S. Lim, H. Park, S.E. Lee, S. Chang, B. Sim, J.C. Ye, CycleGAN with a blur kernel for deconvolution microscopy: optimal transport geometry, IEEE Transactions on Computational Imaging 6 (2020) 1127–1138.

[11] C. Villani, Optimal Transport: Old and New, vol. 338, Springer Science & Business Media, 2008.

[12] Y. Choi, M. Choi, M. Kim, J.W. Ha, S. Kim, J. Choo, Stargan: unified generative adversarial networks for multi-domain image-to-image translation, in: Proceedings of the IEEE Conference on Computer Vision and Pattern Recognition, 2018, pp. 8789–8797.

[13] D. Lee, J. Kim, W.J. Moon, J.C. Ye, CollaGAN: collaborative GAN for missing image data imputation, in: Proceedings of the IEEE/CVF Conference on Computer Vision and Pattern Recognition, 2019, pp. 2487–2496.

[14] S.U. Dar, M. Yurt, L. Karacan, A. Erdem, E. Erdem, T. Çukur, Image synthesis in multi-contrast MRI with conditional generative adversarial networks, IEEE Transactions on Medical Imaging 38 (10) (2019) 2375–2388.

[15] E.K. Cole, F. Ong, S.S. Vasanawala, J.M. Pauly, Fast unsupervised mri reconstruction without fully-sampled ground truth data using generative adversarial networks, in: Proceedings of the IEEE/CVF International Conference on Computer Vision, 2021, pp. 3988–3997.

[16] E. Kang, H.J. Koo, D.H. Yang, J.B. Seo, J.C. Ye, Cycle-consistent adversarial denoising network for multiphase coronary CT angiography, Medical Physics 46 (2) (2019) 550–562.

[17] G. Oh, B. Sim, H. Chung, L. Sunwoo, J.C. Ye, Unpaired deep learning for accelerated MRI using optimal transport driven CycleGAN, IEEE Transactions on Computational Imaging 6 (2020) 1285–1296.

[18] D. Lee, W.J. Moon, J.C. Ye, Assessing the importance of magnetic resonance contrasts using collaborative generative adversarial networks, Nature Machine Intelligence 2 (1) (2020) 34–42.

Deep learning for medical image reconstruction

9

Focus on MRI, CT and PET

Jun Zhao[a], **Qiu Huang**[a], **Dong Liang**[b], **Yang Chen**[c], **and Ge Wang**[d]

[a]*Shanghai Jiao Tong University, Shanghai, China*
[b]*Shenzhen Institute of Advanced Technology, Chinese Academy of Sciences, Shenzhen, China*
[c]*Southeast University, Nanjing, China*
[d]*Rensselaer Polytechnic Institute, Troy, NY, United States*

9.1 Introduction

Magnetic Resonance Imaging (MRI), Computed Tomography (CT) and Positron Emission Tomography (PET) are the common medical imaging modalities. The image intensity of these three modalities represents anatomical or functional information of the human body, which can aid in the diagnosis of diseases. Therefore, it is very important to get high-quality medical images from the measured data by detectors, which is called the reconstruction process. The reconstruction tasks for MRI, CT and PET have similarities. They all involve a forward imaging model, i.e., a physical description of how the measurement is generated by spatial information in the image. Since the model is based on a rigorous mathematical deduction, analytic algorithms have been first proposed to solve the inverse problem. Although analytic methods can fast reconstruct images, they are noise-sensitive and have limited effectiveness in handling under-sampled or inconsistent data. Iterative methods are thus proposed to reduce noise and suppress artifacts with the regularization of prior information or statistical model, though they are complex and time-consuming to optimize. Recently, with the development of big data technology, deep learning (DL) has shown great potential. DL is first applied in the medical image processing and does a good job in tasks such as organ segmentation, image registration, lesion detection and prognosis prediction. Then, it is generalized to the image reconstruction field. Deep learning reconstruction methods for MRI, CT and PET enrich the medical imaging techniques.

9.2 Deep learning for MRI reconstruction
9.2.1 Introduction

Since its inception in the early 1970s, MRI has revolutionized radiology and medicine [1]. However, MRI is known to be a slow imaging modality, and many techniques have been developed to reconstruct the desired image from under-sampled measured data to improve the imaging speed. In past decades, Compressed Sensing (CS) has become an important strategy for fast MR imaging based on the sparsity prior [2,3]. However, it takes a relatively long time for the iterative solution procedure to achieve high-quality reconstruction, and the selection of the regularization parameter is empirical. Although some numerical methods have been proposed to optimize the free parameters in MR imaging [4], these methods are burdened with high-computational complexity. Additionally, most approaches only exploit prior information, either directly from the to-be-reconstructed images or with very few reference images involved.

Deep learning has shown great potential in fast MR imaging. In contrast to CS and other constrained reconstruction methods, deep learning avoids complicated optimization-parameter tuning and performs superfast online reconstruction with the aid of offline training using enormous data. In deep learning-based reconstruction, the prior information is exploited by the deep neural network from abundant MR data.

According to the training data requirement, DL-based MRI reconstruction methods can be approximately divided into two categories: supervised learning [8–52] and unsupervised learning [53–73]. Supervised learning uses the known ground-truth data to learn the mapping between data pairs, while unsupervised learning infers the structures within the samples without labeled outputs. Currently, most applications in MRI reconstruction use supervised learning, however, unsupervised techniques remain an area of active research.

The main purpose of this section is to give an overview of the DL-based MR image reconstruction methods, with an effort to highlight their unique properties and similarities between them. This section by no means includes a complete list of references of all contributions, as the field is fast-growing, but the methods introduced herein should serve as good examples for understanding the field. For more details on deep learning developments for MRI reconstruction, we refer the interested reader to survey papers [5–7].

9.2.2 Basic of MR reconstruction

In MRI, spatial information of the subject, such as the spin density and relaxation parameters, is encoded in the measured data in a variety of ways. Typically, a forward imaging model is a mathematical description of how the measured data is related to the spatial information (i.e., image). A linear imaging model is typically used after some approximation and can be written as

$$\mathbf{f} = \mathbf{Am} + \boldsymbol{\epsilon} \tag{9.1}$$

where $\mathbf{A} : \mathbb{C}^N \to \mathbb{C}^M$ is the encoding matrix, $\mathbf{f} \in \mathbb{C}^M$ is the acquired k-space data, $\mathbf{m} \in \mathbb{C}^N$ is the image to be reconstructed and $\boldsymbol{\epsilon}$ is the measurement noise, which can be well modeled as complex additive Gaussian white noise under the assumption that the noise equally affects the entire frequency (i.e., all the samples in k-space).

During data acquisition, the measured data $\mathbf{f}$ and the imaging model captured in the encoding matrix $\mathbf{A}$ are both known. The problem of image reconstruction is to recover the desired image $\mathbf{m}$ from the measurements $\mathbf{f}$.

There are several methods of solving for $\mathbf{m}$ in Eq. (9.1), such as obtaining the least-squares solution directly or through an iterative procedure. If the acquired data (so-called k-space data) is sampled on a Cartesian grid and satisfies the Nyquist sampling criterion, the image can be reconstructed directly by applying a fast Fourier transform (FFT). Multichannel acquisition entails more complicated encoding matrices but they can also be reconstructed by direct matrix inversion for Cartesian sampling. On the other hand, for sub-Nyquist sampling, iterative reconstruction is typically used to solve the underdetermined inverse problem. In such scenarios, additional prior information is often incorporated into the imaging model to facilitate the reconstruction. In general, the imaging model of the sub-Nyquist data can be written as

$$\hat{\mathbf{m}} = \underset{\mathbf{m}}{\arg\min}\, F(\mathbf{Am}, \mathbf{f}) + G(\mathbf{m}), \tag{9.2}$$

where $F(\mathbf{Am}, \mathbf{f})$ is the data fidelity term depending on the system noise distribution, $F(\mathbf{Am}, \mathbf{f}) = \frac{1}{2}\|\mathbf{Am} - \mathbf{f}\|_2^2$ if the noise is assumed to be normal distributed. $G(\mathbf{m})$ denotes the regularization term relating to the prior information, such as the l_1 regularization according to the sparse prior.

9.2.3 Deep learning MRI reconstruction with supervised learning

The supervised learning methods learn the mapping between the input and output from the training data set, consisting of paired data. This requires a ground-truth fully sampled data set (k-space or images, used as the desired output) and the paired under-sampled data (used as the input). With the training data pairs, the supervised reconstruction requires a qualitative metric—also known as loss function—to evaluate how close the output of the network is to the target one.

From the perspective of the imaging model in network design, supervised MR reconstruction methods can be roughly divided into two categories, purely data-driven [8–31] and unrolling-based [32–52].

9.2.3.1 Purely data-driven methods

Data-driven methods employ certain standard neural networks to learn the nonlinear mapping between input and output on the paired data without any knowledge of the imaging model.

The idea of using the convolutional neural network (CNN) for MR imaging was first proposed by Wang et al. [8]. This method directly uses a standard CNN to learn the network-based mapping between the aliased images and the clean images. In most existing works, the aliased image, the inverse Fourier transform from undersampled k-space data, is used as the network input, and the desired image from the fully sampled k-space data is used as output. The mapping is learned through standard networks, such as MLP [9], U-Net [10–16] and GAN [17–19].

Some methods try to enhance the k-space performance through k-space interpolation [20–23]. RAKI uses a 3-layer CNN to learn the k-space interpolation for parallel imaging, like GRAPPA, and then obtains the reconstructed image from the interpolated full k-space data [20]. Alternative methods exploit the low-rankness of the MRI signal and use the deep networks to exploit the signal representation in k-space [22,23].

AutoMap has shown the possibility to directly learn the transformation between under-sampled k-space data and the reconstructed image [24]. It uses fully connected layers to perform the encoding such as Fourier transform, which unfortunately results in a large number of parameters and is burdened with high computational complexity. To reduce the computational complexity, MLP is used to learn the 1D inverse Fourier transform in phase-encoding direction rather than the whole image [25].

Since k-space and image domain exhibit different properties, and some information is already lost if the network is only trained separately, some cross-domain methods operate in both k-space and image domain to address this issue [26,27].

Deep networks are also used to estimate the quantitative tissue parameters from recorded complex-valued data [28–31]. For example, in MR quantitative parameter mapping, 3D CNN with the architecture of U-Net is constructed to generate high-quality susceptibility maps/parametric maps from single orientation data/under sampled parameter weighted images.

9.2.3.2 Unrolling-based methods

Unrolling-based methods are inspired by the iterative optimization algorithm. Specifically, a regularized objective function—as in (9.2)—is solved by an optimization algorithm, then the iterations of such algorithm are unrolled to an end-to-end network, mapping the measured k-space to the corresponding reconstructed image. The regularization term and the hyper-parameters can be trained explicitly or implicitly through the back-propagation on the training data. In this way, the topology of the deep network is determined by the iterations of the algorithm, and because of the fewer iterations, the reconstruction of unrolling is faster.

Several optimization algorithms have been successfully unrolled into networks, including gradient descent (GD) [32–34], proximal gradient descent (PGD) [35–37], the iterative shrinkage-thresholding algorithm (ISTA) [38], the alternating minimization algorithm (AMA) [39–49], the alternating direction method of multipliers (ADMM) [50] and the primal dual hybrid gradient (PDHG) [51,52]. All unrolled methods solve some form of the optimization problem (9.2). The definitions of the data consistency term F and regularization term G, together with optimization strategy, determine the fundamental structure of the resulting deep networks. A summary of the unrolled methods is presented in Table 9.1, which the readers are encouraged to use for reference.

Most unrolled methods define the data consistency term F in the form of least-square $F(\mathbf{Am}, \mathbf{f}) = \frac{1}{2} \|\mathbf{Am} - \mathbf{f}\|_2^2$, assuming that the measurement noise is normal distributed. The variability of the reconstruction model lies in the regularization term. Some methods consider the explicit expression of $G(\mathbf{m})$. Many methods use the gen-

Table 9.1 Summary of some unrolling-based methods.

	Method	$G(\mathbf{m})$	$F(\mathbf{Am}, \mathbf{f})$	Algorithm	Network	Learning issues	Application
Unrolling-based methods	ADMM-CSNet [50]	$\sum_{l=1}^{L} \lambda_l g(\mathbf{D}_l \mathbf{m})$	$\|\mathbf{Am} - \mathbf{f}\|_2^2$	ADMM	CNN	Hyper-parameters, $\mathbf{D}_l$, g	Single-coil imaging
	VN [32]	$\sum_{l=1}^{L} \langle g_l(\mathbf{D}_l \mathbf{m}), 1 \rangle$		GD	CNN	Hyper-parameters, $\mathbf{D}_l$, g_l	Multi-coil imaging
	ISTA-Net [38]	$\lambda \|\mathbf{Dm}\|_1$		ISTA	CNN	Hyper-parameters, $\mathbf{D}$	Single-coil imaging
	DC-CNN [41]	$\lambda \|\mathbf{m} - C(\mathbf{m})\|_2^2$		AMA	CNN	CNN denoiser	Single-coil imaging
	MoDL [39]	$\lambda \|\mathbf{m} - C(\mathbf{m})\|_2^2$		AMA	CNN	Hyper-parameters, CNN denoiser	Multi-coil imaging
	CRNN [42]	$G(\mathbf{m})$		AMA	CRNN	Hyper-parameters, Proximal operator	Single-coil dynamic imaging
	VS-Net [43]	$G(\mathbf{m})$		AMA	CNN	Hyper-parameters, Proximal operator	Multi-coil imaging
	Learned DC [36]	$G(\mathbf{m})$	$F(\mathbf{Am}, \mathbf{f})$	PGD	CNN	$\nabla F(\mathbf{Am}, \mathbf{f})$ Proximal operator	Multi-coil dynamic imaging

eralized CS model, in which the regularization term is expressed as

$$G(\mathbf{m}) = \sum_{l=1}^{L} \lambda_l g(\mathbf{D}_l \mathbf{m}) \tag{9.3}$$

where the regularization term is extended to L terms, and $\mathbf{D}_l$ is a transformation matrix; $g(.)$ is a nonlinear operator (e.g., l_q-regularizer ($q \in [0, 1]$) to promote sparsity); and λ_l is the regularization parameter. ADMM-CSNet [50], VN [32] and ISTA-Net [38], which unroll ADMM, GD and ISTA, respectively, use this formulation. The parameter λ_l and the linear sparsifying transforms $\mathbf{D}_l$ are learned by convolutional layers. Different parameterizations of the nonlinear sparsity-promoting functions $g(.)$ are used: ADMM-CSNet uses piecewise linear functions, VN uses radial basis functions and ISTA-Net uses the fixed l_1-norm instead of learning functions. Some methods explicitly express the $G(\mathbf{m})$ as the de-noising model:

$$G(\mathbf{m}) = \lambda \|\mathbf{m} - C(\mathbf{m})\|_2^2 \tag{9.4}$$

where $C(\mathbf{m})$ is the "de-noised" version of $\mathbf{m}$ with removed aliasing artifacts and noise, which can be obtained by a CNN unit. Methods in this class include DC-CNN [41] and MoDL [39].

There are some methods that consider a general form of $G(\mathbf{m})$ instead of using the explicit expression. The deep network is used to parameterize the proximal operator of $G(\mathbf{m})$ and the formulation of the regularizer is not constrained. These are the cases of CRNN [42], VS-Net [43], L+S-Net [47] and PDHG-CSNet [52].

Although most methods use the l_2-norm data consistency, other approaches have been proposed. In CP-Net [52] and Learned DC [36], the data consistency term is relaxed to a generic form $F(\mathbf{Am}, \mathbf{f})$ based on the assumption that the measurement noise distribution satisfies a more general exponential form distribution after a nonlinear transform. This may increase the generality of the reconstruction model and improve the reconstruction quality.

The different reconstruction models and optimizations lead to significant variability in the resulting network architectures, which cannot be fully covered in this section. However, the unrolling methods have common alternating blocks: a model-driven data consistency block and a learned prior block. They are often truncated to a fixed fewer number of iterations compared to traditional optimization methods and trained in an end-to-end fashion. They may share weights across the iterations or not and rely on training data to different extents. Model-driven approaches might use a more constrained formulation and shallower priors and have a smaller number of parameters. Such methods may be easier to interpret and validate and require less training data. As constraints are relaxed and deeper priors are used, methods become more data-driven and may have more parameters. Such methods have a looser connection to the physics-driven model, but given enough training data, they might outperform more model-driven approaches on a particular task due to increased representational power.

9.2.4 **Deep learning MRI reconstruction with unsupervised learning**

Most of the deep learning approaches follow supervised learning frameworks where a large number of matched fully sampled scans must be provided to train the neural network properly. This imposes challenges in practice since the matched fully sampled reference data are unavailable and difficult or impossible to acquire. In this circumstance, unsupervised learning techniques provide a promising alternative. In unsupervised learning, methods try to find patterns in data without any ground-truth data. Hence, how to better discover effective prior information is very important for unsupervised learning.

Starting with Deep image prior (DIP) [53], several works have demonstrated that the architecture of a network can act as a strong prior to enable image reconstruction, even without any training data [54–56]. Network architectures may be re-designed to accommodate different imaging scenarios, and the inference process is also the network training process, which is why these methods are also called "un-trained networks."

Given pairs of noisy images arising from the same clean target image, each with its own independent identically distributed, zero-mean, random noise components, Noise2Noise can train a de-noising network with the noisy image pairs [57]. Inspired by Noise2Noise, RARE trains the neural network on artifact image pairs from under-sampled measurements [58]. These noisy or artifact data training methods are based on the assumption that the expected value of the noisy/artifact image pairs with various acquisition times is equivalent to the clean image. Although these methods eliminate acquiring fully sampled data, the requirement of data pairs may be challenging in some imaging applications. EDAEP uses the de-noising autoencoder as the deep de-noiser for MR reconstruction [59].

Some works try to guide the network training using the sampled data. RELAX [60] uses the data consistency term in (9.2) with two MR physical models, including an MR quantitative signal model and an MR imaging model, as the loss function to train the network for quantitative MR imaging. Additional regularizations that do not rely on references can be further added as complementary constraints to improve the training performance. Different from DIP-based methods, RELAX needs training data. Yaman et al. [61] divided the sampled k-space data into two disjoint subsets, one was used as network input and the other to calculate the loss function, which could be called self-supervised learning via data under-sampling (SSDU). Since the under-sampled data needs to be divided, the information provided to the network for learning is further reduced, which will result in a poor reconstruction for highly under-sampled data. In some special imaging scenarios, such as dynamic imaging, the under-sampled k-space data can be used to simulate fully sampled data through the predefined imaging trajectory. Ke et al. [62] built fully encoded data as the reference to train the network for dynamic cardiac cine by merging the under-sampled k-space data along temporal dimension with a time-interleaved data acquisition scheme. Although this data merging operation could synthesize fully sampled data to train the network, the correlations along temporal dimension were erased, which would affect the performance of dynamic information reconstruction, especially at high acceleration factors.

Other works aim to reconstruct images through generative models. In MR reconstruction, generative models can be used as the prior models, regardless of the data acquisition settings, thus providing an unsupervised learning reconstruction. The generative model represents the probability distributions with two different models, one is the explicit model that represents a probability density or mass function [63,64], such as autoregressive models and variable autoencoder (VAE), the other is the implicit model that directly represents a sampling process where the distribution is defined implicitly [65–73], such as GAN and its variations.

Deep density prior (DDP) is one of the probabilistic methods that employed a network as an explicit prior for MR reconstruction [63]. It uses the VAEs to approximate the distribution of MR image patches and the likelihood of a previously unseen image by maximizing the evidence lower bound (ELBO). The learned distribution is used as a probabilistic prior in a Bayesian reconstruction framework to provide an unsupervised reconstruction. Unlike DDP, which uses an approximation density model, Luo et al. estimate the distribution of MR images through a mixture of the logistic distribution [64]. The mixture distribution model was then used to compute the likelihood of images, serving as a prior model for reconstruction.

WGAN introduces an unpaired training scheme for MR reconstruction by leveraging adversarial training based on the Wasserstein distance and the data consistency [66]. The generator performs the reconstruction by taking in the under-sampled k-space and outputting the reconstructed images. The discriminator takes in the image reconstructed by the generator and the image in the label set and outputs a real number that reflects the Wasserstein distance between the two. It does not require pairing between the input and label. CycleGAN attempts to minimize the statistic distance in both measurement and image domains, making the algorithm more stable [67,68]. With the optimal transport (OT) theory, OT-cycleGAN, a generalization of cycle-GAN, is introduced in MR reconstruction to improve the stability of network training and reduce training time [69,70]. In OT-cycleGAN, a novel compositional discriminator and a cycle-consistency term with the square-root of sum-of-the squares (SSoS) operation are used, and a mathematical theory is provided to guarantee that it is still a valid dual formulation from optimal transport problem. The OT-cycleGAN can outperform the conventional cycleGAN and achieve competitive performance to supervised learning approaches in MR reconstruction.

Some research use the score-based generative model for medical imaging without any assumptions on the measurement scheme [71–73]. The score function is the gradient of the data distribution and can be estimated by de-noising score matching. With the trained score function, given measurements and the physical model of the measurement process at the inference stage, the solver of the stochastic differential equation (SDE), which enables the sample from the posterior distribution, could generate the reconstruction consistent with both the prior and observed measurements.

9.2.5 **Outlook**

Unlike traditional constrained reconstruction with hand-crafted priors, a theoretical analysis for deep reconstruction is largely unexplored. Only a few works mention theoretic convergence and have analyzed the convergence behavior in theory. Liu et al. [74] developed a generic paradigm to unroll nonconvex optimization and proved in theory that the propagation could globally converge to the critical point of the original optimization model. Cheng et al. [36] and Huang et al. [47] also gave the convergence analysis of the proposed method in the main context. Ye et al. [75] provided a preliminary theoretical rationale for some existing deep learning architectures and components. Greater effort should be made to achieve rigorous mathematical derivations and analysis.

Although DL-based MR imaging has advanced rapidly, it still suffers from some limitations, such as the interpretability, robustness and the generalization of the neural networks. The progress in this field will be important to increase trust in the results obtained. In normal conditions, the performance of supervised learning is better than that of network learning without labels. For the best performance, current supervised deep learning techniques for image reconstruction are specifically trained for the sampling trajectory, acceleration factor, coil configuration, image contrast or body region used. A variational network, for example, has been shown to be quite sensitive to differing signal-to-noise ratios between training and test data sets but less sensitive to different imaging contrasts [76]. Training on heterogeneous data helps to generalize better, but it is not yet clear if it is possible to train one algorithm generalizing well enough to all different imaging scenarios. The first instability analysis of neural networks for image reconstruction was studied by Antun et al. [77]. Hammernik et al. [78] conducted a different instability analysis, which studied the influence of regularization networks, DC layers and variations in the data in a controlled experimental setup. Transfer learning provides an alternative way when training is insufficient [79,80]. Moreover, open data sets and challenges, such as the fast MRI challenge [81], provide a way for more training data, especially the raw k-space measurements, making it possible to benchmark and compare different networks in the same settings and to better evaluate the performance of each network. The community is also working on characterizing the uncertainty in deep MRI reconstruction [82,83]. These uncertainty estimates may be helpful in diagnosis or automated image quality assessment.

Loss function plays an important role in driving the direction of network learning. The most commonly used loss functions in deep MRI reconstruction are pixelwise mean square error (MSE) and mean absolute error (MAE). However, these metrics do not reflect a radiologist's perspective well and are generally not good at representing small structures. The development of new loss functions, including feature losses, remains an active research area.

9.2.6 Conclusion

With the rapid development of deep learning, the past 5 years have witnessed substantial changes in MR reconstruction. We have provided a comprehensive introduction on deep learning-based MRI reconstruction and summarized the typical networks in this field. In only a few years, various networks have already been developed to take advantage of the unique properties of MRI. The methods in this field not only pursue a faster and more accurate reconstruction performance, but also inspire unexplored MRI applications. It is foreseeable that the development of DL-MRI will usher in a new era of digital healthcare and personalized medicine.

9.3 Deep learning for CT reconstruction

When it comes to computed tomography (CT) imaging modality, the data measured by the sensors is vastly different from the human-interpretable images. CT reconstruction is the process of computing image voxels from these measured data. In this case, each sensor measurement can help us define thousands of image voxel values, and each voxel value corresponds to thousands of sensor measurements. Therefore the reconstruction problem is more complex than the conventional image-to-image processing tasks. In the past several decades, extensive efforts have been made to improve the quality of the reconstructed CT images. The conventional reconstruction methods can be classified as analytic reconstruction and iterative reconstruction, which depend on the mathematical inverse of the forward model and the numerical forward model combined with a feedback loop, respectively. In the ideal case, conventional methods could reconstruct satisfying images. However, low-dose sampling is a generally accepted way of radiation reduction, which reduces the probability of radiation-induced diseases [84,85]. Decreasing the X-ray flux of detectors and the projection views are two ways to reduce the radiation dose. The former directly reduces the quality of the sampled data, and the latter results in an imaging system with fewer data points than unknown voxels, which also degrades the quality of the reconstructed images. Moreover, the sensor data may deviate from the original predictions of the model for various factors, such as the scattering effect, photon starvation and beam hardening. In this case, conventional analytical and iterative methods based on accurate mathematical models may produce severe noise and artifacts.

Recently, deep learning technology has revealed great potential in image processing. Researchers proposed a data-driven reconstruction method based on deep learning. It has become the most concerned method in the field of CT imaging. Compared with conventional methods, the deep learning-based reconstruction method does not entirely rely on accurate mathematical models, and it trains a neural network through big data for superior tomographic reconstruction. In other words, deep learning-based CT reconstruction is a data-driven way to find the optimal solution, which makes the development of the algorithm simpler in concept and more effective in practical application. Recent studies reported that deep learning-based reconstruction significantly outperforms conventional iterative reconstruction in terms of noise reduction while maintaining a good image texture [86,87]. Some typical reconstruction results are shown in Fig. 9.1. We can see that the images reconstructed by the iterative reconstruction method Total Variation (TV) are degraded by artifacts, while the ones generated by the deep-learning method DDNet [88] have a good visual perception, as pointed by the yellow arrow in Fig. 9.1(d).

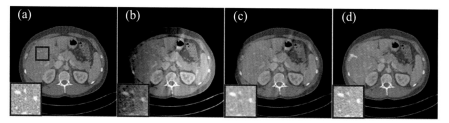

FIGURE 9.1

Image reconstruction via conventional methods and deep learning. (a) Normal-dose CT (NDCT), (b) Low-dose CT (LDCT), (c) Iterative reconstruction (TV) and (d) Deep-learning method (DDNet).

The deep learning-based CT reconstruction methods can be grouped into four categories: image domain post-processing, hybrid domain-based processing, deep learning-based iterative reconstruction and deep learning-based direct reconstruction. The first category focuses on restoring CT images in a single domain. These methods are designed to train an image-to-image mapping network, which converts degraded images into acceptable high-quality images without accessing the raw projection data. There are also some opportunities to enhance the projection domain data using deep learning, such as de-noising and corrections. The second category processes the data in both image and projection domains. The quality of the reconstruction images can be further improved by processing projection data. The third category combines the conventional iterative reconstruction with deep learning to achieve better results. The fourth category explores a direct mapping from projection data to images via deep neural networks. Currently, deep learning is a very popular research topic in the field of medical imaging. Some methods have been applied in commercial CT scanners for their impressive reconstruction results.

9.3.1 Image domain post-processing

In imaging systems, the reconstructed images are often accompanied by artifacts and noise due to sampling, dose limitations and physical defects, which may seriously affect the diagnosis results. The post-processing algorithm based on the image domain can make the reconstructed image close to, or even equal to a noise-free and artifact-free image with the maximum probability. Because it is difficult to determine the noise distribution and artifact range in the image domain, the conventional image domain processing algorithm cannot achieve satisfying results in image de-noising and artifact removal. However, once sufficient and good training samples are provided, deep learning techniques can effectively solve this problem by using their strong ability on learning prior information [89]. Such problems can be solved by optimizing the following objective functions to obtain high-quality reconstructed images:

$$\hat{g} = \arg\min_{g} \left\| g(x) - x^* \right\|_2^2 + p\left(x^*\right) \tag{9.5}$$

where x is the image with noise and artifacts and x^* is the ideal reconstructed image, $g(x)$ represents the image reconstructed by deep learning operator, the prior constraint $p\left(x^*\right)$ can be learned from training data using a neural network. Continuously optimizing the image processing operator $g(x)$ through deep learning makes the processed image close to the ground truth image with the maximum probability.

The convolutions, pooling operations and nonlinearities are three basic elements of deep neural networks. The combination of these elements yields a powerful tool for medical imaging. Noise is usually represented as an isolated pixel or pixel block that causes a strong visual effect on the image. The convolutional kernel of the deep neural network is equivalent to the filter operator in digital image processing. Fig. 9.2 shows a convolutional neural network (CNN)-based method for LDCT de-noising [86], which utilized multi-layer convolutions to map LDCT images to the corresponding NDCT counterparts. "ReLU" represents the rectified linear unit, which is an activation function commonly used in artificial neural networks. The residual connection prevents the loss of information in the feature extraction stage. In 2016, Kang et al. [90] proposed a similar CNN-based architecture for LDCT de-noising. These simpler structures can also work well as networks are trained with larger, more representative data sets. In the following years, researchers focused on improving the network structures and loss functions [91]. For example, Chen et al. [92] adopted the deconvolution layers and skip connections to construct an encoder–decoder architecture (RED-CNN), which can maintain more image details.

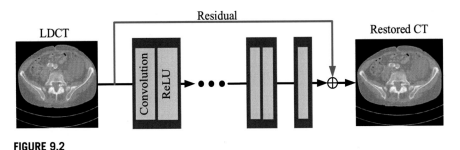

FIGURE 9.2

A CNN-based method for LDCT processing.

It should be noted that the process of training a neural network is actually feature learning. To further improve the performance of RED-CNN, Zhang et al. [93] replaced all the convolution layers with a dense block [94]. This modification of enhancing image features has been proved to be effective. Preserving useful image features to the greatest extent, such as edges and textures, is the key to obtaining high-quality reconstructed images. In reference to the recent works using dictionary learning to distinguish positive features (tissue relevant features) and negative features (noise and artifacts) in CT images [95,96], Liu et al. [97] extended the idea of feature extraction to three dimensions. In this work, a deep 3D iterative reconstruction estimation (DIRE) strategy was proposed to estimate noise and artifacts in LDCT.

9.3.2 Hybrid domain-based processing

In the projection domain, conventional methods design filters according to the statistical characteristics of noise. In the past few years, deep learning has been developed extensively to process corrupted projection data. Claus et al. [98] introduced a network consisting of three fully connected layers to reduce the metal artifacts in the projection domain. Park et al. [99] utilized the U-Net to learn the consistency of projection data.

Since the side effects caused by the operation in the projection domain can introduce secondary image artifacts, the methods based on the projection domain and image domain should be combined to eliminate artifacts and improve image quality. A common path toward the hybrid domain-based CT reconstruction is illustrated in Fig. 9.3. First, a deep neural network can be used to restore the missing projection data. Second, we can obtain the reconstructed CT images by using the filtered back projection (FBP) algorithm. Finally, the CT images with high quality are obtained by using a deep neural network to further suppress noise.

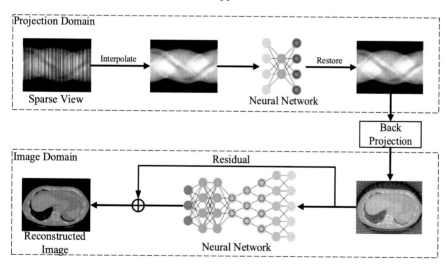

FIGURE 9.3

A hybrid domain-based deep-learning method for sparse view CT reconstruction.

Recently, the problem of joint optimization in the hybrid domain has attracted extensive attention. In [100], to improve image quality and shorten algorithm processing time, Yin et al. proposed a Domain Progressive 3D Residual Convolution Network (DP-ResNet) to remove the noise of LDCT in the image domain and projection domain, respectively. The algorithm was composed of projection domain subnetwork, FBP reconstruction and image domain subnetwork. It can represent the data information of projection space and image domain at a different depth and obtain better results than single domain processing. Dual spatial network synergistic constraints help to improve image quality and shorten algorithm processing time. Some representative results are shown in Fig. 9.4. We can observe that all the methods have shown good de-noising and detail restoration capacity. Overall, images produced by the hybrid domain-based method can mitigate the blurring effect and restore more structural details, as pointed out by the red arrow in Fig. 9.4 (e). Zhang et al. [101] used GAN in their hybrid domain method to improve the edges, textures and other details in LDCT images. This method was composed of a projection domain generator (PD-Net), image domain generator (ID-Net) and image domain discriminator. Both generators were composed of 3D Res-UNet. In addition, a differentiable FBP operator was introduced to combine the two domains. The operator was compatible with the back-propagation algorithm and could propagate the image gradient to the projection domain.

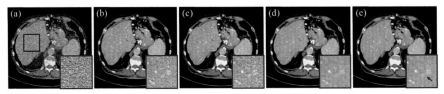

FIGURE 9.4

Representative results selected from [100]. (a) LDCT, (b) Ground-truth, (c) Projection domain-based reconstruction, (d) Image domain-based reconstruction, (e) Hybrid domain-based reconstruction.

In addition to LDCT reconstruction, deep learning-based approaches are also very effective in solving the reconstruction problem of missing data. Since the measurement consistency can provide robust guarantees for the worst-case performance, they applied the FDK algorithm as a correction operator to get error images [102].

Dual-energy computed tomography (DECT) has the unique advantages of fast imaging speed, superior diagnostic quality and material identification. However, DECT has obvious information redundancy. First, the anatomical structures of low-energy and high-energy CT images are consistent. Second, the images in the energy domain are also correlated with each other. To deal with this problem, we can still accurately restore the image while reducing the number of samples (avoid collecting redundant information) with the help of deep learning. Zhang et al. [103] applied the hybrid domain learning to DECT sparse-view reconstruction. They proposed a Comprehensive Domain Network (CD-Net) for DECT sparse-view reconstruction, which could provide the simultaneous and effective reconstruction of two energy levels in a single scan. Lyu et al. [104] designed a hybrid domain material decomposition network to estimate DECT images from single-energy CT data.

9.3.3 Iterative reconstruction via deep learning

Due to the long computation time and high-computational complexity of the conventional iterative reconstruction, the earlier algorithms were only used in the field of nuclear imaging. In recent years, with the development of computer technology, deep learning and the growing demand for LDCT imaging, iterative reconstruction algorithms using deep learning have received renewed attention in the field of CT imaging. This type of method replaces the regular term of the conventional iterative reconstruction with a deep neural network to learn the prior information. It is still based on the framework of the iterative reconstruction. Fig. 9.5 illustrates a common iterative reconstruction method using deep learning. The deep-learning networks can be embedded in the projection domain and image domain to optimize the intermediate image.

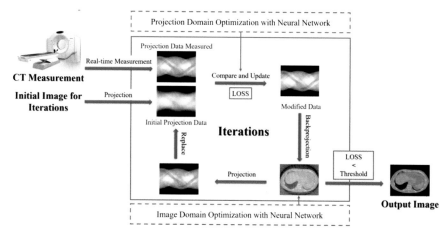

FIGURE 9.5

Iterative reconstruction flow via deep learning.

Considering that CNN can introduce prior knowledge of images through the training process, Chen et al. [105] constructed a Learned Experts' Assessment-based Reconstruction Network (LEARN) based on compressed sensing for data-driven training. The Field of Experts (FoE) model was introduced to construct regularization terms. Moreover, the latest iterative reconstruction technology performs iterative calculation in the projection domain and image domain through forward and backward reconstruction. It utilizes a statistical model for comparison and correction, finally obtaining clearer low-noise and high-resolution CT images. This requires the introduction of appropriate prior knowledge in both domains and involves tedious manual optimization of multiple parameters. To this end, He et al. [106] proposed a plug-and-play method for alternating direction method of multipliers 3pADMM. The deep-learning strategy was introduced to solve the problems of prior knowledge design and parameter selection in an optimization framework. In addition, Bubba et al. [107] introduced a framework, which combined the model-based sparse regularization with U-Net. Specifically, they divided the original data into visible and invisible parts. The conventional sparse regularization was used to deal with the visible part, and the U-Net was employed to predict the invisible part. Hu et al. [108] proposed a hybrid domain reconstruction method called SPECIAL (Single-Shot Projection Error Correction Integrated Adversarial Learning) for Limited-Angle CT. They introduced a Dense Encoder-Decoder Network (DEDN) to obtain the complementary information contained in the image and projection domains. Xiang et al. [109] unfolded the model-based Fast Iterative Shrinkage/Thresholding Algorithm (FISTA) into a deep neural network to update the gradient matrix during iteration.

9.3.4 Direct reconstruction via deep learning

Before the explosion of deep learning, neural networks were used for CT reconstruction work. Due to hardware limitations at that time, the original network only had several hidden layers. With the development of deep learning, researchers began to explore direct mapping from projection data to the final reconstructed images with deeper networks.

In 2018, Zhu et al. [24] presented a direct reconstruction network, named automated transform by manifold approximation (AutoMap), which employed a series of fully connected layers to learn the whole mapping process. Then the fully connected layers, two convolutional layers and one deconvolutional layer were adopted to reduce the noise and artifacts. Fu et al. [110] simplified the fully connected method into a sparse matrix by using the data correlation. Due to the huge number of trainable parameters of AutoMap caused by the fully connected layer, the limitation of this direction is its computational cost during network training. For example, given a feature map with a size of $7 \times 7 \times 64$, the fully connected layer flattens the feature map into a 2D vector with a size of 1×1024. The number of parameters in this layer is $7 \times 7 \times 64 \times 1024$, which has exceeded 3 million. To this end, some works [111,112] introduced analytic transform, such as the Radon transform, in neural networks as their physical basis to simulate the reconstruction process and reconstruct more accurately, even with the limited angles problems and sparse views problems.

Fig. 9.6 shows a common deep-learning network that simulates FBP. L1-L5 suppresses noise and converts sparse view sinogram into a dense view sinogram, corresponding to the signal correction step in conventional FBP. L6-L9 learns high-level feature representations from the output data of the L5 layer, corresponding to the filtering step. L10 performs a domain transform from the extracted data feature space to image space and L11-L12 learn a combination of the partial image from each view angle to generate a final image, corresponding to the back projection and summation steps.

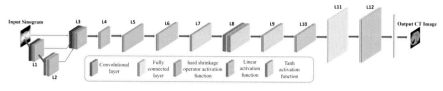

FIGURE 9.6

A common deep learning network that simulates FBP [112], in which each stage of FBP corresponds to part of the network.

9.3.5 Conclusion

Recently, deep learning-based CT reconstruction methods have achieved great success. Until now, most of them are supervised learning, which means that sufficient one-to-one corresponding data are needed for network training. However, it is impractical to obtain the NDCT and LDCT scans on the same patient. Clinical tomographic images and projection data for network training are generally limited, and their labels are typically unavailable or inaccurate.

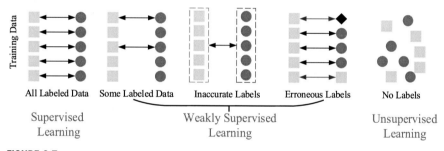

FIGURE 9.7

Training data labeled in different forms. All labeled data allow supervised learning, and unlabeled data can only be used for unsupervised learning.

As shown in Fig. 9.7, clinical data sets are incomplete or inaccurate in most cases, which means that the supervised learning mentioned is no longer applicable. Extensive efforts have been made to handle this problem. For example, Kang et al. [113] introduced cycleGAN for unlabeled LDCT reconstruction. Liao et al. [114] employed an unsupervised learning strategy for CT metal artifact reduction. It is essential for us to combine various kinds of prior knowledge when using weakly supervised or unsupervised learning.

Although deep learning-based reconstruction algorithms have emerged in recent years, they are still in their infancy. The computational cost and the difficulty in obtaining complete clinical data greatly hinder their implementation in clinical practice. However, with the orderly advancement of research, various problems have been gradually solved, and the level of reconstruction has been continuously improved.

We believe that research in this field will transform current CT diagnostics into smart, affordable, preventive and precision medicine.

9.4 Deep learning for PET reconstruction

9.4.1 Introduction

Positron Emission Tomography (PET) is a molecular imaging technique commonly used in clinic applications such as disease diagnosis, radiation therapy planning and prognosis evaluation. The procedure of PET imaging is illustrated in Fig. 9.8. Prior to a PET scan, a tracer compound labeled with a positron emitting radionuclide is administered into a patient (or a research subject). The radionuclide decays by emitting positrons (hence the name of PET). Positrons annihilate on contact with electrons, subsequently with two 511 keV γ photons produced traveling in the opposite directions. During the PET scan, these photons are registered by external detectors positioned surrounding the patient. Detector electronics are designed to determine whether a pair of photons reach the detector simultaneously (more precisely, within a particular time window). The process is called annihilation coincidence detection. Information about coincident photons is then stored for computer algorithms to reconstruct the tracer distribution throughout the patient. With the distribution, one can quantitatively assess metabolism, receptor binding and other physiological activities *in vivo*.

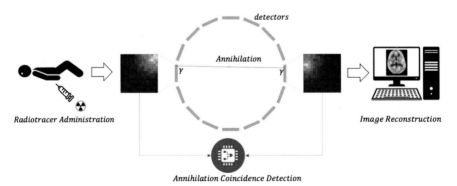

FIGURE 9.8

The procedure of PET imaging. Positron emitting radiotracers are administrated into the subject; then pairs of γ photons that have been produced from the annihilation of positrons and electrons are registered via the annihilation coincidence detection. An image reconstruction algorithm provides the cross-sectional images of radioactive intensity from acquired coincident photons.

9.4.2 **Conventional PET reconstruction**

Numerous research efforts have been devoted to the developing of PET image reconstruction methods for better performance since the introduction of PET in the 1970s. PET image reconstruction aims to obtain cross-sectional maps of radioactive intensity from coincident γ photons recorded.

A simple analytic model in PET sees the number of coincident photons traveling along a specific line as a value proportional to a line integral of the tracer activity along that line, which is similar to the model in CT imaging. Parallel sets of such line integrals are called projections, or sinograms in a 2D case arranged for different angles of line integrals. The most well-known algorithm for reconstruction is the analytical method called Filtered Back-Projection (FBP). FBP reconstruction is essentially a direct inverse of the integral, and thus involves some differentiation, which amplifies noise in the data. Besides, the mathematic model ignores physical effects such as attenuation of photons in the patient, scatter coincidence and random coincidence.

Statistical models are developed to account for the counting noise as Poisson distributed noise and incorporate more physical effects to improve the reconstruction performance. Iterative reconstruction algorithms are usually designed to invert these statistical models. The most commonly used iterative algorithms are the Maximum Likelihood Expectation Maximization (MLEM) algorithm [115] and its extension with higher-computational efficiency the Ordered Subsets Expectation Maximization (OSEM) algorithm [116]. Compared to the analytical algorithms, the iterative algorithms can provide reconstructed images with a lower noise level but at the cost of a higher-computational burden.

Combining analytic models with iterative methods takes the advantage of both categories of reconstruction methods. For the fully 3D reconstruction, the Reprojection and Filtered Back-projection (3D-RP) [117] was widely used, until Fourier Rebinning [118] reduces the 3D reconstruction problem to a series of 2D reconstruction problems. The hybrid method combining Fourier rebinning and iterative methods provides comparable images as 3D-RP but significantly reduces the computational burden.

To further improve the performance of the statistical model, Bayesian methodology is used to incorporate a priori information about the PET image into reconstruction [119]. It turns the maximum likelihood estimation to the maximum a posterior (MAP) estimation. Most MAP-EM algorithms choose smoothing priors to suppress the noise and simultaneously reserve the edge. Another approach is the kernelized EM [120], which models the image as features based on specific kernels and provides better noise property for low-count data. However, PET images are still associated with relatively poor spatial resolution and high-noise levels due to the photon-limited acquisition procedure.

9.4.3 Deep learning-based algorithms in PET imaging

In recent years, machine learning (more specifically its subfield deep learning) has widely impacted many diverse fields. It has not surprisingly become one of the most popular techniques used in image reconstruction. The data-driven characteristic of deep-learning reconstruction saves the efforts of deriving the explicit model for imaging. And since the neural network (the backbone of deep learning) is trained beforehand in an iterative way, and then infers the image as an analytic algorithm does, deep-learning reconstruction has high-computational efficiency. Furthermore, reducing the radiation dose in PET results in more noisy measured data. The excellent performance of various de-noising networks becomes especially crucial in PET reconstruction at suppressing noise.

Some research adopted direct deep-learning methods for PET reconstruction to learn a direct mapping between projection domain and image domain, for example, with fully connected layers [24,121] or convolutional neural networks [122]. Direct learning relies highly on measured data and does not assume knowledge of data acquisition.

To reduce the requirements on training data, some works designed model-based methods combining deep learning with the traditional iterative reconstruction method. Lim et al. [123] proposed a BCD-Net to unfold a block coordinate descent algorithm using learned convolutional analysis operators. Gong et al. proposed an EM-net [124] and a MAPEM-Net [125] to incorporate the popular penalized MLEM and MAPEM algorithm. Mehranian and Reader [126] unrolled the forward–backward split EM algorithm into a recurrent neural network. In these methods, the convolutional neural network (CNN) replaces the regularization term in the iterative methods, which extracts more powerful prior information from the training data set. However, the reconstruction speed is limited by the iterative algorithm.

The model-based deep-learning method can also be combined with analytical reconstruction algorithms to speed up the reconstruction. Würfl et al. [111] mapped the FBP algorithm to neural network and proposed a new back-projection layer to replace the fully connected layer. Ge et al. [127] first implemented a BPF-type CT reconstruction strategy (that may apply to PET data) using the deep-learning approach in the image domain to learn a close approximation of the theoretical deconvolution kernel. Wang and Liu [128] proposed the FBP-Net, which contains the FBP module to adaptively learn the frequency filter and the de-noiser module to merge the information of all time frames to improve the dynamic PET image quality. It requires only a small data size to achieve comparable results with the DeepPET. Also, several works [129–131] used back-projection-like histo-images as the network input for direct reconstruction, where the histo-image is an intermediate image between projected data and reconstructed image.

Recent work about a BPF-like deep learning algorithm is presented to reconstruct the time-of-flight (TOF) PET data. Each coincidence in the listmode data is back-projected into the image space with a Gaussian kernel determined by the TOF resolution. The back-projected image is proved to be related to the original image via an explicit filter. Then a modified U-Net that learns the inverse of the filter outputs the estimated image. This method performs on-the-fly back-projection while collecting the listmode data and restores only the back-projected image to reduce the storage space. It shows a good generative ability from one type of phantom to another [132]. See Fig. 9.9.

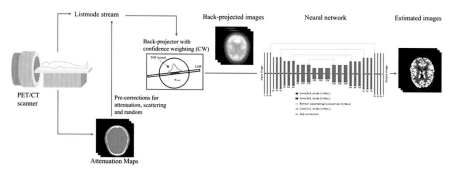

FIGURE 9.9

The BPF-like deep-learning algorithm for PET imaging. Compared to the conventional U-Net, the proposed deep filter network uses a convolution kernel with stride 2 × 2 for down-sampling instead of the max pooling module; removes the BN module; uses a 2 × 2 bi-linear up-sampling module for up-sampling instead of a deconvolution module; and uses a copy-and-add operation for shortcut instead of concatenating [132].

Different review articles have been published on deep learning in PET reconstruction [133–137]. Even more summations and surveys can be found in the broader area of artificial intelligence in medical imaging and medical image analysis [138–147]. Readers are suggested to refer to these extensive works for more details. Besides, AI for CT reconstruction in Section 9.3 is also a good reference where some algorithms are also applicable to PET reconstruction, due to the similar analytical model for PET and CT acquisitions.

Generally, the endeavor to improve PET image reconstruction aims to increase overall image quality that could potentially be translated to better diagnostic confidence or lower dose level. Other than using deep learning on reconstruction algorithms, there are many more that can be done to achieve this goal.

For instance, the detection of γ photons can be improved in terms of both the time and position of interaction. Deep-learning technology has been used to detect the time resolution in the coincidence of γ photons. The timing information can be learned from the coincident detector waveforms acquired by fast waveform digitizers with the deep CNN. This direct estimation of time-of-flight improves timing resolution by 20% compared to conventional methods [148]. For more accurate position information about the γ photon interaction, researchers use neural networks to estimate the inter-crystal scattering [149–151], with the potential to increase the detection efficiency and spatial resolution. Another scenario for deep learning to improve the detection accuracy is positioning the actual positron, instead of the coincidence of γ photons. In PET imaging, some radionuclides emit high-energy positrons that travel a long distance (known as the positron range) before annihilation. Herraiz et al. designed a U-Net to correct the blurring in reconstructed images caused by the long positron range [152].

There are also efforts on training a deep network to solve the problems faced in developing novel PET systems. At the detector level, CNNs are designed for location estimation of γ photon interactions in coarse [153] and monolithic [154] scintillation crystal detectors, increasing the cost performance. These approaches may also improve simultaneously the sensitivity and resolution of PET imaging. As for the system design, research works have shown that CNN works better than model-based methods in recovering missing data in the sinograms and restoring artifact-free images, for the PET system with sparse detectors [155–157] and irregular geometric PET systems such as the C-arm PET [158].

9.4.4 Conclusion

As reviewed here and in many other review articles, machine learning in PET imaging has become an exciting topic in the last 5 years. Learning strategy can be used either directly on the measured PET data to obtain reconstructed images, as a component or a replacement of conventional reconstruction, or on corrections for physical effects such as attenuation and scattering. Marvelous algorithms have been demonstrated in improving the image quality and reducing the computational load. Besides the image reconstruction, deep-learning finds its application everywhere else on the chain of PET imaging. At the end of signal detection, deep learning can be used to design better detectors and systems. Moving to the end after reconstruction, deep learning finds its application on quantitation and image processing. Although there are concerns about ethics and safety, we believe once properly utilized the deep-learning technology can be translated to solid clinical applications with PET imaging and benefit both physicians and patients.

9.5 Discussion and conclusion

We have given a comprehensive review on deep learning-based MRI, CT and PET reconstruction and summarized the typical networks in this field. We refer interested readers to another review on deep learning for tomographic image reconstruction [159]. In only a few years, various networks have already been developed to take advantage of the unique properties of MRI, CT or PET. Implicit neural representation (INR), which is first introduced in computer vision to reconstruct complex scenes, has been further developed in medical image reconstruction. With the continuous representation of the object, INR reconstructs images with high quality and fewer artifacts in sparse-view CT or accelerated MRI [160,161]. Diffusion models have emerged as a recent and burgeoning trend in the last few years. Initially, diffusion models achieved impressive performance in the task of natural image generation, and subsequently, they were quickly adopted in the field of medical imaging. Studies have been proposed to accomplish data set synthesis [162] and image reconstruction tasks [163], leveraging the powerful generative capacity and controllable generation approach of diffusion models. As the Transformer, Diffusion model and ChatGPT have become more and more popular, deep learning-based MRI, CT and PET reconstruction will be more powerful.

References

[1] Z.-P. Liang, F.E. Boada, R.T. Constable, E.M. Haacke, P.C. Lauterbur, M.R. Smith, Constrained reconstruction methods in MR imaging, Reviews of Magnetic Resonance in Medicine 4 (1992) 67–185.

[2] M. Lustig, J.M. Pauly, Sparse MRI: the application of compressed sensing for rapid MR imaging, Magnetic Resonance in Medicine 58 (6) (2007) 1182–1195.

[3] M. Lustig, D.L. Donoho, J.M. Santos, J.M. Pauly, Compressed sensing MRI, IEEE Signal Processing Magazine 25 (2008) 72–82.

[4] S. Ramani, Z.H. Liu, J. Rosen, J.F. Nielsen, J.A. Fessler, Regularization parameter selection for nonlinear iterative image restoration and MRI reconstruction using GCV and SURE-based methods, IEEE Transactions on Image Processing 21 (2012) 3659–3672.

[5] D. Liang, J. Cheng, Z. Ke, L. Ying, Deep magnetic resonance image reconstruction: inverse problems meet neural networks, IEEE Signal Processing Magazine 37 (1) (2020) 141–151.

[6] J. Montalt-Tordera, V. Muthurangu, A. Hauptmann, J.A. Steeden, Machine learning in magnetic resonance imaging: image reconstruction, Physica Medica 83 (2021) 79–87.

[7] F. Knoll, K. Hammernik, C. Zhang, S. Moeller, T. Pock, D.K. Sodickson, M. Akçakaya, Deep-learning methods for parallel magnetic resonance imaging reconstruction: a survey of the current approaches, trends, and issues, IEEE Signal Processing Magazine 37 (1) (2020) 128–140.

[8] S. Wang, Z. Su, L. Ying, X. Peng, S. Zhu, F. Liang, D. Feng, D. Liang, Accelerating magnetic resonance imaging via deep learning, in: Proc in IEEE Int Symp Biomed Imaging, 2016, pp. 514–517.

[9] K. Kwon, D. Kim, H. Park, A parallel MR imaging method using multilayer perceptron, Medical Physics 44 (12) (2017) 6209–6224.

[10] D. Lee, J. Yoo, S. Tak, J.C. Ye, Deep residual learning for accelerated MRI using magnitude and phase networks, IEEE Transactions on Bio-Medical Engineering 65 (9) (2018) 1985–1995.

[11] A. Hauptmann, S. Arridge, F. Lucka, V. Muthurangu, J.A. Steeden, Real-time cardiovascular MR with spatio-temporal artifact suppression using deep learning–proof of concept in congenital heart disease, Magnetic Resonance in Medicine 81 (2) (2019) 1143–1156.

[12] R. Souza, M. Bento, N. Nogovitsyn, K.J. Chung, W. Loos, R.M. Lebel, R. Frayne, Dual-domain cascade of U-nets for multi-channel magnetic resonance image reconstruction, Magnetic Resonance Imaging 71 (2020) 140–153.

[13] E. Cole, J. Cheng, J. Pauly, S. Vasanawala, Analysis of deep complex-valued convolutional neural networks for MRI reconstruction and phase-focused applications, Magnetic Resonance in Medicine 86 (2) (2021) 1093–1109.

[14] W.J. Do, S. Seo, Y. Han, J.C. Ye, S.H. Choi, S.H. Park, Reconstruction of multicontrast MR images through deep learning, Medical Physics 47 (3) (2020) 983–997.

[15] X. Peng, B.P. Sutton, F. Lam, Z.P. Liang, DeepSENSE: learning coil sensitivity functions for SENSE reconstruction using deep learning, Magnetic Resonance in Medicine 87 (4) (2022) 1894–1902.

[16] E.Z. Chen, P. Wang, X. Chen, T. Chen, S. Sun, Pyramid convolutional RNN for MRI image reconstruction, IEEE Transactions on Medical Imaging 41 (8) (2022) 2033–2047.

[17] M. Mardani, E. Gong, J.Y. Cheng, S.S. Vasanawala, G. Zaharchuk, L. Xing, J.M. Pauly, Deep generative adversarial neural networks for compressive sensing MRI, IEEE Transactions on Medical Imaging 38 (1) (2019) 167–179.

[18] G. Yang, S. Yu, H. Dong, G. Slabaugh, P.L. Dragotti, X. Ye, F. Liu, S. Arridge, J. Keegan, Y. Guo, D. Firmin, DAGAN: deep de-aliasing generative adversarial networks for fast compressed sensing MRI reconstruction, IEEE Transactions on Medical Imaging 37 (6) (2017) 1310–1321.

[19] T.M. Quan, T. Nguyen-Duc, W.K. Jeong, Compressed sensing MRI reconstruction using a generative adversarial network with a cyclic loss, IEEE Transactions on Medical Imaging 37 (2018) 1488–1497.

[20] M. Akçakaya, S. Moeller, S. Weingärtner, K. Uğurbil, Scan-specific robust artificial-neural-networks for k-space interpolation (RAKI) reconstruction: database-free deep learning for fast imaging, Magnetic Resonance in Medicine 81 (1) (2019) 439–453.

[21] Y. Arefeen, O. Beker, J. Cho, H. Yu, E. Adalsteinsson, B. Bilgic, Scan-specific artifact reduction in k-space (SPARK) neural networks synergize with physics-based reconstruction to accelerate MRI, Magnetic Resonance in Medicine 87 (2) (2022) 764–780.

[22] A. Pramanik, H.K. Aggarwal, M. Jacob, Deep generalization of structured low-rank algorithms (Deep-SLR), IEEE Transactions on Medical Imaging 39 (12) (2020) 4186–4197.

[23] Y. Han, L. Sunwoo, J.C. Ye, K-space deep learning for accelerated MRI, IEEE Transactions on Medical Imaging 39 (2) (2020) 377–386.

[24] B. Zhu, J.Z. Liu, S.F. Cauley, B.R. Rosen, M.S. Rosen, Image reconstruction by domain-transform manifold learning, Nature 555 (7697) (2018) 487–492.

[25] T. Eo, H. Shin, Y. Jun, T. Kim, D. Hwang, Accelerating Cartesian MRI by domain-transform manifold learning in phase-encoding direction, Medical Image Analysis 101689 (2020).

[26] S. Wang, Z. Ke, H. Cheng, S. Jia, L. Ying, H. Zheng, D. Liang, DIMENSION: dynamic MR imaging with both k-space and spatial prior knowledge obtained via multi-supervised network training, NMR in Biomedicine (2019) e4131.

[27] T. Eo, Y. Jun, T. Kim, J. Jang, H.J. Lee, D. Hwang, KIKI-Net: cross-domain convolutional neural networks for reconstructing undersampled magnetic resonance images, Magnetic Resonance in Medicine 80 (5) (2018) 2188–2201.

[28] C. Cai, C. Wang, Y. Zeng, S. Cai, D. Liang, Y. Wu, Z. Chen, X. Ding, J. Zhong, Single-shot T2 mapping using overlapping-echo detachment planar imaging and a deep convolutional neural network, Magnetic Resonance in Medicine 80 (5) (2018) 2202–2214.

[29] F. Liu, L. Feng, R. Kijowski, MANTIS: Model-Augmented Neural neTwork with Incoherent k-space Sampling for efficient MR parameter mapping, Magnetic Resonance in Medicine 82 (1) (2019) 74–188.

[30] J. Yoon, E. Gong, I. Chatnuntawech, B. Bilgic, J. Lee, W. Jung, J. Ko, H. Jung, K. Setsompop, G. Zaharchuk, E.Y. Kim, J. Pauly, J. Lee, Quantitative susceptibility mapping using deep neural network: QSMnet, NeuroImage 179 (2018) 199–206.

[31] O. Cohen, B. Zhu, M.S. Rosen, MR fingerprinting Deep RecOnstruction NEtwork (DRONE), Magnetic Resonance in Medicine 80 (3) (2018) 885–894.

[32] K. Hammernik, T. Klatzer, E. Kobler, M.P. Recht, D.K. Sodickson, T. Pock, F. Knoll, Learning a variational network for reconstruction of accelerated MRI data, Magnetic Resonance in Medicine 79 (6) (2018) 3055–3071.

[33] V. Vishnevskiy, J. Walheim, S. Kozerke, Deep variational network for rapid 4D flow MRI reconstruction, Nature Machine Intelligence 2 (4) (2020) 228–235.

[34] D. Polak, S. Cauley, B. Bilgic, et al., Joint multi-contrast variational network reconstruction (jVN) with application to rapid 2D and 3D imaging, Magnetic Resonance in Medicine 84 (2020) 1456–1469.

[35] S.A.H. Hosseini, B. Yaman, S. Moeller, M. Hong, M. Akçakaya, Dense recurrent neural networks for accelerated MRI: history-cognizant unrolling of optimization algorithms, IEEE Journal of Selected Topics in Signal Processing 14 (2020) 1280–1291.

[36] J. Cheng, Z.X. Cui, W. Huang, Z. Ke, L. Ying, H. Wang, Y. Zhu, D. Liang, Learning data consistency and its application to dynamic MR imaging, IEEE Transactions on Medical Imaging 40 (11) (2021) 3140–3153.

[37] C.M. Sandino, P. Lai, S.S. Vasanawala, J.Y. Cheng, Accelerating cardiac cine MRI using a deep learning-based ESPIRiT reconstruction, Magnetic Resonance in Medicine 85 (1) (2021) 152–167.

[38] J. Zhang, B. Ghanem, ISTA-Net: interpretable optimization-inspired deep network for image compressive sensing, in: Proc. IEEE Comput. Soc. Conf. Comput. Vis. Pattern Recognit., 2018, pp. 1828–1837.

[39] H.K. Aggarwal, M.P. Mani, M. Jacob, MoDL: model-based deep learning architecture for inverse problems, IEEE Transactions on Medical Imaging 38 (2) (2019) 394–405.

[40] S. Biswas, H.K. Aggarwal, M. Jacob, Dynamic MRI using model-based deep learning and SToRM priors: MoDL-SToRM, Magnetic Resonance in Medicine 82 (2019) 485–494.

[41] J. Schlemper, J. Caballero, J.V. Hajnal, A.N. Price, D. Rueckert, A deep cascade of convolutional neural networks for dynamic MR image reconstruction, IEEE Transactions on Medical Imaging 37 (2) (2018) 491–503.

[42] C. Qin, J. Schlemper, J. Caballero, A.N. Price, J.V. Hajnal, D. Rueckert, Convolutional recurrent neural networks for dynamic MR image reconstruction, IEEE Transactions on Medical Imaging 38 (1) (2019) 280–290.

[43] J. Duan, Jo Schlemper, C. Qin, C. Ouyang, Wenjia Bai, C. Biffi, G. Bello, B. Statton, D. O'Regan, D. Rueckert, VS-Net: variable splitting network for accelerated parallel MRI reconstruction, in: MICCAI, 2019, pp. 713–722.

[44] Z. Ke, W. Huang, Z.X. Cui, J. Cheng, S. Jia, H. Wang, X. Liu, H. Zheng, L. Ying, Y. Zhu, D. Liang, Learned low-rank priors in dynamic MR imaging, IEEE Transactions on Medical Imaging 40 (12) (2021) 3698–3710.

[45] Y. Liu, Q. Liu, M. Zhang, Q. Yang, S. Wang, D. Liang, IFR-Net: iterative feature refinement network for compressed sensing MRI, IEEE Transactions on Computational Imaging 6 (2019) 434–446.

[46] Z. Ke, Z.X. Cui, W. Huang, J. Cheng, S. Jia, L. Ying, Y. Zhu, D. Liang, Deep manifold learning for dynamic MR imaging, IEEE Transactions on Computational Imaging 7 (2021) 1314–1327.

[47] W. Huang, Z. Ke, Z. Cui, J. Cheng, Z. Qiu, S. Jia, L. Ying, Y. Zhu, D. Liang, Deep low-rank plus sparse network for dynamic MR imaging, Medical Image Analysis 73 (2021) 102190.

[48] L. Sun, Z. Fan, X. Fu, Y. Huang, X. Ding, J. Paisley, A deep information sharing network for multi-contrast compressed sensing MRI reconstruction, IEEE Transactions on Image Processing 28 (2019) 6141–6153.

[49] S. Wang, H. Cheng, L. Ying, T. Xiao, Z. Ke, H. Zheng, D. Liang, DeepcomplexMRI: exploiting deep residual network for fast parallel MR imaging with complex convolution, Magnetic Resonance Imaging 68 (2020) 136–147.

[50] Y. Yang, J. Sun, H. Li, Z. Xu, ADMM-CSNet: a deep learning approach for image compressive sensing, IEEE Transactions on Pattern Analysis and Machine Intelligence 42 (3) (2020) 521–538.

[51] J. Adler, J. Adler, Learned primal-dual reconstruction, IEEE Transactions on Medical Imaging 37 (6) (2018) 1322–1332.

[52] J. Cheng, H. Wang, L. Ying, D. Liang, Model learning: primal dual networks for fast MR imaging, in: MICCAI, 2019, pp. 21–29.

[53] D. Ulyanov, A. Vedaldi, V. Lempitsky, Deep image prior, in: IEEE Computer Society Conference on Computer Vision and Pattern Recognition (CVPR), 2018, pp. 9446–9454.

[54] J. Yoo, K.H. Jin, H. Gupta, J. Yerly, M. Stuber, M. Unser, Time-dependent deep image prior for dynamic MRI, IEEE Transactions on Medical Imaging 40 (12) (2021) 3337–3348.

[55] M.Z. Darestani, R. Heckel, Accelerated MRI with un-trained neural networks, IEEE Transactions on Computational Imaging 7 (2021) 724–733.

[56] R. Heckel, M. Soltanolkotabi, Compressive sensing with un-trained neural networks: gradient descent finds the smoothest approximation, in: Proc. Int. Conf. Mach. Learn., 2020, pp. 4149–4158.

[57] J. Lehtinen, J. Munkberg, J. Hasselgren, S. Laine, T. Karras, M. Aittala, T. Aila, Noise2Noise: learning image restoration without clean data, in: ICML, 2018, pp. 2965–2974.

[58] J. Liu, Y. Sun, C. Eldeniz, W. Gan, H. An, U.S. Kamilov, RARE: image reconstruction using deep priors learned without groundtruth, IEEE Journal of Selected Topics in Signal Processing 14 (6) (2020) 1088–1099.

[59] Q. Liu, Q. Yang, H. Cheng, S. Wang, M. Zhang, D. Liang, Highly undersampled magnetic resonance imaging reconstruction using autoencoding priors, Magnetic Resonance in Medicine 83 (1) (2020) 322–336.

[60] F. Liu, R. Kijowski, G. El Fakhri, L. Feng, Magnetic resonance parameter mapping using model-guided self-supervised deep learning, Magnetic Resonance in Medicine 85 (6) (2021) 3211–3226.

[61] B. Yaman, S.A.H. Hosseini, S. Moeller, J. Ellermann, K. Uğurbil, M. Akçakaya, Self-supervised learning of physics-guided reconstruction neural networks without fully sampled reference data, Magnetic Resonance in Medicine 84 (6) (2020) 3172–3191.

[62] Z. Ke, J. Cheng, L. Ying, H. Zheng, D. Liang, An unsupervised deep learning method for multi-coil cine MRI, Physics in Medicine and Biology 65 (23) (2020) 235041.

[63] K.C. Tezcan, C.F. Baumgartner, R. Luechinger, K.P. Pruessmann, E. Konukoglu, MR image reconstruction using deep density priors, IEEE Transactions on Medical Imaging 38 (7) (2019) 1633–1642.

[64] G. Luo, N. Zhao, W. Jiang, E.S. Hui, P. Cao, MRI reconstruction using deep Bayesian estimation, Magnetic Resonance in Medicine 84 (4) (2020) 2246–2261.

[65] S.U. Dar, M. Yurt, M. Shahdloo, M.E. Ildız, B. Tınaz, T. Çukur, Prior-guided image reconstruction for accelerated multi-contrast MRI via generative adversarial networks, IEEE Journal of Selected Topics in Signal Processing 14 (6) (2020) 1072–1087.

[66] K. Lei, M. Mardani, J.M. Pauly, S.S. Vasanawala, Wasserstein GANs for MR imaging: from paired to unpaired training, IEEE Transactions on Medical Imaging 40 (1) (2021) 105–115.

[67] J.Y. Zhu, T. Park, P. Isola, A.A. Efros, Unpaired image-to-image translation using cycle-consistent adversarial networks, in: Proceedings of the IEEE International Conference on Computer Vision (ICCV), 2017, pp. 2223–2232.

[68] H. Chung, E. Cha, L. Sunwoo, J.C. Ye, Two-stage deep learning for accelerated 3D time-of-flight MRA without matched training data, Medical Image Analysis 71 (2021) 102047.

[69] G. Oh, B. Sim, H. Chung, L. Sunwoo, J.C. Ye, Unpaired deep learning for accelerated MRI using optimal transport driven CycleGAN, IEEE Transactions on Computational Imaging 6 (2020) 1285–1296.

[70] B. Sim, G. Oh, J. Kim, C. Jung, J.C. Ye, Optimal transport driven CycleGAN for unsupervised learning in inverse problems, SIAM Journal on Imaging Sciences 13 (4) (2020) 2281–2306.

[71] C. Quan, J. Zhou, Y. Zhu, Y. Chen, S. Wang, D. Liang, Q. Liu, Homotopic gradients of generative density priors for MR image reconstruction, IEEE Transactions on Medical Imaging 40 (12) (2021) 3265–3278.

[72] A. Jalal, M. Arvinte, G. Daras, E. Price, A. Dimakis, J. Tamir, Robust compressed sensing MRI with deep generative priors, in: NeurIPS 2021, 2021.

[73] Y. Song, L. Shen, L. Xing, S. Ermon, Solving inverse problems in medical imaging with score-based generative models, in: ICLR2022, 2022.

[74] R. Liu, S. Cheng, L. Ma, X. Fan, Z. Luo, Deep proximal unrolling: algorithmic framework, convergence analysis and applications, IEEE Transactions on Image Processing 28 (10) (2019) 5013–5026.

[75] J.C. Ye, Y. Han, E. Cha, Deep convolutional framelets: a general deep learning framework for inverse problems, SIAM Journal on Imaging Sciences 11 (2) (2018) 991–1048.

[76] F. Knoll, K. Hammernik, E. Kobler, T. Pock, M.P. Recht, D.K. Sodickson, Assessment of the generalization of learned image reconstruction and the potential for transfer learning, Magnetic Resonance in Medicine 81 (2019) 116–128.

[77] V. Antun, F. Renna, C. Poon, B. Adcock, A.C. Hansen, On instabilities of deep learning in image reconstruction and the potential costs of AI, Proceedings of the National Academy of Sciences 117 (48) (2020) 30088–30095.

[78] K. Hammernik, J. Schlemper, C. Qin, J. Duan, R.M. Summers, D. Rueckert, Systematic evaluation of iterative deep neural networks for fast parallel MR image reconstruction, Magnetic Resonance in Medicine 86 (4) (2021) 1859–1872.

[79] S.U.H. Dar, M. Özbey, A.B. Çatlı, T. Çukur, A transfer-learning approach for accelerated MRI using deep neural networks, Magnetic Resonance in Medicine 84 (2) (2020) 663–685.

[80] Y. Han, J. Yoo, H.H. Kim, H.J. Shin, K. Sung, J.C. Ye, Deep learning with domain adaptation for accelerated projection-reconstruction MR, Magnetic Resonance in Medicine 80 (3) (2018) 1189–1205.

[81] F. Knoll, T. Murrell, A. Sriram, N. Yakubova, J. Zbontar, M. Rabbat, A. Defazio, M.J. Muckley, D.K. Sodickson, C.L. Zitnick, M.P. Recht, Advancing machine learning for MR image reconstruction with an open competition: overview of the 2019 fastMRI challenge, Magnetic Resonance in Medicine 84 (2020) 3054–3070.

[82] V. Edupuganti, M. Mardani, S. Vasanawala, J. Pauly, Uncertainty quantification in deep MRI reconstruction, IEEE Transactions on Medical Imaging 40 (1) (2021) 239–250.

[83] D. Narnhofer, A. Effland, E. Kobler, K. Hammernik, F. Knoll, T. Pock, Bayesian uncertainty estimation of learned variational MRI reconstruction, IEEE Transactions on Medical Imaging 41 (2) (2021) 279–291.

[84] D.J. Brenner, E.J. Hall, Computed tomography-an increasing source of radiation exposure, The New England Journal of Medicine 357 (2007) 2277–2284.

[85] I. Shuryak, R.K. Sachs, D.J. Brenner, Cancer risks after radiation exposure in middle age, Journal of the National Cancer Institute 102 (21) (11 2010) 1628–1636.

[86] H. Chen, Y. Zhang, W. Zhang, P. Liao, K. Li, J. Zhou, G. Wang, Low-dose CT via convolutional neural network, Biomedical Optics Express 8 (2) (2017) 679–694.

[87] H. Shan, A. Padole, F. Homayounieh, U. Kruger, R.D. Khera, C. Nitiwarangkul, M.K. Kalra, G. Wang, Competitive performance of a modularized deep neural network compared to commercial algorithms for low-dose CT image reconstruction, Nature Machine Intelligence 1 (6) (2019) 269–276.

[88] Z.C. Zhang, X.K. Liang, X. Dong, Y. Xie, G. Cao, A sparse-view CT reconstruction method based on combination of densenet and deconvolution, IEEE Transactions on Medical Imaging 37 (6) (Jun 2018) 1407–1417.

[89] H. Wang, Y. Li, N. He, K. Ma, D. Meng, Y. Zheng, DICDNet: deep interpretable convolutional dictionary network for metal artifact reduction in CT images, IEEE Transactions on Medical Imaging 41 (4) (2022) 869–880, https://doi.org/10.1109/TMI.2021.3127074.

[90] E. Kang, J. Min, J.C. Ye, A deep convolutional neural network using directional wavelets for low-dose x-ray CT reconstruction, Medical Physics 44 (10) (2017).

[91] J.M. Wolterink, T. Leiner, M.A. Viergever, I. Isgum, Generative adversarial networks for noise reduction in low-dose CT, IEEE Transactions on Medical Imaging 36 (12) (2017) 2536–2545.

[92] H. Chen, Y. Zhang, M.K. Kalra, F. Lin, Y. Chen, P. Liao, J. Zhou, G. Wang, Low-dose CT with a residual encoder–decoder convolutional neural network, IEEE Transactions on Medical Imaging 36 (2017) 2524–2535.

[93] Y. Zhang, H. Yu, Convolutional neural network based metal artifact reduction in X-ray computed tomography, IEEE Transactions on Medical Imaging 37 (6) (June 2018) 1370–1381.

[94] G. Huang, Z. Liu, L. Van Der Maaten, K.Q. Weinberger, Densely connected convolutional networks, in: 2017 IEEE Conference on Computer Vision and Pattern Recognition (CVPR), 2017, pp. 2261–2269.

[95] Y. Chen, J. Liu, J. Hu, et al., Discriminative feature representation: an effective postprocessing solution to low dose CT imaging, Physics in Medicine and Biology 62 (6) (2017) 2103.

[96] Jin Liu, Yining Hu, Jian Yang, Yang Chen, Huazhong Shu, Limin Luo, Qianjing Feng, Zhiguo Gui, Gouenou Coatrieux, 3D feature constrained reconstruction for low dose CT imaging, IEEE Transactions on Circuits and Systems for Video Technology 28 (5) (2018) 1232–1247.

[97] J. Liu, Y. Zhang, Q. Zhao, et al., Deep iterative reconstruction estimation (DIRE): approximate iterative reconstruction estimation for low dose CT imaging, Physics in Medicine and Biology 64 (13) (2019) 135007.

[98] B.E. Claus, Y. Jin, L.A. Gjesteby, G. Wang, B. De Man, Metal-artifact reduction using deep-learning based sinogram completion: initial results, in: Proc. 14th Int. Meeting Fully Three Dimensional Image Reconstruction Radiol. Nucl. Med., 2017, pp. 631–634.

[99] H.S. Park, H.S. Park, S.M. Lee, H.P. Kim, J.K. Seo, Y.E. Chung, CT sinogram-consistency learning for metal-induced beam hardening correction, Medical Physics 45 (2018) 5376–5384.

[100] X. Yin, et al., Domain progressive 3D residual convolution network to improve low-dose CT imaging, IEEE Transactions on Medical Imaging 38 (12) (2019) 2903–2913.

[101] Y. Zhang, et al., CLEAR: comprehensive learning enabled adversarial reconstruction for subtle structure enhanced low-dose CT imaging, IEEE Transactions on Medical Imaging 40 (11) (2021) 3089–3101.

[102] K.H. Jin, M.T. McCann, E. Froustey, M. Unser, Deep convolutional neural network for inverse problems in imaging, IEEE Transactions on Image Processing 26 (9) (2017) 4509–4522.

[103] Y. Zhang, et al., CD-Net: comprehensive domain network with spectral complementary for DECT sparse-view reconstruction, IEEE Transactions on Computational Imaging 7 (2021) 436–447.

[104] T. Lyu, W. Zhao, Y. Zhu, et al., Estimating dual-energy CT imaging from single-energy CT data with material decomposition convolutional neural network, Medical Image Analysis 70 (5) (2021) 102001.

[105] H. Chen, Y. Zhang, Y. Chen, J. Zhang, W. Zhang, H. Sun, et al., LEARN: learned experts' assessment-based reconstruction network for sparse-data CT, IEEE Transactions on Medical Imaging 37 (6) (2018) 1333–1347.

[106] J. He, Y. Yang, Y. Wang, D. Zeng, Z. Bian, H. Zhang, et al., Optimizing a parameterized plug-and-play ADMM for iterative low-dose CT reconstruction, IEEE Transactions on Medical Imaging 38 (2) (2019) 371–382.

[107] T.A. Bubba, G. Kutyniok, M. Lassas, M. Maerz, W. Samek, S. Siltanen, V. Srinivasan, Learning the invisible: a hybrid deep learning-shearlet framework for limited angle computed tomography, Inverse Problems 35 (2019) 064002.

[108] D. Hu, et al., SPECIAL: single-shot projection error correction integrated adversarial learning for limited-angle CT, IEEE Transactions on Computational Imaging 7 (2021) 734–746.

[109] J. Xiang, Y. Dong, Y. Yang, FISTA-Net: learning a fast iterative shrinkage thresholding network for inverse problems in imaging, IEEE Transactions on Medical Imaging 40 (5) (2021) 1329–1339.

[110] L. Fu, B. De Man, A hierarchical approach to deep learning and its application to tomographic reconstruction, in: 15th International Meeting on Fully Three-Dimensional Image Reconstruction in Radiology and Nuclear Medicine, vol. 11072, International Society for Optics and Photonics, 2019, p. 1107202.

[111] T. Wurfl, M. Hoffmann, V. Christlein, K. Breininger, Y. Huang, M. Unberath, A.K. Maier, Deep learning computed tomography: learning projection-domain weights from image domain in limited angle problems, IEEE Transactions on Medical Imaging 37 (6) (2018) 1454–1463.

[112] Y. Li, K. Li, C. Zhang, et al., Learning to reconstruct computed tomography images directly from sinogram data under a variety of data acquisition conditions, IEEE Transactions on Medical Imaging 38 (10) (2019) 2469–2481.

[113] E. Kang, H.J. Koo, D.H. Yang, J.B. Seo, J.C. Ye, Cycle-consistent adversarial denoising network for multiphase coronary CT angiography, Medical Physics 46 (2) (2019) 550–562.

[114] H. Liao, W.-A. Lin, S.K. Zhou, J. Luo, ADN: artifact disentanglement network for unsupervised metal artifact reduction, IEEE Transactions on Medical Imaging (2019).

[115] L.A. Shepp, Yehuda Vardi, Maximum likelihood reconstruction for emission tomography, IEEE Transactions on Medical Imaging 1 (2) (1982) 113–122.

[116] H.M. Hudson, R.S. Larkin, Accelerated image reconstruction using ordered subsets of projection data, IEEE Transactions on Medical Imaging 13 (4) (1994) 601–609.

[117] P.E. Kinahan, J.G. Rogers, Analytic 3D image reconstruction using all detected events, IEEE Transactions on Nuclear Science 36 (1) (1989) 964–968.

[118] M. Defrise, P.E. Kinahan, D.W. Townsend, C. Michel, M. Sibomana, D.F. Newport, Exact and approximate rebinning algorithms for 3-D PET data, IEEE Transactions on Medical Imaging 16 (2) (1997) 145–158.

[119] Vardi Yehuda, Larry A. Shepp, Linda Kaufman, A statistical model for positron emission tomography, Journal of the American Statistical Association 80 (389) (1985) 8–20.

[120] Wang Guobao, Qi Jinyi, PET image reconstruction using kernel method, IEEE Transactions on Medical Imaging 34 (1) (2015) 61–71.

[121] He Ji, Yongbo Wang, Jianhua Ma, Radon inversion via deep learning, IEEE Transactions on Medical Imaging 39 (6) (2020) 2076–2087.

[122] Ida Häggström, Schmidtlein C. Ross, Campanella Gabriele, Fuchs Thomas, Deep PET: a deep encoder–decoder network for directly solving the PET image reconstruction inverse problem, Medical Image Analysis 54 (2019) 253–262.

[123] H. Lim, I.Y. Chun, Y.K. Dewaraja, J.A. Fessler, Improved low-count quantitative PET reconstruction with an iterative neural network, IEEE Transactions on Medical Imaging 39 (11) (2020) 3512–3522.

[124] K. Gong, D. Wu, K. Kim, J. Yang, G. El Fakhri, Y. Seo, Q. Li, EMnet: an unrolled deep neural network for PET image reconstruction, Medical Imaging 2019: Physics of Medical Imaging 10948 (2019) 1203–1208.

[125] K. Gong, D. Wu, K. Kim, J. Yang, T. Sun, G. El Fakhri, Y. Seo, Q. Li, MAPEM-Net: an unrolled neural network for fully 3D PET image reconstruction, in: 15th International Meeting on Fully Three-Dimensional Image Reconstruction in Radiology and Nuclear Medicine, vol. 11072, International Society for Optics and Photonics, 2019, p. 110720O.

[126] Mehranian Abolfazl, Andrew J. Reader, Model-based deep learning PET image reconstruction using forward–backward splitting expectation–maximization, IEEE Transactions on Radiation and Plasma Medical Sciences 5 (1) (2020) 54–64.

[127] Ge Yongshuai, Zhang Qiyang, Hu Zhanli, Chen Jianwei, Shi Wei, Zheng Hairong, Liang Dong, Deconvolution-based backproject-filter (BPF) computed tomography image reconstruction method using deep learning technique, arXiv preprint, arXiv:1807.01833.

[128] Wang Bo, Huafeng Liu, FBP-Net for direct reconstruction of dynamic PET images, Physics in Medicine and Biology 65 (23) (2020) 1–16.

[129] W. Whiteley, V. Panin, C. Zhou, J. Cabello, D. Bharkhada, J. Gregor, FastPET: near real-time reconstruction of PET histo-image data using a neural network, IEEE Transactions on Radiation and Plasma Medical Sciences 5 (1) (2020) 65–77.

[130] Feng Tao, Yao Shulin, Xi Chen, Zhao Yizhang, Wang Ruimin, Wu Shina, Li Can, Xu Baixuan, Deep learning-based image reconstruction for TOF PET with DIRECT data partitioning format, Physics in Medicine and Biology 66 (16) (2021) 165007.

[131] Yusheng Li, Samuel Matej, DeepDIRECT: deep direct image reconstruction from multi-view TOF PET histoimages using convolutional LSTM, in: 16th International Meeting on Fully 3D Image Reconstruction in Radiology and Nuclear Medicine, 2021, pp. 111–115.

[132] L. Lv, G.L. Zeng, Y. Zan, X. Hong, M. Guo, G. Chen, W. Tao, W. Ding, Q. Huang, A back-projection-and-filtering-like(BPF-like) reconstruction method with the deeplearning filtration from listmode data in TOF-PET, Medical Physics (2022) 1–14.

[133] Kuang Gong, Eric Berg, Simon R. Cherry, Jinyi Qi, Machine learning in PET: from photon detection to quantitative image reconstruction, Proceedings of the IEEE 108 (1) (2019) 51–68.

[134] Andrew J. Reader, Guillaume Corda, Abolfazl Mehranian, Casper da Costa-Luis, Sam Ellis, Julia A. Schnabel, Deep learning for PET image reconstruction, IEEE Transactions on Radiation and Plasma Medical Sciences 5 (1) (2020) 1–25.

[135] Tonghe Wang, Yang Lei, Yabo Fu, Walter J. Curran, Tian Liu, Jonathon A. Nye, Xiaofeng Yang, Machine learning in quantitative PET: a review of attenuation correction and low-count image reconstruction methods, Physica Medica 76 (2020) 294–306.

[136] Kuang Gong, Kyungsang Kim, Jianan Cui, Dufan Wu, Quanzheng Li, The evolution of image reconstruction in PET: from filtered back-projection to artificial intelligence, PET Clinics 16 (4) (2021) 533–542.

[137] Keisuke Matsubara, Masanobu Ibaraki, Mitsutaka Nemoto, Hiroshi Watabe, Yuichi Kimura, A review on AI in PET imaging, Annals of Nuclear Medicine 36 (2) (2022) 133–143.

[138] Ge Wang, Jong Chu Ye, Klaus Mueller, Jeffrey A. Fessler, Image reconstruction is a new frontier of machine learning, IEEE Transactions on Medical Imaging 37 (6) (2018) 1289–1296.

[139] Haimiao Zhang, Bin Dong, A review on deep learning in medical image reconstruction, Journal of the Operations Research Society of China 8 (2) (2020) 311–340.

[140] S. Kevin Zhou, Hayit Greenspan, Christos Davatzikos, James S. Duncan, Bram van Ginneken, Anant Madabhushi, Jerry L. Prince, Daniel Rueckert, Ronald M. Summers, A review of deep learning in medical imaging: imaging traits, technology trends, case studies with progress highlights, and future promises, arXiv:2008.09104, 2020.

[141] Maribel Torres-Velázquez, Wei-Jie Chen, Xue Li, Alan B. McMillan, Application and construction of deep learning networks in medical imaging, IEEE Transactions on Radiation and Plasma Medical Sciences 5 (2) (2021) 137–159.

[142] Hanene Ben Yedder, Ben Cardoen, Ghassan Hamarneh, Deep learning for biomedical image reconstruction: a survey, Artificial Intelligence Review 54 (1) (2021) 215–251.

[143] Emmanuel Ahishakiye, Martin Bastiaan Van Gijzen, Julius Tumwiine, Ruth Wario, Johnes Obungoloch, A survey on deep learning in medical image reconstruction, Intelligent Medicine 1 (3) (2021) 118–127.

[144] Shanshan Wang, Guohua Cao, Yan Li Wang, Shu Liao, Qiang Wang, Junjie Shi, Cheng Li, Dinggang Shen, Review and prospect: artificial intelligence in advanced medical imaging, Frontiers in Radiology 1 (2021) 1.

[145] Ge Wang, Mathews Jacob, Xuanqin Mou, Yongyi Shi, Yonina.C. Eldar, Deep tomographic image reconstruction: yesterday, today, and tomorrow—editorial for the 2nd special issue "machine learning for image reconstruction", IEEE Transactions on Medical Imaging 40 (11) (2021) 2956–2964.

[146] Zhibiao Cheng, Junhai Wen, Gang Huang, Jianhua Yan, Applications of artificial intelligence in nuclear medicine image generation, Quantitative Imaging in Medicine and Surgery 11 (6) (2021) 2792–2822.

[147] Hossein Arabi, Azadeh AkhavanAllaf, Amirhossein Sanaat, Isaac Shiri, Habib Zaidi, The promise of artificial intelligence and deep learning in PET and SPECT imaging, Physica Medica 83 (2021) 122–137.

[148] E. Berg, S.R. Cherry, Using convolutional neural networks to estimate time-of-flight from PET detector waveforms, Physics in Medicine and Biology 63 (2) (2018) 02LT01.

[149] J.B. Michaud, M.A. Tetrault, J.F. Beaudoin, J. Cadorette, J.D. Leroux, C.A. Brunet, R. Lecomte, R. Fontaine, Sensitivity increase through a neural network method for LOR recovery of ICS triple coincidences in high-resolution pixelated-detectors PET scanners, IEEE Transactions on Nuclear Science 62 (1) (2014) 82–94.

[150] P. Peng, M.S. Judenhofer, A.Q. Jones, S.R. Cherry, Compton PET: a simulation study for a PET module with novel geometry and machine learning for position decoding, Biomedical Physics & Engineering Express 5 (1) (2018) 015018.

[151] Lee Seungeun, Lee Jae Sung, Inter-crystal scattering recovery of light-sharing PET detectors using convolutional neural networks, Physics in Medicine and Biology 66 (18) (2021) 185004.

[152] J.L. Herraiz, A. Bembibre, A. López-Montes, Deep-learning based positron range correction of PET images, Applied Sciences 11 (1) (2021) 266.

[153] Hong Xiang, Zan Yunlong, Weng Fenghua, Tao Weijie, Peng Qiyu, Huang Qiu, Enhancing the image quality via transferred deep residual learning of coarse PET sonograms, IEEE Transactions on Medical Imaging 37 (10) (2018) 2322–2332.

[154] L. Tao, X. Li, L.R. Furenlid, C.S. Levin, Deep learning based methods for γ ray interaction location estimation in monolithic scintillation crystal detectors, Physics in Medicine and Biology 65 (11) (2020) 115007.

[155] Feng Tao, Wang Jizhe, Li Hongdi, Sensitivity estimation and image reconstruction for sparse PET with deep learning, in: 2018 IEEE Nuclear Science Symposium and Medical Imaging Conference Proceedings, 2018, pp. 1–4.

[156] W. Whiteley, J. Gregor, CNN-based PET sinogram repair to mitigate defective block detectors, Physics in Medicine and Biology 64 (23) (2019) 235017.

[157] Amirrashedi Mahsa, Sarkar Saeed, Ghadiri Hossein, Ghafarian Pardis, Zaidi Habib, Ay Mohammad Reza, A deep neural network to recover missing data in small animal pet imaging: comparison between sinogram-and image-domain implementations, in: 2021 IEEE 18th International Symposium on Biomedical Imaging, 2021, pp. 1365–1368.

[158] C.C. Liu, H.M. Huang, Partial-ring PET image restoration using a deep learning based method, Physics in Medicine and Biology 64 (22) (2019) 225014.

[159] G. Wang, J.C. Ye, B. De Man, Deep learning for tomographic image reconstruction, Nature Machine Intelligence 2 (12) (2020) 737–748.

[160] J. Koo, E.O. Brenne, A.B. Dahl, V.A. Dahl, A tomographic reconstruction method using coordinate-based neural network with spatial regularization, in: Proceedings of the Northern Lights Deep Learning Workshop, 2021.

[161] L. Shen, P. Jonh, L. Xing, NeRP: implicit neural representation learning with prior embedding for sparsely sampled image reconstruction, IEEE Transactions on Neural Networks and Learning Systems (2022).

[162] Y. Shi, G. Wang, Conversion of the Mayo LDCT data to synthetic equivalent through the diffusion model for training denoising networks with a theoretically perfect privacy, arXiv preprint, arXiv:2301.06604.

[163] H. Chung, JC. Ye, Score-based diffusion models for accelerated MRI, Medical Image Analysis 80 (2022) 102479.

Medical image segmentation, registration, and applications

Dynamic inference using neural architecture search in medical image segmentation

10

From a novel adaptation perspective

Dong Yang, Holger R. Roth, Xiaosong Wang, Ziyue Xu, and Daguang Xu

NVIDIA, Santa Clara, CA, United States

10.1 Introduction

Nowadays, medical image processing has become a critical step for disease understanding, clinical diagnosis and treatment planning, given the technology advances in both algorithmic designs (e.g., deep learning) and hardware platforms (e.g., GPU). During the process, the majority of the challenges in medical imaging are inevitably introduced through the scanning/imaging procedures. One of the most common challenges is image data inconsistency, which likely causes difficulties for computational processing or deployment of machine learning models when facing unknown data. The source of data inconsistency may come from scanners from different vendors, inconsistent scanning protocols, anatomy difference among populations, artifacts introduced at imaging and other related factors. For instance, large appearance variance may exist among the regular 3D T2-weighted brain MRI from different institutions and hospitals. As a result, performance of machine learning models can be significantly downgraded when they are deployed at unknown image domains.

Researchers has proposed several domain adaptation approaches to address the issue of data inconsistency raised from the unknown data/domain. One major prerequisite for the existing approaches is that the potential testing images must be available before the deployment of machine learning models [21]. The weights of the deployed models require necessary updates using images from both the training (known) and testing (unknown) data, which follow a semi-supervised fashion to reduce the performance gap between domains. However, the deployment of machine learning models should not fully rely on the assumptions that the testing data is always available, or that model fine-tuning is possible. In practice, the quantity and

Deep Learning for Medical Image Analysis. https://doi.org/10.1016/B978-0-32-385124-4.00021-0

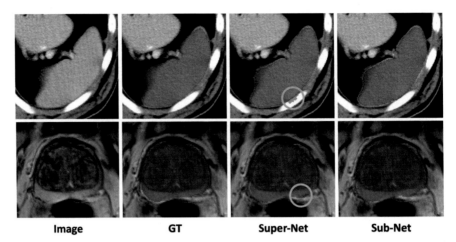

| Image | GT | Super-Net | Sub-Net |

FIGURE 10.1

Sample appearance for spleen segmentation in 3D CT (up) and prostate segmentation in 3D MRI. We compared the results from super-net with equally weighted candidates and sub-network, which is searched during inference for individual data points. The sub-network is capable to correct erroneous parts of prediction with its unique feature representation.

quality of unknown data may not be certain most of the time. Thus the fine-tuned models with all data points may not be feasible for the unknown data.

Recently, "AutoML"-type of work in deep learning has been largely explored for various applications, such as image recognition, semantic segmentation, object detection, natural image generation, etc. One of the most popular tasks in AutoML is neural architecture search (NAS) [52]. The objective of NAS is to design neural network architectures automatically without much of human heuristics or assumptions. Besides the model weights, the model structure itself becomes fitted for the task after searching, and even transferable for different applications [53]. Additional constraints, such as latency or parameter quantity of models, can be added as searching objectives to fit the models into different platforms. Several work [42] has achieved the state-of-the-art performance in large-scale image recognition (e.g., ImageNet database [9]).

In this paper, we propose a new approach to improve model generalization and reduce the performance gap of machine learning models, especially for convolution neural networks (CNN), between known and unknown data points. At first, a "super-net" is constructed to enable a mixture of candidate modules in parallel to represent multi-scale appearance features at different network levels, respectively. Once the super-net has been trained sufficiently, the optimal sub-network for each unseen data point can be determined with the guidance of additional unsupervised loss functions at inference. As a result, each domain, or even each data point, would have its specific neural architecture during deployment. Compared to the super-net, the feature representations from the sub-network are more suitable for different data points. See Fig. 10.1.

The contributions of our proposed work can be summarized as follows:

1. Our proposed approach increases the generalizability and transferability of neural network models when processing unseen data points;
2. The deployment of the proposed approach is efficient and effective even without further fine-tuning (using both seen and unseen data);
3. We propose a novel path sampling strategy to speed up model convergence with "fair" super-net training;
4. To the best of our knowledge, it is the first time that neural architecture search is applied on data points or domain adaptation in medical imaging.

The remaining sections are arranged as follows. Section 10.2 summarizes the previous works in the related areas of the proposed approach. Section 10.3 describes technical details and research motivation. Next, Section 10.4 explains experiments and ablation study and Section 10.5 shows validity of the proposed approach with tasks of 3D medical image segmentation, and explores the design choices. Lastly, Section 10.7 concludes the paper and discusses the future directions.

10.2 Related works
10.2.1 Efficient ConvNet models for medical imaging

Deep convolutional neural networks have been successfully applied for medical image analysis recently. One of the most influential works in medical image segmentation using deep neural networks is U-Net [40,7]. U-Net has found to be more effective and efficient compared to the previous learning-based approaches. Researchers have adopted the design concepts of U-Net ("U"-shape convolutional encoder-decoder with skip connections), and further extended it into novel and effective neural network architectures [35,29,34,38,2,49,51,37,33,43]. For example, 2D/3D U-Net is considered as the common baseline model for most segmentation tasks. And the state-of-the-art performance of several tasks is reached via using variants of U-Net with model ensembling [24,23,25]. However, one potential downside of U-net is that once the U-shape models are trained properly, their weights cannot be updated at inference given validation or testing data. The performance may drop significantly when the domain of the testing data is far away from the training data. Our proposed approach can adjust models after training, depending on targeting data points or domains.

10.2.2 Domain adaptation

Data or domain inconsistency is a common issue for medical images from various resources. To mitigate domain discrepancy, transfer learning is mostly proposed to fit pre-trained models into new data domains with necessary model fine-tuning. But the connection between the source and target domains is weak during transfer learning, since fine-tuning is only conducted with data from the targeting domain. Recently,

"Pix2Pix" and "CycleGAN" are the pioneering works with great success in area of natural image translation from one domain to another, using either paired or non-paired images from two domains for training [26,51]. Inspired by those works, the similar strategy has been applied to specific applications such as semantic segmentation [21,50,22]. The main idea among those works is to use cycle consistency to build up relationships between two domains, and have the application-specific sub-networks and training objectives embedded into the framework. Other works like [27] propose the use of adversarial loss feature-level gap between different domains. Xia et al. introduced the co-training concept to add training objectives for unlabeled data in a semi-supervised learning way [45]. Meanwhile, domain adaptation can be also achieved with gradient back-propagation in adversarial training [12,13]. The idea of adversarial training suggests that the gradients from additional constraints are able to help align different domains and adjust feature representation of neural networks. However, without any exception, the methods mentioned above require that "unseen" images are available before model deployment for essential model training or fine-tuning to guarantee proper performance. By contrast, our proposed approach does not require seeing testing image before deployment, because the dedicated selection of sub-network is able to minimize domain variance.

Another seemly related area is domain generalization [36,15,28,30], which aims to train models that can be generalized to new domains without requiring the data from targeting domain, as well as the need of retraining. The model is fixed after the training step. In contrary, our model is on-the-fly adapted to new domain or data point, which shall have better flexibility and specificity.

10.2.3 Neural architecture search

Neural architecture search (NAS) is commonly used to design neural network automatically with limited human heuristics to meet different user requirements (e.g., lightweight model or small amount of computation) [11]. Zoph and Le first introduced a novel framework to conduct neural architecture search using reinforcement learning for large-scale image recognition [52,53,39]. Specifically, they formulated the NAS problem as searching convolutional layers for repeated modules inside the entire networks, which is capable to reduce the searching space and cost to a great extent, since the same module structure is applied for several modules. To simplify the searching operations, they intentionally encode the architecture candidates as one-dimensional vectors. Then another controller network (mostly recurrent neural network) is capable to directly take the previous architecture code as input, generate code for new architectures, collect reward (validation scores) after training of the candidates and update its own weights. The whole procedure is iterated for several times. Their searched networks after training is able to achieve the state-of-the-art performance on ImageNet database [9]. Others followed the similar idea to adopt reinforcement learning (RL) to tune the hyper-parameters of training settings or to find optimal data augmentation solutions [8,48]. Using newly searched neural networks, researchers have improved the performance of various computer vision applications (semantic segmentation, object detection, design of loss function, etc.) in

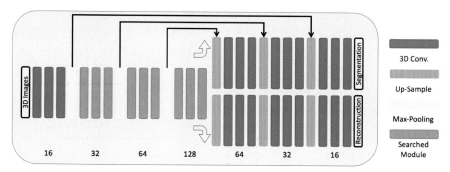

FIGURE 10.2

Overall framework (best view in color).

the challenging data sets [3,5,47,10,14]. Meanwhile, researchers have explored other concepts of NAS: "super-net" and one-shot NAS [4,32,45,31,19,44,41,46,17]. The idea of super-net is to create a large neural network with candidate modules in parallel at different levels of the network. The network can be trained jointly or with sampled paths/modules from the entire network, using RL, generic algorithms, or uniform sampling to choose one sub-network for training. And the final architectures at deployment are the sub-networks with selected modules/paths from the super-net based on the scalar weights of paths/modules. Compared to the conventional NAS, our proposed approach has better flexibility at inference, because our approach collects a pool of candidate networks during training, and selects optimal network for each data point at inference following certain criteria.

10.3 Data oriented medical image segmentation

The proposed approach consists of two consecutive steps: super-net training and deployment, which are mainly designed for 3D medical image segmentation. At first, we construct a super-net containing various module candidates in parallel at different levels/scales. Then the super-net is trained with arbitrary paths from uniform sampling of module candidates. Once the training is accomplished, a sub-network/path for each data point can be determined on-the-fly with auxiliary constraints at deployment. The details of two steps are discussed as follows, and the overview of the framework shown in Fig. 10.2.

10.3.1 Super-net design and training

Following the intuition of network designs from [40,7], we construct a super-net with an encoder–decoder macro-structure. The multi-level features of encoder and decoder are concatenated via skip connections. Then the input images are fed into the encoder, and the decoder generates segmentation masks accordingly. Moreover,

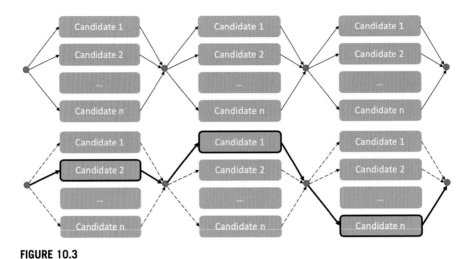

FIGURE 10.3

First row is three consecutive searched modules (part of super-net); second row is one sampled path from the super-net for training and validation.

we add another reconstruction decoder at the end of the encoder to restore the input appearance. The reason why we add such reconstruction decoder is to have better feature representation at the encoder part. We optimize the loss functions for bother decoder and reconstruction decoder, which are defined as follows:

$$\min_{a \in \mathcal{A}} \mathcal{L}_a = \min_{a \in \mathcal{A}} \left(\mathcal{L}_{seg} + \mathcal{L}_{recon} \right) \tag{10.1}$$

$\mathcal{A}$ represents the overall super-net, and $a \in \mathcal{A}$ is the sampled sub-network from super-net. $\mathcal{L}_{seg}$ is soft dice loss [35] on prediction masks and segmentation labels, and $\mathcal{L}_{seg}$ is $\mathcal{L}_2$ loss to quantify similarity between input images and reconstructed images.

Several NAS works search for the cell-level components, and repeat the cell structures several times in one network [52,53]. Although the cell-level search can significantly reduce the searching space, the same structure used at different network levels may limit model capacity and performance [44]. Instead, we choose to use a layerwise searching space for the super-net, and fix the macro-structure of the network. The searched layers are the ones in the encoder, because the feature maps of encoder capture low- and high-level image contextual information, which is critical for model capacity. At each searched layer, N candidates are in parallel with N individual paths. Each path has a positive weight $w_{n \in N}$, and $\sum_{n=1}^{N} w_n = 1$. The output of the searched layer is a weighted sum. And the number of input and output channels of layers are fixed. The lower level layers has less channels, and the number of feature maps at each layer increases as the layer level goes higher. The spatial dimension remains the same with necessary padding operations. The down-sampling and up-sampling layers in super-net is max-pooling and trilinear interpolation, respectively.

During training, we sample single path from each searched layer of the super-net at each iteration, and update the parameters of the new sub-networks during gradient back-propagation, shown in Algorithm 10.1. Sampling one path can be achieved by setting the weights of the selected path to 1, and the rest to 0. And the path weights are fixed tensors during training, which do not require gradients. Such operation largely reduces the GPU memory consumption, since training large 3D networks is expensive in time and computation resources. Then all other weights in the encoder, decoder and reconstruction decoders are jointly updated. In [4], the weights of paths are also updated during training. However, super-net would be trained with a large bias because the weights also determine how possible each path get sampled. The path with a large weight will have enough updates, and the ones with less weight did not see enough training samples. Thus the model initialization is critical and largely determines the final searched architecture.

Stochastic sampling We propose a novel path sampling strategy to maintain the sample balance between candidates at searching layers for model training. For each candidate operations op, its total amount of sampled times c_{op} is tracked dynamically at training. Then a dynamic weights $w_{op,i}$ of each op at layer level i is computed as follows:

$$w_{op,i} = \frac{1}{c_{op,i}^{\gamma}} \tag{10.2}$$

Here, the floating number γ is positive. Accordingly, the estimated sampling probability p_{op} for next iteration is further calculated:

$$p_{op} = \frac{w_{op}}{\sum_{op} w_{op}} \tag{10.3}$$

During next iteration, the candidates op is selected based on the distribution of the probability p_{op} before each iteration starts. For each mini-batch, we can control the number of how many sampled paths would be trained. The op with smaller amounts of sampling times has larger chance to be sampled during the next iterations. Similarly, [6] introduced a "fair" way to sample paths, which randomly generates possible paths during training covering all candidates without overlapping. And all sampled paths would be trained with the same mini-batch sequentially at each "iteration," which is designed to make sure each candidate op has been trained "fairly." However, such method cannot handle the situation that layers have different amount of candidate op, because the all sampled paths cannot cover all candidates without overlapping.

Normally, super-net cannot be trained with all candidate modules simultaneously. Because training such super-net would consume vast amount of GPU memory, especially for 3D medical images. Frequently, even training with one patch would cause issues "out of GPU memory". Training with sampled paths would reduce GPU memory consumption, but it takes much longer time for convolution kernels to be converged.

Algorithm 10.1: Training super-net and stochastic path sampling

---

Data: mini-batches $\{(X_i, Y_i) : i = 1, 2, \cdots\}$ from training data set, n candidates per searching layer, maximum epoch number MAX_EPOCH, and number of sampled paths per mini-batch NUM_PATHS;

Result: The super-net $\mathcal{F}_A$, and model parameters θ;

1 **for** $i = 1, 2, \cdots, $ MAX_EPOCH **do**

2   **for** $j = 1, 2, \cdots, $ NUM_PATHS **do**

3   Samples paths at each searching level regarding probability distribution $p_{op,n}$;

4   Fix weights of selected candidates $w_k = 1$, and $w_k = 0$ for the rest candidates within current iteration i;

5          $\theta \leftarrow \theta + \nabla_\theta \mathcal{L}_{\text{seg}}\left((X_i, Y_i); w_n, n = 1 \cdots N\right) +$ $\lambda \nabla_\theta \mathcal{L}_{\text{recon}}\left(X_i; w_n, n = 1 \cdots\right)$;

6   Update total samples number $c_{op,n}$ for each candidate;

7   Update probability distribution $p_{op,n}$ for each candidate with Eq. (10.2);

8   **end**

9 **end**

10.3.2 Data adaptation with super-net

Modern neural architecture search methods finalize network structures when the searching period is done. The final network is either directly applied for test data, or fine-tuned with all training data before deployment. The history or knowledge learned during the searching process would be mostly abandoned at deployment. For example, the paths with lower weights at each layer would be trimmed to achieve a slim final network [4,41]. However, such abandoned knowledge represents the preference of original super-net given training data. And candidate sub-networks perform differently because layer candidates at the same level actually capture varied contextual features. Therefore it would be helpful to leverage the "abandoned" knowledge from searching processing for model inference.

Actually, we apply it to the testing data, and choose the optimal sub-networks on-the-fly, once the training of super-net is accomplished. When each testing data point is fed into the super-net, the optimal module/path at each searching layer would be determined at the same time using additional constraints. The prediction of the specific data point is computed solely based on the newly selected architectures with pre-trained weights. Moreover, each data points has its own architecture at inference, and data preference learned from searching can be applied effectively.

In order to achieve on-the-fly architecture selection, we utilize the additional information from reconstruction branch. The outline of our proposed approach is shown in Algorithm 10.2. When feeding a new testing data point x, we can compute the reconstruction loss $\mathcal{L}_{\text{recon}}$ via the reconstruction decoder. The loss indicates the sim-

---

Algorithm 10.2: Data adaptation with super-net

Result: A data dependent sub-network $\mathcal{F}_x \in \mathcal{F}_{\mathcal{A}}$, given a data point x, and corresponding prediction y'

1 Set all path/candidate weights w_n equal to $\frac{1}{n}$;
2 Feed x to super-net $\mathcal{F}$;
3 Compute reconstruction loss $\mathcal{L}_{\text{recon}}$ through encoder and reconstruction decoder;
4 $w'_n \leftarrow w_n + \lambda \nabla_{w_n} \mathcal{L}_{\text{recon}}(x; w_n, n = 1 \cdots N)$;
5 Select path $n' \leftarrow \text{argmax}_n \{w_n; n \in N\}$;
6 Construct sub-network $\mathcal{F}_x$;
7 Compute segmentation prediction $y' \leftarrow \mathcal{F}_x(x)$;
8 Repeat steps above when feeding new x;

---

ilarity between testing data and reconstructed testing data. Meanwhile, updating the loss propagates the gradients back to previous layers. And we fix the weights of all modules in the encoder, decoder and reconstruction decoder, and enable the path weights w_n to be trainable. w_n would be updated after training with one iteration using the specific testing data point.

$$w'_n \leftarrow w_n + \lambda \nabla_{w_n} \mathcal{L}_{\text{recon}}(x; w_n, n = 1 \cdots N) \qquad (10.4)$$

λ is the learning rate. Once updating is done, the optimal path at each level can be simply chosen by taking the one with the largest w_n. The overall optimal architecture is finalized with all optimal paths determined. Next, the prediction for that data point can be generated via feeding it into the finalized network structure. For the next data point, w_n is reset to $\frac{1}{n}$, and the weight updating repeats again. It makes sure that the decision of each data-driven sub-network is independent.

During updating of path weights w_n, no other module in the super-net is going to be updated. Thus the knowledge from searching/training process is well preserved. Different data points at inference can benefit from its own feature extractor. Meanwhile, updating path weight w_n is very efficient, because they are only vector variables, and they are the only layers requiring gradient computation. Moreover, inference with sub-network is much faster than that with the entire super-net.

Our proposed approach is similar with the "Fast Gradient Sign Attack" (FGSA) in [18], which is a one-step updating method to compute adversarial examples with on-the-fly gradient back-propagation on top of a pre-trained neural network classifier. The updated image is able to fool the pre-trained classifier with incorrect class prediction. And another work [12] showed domain adaptation can be done using unsupervised learning together with gradient back-propagation. Both of works validate the benefits of using gradients for domain understanding. Furthermore, inspired by those works, our approach leverages the gradient information as well, to guide the sub-network determination with unsupervised loss functions on-the-fly.

Table 10.1   Comparison of average Dice scores on validation sets for task.

Task 04 - Hippocampus Segmentation			
Classes	**1**	**2**	**Avg.**
[33]	0.858	0.846	0.852
Ours (Super-Net)	0.865	0.828	0.847
Ours (Sub-Network)	**0.878**	**0.862**	**0.870**

Task 05 - Prostate Segmentation				
Classes	**1**	**2**	**Avg.**	**1 + 2**
[33]	**0.467**	0.519	0.493	0.896
Ours (Super-Net)	0.236	0.574	0.405	0.907
Ours (Sub-Network)	0.410	**0.602**	**0.506**	**0.908**

Task 09 - Spleen Segmentation	
Classes	**1**
[33]	**0.957**
Ours (Super-Net)	0.948
Ours (Sub-Network)	0.952

10.4 **Experiments**

Data sets The medical decathlon challenge (MSD) hosts several tasks of 3D medical image segmentation [1]. To cover various objects and image modalities, the data sets of task 04 (hippocampus segmentation), task 05 (prostate segmentation) and task 09 (spleen segmentation) are adopted for experiments with our own data split for training/validation (ratio 4/1). For task 04, 208 mono-modal MRI volumes for training, 52 for validation; for task 05, 25 multi-modal MR (T2, ADC) volumes for training, 7 for validation; for task 09, 32 CT volumes for training, 9 for validation. All data sets except hippocampus MRI are re-sampled into the isotropic voxel spacing 1.0 mm. For hippocampus MRI, all data volumes (including images and labels) are re-sampled to the same shape $96 \times 96 \times 96$. For tasks with MRI images, the voxel intensities are pre-processed with standard normalization. For tasks with CT images, the voxel intensities of the images are normalized to the range [0, 1] according to 5th and 95th percentile of overall foreground intensities. For task 05, we also compare the performance of whole prostate segmentation, denoted as "1+2" in Table 10.1. The whole prostate segmentation is single-class segmentation merging two-class annotation.

Implementation Our baseline neural network is shown in Fig. 10.3. During training, the input of the network are patches with size $96 \times 96 \times 96$, randomly cropped from images. The learning rate for optimizer for training is 0.001, and the learning rate for final architecture determination is 0.1. λ in Eq. (10.4) is 0.1. All training jobs use the NovoGrad optimizer, which has been proved to have faster convergence rates during training compared to Adam optimizer [16]. Necessary data augmentation techniques, e.g., random intensity shift, are used for training. Padding input volumes is necessary when the dimension of the volume is not a multiple of 16. The validation accuracy is measured with the Dice

Table 10.2 Candidate layers.

Index	Convolutional Operations
1	$3 \times 3 \times 3$ $3\mathcal{D}$ convolution
2	$5 \times 5 \times 5$ $3\mathcal{D}$ convolution
3	$7 \times 7 \times 7$ $3\mathcal{D}$ convolution
4	3×3 $2\mathcal{D}$ convolution on $\mathcal{X}$-direction
5	3×3 $2\mathcal{D}$ convolution on $\mathcal{Y}$-direction
6	3×3 $2\mathcal{D}$ convolution on $\mathcal{Z}$-direction
7	One $3 \times 3 \times 3$ $3\mathcal{D}$ residual block
8	Two $3 \times 3 \times 3$ $3\mathcal{D}$ residual blocks
9	Three $3 \times 3 \times 3$ $3\mathcal{D}$ residual blocks

score after inference. The total training epoch is 1000, the number of paths for each mini-batch is 6, and γ is 1.0. And our proposed approach is implemented with PyTorch and trained on NVIDIA V100 GPUs with 32 GB memory.

Layer candidates Our baseline neural network is a U-shape network with one encoder branch and two decoder branches shown in Fig. 10.3. Skip connections concatenate multi-level features from the encoder to the decoder. And there is no skip connection between encoder and reconstruction decoder because the reconstruction procedure focuses on learning feature representation as in an auto-encoder. We choose 6 different convolutional operations as the candidate layers for all searched modules shown in Table 10.2. The input and output of the convolutional operations share the same spatial shape. The quantity of convolutional kernels is doubled after max-pooling layers or halved after up-sampling layers. The initial quantity at the first convolutional layer is 16. The activation functions of the last convolutional layers for decoder and reconstruction decoders are softmax and linear functions. We add the residual blocks [20] with different hyper-parameters (e.g., quantity) into the candidate pool as parts of the searched layers. For instance, the depth of the sampled network varies by changing the number of residual blocks (1, 2, or 3). Different network depths would correspond to unique feature representations.

The final performance is shown in Table 10.1. We can clearly see that our proposed approach has improved the baseline method [33] significantly. In the table, "super-net" means setting up all path weights as $\frac{1}{6}$, which means each candidate contributes equally. "Sub-network" denotes the performance using the finalized single-path network architecture.

Fig. 10.4 shows that the data-driven sub-network performs better that super-net for almost all the time during training, in terms of validation accuracy. It fits the intuition that the super-net is trained with a single path instead of jointly. Inference jointly would hurt the overall performance by adding useless information into each other's feature maps.

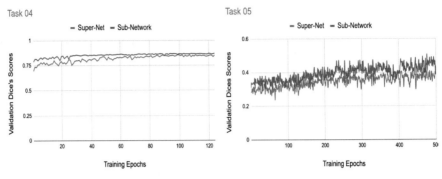

FIGURE 10.4

Validation Dice scores for super-net and sub-network during super-net training.

Table 10.3 The accuracy of different amounts of candidates sampled at each level during inference of whole prostate segmentation. Because the super-net is trained with a single path, the single path performs best compared with multi-path sampling. "All" means all candidates are in use with equal weights, and "majority" denotes all candidates selected with weight increasing during inference.

Number of Candidates	1	2	3	6	all	majority
Validation Accuracy	0.908	0.903	0.904	0.903	0.907	0.903

10.5 Ablation study
10.5.1 Validation with single path or multiple paths

We compare our proposed approach to the sub-network with multiple paths at each level instead of choosing one with the largest weights. The criterion is to check the sign of gradient for path weights during inference. If the sign is positive, we keep the path; but if the sign is negative, we remove the path from the searched layers. We run experiments on prostate multi-class segmentation and obtain the average Dice score 0.469. Although it is better than the results using super-net, it cannot be compared to the one using a single-path sub-network.

Furthermore, we compare the validation accuracy with different amounts of candidates sampled at each searching level in Table 10.3. The comparison is conducted with the whole prostate segmentation in 3D MRI. The path with all single candidates performs the best. Because our model is trained with single-path sampled from the super-net. And super-net with equally weighted candidates performs good leveraging all various information from different candidates but with much more GPU computation and large latency. "Majority" denotes all candidates selected with weight increasing during inference. But it did not improve the accuracy.

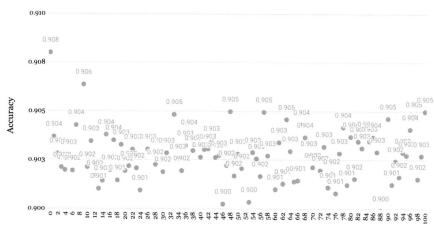

Network Index

FIGURE 10.5

The accuracy comparison between the search networks for each data point, and randomly sampled networks for each data point. The horizontal axis denotes the indices of the different random sampling trials. The network with index 0 is the sub-network from the proposed approach.

10.5.2 Guided search and random search

To further validate the effectiveness of our proposed searching approach, we compare the accuracy (in terms of Dice score) between the search network for each data point, and randomly sampled networks for each data point shown in Fig. 10.5. Since we are searching 9 layers with 9 different candidates of operations, the total amount possible path is $9^9 = 387,420,489$. It is a huge amount that we cannot easily enumerate all possibilities. Instead, we randomly sample networks during inference for each data points with 100 independent trials. Our searched sub-network (index 0) for each data point shows clear advantage.

10.5.3 Training with single path or multiple paths

The curves of training loss using different path quantities for each mini-batch for training are compared. We vary the value of path numbers in line 2 of Algorithm 10.1 (as 1, 2, 4, 8). The proposed path sampling strategy would benefit from the multi-path training with the same mini-batch, because the multiple *op* candidates is able to see through the same mini-batch. One path per mini-batch is the standard way of training strategy following [4]. But the training convergence is much faster when the number of paths increases, which demonstrates the effectiveness of our proposed sampling strategy, shown in Fig. 10.6.

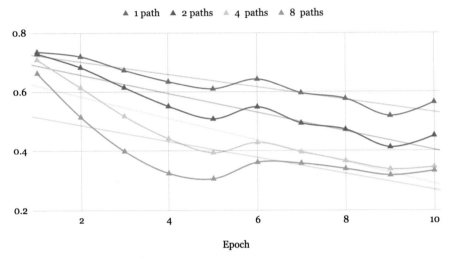

FIGURE 10.6

The training loss comparison when using different quantity of paths for each mini-batch for training.

Table 10.4 Comparison of average Dice scores on validation sets for task 02.

Task 02 - Left Atrium MRI Segmentation	
Classes	**1**
[33]	0.912
Ours (Super-Net)	0.928
Ours (Sub-Network)	**0.928**

10.6 Additional experiments

We have validated our proposed approach on the additional task, 3D left atrium MRI segmentation. The model is trained using the data set (task 02) of the "Medical Segmentation Decathlon Challenge 2018" with 16 training volumes and 4 validation volumes. The accuracy comparison is shown in Table 10.4. Based on Fig. 10.7, we can see the proposed "sub-network" is capable to avoid the errors from the "super-net" prediction.

10.7 Discussions

In the paper, we proposed a novel approach to adapt neural network models according to data points or domains for 3D medical image segmentation. The proposed approach utilizes the super-net to increase representation capacities at multiple scales.

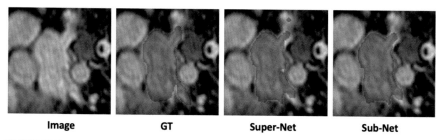

| Image | GT | Super-Net | Sub-Net |

FIGURE 10.7

Sample appearance for left atrium segmentation in 3D MRI. We compared the results from super-net with equally weighted candidates and sub-network, which is searched at inference for individual data points. The sub-network is capable to correct erroneous parts of prediction with its unique feature representation.

Then the optimal architecture can be further determined for each data point based on the reconstruction loss at inference. Meanwhile, we proposed a novel path-sampling strategy for "fair" model training. The experiments showed that using a data-driven sub-network can achieve better performance with data-dependent feature representation compared to the baseline methods.

One potential issue with the proposed approach is that training super-net requires much longer time due to the sampling strategy compared to training a feed-forward CNN. Because each convolutional kernel requires a sufficient amount of training iterations for convergence, the total iteration amount tends to be larger compared to the amount for each kernel. Future studies that can further reduce the training time of the process is strongly encouraged.

References

[1] Medical decathlon challenge, http://medicaldecathlon.com, 2018.
[2] V. Badrinarayanan, A. Kendall, R. Cipolla, Segnet: a deep convolutional encoder-decoder architecture for image segmentation, IEEE Transactions on Pattern Analysis and Machine Intelligence 39 (12) (2017) 2481–2495.
[3] I. Bello, B. Zoph, V. Vasudevan, Q.V. Le, Neural optimizer search with reinforcement learning, in: Proceedings of the 34th International Conference on Machine Learning-Volume 70, JMLR.org, 2017, pp. 459–468.
[4] H. Cai, L. Zhu, S. Han, Proxylessnas: direct neural architecture search on target task and hardware, arXiv preprint, arXiv:1812.00332, 2018.
[5] L.C. Chen, M. Collins, Y. Zhu, G. Papandreou, B. Zoph, F. Schroff, H. Adam, J. Shlens, Searching for efficient multi-scale architectures for dense image prediction, in: Advances in Neural Information Processing Systems, 2018, pp. 8699–8710.
[6] X. Chu, B. Zhang, R. Xu, J. Li, Fairnas: rethinking evaluation fairness of weight sharing neural architecture search, CoRR, arXiv:1907.01845 [abs], 2019, http://arxiv.org/abs/1907.01845.

[7] Ö. Çiçek, A. Abdulkadir, S.S. Lienkamp, T. Brox, O. Ronneberger, 3d u-net: learning dense volumetric segmentation from sparse annotation, in: International Conference on Medical Image Computing and Computer-Assisted Intervention, Springer, 2016, pp. 424–432.

[8] E.D. Cubuk, B. Zoph, D. Mane, V. Vasudevan, Q.V. Le, Autoaugment: learning augmentation policies from data, arXiv preprint, arXiv:1805.09501, 2018.

[9] J. Deng, W. Dong, R. Socher, L.J. Li, K. Li, L. Fei-Fei, Imagenet: a large-scale hierarchical image database, in: 2009 IEEE Conference on Computer Vision and Pattern Recognition, IEEE, 2009, pp. 248–255.

[10] N. Dong, M. Xu, X. Liang, Y. Jiang, W. Dai, E. Xing, Neural architecture search for adversarial medical image segmentation, in: International Conference on Medical Image Computing and Computer-Assisted Intervention, Springer, 2019, pp. 828–836.

[11] T. Elsken, J.H. Metzen, F. Hutter, Neural architecture search: a survey, arXiv preprint, arXiv:1808.05377, 2018.

[12] Y. Ganin, V. Lempitsky, Unsupervised domain adaptation by backpropagation, in: Proceedings of the 32nd International Conference on International Conference on Machine Learning-Volume 37, JMLR.org, 2015, pp. 1180–1189.

[13] Y. Ganin, E. Ustinova, H. Ajakan, P. Germain, H. Larochelle, F. Laviolette, M. Marchand, V. Lempitsky, Domain-adversarial training of neural networks, The Journal of Machine Learning Research 17 (1) (2016) 2096–2130.

[14] G. Ghiasi, T.Y. Lin, Q.V. Le, Nas-fpn: learning scalable feature pyramid architecture for object detection, in: Proceedings of the IEEE Conference on Computer Vision and Pattern Recognition, 2019, pp. 7036–7045.

[15] M. Ghifary, W. Bastiaan Kleijn, M. Zhang, D. Balduzzi, Domain generalization for object recognition with multi-task autoencoders, in: Proceedings of the IEEE International Conference on Computer Vision, 2015, pp. 2551–2559.

[16] B. Ginsburg, P. Castonguay, O. Hrinchuk, O. Kuchaiev, V. Lavrukhin, R. Leary, J. Li, H. Nguyen, J.M. Cohen, Stochastic gradient methods with layer-wise adaptive moments for training of deep networks, arXiv preprint, arXiv:1905.11286, 2019.

[17] X. Gong, S. Chang, Y. Jiang, Z. Wang, Autogan: neural architecture search for generative adversarial networks, in: Proceedings of the IEEE International Conference on Computer Vision, 2019, pp. 3224–3234.

[18] I.J. Goodfellow, J. Shlens, C. Szegedy, Explaining and harnessing adversarial examples, arXiv preprint, arXiv:1412.6572, 2014.

[19] Z. Guo, X. Zhang, H. Mu, W. Heng, Z. Liu, Y. Wei, J. Sun, Single path one-shot neural architecture search with uniform sampling, arXiv preprint, arXiv:1904.00420, 2019.

[20] K. He, X. Zhang, S. Ren, J. Sun, Deep residual learning for image recognition, in: Proceedings of the IEEE Conference on Computer Vision and Pattern Recognition, 2016, pp. 770–778.

[21] J. Hoffman, E. Tzeng, T. Park, J.Y. Zhu, P. Isola, K. Saenko, A. Efros, T. Darrell, Cycada: cycle-consistent adversarial domain adaptation, in: International Conference on Machine Learning, 2018, pp. 1994–2003.

[22] Y. Huo, Z. Xu, S. Bao, A. Assad, R.G. Abramson, B.A. Landman, Adversarial synthesis learning enables segmentation without target modality ground truth, in: 2018 IEEE 15th International Symposium on Biomedical Imaging (ISBI 2018), IEEE, 2018, pp. 1217–1220.

[23] F. Isensee, P. Kickingereder, W. Wick, M. Bendszus, K.H. Maier-Hein, No new-net, in: International MICCAI Brainlesion Workshop, Springer, 2018, pp. 234–244.

[24] F. Isensee, J. Petersen, A. Klein, D. Zimmerer, P.F. Jaeger, S. Kohl, J. Wasserthal, G. Koehler, T. Norajitra, S. Wirkert, et al., nnu-net: self-adapting framework for u-net-based medical image segmentation, arXiv preprint, arXiv:1809.10486, 2018.

[25] F. Isensee, J. Petersen, S.A. Kohl, P.F. Jäger, K.H. Maier-Hein, nnu-net: breaking the spell on successful medical image segmentation, arXiv preprint, arXiv:1904.08128, 2019.

[26] P. Isola, J.Y. Zhu, T. Zhou, A.A. Efros, Image-to-image translation with conditional adversarial networks, in: Proceedings of the IEEE Conference on Computer Vision and Pattern Recognition, 2017, pp. 1125–1134.

[27] K. Kamnitsas, C. Baumgartner, C. Ledig, V. Newcombe, J. Simpson, A. Kane, D. Menon, A. Nori, A. Criminisi, D. Rueckert, et al., Unsupervised domain adaptation in brain lesion segmentation with adversarial networks, in: International Conference on Information Processing in Medical Imaging, Springer, 2017, pp. 597–609.

[28] H. Li, S. Jialin Pan, S. Wang, A.C. Kot, Domain generalization with adversarial feature learning, in: Proceedings of the IEEE Conference on Computer Vision and Pattern Recognition, 2018, pp. 5400–5409.

[29] X. Li, H. Chen, X. Qi, Q. Dou, C.W. Fu, P.A. Heng, H-denseunet: hybrid densely connected unet for liver and tumor segmentation from ct volumes, IEEE Transactions on Medical Imaging 37 (12) (2018) 2663–2674.

[30] Y. Li, X. Tian, M. Gong, Y. Liu, T. Liu, K. Zhang, D. Tao, Deep domain generalization via conditional invariant adversarial networks, in: Proceedings of the European Conference on Computer Vision (ECCV), 2018, pp. 624–639.

[31] C. Liu, L.C. Chen, F. Schroff, H. Adam, W. Hua, A.L. Yuille, L. Fei-Fei, Auto-deeplab: hierarchical neural architecture search for semantic image segmentation, in: Proceedings of the IEEE Conference on Computer Vision and Pattern Recognition, 2019, pp. 82–92.

[32] H. Liu, K. Simonyan, Y. Yang, Darts: differentiable architecture search, arXiv preprint, arXiv:1806.09055, 2018.

[33] S. Liu, D. Xu, S.K. Zhou, O. Pauly, S. Grbic, T. Mertelmeier, J. Wicklein, A. Jerebko, W. Cai, D. Comaniciu, 3d anisotropic hybrid network: transferring convolutional features from 2d images to 3d anisotropic volumes, in: International Conference on Medical Image Computing and Computer-Assisted Intervention, Springer, 2018, pp. 851–858.

[34] J. Merkow, A. Marsden, D. Kriegman, Z. Tu, Dense volume-to-volume vascular boundary detection, in: International Conference on Medical Image Computing and Computer-Assisted Intervention, Springer, 2016, pp. 371–379.

[35] F. Milletari, N. Navab, S.A. Ahmadi, V-net: fully convolutional neural networks for volumetric medical image segmentation, in: 2016 Fourth International Conference on 3D Vision (3DV), IEEE, 2016, pp. 565–571.

[36] K. Muandet, D. Balduzzi, B. Schölkopf, Domain generalization via invariant feature representation, in: International Conference on Machine Learning, 2013, pp. 10–18.

[37] A. Myronenko, 3d mri brain tumor segmentation using autoencoder regularization, in: International MICCAI Brainlesion Workshop, Springer, 2018, pp. 311–320.

[38] A. Newell, K. Yang, J. Deng, Stacked hourglass networks for human pose estimation, in: European Conference on Computer Vision, Springer, 2016, pp. 483–499.

[39] H. Pham, M. Guan, B. Zoph, Q. Le, J. Dean, Efficient neural architecture search via parameter sharing, in: International Conference on Machine Learning, 2018, pp. 4092–4101.

[40] O. Ronneberger, P. Fischer, T. Brox, U-net: convolutional networks for biomedical image segmentation, in: International Conference on Medical Image Computing and Computer-Assisted Intervention, Springer, 2015, pp. 234–241.

[41] A. Shaw, D. Hunter, F. Landola, S. Sidhu, Squeezenas: fast neural architecture search for faster semantic segmentation, in: Proceedings of the IEEE International Conference on Computer Vision Workshops, 2019.

[42] M. Tan, Q. Le, Efficientnet: rethinking model scaling for convolutional neural networks, in: International Conference on Machine Learning, 2019, pp. 6105–6114.

[43] Y. Weng, T. Zhou, Y. Li, X. Qiu, Nas-unet: neural architecture search for medical image segmentation, IEEE Access 7 (2019) 44247–44257.

[44] B. Wu, X. Dai, P. Zhang, Y. Wang, F. Sun, Y. Wu, Y. Tian, P. Vajda, Y. Jia, K. Keutzer, Fb-net: hardware-aware efficient convnet design via differentiable neural architecture search, in: Proceedings of the IEEE Conference on Computer Vision and Pattern Recognition, 2019, pp. 10734–10742.

[45] Y. Xia, F. Liu, D. Yang, J. Cai, L. Yu, Z. Zhu, D. Xu, A. Yuille, H. Roth, 3d semi-supervised learning with uncertainty-aware multi-view co-training, arXiv preprint, arXiv: 1811.12506, 2018.

[46] S. Xie, A. Kirillov, R. Girshick, K. He, Exploring randomly wired neural networks for image recognition, arXiv preprint, arXiv:1904.01569, 2019.

[47] H. Xu, H. Zhang, Z. Hu, X. Liang, R. Salakhutdinov, E. Xing, Autoloss: learning discrete schedules for alternate optimization, arXiv preprint, arXiv:1810.02442, 2018.

[48] D. Yang, H. Roth, Z. Xu, F. Milletari, L. Zhang, D. Xu, Searching learning strategy with reinforcement learning for 3d medical image segmentation, in: International Conference on Medical Image Computing and Computer-Assisted Intervention, Springer, 2019, pp. 3–11.

[49] D. Yang, D. Xu, S.K. Zhou, B. Georgescu, M. Chen, S. Grbic, D. Metaxas, D. Comaniciu, Automatic liver segmentation using an adversarial image-to-image network, in: International Conference on Medical Image Computing and Computer-Assisted Intervention, Springer, 2017, pp. 507–515.

[50] Z. Zhang, L. Yang, Y. Zheng, Translating and segmenting multimodal medical volumes with cycle-and shape-consistency generative adversarial network, in: Proceedings of the IEEE Conference on Computer Vision and Pattern Recognition, 2018, pp. 9242–9251.

[51] J.Y. Zhu, T. Park, P. Isola, A.A. Efros, Unpaired image-to-image translation using cycle-consistent adversarial networks, in: Proceedings of the IEEE International Conference on Computer Vision, 2017, pp. 2223–2232.

[52] B. Zoph, Q.V. Le, Neural architecture search with reinforcement learning, arXiv preprint, arXiv:1611.01578, 2016.

[53] B. Zoph, V. Vasudevan, J. Shlens, Q.V. Le, Learning transferable architectures for scalable image recognition, in: Proceedings of the IEEE Conference on Computer Vision and Pattern Recognition, 2018, pp. 8697–8710.

Multi-modality cardiac image analysis with deep learning

11

Lei Li[a], Fuping Wu[a], Sihang Wang[a], and Xiahai Zhuang[a]

School of Data Science, Fudan University, Shanghai, China

11.1 Introduction

Multi-modality cardiac images are widely utilized to assist the diagnosis and treatment management of patients [1]. Cardiac computed tomography (CT) is generally fast, low cost and with high quality for cardiac imaging. Magnetic resonance imaging (MRI) can provide important anatomical and function information of the heart, and different sequences of MRI can further capture different information. For example, the LGE MRI sequence has been widely used to visualize myocardial infarction (MI) as well as left atrial (LA) fibrosis and scars; the balanced-steady-state-free procession (bSSFP) cine sequence can present clear cardiac boundaries and captures cardiac motions in different phases; the T2-weighted MRI sequence can display the acute injury and ischemic regions. Combining multi-modality/sequence cardiac images is a promising research direction in the literature, such as multi-modality registration [2], multi-modality/sequence fusion [3,4] and domain adaptation [5].

In this chapter, we will present three topics related to the multi-modality cardiac image processing. Section 11.2 presents two challenges for multi-sequence cardiac MRI-based myocardial and pathology segmentation. Section 11.3 presents two novel frameworks, namely, LearnGC and AtrialJSQnet, for left atrial scar segmentation and quantification from LGE MRI (with the assist of an additional nonenhanced MRI). Section 11.4 introduces three unsupervised domain adaptation algorithms for cross-modality cardiac image segmentation.

11.2 Multi-sequence cardiac MRI based myocardial and pathology segmentation

11.2.1 Introduction

Cardiovascular disease is one of the leading causes of global death, among which MI is the most acute and deadly one [6]. Early diagnosis as well as prompt treatment

---

[a] All authors contribute to this chapter equally.

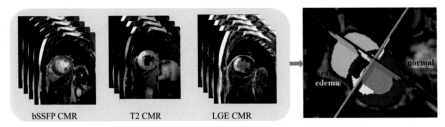

FIGURE 11.1

Visualization of myocardial pathology segmentation combining multi-sequence CMR images acquired from the same patient. Image adopted from the website of MyoPS 2020 challenge: http://www.sdspeople.fudan.edu.cn/zhuangxiahai/0/myops20/.

are the key to prevent the poor prognosis. Among the imaging modalities available in clinical routines for MI, cardiac magnetic resonance (CMR) imaging becomes the gold-standard technique. The functional cardiac indexes, i.e., left ventricular (LV), ejection fraction (EF), LV volumes, myocardium mass as well as precise location of lesion could be obtained from the analysis of MRI. However, one MRI sequence could provide limited clinic information. In clinic practice, multi-modality would be simultaneously utilized, since the complementary information from multi-sequences can assist the diagnosis and location of lesion. Whereas the misalignment among multi-modalities caused by the different scanning orientations, the various sequences characteristic and the low tissue contrast in special modalities (such as T2 and LGE CMR) make it challenging to handle multi-modality tasks.

To boost the study in this field, in recent years, we have organized two challenges, providing a fair and unified platform and open benchmark data set for researches around the world. We first held MS-CMRSeg challenge event [7] for LGE CMR image segmentation with multi-sequence CMR available, segmenting the anatomical structure (i.e., left ventricle, right ventricle and myocardium). Fig. 11.1 provides an example of multi-sequence images from one subject, including bSSFP, T2 and LGE CMR. One can see that there exist misalignment, vast image intensity distribution gap and various pathology region shape among them. These differences are the main obstacles for image analysis. As an extension, we then organized myocardial pathology segmentation (MyoPS) challenge event [8] for the myocardial pathology segmentation, including scar and edema. In the following, we summarize the top-performed methods in the two challenges.

11.2.2 Methodology summary for challenge events

11.2.2.1 MS-CMRSeg challenge: cardiac segmentation on late gadolinium enhancement MRI

We organized multi-sequence cardiac MR segmentation (MS-CMRSeg) challenge, in conjunction with MICCAI 2019. The challenge mainly focused on the anatomical structure (ventricles and myocardium) segmentation of LGE sequence with complementary information from the other two sequences (bSSFP and T2 sequence). Sixty-five teams from all over the world participated in the challenge, twenty three of which submitted results for evaluation before the submission deadline. To keep the chapter concise, only the top nine methods will be discussed. These nine methods could roughly be divided into two categories. The first one is training without LGE annotation, namely an unsupervised domain adaptation (UDA) problem, and three teams focused on this task; the other six teams trained their models with a few LGE ground-truth, considered as supervised methods.

For UDA methods, two teams, i.e., ICL [9] and INRIA [10], adopted image translation scheme via the style-transfer. ICL leveraged multi-modal unsupervised image-to-image translation network [11] to implement style transfer. In their framework, the encoder extracts style information and structure information from image separately, while decoders reconstruct the image using the extracted features. INRIA adopts conventional style transformation, i.e., histogram matching toward LGE, and also employs some data augmentation schemes including adaptive histogram equalization and intensity inversion. As for the network structure, ICL adopts two stage cascaded network to extract "coarse to fine" features, while INRIA utilizes a dual U-Net [12]. Instead of using image translation, XMU [13] performs feature alignment to achieve UDA optimization. The alignment is achieved via a discriminator, which can minimize the distribution discrepancy between the two domains in both feature and output spaces.

Among the supervised-learning based methods, UB [14] and HIT [15] mainly adopted several date augmentation strategies to avoid over-fitting, while the other teams try to design effective model structures for LGE MRI segmentation. For data augmentation, UB leverages CycleGAN strategy [16] to convert bSSFP images into LGE-like ones and utilizes region rotation of scars, while HIT uses histogram matching for augmentation. For model structure, only NVIDIA [10] leverages conventional multi-atlas segmentation (MAS) framework, while the other teams, i.e., FAU [17], SUST [18] and SCU [19] employs deep neural networks. SCU [19] redesigns the baseline U-Net with the squeeze-and-excitation residual module and the selective kernel module [20] to recalibrate channelwise feature responses and adjust the size of its receptive field, respectively. FAU [17] uses transfer-learning to facilitate modeling ability with complementary modality information for bSSFP and T2. SUST utilizes generator and discriminator to generate segmentation masks from LGE CMR image.

11.2.2.2 MyoPS: myocardial pathology segmentation from multi-sequence cardiac MRI

We further organized MyoPS challenge as the extension of MS-CMRSeg challenge, in conjunction with MICCAI 2020, to focus on the pathology segmentation instead of the anatomical structure segmentation. Up to now, MyoPS challenge has received seventy-six requests of registration around world, among which twenty-three teams submitted results for evaluation. As mentioned before, one of the major challenges of multi-modal image analysis is the misalignment between different modalities. To alleviate this, in this challenge we pre-processed the MS-CMR data set via the MvMM algorithm [21] for inter-sequence registration. In this section, we will summarize useful training strategies and trends observed from 15 approaches submitted to MyoPS, in terms of preprocessing, data augmentation, segmentation model architecture and post-processing.

Preprocessing. Preprocessing is a crucial technique to mitigate undesirable variations from raw data and reduce modeling complexity. Since the region of interest (edema and scar) of CMR is relatively small compared to background, all approaches crops the training images as a preprocessing. Most of them roughly crops the training images to generate the center of heart. For example, USTB [22] simply crops the images into the ROI with 256×256 pixels. Besides, several teams employs prior segmentation network to automatically localize the position of LV and myocardium for ROI extraction. For example, UBA [23] leverages U-Net to segment myocardium and crops the smallest bounding box containing the prediction. In this way, one could obtain an ROI and dramatically reduce the useless information for the following pathology segmentation. Moreover, data normalization is also a vital data preprocessing technique to reduce data variations, due to the large domain shift among different modalities. The majority of algorithms adopts the z-score normalization, while several teams simply scales the value to [0, 1].

Data augmentation. Data augmentation schemes are widely used to facilitate model generalization ability. The augmentation strategies utilized in the challenge methods could be roughly categorized into two parts, online transformation and offline data augmentation. Online transformation mainly contains several conventional augmentation schemes, such as randomly rotation, scaling, shifting, brightness, nonrigid transformations and contrast adjustment. For example, USTB [22] transforms the original images nonrigidly with elastic-transform, grid-distortion and optical-distortion. Offline augmentation mainly refers to data generation. UBA [23] adopts spatially-adaptive normalization [24] for style transfer, pathology rotation and dilation/erosion.

Model architectures. The design of model architecture is another determinant for the prediction results. The most prevailing backbone utilized by these methods is U-Net, which includes elegant symmetric encoder and decoder structure with multi-scale feature and skip-connection strategy. UESTC [25] utilizes U-Net for both coarse and fine segmentation networks. Moreover, dense connection and attention are useful techniques. UBA [23] utilized an U-Net variant, termed as BCDU-Net [26], which reuses feature maps via dense convolutions. USTB [22] adopts channel and space attention modules at the basis of U-Net. As for loss functions, most teams employ the Dice loss and the cross-entropy loss. Also, FZU [27] utilizes boundary loss to enforce the model to focus on the boundary regions.

Post-processing. Among all teams, only four of them utilized post-processing to refine the predictions. UBA [23] adopts the most complicated post-processing scheme. They first constrains the myocardium into a ring shape, and then calculates the distances of the pixels, which are predicted as nonbackground to the Myo. In addition,

Table 11.1 Image acquisition parameters of the original multi-sequence data. ED: end-diastolic [7].

Sequence	Imaging type	No. slices	TR/TE (ms)	Slice thickness	In-plane resolution
LGR CMR	T1-weighted	10–18	3.6/1.8	5 mm	0.75×0.75 mm²
T2 CMR	T2-weighted	3–7	2000/90	12–20 mm	1.35×1.35 mm²
bSSFP CMR	Cine sequence	8–12	2.7/1.4	8–13 mm	1.25×1.25 mm²

NPU [28] and USTB [22] simply removes the isolated regions. UOA [29] solely retains the largest connected component of predicted LV and then fills the holes.

11.2.3 Data and results

11.2.3.1 Data

The data sets of two challenges were collected from the same patient group, but with different annotations. The data sets includes multi-CMR sequences (bSSFP, T2 and LGE), taken from 45 subjects who underwent cardiomyopathy, and were annotated by at least three experts. They had been collected with institutional ethics approval and underwent anonymization. Moreover, multi-sequences were pre-aligned by MvMM algorithm [21] in the MyoPS challenge. The details of three sequences are shown in Table 11.1.

11.2.3.2 Evaluation metrics

For evaluation, Dice score was applied in both MS-CMRSeg and MyoPS challenges,

$$Dice(V_{seg}, V_{GD}) = \frac{2|V_{seg} \ \& \ V_{GD}|}{|V_{seg}| + |V_{GD}|}, \tag{11.1}$$

where V_{GD} and V_{seg} denote the gold standard and automatic segmentation, respectively. Moreover, MS-CMRSeg used average surface distance (ASD) and Hausdorff distance (HD) as supplementary metrics, which can be defined as

$$HD(X, Y) = max[\sup_{x \in X} \inf_{y \in Y} d(x, y), \sup_{y \in Y} \inf_{x \in X} d(x, y)], \tag{11.2}$$

$$ASD(X, Y) = \frac{1}{2} \left(\frac{\sum_{x \in X} \min_{y \in Y} d(x, y)}{\sum_{x \in X} 1} + \frac{\sum_{y \in Y} \min_{x \in X} d(x, y)}{\sum_{y \in Y} 1} \right), \tag{11.3}$$

where X and Y represent two sets of contour points, and $d(x, y)$ indicates the distance between the two points x and y.

11.2.3.3 Results from MS-CMRSeg challenge event

Table 11.2 and Table 11.3 present the quantitative results of the nine evaluated algorithms. The mean Dice scores of Myo, LV and RV segmentation were 0.766 ± 0.104, 0.891 ± 0.056 and 0.822 ± 0.116, respectively, and the mean volumetric HD values

Table 11.2 Dice score of the evaluated algorithms on the LGE MRI segmentation [7]. UDA: unsupervised domain adaptation; teams updating their results after the challenge deadline are indicated with an asterisk (*), and teams using the unlabeled LGE images (I^{unl}) for training are indicated with a dagger (†).

Teams	Volumetric Dice			Training
	Myo	**LV**	**RV**	
ICL† [9]	0.826 ± 0.035	0.919 ± 0.026	0.875 ± 0.050	UDA
XMU† [13]	0.796 ± 0.059	0.896 ± 0.047	0.846 ± 0.086	UDA
INRIA* [30]	0.705 ± 0.115	0.870 ± 0.051	0.762 ± 0.150	UDA
SCU* [19]	0.843 ± 0.048	0.926 ± 0.028	0.890 ± 0.044	Supervised
UB† [14]	0.810 ± 0.061	0.898 ± 0.045	0.866 ± 0.050	Supervised
FAU [17]	0.789 ± 0.073	0.912 ± 0.034	0.833 ± 0.084	Supervised
NVIDIA† [10]	0.780 ± 0.047	0.890 ± 0.043	0.844 ± 0.063	Supervised
HIT† [15]	0.751 ± 0.119	0.884 ± 0.070	0.791 ± 0.165	Supervised
SUSTech [18]	0.610 ± 0.102	0.824 ± 0.068	0.710 ± 0.135	Supervised
	0.775 ± 0.093	0.895 ± 0.047	0.828 ± 0.114	UDA
Average	0.764 ± 0.109	0.889 ± 0.060	0.822 ± 0.117	Supervised
	0.766 ± 0.104	0.891 ± 0.056	0.822 ± 0.116	All
Inter-Ob	0.764 ± 0.069	0.881 ± 0.064	0.816 ± 0.084	

Table 11.3 HD of the evaluated algorithms on the LGE MRI segmentation [7].

Teams	Volumetric HD (mm)			Training
	LV Endo	**LV Epi**	**RV Endo**	
ICL† [9]	10.28 ± 3.376	12.45 ± 3.142	15.38 ± 6.942	UDA
XMU† [13]	13.59 ± 5.206	15.70 ± 5.814	15.21 ± 6.327	UDA
INRIA* [30]	41.74 ± 7.696	42.79 ± 13.26	34.38 ± 8.065	UDA
SCU* [19]	9.748 ± 3.280	11.65 ± 4.002	13.34 ± 4.615	Supervised
UB† [14]	10.78 ± 4.066	11.96 ± 3.620	15.91 ± 6.895	Supervised
FAU [17]	11.29 ± 4.559	12.54 ± 3.379	17.11 ± 6.141	Supervised
NVIDIA† [10]	11.58 ± 7.524	16.25 ± 6.336	18.12 ± 9.262	Supervised
HIT† [15]	14.30 ± 8.170	14.75 ± 7.823	17.87 ± 9.322	Supervised
SUSTech [18]	23.69 ± 14.66	24.62 ± 12.66	23.46 ± 7.596	Supervised
	21.87 ± 15.23	23.65 ± 16.07	21.66 ± 11.49	UDA
Average	13.56 ± 9.316	15.30 ± 8.389	17.64 ± 8.092	Supervised
	16.37 ± 12.27	18.06 ± 12.18	19.35 ± 9.587	All
Inter-Ob	12.03 ± 4.443	14.32 ± 5.164	21.53 ± 9.460	

were 16.37 ± 12.27 mm (LV Endo), 18.06 ± 12.18 mm (LV Epi) and 19.35 ± 9.587 mm, respectively. Interestingly, the unsupervised domain adaptation models performed comparably to supervised ones, thanks to the style-translation data synthesis. As shown in Table 11.2, the Dice scores of LV were evidently better than that of

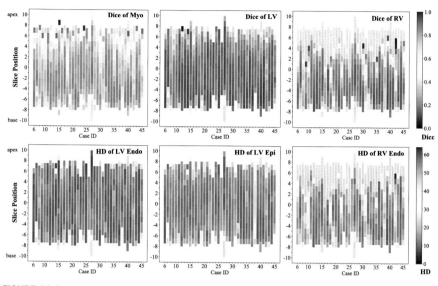

FIGURE 11.2

The average Dice score of the nine evaluated methods on each slice of the 40 test LGE CMR images. Image adopted from Zhuang et al. [7].

RV and Myo. Similarly, the HD values of myocardium, including LV Endo and Epi, were generally better than that of RV Endo. One reasonable explanation is that the variance of the shape of RV is larger than that of LV, which commonly presents a ring-like structure. Moreover, the segmentation results were related to spatial position. Fig. 11.2 presents the accuracy of different slices. One can see that the accuracy on apical slices were generally worse than that on midden and basal slices, which may be due to the shape variance.

11.2.3.4 Results from MyoPS challenge event

The mean Dice scores of the scar and edema were 0.634 ± 0.225 and 0.665 ± 0.146, respectively, and the best Dice scores for both scar and edema were achieved by ESTC. The results indicated that the Dice scores of edema are higher than that of scars, maybe due to the larger extent percentage of edema. Moreover, the segmentation precise is also related with slice position, as we found that the accuracy of midden and basal slices are relatively higher than that of apical slices. One possible reason is that the large variation of both anatomical and pathological shapes on apical slices. To figure out the correlation between the accuracy and pathology regional position, we also generated the bulls-eye maps to visualize the segmentation accuracy per region. The maps show that the inaccurate segmentation of scars and edema mainly occurs at the basal and inferior regions.

11.2.4 Discussion and conclusion

Intrinsically, the aforementioned works are trying to explore and analyze the same data set progressively. First, the inherent challenge for the multi-sequence task is that the images obtained from different sequences or even from the same center are generally not well aligned. MS-CMRSeg challenge focused on the anatomical structure segmentation, while the MyoPS challenge was an extent of the MS-CMRSeg for the pathology segmentation. Observed from the evaluated methods, scar and edema segmentation will be benefited from cardiac structure information, hence the majority of methods leveraged "coarse to fine" strategy. Note that the MS-CMRSeg and MyoPS data set and corresponding evaluation tool are still available for researchers upon request and registration via the challenge homepage https://zmi-clab.github.io/index.html.

11.3 LGE MRI based left atrial scar segmentation and quantification

11.3.1 Introduction

Atrial fibrillation (AF) is the most common type of arrhythmia and a severe public health concern. The identification of fibrosis and scarring region in left atrium (LA) is important for AF diagnosis, treatment and prognosis. Late gadolinium enhancement magnetic resonance imaging (LGE MRI) has been shown to be an noninvasive tool for left atrial (LA) fibrosis and scar assessment and quantification. However, LGE MRI usually has poor image quality, mainly due to its residual respiratory motion, variability in the heart rate and gadolinium wash-out during the long acquisition time. Moreover, LA wall is thin (mean thickness: 1.89 ± 0.48 *mm* [31]) with regional wall thickness variations. Various shapes of LA and pulmonary veins (PV) introduce additional challenges for scar segmentation of LGE MRI. Fig. 11.3 visualizes the major challenges.

Most methods for scar segmentation and quantification mainly based on thresholding [32]. Recently, with the development of deep learning (DL) in medical image computing, several DL-based algorithms have been proposed for automatic scar segmentation and quantification [33,34]. One could refer to the review papers [32,35] for the literature of LA and scar segmentation from LGE MRI. Next, we will introduce our two state-of-the-art framework for LA LGE MRI computing. Our first work mainly aims to solve the challenging of thin thickness in scar quantification, and we proposed a surface projection scheme (see Section 11.3.2.1). The second work focuses on the joint optimization of LA segmentation and scar quantification, and we designed a multi-task learning based network (see Section 11.3.2.2).

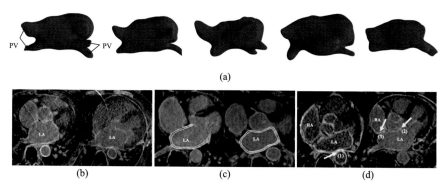

(a)

(b)   (c)   (d)

FIGURE 11.3

The challenges of automatic scar quantification from LGE MRI: (a) various LA and pulmonary vein (PV) shapes; (b) two typical LGE MRIs with poor quality; (c) thin atrial walls highlighted using bright white color; (d) surrounding enhanced regions pointed out by the arrows, where (1) and (2) indicate the enhanced walls of descending and ascending aorta, respectively and (3) denotes the enhanced walls of right atrium. Images adopted from Li et al. [35].

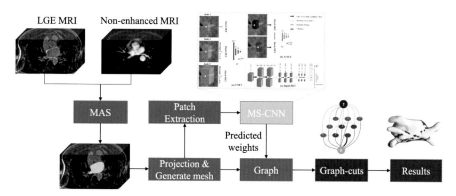

FIGURE 11.4

The proposed LearnGC framework for scar quantification. The images are modified from Li et al. [33,34].

11.3.2 Method

11.3.2.1 LearnGC: atrial scar segmentation via potential learning in the graph-cut framework

Fig. 11.4 presents the proposed LearnGC framework. First, we employ the multi-atlas segmentation (MAS) algorithm for whole heart segmentation, and then extract LA segmentation as an initialization. Then we generate a surface mesh based on the LA endocardium to perform the scar quantification on it via graph-cuts algorithm. The edge weights of graph-cuts are predicted by the proposed multi-scale convolution network (MS-CNN). Note that the scar quantification is performed on the generated surface mesh, to avoid the challenging segmentation task, i.e., thin LA wall segmentation. Moreover, it could be effective to reduce the computational cost.

LA segmentation via MAS. As LGE MRI covers the whole heart, we propose to employ multi-atlas whole heart segmentation (MA-WHS) to obtain the geometrical information of the LA. MAS algorithm can be separated into two steps: registration between atlases and the target image; label fusion of transformed atlases. Considering the poor image quality of LGE MRI, we employ an nonenhanced MRI from the same patient to assist its segmentation. The nonenhanced MRI normally has higher quality, and shares the anatomical structures with LGE MRI. With the WHS results, we employ marching cube algorithm to obtain a surface mesh of the LA endocardium.

Projection and graph formulation. In the clinic, the location and extent of scars are the main concern. Inspired by this, we project the LA endocardium onto a surface mesh, and then performed the scar quantification on the surface via graph-cuts. Moreover, the projection mitigates the effect of LA wall thickness and inaccurate LA segmentation, and also reduces dramatically the computational complexity. The projection is equidistant to preserve the geodesic distances between two nodes in the graph-cuts framework. Instead of using single pixel on the surface, we extract a profile via multi-scale patch to incorporate both global and local texture information of scars.

The scar quantification is formulated as an energy minimization problem in the graph-cuts framework. The edge weights of graph include the regional term E_R and the boundary term E_B, which encodes the intensity distributions of two classes and ensures the continuity between neighbors. One can denote the graph as $G = \{\mathcal{X}, \mathcal{N}\}$, where $\mathcal{X} = \{x_i\}$ is the set of graph nodes and $\mathcal{N} = \{< x_i, x_j >\}$ indicates the set of edges connecting graph nodes. Each graph has two terminals, which denote the scars (foreground) and normal myocardium (background), respectively. There are two kinds of edges, i.e., t-link that connects graph nodes to the terminals and n-link connecting neighboring nodes [36]. Therefore, the segmentation energy can be defined as follows:

$$E(l) = E_R(l) + \lambda E_B(l)$$
$$= \sum_{x_i \in \mathcal{X}} W_{x_i}^{t\text{-}link}(l_{x_i}) + \lambda \sum_{(x_i,x_j) \in \mathcal{N}} W_{\{x_i,x_j\}}^{n\text{-}link}(l_{x_i}, l_{x_j}), \qquad (11.4)$$

where $W_{x_i}^{t\text{-}link}$ and $W_{\{x_i,x_j\}}^{n\text{-}link}$ are the t-link and n-link weight, respectively; $l_{x_i} \in \{0, 1\}$ is the label value of x_i; and λ is a balancing parameter. Different from conventional graph-based segmentation, we directly predict the t/n-link weights for the regional and boundary terms. In this way, we can represent each graph node using a multi-scale patch (MSP), and then learn the weighs using the proposed MS-CNN. These patches are defined along the normal direction of the LA endocardial surface with an elongate shape. We further adjust the sample spacing to generate MSPs on the LGE MRI with different resolutions.

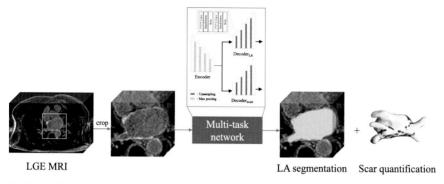

FIGURE 11.5

The proposed AtrialJSQnet framework for the simultaneous LA segmentation, scar projection onto LA surface and scar quantification. The images are modified from Li et al. [34].

Edge weight prediction via MS-CNN. To predict the edge weights in Eq. (11.4), we design two networks, i.e., T-NET and N-NET. T-NET is designed to predict the t-link weights, i.e., the probabilities of a node belonging to scarring and normal regions, respectively; N-NET aims to calculate the n-link weights, defined based on the similarity of two neighbor nodes and their distance. To embed the MSP into the networks, we adopt parallel convolutional pathways for multi-scale training, namely, MS-CNN. In the training phase of MS-CNN, we adopt a weight sampling strategy to mitigate the class imbalance problem. Specifically, instead of extracting the patches of all nodes for training, we randomly select the similar number of nodes from the normal wall and scars. Besides, we use a random shift strategy when extracting the MSPs to mitigate the effect of inaccurate LA segmentation. Note that the weight sampling and random shift strategy are not required in the testing phase. After obtaining the weights, one can obtain the scar quantification result by optimizing the graph-cuts framework.

11.3.2.2 AtrialJSQnet: a new framework for joint segmentation and quantification of left atrium and scars incorporating spatial and shape information

Fig. 11.5 presents the overview of the proposed joint segmentation and quantification framework, i.e., AtrialJSQnet. One can see that AtrialJSQnet is a two-task network consisting of two decoders for LA segmentation and scar quantification, respectively. We proposed a spatial encoding (SE) loss as to learn the spatial information of the LA cavity and scars. Moreover, we employ a shape attention (SA) scheme to utilize the spatial relationship between LA and scar. The SA scheme is also helpful to achieve an end-to-end scar projection.

Spatially encoded constraint in the AtrialJSQnet framework. We introduce a novel SE loss, which incorporates spatial information in the pipeline without any modifications of networks. The SE loss is designed based on the distance transform maps (DTM), a continuous representation of the target label. The signed DTM can be defined as

$$\phi(x_i) = \begin{cases} -d^\beta & x_i \in \Omega_{in} \\ 0 & x_i \in S \\ d^\beta & x_i \in \Omega_{out} \end{cases} \tag{11.5}$$

where Ω_{in} and Ω_{out} indicate the region inside and outside the target label, respectively; S denotes the surface boundary, d represents the distance from pixel x_i to the nearest point on S and β is a hyper-parameter.

For LA segmentation, the SE loss is defined as

$$\mathcal{L}_{LA}^{SE} = \sum_{i=1}^{N} (\hat{y}(x_i; \theta) - T_{LA}) \cdot \phi(x_i), \tag{11.6}$$

where $\hat{y}$ and y ($y \in \{0, 1\}$) are the prediction of LA and its ground truth, respectively; N is the number of pixels, T_{LA} is the threshold for LA segmentation, and $\cdot$ denotes the dot product. One can see the main idea of $\mathcal{L}_{LA}^{SE}$ is to assign different penalties to a false classification of each pixel based on its distance to the target boundary, i.e., the DTM value. The final loss for LA segmentation can be defined as

$$\mathcal{L}_{LA} = \mathcal{L}_{LA}^{BCE} + \lambda_{LA}\mathcal{L}_{LA}^{SE}, \tag{11.7}$$

where $\mathcal{L}_{LA}^{BCE}$ is the conventional binary cross-entropy (BCE) loss, and λ_{LA} is a balancing parameter.

For scar quantification, we first obtain the DTM of scars and normal wall, and then calculate the corresponding probability maps based on DTMs, i.e., $p = exp^{-|\phi(x)|}$ and $p = [p_{normal}, p_{scar}]$. Therefore the SE loss for scar quantification is defined as

$$\mathcal{L}_{scar}^{SE} = \sum_{i=1}^{N} \|\hat{p}(x_i; \theta) - p(x_i)\|_2^2, \tag{11.8}$$

where $\hat{p}$ ($\hat{p} = [\hat{p}_{normal}, \hat{p}_{scar}]$) is the predicted probability maps of normal wall and scars. Note that here we did not consider the probability map of background (pixels not belong to scars neither normal wall), as we quantify the scars on the LA surface. However, the predicted LA surface can be inaccurate, so we did not employ a fixed threshold on $\hat{p}_{normal}$ or $\hat{p}_{scar}$. Instead, we propose to compare the probabilities of each pixel belonging to scars and normal wall for final scar quantification results.

End-to-end trainable shape attention via multi-task learning. For joint optimization, we develop a multi-task network where segmentation and quantification of LGE MRI are simultaneously achieved. To further learn the spatial relationship between LA and scars, we introduce an attention mask, which is represented by the LA boundary from the predicted LA segmentation. The attention mask not only can alleviate the class imbalance problem, but also contributes to the end-to-end surface projection. To achieve this, we design a SA loss, which is defined as follows:

$$\mathcal{L}^{SA}_{scar} = \sum_{i=1}^{N} (M \cdot (\nabla \hat{p}(x_i; \theta) - \nabla p(x_i)))^2,$$ (11.9)

where $\nabla \hat{p} = \hat{p}_{normal} - \hat{p}_{scar}$, $\nabla p = p_{normal} - p_{scar}$ and $M = \{M_1, M_2\}$ is the attention mask. Here, M_1 and M_2 refer to the gold standard LA wall segmentation and the predicted LA boundary, respectively.

Therefore we can combine these loss functions for the final optimization of AtrialJSQnet as follows:

$$\mathcal{L} = \mathcal{L}_{LA} + \lambda_{scar}\mathcal{L}^{SE}_{scar} + \lambda_{M_1}\mathcal{L}^{SA}_{scar\,M_1} + \lambda_{M_2}\mathcal{L}^{SA}_{scar\,M_2},$$ (11.10)

where λ_{scar}, λ_{M_1} and λ_{M_2} are balancing parameters.

11.3.3 Data and results

11.3.3.1 Data acquisition

For the proposed methods, we evaluated them via two different data set, separately. For LearnGC, we employed 58 post-ablation LGE MRIs from longstanding persistent AF patients. All images were acquired from 1.5T Siemens Magnetom Avanto scanner (Siemens Medical Systems, Erlangen, Germany), using an inversion prepared segmented gradient echo sequence (TE/TR 2.2/5.2 ms), and were acquired 15 min after gadolinium administration. The acquisition resolution is (1.4-1.5)×(1.4-1.5)×4 mm, and is reconstructed to (0.7-0.75)×(0.7–0.75)×2 mm. For AtrialJSQnet, we adopted a public data from the *MICCAI2018 Atrial Segmentation Challenge* [37], which released 60 post-ablation LGE MRIs with manual LA segmentation results. The public LGE MRIs were acquired from 1.5T Siemens Avanto or 3T Siemens Vario (Siemens Medical Solutions, Erlangen, Germany), with a resolution of 1.25×1.25×2.5 mm. All images were acquired approximately 20–25 min after gadolinium administration, using a 3D respiratory navigated, inversion recovery prepared gradient echo pulse sequence (TE/TR 2.3/5.4 ms).

11.3.3.2 Gold standard and evaluation

All the images were manually segmented by a well-trained expert, which were regarded as the gold standard for evaluation. For LA segmentation, we employed Dice score, ASD and HD for evaluation. For scar quantification evaluation, we first projected manual and (semi-) automatic scar segmentation results onto the surface of manual LA segmentation. Then we used the *Accuracy*, Dice score and generalized Dice (GDice) score for the evaluation of scar quantification.

$$Accuracy = \frac{TP + TN}{TP + FP + FN + TN},$$ (11.11)

Table 11.4 Summary of the quantitative evaluation results of scar quantification. Here, LA_M denotes the manual LA segmentation, while LA_{auto} refers to the automatically segmented LA using MA-WHS. ^{0} means that the methods did not employ random shift scheme ($\gamma = 0$). MS-CNN refers to the learning based method only using the two t-link weights estimated from T-NET to classify scars. The asterisk (*) in column $Dice_{scar}$ indicates the methods performed statistically poorer ($p < 0.01$) compared to the proposed LA_{auto} + LearnGC.

Method	Accuracy	$Dice_{scar}$	GDice
LA_M + 2SD [38]	0.809 ± 0.074	0.275 ± 0.091*	0.758 ± 0.098
LA_M + Otsu [39]	0.763 ± 0.188	0.396 ± 0.090*	0.726 ± 0.207
LA_M + MGMM [40]	0.708 ± 0.160	0.545 ± 0.101*	0.716 ± 0.190
LA_M + MGMM + GC	0.716 ± 0.162	0.562 ± 0.102*	0.721 ± 0.192
LA_M + U-Net [41]	0.832 ± 0.046	0.568 ± 0.083*	0.826 ± 0.052
LA_M + MS-CNN^0	0.798 ± 0.051	0.615 ± 0.083*	0.811 ± 0.047
LA_{auto} + MS-CNN^0	0.806 ± 0.052	0.631 ± 0.080*	0.814 ± 0.047
LA_{auto} + MS-CNN	0.846 ± 0.032	0.692 ± 0.069*	0.851 ± 0.030
LA_{auto} + LearnGC	0.856 ± 0.033	0.702 ± 0.071	0.859 ± 0.031

where TP, TN, FN and FP stand for the number of true positives, true negatives, false negatives and false positives, respectively.

$$\text{GDice} = \frac{2 \sum_{k=0}^{N_k-1} \left| S_k^{auto} \cap S_k^{manual} \right|}{\sum_{k=0}^{N_k-1} \left(\left| S_k^{auto} \right| + \left| S_k^{manual} \right| \right)}, \tag{11.12}$$

where S_k^{auto} and S_k^{manual} indicate the segmentation results of label k from the automatic method and manual delineation on the LA surface, respectively, N_k is the number of labels and $N_k = 2$ here to represent scarring ($k = 1$) and normal wall ($k = 0$) regions.

11.3.3.3 Performance of the proposed method

Here, we will present the results for testing LearnGC and AtrialJSQnet algorithms, respectively.

LearnGC. Table 11.4 presents the LearnGC quantification results, which includes the results of both comparison and ablation study. The proposed method is LA_{auto} + LearnGC, where the LA segmentation was performed via MA-WHS, the weights of the graph were predicted using MS-CNN, and the balancing parameter λ was set to 0.4. One can see that proposed LearnGC method obtained the best performance compared to other comparison methods. It indicated that the proposed method can obtain the state-of-the-art performance, and also proved the effect of the proposed schemes, such as MS-CNN, random shift and graph-cuts.

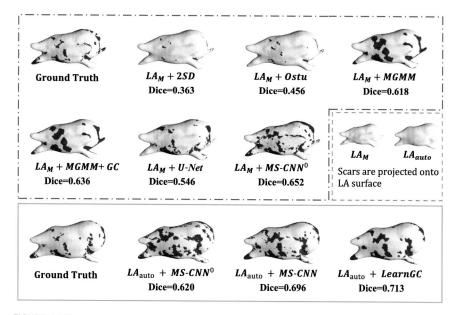

FIGURE 11.6

3D visualization of the LA scar classification results using the nine methods. This is the median case selected from the test set in terms of the Dice score of scars by the proposed method. The scarring areas are red-colored on the LA surface mesh, which can be constructed either from LA_M (LA surface in white) or from LA_{auto} (LA surface in light yellow). The image was adopted from Li et al. [33].

Fig. 11.6 presents the 3D visualization of scar quantification results by the nine methods. One can see that the 3D visualization results were consistent with the above quantitative analysis. The predicted scars based on LA_M and LA_{auto} were projected onto two surfaces, i.e., GT_M and GT_{auto}. However, one can see that GT_M and GT_{auto} have similar scar distribution. Compared to other methods, the proposed LearnGC obtained the most accurate and smooth scar quantification results. Fig. 11.7 visualizes the axial view of three representative cases. The illustration further proved that the proposed method could obtain promising scar quantification results, though with some minor errors. The mis-classification indicates the major challenges of automatic scar quantification, contributed to the major errors of scar quantification.

AtrialJSQnet. Table 11.5 and Table 11.6 present the LA segmentation and scar quantification results of different methods, respectively. For the LA segmentation, the proposed SE loss performed better than the conventional losses, such as BCE and Dice loss. For the scar quantification, the SE loss also obtained promising performance compared to the conventional losses in terms of $Dice_{scar}$. The three (semi-) automatic scar quantification methods generally obtained acceptable results, but relied on an accurate initialization of LA. LearnGC had a similar result compared to

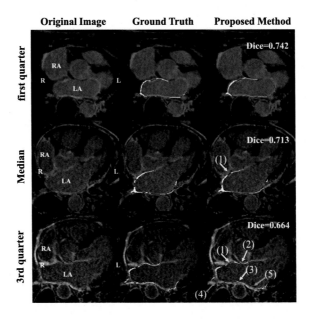

FIGURE 11.7

Axial view of the images, the ground truth scar segmentation and the results by the proposed method. The red and white color labels represent the scar and normal wall, respectively. Arrow (1), (2) and (3) indicate the major classification errors of the proposed method caused by the surrounding enhanced regions, respectively, from the right atrium wall, ascending aorta wall and descending aorta wall; arrow (4) shows an error from the misalignment between the automatic LA segmentation and the ground truth; arrow (5) illustrates that the proposed method can still perform well, even though the automatic LA segmentation contains obvious errors.

Table 11.5 Summary of the quantitative evaluation results of LA segmentation. Here, U-Net$_{LA}$ uses the original U-Net architecture for LA segmentation; BCE, SE, SA and SESA refer to the different loss functions. The proposed method is denoted as AJSQnet-SESA.

Method	Dice$_{LA}$	ASD (mm)	HD (mm)
U-Net$_{LA}$-BCE	0.889 ± 0.035	2.12 ± 0.797	36.4 ± 23.6
U-Net$_{LA}$-Dice	0.891 ± 0.049	2.14 ± 0.888	35.0 ± 17.7
U-Net$_{LA}$-SE	0.880 ± 0.058	2.36 ± 1.49	25.1 ± 11.9
AJSQnet-BCE	0.890 ± 0.042	2.11 ± 1.01	28.5 ± 14.0
AJSQnet-SE	0.909 ± 0.033	1.69 ± 0.688	22.4 ± 9.80
AJSQnet-SESA	0.913 ± 0.032	1.60 ± 0.717	20.0 ± 9.59
Inter-ob	0.894 ± 0.011	1.81 ± 0.272	17.0 ± 5.50

Table 11.6 Summary of the quantitative evaluation results of scar quantification. Here, LA_M denotes that scar quantification is based on the manually segmented LA, while LA_{U-Net} indicates that it is based on the U-Net$_{LA}$-BCE segmentation; U-Net$_{scar}$ is the scar segmentation directly based on the U-Net architecture with different loss functions; The inter-observer variation (Inter-Ob) is calculated from randomly selected twelve subjects.

Method	Accuracy	Dice$_{scar}$	GDice
LA_M+Otsu [42]	0.750 ± 0.219	0.420 ± 0.106	0.750 ± 0.188
LA_M+MGMM [40]	0.717 ± 0.250	0.499 ± 0.148	0.725 ± 0.239
LA_M+LearnGC [33]	0.868 ± 0.024	0.481 ± 0.151	0.856 ± 0.029
LA_{U-Net}+Otsu	0.604 ± 0.339	0.359 ± 0.106	0.567 ± 0.359
LA_{U-Net}+MGMM	0.579 ± 0.334	0.430 ± 0.174	0.556 ± 0.370
U-Net$_{scar}$-BCE	0.866 ± 0.032	0.357 ± 0.199	0.843 ± 0.043
U-Net$_{scar}$-Dice	0.881 ± 0.030	0.374 ± 0.156	0.854 ± 0.041
U-Net$_{scar}$-SE	0.868 ± 0.026	0.485 ± 0.129	0.863 ± 0.026
AJSQnet-BCE	0.887 ± 0.023	0.484 ± 0.099	0.872 ± 0.024
AJSQnet-SE	0.882 ± 0.026	0.518 ± 0.110	0.871 ± 0.024
AJSQnet-SESA	0.867 ± 0.032	0.543 ± 0.097	0.868 ± 0.028
Inter-Ob	0.891 ± 0.017	0.580 ± 0.110	0.888 ± 0.022

MGMM in Dice$_{scar}$, but its *Accuracy* and *G*Dice were higher. The proposed method performed statistically significant better than all the automatic methods in terms of Dice$_{scar}$ ($p \leq 0.001$). Both the LA segmentation and scar quantification benefited from the proposed joint optimization scheme comparing to separately optimize the two tasks. After introducing the new SA loss, the results were further improved in terms of Dice$_{scar}$ ($p \leq 0.001$), but with a slightly worse *Accuracy* ($p \leq 0.001$) and *G*Dice ($p > 0.1$). Moreover, with the SA loss some small and discrete scars could be detected, and an end-to-end scar quantification and projection were achieved.

11.3.4 Conclusion and future work

In this sub-chapter, we present two approaches for scar quantification from LGE MRI. The first approach combines graph-cuts and MS-CNN, referred to as LearnGC, which integrates the multi-scale information of scars and ensures a smooth segmentation results. More importantly, LearnGC is trying to ignore the wall thickness and project the extracted scars onto the LA surface. Therefore it converted the challenging volume-based scar segmentation problem into the relatively easy surface-based scar quantification problem. However, the pixel-wise quantification on the surface only includes limited information, and tends to be affected by the misalignment between the predicted endocardial surface and the corresponding ground truth. Therefore the proposed random shift scheme and MS-CNN are effective to improve the robustness of the proposed method against the LA segmentation errors. A major limitation of the LearnGC method is the lack of an end-to-end training scheme, i.e., MS-CNN and graph-cuts were separately achieved. We therefore proposed another approach, i.e., AtrialJSQnet, which can simultaneously achieved LA segmentation and scar quantification. To eliminate the effect of inaccurate LA segmentation, we learn the spatial information of each pixel on the surface via a newly designed SE loss. The SE loss and joint optimization were both proved to be effective by observing our experimental results.

A limitation of the two works is that the gold standard was constructed from the manual delineation of only one expert. Besides, the subjects included in this study are only post-ablation AF patients. In future work, we will combine multiple experts to construct the gold standard, and consider both pre- and post-ablation data. Moreover, we will collect multi-center LGE MRI to explore the generalization ability of LGE MRI segmentation and quantification models.

11.4 Domain adaptation for cross-modality cardiac image segmentation

11.4.1 Introduction

The capacity of model generalization is essential for the application of computer-aided-diagnosis (CAD) system on cardiac image analysis. In practice, a cardiac segmentation model trained on a specific modality could perform poorly on images from other modalities [43]. The reason is that there exists nonnegligible gap between the distributions of test and training data, which is known as domain shift [44]. How to transfer the learned anatomical knowledge from one domain to others without labeling new data is an interesting and open problem. An important research direction is domain adaptation, which aims to reduce the domain discrepancy between the labeled source and unlabeled target data [45].

To date, many domain adaptation approaches have been proposed for cardiac image segmentation. Most of them learned modality-invariant features via adversarial training [46,47]. For example, Dou et al. [43] designed a dilated fully convolutional network (denoted as PnP-AdaNet), which consists of a plug-and-play domain adaptation module to map two domains into a common space. It adopted the training scheme of domain adversarial neural networks (DANN) [48]. The method was validated on MRI-CT cross-modality cardiac segmentation for 2D images. While PnP-AdaNet extracted domain-invariant latent features from middle layers and achieved promising results, Chen et al. [49] proposed to implement domain adaptation on both feature and image levels. Their method, referred to as SIFA, translated images between two domains, and used the cycle-consistency loss for model constrain. This work was validated to outperform peer methods on cardiac cross-modality segmentation. In addition, Ouyang et al. [50] introduced a VAE-based feature prior matching to further adapt their features, and proposed a data efficient method for multi-domain medical image segmentation.

Although adversarial training has shown great potential in domain adaptation, especially for image translation, there still exist drawbacks which degrade its effectiveness and efficiency. First, the extracted domain-invariant features (DIFs) may not be pure. They could contain specific domain information and lead to biased results [51]. For image translation, no attention has been paid on domain-specific features (DSFs), which might be useful to improve the quality of the reconstructed images. Second, adversarial training reduces the discrepancy implicitly. It suffers from problems originated from the generative adversarial network (GAN) [52], such as the extra discriminators, complex training process and difficulty of obtaining the Nash equilibrium point [53]. While many explicit measurements for distribution discrepancy have been designed, such as the Maximum Mean Discrepancy (MMD) [54] and the moment distance [55], all of them were proposed for classification tasks, and no work has been validated for segmentation, to the best of our knowledge. What kind of explicit metric is efficient for cross-modality segmentation remains an important and open problem.

To tackle these issues, we proposed three domain adaptation frameworks for cardiac segmentation, which are termed as DDFSeg [56], CFDNet [57] and VarDA [58], respectively. Specifically, we first studied feature disentanglement for domain adaptation, and constrained DIFs and DSFs by introducing self-attention and zero-loss. It uses adversarial training for model optimization, thus can be categorized into Type I, as Fig. 11.8 (a) illustrated. Next, we studied the effectiveness of explicit discrepancy metrics for domain adaptation. A new metric based on the distance between characteristic functions is proposed, and it was validated to be effective in cardiac segmentation tasks. This metric is denoted as CF distance, and its minimization leads to the reduction of domain discrepancy and the extraction of domain-invariant features. This method avoids adversarial training, and has a simpler training process and faster model convergence. As Fig. 11.8 (a) illustrated, it can be classified as type II approaches. For both type I and II methods, the domains were mapped into a common latent feature variable z. The domain discrepancy was then either reduced by adversarial training or explicitly minimization of discrepancy metrics. While type II methods were validated to be useful for cross-modality cardiac segmentation, especially using the proposed CFDNet, we found that the computation of these metrics are complex. In practice, we calculate these metrics with marginal distributions instead of joint ones. This substitution weakens the constraint for domain-invariant features. Based on this consideration, we further proposed another type of methods. As illustrated in Fig. 11.8 (b), method of Type III drives two domains toward a common parameterized distribution, i.e., $q_\phi(z)$, in a latent feature z. As q_ϕ can be set to independent among its element variables, such as Gaussian distributions, the effect of the aforementioned substitution for metric calculation could be alleviated significantly. We achieve this approximation using variational auto-encoders, and thus denote the proposed framework as VarDA. In the following, we will describe the three methods in detail, and present their performances on the cardiac segmentation.

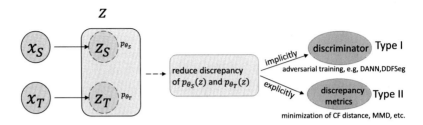

(**a**) The framework of previous researches of domain adaptation in a latent feature space.

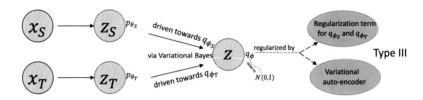

(**b**) The idea of the proposed variational approximation method for domain adaptation.

FIGURE 11.8

Illustration of the difference among three types of methods for domain adaptation. The proposed three frameworks refer to the three types, respectively. Images are adopted from Wu et al. [58].

11.4.2 Method

Let $X_S = \{x_S^i\}_{i=1}^{N_S}$ be the set of labeled source data, which are independent and identically distributed (*i.i.d.*) samples collected from source domain x_S with distribution $p_{\theta_S}(x)$, and θ_S is model parameter. $Y_S = \{y_S^i\}_{i=1}^{N_S}$ denotes the corresponding label of X_S. With X_S and Y_S, we can learn a segmentation model for this source domain. We further collect target data samples from target domain x_T, denoted by $X_T = \{x_T^i\}_{i=1}^{N_T}$, from a different distributions $p_{\theta_T}(x)$. The goal of domain adaptation is to transfer the knowledge from the source data, and train a segmentation model for the target data.

11.4.2.1 DDFSeg: disentangle domain features for domain adaptation and segmentation

We first study domain adaptation via image translation. Taking DSFs into account, we propose a new framework. As Fig. 11.9 illustrated, we use four encoders, i.e., E_S^{styl} and E_S^{cont} for source domain, E_T^{styl} and E_T^{cont} for target domain, to disentangle each domain into their DIFs and DSFs. These features are denoted as $z_d^c = E_d^c(x_d)$, where $c \in \{styl, cont\}$ and $d \in \{S, T\}$. These features are then swapped and decoded into images with the anatomical structures maintained and the style exchanged, using two decoders D_S and D_T. Mathematically, the new generated images can be expressed as $x_S^{fake} = D_S(z_S^{styl}, z_T^{cont})$, and $x_T^{fake} = D_T(z_T^{styl}, z_S^{cont})$. x_S^{fake} and x_T^{fake} are further encoded and decoded again for image reconstruction, which can be seen as a modified version of CycleGAN [16]. The reconstructed images are denoted as x_S^{recon} and x_T^{recon}, with $x_S^{recon} = D_S(E_S^{styl}(x_S^{fake}), E_T^{cont}(x_T^{fake}))$ and $x_T^{recon} = D_T(E_T^{styl}(x_T^{fake}), E_S^{cont}(x_S^{fake}))$. To enhance the DIFs and DSFs, we introduce the techniques of self-attention and zero-loss. In addition, extra discriminator is used to constrain the anatomical shape of segmentation output. Hence, the total loss function consists of three parts, i.e., image translation loss, zero-loss and segmentation loss.

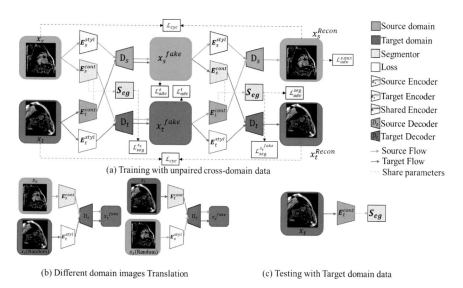

(a) Training with unpaired cross-domain data

(b) Different domain images Translation   (c) Testing with Target domain data

FIGURE 11.9

(a) Overview of the framework. (b) Illustration of different domain images translation. (c) Illustration of the segment with the target domain image at test time. Images are adopted from Pei et al. [56].

For image translation, we adopt cycle consistency loss to achieve image reconstruction, and use several discriminators to force the generated images to be as real as possible. The cycle consistency loss is defined as follows:

$$\mathcal{L}_{cyc}\left(E_S^{cont}, E_S^{styl}, E_T^{cont}, E_T^{styl}, D_S, D_T\right)$$
$$=\mathbb{E}_{x_S,x_T \sim P(X_S,X_T)} \left\| x_S^{recon} - x_S \right\|_1 + \mathbb{E}_{x_S,x_T \sim P(X_S,X_T)} \left\| x_T^{recon} - x_T \right\|_1. \tag{11.13}$$

To force x_S^{fake} and x_T^{fake} to be real, we introduce two discriminators Dis_S and Dis_T for source and target domains, respectively. The objective functions for adversarial training can be formulated as follows:

$$\min_{\left(E_S^{cont}, E_T^{styl}, D_T\right)} \max_{Dis_T} \mathcal{L}_{adv}^T = \mathbb{E}_{x_T \sim P(X_T)} \left[\log Dis_T\left(x_T\right)\right] +$$

$$\mathbb{E}_{x_S, x_T \sim P(X_S, X_T)} \left[\log\left(1 - Dis_T\left(x_T^{fake}\right)\right)\right], \quad (11.14)$$

$$\min_{\left(E_T^{cont}, E_S^{styl}, D_S\right)} \max_{Dis_S} \mathcal{L}_{adv}^S = \mathbb{E}_{x_S \sim P(X_S)} \left[\log Dis_S\left(x_S\right)\right] +$$

$$\mathbb{E}_{x_S, x_T \sim P(X_S, X_T)} \left[\log\left(1 - Dis_S\left(x_S^{fake}\right)\right)\right]. \quad (11.15)$$

Moreover, to further enhance the extracted DIFs to be domain-invariant, we add an auxiliary task to the source discriminator Dis_S to differentiate x_S^{fake} and x_S^{recon}. The objective function is defined as follows:

$$\min_{E_T^{cont}} \max_{Dis_S} \mathcal{L}_{adv}^{S.aux} = \mathbb{E}_{x_S^{recon} \sim P\left(x_S^{recon}\right)} \left[\log Dis_S\left(x_S^{recon}\right)\right] +$$

$$\mathbb{E}_{x_S^{fake} \sim P\left(x_S^{fake}\right)} \left[\log\left(1 - Dis_S\left(x_S^{fake}\right)\right)\right]. \quad (11.16)$$

The zero-loss is used to constrain the encoders E_S^{styl} and E_T^{styl} to force the extracted information from target and source images to be zero. Hence, the losses can be formulated as follows:

$$\mathcal{L}_{zero}^T\left(E_T^{styl}\right) = \mathbb{E}_{x_S \sim P(X_S)} \left[\left\|E_T^{styl}\left(x_S\right)\right\|_1\right], \quad (11.17)$$

and

$$\mathcal{L}_{zero}^S\left(E_S^{styl}\right) = \mathbb{E}_{x_T \sim P(X_T)} \left[\left\|E_S^{styl}\left(x_T\right)\right\|_1\right]. \quad (11.18)$$

Combining (11.17) and (11.18), we have the total zero-loss,

$$\mathcal{L}_{zero} = \mathcal{L}_{zero}^T + \mathcal{L}_{zero}^S. \quad (11.19)$$

The third type of loss is designed for semantic segmentation. The segmentation module predicts the labels from the latent features z_S^{cont} and z_T^{cont}. The first segmentation loss can be formulated as follows:

$$\mathcal{L}_{seg}^{x_S}\left(E_S^{cont}, S_{seg}\right) = \mathbb{E}_{x_S, y_S \sim P(X_S, Y_S)} \left[C\left(y_S, \widehat{y}_S\right) + \alpha \cdot Dice\left(y_S, \widehat{y}_S\right)\right], \quad (11.20)$$

where $\widehat{y}_S$ is the prediction of x_S, $\widehat{y}_S = S_{seg}(z_S^{cont})$, $C\left(y_S, \widehat{y}_S\right)$ is the cross-entropy loss, $Dice\left(y_S, \widehat{y}_S\right)$ the Dice loss and α is the hyper-parameter.

We further use the generated images x_t^{fake}, which contains the same anatomical information as x_S, to train the segmentation module. The loss is then formulated as follows:

$$
\begin{aligned}
&\mathcal{L}_{seg}^{x_T^{fake}}\left(E_T^{cont}, S_{seg}\right)\\
&=\mathbb{E}_{x_T^{fake}, y_S \sim P\left(x_T^{fake}, Y_S\right)}\left[C\left(y_S, \widehat{y}_S^{fake}\right) + \alpha \cdot Dice\left(y_S, \widehat{y}_S^{fake}\right)\right],
\end{aligned}
\tag{11.21}
$$

where $\widehat{y}_S^{fake}$ is the prediction of x_T^{fake}.

We have the total segmentation loss as follows:

$$
\mathcal{L}_{seg} = \mathcal{L}_{seg}^{x_S} + \mathcal{L}_{seg}^{x_T^{fake}}.
\tag{11.22}
$$

In addition, we introduce another discriminator Dis^{seg} to constrain the shape of the segmentation output of target images to be similar to that of source images. The objective function is defined as follows:

$$
\begin{aligned}
\min_{\left(E_T^{cont}, S_{seg}\right)} \max_{Dis^{seg}} \mathcal{L}_{adv}^{seg} &= \mathbb{E}_{x_T^{fake} \sim P\left(x_T^{fake}\right)}\left[\log Dis^{seg}\left(S_{seg}\left(E_T^{cont}\left(x_T^{fake}\right)\right)\right)\right]+\\
&\mathbb{E}_{x_T \sim P(X_T)}\left[\log\left(1 - Dis^{seg}\left(S_{seg}\left(E_T^{cont}(x_T)\right)\right)\right)\right].
\end{aligned}
\tag{11.23}
$$

Combining all the aforementioned losses, we have the total loss as follows:

$$
\begin{aligned}
\mathcal{L} =\;& \lambda_1 \mathcal{L}_{adv}^{t}\left(E_s^{cont}, E_t^{styl}, D_t, Dis_t\right)+\\
& \lambda_2 \mathcal{L}_{adv}^{s}\left(E_t^{cont}, E_s^{styl}, D_s, Dis_s\right)+\\
& \lambda_3 \mathcal{L}_{cyc}\left(E_s^{cont}, E_s^{styl}, E_t^{cont}, E_t^{styl}, D_s, D_t\right)+\\
& \lambda_4 \mathcal{L}_{adv}^{s.aux}\left(E_t^{cont}, Dis_s\right) + \lambda_5 \mathcal{L}_{zero}\left(E_t^{styl}, E_s^{styl}\right)+\\
& \lambda_6 \mathcal{L}_{seg}\left(E_s^{cont}, E_t^{cont}, S\right) + \lambda_7 \mathcal{L}_{adv}^{seg}\left(E_t^{cont}, S, Dis^{seg}\right).
\end{aligned}
\tag{11.24}
$$

In experiments, we set $\lambda_{adv}^{1} = 1.0$, $\lambda_{adv}^{2} = 1.0$, $\lambda_3 = 1.0$, $\lambda_4 = 0.1$, $\lambda_5 = 0.01$, $\lambda_6 = 0.1$ and $\lambda_7 = 0.1$.

11.4.2.2 CFDNet: characteristic function distance for unsupervised domain adaptation

Beside the adversarial training, we further study the effectiveness of an explicit metric for domain adaptation. We propose a new metric, which measures the distance between the characteristic functions of the latent features from source and target domains. Based on this CF distance, we propose a framework for cardiac segmentation, denoted as CFDNet. Fig. 11.10 illustrates the whole framework. The encoder extracts the latent features $z_S \in \mathbb{R}^n$ and $z_T \in \mathbb{R}^n$, respectively, from the source and target data. The segmentor module outputs the segmentation results from the latent features. The reconstructor module reconstructs the target images. The prior matching module regularizes the prior distributions of z_S and z_T to be close to $\mathcal{N}(0, I)$.

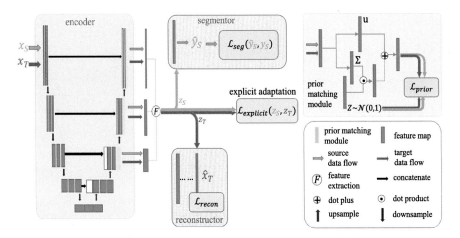

FIGURE 11.10

Framework of the proposed domain adaptation method for medical image segmentation. Images are adopted from Wu et al. [57].

The explicit adaptation module computes the domain discrepancy explicitly. Next, we describe each module in detail.

Calculating the discrepancy between the distributions of two domains in the latent feature space, i.e., $p_{z_S}(z)$ and $p_{z_T}(z)$, is difficult, because they are unknown. We instead estimate the distance of their CFs, $f_{z_S}(\vec{t})$ and $f_{z_T}(\vec{t})$. The loss function is given by

$$\mathcal{D}_{CF}(z_S, z_T; U) = \int_{-U}^{U} ||f_{z_S}(\vec{t}) - f_{z_T}(\vec{t})||^2 dt, \tag{11.25}$$

where $U \in \mathbb{R}_+{}^n$.

In practice, we solely compute the loss for a single point $U_a = [a, \cdots, a] \in \mathbb{R}_+{}^n$ using the mini-batch of samples. The CF distance is then estimated by

$$\mathcal{D}_{CF}(z_S, z_T; U_a) \approx \frac{1}{M^2} \sum_{p=1}^{M} \sum_{q=1}^{M} k(z_S^p, z_S^q) +$$

$$\frac{1}{M^2} \sum_{p=1}^{M} \sum_{q=1}^{M} k(z_T^p, z_T^q) - \frac{2}{M^2} \sum_{p=1}^{M} \sum_{q=1}^{M} k(z_S^p, z_T^q), \tag{11.26}$$

where $k(z_S, z_T) = \prod_{k=1}^{n} \frac{2\sin[(z_{S_k} - z_{T_k})a]}{z_{S_k} - z_{T_k}}$, for $\forall z_S, z_T \in \mathbb{R}^n$; z_{S_k} is the kth element of z_S, and likewise for z_{T_k}; M is the number of samples.

To simplify the calculation, we adopt a sliced version of CFD distance as a substitution, which is defined as follows:

$$\mathcal{L}_{SCF}(z_S, z_T; U) \approx \frac{1}{n} \sum_{i=1}^{n} \mathcal{D}_{CF}(z_{S_i}, z_{T_i}; U). \tag{11.27}$$

We further introduce the mean value matching to enforce domain adaptation. The mean loss is defined as follows:

$$\mathcal{L}_{mean} = \| \mathbb{E}_{p_{z_S}(z)}(z) - \mathbb{E}_{p_{z_S}(z)}(z) \|^2. \tag{11.28}$$

Combining the sliced CF distance with the mean loss, we have the explicit domain discrepancy loss,

$$\mathcal{L}_{explicit} = \mathcal{L}_{CFD} = \beta_1 \mathcal{L}_{SCF} + \beta_2 \mathcal{L}_{mean}, \tag{11.29}$$

where β_1 and β_2 are hyper-parameters.

Moreover, we introduce the technique of prior matching. We use a variational auto-encoder to map two domains into a common latent space z, with posterior distributions being subject to $q_{\phi_{S/T}}(z|x) = \mathcal{N}(u_{S/T}, \Sigma_{S/T})$, where $u_{S/T} = (u_{S/T}^1, \cdots, u_{S/T}^n) \in \mathbb{R}^n$, $\Sigma_{S/T} = \mathrm{diag}(\lambda_{S/T}^1, \cdots, \lambda_{S/T}^n) \in \mathbb{R}^{n \times n}$. The prior matching loss is formulated as follows:

$$\mathcal{L}_{prior} = E_{p_{x_S}(x)}[KL(q_{\phi_S}(z|x)\|\mathcal{N}(\mathbf{0}, I))] + E_{p_{x_T}(x)}[KL(q_{\phi_T}(z|x)\|\mathcal{N}(\mathbf{0}, I))], \tag{11.30}$$

where $KL(\cdot\|\cdot)$ denotes the Kullback–Leibler (KL) divergence, and $\mathbf{0} \in \mathbb{R}^n$ is a zero vector.

To constrain the feature of target images, we add a reconstruction loss, denoted as $\mathcal{L}_{recon}$. We use the cross-entropy loss for the segmentation loss from the labeled source domain, and denote it as $\mathcal{L}_{seg}(\widehat{y}_S, y_S)$. Then the total loss of the proposed CFDNet is formulated as follows:

$$\mathcal{L} = \alpha_1 \mathcal{L}_{seg} + \alpha_2 \mathcal{L}_{prior} + \alpha_3 \mathcal{L}_{recon} + \alpha_4 \mathcal{L}_{explicit}, \tag{11.31}$$

where α_1, α_2, α_3 and α_4 are the parameters.

11.4.2.3 VarDA: domain adaptation via variational approximation

Although the proposed CF distance is validated to be effective for domain adaptation, the substitution of its calculation using marginal distributions leads to a weaker constraint on the features. Moreover, the prior matching technique is not very useful as expected, due to the two-step sampling for estimation of the CF distance. Based on these observations, we further proposed another domain adaptation framework, which drives two domains toward a common parameterized distribution via variational approximation.

As Fig. 11.11 illustrated, the proposed VarDA framework consists of three modules, i.e., two VAE for each domains, and a module to compute the regularization

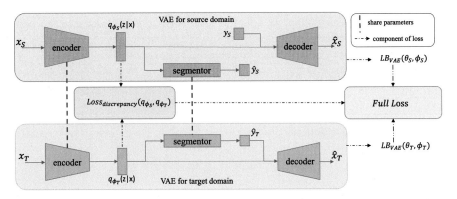

FIGURE 11.11

Framework of the proposed VarDA. This image is adopted from Wu et al. [58].

term on domain discrepancy. The objective functions of the two VAEs are denoted as $LB_{VAE}(\theta_S, \phi_S)$ and $LB_{VAE}(\theta_T, \phi_T)$, respectively. The regularization term for $q_{\phi_S}(z)$ and $q_{\phi_T}(z)$ is denoted as $Loss_{discrepancy}(q_{\phi_S}, q_{\phi_T})$. The total loss function of VarDA is then formulated by

$$
\begin{aligned}
Full\ Loss(\omega) = &-\alpha_1 LB_{VAE}(\theta_S, \phi_S) - \alpha_2 LB_{VAE}(\theta_T, \phi_T) \\
&+\alpha_3 Loss_{discrepancy}(q_{\phi_S}, q_{\phi_T}),
\end{aligned}
\tag{11.32}
$$

where $\omega = (\theta_S, \phi_S, \theta_T, \phi_T)$ are the parameters to be optimized, and $\alpha_1, \alpha_2, \alpha_3$ are the trade-off parameters.

Similar to the original VAE, we have the following objective function for the source domain:

$$
\begin{aligned}
LB_{VAE}(\theta_S, \phi_S) = &-D_{KL}(q_{\phi_S}(z|x) \parallel p_{\theta_S}(z)) \\
&+ E_{\log q_{\phi_S}(z|x)}[p_{\theta_S}(x|y, z)] + E_{q_{\phi_S}(z|x)}[\log p_{\theta_S}(y|z)],
\end{aligned}
\tag{11.33}
$$

where $D_{KL}(q\|p)$ is the KL divergence of q and p. The second term $E_{q_{\phi_S}(z|x)}[\log p_{\theta_S}(x|y, z)]$ can be modeled by the image reconstruction. The third term $E_{q_{\phi_S}(z|x)}[\log p_{\theta_S}(y|z)]$ is modeled by the segmentor.

We estimate $LB_{VAE}(\theta_S, \phi_S)$ using mini-batch samples as follows:

$$
\begin{aligned}
\widetilde{\mathcal{L}}_S(\theta_S, \phi_S; x^i, y^i) = &-D_{KL}(q_{\phi_S}(z^i|x^i) \parallel p_{\theta_S}(z^i)) \\
&+ \frac{1}{L} \sum_{l=1}^{L} \left[\log p_{\theta_S}(x^i|y^i, z^{(i,l)}) + \log p_{\theta_S}(y^i|z^{(i,l)}) \right],
\end{aligned}
\tag{11.34}
$$

where $z^{(i,l)} = g_{\phi_S}(\epsilon^{(i,l)}, x^i)$, with $\epsilon^{(i,l)} \sim p(\epsilon)$, L is the number of samples, and $z = g_{\phi_S}(\epsilon, x)$ is a differentiable transformation with $\epsilon \sim p(\epsilon)$.

Similarly, we have the variational lower bound for the target domain as follows:

$$LB_{VAE}(\theta_T, \phi_T) = -D_{KL}(q_{\phi_T}(z|x) \| p_{\theta_T}(z))$$
$$+ E_{q_{\phi_T}(z|x)}[\log p_{\theta_T}(x|\widehat{y}, z)] + E_{q_{\phi_T}(z|x)}[\log p_{\theta_T}(\widehat{y}|z)]. \qquad (11.35)$$

Finally, we force the approximations $q_{\phi_S}(z)$ and $q_{\phi_T}(z)$ to be the same one, and thus have the regularization term using l_2 norm of their distance as follows:

$$D(\phi_S, \phi_T) = \int [q_{\phi_S}(z) - q_{\phi_T}(z)]^2 dz$$

$$\approx \int \left[\frac{1}{M} \sum_{i=1}^{M} q_{\phi_S}(z|x_S^i) - \frac{1}{M} \sum_{j=1}^{M} q_{\phi_T}(z|x_T^j) \right]^2 dz$$

$$= \frac{1}{M^2} \sum_{i=1}^{M} \sum_{j=1}^{M} \left[k(x_S^i, x_S^j) + k(x_T^i, x_T^j) - 2k(x_S^i, x_T^j) \right], \qquad (11.36)$$

where $k(x_S^i, x_T^j) = \int q_{\phi_S}(z|x_S^i) \cdot q_{\phi_T}(z|x_T^j) dz$. Let $q_{\phi_S}(z|x_S^i)$ and $q_{\phi_T}(z|x_T^j)$ subject to $N(u_S^i, \Sigma_S^i)$ or $N(u_T^j, \Sigma_T^j)$, one can obtain that

$$k(x_S^i, x_T^j) = \frac{e^{-\frac{1}{2}\sum_{l=1}^{n} \frac{(u_{S_l}^i - u_{T_l}^j)^2}{\lambda_{S_l}^i + \lambda_{T_l}^j}}}{(2\pi)^{\frac{n}{2}} \cdot (\prod_{l=1}^{n}(\lambda_{S_l}^i + \lambda_{T_l}^j))^{\frac{1}{2}}}, \qquad (11.37)$$

where $u_{S_l}^i$ is the lth element of u_S^i.

As the computation for this regularization term is complex, similar to the sliced CF distance, we use the marginal distributions of z_S and z_T to calculate the distance. The substitution is as follows:

$$\widetilde{D}(\phi_S, \phi_T) = \sum_{i=1}^{n} \int [q_{\phi_S}(z_i) - q_{\phi_T}(z_i)]^2 dz. \qquad (11.38)$$

Based on the three loss functions discussed above, we have the total loss of VarDA as follows:

$$\widetilde{\mathcal{H}}(\omega) = - \alpha_1 \cdot \widetilde{\mathcal{L}}_S(\theta_S, \phi_S; X_S, Y_S)$$
$$- \alpha_2 \cdot \widetilde{\mathcal{L}}_T(\theta_T, \phi_T; X_T, \widehat{Y}_T) + \alpha_3 \cdot \widetilde{D}(\phi_S, \phi_T). \qquad (11.39)$$

11.4.3 Data and results

In this section, we present performances of the three proposed frameworks on two cardiac segmentation tasks, i.e., CT-MR cross-modality cardiac segmentation and C0-LGE multi-sequence CMR segmentation.

11.4.3.1 Data

We used two data sets from two public challenges, i.e., the CT-MR data set from the MM-WHS challenge [59,60], and the bSSFP and LGE CMR images from the MS-CMRSeg challenge.[1] The former data set was from different subjects, while the later was paired images from the same subjects and we shuffled them to be unpaired.

CT-MR data set: This data set consists of 52 cardiac CT images and 45 MR images, of which 20 CT images and 20 MR images were from the MM-WHS challenge, and the others were from an open data source [61]. For each 3D image, 16 slices from the long-axis view around the center of left ventricular cavity were selected, cropped with the size of 192×192 pixels around the center of the heart. All methods were validated on these 2D slices for the segmentation of left ventricular cavity (LV) and left ventricular myocardium (MYO).

MS-CMRSeg data set: This data set consists of 45 paired bSSFP CMR and LGE CMR images, among which 5 LGE CMR images were provided with labels for validation, and the ground truths of other 40 images were not available. The target is to learn knowledge from the labeled bSSFP CMR, and transfer it to LGE CMR images for the prediction of LV, MYO and RV.

11.4.3.2 Comparison study for DDFSeg

We compared DDFSeg with other four methods: (1) **Unet(supervised):** A U-net was trained with labeled target data in a supervised manner. (2) **Unet(NoAdapt):** A U-net was trained with the source data, and then applied directly on the target images. (3) **CycleSeg:** We used CycleGAN [16] for image translation. The generated fake target images were then used for model training and (4) **SIFA** [49].

Table 11.7 presents the comparison results on CT-MR cross-modality segmentation. One can see that U-Net (NoAdapt) performed poorly on both tasks because of the domain shift. When MR images were taken as the target data with CT as the source domain, DDFseg achieved the best Dice and ASD values among all UDA methods on both tasks. Particularly on MYO, when compared to SIFA, it obtained more than 4% higher Dice score for MR segmentation and more than 10% for CT segmentation.

For LGE CMR segmentation, we present the comparison results in Table 11.8. One can see that U-Net (NoAdapt) failed on this task, especially on the myocardium. This indicates the large domain shift between the two domains. Among all three UDA methods, DDFSeg achieved the best results, with 7.6% higher average Dice score than SIFA. Cycleseg and SIFA obtained comparable Dice scores on RV and LV, but the Dice scores were much lower than that of DDFSeg. The reason could be that their performances were heavily dependent on the generated fake images. However, they did not pay attention on the DSFs to enhance the translation process, while we introduced the zero-loss, which led to better image disentanglement and higher-image quality of translated images.

---

[1] http://www.sdspeople.fudan.edu.cn/zhuangxiahai/0/mscmrseg19/.

Table 11.7 Comparison results for DDFSeg on the CT-MR cardiac data set in both directions of domain adaptation. This table is adopted from Pei et al. [56].

	CT→MR							
	MYO		RV		LV		Mean	
Method	Dice (%)	ASD (mm)	Dice (%)	ASD (mm)	Dice (%)	ASD (mm)	Dice (%)	ASD (mm)
Unet(supervised)	77.1±10.2	8.6±5.4	86.8±11.2	4.9±3.1	90.3±8.4	2.5±5.4	84.8±11.4	5.3±4.5
Unet(NoAdapt)	23.8±24.1	17.2±8.5	64.7±22.1	12.6±7.9	72.0±19.7	8.7±5.1	53.4±30.6	12.8±8.1
CycleSeg	53.2±17.1	11.8±5.1	79.2±13.1	8.9±4.7	81.3±11.8	6.6±3.6	71.2±19.1	9.1±5.0
SIFA	67.3±11.4	8.2±5.3	84.2±11.5	5.3±2.8	87.6±8.9	4.6±2.3	79.6±13.9	6.0±4.0
DDFseg	71.3±10.6	9.7±5.7	83.2±11.7	4.6±2.4	87.7±10.4	3.8±1.9	80.7±12.9	6.0±4.5

	MR→CT							
	MYO		RV		LV		Mean	
Method	Dice (%)	ASD (mm)	Dice (%)	ASD (mm)	Dice (%)	ASD (mm)	Dice (%)	ASD (mm)
Unet(supervised)	84.1±5.0	3.2±2.4	89.2±6.7	3.9±2.3	90.6±10.6	3.9±3.3	88.0±8.3	3.6±2.7
Unet(NoAdapt)	10.6±9.1	22.2±8.0	56.0±12.4	18.3±7.0	56.2±16.7	17.0±5.0	40.9±25.1	19.2±7.1
CycleSeg	51.3±15.4	6.6±3.8	83.3±7.7	8.4±2.9	79.3±15.3	8.3±3.9	71.3±19.5	7.8±3.7
SIFA	56.6±12.4	6.8±3.8	80.0±8.3	8.0±2.7	82.6±12.6	7.8±3.0	73.1±16.3	7.5±3.3
DDFseg	66.9±11.0	6.8±4.6	79.1±6.7	6.6±3.9	83.5±16.0	8.3±4.2	76.5±13.8	7.3±4.3

Table 11.8 Comparison results for DDFSeg on LGE CMR segmentation. This table is adopted from Pei et al. [56].

	MYO		RV		LV		Mean	
Method	Dice (%)	ASD (mm)	Dice (%)	ASD (mm)	Dice (%)	ASD (mm)	Dice (%)	ASD (mm)
Unet(supervised)	74.4±10.0	2.0±1.8	78.6±12.0	1.8±1.0	87.1±9.0	1.1±0.5	80.0±11.6	1.7±1.3
Unet(NoAdapt)	29.6±19.5	5.4±5.3	48.1±20.2	3.5±1.9	62.7±18.0	3.4±1.8	46.8±23.5	4.1±3.5
CycleSeg	57.1±14.9	2.6±1.7	75.7±15.3	2.5±2.1	82.2±9.3	2.2±1.2	71.1±17.1	2.4±1.7
SIFA	68.1±15.0	2.2±1.9	73.6±18.7	1.7±1.2	83.5±13.0	1.6±0.8	75.1±16.9	1.8±1.4
CFDnet	69.5±9.2	2.5±1.8	77.6±8.8	1.9±1.4	86.4±5.6	1.9±0.9	77.8±10.6	2.1±1.4
DDFseg	75.0±7.3	1.4±1.3	84.5±7.0	1.3±0.8	88.6±5.0	1.4±0.9	82.7±8.6	1.3±1.0

Table 11.9 Performance comparisons for CFDNet on the CT-MR cross-modality cardiac segmentation task. This table is adopted from Wu et al. [57].

Segmentation task	Methods	LV		MYO	
		Dice (%)	ASSD (mm)	Dice (%)	ASSD (mm)
Target: MR seg	NoAdapt	44.4±13.9	19.1±6.52	24.4±9.11	17.3±2.70
Source: CT	PnP-AdaNet	86.2±6.46	**2.74±1.04**	57.9±8.43	**2.46±0.661**
	AdvLearnNet	83.8±10.3	5.76±6.07	61.9±15.2	3.79±2.23
	CORALnet	88.4±7.11	3.02±2.45	67.7±10.8	3.18±1.65
	MMDnet	86.7±8.65	3.64±3.47	64.4±12.0	3.85±2.39
	CFDnet	**88.7±10.6**	2.99±2.79	**67.9±8.62**	3.40±2.75
Target: CT seg	NoAdapt	30.3±27.7	N/A	0.140±0.130	N/A
Source: MR	PnP-AdaNet	78.3±18.4	3.88±4.09	62.8±8.24	**3.09±1.59**
	AdvLearnNet	77.7±18.0	4.56±3.68	54.7±9.51	3.65±1.31
	CORALnet	76.1±16.9	12.2±10.2	58.1±10.9	5.89±2.97
	MMDnet	77.7±18.2	5.62±4.86	57.1±12.0	4.13±1.70
	CFDnet	**81.9±18.2**	**3.64±3.94**	**62.9±10.9**	3.16±1.18

11.4.3.3 Comparison study for CFDNet

We compared the proposed CFDnet with five other methods: (1) NoAdapt, (2) PnP-AdaNet, (3) AdvLearnNet: We used the same network via adversarial training, (4) CORALnet: This method is the same as CFDNet except using the distance between the second-order statistics (covariances) of the source and target features as the explicit metric, which was proposed by [55] and (5) MMDnet: This method is the same as CFDNet except using MMD with the Gaussian kernel function as the explicit metric.

Table 11.9 presents the comparison results on CT-MR cross-modality cardiac segmentation. When we took MR images as the target domain and CT as the source one, CFDNet achieved comparable results with PnP-AdaNet, though worse in terms of ASSD values. When tested on CT images with MR as the source domain, CFDnet obtained higher Dice scores, especially significantly better on the LV ($p < 0.01$). These results indicated that the proposed CF distance was effective for domain adaptation on segmentation tasks, and could achieve no worse prediction than the conventional adversarial training methods.

For LGE CMR segmentation, as shown in Table 11.10, CFDNet obtained much better accuracies on all structures in all metrics compared to PnP-AdaNet and AdvLearnNet. This results further demonstrated the effectiveness of an explicit metric for domain adaptation. Compared to other explicit metrics, CF distance obtained a higher score on RV, and comparable results on LV and MYO. This might be due to the substitution process for the computation of CF distance, which used the marginal distributions instead of joint ones. This substitution leaded to a weaker constraint for feature extraction. We further provided their visual comparison in Fig. 11.12. One can see that CFDNet can achieve better prediction, while the shapes of the segmentation results were not satisfactory as expected.

Table 11.10 Performance comparison for CFDNet on LGE CMR images with bSSFP CMR as the source domain. This table is adopted from Wu et al. [57].

Methods	Dice (%)			ASSD (mm)		
	MYO	**LV**	**RV**	**MYO**	**LV**	**RV**
NoAdapt	14.5±20.12	34.5±31.6	31.1±26.3	21.6±19.4	11.3±13.1	14.5±17.3
PnP-AdaNet	64.6±16.4	78.4±16.2	72.6±19.0	4.64±6.41	13.8±10.3	5.30±5.33
AdvLearnNet	65.5±13.7	84.6±8.26	75.2±16.5	2.68±1.23	3.70±2.33	**4.08±2.65**
CORALnet	68.0±10.4	85.2±6.41	73.8±11.7	**2.30±0.831**	3.43±1.66	5.44±2.55
MMDnet	67.0±9.83	84.8±6.26	72.3±11.4	2.32±0.664	3.26±1.27	5.74±2.46
CFDnet	**69.1±9.69**	**86.4±5.62**	**76.0±10.9**	2.46±0.840	**3.07±1.66**	4.50±2.13

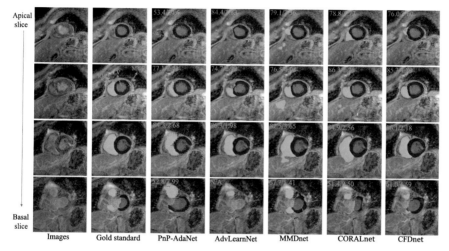

FIGURE 11.12

Visualization of 2D LGE CMR slices and segmentation results from a comparison study for CFDNet. These are extracted from the test subject with a median Dice score by CFDnet. The image is adopted from Wu et al. [57].

11.4.3.4 Comparison study for VarDA

We compared the proposed VarDA with three state-of-the-art methods, i.e., PnP-AdaNet (also denoted as PnP-Ada for short) [43], SIFA [49] and CFDNet.

Table 11.11 presents the comparison results on LGE CMR segmentation. The segmentation was done slice-by-slice in a 2D manner. Fig. 11.13 provides the visualization of the segmentation results of a subject, which was the median case of VarDA according to the average Dice score. One can see that the proposed VarDA performed much better than the CFDNet, which also used an explicit metric for domain adaptation. The reason could be that it used variational approximation, which forced the correlations between the elements of the latent features to be weak, and thus led to a reasonable substitution of the metric calculation. When compared to

Table 11.11 Performance comparison for VarDA on LGE CMR images. This table is adopted from Wu et al. [58].

Methods	Dice (%)			ASSD (mm)		
	MYO	**LV**	**RV**	**MYO**	**LV**	**RV**
NoAdapt	14.50±20.18	34.51±31.62	31.10±26.30	21.6±19.4	11.3±13.1	14.5±17.3
PnP-AdaNet	64.64±16.41	78.43±16.24	72.66±19.04	4.64±6.41	13.8±10.3	5.30±5.33
CFDnet	69.1±9.69	86.4±5.62	76.0±10.9	2.46±0.840	3.07±1.66	4.50±2.13
SIFA	70.66±9.689	84.62±7.760	**83.99±6.821**	2.40±1.22	2.68±1.14	**2.05±1.19**
VarDA	**73.03±8.316**	**88.06±4.832**	78.47±14.86	**1.73±0.560**	**2.55±1.18**	3.51±2.24

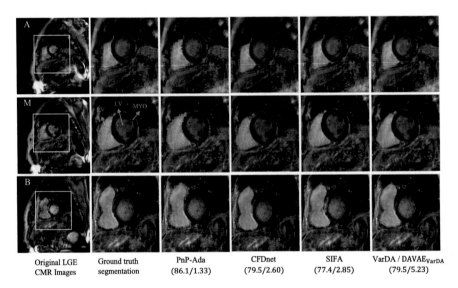

Original LGE CMR Images | Ground truth segmentation | PnP-Ada (86.1/1.33) | CFDnet (79.5/2.60) | SIFA (77.4/2.85) | VarDA / DAVAE$_{VarDA}$ (79.5/5.23)

FIGURE 11.13

Visualization of 2D LGE MR cardiac image segmentation results for a comparison study for VarDA. The cardiac structure of MYO, LV, RV are indicated in the blue, red and green color, respectively. Note that VarDA is the same as DAVAE$_{VarDA}$. The image is adopted from Wu et al. [58].

SIFA, VarDA obtained better accuracies on MYO and LV segmentation but worse on RV segmentation.

11.4.4 Conclusion

The three proposed domain adaptation frameworks investigated different aspects. DDFSeg studied the technique of feature disentanglement by paying more attention on DSFs, and demonstrated that DSFs are useful for image translation, and thus for domain adaptation. CFDNet proposed a new metric for domain discrepancy, and was effective in cross-modality segmentation, with comparable results as the conventional adversarial training methods. Based on CFDNet, we further proposed VarDA, which improved the effectiveness and performance of the explicit metric for domain adaptation.

References

[1] L. Li, W. Ding, D. Huang, X. Zhuang, V. Grau, Multi-modality cardiac image computing: A survey, Medical Image Analysis 88 (2023) 102869.

[2] A. Collignon, F. Maes, D. Delaere, D. Vandermeulen, P. Suetens, G. Marchal, Automated multi-modality image registration based on information theory, in: Information Processing in Medical Imaging, vol. 3, 1995, pp. 263–274.

[3] B.H. Menze, A. Jakab, S. Bauer, J. Kalpathy-Cramer, K. Farahani, J. Kirby, Y. Burren, N. Porz, J. Slotboom, R. Wiest, et al., The multimodal brain tumor image segmentation benchmark (BRATS), IEEE Transactions on Medical Imaging 34 (10) (2014) 1993–2024.

[4] T. Zhou, S. Ruan, S. Canu, A review: deep learning for medical image segmentation using multi-modality fusion, Array 3 (2019) 100004.

[5] N. Tajbakhsh, L. Jeyaseelan, Q. Li, J.N. Chiang, Z. Wu, X. Ding, Embracing imperfect datasets: a review of deep learning solutions for medical image segmentation, Medical Image Analysis 63 (2020) 101693.

[6] K. Thygesen, J.S. Alpert, H.D. White, Universal definition of myocardial infarction, Journal of the American College of Cardiology 50 (22) (2007) 2173–2195.

[7] X. Zhuang, J. Xu, X. Luo, C. Chen, C. Ouyang, D. Rueckert, V.M. Campello, K. Lekadir, S. Vesal, N. RaviKumar, et al., Cardiac segmentation on late gadolinium enhancement MRI: a benchmark study from multi-sequence cardiac MR segmentation challenge, Medical Image Analysis 81 (2022) 102528.

[8] L. Li, F. Wu, S. Wang, et al., MyoPS: A benchmark of myocardial pathology segmentation combining three-sequence cardiac magnetic resonance images, Medical Image Analysis 87 (2023) 102808.

[9] C. Chen, C. Ouyang, G. Tarroni, J. Schlemper, H. Qiu, W. Bai, D. Rueckert, Unsupervised multi-modal style transfer for cardiac MR segmentation, in: International Workshop on Statistical Atlases and Computational Models of the Heart, Springer, 2019, pp. 209–219.

[10] H. Roth, W. Zhu, D. Yang, Z. Xu, D. Xu, Cardiac segmentation of LGE MRI with noisy labels, in: International Workshop on Statistical Atlases and Computational Models of the Heart, Springer, 2019, pp. 228–236.

[11] X. Huang, M.-Y. Liu, S. Belongie, J. Kautz, Multimodal unsupervised image-to-image translation, in: Proceedings of the European Conference on Computer Vision (ECCV), 2018, pp. 172–189.

[12] S. Jia, A. Despinasse, Z. Wang, H. Delingette, X. Pennec, P. Jaïs, H. Cochet, M. Sermesant, Automatically segmenting the left atrium from cardiac images using successive 3D U-nets and a contour loss, in: International Workshop on Statistical Atlases and Computational Models of the Heart, Springer, 2018, pp. 221–229.

[13] J. Wang, H. Huang, C. Chen, W. Ma, Y. Huang, X. Ding, Multi-sequence cardiac MR segmentation with adversarial domain adaptation network, in: M. Pop, M. Sermesant, O. Camara, X. Zhuang, S. Li, A. Young, T. Mansi, A. Suinesiaputra (Eds.), Statistical Atlases and Computational Models of the Heart. Multi-Sequence CMR Segmentation,

CRT-EPiggy and LV Full Quantification Challenges, Springer International Publishing, Cham, 2020, pp. 254–262.

[14] V.M. Campello, C. Martín-Isla, C. Izquierdo, S.E. Petersen, M.A.G. Ballester, K. Lekadir, Combining multi-sequence and synthetic images for improved segmentation of late gadolinium enhancement cardiac MRI, in: M. Pop, M. Sermesant, O. Camara, X. Zhuang, S. Li, A. Young, T. Mansi, A. Suinesiaputra (Eds.), Statistical Atlases and Computational Models of the Heart. Multi-Sequence CMR Segmentation, CRT-EPiggy and LV Full Quantification Challenges, Springer International Publishing, Cham, 2020, pp. 290–299.

[15] Y. Liu, W. Wang, K. Wang, C. Ye, G. Luo, An automatic cardiac segmentation framework based on multi-sequence MR image, in: International Workshop on Statistical Atlases and Computational Models of the Heart, Springer, 2019, pp. 220–227.

[16] J.-Y. Zhu, T. Park, P. Isola, A.A. Efros, Unpaired image-to-image translation using cycle-consistent adversarial networks, in: Proceedings of the IEEE International Conference on Computer Vision, 2017, pp. 2223–2232.

[17] S. Vesal, N. Ravikumar, A. Maier, Automated multi-sequence cardiac MRI segmentation using supervised domain adaptation, in: International Workshop on Statistical Atlases and Computational Models of the Heart, Springer, 2019, pp. 300–308.

[18] J. Chen, H. Li, J. Zhang, B. Menze, Adversarial convolutional networks with weak domain-transfer for multi-sequence cardiac MR images segmentation, in: M. Pop, M. Sermesant, O. Camara, X. Zhuang, S. Li, A. Young, T. Mansi, A. Suinesiaputra (Eds.), Statistical Atlases and Computational Models of the Heart. Multi-Sequence CMR Segmentation, CRT-EPiggy and LV Full Quantification Challenges, Springer International Publishing, Cham, 2020, pp. 317–325.

[19] X. Wang, S. Yang, M. Tang, Y. Wei, X. Han, L. He, J. Zhang, SK-Unet: an improved U-net model with selective kernel for the segmentation of multi-sequence cardiac MR, in: M. Pop, M. Sermesant, O. Camara, X. Zhuang, S. Li, A. Young, T. Mansi, A. Suinesiaputra (Eds.), Statistical Atlases and Computational Models of the Heart. Multi-Sequence CMR Segmentation, CRT-EPiggy and LV Full Quantification Challenges, Springer International Publishing, Cham, 2020, pp. 246–253.

[20] J. Hu, L. Shen, G. Sun, Squeeze-and-excitation networks, in: Proceedings of the IEEE Conference on Computer Vision and Pattern Recognition, 2018, pp. 7132–7141.

[21] X. Zhuang, Multivariate mixture model for myocardial segmentation combining multi-source images, IEEE Transactions on Pattern Analysis and Machine Intelligence 41 (12) (2018) 2933–2946.

[22] H. Yu, S. Zha, Y. Huangfu, C. Chen, M. Ding, J. Li, Dual attention U-Net for multi-sequence cardiac MR images segmentation, in: Myocardial Pathology Segmentation Combining Multi-Sequence CMR Challenge, Springer, 2020, pp. 118–127.

[23] C. Martín-Isla, M. Asadi-Aghbolaghi, P. Gkontra, V.M. Campello, S. Escalera, K. Lekadir, Stacked BCDU-Net with semantic CMR synthesis: application to myocardial pathology segmentation challenge, in: Myocardial Pathology Segmentation Combining Multi-Sequence CMR Challenge, Springer, 2020, pp. 1–16.

[24] T. Park, M.-Y. Liu, T.-C. Wang, J.-Y. Zhu, Semantic image synthesis with spatially-adaptive normalization, in: Proceedings of the IEEE/CVF Conference on Computer Vision and Pattern Recognition, 2019, pp. 2337–2346.

[25] S. Zhai, R. Gu, W. Lei, G. Wang, Myocardial edema and scar segmentation using a coarse-to-fine framework with weighted ensemble, in: Myocardial Pathology Segmentation Combining Multi-Sequence CMR Challenge, Springer, 2020, pp. 49–59.

[26] M. Tan, Q. Le, Efficientnet: rethinking model scaling for convolutional neural networks, in: International Conference on Machine Learning, PMLR, 2019, pp. 6105–6114.

[27] Z. Zhang, C. Liu, W. Ding, S. Wang, C. Pei, M. Yang, L. Huang, Multi-modality pathology segmentation framework: application to cardiac magnetic resonance images, in: Myocardial Pathology Segmentation Combining Multi-Sequence CMR Challenge, Springer, 2020, pp. 37–48.

[28] J. Zhang, Y. Xie, Z. Liao, J. Verjans, Y. Xia, Efficientseg: a simple but efficient solution to myocardial pathology segmentation challenge, in: Myocardial Pathology Segmentation Combining Multi-Sequence CMR Challenge, Springer, 2020, pp. 17–25.

[29] X. Zhang, M. Noga, K. Punithakumar, Fully automated deep learning based segmentation of normal, infarcted and edema regions from multiple cardiac MRI sequences, in: Myocardial Pathology Segmentation Combining Multi-Sequence CMR Challenge, Springer, 2020, pp. 82–91.

[30] B. Ly, H. Cochet, M. Sermesant, Style data augmentation for robust segmentation of multi-modality cardiac MRI, in: M. Pop, M. Sermesant, O. Camara, X. Zhuang, S. Li, A. Young, T. Mansi, A. Suinesiaputra (Eds.), Statistical Atlases and Computational Models of the Heart. Multi-Sequence CMR Segmentation, CRT-EPiggy and LV Full Quantification Challenges, Springer International Publishing, Cham, 2020, pp. 197–208.

[31] R. Beinart, S. Abbara, A. Blum, M. Ferencik, K. Heist, J. Ruskin, M. Mansour, Left atrial wall thickness variability measured by CT scans in patients undergoing pulmonary vein isolation, Journal of Cardiovascular Electrophysiology 22 (11) (2011) 1232–1236.

[32] G. Pontecorboli, R.M. Figueras i Ventura, A. Carlosena, E. Benito, S. Prat-Gonzales, L. Padeletti, L. Mont, Use of delayed-enhancement magnetic resonance imaging for fibrosis detection in the atria: a review, Europace 19 (2) (2017) 180–189.

[33] L. Li, F. Wu, G. Yang, L. Xu, T. Wong, R. Mohiaddin, D. Firmin, J. Keegan, X. Zhuang, Atrial scar quantification via multi-scale cnn in the graph-cuts framework, Medical Image Analysis 60 (2020) 101595.

[34] L. Li, V.A. Zimmer, J.A. Schnabel, X. Zhuang, AtrialJSQnet: a new framework for joint segmentation and quantification of left atrium and scars incorporating spatial and shape information, Medical Image Analysis 76 (2022) 102303.

[35] L. Li, V.A. Zimmer, J.A. Schnabel, X. Zhuang, Medical image analysis on left atrial LGE MRI for atrial fibrillation studies: a review, Medical Image Analysis 77 (2022) 102360.

[36] Y.Y. Boykov, M.-P. Jolly, Interactive graph cuts for optimal boundary & region segmentation of objects in nd images, in: IEEE International Conference on Computer Vision, vol. 1, 2001, pp. 105–112.

[37] J. Zhao, Z. Xiong, MICCAI 2018: atrial segmentation challenge, http://atriaseg2018.cardiacatlas.org/, 2018.

[38] R. Karim, R.J. Housden, M. Balasubramaniam, Z. Chen, D. Perry, A. Uddin, Y. Al-Beyatti, E. Palkhi, P. Acheampong, S. Obom, et al., Evaluation of current algorithms for segmentation of scar tissue from late gadolinium enhancement cardiovascular magnetic resonance of the left atrium: an open-access grand challenge, Journal of Cardiovascular Magnetic Resonance 15 (1) (2013) 105.

[39] N. Otsu, A threshold selection method from gray-level histograms, IEEE Transactions on Systems, Man and Cybernetics 9 (1) (1979) 62–66.

[40] J. Liu, X. Zhuang, L. Wu, D. An, J. Xu, T. Peters, L. Gu, Myocardium segmentation from DE MRI using multicomponent Gaussian mixture model and coupled level set, IEEE Transactions on Biomedical Engineering 64 (11) (2017) 2650–2661.

[41] O. Ronneberger, P. Fischer, T. Brox, U-net: convolutional networks for biomedical image segmentation, in: International Conference on Medical Image Computing and Computer-Assisted Intervention, Springer, 2015, pp. 234–241.

[42] D. Ravanelli, E.C. dal Piaz, M. Centonze, G. Casagranda, M. Marini, M. Del Greco, R. Karim, K. Rhode, A. Valentini, A novel skeleton based quantification and 3-D volumetric visualization of left atrium fibrosis using late gadolinium enhancement magnetic resonance imaging, IEEE Transactions on Medical Imaging 33 (2) (2013) 566–576.

[43] Q. Dou, C. Ouyang, C. Chen, H. Chen, B. Glocker, X. Zhuang, P. Heng, PnP-AdaNet: plug-and-play adversarial domain adaptation network at unpaired cross-modality cardiac segmentation, IEEE Access 7 (2019) 99065–99076.

[44] H. Shimodaira, Improving predictive inference under covariate shift by weighting the log-likelihood function, Journal of Statistical Planning and Inference 90 (2) (2000) 227–244.

[45] G. Csurka, A Comprehensive Survey on Domain Adaptation for Visual Applications, Springer International Publishing, Cham, 2017, pp. 1–35.

[46] A. Chartsias, G. Papanastasiou, C. Wang, S. Semple, D.E. Newby, R. Dharmakumar, S.A. Tsaftaris, Disentangle, align and fuse for multimodal and semi-supervised image segmentation, IEEE Transactions on Medical Imaging 40 (3) (2020) 781–792.

[47] Q. Dou, L. Yu, H. Chen, Y. Jin, X. Yang, J. Qin, P.-A. Heng, 3D deeply supervised network for automated segmentation of volumetric medical images, Medical Image Analysis 41 (2017) 40–54.

[48] Y. Ganin, E. Ustinova, H. Ajakan, P. Germain, H. Larochelle, F. Laviolette, M. Marchand, V. Lempitsky, Domain-adversarial training of neural networks, Journal of Machine Learning Research 17 (1) (2016) 2096–2130.

[49] C. Chen, Q. Dou, H. Chen, J. Qin, P.A. Heng, Unsupervised bidirectional cross-modality adaptation via deeply synergistic image and feature alignment for medical image segmentation, IEEE Transactions on Medical Imaging 39 (7) (2020) 2494–2505.

[50] C. Ouyang, K. Kamnitsas, C. Biffi, J. Duan, D. Rueckert, Data efficient unsupervised domain adaptation for cross-modality image segmentation, in: Medical Image Computing and Computer Assisted Intervention - MICCAI 2019 - 22nd International Conference, Shenzhen, China, October 13-17, 2019, Proceedings, Part II, 2019, pp. 669–677.

[51] R. Cai, Z. Li, P. Wei, J. Qiao, K. Zhang, Z. Hao, Learning disentangled semantic representation for domain adaptation, in: IJCAI: Proceedings of the Conference, vol. 2019, NIH Public Access, 2019, p. 2060.

[52] I. Goodfellow, et al., Generative adversarial nets, in: Advances in Neural Information Processing Systems, 2014, pp. 2672–2680.

[53] M. Heusel, H. Ramsauer, T. Unterthiner, B. Nessler, S. Hochreiter, GANs trained by a two time-scale update rule converge to a local Nash equilibrium, in: Advances in Neural Information Processing Systems, vol. 30, Curran Associates, Inc., 2017, pp. 6626–6637.

[54] E. Tzeng, J. Hoffman, N. Zhang, K. Saenko, T. Darrell, Deep domain confusion: maximizing for domain invariance, CoRR, arXiv:1412.3474 [abs].

[55] B. Sun, K. Saenko, Deep CORAL: correlation alignment for deep domain adaptation, in: European Conference on Computer Vision, Springer, 2016, pp. 443–450.

[56] C. Pei, F. Wu, L. Huang, X. Zhuang, Disentangle domain features for cross-modality cardiac image segmentation, Medical Image Analysis 71 (2021) 102078.

[57] F. Wu, X. Zhuang, CF distance: a new domain discrepancy metric and application to explicit domain adaptation for cross-modality cardiac image segmentation, IEEE Transactions on Medical Imaging 39 (12) (2020) 4274–4285.

[58] F. Wu, X. Zhuang, Unsupervised domain adaptation with variational approximation for cardiac segmentation, IEEE Transactions on Medical Imaging (2021) 1–13.

[59] X. Zhuang, J. Shen, Multi-scale patch and multi-modality atlases for whole heart segmentation of MRI, Medical Image Analysis 31 (2016) 77–87.

[60] X. Zhuang, et al., Evaluation of algorithms for multi-modality whole heart segmentation: an open-access grand challenge, Medical Image Analysis 58 (2019) 101537–101550.

[61] M. Schaap, et al., Standardized evaluation methodology and reference database for evaluating coronary artery centerline extraction algorithms, Medical Image Analysis 13 (5) (2009) 701–714.

Deep learning-based medical image registration

12

**Xiaohuan Cao[a], Peng Xue[b], Jingfan Fan[c], Dingkun Liu[c], Kaicong Sun[b],
Zhong Xue[a], and Dinggang Shen[a,b]**

[a]*Shanghai United Imaging Intelligence, Co., Ltd., Shanghai, China*
[b]*School of Biomedical Engineering, ShanghaiTech University, Shanghai, China*
[c]*School of Optics and Photonic, Beijing Institute of Technology, Beijing, China*

12.1 Introduction

Medical image registration aims to establish anatomical correspondences between images of different subjects or the same subject acquired at different time points or between images of different imaging modalities. It is a critical technique used in many clinical applications, such as population analysis, longitudinal studies, multimodal image fusion and image-guided intervention. In recent years, deep learning, especially deep convolutional neural networks (CNNs), has shown great success in medical image registration [1–5]. In this chapter, we introduce the recent development of deep learning-based medical image registration methods. Conventional and machine learning-based registration methods will also be introduced briefly.

Image registration can be classified as *linear* and *deformable* registration according to the transformation model. Linear registration aims to estimate global rigid or affine transformation parameters, including translation, rotation, scale and shearing [6]. Deformable registration estimates local nonrigid deformation, i.e., voxel-to-voxel correspondences [7]. Formally, given a pair of fixed image I_F and moving image I_M, image registration can be formulated as a typical optimization problem, with the objective function generally defined as

$$\phi^* = argmin D(I_F, \phi(I_M)) + \alpha R(\phi). \tag{12.1}$$

It consists of two terms: 1) a data fitting term $D(I_F, \phi(I_M))$ that minimizes image dissimilarity between fixed image I_F and the transformed moving image $\phi(I_M)$; and 2) a regularization term $R(\phi)$ that imposes a smoothness constraint on the transformation. α is a weighting parameter used to balance the two terms. For linear registration, the regularization terms can be used to limit possible ranges of the transformation; while for deformable registration, it usually serves to preserve certain topological characteristics to yield plausible and realistic transformations.

Conventional registration methods can be categorized as intensity-based and feature-based registration. The most commonly-used image similarity metrics include Mean Square Error (MSE) [8], Sum of Squared Distance (SSD) [9], Normalized Cross-Correlation (NCC) [10], Mutual Information (MI) [11] and Correlation Ratio (CR) [12]. Deformation fields are often modeled by spline functions [13] to guarantee spatial smoothness, or using diffeomorphic models to enforce differentiability [10], or modeled by another displacement field constrained by Gaussian smoothing or bending energy [14]. A variety of optimization algorithms have been applied to transformation estimation after defining the registration problem. Some comprehensive reviews of the conventional registration algorithms can be found in [15–18].

Despite advantages of conventional registration methods such as promising accuracy, there are still challenges to be solved particularly for deformable registration. First, it is difficult to tradeoff between image similarity and deformation topology, especially for large deformations. Second, registration between multi-modal images with a large appearance difference needs to be further explored. Third, conventional optimization-based methods are usually computationally expensive, and cannot fulfill clinical demands, which limits their applications in routine clinical practice.

Machine learning-based algorithms have been proposed to tackle the aforementioned challenges [5]. Taking advantage of prior knowledge from an existing data set, different algorithms, based on sparse learning, random forest and support vector machine, have been used to make registration more efficient and accurate. For example, more appropriate initialization [19–21] or an intermediate template [21–23] between fixed and moving images are employed through learning the prior distributions based on the Support Vector Machine (SVM) or Random Forest (RF). To alleviate appearance differences between multi-modal images, some image appearance mapping models [24–27] are established by using the random forest with the auto-context model. Additionally, in [24,28–30], joint intensity distribution of different modalities is learned based on which proper metrics are defined to effectively register images across modalities. It can be seen that machine learning-based methods are mainly used for improving registration accuracy and robustness, either by modeling the deformation field or image priors, or by modeling cross-modality metrics. However, well-prepared training data sets with known transformations is required, and conventional optimization is still used required to get the final registration results.

Recently, deep learning-based registration has attracted enormous attention, and has shown remarkable success in medical image registration [3]. Different from other medical image analysis tasks, the deformable registration model aims to construct voxelwise dense correspondences between fixed and moving images, which is highly nonlinear and complex. Many works have been proposed, ranging from supervised learning [31] to unsupervised [32] and semi-supervised learning [33]. The results indicate that deep learning-based registration can achieve better registration accuracy, with significantly improved computational efficiency. To further facilitate registration accuracy and clinical applications, more advanced learning frameworks are investigated, where the smoothness property or semantic information are involved in the deep learning-based registration framework [34,35] to better preserve topology consistency. By using these strategies, deep learning-based registration models have already shown great potential for solving challenging scenarios, e.g., registration of images with large local deformation or subtle anatomies.

The rest of this chapter is organized as follows. Section 12.2 mainly covers the representative learning-based methods, including supervised learning, unsupervised learning and semi-supervised learning. Section 12.3 introduces semantic-aware registration algorithms applied in typical clinical scenarios to show current applications of deep learning-based registration. Section 12.4 summarizes the entire chapter.

12.2 Deep learning-based medical image registration methods

Convolutional neural networks are designed to learn the parameters of a transformation or a deformation field between an image pair. Basically, the input of the network consists of two images, and the output is the deformation field. Based on how the registration network is trained, deep learning-based registration can be categorized into three types: 1) supervised learning, where ground-truth transformations or deformations are available; 2) unsupervised learning, where similarity measure between fixed and transformed, moving images are used to estimate deformation field and 3) semi-supervised learning, which combines the above two learning strategies. Besides different learning strategies, other constraints such as deformation field smoothness, inverse consistency and topological correctness, can be imposed into the network by *either* additional regularization *or* specially-designed network architecture.

12.2.1 Deep learning-based medical image registration: supervised learning

Supervised learning is the most intuitive and straightforward training strategy for deep learning-based registration. The ground truth of registration is *either* the transformation parameters *or* the deformation fields between the input image pairs. Fig. 12.1 shows the framework of supervised learning-based image registration, and Table 12.1 lists some related works. The registration network takes fixed and moving images as the input, and predicts the transformation parameters or deformation field. In supervised learning, we assume that the ground-truth transformation is available, and the error between the output transformation and the ground truth is defined as the loss function. The challenge for supervised learning-based registration is to acquire or simulate the ground truth, whose quality can highly affect accuracy of the trained model [5]. Due to complexity of transformations, it is difficult to obtain the ground truth manually. In fact, they can be generated either by applying a conventional registration method with careful parameter tuning or using simulated images with synthesized transformations or deformation fields.

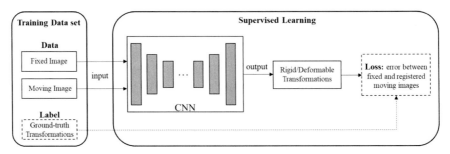

FIGURE 12.1

The framework of supervised deep learning-based image registration.

Table 12.1 Deep learning-based medical image registration methods: Supervised learning.

Transform	Modality	Organ	Supervision	Model	Reference
Rigid	X-ray/DDR	Bone	Synthetic transforms	6-layer CNN	[36]
Rigid	X-ray	Bone	Synthetic transforms	17-layer CNN + PDA module	[37]
Rigid	MR	Brain	Synthetic transforms	6-layer CNN + 10-layer FCN	[38]
Rigid	MR	Brain	Synthetic transforms	AIRNet	[39]
Rigid	MR	Brain	Synthetic transforms	11-layer CNN + ResNet-18	[40]
Deformable	MR	Abdominal	Real transforms	CNN	[41]
Deformable	MR	Brain	Real transforms	9-layer CNN	[26]
Deformable	CT	Chest	Real transforms	RegNet	[42]
Deformable	MR	Brain	Real transforms	U-net	[43]
Deformable	MR	Cardiac	Real transforms	SVF-net	[44]
Deformable	MR	Brain	Real transforms	FCN	[45]
Deformable	MR	Brain	Real transforms	CNN + FCN	[46]
Deformable	CT	Lung	Synthetic transforms	U-net	[47]
Deformable	MR	Brain/Cardiac	Synthetic transforms	FlowNet	[48]
Deformable	MR	Brain	Synthetic transforms	GoogleNet	[49]

For linear registration, the registration network is designed to predict transformation matrix, and the loss function is defined by a distance measure between the predicted and the ground-truth transformation. MSE and SSD losses are commonly used as distance metrics. Miao et al. [36] use a deep learning network to predict rigid transformation matrix and apply it to the fusion of 2D X-ray images and 3D CT images. With regard to the training data set, the target transformations are predefined and the training image pairs are obtained by transforming images using the predefined transformations. From the experimental result, this method outperforms traditional registration methods using MI, CC and gradient correlation (GC) as similarity metrics, in terms of both accuracy and computational efficiency. Later, Zheng et al. [37] apply deep learning networks to achieve rapid alignment from preoperative 3D X-ray image to intraoperative 2D X-ray image for image-guided therapy. In particular, a pairwise domain adaptation module is proposed to handle difference between real and ground-truth transformations. Recently, more generic supervised rigid registration networks have been proposed. These methods show superior performance compared to the traditional registration methods in 3D-to-3D [40], unimodal [39] and multimodal [38] registration tasks.

For deformable registration, the ground-truth deformation fields are more difficult to simulate or manually annotated. A common practice of obtaining ground-truth deformations is to conduct a state-of-the-art conventional registration method with careful parameter tuning. These expected deformations can be directly adopted as the ground truth or used to simulate other deformations and corresponding images for training. Cao et al. [26] use a CNN to predict displacement vectors of key points, which represent key anatomical structures. The final dense deformation field is interpolated through the predicted displacement vectors of key points. Jun et al. [41] utilize a similar way to train a CNN model to compensate respiratory motion. Sokooti et al. [42] propose a multiscale CNN to predict corresponding displacement vectors of patches at different scales by applying random nonlinear deformations for data augmentation. The performance is comparable to that of the B-Spline registration method. Later on, U-Net-based [43,44] or FCN-based [45,46] models are proposed to directly predict dense deformation fields rather than displacement vectors at selected points, which turns out to be more effective to perform registration for the whole images.

Although the results of such methods are encouraging, the performance is limited by the quality of ground-truth deformation fields and also the size of training data. To tackle this issue, Eppenhof et al. [47] use a large number of random multiscale deformation fields to warp images, and these deformation fields are regarded as the ground truth for transformed images. In addition to generating ground-truth deformation fields by random transformation, Uzunova et al. [48] employ a statistical appearance model to generate deformation fields. Their experimental results show that the ground truth generated with this model can train the network more effectively and obtain better registration accuracy. Ito et al. [49] propose to train a deep learning model to generate more plausible deformation fields. By using this model, more synthesized image data and ground-truth deformations can be used to train a more generalized registration model.

In summary, supervised learning strategy requires ground-truth transformations, and registration performance is highly dependent on the feasibility of these transformations. However, ground-truth transformations are difficult to obtain in practice since it is not possible to do large sets of manual annotations, especially for deformable registration. In fact, if ground-truth transformations are obtained by an existing registration algorithm, its performance might be limited to that specific algorithm. Therefore, registration methods based on unsupervised learning are more commonly investigated recently to circumvent the requirement of ground-truth deformations when training the registration model.

12.2.2 Deep learning-based medical image registration: unsupervised learning

Unsupervised learning has attracted more attention recently than supervised learning in the image registration community, since it does not need ground-truth transformations. The training pipeline for unsupervised learning is illustrated in Fig. 12.2. The loss function mainly consists of two terms: 1) the data fitting term, which measures dissimilarity between fixed and transformed moving images and 2) the regularization term, which constrain the field smoothness. Different from supervised learning, unsupervised registration model is evaluated by dissimilarities between images, rather than differences between predicted and ground-truth deformations. Specially, the transformed moving image is obtained by warping the moving image using the predicted deformation field. A spatial transformation operator, i.e., spatial transformer network (STN) [50], is adopted to perform warping of the moving image according to deformation field. It is worth noting that there are no trainable parameters in STN. A summary of representative unsupervised registration methods is given in Table 12.2.

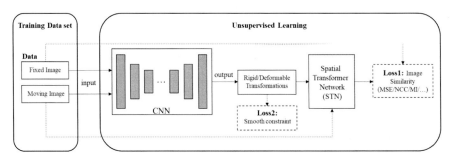

FIGURE 12.2

The framework of unsupervised deep learning-based medical image registration.

For most unsupervised registration methods, the backbone of the network architecture is based on FCN [51–56] or U-Net [31,35,57,58]. Li et al. [51] use NCC as a loss function to train FCN to perform deformable registration of brain MR images. Similarly, de Vos et al. [52] propose DIRNet to track 4D motion of cardiac cine, and also use FCN with the NCC loss. Similar FCN-based registration models [53–56] have achieved superior registration performance, compared with conventional registration methods for different applications.

On the other hand, the U-Net-based network has been widely applied to deformable image registration, since the encoder and decoder enable multi-resolution image registration, and more hierarchical feature representations can be incorporated during the model training. A representative U-Net-based network is VoxelMorph [35,57], which predicts deformation field and maintains diffeomorphism of defor-

Table 12.2 Deep learning-based medical image registration methods: Unsupervised learning.

Modality	Organ	Transform	Loss term	Model	Reference
MR	Brain	Deformable	NCC	8-layer FCN	[51]
MR	Cardiac cine	Deformable	NCC	DIRNet	[52]
CT	Head	Deformable	Predicted TRE	FCN	[53]
MR, US	Brain	Deformable	L2 + image gradient	FCN	[54]
MR	Brain	Deformable	UB SSD	19-layer FCN	[55]
MR	Cardiac cine	Deformable	MSE	8-layer FCNet	[56]
MR	Brain	Deformable	MSE	VoxelMorph	[35]
MR	Brain	Deformable	CC	VoxelMorph	[57]
CT, MR	Pelvis	Deformable	NCC	U-Net	[31]
X-ray, MR	Bone	Deformable	NCC	U-Net STN	[58]
MR	Brain	Deformable	BCE	GAN	[32]
CT, MR	Brain, Prostate	Deformable	BCE + anti-folding	GAN	[59]
MR	Brain	Deformable	BCE + CC	GAN	[60]

mation field by integration of velocity fields. In [57], the authors employ MSE was used as the loss function. Then Balakrishnan et al. [35] changed the loss function to CC to make the model more robust. VoxelMorph achieved better results than traditional registration methods on MR images. Other U-Net-based registration networks have also been successfully applied to CT [31] and X-ray [58] images. In summary, these methods do not rely on ground-truth deformations and both the accuracy and efficiency can be improved. However, a specific similarity metric needs to be chosen, and for different registration tasks, the choice of the similarity metric may also influence final registration performance. To tackle this issue, GAN-based unsupervised registration methods have been proposed, where image similarity is measured by a trainable network, rather than a pre-defined similarity metric.

Fan et al. [32] use binary cross-entropy (BCE) as a loss function to train a GAN model for 3D brain MR deformable registration. In this work, the generator is designed to perform deformable registration, and the discriminator is used to measure image similarity. Based on experimental results, the performance of the GAN-based model is better than those with a specific similarity metric, such as CC and SSD. Later, GAN-based model is extended from mono-modal to multi-modal registration problems.

In summary, unsupervised image registration has yielded great success. This is mainly because it does not require extensive data annotation, thus registration accuracy is not limited by the quality of the provided "ground-truth" and can be used in a wide variety of clinical applications. Unsupervised image registration is still an attractive research field, and more significant progress is expected.

12.2.3 Deep learning-based medical image registration: weakly-supervised learning

Weakly-supervised learning can be formulated as 1) training the registration model using both labeled (with ground-truth deformations) and unlabeled data (i.e., the combination of Fig. 12.1 and Fig. 12.2) or 2) using certain auxiliary information such as organ segmentation as the guidance to train the model more accurately as shown in Fig. 12.3. Some representative weakly-supervised registration methods are listed in Table 12.3.

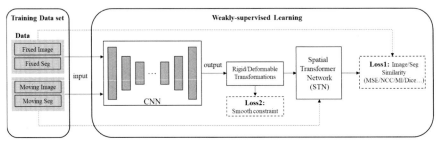

FIGURE 12.3

Weakly supervised deep learning-based image registration.

Table 12.3 Deep learning-based medical image registration methods: Weakly-supervised learning.

Modality	Organ	Transform	Supervision	Model	Reference
MR/US	Prostate	Deformable	Segmentations	30-layer FCN	[61]
MR/US	Prostate	Deformable	Segmentations + adversarial loss	GAN	[62]
MR	Brain	Deformable	Real transforms + similarity metric	U-net	[33]
MR/US	Prostate	Rigid	Synthetic transforms + adversarial loss	GAN	[63]
MR	Brain	Deformable	Real transforms + similarity metric	U-net	[64]
MR/US	Prostate	Deformable	Segmentations + similarity metric	U-net GAN	[65]

The loss functions are defined by combining supervised and unsupervised strategies using both labeled and unlabeled data. Some works refer these weakly-supervised methods as dual-supervised ones, and during the training both labeled and unlabeled data can be used simultaneously, sequentially or alternatively. Fan et al. [33] propose a modified U-Net architecture, which leverages hierarchical image and deformation field similarity matching, and the registration accuracy is better than the traditional U-Net-based registration methods. Yan et al. [63] propose a dual-supervised rigid registration method based on GAN, where the generator is trained to generate a rigid transformation and the discriminator is trained to discern whether the images are well registered. Unlike the above methods, Hering et al. [65] use both weakly and dual supervision by incorporating segmentation similarity and image similarity in the loss function for cardiac motion tracking.

By introducing auxiliary information, the registration performance can be further enhanced. Hu et al. [61] propose an end-to-end network to predict both affine transformation and local deformations, and the network is trained by the overlap ratio of the segmentations. Further, they added an adversarial term to the loss function to regularize the network and obtain more realistic prediction results for the deformation fields [62]. Weakly supervised learning is more flexible to train the registration network. By introducing the auxiliary information, it can further enhance the registration performance compared with the pure unsupervised training strategy.

12.2.4 Deep learning-based registration: smoothness, consistency and other properties

A comprehensive evaluation of registration performance should consider both accuracy and topology preservation. For deformable registration, the smoothness of deformation field is important, since it can help avoid distortion and preserve topology of anatomies. For deep learning-based registration, in the early stage, most of the registration methods focus on registration accuracy and do not pay much attention to topological correctness of deformations, i.e., smoothness or consistency of the predicted deformation field. Total gradients of the deformation field is often used as regularization for constraining smoothness on deformation field. Several representative models have been proposed to maintain registration consistency or deformation field smoothness, including symmetric registration [66,67], diffeomorphic registration [66,68], inverse-consistent registration [34,69], cycle-consistent registration [37,70] and hierarchical registration [33,71–73] as listed in Table 12.4.

Table 12.4 Representative works considering different registration properties.

Registration properties	Supervision	Organ	Reference
Symmetry	Unsupervised	Brain MRI	[66,67]
Diffeomorphism	Unsupervised	Brain T1 MRI	[66,68]
Inverse-consistency	Unsupervised	Brain MRI	[34]
		T1 MRI	[69]
Cycle-consistency	Unsupervised	Facial expression image	[37,70]
		Brain MRI	
		Liver CT	
Multi-scale	Unsupervised	Pulmonary CT	[73]
	Unsupervised	Knee MRI	[72]
	Semi-supervised	Brain MRI	[33]

Symmetric registration. Registering images with large anatomical variations is always challenging, since large deformation is difficult to estimate and the smoothness

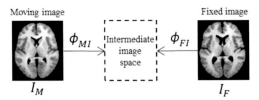

(a) Symmetric registration

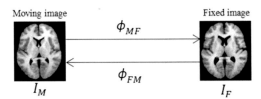

(b) Inverse-consistent registration

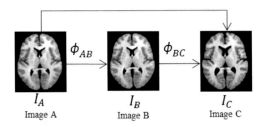

(c) Cycle-consistent registration

FIGURE 12.4

Different deep learning-based registration strategies.

of the local deformation is hard to preserve. To tackle this issue, symmetric registration has been proposed in the conventional registration methods [7,10], and recently, symmetric registration is also implemented using deep learning. As shown in Fig. 12.4(a), different from directly estimating the deformation pathway from the fixed image to the moving image, symmetric registration estimates bi-directional deformation pathways, i.e., ϕ_{MI} from moving image space to intermediate image space, and ϕ_{FI} from fixed space to intermediate space with $\phi_{MI}=-\phi_{FI}$. Herein, the intermediate image is a pseudo space, which lies between the manifolds of the fixed and the moving image spaces. Sui et al. [67] have applied this symmetric strategy to deep learning-based registration. In the training stage, the output of the network is the halfway deformation ϕ_{MI} and the dissimilarity measure is calculated in the intermediate space by simultaneously warping the fixed and moving images. By resorting to the symmetric constraint, registration can be more accurate and robust particularly on the images with large anatomical variations. Moreover, it can effectively avoid the distortion problem when estimating large deformations, so that registration performance can be comprehensively improved. In another study, Mok et al. [66] propose a fast symmetric diffeomorphic approach for deformable image registration, which learns the symmetric deformation field that align the pair of images to their mean shape within the space of diffeomorphic maps. The results demonstrate that this method *not only* achieves state-of-the-art registration accuracy, *but also* turns to be more consistent with the diffeomorphic property compared with the state-of-the-art deep learning-based registration methods.

Inverse-consistent registration. Although deep learning-based registration methods achieve comparable accuracy and are much faster than traditional registration in the application stage, the estimated deformation fields do not necessarily possess inverse consistency, which means when swapping the order of the input image pair, the estimated deformation should be inverse of each other. Mathematically, the composition of forward and backward deformations should be identical or close to identity: $\phi_{MF} \circ \phi_{FM} = Id$, as shown in Fig. 12.4(b). ϕ_{MF} is the forward deformation that aligns the moving image I_M to the fixed image I_F. ϕ_{FM} is the backward deformation that aligns the fixed image I_F to the moving image I_M. By using deep learning, ϕ_{MF} and ϕ_{FM} can be obtained through the same network by changing the input order of I_F and I_M. If the forward and backward deformations are inverse-consistent, the composition of these two deformations should be an identical transformation, and this can be applied as an additional regularization term. Gu et al. [34] propose a deep learning-based registration method to maintain the property of inverse-consistency such that the forward and backward deformations can align anatomical structures consistently. In addition, Zhang et al. [69] propose an Inverse-Consistent deep Network (IC-Net), where a pair of images are symmetrically deformed toward each other with inverse-consistent constraint until the bi-directionally warped images are well aligned. Experiments show that the inverse-consistent registration can reduce bias caused by the order of input images, increase registration robustness and improve the reliability of subsequent quantitative analysis.

Cycle-consistent registration. In addition to inverse consistency, the use of cycle-consistency strategy can also maintain topological structure of the deformation field, especially for registration of a group of images. The cycle consistency enhances image registration performance by providing an implicit regularization to preserve topology during the deformation. As shown in Fig. 12.4(c), for a group of images I_A, I_B and I_C, the composition of deformation ϕ_{AB} and deformation ϕ_{BC} should be equal to the deformation ϕ_{AC}, i.e., $\phi_{AB} \circ \phi_{BC} = \phi_{AC}$. Here, "$\circ$" indicates the composition of deformation field. In [37], Kim et al. [37] adopt the cycle-consistent constraint between two images in such a way that the deformed images are given as the inputs to the networks again by switching their order to impose the cycle consistency. This constraint ensures that the shape of the deformed images can turn back to the original one, and the results show that the cycle-consistency strategy can maintain topology and reduce deformation folding problem. In their later work, CycleMorph, Kim et al. [70] extend their previous work from single-scale to multi-scale registration where an imagewise registration is followed by a patchwise registration for fine-grained registration performance. The cycle consistency enhances image registration performance by providing an implicit regularization to preserve topology during the deformation. In their experiments, CycleMorph provides topology-preserved image deformation with less folding problem.

Generally, the smoothness of deformation field can be preserved by using symmetric constraint, inverse-consistent constraint, and/or cycle-consistent constraint. Another import constraint on the deformation field is diffeomorphism [66], which requires the deformation to be invertible and also the deformation and its inverse to be differentiable. This is an important property of the deformation in many medical applications.

Diffeomorphic registration. Diffeomorphic deformable image registration [10,74, 75] requires invertible and differentiable deformations, which guarantees smoothness and one-to-one mapping. Therefore, diffeomorphism also preserves topology. In learning-based methods [66,68], it is usually achieved by integrating the SVF (stationary velocity field) using the scaling and squaring method. Typically, conventional diffeomorphic registration methods are computationally intensive and time-consuming. Getting rid of the iterative optimization paradigm, deep learning-based registration models can greatly improve computational efficiency. Researchers have proposed diffeomorphic training strategies along with other smoothness and consistency strategies. To achieve unsupervised and end-to-end learning for diffeomorphic registrations, Mok et al. [66] propose to learn the symmetric registration function from a collection of an n-D data set and output a pair of diffeomorphic maps that map the input images to the middle from both geodesic paths. Consequently, the forward mapping from one image to another image can be obtained by composing the output diffeomorphic map and the inverse of the other diffeomorphic map. In addition, Dalca et al. [68] introduce diffeomorphic integration layers combined with a transform layer in the *Voxelmorph* registration framework. Registration results in 3D brain data set show that this method achieves state-of-the-art registration accuracy with the property of diffeomorphism.

Multi-scale strategy. In general, for an unsupervised end-to-end deep learning framework, as shown in Fig. 12.2, it is challenging to align images (with fine structures) with large deformations in one step using a global loss function. To solve this problem, recent studies [33,71–73] employ a multi-scale training strategy. Multi-scale is a common strategy for image registration, since it can perform registration from coarse-to-fine, and the registration accuracy can be improved hierarchically. For the U-Net-based registration framework, the paired images need to be down-sampled and up-sampled several times to extract the features between paired images from multiple scales. Therefore, hierarchical loss based on multiple scales can be employed for the U-Net based framework to provide more constraints for registration.

For example, Shen et al. [72] propose an end-to-end 3D image registration method consisting of a multi-step affine network and a deformable registration network using a momentum-based SVF (Stationary Velocity Field) algorithm. Experimental results have shown that this proposed method achieves comparable performance to the state-of-the-art registration methods, but it is much faster with better transformation properties including the ability to produce approximately symmetric transformations.

In the conventional U-Net, the loss is calculated only in the final layer, leading to suboptimal update of the parameters in the frontal convolution layers. In this way, the parameters of the first half convolution layers are not well updated as the latter half. This *not only* causes slow convergence, *but also* leads to over-fitting problem. Therefore, Fan et al. [33] employ hierarchical loss in the up-sampling path of the U-Net, giving multi-scale constraints on the frontal convolution layers for easier convergence.

In summary, most deep learning-based deformable registration methods have achieved promising registration efficiency. However, these models usually ignore desirable properties of the transformation such as topology preservation and invertibility of the transformation. To obtain these properties, in addition to integrating associated regularization terms into the loss function, it is also encouragable to adapt the architecture of networks as described in this section.

12.3 Deep learning-based registration with semantic information

Registration of subtle and complicated anatomies is always challenging. To satisfy the demands in clinical practice, more anatomical information is incorporated into the registration framework for better registration accuracy. By using semantic-aware registration, complicated anatomies, e.g., lesions or vessels, can be well registered and analyzed.

Deep learning is an effective technique to better understand anatomical structures, defined by organ/lesion segmentation, landmark detection and vessel extraction. The semantic understanding can bring more information into the registration pipeline. With this rich semantic information, we can explore more challenging registration tasks, e.g., for registration of images with complicated lesions (brain tumor, lung nodule and infection area), or images from multi-modalities or multi-phases. In this section, we will introduce some semantic-aware registration methods. A summary of these categories can be found in Table 12.5.

Table 12.5 Summary of semantic-aware registration methods.

Application	Modality	Anatomy	Reference
Segmentation-guided registration	CT-CT	Airways, lobules, and pulmonary vessel structures	[76]
	CT-CT	Tube structure, vessel skeleton	[78]
Lesion image registration	MRI-MRI	Brain tumor	[80]
	CT-CT	Lung infection	[81]
	DCE-MRI	Liver tumor	[81]
	CT-MR	Liver tumor	[77]
Groupwise registration	MR-MR	Brain	[64]

Organ segmentation as a critical task for medical image analysis provides rich boundary information, which can be used to guide image registration. Chen et al. [76] propose a semantic-aware registration network for longitudinal pulmonary CT image registration. In this work, the airways, lobules and pulmonary vessel structures are considered during lung CT registration, and a coarse-to-fine hierarchy is applied using two networks. Different from the multi-scale strategy in conventional registration, the "coarse" and "fine" do not indicate the image resolution but represent the semantic information. The first hierarchy mainly focuses on large volume with simple anatomical structures, and the second hierarchy focuses on subtle anatomy with complicated semantic information such as vessels by using the result from the first hierarchy as an initialization. Combining the two networks, both global and local anatomy can be well aligned. It achieves better registration performance than competitive models especially on critical structures. Based on experimental results, this model facilitates a more accurate follow-up study for treatment assessment of CT lung nodules. It is worth noting that accurate segmentation supports the registration task, and registration task can also improve segmentation performance in return. A joint registration and segmentation framework is proposed in [77] by using shape prior as guidance. Lee et al. [78] propose a template transformer network for image segmentation by registering the template image to the subject image. A spatial transformer is designed to deform a shape template to match the underlying structure of interest via an end-to-end training strategy. The shape prior and semantic information can be represented by the vessel structure or the skeleton of tube structure, such as centerline. Based on this framework, the real topology of tube structure is preserved. Zotti et al. [79] also use shape prior and registration to facilitate cardiac MRI segmentation.

Another problem is to register images with lesions. Many images acquired in hospitals may have lesions. MRI and CT are the most commonly-used imaging techniques in hospitals for image-guided diagnosis. The registration of CT or MR images with lesion is difficult, since morphology and appearance of lesions are variable, which often introduces distortion and artifacts during registration. For brain tumor images, accurately analyzing the tumor region in the brain is crucial to assess the patient's condition or perform surgical planning. Liu et al. [80] propose a registration framework to tackle this tumor brain image registration problem by recovering tumor region from normal brain tissue. Specifically, U-Net is first applied to segment tumor, and then a partial convolutional network [61] is leveraged to replace tumor region with normal brain tissue. After that, registration can be performed on the tumor-free images, and the brain label information can be accurately transformed from brain atlas to the tumor image. This method relieves large distortions and uncertainty when performing registration between normal and tumor images.

Gu et al. [81] use lung lobe and segmented structures to guide registration of a large group of CT images with pneumonia, for tracking longitudinal evolution of pneumonia in lung CT images. Directly registering the original CT images with large infection region may mislead anatomical correspondence. By using detailed lung anatomy, registration can be performed on organ structures and eliminate the influence of the infection region. In this way, more promising longitudinal and population analysis can be achieved. A similar strategy is applied in [76] for population-based lung nodule analysis. In particular, stable organ structures are used for initial registration, thus reducing the influence from the lesion area. In this way, analysis on the lesion areas can be more effective and meaningful.

Some multi-modal or multi-phase image registration approaches are also investigated with deep learning. Multi-modal and multi-phase images can provide complementary information to help clinicians better diagnose the disease. Qian et al. [81] propose a cascaded network for integrated registration of liver hepatic dynamic contrast-enhanced magnetic resonance images (DCE-MRIs) and apply it for evaluation of trans-arterial chemoembolization or radiofrequency ablation by quantifying viable residual tumor against necrosis. To achieve precise analysis, multi-phase DCE-MRIs should be well aligned to eliminate liver deformation caused by breathing movement, so that tumor regions at different phases can be fused for subsequent analysis. Note that the intensities of different phases are changed due to contrast agents, especially for tumors and lesions. In this work, a cascaded registration framework is proposed, where a de-enhancement network is used to eliminate appearance difference between multi-phase images, and a registration network is then trained by using the images with the removed contrast enhancement. From experimental results, the registration efficiency is improved, and tumor regions can be more accurately diagnosed by fusing the multi-phase DCE-MRIs. Wei et al. [77] introduce another deep learning-based multi-modal (CT-MR) registration method for image-guided thermal ablation of liver tumors. A Cycle-GAN model with mutual information constraint is leveraged to synthesize a pseudo-CT image from MRI, and then the registration network is trained based on the CT and the pseudo-CT images. In this way, the multi-modal registration problem becomes a mono-modal registration problem. Moreover, a partial convolutional network [61] is applied to inpaint the probe and other artifacts with the normal tissue in real CT images, which can further simplify image registration. In this work, before performing registration, deep learning is applied to eliminate appearance difference across images and also artifacts in CT images, so that the registration performance can be highly improved.

Groupwise registration is an important branch of image registration [82]. It is widely used for population analysis or atlas construction, which can eliminate biases that potentially arise from inappropriate template selection. Typically, it involves simultaneous pairwise registration of a cohort of images to a common space. Thus, conventional groupwise registration is computationally complex. Ahmad et al. [64] propose a deep learning-based deformation initialization for fast groupwise registration. In their work, the image group is first separated into different clusters, and a deep learning framework is applied to rapidly estimate large deformations to reduce structural variation. Then a conventional groupwise registration is applied. By using this fast deformation initialization, more accurate and efficient groupwise registration results can be achieved.

12.4 Concluding remarks

This chapter presents various deep learning-based medical image registration methods. To train a deep learning-based registration network, some supervised, unsupervised and weakly-supervised learning strategies can be utilized in an end-to-end manner. Important biomedical properties, including symmetry, inverse consistency, topology preservation and diffeomorphism, are encouraged to consider during the design of the registration networks. Besides, semantic or anatomical information can also be utilized for better registration accuracy, particularly for registering subtle anatomy or images with lesion/tumor. Compared to conventional registration methods, deep learning-based models *not only* obtain superior registration accuracy, *but also* boost computational efficiency significantly. Properly-designed models can be practically deployed in different clinical applications. Future works are mainly focused on application-specific model fine-tuning, multi-modality registration, longitudinal registration and groupwise registration.

References

[1] J. Ker, et al., Deep learning applications in medical image analysis, IEEE Access 6 (2017) 9375–9389.

[2] D. Shen, G. Wu, H.-I. Suk, Deep learning in medical image analysis, Annual Review of Biomedical Engineering 19 (2017) 221–248.

[3] G. Haskins, U. Kruger, P. Yan, Deep learning in medical image registration: a survey, Machine Vision and Applications 31 (1) (2020) 1–18.

[4] Y. Fu, et al., Deep learning in medical image registration: a review, Physics in Medicine and Biology 65 (20) (2020) 20TR01.

[5] X. Cao, et al., Image registration using machine and deep learning, in: Handbook of Medical Image Computing and Computer Assisted Intervention, Elsevier, 2020, pp. 319–342.

[6] B. Fischer, J. Modersitzki, FLIRT: a flexible image registration toolbox, in: International Workshop on Biomedical Image Registration, Springer, 2003.

[7] D. Shen, C. Davatzikos, HAMMER: hierarchical attribute matching mechanism for elastic registration, IEEE Transactions on Medical Imaging 21 (11) (2002) 1421–1439.

[8] L.G. Brown, A survey of image registration techniques, ACM Computing Surveys 24 (4) (1992) 325–376.

[9] D. Rueckert, et al., Nonrigid registration using free-form deformations: application to breast MR images, IEEE Transactions on Medical Imaging 18 (8) (1999) 712–721.

[10] B.B. Avants, et al., Symmetric diffeomorphic image registration with cross-correlation: evaluating automated labeling of elderly and neurodegenerative brain, Medical Image Analysis 12 (1) (2008) 26–41.

[11] P. Viola, W.M. Wells III, Alignment by maximization of mutual information, International Journal of Computer Vision 24 (2) (1997) 137–154.

[12] A. Roche, et al., The correlation ratio as a new similarity measure for multimodal image registration, in: International Conference on Medical Image Computing and Computer-Assisted Intervention, Springer, 1998.

[13] R. Szeliski, J. Coughlan, Spline-based image registration, International Journal of Computer Vision 22 (3) (1997) 199–218.

[14] G. Wu, et al., Hierarchical attribute-guided symmetric diffeomorphic registration for MR brain images, in: International Conference on Medical Image Computing and Computer-Assisted Intervention, Springer, 2012.

[15] A. Sotiras, C. Davatzikos, N. Paragios, Deformable medical image registration: a survey, IEEE Transactions on Medical Imaging 32 (7) (2013) 1153–1190.

[16] M.A. Viergever, et al., A Survey of Medical Image Registration–Under Review, Elsevier, 2016.

[17] Y. Ou, et al., Comparative evaluation of registration algorithms in different brain databases with varying difficulty: results and insights, IEEE Transactions on Medical Imaging 33 (10) (2014) 2039–2065.

[18] A. Klein, et al., Evaluation of 14 nonlinear deformation algorithms applied to human brain MRI registration, NeuroImage 46 (3) (2009) 786–802.

[19] D. Han, et al., Robust anatomical landmark detection with application to MR brain image registration, Computerized Medical Imaging and Graphics 46 (2015) 277–290.

[20] M. Kim, et al., A general fast registration framework by learning deformation–appearance correlation, IEEE Transactions on Image Processing 21 (4) (2011) 1823–1833.

[21] Q. Wang, et al., Predict brain MR image registration via sparse learning of appearance and transformation, Medical Image Analysis 20 (1) (2015) 61–75.

[22] S. Tang, et al., RABBIT: rapid alignment of brains by building intermediate templates, NeuroImage 47 (4) (2009) 1277–1287.

[23] P. Dong, et al., Scalable joint segmentation and registration framework for infant brain images, Neurocomputing 229 (2017) 54–62.

[24] R.W. So, A.C. Chung, A novel learning-based dissimilarity metric for rigid and non-rigid medical image registration by using Bhattacharyya Distances, Pattern Recognition 62 (2017) 161–174.

[25] L. Wei, et al., Learning-based deformable registration for infant MRI by integrating random forest with auto-context model, Medical Physics 44 (12) (2017) 6289–6303.

[26] X. Cao, et al., Deformable Image Registration Based on Similarity-Steered CNN Regression, Springer International Publishing, Cham, 2017.

[27] X. Cao, et al., Learning-based multimodal image registration for prostate cancer radiation therapy, in: International Conference on Medical Image Computing and Computer-Assisted Intervention, Springer, 2016.

[28] M.E. Leventon, W.E.L. Grimson, Multi-modal volume registration using joint intensity distributions, in: International Conference on Medical Image Computing and Computer-Assisted Intervention, Springer, 1998.

[29] A.C. Chung, et al., Multi-modal image registration by minimising Kullback-Leibler distance, in: International Conference on Medical Image Computing and Computer-Assisted Intervention, Springer, 2002.

[30] M.R. Sabuncu, P. Ramadge, Using spanning graphs for efficient image registration, IEEE Transactions on Image Processing 17 (5) (2008) 788–797.

[31] X. Cao, et al., Deep Learning Based Inter-Modality Image Registration Supervised by Intra-Modality Similarity, Springer International Publishing, Cham, 2018.

[32] J. Fan, et al., Adversarial similarity network for evaluating image alignment in deep learning based registration, in: International Conference on Medical Image Computing and Computer-Assisted Intervention, Springer, 2018.

[33] J. Fan, et al., BIRNet: brain image registration using dual-supervised fully convolutional networks, Medical Image Analysis 54 (2019) 193–206.

[34] D. Gu, et al., A consistent deep registration network with group data modeling, Computerized Medical Imaging and Graphics 90 (2021) 101904.

[35] G. Balakrishnan, et al., Voxelmorph: a learning framework for deformable medical image registration, IEEE Transactions on Medical Imaging 38 (8) (2019) 1788–1800.

[36] S. Miao, et al., Real-time 2D/3D registration via CNN regression, in: 2016 IEEE 13th International Symposium on Biomedical Imaging (ISBI), 2016.

[37] B. Kim, et al., Unsupervised deformable image registration using cycle-consistent CNN, in: 10th International Workshop on Machine Learning in Medical Imaging (MLMI) / 22nd International Conference on Medical Image Computing and Computer-Assisted Intervention (MICCAI), Shenzhen, Peoples R China, 2019.

[38] J.M. Sloan, K.A. Goatman, J.P. Siebert, Learning rigid image registration - utilizing convolutional neural networks for medical image registration, in: International Conference on Bioimaging, 2018.

[39] E. Chee, Z. Wu, AIRNet: self-supervised affine registration for 3D medical images using neural networks, arXiv:1810.02583, 2018.

[40] S.S.M. Salehi, et al., Real-time deep pose estimation with geodesic loss for image-to-template rigid registration, IEEE Transactions on Medical Imaging 38 (2) (2019) 470–481.

[41] J. Lv, et al., Respiratory motion correction for free-breathing 3D abdominal MRI using CNN-based image registration: a feasibility study, British Journal of Radiology 91 (1083) (2018).

[42] H. Sokooti, et al., Nonrigid Image Registration Using Multi-Scale 3D Convolutional Neural Networks, Springer International Publishing, Cham, 2017.

[43] X. Yang, R. Kwitt, M. Niethammer, Fast Predictive Image Registration, Springer International Publishing, Cham, 2016.

[44] M.-M. Rohé, et al., SVF-Net: Learning Deformable Image Registration Using Shape Matching, Springer International Publishing, Cham, 2017.

[45] X. Yang, et al., Quicksilver: fast predictive image registration – a deep learning approach, NeuroImage 158 (2017) 378–396.

[46] X. Cao, et al., Non-rigid brain MRI registration using two-stage deep perceptive networks, in: Proceedings of the International Society for Magnetic Resonance in Medicine ... Scientific Meeting and Exhibition. International Society for Magnetic Resonance in Medicine, Scientific Meeting and Exhibition, 2018, 2018.

[47] K.A.J. Eppenhof, J.P.W. Pluim, Pulmonary CT registration through supervised learning with convolutional neural networks, IEEE Transactions on Medical Imaging 38 (5) (2019) 1097–1105.

[48] H. Uzunova, et al., Training CNNs for image registration from few samples with model-based data augmentation, in: International Conference on Medical Image Computing and Computer-Assisted Intervention, 2017.

[49] M. Ito, F. Ino, An automated method for generating training sets for deep learning based image registration, in: 5th International Conference on Bioimaging, BIOIMAGING 2018 - Part of 11th International Joint Conference on Biomedical Engineering Systems and Technologies, BIOSTEC 2018, January 19, 2018 - January 21, 2018, SciTePress, Funchal, Madeira, Portugal, 2018.

[50] M. Jaderberg, et al., Spatial transformer networks, arXiv:1506.02025, 2015.

[51] H.M. Li, Y. Fan, IEEE, Non-rigid image registration using self-supervised fully convolutional networks without training data, in: 15th IEEE International Symposium on Biomedical Imaging (ISBI), Washington, DC, 2018.

[52] B.D. de Vos, et al., End-to-End Unsupervised Deformable Image Registration with a Convolutional Neural Network, Springer International Publishing, Cham, 2017.

[53] J. Neylon, et al., A neural network approach for fast, automated quantification of DIR performance, Medical Physics 44 (8) (2017) 4126–4138.

[54] L. Sun, S.T. Zhang, Deformable MRI-ultrasound registration using 3D convolutional neural network, in: Int Workshop on Point-of-Care Ultrasound / Int Workshop on Bio-Imaging and Visualizat for Patient-Customized Simulat / Int Workshop on Correct of Brainshift with Intra-Operat Ultrasound / Int Workshop on Computat Precis Med, Med Image Comp & Comp Assisted Intervent Soc, Granada, Spain, 2018.

[55] S. Ghosal, N. Rayl, Deep deformable registration: enhancing accuracy by fully convolutional neural net, Pattern Recognition Letters 94 (2017) 81–86.

[56] A. Sheikhjafari, et al., Unsupervised deformable image registration with fully connected generative neural network, 2018.

[57] G. Balakrishnan, et al., An unsupervised learning model for deformable medical image registration, CoRR, arXiv:1802.02604 [abs], 2018.

[58] E. Ferrante, et al., On the Adaptability of Unsupervised CNN-Based Deformable Image Registration to Unseen Image Domains, Springer International Publishing, Cham, 2018.

[59] J. Fan, et al., Adversarial learning for mono- or multi-modal registration, Medical Image Analysis 58 (2019) 101545.

[60] X. Zhang, et al., Deform-GAN: an unsupervised learning model for deformable registration, arXiv:2002.11430, 2020.

[61] G. Liu, et al., Image inpainting for irregular holes using partial convolutions, in: Proceedings of the European Conference on Computer Vision (ECCV), 2018.

[62] Y.P. Hu, et al., Adversarial deformation regularization for training image registration neural networks, in: 21st International Conference on Medical Image Computing and Computer-Assisted Intervention (MICCAI) / 8th Eurographics Workshop on Visual Computing for Biology and Medicine (VCBM) / International Workshop on Computational Diffusion MRI (CDMRI), Granada, SPAIN, 2018.

[63] P. Yan, et al., Adversarial Image Registration with Application for MR and TRUS Image Fusion, Springer International Publishing, Cham, 2018.

[64] S. Ahmad, et al., Deep learning deformation initialization for rapid groupwise registration of inhomogeneous image populations, Frontiers in Neuroinformatics 13 (2019) 34.

[65] A. Hering, et al., Enhancing Label-Driven Deep Deformable Image Registration with Local Distance Metrics for State-of-the-Art Cardiac Motion Tracking, Springer Fachmedien Wiesbaden, Wiesbaden, 2019.

[66] T.C.W. Mok, A.C.S. Chung, IEEE, Fast Symmetric diffeomorphic image registration with convolutional neural networks, in: IEEE/CVF Conference on Computer Vision and Pattern Recognition (CVPR), Electr Network, 2020.

[67] X.D. Sui, et al., Symmetric deformable registration via learning a pseudomean for MR brain images, Journal of Healthcare Engineering 2021 (2021).

[68] A.V. Dalca, et al., Unsupervised learning for fast probabilistic diffeomorphic registration, in: 21st International Conference on Medical Image Computing and Computer Assisted Intervention (MICCAI), Granada, Spain, 2018.

[69] J. Zhang, Inverse-consistent deep networks for unsupervised deformable image registration, arXiv:1809.03443, 2018.

[70] B. Kim, et al., CycleMorph: cycle consistent unsupervised deformable image registration, Medical Image Analysis 71 (2021).

[71] A.V. Dalca, et al., Unsupervised learning of probabilistic diffeomorphic registration for images and surfaces, Medical Image Analysis 57 (2019) 226–236.

[72] Z.Y. Shen, et al., Networks for joint affine and non-parametric image registration, in: IEEE/CVF Conference on Computer Vision and Pattern Recognition (CVPR), Long Beach, CA, 2019.

[73] L. Chen, et al., Semantic Hierarchy Guided Registration Networks for Intra-Subject Pulmonary CT Image Alignment, Springer International Publishing, Cham, 2020.

[74] T. Vercauteren, et al., Diffeomorphic demons: efficient non-parametric image registration, NeuroImage 45 (1) (2009) S61–S72.

[75] J. Du, A. Goh, A. Qiu, Large Deformation Diffeomorphic Metric Mapping of Orientation Distribution Functions, Springer Berlin Heidelberg, Berlin, Heidelberg, 2011.

[76] L. Chen, et al., An artificial-intelligence lung imaging analysis system (ALIAS) for population-based nodule computing in CT scans, Computerized Medical Imaging and Graphics 89 (2021) 101899.

[77] D. Wei, et al., Synthesis and inpainting-based mr-ct registration for image-guided thermal ablation of liver tumors, in: International Conference on Medical Image Computing and Computer-Assisted Intervention, Springer, 2019.

[78] M.C.H. Lee, et al., Tetris: template transformer networks for image segmentation with shape priors, IEEE Transactions on Medical Imaging 38 (11) (2019) 2596–2606.

[79] C. Zotti, et al., GridNet with automatic shape prior registration for automatic MRI cardiac segmentation, in: International Workshop on Statistical Atlases and Computational Models of the Heart, Springer, 2017.

[80] Z. Liu, et al., Automatic segmentation of non-tumor tissues in glioma MR brain images using deformable registration with partial convolutional networks, in: International MICCAI Brainlesion Workshop, Springer, 2020.

[81] L. Qian, et al., A cascade-network framework for integrated registration of liver DCE-MR images, Computerized Medical Imaging and Graphics 89 (2021) 101887.

[82] P. Dong, et al., Fast groupwise registration using multi-level and multi-resolution graph shrinkage, Scientific Reports 9 (1) (2019) 1–12.

Data-driven learning strategies for biomarker detection and outcome prediction in Autism from task-based fMRI

13

James Duncan[a,b], **Lawrence H. Staib**[a,b], **Nicha Dvornek**[a,b], **Xiaoxiao Li**[d], **Juntang Zhuang**[a], **Jiyao Wang**[a], and **Pamela Ventola**[c]

[a]*Department of Biomedical Engineering, New Haven, CT, United States*
[b]*Division of Bioimaging Sciences, Department of Radiology & Biomedical Imaging, New Haven, CT, United States*
[c]*Child Study Center, Yale University, New Haven, CT, United States*
[d]*Department of Electrical & Computer Engineering, University of British Columbia, Vancouver, BC, Canada*

13.1 Introduction

Autism spectrum disorder (ASD) is characterized by impaired communication and social skills, and restricted, repetitive and stereotyped behaviors that result in significant disability [41,42]. The disorder is not singular; it is heterogeneous and the impact can vary greatly. The severity of symptoms interacts with the degree of intellectual disability and co-morbidities. Research aimed at uncovering the pathogenesis of ASD and improved understanding of treatment is of the greatest importance. In addition, co-morbid conditions can compromise daily functioning and exacerbate core ASD symptoms, including impairments in social communication [11].

The work described in this chapter is on machine learning for neuroimage analysis, and aims to identify functional imaging biomarkers of ASD and predict response in children undergoing ASD treatment, including Pivotal Response Treatment (PRT) [59]. This work is focused on children with ASD between the ages of 5 and 18. Given the tremendous variability in ASD and the time and expense of treatment, personalized treatments are critical. Our methods are aimed at understanding this variability from a neuroimaging perspective, and we believe that machine learning and quantitative imaging biomarkers will facilitate early prediction of outcome, helping personalize the therapy.

fMRI provides valuable spatio-temporal functional information. ASD researchers have extracted biomarkers and classified or predicted from resting-state fMRI primarily using neuroanatomical atlases to localize regions of interest (ROIs), connectivity matrices using regional cross-correlations and learning methods, e.g., support vector machines, random forests or ridge regression [1,7,49]. Most often, statistical analysis of the entire rsfMRI time course within each ROI was used to *spatially* localize subnetworks and classify subjects (ASD vs. Typically Developing Control (TDC)), or predict ASD measures (e.g., SRS [37], using linear regression). Indeed, our own efforts on Bayesian community finding [58] were successful in finding communities from tfMRI that serve as *groupwise* biomarkers. While novel spatio-temporal fMRI analysis ideas (e.g., the *chronnectome* [5]) have been proposed and dynamic connectivity analysis is clearly effective for classification of ASD and other brain disorders [63], progress has been limited.

In recent years, deep learning has heavily influenced fMRI analysis. These efforts, including our own, continue to use correlation-based connectivity but have also had success directly using ROI-based, fMRI time series data [14]. Recent work uses publicly-available rsfMRI and a graph convolutional neural network (GNN) to analyze spatial ROI relationships (e.g., [34]), with one approach integrating temporal sub-sequence results in parallel and predicting age and sex [19,20] and combining GNNs, spatio-temporal information and recurrent networks to classify ASD vs. TDC [62].

We address three key issues in this chapter: (i) improved classification of ASD vs. TDC and identification of spatial biomarkers, (ii) ASD severity score prediction from complete time-series data and (iii) improved classification/ prediction by incorporating ROI causality information. In the first subsection below (13.2), we describe our two-module approach to biomarker detection and outcome prediction based on (i) a set of BrainGNN convolutional graph neural networks that take the brain network map within a time series and project it into a reduced dimension space. In the next subsection (13.3), we describe the use of a recurrent neural network (RNN) based on LSTM components that assembles the data from all time points to yield an integrated classification or prediction that also incorporates phenotypic information. Finally, in the last subsection (13.4), we describe an approach based on effective connectivity to incorporate causality into our approach.

13.2 BrainGNN

In this work, we propose a graph neural network-based framework for mapping regional and cross-regional functional activation patterns for classification tasks, such as classifying patients versus healthy control (HC) subjects and performing cognitive task decoding. Unlike the existing work mentioned above, we tackle the limitations of considering graph nodes (brain ROIs) as identical by proposing a novel clustering-based embedding method in the graph convolutional layer. We aim to provide users with the flexibility to interpret different levels of biomarkers through graph node pooling and several innovative loss terms to regulate the pooling operation. In addition, different from much of the GNN literature [46,33] where population-based graphs using fMRI are formed by treating each subject as a node on the graph, we model each subject's brain as one graph and each brain ROI as a node to learn ROI-based graph embeddings. Specifically, our framework jointly learns ROI clustering and whole-brain fMRI prediction. This formulation not only reduces preconceived errors, but also allows the learning of particular clustering patterns associated with other quantitative brain image analysis tasks—from estimated model parameters, we can retrieve ROI clustering patterns. Also, our GNN design facilitates model interpretability by regulating intermediate outputs with a novel loss term for enforcing similarity of pooling scores, which provides the flexibility to choose between individual-level and group-level explanations. The methods discussed in this section are based on prior work [39,38].

13.2.1 Notation

First, we parcellate the brain into N ROIs based on its T1 structural MRI. We define ROIs as graph nodes $\mathcal{V} = \{v_1, \ldots, v_N\}$ and the nodes are preordered. As brain ROIs can be aligned by brain parcellation atlases based on their locations in the structure space, we define the brain graphs as ordered aligned graphs. We define an undirected weighted graph as $G = (\mathcal{V}, \mathcal{E})$, where $\mathcal{E}$ is the edge set, i.e., a collection of (v_i, v_j) linking vertices from v_i to v_j. In our setting, G has an associated node feature set and can be represented as matrix $H = [\mathbf{h}_1, \ldots, \mathbf{h}_N]^\top$, where $\mathbf{h}_i$ is the feature vector associated with node v_i. For every edge connecting two nodes, $(v_i, v_j) \in \mathcal{E}$, we have its strength $e_{ij} \in \mathbb{R}$ and $e_{ij} > 0$. We also define $e_{ij} = 0$ for $(v_i, v_j) \notin \mathcal{E}$ and, therefore, the adjacency matrix $E = [e_{ij}] \in \mathbb{R}^{N \times N}$ is well-defined. We also list all the notation in Table 13.1.

13.2.2 Architecture overview

Classification on graphs is achieved by first embedding node features into a low-dimensional space, then coarsening or pooling nodes and summarizing them. The summarized vector is then fed into a multi-layer perceptron (MLP). We train the graph convolutional/pooling layers and the MLP in an end-to-end fashion. Our proposed network architecture is illustrated in Fig. 13.1. It is formed by three different types of layers: graph convolutional layers, node pooling layers and a readout layer. Generally speaking, GNNs inductively learn a node representation by recursively transforming and aggregating the feature vectors of its neighboring nodes. See Figs. 13.2 and 13.3.

A **graph convolutional layer** is used to probe the graph structure by using edge features, which contain important information about graphs. For example, the weights of the edges in brain fMRI graphs can represent the relationship between different ROIs. See Fig. 13.2.

Following [53], we define $\mathbf{h}_i^{(l)} \in \mathbb{R}^{d^{(l)}}$ as the features for the ith node in the lth layer, where $d^{(l)}$ is the dimension of the lth layer features. The propagation model

Table 13.1 Notation used in this chapter.

Notation	Description
C	number of classes
M	number of samples
N	number of ROIs
v_i	node i (ROI i) in the graph
$\mathcal{N}(i)$	neighborhood of v_i
e_{ij}	edge connecting node v_i and v_j
$\tilde{e}_{ij}$	normalized edge score over $j \in \mathcal{N}(i)$
$\mathcal{V}$	nodes set
$\mathcal{E}$	edge set
G	graph, $G = (\mathcal{V}, \mathcal{E})$
E	adjacency matrix, $E = [e_{ij}] \in \mathbb{R}^{N \times N}$
$d^{(l)}$	node feature dimension of the lth layer
$\mathbf{h}_i$	node feature vector associated with v_i, $\mathbf{h}_i \in \mathbb{R}^d$
H	node feature matrix
$\tilde{\mathbf{h}}_i$	embedded node feature vector associated with v_i before pooling, $\tilde{\mathbf{h}}_i \in \mathbb{R}^d$
$\tilde{H}$	embedded node feature matrix before pooling
$\mathbf{s}_m$	node pooling score vector before normalization of subject m
$\tilde{\mathbf{s}}_m$	node pooling score vector after normalization of subject m
$\mathbf{r}_i$	one-hot encoding vector of v_i, $\mathbf{r}_i \in \mathbb{R}^N$, $\mathbf{r}_{i,j} = 0, \forall j \neq i$
k	number of nodes left after pooling
K	number of ROI communities
α_i	learnable membership score vector of v_i to each community, $\alpha_i \in \mathbb{R}^K$
β_u	learnable filter basis, $\beta_u^{(l)} \in \mathbb{R}^{d^{(l+1)} \cdot d^{(l)}}, \forall u \in \{1, \dots, K^{(l)}\}$
$W_i^{(l)}$	graph kernel for node v_i of the lth layer, $W_i^{(l)} \in \mathbb{R}^{d^{(l+1)} \times d^{(l)}}$
λ	parameter associated with loss function

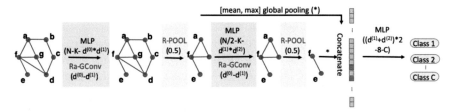

FIGURE 13.1

BrainGNN is composed of blocks of Ra-GConv layers and R-pool layers. It takes graphs as inputs and outputs graph-level predictions.

for the forward-pass update of node representation is calculated as

$$\tilde{\mathbf{h}}_i^{(l+1)} = \text{relu}\left(W_i^{(l)}\mathbf{h}_i^{(l)} + \sum_{j \in \mathcal{N}^{(l)}(i)} e_{ij}^{(l)} W_j^{(l)}\mathbf{h}_j^{(l)}\right), \quad (13.1)$$

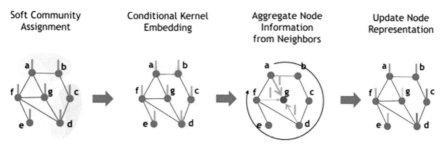

FIGURE 13.2

Operations in the Ra-GConv layer embed node features. First, nodes are softly assigned to communities based on their membership scores to the communities. Each community is associated with a different basis vector. Each node is embedded by the particular basis vectors based on the communities that it belongs to. Then, by aggregating a node's own embedding and its neighbors' embedding, the updated representation is assigned to each node on the graph.

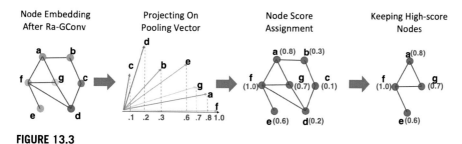

FIGURE 13.3

Operations in the R-pool layer select nodes to keep. All the nodes' representations are projected to a learnable vector. The nodes with large projected values are retained with their corresponding connections.

where $\mathcal{N}^{(l)}(i)$ denotes the set of indices of neighboring nodes of node v_i, $e_{ij}^{(l)}$ denotes the features associated with the edge from v_i to v_j, $W_i^{(l)}$ denote the model's parameters to be learned. The first layer is operated on the original graph, i.e., $\mathbf{h}_i^{(0)} = \mathbf{h}_i$, $e_{ij}^{(0)} = e_{ij}$. To avoid increasing the scale of output features, the edge features need to be normalized, as in GAT [57] and GNN [35]. Due to the aggregation mechanism, we normalize the weights by $e_{ij}^{(l)} = e_{ij}^{(l)} / \sum_{j \in \mathcal{N}^{(l)}(i)} e_{ij}^{(l)}$.

A **node pooling** layer is used to reduce the size of the graph, either by grouping the nodes together or pruning the original graph G to a subgraph G_s by keeping some important nodes only. We will focus on the pruning method, as it is more interpretable and can help detect biomarkers. See Fig. 13.3.

A **readout** layer is used to summarize the node feature vectors $\{\mathbf{h}_i^{(l)}\}$ into a single vector $\mathbf{z}^{(l)}$, which is finally fed into a classifier for graph classification.

In the next sections, we provide details on these layers, the loss functions we use and results.

13.2.3 ROI-aware graph convolutional layer

We propose an ROI-aware graph convolutional layer (Ra-GConv) with two insights. First, when computing the node embedding, we allow Ra-GConv to learn different embedding weights in graph convolutional kernels conditioned on the ROI (geometrically distributed information of the brain), instead of using the same weights W on all the nodes as shown in Eq. (13.1). In our design, the weights W can be decomposed as a linear combination of the basis set, where each basis function represents a community. Second, we include edge weights for message filtering, as the magnitude of edge weights presents the connection strength between two ROIs. We assume that more closely connected ROIs have a larger impact on each other.

Design

We begin by assuming the graphs have additional regional information and the nodes of the same region from different graphs have similar properties. We propose to encode the regional information into the embedding kernel function for the nodes. Given node i's regional information $\mathbf{r}_i$, such as the node's coordinates in a mesh graph, we propose to learn the vectorized embedding kernel $\text{vec}(W_i^{(l)})$ based on $\mathbf{r}_i$ for the lth Ra-GConv layer:

$$\text{vec}(W_i^{(l)}) = f_{MLP}^{(l)}(\mathbf{r}_i) = \Theta_2^{(l)}\text{relu}(\Theta_1^{(l)}\mathbf{r}_i) + \mathbf{b}^{(l)}, \qquad (13.2)$$

where the MLP with parameters $\{\Theta_1^{(l)}, \Theta_2^{(l)}\}$ maps $\mathbf{r}_i$ to a $d^{(l+1)} \cdot d^{(l)}$ dimensional vector then reshapes the output to a $d^{(l+1)} \times d^{(l)}$ matrix $W_i^{(l)}$ and $\mathbf{b}^{(l)}$ is the bias term in the MLP.

Given a brain parcellated into N ROIs, we order the ROIs in the same manner for all the brain graphs. Therefore, the nodes in the graphs of different subjects are aligned. However, the convolutional embedding should be independent of the ordering methods. Given an ROI ordering for all the graphs, we use one-hot encoding to represent the ROI's location information, instead of using coordinates, because the nodes in the brain are aligned well. Specifically, for node v_i, its ROI representation $\mathbf{r}_i$ is a N-dimensional vector with 1 in the ith entry and 0 for the other entries. Assume that $\Theta_1^{(l)} = [\boldsymbol{\alpha}_1^{(l)}, \dots, \boldsymbol{\alpha}_{N^{(l)}}^{(l)}]$, where $N^{(l)}$ is the number of ROIs in the lth layer, $\boldsymbol{\alpha}_i^{(l)} = [\alpha_{i1}^{(l)}, \dots, \alpha_{iK^{(l)}}^{(l)}]^\top \in \mathbb{R}^{K^{(l)}}$, $\forall i \in \{1, \dots, N^{(l)}\}$, where $K^{(l)}$ can be seen as the number of clustered communities for the $N^{(l)}$ ROIs. Assume $\Theta_2^{(l)} = [\boldsymbol{\beta}_1^{(l)}, \dots, \boldsymbol{\beta}_{K^{(l)}}^{(l)}]$ with $\boldsymbol{\beta}_u^{(l)} \in \mathbb{R}^{d^{(l+1)} \cdot d^{(l)}}$, $\forall u \in \{1, \dots, K^{(l)}\}$. Then Eq. (13.2) can be rewritten as

$$\text{vec}(W_i^{(l)}) = \sum_{u=1}^{K^{(l)}} (\alpha_{iu}^{(l)})^+ \boldsymbol{\beta}_u^{(l)} + \mathbf{b}^{(l)}. \qquad (13.3)$$

We can view $\{\boldsymbol{\beta}_u^{(l)} : j = 1, \ldots, K^{(l)}\}$ as a basis and $(\alpha_{iu}^{(l)})^+$ as the coordinates. From another perspective, $(\alpha_{iu}^{(l)})^+$ can be seen as the nonnegative assignment score of ROI i to community u. If we train different embedding kernels for different ROIs for the lth layer, the total parameters to be learned will be $N^{(l)}d^{(l)}d^{(l+1)}$. Usually we have $K^{(l)} \ll N^{(l)}$. By Eq. (13.3), we can reduce the number of learnable parameters to $K^{(l)}d^{(l)}d^{(l+1)} + N^{(l)}K^{(l)}$ parameters, while still assigning a separate embedding kernel for each ROI. The ROIs in the same community will be embedded by the similar kernel so that nodes in different communities are embedded in different ways.

As the graph convolution operations in [23], the node features will be multiplied by the edge weights, so that neighbors connected with stronger edges have a larger influence.

13.2.4 ROI-topK pooling layer

To perform graph-level classification, a layer for dimensionality reduction is needed since the number of nodes and the feature dimension per node are both large. Recent findings have shown that some ROIs are more indicative of predicting neurological disorders than the others [30,3], suggesting that they should be kept in the dimensionality reduction step. Therefore the node (ROI) pooling layer (R-pool) is designed to keep the most indicative ROIs while removing *noisy* nodes, thereby reducing the dimensionality of the entire graph.

Design

To make sure that down-sampling layers behave appropriately with respect to different graph sizes and structures, we adopt the approach of Cangea et al. [6] and Gao et al. [22] for reducing graph nodes. The choice of which nodes to drop is determined based on projecting the node features onto a learnable vector $\mathbf{w}^{(l)} \in \mathbb{R}^{d^{(l)}}$. The nodes receiving lower scores will experience less feature retention. We denote $\tilde{H}^{(l+1)} = [\tilde{\mathbf{h}}_1^{(l+1)}, \ldots, \tilde{\mathbf{h}}_{N^{(l)}}^{(l+1)}]^\top$, where $N^{(l)}$ is the number of nodes at the lth layer. Fully written out, the operation of this pooling layer (computing a pooled graph, $(\mathcal{V}^{(l+1)}, \mathcal{E}^{(l+1)})$, from an input graph, $(\mathcal{V}^{(l)}, \mathcal{E}^{(l)})$), is expressed as follows:

$$
\begin{aligned}
\mathbf{s}^{(l)} &= \tilde{H}^{(l+1)}\mathbf{w}^{(l)}/\|\mathbf{w}^{(l)}\|_2 \\
\tilde{\mathbf{s}}^{(l)} &= (\mathbf{s}^{(l)} - \mu(\mathbf{s}^{(l)}))/\sigma(\mathbf{s}^{(l)}) \\
\mathbf{i} &= \text{topk}(\tilde{\mathbf{s}}^{(l)}, k) \\
H^{(l+1)} &= (\tilde{H}^{(l+1)} \odot \text{sigmoid}(\tilde{\mathbf{s}}^{(l)}))_{\mathbf{i},:} \\
E^{(l+1)} &= E_{\mathbf{i},\mathbf{i}}^{(l)}.
\end{aligned}
\tag{13.4}
$$

Here, $\|\cdot\|$ is the L_2 norm, μ and σ take the input vector and output the mean and standard deviation of its elements. The notation top$k$ finds the indices corresponding to the largest k elements in score vector $\tilde{\mathbf{s}}$. $\odot$ is (broadcasted) elementwise multiplication, and $(\cdot)_{\mathbf{i},\mathbf{j}}$ is an indexing operation, which takes elements at row indices specified by $\mathbf{i}$ and column indices specified by $\mathbf{j}$ (colon denotes all indices). The pooling operation retains sparsity by requiring only a projection, a pointwise multiplication and a slicing into the original features and adjacency matrix. Different from [6], we added elementwise score normalization $\tilde{\mathbf{s}}^{(l)} = (\mathbf{s}^{(l)} - \mu(\mathbf{s}^{(l)}))/\sigma(\mathbf{s}^{(l)})$, which is important for calculating the loss functions in Section 13.2.7.

13.2.5 Readout layer

Lastly, we seek a "flattening" operation to preserve information about the input graph in a fixed-size representation. Concretely, to summarize the output graph of the lth conv-pool block, $(\mathcal{V}^{(l)}, \mathcal{E}^{(l)})$, we use

$$\mathbf{z}^{(l)} = \text{mean } H^{(l)} \parallel \text{max } H^{(l)}, \tag{13.5}$$

where $H^{(l)} = [\mathbf{h}_i^{(l)} : i = 1, ..., N^{(l)}]$, mean and max operate elementwisely, and $\parallel$ denotes concatenation. To retain information of a graph in a vector, we concatenate both mean and max summarization for a more informative graph-level representation. The final summary vector is obtained as the concatenation of all those summaries (i.e., $\mathbf{z} = \mathbf{z}^{(1)} \parallel \mathbf{z}^{(2)} \parallel \cdots \parallel \mathbf{z}^{(L)}$) and it is submitted to a MLP for obtaining final predictions.

13.2.6 Putting layers together

The architecture, as shown in Fig. 13.1, consists of two kinds of layers: Ra-GConv layers shown in the pink blocks and R-pool layer shown in the yellow blocks. The input is a weighted graph with its node attributes constructed from fMRI. We form a two-layer GNN block starting with ROI-aware node embedding by the proposed Ra-GConv layer in Section 13.2.3, followed by the proposed R-pool layer in Section 13.2.4. The whole network sequentially concatenates these GNN blocks, and readout layers are added after each GNN block. The final summary vector concatenates all the summaries from the readout layers, and an MLP is applied after that to give final predictions.

13.2.7 Loss functions

The classification loss is the cross-entropy loss:

$$L_{ce} = -\frac{1}{M} \sum_{m=1}^{M} \sum_{c=1}^{C} y_{m,c} \log(\hat{y}_{m,c}), \tag{13.6}$$

where M is the number of instances, C is the number of classes, y_{mc} is the ground truth label and $\hat{y}_{mc}$ is the model output.

Now we describe the loss terms designed to regulate the learning process and control the interpretability.

Unit loss

As we mentioned in Section 13.2.4, we project the node representation to a learnable vector $\mathbf{w}^{(l)} \in \mathbb{R}^{d^{(l)}}$. The learnable vector $\mathbf{w}^{(l)}$ can be arbitrarily scaled while the pooling scores $\mathbf{s}^{(l)} = \tilde{H}^{(l+1)}(a\mathbf{w}^{(l)})/\|a\mathbf{w}^{(l)}\|$ remain the same with non-zero scalar $a \in \mathbb{R}$. This suggests an identifiability issue, i.e., multiple parameters generate the same distribution of the observed data. To remove this issue, we add a constraint that $\mathbf{w}^{(l)}$ is a unit vector. To avoid the problem of identifiability, we propose unit loss:

$$L_{unit}^{(l)} = (\|\mathbf{w}^{(l)}\|_2 - 1)^2. \tag{13.7}$$

Group-level consistency loss

We propose group-level consistency (GLC) loss to force BrainGNN to select similar ROIs in a R-pool layer for different input instances. This is because for some applications, users may want to find the common patterns/biomarkers for a certain neuro-prediction task. Note that $\tilde{\mathbf{s}}^{(l)}$ in Eq. (13.4) is computed from the input $H^{(l)}$ and they change as the layer goes deeper for different instances. Therefore, for different inputs $H^{(l)}$, the selected entries of $\tilde{\mathbf{s}}^{(l)}$ may not correspond to the same set of nodes in the original graph, so it is not meaningful to enforce similarity of these entries. Thus we only use the GLC loss regularization for $\tilde{\mathbf{s}}^{(l)}$ vectors after the first pooling layer.

Now, we mathematically describe the novel GLC loss. In each training batch, suppose there are M instances, which can be partitioned into C subsets based on the class labels, $\mathcal{I}_c = \{m : m = 1, \ldots, M, y_{m,c} = 1\}$, for $c = 1, \ldots, C$. And $y_{m,c} = 1$ indicates the mth instance belongs to class c. We form the scoring matrix for the instances belonging to class c as $S_c^{(1)} = [\tilde{\mathbf{s}}_m^{(1)} : m \in \mathcal{I}_c]^\top \in \mathbb{R}^{M_c \times N}$, where $M_c = |\mathcal{I}_c|$. The GLC loss can be expressed as

$$L_{GLC} = \sum_{c=1}^{C} \sum_{m,n \in \mathcal{I}_c} \| \tilde{\mathbf{s}}_m^{(1)} - \tilde{\mathbf{s}}_n^{(1)} \|^2 = 2 \sum_{c=1}^{C} \mathrm{Tr}((S_c^{(1)})^\top L_c S_c^{(1)}), \tag{13.8}$$

where $L_c = D_c - W_c$ is a symmetric positive semi-definite matrix, W_c is a $M_c \times M_c$ matrix with values of 1, D_c is a $M_c \times M_c$ diagonal matrix with M_c as diagonal elements [61], m and n are the indices for instances. Thus Eq. (13.8) can be viewed as calculating pairwise pooling score similarities of the instances.

TopK pooling loss

We propose TopK pooling (TPK) loss to encourage reasonable node selection in R-pool layers. In other words, we hope the top k selected indicative ROIs should have significantly different scores than those of the unselected nodes. Ideally, the scores for the selected nodes should be close to 1 and the scores for the unselected nodes should be close to 0. To achieve this, we rank sigmoid$(\tilde{\mathbf{s}}_m^{(l)})$ for the mth instance in a descending order, denote it as $\hat{\mathbf{s}}_m^{(l)} = [\hat{s}_{m,1}^{(l)}, \ldots, \hat{s}_{m,N^{(l)}}^{(l)}]$ and apply a constraint to all the M training instances to make the values of $\hat{\mathbf{s}}_m^{(l)}$ more dispersed. In practice, we define TPK loss using binary cross-entropy as

$$L_{TPK}^{(l)} = -\frac{1}{M}\sum_{m=1}^{M}\frac{1}{N^{(l)}}\left(\sum_{i=1}^{k}\log(\hat{s}_{m,i}^{(l)})) + \sum_{i=1}^{N^{(l)}-k}\log(1-\hat{s}_{m,i+k}^{(l)})\right), \quad (13.9)$$

From our experiments, the top 50% selected nodes have significantly higher importance scores than the unselected ones.

Finally, the final loss function is formed as

$$L_{total} = L_{ce} + \sum_{l=1}^{L}L_{unit}^{(l)} + \lambda_1\sum_{l=1}^{L}L_{TPK}^{(l)} + \lambda_2 L_{GLC}, \quad (13.10)$$

where λ's are tunable hyper-parameters, l indicates the lth GNN block and L is the total number of GNN blocks. To maintain a concise loss function, we do not have tunable hyper-parameters for L_{ce} and $L_{unit}^{(l)}$. We observed that the unit loss $L_{unit}^{(l)}$ can quickly decrease to a small number close to zero.

13.2.8 Experiments and results

Biopoint data set. The Biopoint Autism Study Data Set [58] contains task fMRI scans for ASD and neurotypical healthy controls (HCs). The subjects perform the "biopoint" task, viewing point-light animations of coherent and scrambled biological motion in a block design [30] (24s per block). The fMRI data are preprocessed using the pipeline described in [58], and includes the removal of subjects with significant head motion during scanning. This results in 75 ASD children and 43 age-matched ($p > 0.124$) and IQ-matched ($p > 0.122$) neurotypical HCs. We insured that the head motion parameters are not significantly different between the groups. There are more male subjects than female samples, similar to the level of ASD prevalence in the population [17,28]. The first few frames are discarded, resulting in 146 frames for each fMRI sequence.

Experiment setup. The model architecture was implemented with 2 conv layers and 2 pooling layers as shown in Figure (13.1), with parameter $N = 84$, $K^{(0)} = K^{(1)} = 8$, $d^{(0)} = 84$, $d^{(1)} = 16$, $d^{(2)} = 16$, $C = 2$. In our work, we set k in Eq. (13.4) as half of nodes in that layer, namely, the dropout rate is 0.5. The motivation of $K = 8$ comes from the eight functional networks defined by Finn et al. [16], because these 8 networks show key brain functionality relevant to our tasks.

Comparison with baseline methods. We compare our method with traditional machine learning (ML) methods and state-of-the-art deep learning (DL) methods to evaluate the classification accuracy. The ML baseline methods take vectorized correlation matrices as inputs, with dimension N^2, where N is the number of parcellated ROIs. These methods included Random Forest (1000 trees), SVM (RBF kernel) and MLP (2 layers with 20 hidden nodes). A variety of DL methods have been applied to brain connectome data, e.g., long short-term memory (LSTM) recurrent neural network [10] and 2D CNN [32], but they are not designed for brain graph analysis. Here, we choose to compare our method with BrainNetCNN [32], which is designed for fMRI network analysis. We also compare our method with other GNN methods: GAT [57], GraphSAGE [25] and our preliminary version PR-GNN [39]. It is worth noting that GraphSAGE does not take edge weights in the aggregation step of the graph convolutional operation. The inputs of BrainNetCNN are correlation matrices. We follow the parameter settings indicated in the original paper [32]. The inputs and the settings of hidden layer nodes for the graph convolution, pooling and MLP layers of the alternative GNN methods are the same as BrainGNN. We also show the number of trainable parameters required by each method. We repeat the experiment and randomly split independent training, validation and testing sets five times. Hyperparameters for baseline methods are also tuned on the validation sets and we report the results on the five testing sets in Table 13.2.

As shown in Table 13.2, we report the comparison results using four different evaluation metrics, including accuracy, F1-score, recall and precision. We report the mean and standard deviation of the metrics on the five testing sets. We use validation sets to select the early stop epochs for the deep learning methods. As data augmentation are performed on all the data points for the consistency of cross-validation and to improve prediction performance, we report the subjectwise metric through majority-voting on the predicted label from the augmented inputs. BrainGNN is significantly better than most of the alternative methods ($p < 0.05$ under one tail two-sample t-test) except for the previous version of our own work, PR-GNN and BrainGNN, although the mean values of all the metrics are consistently better than PR-GNN and BrainNetCNN. The improvement may result from two causes. First, due to the intrinsic complexity of fMRI, complex models with more parameters are desired, which also explains why CNN and GNN-based methods were better than SVM and random forest. Second, our model utilized the properties of fMRI and community structure in the brain network, and thus potentially modeled the local integration more effectively. Compared to alternative machine learning models, BrainGNN achieved significantly better classification results on two independent task-fMRI data sets. Moreover, BrainGNN does not have the burden of feature selection, which is needed in traditional machine learning methods. Compared with MLP and CNN-based methods, GNN-based methods require less trainable parameters. Specifically, BrainGNN needs only 10%–30% of the parameters of MLP and less than 3% of the parameters of BrainNetCNN. Our method requires less parameters and achieves higher data utility, hence it is more suitable as a deep learning tool for fMRI analysis, when the sample size is limited.

Interpretability of BrainGNN for biomarker discoveries. A compelling advantage of BrainGNN is its *built-in* interpretability. It is essential for a pipeline to be able to discover personal biomarkers and group-level biomarkers in different application scenarios, i.e., precision medicine and disease understanding. In this section, we discuss how to adjust λ_2, the parameter associated with GLC loss, to manipulate the level of biomarker interpretation through training.

Table 13.2 Comparison of the classification performance with different baseline machine learning models and state-of-the-art deep learning models.

	SVM	Random Forest	MLP	BrainNetCNN	GAT	GraphSAGE	PR-GNN	BrainGNN
Accuracy (%)	62.80(4.92) [a]	68.60(3.58)	58.80(1.79)	75.20(3.49)	77.40(3.51)	78.60(5.90)	77.10(8.71)	**79.80(3.63)** [c]
F1 (%)	60.08(3.91)	63.97(4.95)	55.25(9.49)	65.58(14.48)	75.08(5.19)	75.55(7.03)	75.20(7.01)	**75.80(6.03)**
Recall (%)	60.20(4.49)	71.11(8.12)	61.00(4.85)	66.20(10.85)	71.60(6.07)	75.20(6.46)	78.26(10.28)	72.60(5.64)
Precision (%)	60.00(3.81)	67.80(5.36)	53.40(12.52)	65.60(17.95)	79.40(8.02)	76.20(8.11)	76.50(14.32)	**79.60(8.59)**
Parameter (k) [b]	3	3	138	1438	16	6	6	41

[a] Reported in mean (standard deviation) format.
[b] The number of trainable parameters of each model is denoted.
[c] We boldfaced the results generated from our proposed BrainGNN.

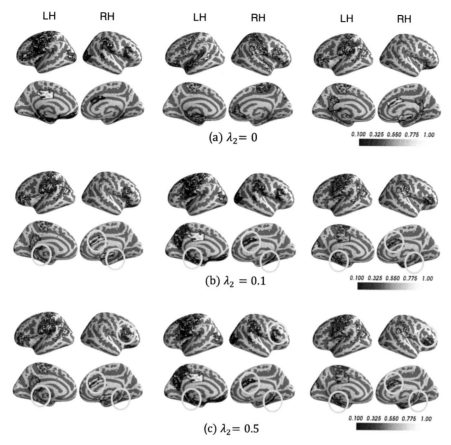

LH   RH   LH   RH   LH   RH

(a) $\lambda_2 = 0$

0.100 0.325 0.550 0.775 1.00

(b) $\lambda_2 = 0.1$

0.100 0.325 0.550 0.775 1.00

(c) $\lambda_2 = 0.5$

0.100 0.325 0.550 0.775 1.00

FIGURE 13.4

Interpretation results of Biopoint task. The selected salient ROIs of three different ASD individuals with different weights λ_2 associated with group-level consistency term L_{GLC}. The color bar ranges from 0.1 to 1. The bright-yellow color indicates a high score, while dark-red color indicates a low score. The commonly detected salient ROIs across different individuals are circled in blue.

Our proposed R-pool can prune the uninformative nodes and their connections from the brain graph based on the learning tasks. In other words, only the salient nodes are kept/selected. Without losing the generalizability, we show the salient ROI detection results of 3 randomly selected ASD instances from the Biopoint data set in Fig. 13.4. We show the remaining 21 ROIs after the 2nd R-pool layer (with pooling ratio = 0.5, 25% nodes left) and corresponding pooling scores. As shown in Fig. 13.4(a), when $\lambda_2 = 0$, "overlapped areas" (defined as spatial areas where saliency values agree) among the three instances are rarely to be found. The various salient brain ROIs are biomarkers specific to each individual. Many clinical

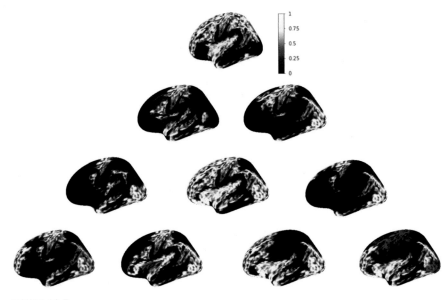

FIGURE 13.5

Biomarkers calculated on fMRI subsequences. The first row shows biomakers identified from full fMRI sequence. The second and third row are results truncating fMRI into 2 and 3 consecutive subsequences of equal length, respectively. In the fourth row, we use subsequence length 2/5 of full sequence and apply a 1/5 overlapping between neighboring subsequences.

applications, such as personalized treatment outcome prediction or disease subtype detection, require learning the individual-level biomarkers to achieve the best predictive performance. However, in some other applications, such as understanding the general pattern or mechanism associated with a cognitive task or disease, group-level biomarkers, which highlight consistent explanations across individuals, are important [2,58,52]. We can increase λ_2 to achieve such group-level explanations. In Fig. 13.4(b-c), we circle the big "overlapped areas" across the three instances. By visually examining the salient ROIs, we find three "overlapped areas" in Fig. 13.4(b) and five "overlapped areas" in Fig. 13.4(c).

13.2.9 Brain-GNN implication for dynamic brain states

In the Brain-GNN project, we leverage the interpretability of GNN and TopK pooling to identify brain regions as ASD biomarkers based on functional connectivity calculated over full fMRI sequence. Similarly, we perform the same operation on truncated fMRI subsequences. As shown in Fig. 13.5, when taking various subsequences, the identified biomarkers are different. This is a potential indication of dynamic brain state changes for task-based fMRI data.

13.3 LSTM-based recurrent neural networks for prediction in ASD

In this section, we propose new strategies that facilitate learning more generalizable neural network models from small fMRI data sets. We first adopt a recurrent neural network with long short-term memory (LSTM) to generate predictions from a whole-brain parcellation of fMRI data. We then use resampling approaches to generate multiple summary time series for each region in the parcellation, augmenting the original data set. Next, we utilize available nonimaging variables to provide subject-specific initialization of the LSTM network. Finally, we describe a criteria for selecting the most generalizable model from many training instances on the same data using only training loss, allowing all available data to be used for model training. We apply the proposed strategies and compare them to other approaches to learn from task-fMRI for one small data example: a regression problem of predicting treatment outcome from 21 children with autism spectrum disorder (ASD).

While we ultimately want to use the region-of-interest (ROI) connectivity-based biomarker work described elsewhere in this chapter to steer our prediction efforts, the work described in this section illustrates an initial approach for analyzing the raw task-based fMRI signal information to do outcome prediction in ASD. The methods and experiments presented here are based on prior work [15].

13.3.1 Basic LSTM architecture for task-based fMRI

LSTMs and related architectures are designed to learn long-term dependencies in time-series data [27]. They have recently been applied to fMRI for modeling brain dynamics [24] and for classification [13]. In addition to the time dependent nature of the model, LSTMs are a nice neural network architecture specifically for small fMRI data sets, since an "unrolled" LSTM with T timesteps can be thought of as a deep network with T layers that share the same parameters across all the layers. This likely considerably reduces the number of model parameters that need to be learned compared to other standard deep neural network architectures.

Standard fMRI whole-brain analysis involves first summarizing the data in a number of regions of interest (ROIs) according to some brain parcellation. While deep networks are able to learn from raw image inputs, the ROI approach is beneficial in our case of dealing with smaller fMRI data sets, as fMRI data is very noisy and the ROI representation greatly reduces the input data dimension.

Our basic LSTM architecture is based on the model in [13], with added regularization and slight changes for regression vs. binary classification. The summary time series from the N ROIs $\{x_1, x_2, ..., x_T\}, x_t \in R^N$ are used as input to an LSTM. For regression, which we focus on for this chapter subsection, we pass the output from the LSTM at the last timestep to a dense layer to produce the predicted value (Fig. 13.6, blue path); thus, the entire task-fMRI sequence is analyzed before providing a final prediction. During training, we include dropout of the LSTM weights [21] and add dropout (with probability 0.5) between the LSTM output and dense layer.

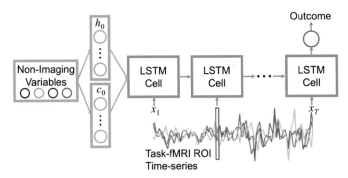

FIGURE 13.6

LSTM-based regression network with initialization using nonimaging variables. Figure is from Dvornek et al. [15].

13.3.2 Strategies for learning from small data sets

Data augmentation by resampling

We propose a resampling approach designed for augmenting fMRI ROI data. Traditional ROI analysis extracts the mean time-series calculated from all voxels in the ROI. Standard image data augmentation techniques such as random croppings or rotations are not appropriate for fMRI ROI time-series data. While we could perform random cropping along the time dimension, LSTMs learn best from long sequences. Another generic approach is to inject random noise into the inputs [16]; however, it is unclear how to choose the best noise model and its associated parameters, and the noise may not be representative of the variation in the fMRI data.

Instead, we propose a resampling approach to inject variation into the ROI time series. We propose sampling all voxels in an ROI with replacement (bootstrapping) and using the average of the sampled data to summarize the time series for the ROI.

LSTM initialization with nonimaging variables

Simple nonimaging subject information (e.g., age, sex) is often available. We propose utilizing such information to perform subject-specific initialization of the LSTM state. An LSTM cell contains two state vectors, the hidden state (i.e., output) h_t and the cell state c_t. The state of an LSTM at time t depends on the current input x_t and the hidden and cell state from the previous timestep h_{t-1} and c_{t-1}.

Unless otherwise specified, the initial state of the LSTM is set to zeros, $h_0 = c_0 = 0$. We propose initializing the LSTM by feeding readily available non-imaging information into 2 dense layers, whose outputs are the initial hidden and cell states (Fig. 13.6, green path). Such initialization approaches have been proposed in other domains, e.g., an LSTM model to generate an image caption was initialized on image features extracted via a convolutional neural network [31]. In our small data setting, conditioning the LSTM on subject-specific parameters helps to incorporate nonimaging variation across subjects with just a small increase in model parameters, unlike other multi-modal fusion techniques for neural networks [45,12].

Model selection from training loss

Neural network training (in the non transfer-learning case) is generally performed using random initialization of model weights. With large amounts of data, several training runs can be performed with different initializations, and a validation data set can be set aside to assist with choosing the best trained model. However, with small data sets, we would prefer to use all available data for training. Furthermore, splitting off a small validation set is likely not representative of the test data, and thus is not appropriate for model selection.

We propose choosing the best model from different initializations based on the training loss curve. The model with the lowest loss is likely to be the most overfit to the small data set. Thus, we propose selecting the model that fits slowest to the data. We quantify this criteria by the following: $\hat{M} = \arg\max_{M} \left[median \left(\triangle L_{M,s} \right) \frac{1}{L_M(0) \times s} \right]$, where L_M is the training loss curve for model M, $L_M(0)$ is the loss after epoch 0, $\triangle L_{M,s}$ are the first differences of the loss curve from epoch 0 to stopping epoch s, and s is the first epoch such that $L_M(s) < \frac{L_M(0)}{e}$. Thus the criteria is looking for the model that learns slowest, measured by 1) how fast the model fits the data in earlier epochs, as measured by the first differences in loss values; 2) the magnitude of the initial loss and 3) how long it takes for the training loss to exponentially decay ("relaxation time").

13.3.3 Prediction of treatment outcome

We investigated the effectiveness of the proposed learning strategies on the following regression problem: to predict the treatment outcome for children with ASD undergoing Pivotal Response Therapy (PRT) from baseline task-fMRI and nonimaging information. We acquired data from 21 children with ASD (ages 6.05 ± 1.24 years) who underwent 16 weeks of PRT, an empirically-supported practice that targets pivotal areas of development, such as motivation and self-initiation [36]. Prior to treatment, each subject underwent a T1-weighted MP-RAGE structural MRI (1 × 1 × 1 mm^3 voxel size) and BOLD T2*-weighted fMRI sequence (3.44 × 3.44 × 4.00 mm^3 acquired voxel size) during a biological motion perception task [30]. The fMRI paradigm involved viewing point light animations of coherent and scrambled biological motion in a block design (24 s per block, 5 min scan). Nonimaging information collected included age, sex, IQ and score on the Social Responsiveness Scale (SRS), 2nd edition [9]. SRS measures severity of social impairment in autism; lower scores signify better social ability. SRS score was measured again at the end of treatment. Treatment outcome was defined as the percent change in SRS.

Images were preprocessed in FSL [29] using the pipeline by Pruim et al. [51], which included motion correction, interleaved slice timing correction, brain extraction, 4D mean intensity normalization, spatial smoothing (5 mm FWHM), data de-noising via ICA-AROMA [51], nuisance regression using white matter and cerebrospinal fluid and high-pass temporal filtering (100 s). Functional MRI were aligned to the standard MNI brain with the aide of the structural MRI. The AAL atlas [55] was applied, resulting in 90 cerebral ROIs from which summary time series (156 timepoints) were extracted, standardized (subtracted mean and divided by standard deviation) and used as input to the LSTM. The data for each non-imaging variable were normalized to the range $[-1,1]$.

Leave-one-out cross-validation (train on 20, test 1) was used to assess model performance. Mean squared error (MSE), standard deviation (SD) of the squared error, and Pearson's correlation coefficient (r) between predicted and true treatment outcome were computed from cross-validation folds. Paired one-tailed t-tests were used to compare the squared errors, and p-values for r provided evidence for nonzero correlation, with a significance level of 0.05. Neural networks were implemented and trained in Keras using the MSE loss function, adadelta optimizer, 8 hidden LSTM units, a maximum of 100 epochs with early stopping (patience of 5 epochs monitoring training loss), and a batch size of 32 unless otherwise specified.

We first directly trained the LSTM network on the 21 fMRI data sets, varying the batch size to try to improve learning. The best result produced a correlation of $r = 0.35$, which was insignificant ($p = 0.1204$), and MSE $= 0.097 \pm 0.160$. We then trained a model using the proposed bootstrap resampling of all voxels from each ROI to compute the summary time series, augmenting each subject's data 50 times, resulting in 1050 samples. The model learned from the bootstrap augmented data produced significant correlation ($r = 0.53$, $p = 0.01$) and significantly reduced MSE $= 0.031 \pm 0.041$.

We next included initialization of the LSTM with nonimaging data. This dramatically improved the correlation ($r = 0.73$) and reduced the MSE by 35% (MSE $= 0.020 \pm 0.025$), at the cost of only a 1% increase in number of parameters. Applying a standard multimodal fusion approach to combine the final fMRI score and nonimaging data in a dense layer, also increasing the number of parameters by 1%, resulted in worse performance ($r = 0.43$, MSE $= 0.035 \pm 0.037$), demonstrating the benefit of our LSTM initialization method.

We tested our model selection approach by assessing the training curves from 2 separate runs, and compared this to averaging the predictions from the 2 runs (bagging). We applied these approaches to the bootstrap with nonimaging model. Model bagging did not produce significantly lower errors compared to the individual models for the bootstrap data set. Our model selection approach resulted in significantly lower MSE compared to at least one of the individual models. Furthermore, applying all three of our proposed learning strategies resulted in significantly more accurate predictions compared to data augmentation alone, with the highest correlation with the true outcomes ($r = 0.77$). The effect of adding each proposed learning strategy is illustrated in Fig. 13.7.

13.4 Causality and effective connectivity in ASD

Connectome analysis in fMRI aims to characterize neural connections in the brain and can be categorized into two types. The *functional connectome (FC)* [56] typically

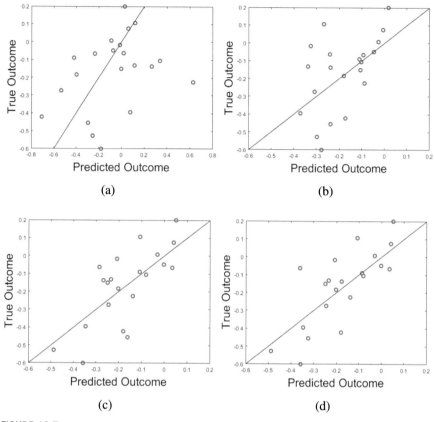

FIGURE 13.7

Plots of true vs. predicted treatment outcome after applying each proposed learning strategy. Perfect predictions would fall on red reference line. (a) Original data ($r = .35$). (b) Data augmentation with bootstrap resampling ($r = 0.53$). (c) Bootstrap resampling and LSTM initialization with nonimaging data ($r = 0.73$). (d) Bootstrap resampling, LSTM initialization with nonimaging data and model selection based on training loss ($r = 0.77$). Plots are from Dvornek et al. [15].

calculates the correlation (or similar measure) between fMRI time series of different regions-of-interest (ROIs) in the brain. The FC is easy to compute and typically robust; however, it does not reveal the underlying dynamics. The *effective connectome (EC)* [18] models the directed influence between ROIs, and provides a richer understanding of the functional network. It is widely used in the analysis of fMRI [54] but it more difficult to compute.

In this section, we propose a framework for fMRI data analysis to estimate the whole-brain EC based on Dynamic Causal Modeling (DCM) using our Multiple-Shooting Adjoint (MSA) method. We first briefly introduce DCM and EC. We then discuss the multiple-shooting method, which is related to the numerical solution of a continuous dynamical system. Next, we introduce the adjoint state method, which efficiently determines the gradient for parameters in continuous dynamical systems. We then discuss the proposed MS-MDL method, which combines multiple-shooting and the adjoint state method, and can be applied with general forward models and gradient-based optimizers. Finally, we demonstrate the power of the MS-MDL method on toy examples with both linear and non-linear models and then apply MSA to the estimation of the whole-brain EC from fMRI and show improved classification of autism spectrum disorder (ASD) vs. control compared to using the functional connectome.

13.4.1 Dynamic causal modeling

Dynamic causal modeling (DCM) [18] is a Bayesian framework to infer directed connections between compartments, and has been used to describe the interactions between neural populations based on functional neuroimaging. DCM is typically analyzed with the expectation-maximization (EM) algorithm [43]. However, because the inversion of a large-scale continuous system is difficult when noisy observations are present, DCM by EM is typically limited to a small number of compartments (<10). Another drawback with the EM formulation is its complexity; when the forward model changes, the posterior mean changes, and we need to re-derive the algorithm for optimization. In this work, we propose the MSA to address these limitations. MSA uses the multiple-shooting method for parameter estimation in ordinary differential equations (ODEs) under noisy observations, and is suitable for large-scale systems such as whole-brain fMRI analysis. Furthermore, MSA uses the adjoint method for accurate gradient estimation in the ODE; since the adjoint method is generic, MSA is a generic method for both linear and nonlinear systems, and does not require re-derivation of the algorithm as in EM.

13.4.2 The effective connectome

The Effective Connectome is typically estimated from DCM. Suppose there are p nodes (ROIs) and denote the observed fMRI time-series signal as $s(t)$, which is a p-dimensional vector at each time t. Denote the hidden neuronal state as $z(t)$. Then $z(t)$ and $s(t)$ are p-dimensional vectors for each time point t. Denote the hemodynamic response function (HRF) [40] as $h(t)$, and denote the external stimulation as $u(t)$, which is an n-dimensional vector for each t. The model is

$$f\left([z(t) \ D(t)]\right) = \begin{bmatrix} dz(t)/dt \\ dD(t)/dt \end{bmatrix} = \begin{bmatrix} D(t)z(t) + Cu(t) \\ Bu(t) \end{bmatrix}, \quad D(0) = A$$

$$s(t) = \left(z(t) + \epsilon(t)\right) * h(t), \quad \widetilde{z(t)} = z(t) + \epsilon(t) = Deconv\left(s(t), h(t)\right) \quad (13.11)$$

where $\epsilon(t)$ is the noise at time t, which is assumed to follow an independent Gaussian distribution, and $*$ represents convolution operation. $D(t)$ is a $p \times p$ matrix for each t, representing the effective connectome between nodes. A is a $p \times p$ matrix representing the interaction between ROIs. B is a tensor of shape $p \times p \times n$, representing the effect of stimulation on the effective connectome. C is a matrix of shape $p \times n$, representing the effect of the stimulus on neuronal state. An example of $n = 1$, $p = 3$ is shown in Fig. 13.8. The task is to estimate parameters A, B, C from noisy observation $s(t)$.

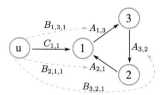

FIGURE 13.8

Toy example of dynamic causal modeling with 3 nodes (labeled 1 to 3). u is a 1-D stimulation signal, so $n = 1$, $p = 3$. A, B, C are defined as in Eq. (13.11). For simplicity, though A is a 3×3 matrix, we assume only three elements $A_{1,3}$, $A_{3,2}$, $A_{2,1}$ are nonzero.

13.4.3 Overcoming long time series and noise with multiple shooting model driven learning (MS-MDL)

While EM is widely used to optimize the DCM model, a drawback is the need to re-derive the algorithm when the forward model changes, which limits its application. Furthermore, current DCMs cannot handle large-scale systems, and thus are unsuitable for whole-brain analysis. Below, we describe our MSA method, which is a generic method for parameter estimation in high-dimensional nonlinear dynamical systems for continuous-time models.

Notations and formulation of problem

We summarize notations here for the ease of reading, which correspond to Fig. 13.9.

- $z(t), \widetilde{z(t)}, \overline{z(t)}$: $z(t)$ is the true time series, $\widetilde{z(t)}$ is the noisy observation and $\overline{z(t)}$ is the estimation. If p time series are observed, then they are p-dimensional vectors for each time t.
- $(t_i, \widehat{z_i})_{i=0}^{N}$: $\{\widehat{z_i}\}_{i=0}^{N}$ are corresponding guesses of states at split time points $\{t_i\}_{i=0}^{N}$. See Fig. 13.9. $\widehat{z_i}$ are discrete points, while $\widetilde{z(t)}, z(t), \overline{z(t)}$ are trajectories.
- f_η: Hidden state $z(t)$ follows the ODE $\frac{dz}{dt} = f(z, t)$, f is parameterized by η.
- θ: $\theta = [\eta, z_0, ...z_N]$. We concatenate all optimizable parameters into one vector for the ease of notation, denoted as θ.
- $\lambda(t)$: Lagrangian multiplier in the continuous case, used to derive the adjoint state equation.

DCM can be viewed as a parameter estimation problem for a continuous dynamical system, and can be formulated as

$$\underset{\eta}{\operatorname{argmin}} \int \left(\overline{z(\tau)} - \widetilde{z(\tau)}\right)^2 d\tau \quad s.t. \quad \frac{d\overline{z(\tau)}}{d\tau} = f_\eta(\overline{z(\tau)}, \tau) \tag{13.12}$$

The goal is to estimate η from observations $\widetilde{z}$.

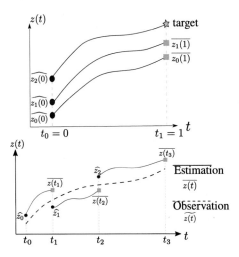

FIGURE 13.9

Top: illustration of the shooting method. Bottom: illustration of the multiple-shooting method. Blue dots represent the guess of the state at split time t_i.

Multiple shooting method

The shooting method is commonly used to fit an ODE under noisy observations, which is crucial for parameter estimation. The *shooting method* typically reduces a boundary-value problem to an initial value problem [26]. An example is shown in Fig. 13.9: to find a correct initial condition (at $t_0 = 0$) that reaches the target (at $t_1 = 1$), the shooting algorithm first takes an initial guess (e.g., $\widehat{z_0(0)}$), then integrates the curve to reach point $(t_1, \overline{z_0(1)})$; the error term $target - z_0(1)$ is used to update the initial condition (e.g., $\widehat{z_1(0)}$) so that the end-time value $\overline{z_1(1)}$ is closer to the target. This process is repeated until convergence. Besides the initial condition, the shooting method can be applied to update other parameters.

The *multiple-shooting method* [4] is an extension of the shooting method to long time series. It splits a long time series into chunks, and applies the shooting method to each chunk. Integration of a dynamical system for a long time is typically subject to noise and numerical error, while solving short time series is generally easier and more robust.

As shown in the bottom sub-figure of Fig. 13.9, a guess of initial condition at time t_0 is denoted as $\widehat{z_0}$, and we can use any ODE solver to get the estimated integral curve $\overline{z(t)}, t \in [t_0, t_1]$. Similarly, we can guess the initial condition at time t_1 as $\widehat{z_1}$, and get $\overline{z(t)}, t \in [t_1, t_2]$ by integration as in Eq. (13.14). Note that each time chunk is shorter than the entire chunk ($|t_{i+1} - t_i| < |t_3 - t_0|, i \in \{1, 2\}$), hence easier to solve. The split causes another issue: the guess might not match estimation at boundary points (e.g., $\overline{z(t_1)} \neq \widehat{z_1}$, $\overline{z(t_2)} \neq \widehat{z_2}$). Therefore we need to consider this error of mismatch when updating parameters, and minimizing this mismatch error is typically easier compared to directly analyzing the entire sequence.

The multiple-shooting method can be written as

$$\underset{\eta, z_0, \ldots z_N}{\mathrm{argmin}} \; J = \underset{\eta, z_0, \ldots z_N}{\mathrm{argmin}} \sum_{i=0}^{N} \int_{t_i}^{t_{i+1}} \left(\overline{z(\tau)} - \widetilde{z(\tau)}\right)^2 d\tau + \alpha \sum_{i=0}^{N} \left(\overline{z(t_i)} - \widehat{z_i}\right)^2 \quad (13.13)$$

$$\overline{z(t)} = \widehat{z_i} + \int_{t_i}^{t} f_\eta\left(\overline{z(\tau)}, \tau\right) d\tau, \quad t_i < t < t_{i+1}, \quad i \in \{0, 1, 2, \ldots N\} \quad (13.14)$$

where N is the total number of chunks discretized at points $\{t_0, \ldots t_N\}$, with corresponding guesses $\{\widehat{z_0}, \ldots \widehat{z_N}\}$. We use $\overline{z(t)}$ to denote the estimated curve as in Eq. (13.14); suppose t falls into the chunk $[t_i, t_{i+1}]$, $z(t)$ is determined by solving the ODE from $(\widehat{z_i}, t_i)$, where $\widehat{z_i}$ is the guess of initial state at t_i. We use $\widetilde{z(t)}$ to denote the observation. The first part in Eq. (13.13) corresponds to the difference between estimation $\overline{z(t)}$ and observation $\widetilde{z(t)}$, while the second part corresponds to the mismatch between estimation (orange square, $\overline{z(t_i)}$) and guess (blue circle, $\widehat{z_i}$) at split time points t_i. The second part is weighted by a hyper-parameter α. The ODE function f is parameterized by η. The optimization goal is to find the best η that minimizes loss in Eq. (13.13), besides model parameters η, we also need to optimize the guess $\widehat{z_i}$ for state at time $t_i, i \in \{0, 1, \ldots N\}$. Note that though previous work typically limits f to have a linear form, we do not have such limitations. Instead, multiple-shooting is generic for general f.

13.4.4 Adjoint state method

Our goal is to minimize the loss function in Eq. (13.13). Let $\theta = [\eta, z_0, \ldots, z_N]$ represent all learnable parameters. After fitting an ODE, we derive the gradient of loss L w.r.t. parameter θ and state guess $\widehat{z_i}$ for optimization.

Adjoint state equation

Note that different from the discrete case, the gradient in the continuous case is slightly complicated. We refer to the adjoint method [50,64,8]. Consider the following problem:

$$\frac{d\overline{z(t)}}{dt} = f_\theta\left(\overline{z(t)}, t\right), \quad s.t. \; \overline{z(0)} = x, \quad t \in [0, T], \quad \theta = [\eta, z_0, \ldots z_N] \quad (13.15)$$

$$\hat{y} = \overline{z(T)}, \quad J\left(\hat{y}, y\right) = J\left(\overline{z(0)} + \int_0^T f_\theta(\bar{z}, t)dt, y\right) \tag{13.16}$$

where the initial condition $z(0)$ is specified by input x, output $\hat{y} = \overline{z(T)}$. The loss function J is applied on $\hat{y}$, with target y. Compared with Eq. (13.12) to Eq. (13.14), for simplicity, we use θ to denote both model parameter η and guess of initial conditions $\{\hat{z}_i\}$. The Lagrangian is

$$L = J\left(\overline{z(T)}, y\right) + \int_0^T \lambda(t)^\top \left[\frac{d\overline{z(t)}}{dt} - f_\theta(\overline{z(t)}, t)\right]dt \tag{13.17}$$

where $\lambda(t)$ is the continuous Lagrangian multiplier. Then we have the following:

$$\frac{\partial J}{\partial \overline{z(T)}} + \lambda(T) = 0 \tag{13.18}$$

$$\frac{d\lambda(t)}{dt} + \left(\frac{\partial f_\theta(\overline{z(t)}, t)}{\partial \overline{z(t)}}\right)^\top \lambda(t) = 0 \ \forall t \in (0, T) \tag{13.19}$$

$$\frac{dL}{d\theta} - \int_T^0 \lambda(t)^\top \frac{\partial f_\theta(\overline{z(t)}, t)}{\partial \theta} dt = 0 \tag{13.20}$$

We skip the proof for simplicity. In general, the adjoint method determines the initial condition $\lambda(T)$ by Eq. (13.18), then solves Eq. (13.19) to get the trajectory of $\lambda(t)$, and finally integrates $\lambda(t)$ as in Eq. (13.20) to get the final gradient. Note that Eq. (13.18) to Eq. (13.20) is generic for general θ, and in case of Eq. (13.13) and Eq. (13.14), we have $\theta = [\eta, z_0, ...z_N]$, and $\nabla\theta = [\frac{\partial L}{\partial \eta}, \frac{\partial L}{\partial z_0}, ... \frac{\partial L}{\partial z_N}]$. Note that we need to calculate $\frac{\partial f}{\partial z}$ and $\frac{\partial f}{\partial \theta}$, which can be easily computed by a single backward pass; we only need to specify the forward model without worrying about the backward, because automatic differentiation is supported in frameworks such as PyTorch and Tensorflow. After deriving the gradient of all parameters, we can update these parameters by gradient descent.

Note that though $J(\overline{z(T)}, y)$ is defined on a single time point in Eq. (13.17), it can extend to the integral form $\int_{t=0}^T loss(t)dt$. We can define F as $\frac{dF(t)}{dt} = loss(t)$, $F(0) = 0$, then $F(T)$ (for a single time point T) equals the integral.

Adaptive checkpoint adjoint

Eq. (13.18) to Eq. (13.20) are the analytical form of the gradient in the continuous case, yet the numerical implementation is crucial for empirical performance. Note that $\overline{z(t)}$ is solved in forward-time (0 to T), while $\lambda(t)$ is solved in reverse-time (T to 0), yet the gradient in Eq. (13.20) requires both $\overline{z(t)}$ and $\lambda(t)$ in the integrand. Memorizing a continuous trajectory $\overline{z(t)}$ requires much memory; to save memory, most existing implementations forget the forward-time trajectory of $\overline{z(t)}$, and instead only record the end-time state $\overline{z(T)}$ and $\lambda(T)$ and solve Eq. (13.15) and Eq. (13.18) to Eq. (13.20) in reverse-time on-the-fly.

Algorithm 13.1: Multiple-Shooting Adjoint (MSA)

Input Observation $\widetilde{z(t)}$, number of chunks N, learning rate lr.
Initialize model parameter η, state $\{\widehat{z}_i\}_{i=0}^N$ at discretized points $\{t_i\}_{i=0}^N$
Repeat until convergence
      (1) Estimate trajectory $\overline{z(t)}$ from current parameters by the multiple
shooting method as in Eq. (13.14).
      (2) Compute the loss J in Eq. (13.13), plug J in Eq. (13.17). Derive the
gradient by ACA.
      (3) Update parameters with first-order gradient optimizers (see [65]).

    While memory cost is low, existing implementations of the adjoint method typ-
ically suffer from numerical error: since the forward-time trajectory (denoted as
$\overrightarrow{z(t)} = \overline{z(t)}$) is deleted, and the reverse-time trajectory (denoted as $\overleftarrow{z(t)}$) is reconstructed from the end-time state $z(T)$ by solving Eq. (13.15) in reverse-time, $\overrightarrow{z(t)}$ and
$\overleftarrow{z(t)}$ cannot accurately overlap due to inevitable errors with numerical ODE solvers.
The error $\overrightarrow{z(t)} - \overleftarrow{z(t)}$ propagates to the gradient in Eq. (13.20) in the $\frac{\partial f(z,t)}{\partial z}$ term.
    To solve this issue, we use the Adaptive Checkpoint Adjoint (ACA) method (see
[65] which records $\overrightarrow{z(t)}$ using a memory-efficient method to guarantee numerical
accuracy.

13.4.5 Multiple-shooting adjoint state method (MSA)

MSA brings in multiple-shooting and is generic for various f. Details are summarized in Algorithm 13.1. MSA iterates over the following steps until convergence:
(1) estimate the trajectory based on the current parameters, using the multiple-shoot
method for integration; (2) compute the loss and derive the gradient using the adjoint
method; (3) update the parameters based on the gradient.
    Previous work has used the multiple-shooting method for parameter estimation
in ODEs [47], yet MSA is different in the following aspects: (A) Suppose the parameters have k dimensions. MSA uses an elementwise update, hence has only $O(k)$
computational cost in each step; yet the method in [47] requires the inversion of a
$k \times k$ matrix, hence might be infeasible for large-scale systems. (B) The implementation of [47] does not tackle the mismatch between forward-time and reverse-time
trajectory, while we use ACA [64] for accurate gradient estimation in step (2) of
Algorithm 13.1. (C) From a practical perspective, our implementation is based on
PyTorch, which supports automatic-differentiation, therefore we only need to spec-
ify the forward model f without the need to manually compute the gradient $\frac{\partial f}{\partial z}$ and
$\frac{\partial f}{\partial \theta}$. Hence, our method is off-the-shelf for general models, while the method of [47]
needs to re-implement $\frac{\partial f}{\partial z}$ and $\frac{\partial f}{\partial \theta}$ for different f, and conventional DCM with EM
needs to re-derive the entire algorithm when f changes.

13.4.6 Validation of MSA on toy examples

We first validate MSA on toy examples of linear dynamical systems, then validate its performance on large-scale systems and nonlinear dynamical systems.

A linear dynamical system with 3 nodes

We first start with a simple linear dynamical system with only 3 nodes. We further simplify the matrix A as in Fig. 13.8, where only three elements in A are nonzero. We set B as a zeros matrix, and $u(t)$ as a 1-dimensional signal. The dynamical system is linear:

$$\begin{bmatrix} dz(t)/dt \\ dD(t)/dt \end{bmatrix} = \begin{bmatrix} D(t)z(t) + Cu(t) \\ 0 \end{bmatrix}, \quad D(0) = A, \quad u(t) = \begin{cases} 1, & floor(\frac{t}{2})\%2 = 0 \\ 0, & otherwise \end{cases}$$

$$\tag{13.21}$$

$$\widetilde{z(t)} = z(t) + \epsilon(t), \quad \epsilon(t) \sim N(0, \sigma^2) \tag{13.22}$$

$u(t)$ is an alternating block function at a period of 2, taking values 0 or 1. The observed function $\widetilde{z(t)}$ suffers from $i.i.d.$ Gaussian noise $\epsilon(t)$ with 0 mean and uniform variance σ^2.

We perform 10 independent simulations and parameter estimations. For estimation of DCM with the EM algorithm, we use the SPM package [48], which is a widely-used standard baseline. The estimation in MSA is implemented in PyTorch, using ACA [64] as the ODE solver. For MSA, we use the AdaBelief optimizer [67] to update parameters with the gradient; though other optimizers such as SGD can be used, we found AdaBelief converges faster in practice.

For each of the nonzero elements in A, we show the boxplot of error in estimation in Fig. 13.10. Compared with EM, the error by MSA is significantly closer to 0 and has a smaller variance. An example of a noisy observation and estimated curves are shown in Fig. 13.10, and the estimation by MSA is visually closer to the ground-truth compared to the EM algorithm. We emphasize that the estimated curve is not a simple smoothing of the noisy observation; instead, after estimating the parameters of the ODE, the estimated curve (for $t > 0$) is generated by solving the ODE using only the initial state. Therefore the match between estimated curve and observation demonstrates that our method learns the underlying dynamics of the system.

13.4.7 Application to large-scale systems

After validation on a small system with only 3 nodes, we validate MSA on large scale systems with more nodes. We use the same linear dynamical system as in Eq. (13.21), but with the node number p ranging from 10 to 100. The dimensions of A and B grow at a rate of $O(p^2)$, and the EM algorithm estimates a covariance matrix of size $O(p^4)$. Hence, the memory for EM method grows extremely fast with p. For various settings, the ground truth parameter is randomly generated from a uniform distribution between -1 and 1, and the variance of measurement noise is set at $\sigma =$

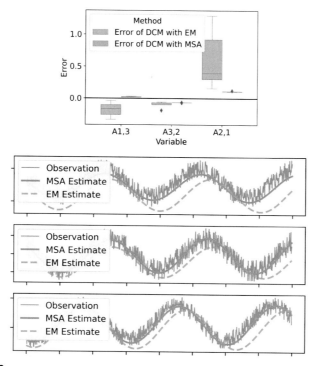

FIGURE 13.10

Results for the toy example of a linear dynamical system in Fig. 13.8. Top: error in esti-mated value of connection $A_{1,3}$, $A_{3,2}$, $A_{2,1}$, other parameters are set as 0 in simulation. Bottom: from top to bottom are the results for node 1, 2, 3, respectively. For each node, we plot the observation and estimated curve from MSA and EM methods. Note that the esti-mated curve is generated by integration of the ODE under-estimated parameters with only the initial condition known, not smoothing of noisy observation.

0.5. For each setting, we perform 5 independent runs, and report the mean squared error (MSE) between estimated parameter and ground truth.

As shown in Table 13.3, for small-size systems (number of nodes $<= 20$), MSA consistently generates a lower MSE than the EM algorithm. For large-scale systems, since the memory cost of the EM algorithm is $O(p^4)$, the algorithm quickly runs out-of-memory. On the other hand, the memory cost for MSA is $O(p^2)$ because it only uses the first-order gradient. Hence, MSA is suitable for large-scale systems such as in whole-brain fMRI analysis.

Application to general non-linear systems

Since neither the multiple-shoot method nor the adjoint state method requires the ODE f to be linear, our MSA can be applied to general nonlinear systems. Further-more, since our implementation is in PyTorch, which supports automatic differentia-

Table 13.3 Mean squared error ($\times 10^{-3}$, **lower** is better) in estimation of parameters for a linear dynamical system with different number of nodes. "OOM" represents "out of memory."

	10 Nodes	20 Nodes	50 Nodes	100 Nodes
EM	3.3 ± 0.2	3.0 ± 0.2	OOM	OOM
MSA	0.7 ± 0.1	0.9 ± 0.3	0.8 ± 0.1	0.8 ± 0.2

tion, we only need to specify f when fitting different models, and the gradient will be calculated automatically. Therefore MSA is an off-the-shelf method, and is suitable for general nonlinear ODEs both in theory and implementation.

We validate MSA on the Lotka–Volterra (L-V) equations [60], a system of nonlinear ODEs describing the dynamics of predator and prey populations. The L-V equation can be written as

$$f\left([z_1(t), z_2(t)]\right) = \begin{bmatrix} dz_1(t)/dt \\ dz_2(t)/dt \end{bmatrix} = \begin{bmatrix} \zeta z_1(t) - \beta z_1(t)z_2(t) \\ \delta z_1(t)z_2(t) - \gamma z_2(t) \end{bmatrix}$$

$$\begin{bmatrix} \widetilde{z_1(t)} \\ \widetilde{z_2(t)} \end{bmatrix} = \begin{bmatrix} z_1(t) + \epsilon_1(t) \\ z_2(t) + \epsilon_2(t) \end{bmatrix} \tag{13.23}$$

where ζ, β, δ, γ are parameters to estimate, $\widetilde{z(t)}$ is the noisy observation and $\epsilon(t)$ is the independent noise. Note that there are nonlinear terms $z_1(t)z_2(t)$ in the ODE, making EM derivation difficult. Furthermore, the EM method needs to explicitly derive the posterior mean, hence needs to be re-derived for every different f; while MSA is generic, and hence does not require re-derivation.

Besides the basic L-V model, we also consider a modified L-V model, defined as

$$dz_1(t)/dt = \zeta z_1(t) - \beta \phi(z_2(t))z_1(t)z_2(t)$$
$$dz_2(t)/dt = \delta \phi(z_1(t))z_1(t)z_2(t) - \gamma z_2(t) \tag{13.24}$$

where $\phi(x) = 1/(1 + e^{-x})$ is the sigmoid function. We use this example to demonstrate the ability of MSA to fit highly nonlinear ODEs.

We compare MSA with LMFIT [44], which is a well-known python package for nonlinear fitting. We use L-BFGS solver in LMFIT, which generates better results than other solvers. We did not compare with original DCM with EM because it is unsuitable for general nonlinear models. The estimation of the curve for $t > 0$ is solved by integrating using the estimated parameters and initial conditions. As shown in Fig. 13.11 and Fig. 13.12, compared with LMFIT, MSA recovers the system accurately. LMFIT directly fits the long sequences, while MSA splits long-sequences into chunks for robust estimation, which may partially explain the better performance of MSA.

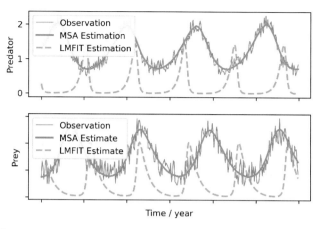

FIGURE 13.11

Results for the L-V model.

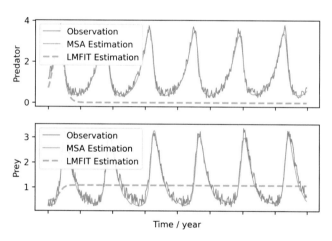

FIGURE 13.12

Results for the modified L-V model.

13.4.8 Apply MDL to identify ASD from fMRI data

We applied EC and FC on the classification task of ASD vs. Control with task-based fMRI. Our results show that combing EC with FC achieves a consistent improvement in classification accuracy.

Task-based fMRI data acquisition and pre-processing

fMRI for 82 children with ASD and 48 age and IQ-matched healthy controls were acquired. The fMRI (BOLD, 132 volumes, TR = 2000 ms, TE = 25 ms, flip angle =

$60°$, voxel size $3.44 \times 3.44 \times 4 \ mm^3$) was acquired on a Siemens MAGNETOM Trio 3T scanner.

A biological motion perception task and a scrambled motion task [30] were presented in alternating blocks (24s). fMRI data was then pre-processed with FSL with the following standard procedures: 1) motion correction, 2) interleaved slice timing correction, 3) brain extraction with BET, 3) spatial smoothing with a full-width at half-maximum (FWHM) of 5 mm, 5) high-pass temporal filtering. For parcellation, we use the AAL atlas [55] containing 116 ROIs.

13.4.9 Improved fitting with ACA and AdaBelief

We compare ACA vs. Adjoint method in the fitting of DCM, and plot the results in Fig. 13.13. We observe that ACA consistently generates a lower training loss than the adjoint method, validating our analysis on the numerical accuracy in gradient estimation (see [65]).

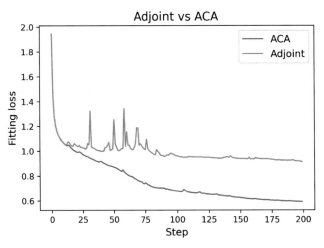

FIGURE 13.13

Compare the fitting loss of ACA and Adjoint method in fitting of DCM. Both curves use the AdaBelief optimizer.

We further compare AdaBelief with Adam in the fitting of DCM, and plot the results in Fig. 13.14. For both experiments, we use the ACA method to derive the gradient accurately, and feed the gradient into different optimizers. We observe that AdaBelief achieves comparable fitting loss as Adam within half the training time.

13.4.10 Estimation of effective connectome and functional connectome

Using the AAL atlas [55] for each subject, the parameters for dynamic causal modeling, as in Eq. (13.11), are estimated using MSA. An example snapshot of the effective

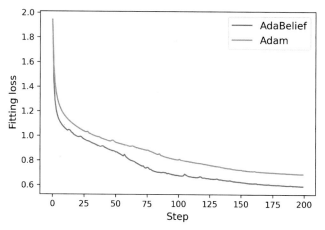

FIGURE 13.14

Compare the fitting loss with different optimizers in fitting of DCM. Both curves use ACA for gradient estimation.

connectome (EC) during the two tasks is shown in Fig. 13.15, showing that MSA captures the dynamic EC. See Fig. 13.16.

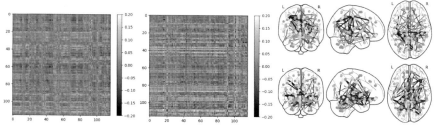

FIGURE 13.15

An example of MSA for one subject in task fMRI. Left: effective connectome during task 1 (biological motion). Middle: effective connectome during task 2 (scrambled motion). Right: top and bottom represents the effective connectome for tasks 1 and 2, respectively. Blue and red edges represent positive and negative connections respectively. Only top 5% strongest connections are visualized.

We estimate the Dynamic Functional Connectome (DFC) using a sliding-window with a window size of 20 time points; every two adjacent windows are separated by 1 time point. We use the AAL atlas and calculate the Pearson Correlation among the atlas regions for each sliding window.

We perform a group comparison between the ASD and control groups, and plot the edges with a p-value smaller than 0.05 (with Bonferroni correction). We plot the results for FC in Fig. 13.17, and plot the results for EC in Fig. 13.18. Despite the

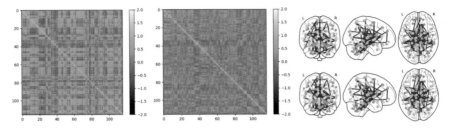

FIGURE 13.16

An example of Dynamic Functional Connectome for one subject in task-based fMRI. Left: functional connectome during task 1. Middle: functional connectome during task 2. Right: top and bottom represents the functional connectome for tasks 1 and 2, respectively. Blue and red edges represent positive and negative connections respectively. Only top 5% strongest connections are visualized.

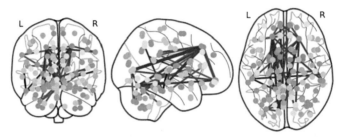

FIGURE 13.17

FC edges (blue=positive, red=negative) that are significantly different between ASD and control groups.

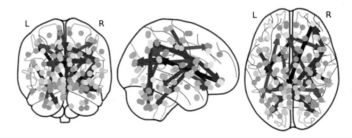

FIGURE 13.18

EC edges that are significantly different between ASD and control groups.

difference, both FC and EC edges include regions in the frontal lobe and the temporal lobe, which match previous findings in the literature on ASD.

13.4.11 **Classification results for task fMRI**

We conduct classification experiments for ASD vs. control using EC, FC and EC-FC concatenated together as the predictor. The classification of a subject is based on the majority vote of the predictions across all time points. We experimented with an In-vNet [66] of 20 layers and a feature dimension of 32. Results for 10-fold subjectwise cross-validation are shown in Fig. 13.19. For classification using task-based fMRI data, using EC generates slightly better accuracy, F1 score, AUC and Precision than using FC as the predictor. Using EC-FC as input consistently improves the classification performance.

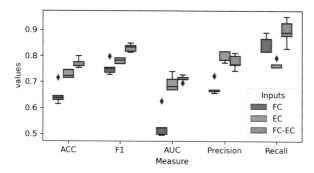

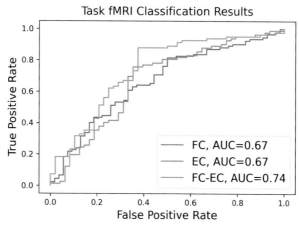

FIGURE 13.19

Classification results on task fMRI data.

13.5 **Conclusion**

Deep learning methods for the analysis of fMRI in ASD have great potential for accurately characterizing individuals and ultimate incorporation into clinical decision-making. These methods have already demonstrated their power as seen in the examples shown in this chapter. Clearly, both spatial and temporal image characteristics are important and analysis methods that exploit these factors effectively will have improved accuracy. Modeling the brain as a network as well as incorporating careful consideration of causality enable further improvements. In addition, the imaging biomarkers generated provide interpretability for the functioning of the methods themselves as well as deeper insight into the underlying functional changes associated with ASD.

References

[1] A. Abraham, M. Milham, A. Martino, R. Craddock, D. Samaras, T. B, G. Varoquaux, Deriving reproducible biomarkers from multi-site resting-state data: an autism-based example, NeuroImage 147 (2017) 736–745.

[2] E. Adeli, Q. Zhao, N.M. Zahr, A. Goldstone, A. Pfefferbaum, E.V. Sullivan, K.M. Pohl, Deep learning identifies morphological determinants of sex differences in the preadolescent brain, NeuroImage 223 (2020) 117293.

[3] J.T. Baker, A.J. Holmes, G.A. Masters, B.T. Yeo, F. Krienen, R.L. Buckner, D. Ongur, Disruption of cortical association networks in schizophrenia and psychotic bipolar disorder, JAMA Psychiatry 71 (2) (2014) 109–118.

[4] H.G. Bock, K.-J. Plitt, A multiple shooting algorithm for direct solution of optimal control problems, in: IFAC Proceedings Volumes, 1984.

[5] V. Calhoun, R. Miller, G. Pearlson, T. Adali, The chronnectome: time-varying connectivity networks as the next frontier in fMRI data discovery, Neuron 84 (October 2014) 262–274.

[6] C. Cangea, P. Velickovic, N. Jovanovic, T. Kipf, P. Lio, Towards sparse hierarchical graph classifiers, arXiv preprint, arXiv:1811.01287, 2018.

[7] C. Chen, C. Keown, A. Jahedi, A. Nair, M. Pflieger, B. Bailey, R. Muller, Diagnostic classification of intrinsic functional connectivity highlights somatosensory, default mode, and visual regions in autism, Neuroimage: Clinical 8 (2015) 238–245.

[8] R.T. Chen, Y. Rubanova, J. Bettencourt, D.K. Duvenaud, Neural ordinary differential equations, in: Advances in Neural Information Processing Systems, 2018.

[9] J.N. Constantino, C.P. Gruber, The Social Responsiveness Scale, second edition (SRS-2), Western Psychological Services, 2012.

[10] J. Dakka, P. Bashivan, M. Gheiratmand, I. Rish, S. Jha, R. Greiner, Learning neural markers of schizophrenia disorder using recurrent neural networks, arXiv preprint, arXiv:1712.00512, 2017.

[11] J. Duvekot, J. van der Ende, F.C. Verhulst, K. Greaves-Lord, Examining bidirectional effects between the autism spectrum disorder (ASD) core symptom domains and anxiety in children with ASD, Journal of Child Psychology and Psychiatry 59 (2018) 277–284.

[12] N.C. Dvornek, P. Ventola, J.S. Duncan, Combining phenotypic and resting- state fmri data for autism classification with recurrent neural networks, in: 5th International IEEE International Symposium on Biomedical Imaging (ISBI2018), April 2018, pp. 725–728.

[13] N.C. Dvornek, P. Ventola, K.A. Pelphrey, J.S. Duncan, Identifying autism from resting-state fmri using long short-term memory networks, in: International Workshop on Machine Learning in Medical Imaging, Springer, 2017, pp. 362–370.

[14] N.C. Dvornek, D. Yang, P. Ventola, J.S. Duncan, Learning generalizable recurrent neural networks from small task-fMRI datasets, in: A.F. Frangi, et al. (Eds.), International Conference on Medical Image Computing and Computer-Assisted Intervention (MICCAI), vol. LNCS11072, Springer, 2018, pp. 329–337.

[15] N.C. Dvornek, D. Yang, P. Ventola, J.S. Duncan, Learning generalizable recurrent neural networks from small task-fmri datasets, in: International Conference on Medical Image Computing and Computer-Assisted Intervention, Springer, 2018, pp. 329–337.

[16] E.S. Finn, X. Shen, D. Scheinost, M.D. Rosenberg, J. Huang, M.M. Chun, X. Papademetris, R.T. Constable, Functional connectome fingerprinting: identifying individuals using patterns of brain connectivity, Nature Neuroscience 18 (11) (2015) 1664.

[17] E. Fombonne, Epidemiology of pervasive developmental disorders, Pediatric Research 65 (6) (2009) 591–598.

[18] K.J. Friston, L. Harrison, Dynamic causal modelling, NeuroImage (2003).

[19] S. Gadgil, Q. Zhao, A. Pfefferbaum, E. Sullivan, E. Adeli, K. Pohl, Spatio-temporal graph convolution for functional MRI analysis, arXiv:2003.10613v2, 2020.

[20] S. Gadgil, Q. Zhao, A. Pfefferbaum, E.V. Sullivan, E. Adeli, K.M. Pohl, Spatio-temporal graph convolution for resting-state fMRI analysis, in: Proceedings of the International Conference on Medical Image Computing and Computer-Assisted Intervention (MICCAI), 2020.

[21] Y. Gal, Z. Ghahramani, A theoretically grounded application of dropout in recurrent neural networks, in: Proceedings of Neural Information Processing Systems (NIPS), 2016.

[22] H. Gao, S. Ji, Graph u-nets, arXiv preprint, arXiv:1905.05178, 2019.

[23] L. Gong, Q. Cheng, Exploiting edge features for graph neural networks, in: Proceedings of the IEEE Conference on Computer Vision and Pattern Recognition, 2019, pp. 9211–9219.

[24] U. Güçlü, M.A. Van Gerven, Modeling the dynamics of human brain activity with recurrent neural networks, Frontiers in Computational Neuroscience 11 (7) (2017).

[25] W. Hamilton, Z. Ying, J. Leskovec, Inductive representation learning on large graphs, in: Advances in Neural Information Processing Systems, 2017, pp. 1024–1034.

[26] F. Hildebrand, Introduction to Numerical Analysis, Courier Corporation, 1987.

[27] S. Hochreiter, J. Schmidhuber, Long short-term memory, Neural Computation 9 (8) (1997) 1735–1780.

[28] L. Hull, K. Petrides, W. Mandy, The female autism phenotype and camouflaging: a narrative review, Review Journal of Autism and Developmental Disorders (2020) 1–12.

[29] M. Jenkinson, C.F. Beckmann, T.E. Behrens, M.W. Woolrich, S.M. Smith, Fsl, NeuroImage 62 (2) (2012) 782–790.

[30] M.D. Kaiser, C.M. Hudac, S. Shultz, S.M. Lee, C. Cheung, A.M. Berken, B. Deen, N.B. Pitskel, D.R. Sugrue, A.C. Voos, Neural signatures of autism, Proceedings of the National Academy of Sciences 107 (49) (2010) 21223–21228.

[31] A. Karpathy, L. Fei-Fei, Deep visual-semantic alignments for generating image descriptions, IEEE Transactions on Pattern Analysis and Machine Intelligence 39 (4) (2017) 664–676.

[32] J. Kawahara, C.J. Brown, S.P. Miller, B.G. Booth, V. Chau, R.E. Grunau, J.G. Zwicker, G. Hamarneh, Brainnetcnn: convolutional neural networks for brain networks; towards predicting neurodevelopment, NeuroImage 146 (2017) 1038–1049.

[33] A. Kazi, S. Shekarforoush, S. Arvind Krishna, H. Burwinkel, G. Vivar, K. Kortüm, S.-A. Ahmadi, S. Albarqouni, N. Navab, Inceptiongcn: receptive field aware graph convolutional network for disease prediction, in: International Conference on Information Processing in Medical Imaging, Springer, 2019, pp. 73–85.

[34] B.-H. Kim, J.C. Ye, Understanding graph isomorphism network for rs-fmri functional connectivity analysis, Frontiers in Neuroscience 14 (2020) 630.

[35] T.N. Kipf, M. Welling, Semi-supervised classification with graph convolutional networks, arXiv preprint, arXiv:1609.02907, 2016.

[36] R. Koegel, L. Koegel, Pivotal Response Treatments for Autism: Communication, Social, and Academic Development, Brookes Publishing Company, Baltimore, MD, 2006.

[37] E. Lake, E. Finn, S. Noble, T. Vanderwal, X. Shen, M. Rosenberg, M. Spann, M. Chun, D. Scheinost, R. Constable, The functional brain organization of an individual allows prediction of measures of social abilities transdiagnostically in autism and attention-deficit/hyperactivity disorder, Biological Psychiatry 86 (2019) 315–326.

[38] X. Li, Y. Zhou, N. Dvornek, M. Zhang, S. Gao, J. Zhuang, D. Scheinost, L. Staib, P. Ventola, J. Duncan, BrainGNN: interpretable brain graph neural network for fMRI analysis, Medical Image Analysis 74 (December 2021) 1–18.

[39] X. Li, Y. Zhou, N.C. Dvornek, M. Zhang, J. Zhuang, P. Ventola, J.S. Duncan, Pooling regularized graph neural network for fmri biomarker analysis, in: International Conference on Medical Image Computing and Computer-Assisted Intervention, Springer, 2020, pp. 625–635.

[40] M.A. Lindquist, J.M. Loh, L.Y. Atlas, T.D. Wager, Modeling the hemodynamic response function in fmri: efficiency, bias and mis-modeling, NeuroImage 45 (2009).

[41] M. Maenner, K. Shaw, A. Bakvian, et al., Prevalence and characteristics of autism spectrum disorder among children aged 8 years — autism and developmental disabilities monitoring network, 11 sites, United States, 2018, MMWR Surveillance Summaries 70 (SS-11) (2021) 1–16, https://doi.org/10.15585/mmwr.ss7011a1.

[42] M. Maenner, K.A. Shaw, J. Baio, et al., Prevalence of autism spectrum disorder among children aged 8 years – autism and developmental disabilities monitoring network, 11 sites, United States, 2016, MMWR Surveill Summ 2020 69 (SS-4) (2020) 1–12.

[43] T.K. Moon, The expectation-maximization algorithm, in: ISPM, 1996.

[44] M. Newville, T. Stensitzki, D.B. Allen, M. Rawlik, A. Ingargiola, A. Nelson, Lmfit: nonlinear least-square minimization and curve-fitting for python, Astrophysics Source Code Library ascl-1606 (2016).

[45] J. Ngiam, A. Khosla, M. Kim, J. Nam, H. Lee, A.Y. Ng, Multimodal deep learning, in: The 28th International Conference on Machine Learning, 2011.

[46] S. Parisot, S.I. Ktena, E. Ferrante, M. Lee, R. Guerrero, B. Glocker, D. Rueckert, Disease prediction using graph convolutional networks: application to autism spectrum disorder and Alzheimer's disease, Medical Image Analysis 48 (2018) 117–130.

[47] M. Peifer, J. Timmer, Parameter estimation in ordinary differential equations for biochemical processes using the method of multiple shooting, IET Systems Biology 1 (2) (2007) 78–88.

[48] W. Penny, K. Friston, J. Ashburner, S. Kiebel, T. Nichols, Statistical Parametric Mapping: the Analysis of Functional Brain Images, Elsevier, 2011.

[49] M. Plitt, K. Barnes, G. Wallace, L. Kenworthy, A. Martin, Resting-state functional connectivity predicts longitudinal change in autistic traits and adaptive functioning in autism, Proceedings of the National Academy of Sciences 112 (48) (2015) E6699–E6706.

[50] L. Pontryagin, Mathematical Theory of Optimal Processes, CRC Press, 2018.

[51] R.H. Pruim, M. Mennes, D. van Rooij, A. Llera, J.K. Buitelaar, C.F. Beckmann, ICA-AROMA: a robust ICA-based strategy for removing motion artifacts from fMRI data, NeuroImage 112 (2015) 267–277.

[52] M.S. Salman, Y. Du, D. Lin, Z. Fu, A. Fedorov, E. Damaraju, J. Sui, J. Chen, A.R. Mayer, S. Posse, et al., Group ica for identifying biomarkers in schizophrenia: 'adaptive' networks via spatially constrained ica show more sensitivity to group differences than spatio-temporal regression, NeuroImage: Clinical 22 (2019) 101747.

[53] M. Schlichtkrull, T.N. Kipf, P. Bloem, R. Van Den Berg, I. Titov, M. Welling, Modeling relational data with graph convolutional networks, in: European Semantic Web Conference, Springer, 2018, pp. 593–607.

[54] M.L. Seghier, P. Zeidman, A.P. Leff, C. Price, Identifying abnormal connectivity in patients using dynamic causal modelling of fmri responses, Frontiers in Neuroscience (2010).

[55] N. Tzourio-Mazoyer, B. Landeau, D. Papathanassiou, F. Crivello, O. Etard, et al., Automated anatomical labeling of activations in spm using a macroscopic anatomical parcellation of the mni mri single-subject brain, NeuroImage (2002).

[56] M.P. Van Den Heuvel, H.E.H. Pol, Exploring the brain network: a review on resting-state fmri functional connectivity, European Neuropsychopharmacology (2010).

[57] P. Veličković, G. Cucurull, A. Casanova, A. Romero, P. Lio, Y. Bengio, Graph attention networks, in: International Conference on Learning Representations (ICLR), 2018.

[58] A. Venkataraman, D. Yang, K. Pelphrey, J. Duncan, Bayesian community detection in the space of group-level functional differences, IEEE Transactions on Medical Imaging 35 (8) (2016) 1866–1881.

[59] P. Ventola, H. Friedman, L. Anderson, J. Wolf, D. Oosting, J. Foss-Feig, N. McDonald, F. Volkmar, K. Pelphrey, Improvements in social and adaptive functioning following short-duration PRT program: a clinical replication, Journal of Autism and Developmental Disorders 44 (11) (2014) 2862–2870.

[60] V. Volterra, Variations and fluctuations of the number of individuals in animal species living together, ICES Journal of Marine Science 3 (1928).

[61] U. Von Luxburg, A tutorial on spectral clustering, Statistics and Computing 17 (4) (2007) 395–416.

[62] L. Wang, K. Li, X.P. Hu, Graph convolutional network for fMRI analysis based on connectivity neighborhood, Network Neuroscience 5 (1) (2021) 83–95.

[63] C.-Y. Wee, P.-T. Yap, D. Shen, Diagnosis of autism spectrum disorders using temporally distinct resting-state functional connectivity networks, CNS Neuroscience & Therapeutics 22 (3) (March 2016) 212–219.

[64] J. Zhuang, N. Dvornek, X. Li, S. Tatikonda, X. Papademetris, J. Duncan, Adaptive checkpoint adjoint for gradient estimation in neural ODE, in: ICML, 2020.

[65] J. Zhuang, N.C. Dvornek, X. Li, S. Tatikonda, X. Papademetris, J. Duncan, Adaptive checkpoint adjoint method for gradient estimation in neural ODE, in: Proceedings of the 37th International Conference on Machine Learning, vol. PLMR 119, 2020, pp. 11639–11649.

[66] J. Zhuang, N.C. Dvornek, X. Li, P. Ventola, J.S. Duncan, Invertible network for classification and biomarker selection for asd, in: MICCAI, 2019.

[67] J. Zhuang, T. Tang, Y. Ding, S.C. Tatikonda, N. Dvornek, X. Papademetris, J. Duncan, Adabelief optimizer: adapting stepsizes by the belief in observed gradients, in: NeurIPS, 2020.

Deep learning in functional brain mapping and associated applications

Ning Qiang[a], Qinglin Dong[b], Heng Huang[c], Han Wang[d], Shijie Zhao[e], Xintao Hu[e], Qing Li[f], Wei Zhang[g], Yiheng Liu[a], Mengshen He[a], Bao Ge[a], Lin Zhao[b], Zihao Wu[b], Lu Zhang[h], Steven Xu[b], Dajiang Zhu[h], Xi Jiang[i], and Tianming Liu[b]

[a]School of Physics and Information Technology, Shaanxi Normal University, Xi'an, China
[b]Cortical Architecture Imaging and Discovery Lab, School of Computing, The University of Georgia, Athens, GA, United States
[c]College of Mathematical Medicine, Zhejiang Normal University, Jinhua, China
[d]College of Biomedical Engineering and Instrument Science, Zhejiang University, Hangzhou, China
[e]School of Automation, Northwestern Polytechnical University, Xi'an, China
[f]State Key Laboratory of Cognitive Neuroscience and Learning, Beijing Normal University, Beijing, China
[g]School of Computer and Cyber Sciences, Augusta University, Augusta, GA, United States
[h]Computer Science and Engineering, University of Texas at Arlington, Arlington, TX, United States
[i]MOE Key Lab for Neuroinformation, School of Life Science and Technology, University of Electronic Science and Technology of China, Chengdu, China

14.1 Introduction

The human brain is the most complex part of the human nervous system. Hundreds of billions of neurons are connected through synapses and form a highly complex brain network, which is the physiological basis for brain information processing and cognitive expression. As one of the most popular noninvasive brain imaging techniques, functional magnetic resonance imaging (fMRI) has been studied for decades to reveal the functional architecture of the human brain, based on measuring blood oxygenation level dependent (BOLD) of each voxel in the brain space. By revealing the synchronization of distant neural systems via correlations in neurophysiological measures of brain activity, functional brain networks (FBN) have been considered as fundamental, organizational elements of human brain architecture [1,2]. The brain regions in a specific FBN have similar temporal patterns. Thus the original 4-dimensional fMRI can be decomposed into temporal and spatial features (FBNs). To understand the mapping of mind and brain, learning brain representation from fMRI, both temporal features and spatial features, has been under extensive active research in the past decade.

In previous studies, researchers have proposed a variety of computational methods and tools for brain network mapping, such as the general linear model (GLM) [3,4], independent component analysis (ICA) [5–8], and sparse dictionary learning (SDL) [9–11]. Among these methods, GLM is widely known in task-based fMRI data analysis, and ICA is dominant in resting-state fMRI data analysis. SDL has also been widely used in modeling both task-based fMRI data and resting-state fMRI data. Although many meaningful results have been achieved by these methods, they are still limited by some assumptions, such as the linear superposition hypothesis and independence hypothesis. Besides, other machine learning methods such as partial least squares regression (PLS) [12], support vector machines (SVM) and principal component analysis (PCA) [13] have also been successfully applied to fMRI analysis [14].

Recently, deep learning has attracted much attention in the fields of fMRI, and there have been growing research studies that applied deep learning to fMRI modeling and associated applications. A deep learning model is a multi-layer neural network that is stacked by multiple similar building blocks. The input layer receives the original data then passes the transformed data to hidden layers, and finally to the output layer. As a result, the deep learning model acts as a hierarchical feature extractor with the power of mining more latent resources from low-level data. In the field of fMRI, deep learning models can extract hierarchical temporal features and spatial features (FBNs), which may contain more potential information than traditional shallow models. In the last decade, researchers have proposed various deep learning models that were applied to fMRI, such as deep belief networks (DBN) [15–17], convolutional neural networks (CNN) [18,19], recurrent neural networks (RNN) [20–23], variational auto-encoders (VAE) [22,24–26], graph neural networks (GNN) [27], attention neural networks [27,28] and transfer learning. However, there are still some challenges to be addressed. The first one is the overfitting problem. As widely known, the training of deep learning models depends on sufficient data, especially training on the fMRI volumes, which contain a large number of voxels. Considering the tremendous dimension of fMRI volumes, most fMRI data sets are not big enough, especially some brain disorder data sets. To cope with the challenge of insufficient data, generative models such as variational auto-encoder (VAE) and generative adversarial net (GAN) are proposed to generate synthetic data in the field of natural images. However, their powerful ability of feature extraction is still overlooked. The second one is the lack of high-quality labels. The fMRI data is weakly-supervised since the psychological label is coarse-grained and no framewise label is given, in addition to the complex co-activities of multiple FBNs. Thus unsupervised or self-supervised architectures of deep learning are desired. The third one is the spatio-temporal modeling of fMRI. The original 4D fMRI data contains complex and rich information in both brain 3D space and time series of each voxel. Although recurrent neural networks and attention networks have been successfully applied for the spatio-temporal modeling of fMRI, it is still challenging to simultaneously model the spatial and temporal features of fMRI. The fourth one is the neural architecture search of deep learning models. It has been shown that deep neural networks are powerful and flexible models that can be applied to fMRI data with superb representation ability over traditional methods. However, a challenge of neural network architecture design has also attracted attention: due to the high dimension of fMRI volume images, the manual process of network model design is very time-consuming and not optimal. Although many existing NAS methods can learn network architectures that outperform manual designs, most of them were designed for image classification problems, which usually have high-quality labels. The fifth one represents the regularity and variability of different brains under different conditions. The organization of brain function and its structural substrate, such as cortical folding pattern and the neuronal connections, vary drastically across populations while still demonstrating the homogeneity. How to effectively represent both regularity and variability of different brains from fMRI is still a challenging problem. The last one is developing effective multi-modal fusion methods to integrate multiple types of network connectome. Multi-modal fusion of different types of neural image data provides an irreplaceable opportunity to take advantages of complementary cross-modal information that may only partially be contained in single modality. However, because of the intrinsic complex relations of brain networks, how to effectively incorporate multi-modal brain networks remains an open question.

This chapter presents a comprehensive review of deep learning models for mapping functional brain activity and associated applications and provides new perspectives and future directions.

14.2 Deep learning models for mapping functional brain networks

14.2.1 Convolutional auto-encoder (CAE)

Among all available deep learning models, the convolutional neural network (CNN) is one of the most popular methods. CNN has been successfully used for hierarchical feature extraction in natural image data. CNN is a variant of the feed-forward artificial neural network, and its connectivities between layers are inspired by the cat's visual cortex. A recent study on neuroimaging data found similar structures in human brains, which suggested that CNN might be naturally suitable for modeling fMRI data.

Fig. 14.1 shows the deep convolutional auto-encoder (DCAE) for modeling tfMRI time series data. The DCAE model consists of two main components, the encoder and the decoder, to model tfMRI time series data hierarchically. Specifically, after data pre-processing, the whole-brain tfMRI signals in each subject are extracted and normalized (with zero mean and standard deviation). For each voxel's signal, the encoder represents it as mid-level and high-level feature maps as the layer goes deeper, and then the decoder decodes these feature maps layer by layer, and finally reconstructs the original signal at its last layer. The objective of the DCAE is to minimize

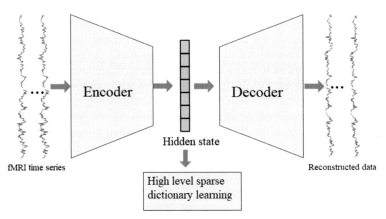

FIGURE 14.1

Illustration of the DCAE structure.

the reconstruction errors of the entire training data sets (voxels' signals from multiple subjects), and the whole training process is completely unsupervised. The DCAE encoder is responsible for mapping the input fMRI time series into higher-level feature maps, and the decoder does the opposite reconstruction work. The rectified nonlinearity unit (Relu) was used as the activation function. The Relu activation function first reduces the possibility of a vanishing gradient (which will most likely happen when the model is deep). Then it interprets the representation in a more neuroscientifically meaningful way given its intrinsic sparse representation. There are one-dimensional convolutional layers and fully-connected layers in both the encoder and decoder. The fully connected layer is used to keep the final hidden state in the encoder to have the same feature size as the input, and at the same time to ensure that the hidden states are learned with a full receptive field of the input (the hidden states will be used to perform the high-level dictionary learning in validation studies). When the DCAE model goes deeper (with more convolutional layers connected to previous layers), the computation pipeline is the same as its shallow form. The difference is that when there are more than one convolutional layer, the input will be transformed by different convolutional layers into different feature maps by a chain rule. The parameters in the whole DCAE are optimized to minimize the mean square error between fMRI signals and their reconstructions. It should be noted that an additional L2 regularization term between feature maps in the encoder and decoder is added to the cost function, which ensures that the fully connected layer does not randomly shuffle the timing order when reconstructing feature maps in the decoder.

This work proposes a novel deep convolutional autoencoder (DCAE) that hierarchically models tfMRI time series data in an unsupervised manner [18]. The HCP motor task fMRI data was used as a testing bed in this study, and the experiments showed promising results, which are summarized as three interesting observations. 1) By visualizing the DCAE model, the feature maps gain a higher-level abstraction of the tfMRI signal along with the model depth increasing. 2) By using theoretical models of brain responses, the feature maps are not randomly generated, and the depth greatly influences the chance to find these theoretical models. 3) The comparison study of shallow sparse dictionary learning and high-level dictionary learning showed that the high-level features are superior in task-related regions detection. At the same time, more intrinsic networks can be detected compared to traditional shallow sparse dictionary learning. Furthermore, spatial distributions of theoretical models in the human brain were investigated. The results showed that the average fMRI signals are highly correlated with theoretical models of brain responses. Through the experiment results, the time shift phenomenon is confirmed and the DCAE has a better performance compared to traditional shallow methods in interpreting rich and diverse neural activities. The investigation of spatial maps further confirmed the powerful feature learning ability of DCAE. Finally, the DCAE was evaluated in discriminating the AD patient from normal based on resting state fMRI data. The results showed the powerful ability of DCAE in modeling resting state fMRI data, in addition to task fMRI data, by extracting descriptive and discriminative features. After the unsupervised training of the DCAE model, each filter represents one kind of local time-series pattern in fMRI signals. If two voxels' (or regions') signals have the same or similar activations (feature maps) on the filter, this means these two voxels have the same or similar local patterns, and they are correlated in time series. In other words, they have dynamic functional connectivity. In DCAE, the lower layer has restricted receptive fields (restricted by filter length or "window size"), thus the lower layer captures the functional connectivity pattern in a smaller window size. As the depth increases, the higher layer will have larger receptive fields (due to the max pooling), and thus capture the high-level functional connectivity pattern based on the low-level activations (feature maps). In this aspect, the whole DCAE model would act as a hierarchical, dynamical, functional, connectivity extractor. In general, this work contributes a novel deep convolution autoencoder framework for fMRI data modeling with significant application potentials in cognitive and clinical neuroscience in the future.

The DCAE is an early attempt of using deep learning to model functional brain activity. However, it models fMRI time series, not volumes. The auto-encoder framework of DCAE inspired a lot of later works and constantly improved the deep learning models of fMRI based on the auto-encoder framework.

14.2.2 Recurrent neural network (RNN)

In previous studies, it was assumed that the brain networks and activation patterns/states are temporally stationary across the entire fMRI scan session. However, there is accumulating evidence indicating that brain activities and states are under dramatic temporal changes at various time scales. For instance, it has been found that each cortical brain area runs different "programs" according to the cognitive context and the current perceptual requirements, and the intrinsic cortical circuits mediate the moment-by-moment functional state changes in the brain. That is, in the brain's dynamic functional process, parts of the brain engage and disengage in time, allowing a person to perceive objects or scenes, and separate remembered parts of an experience, and bind them all together into a coherent whole. What's more, it is still under dynamic changes even in a resting state within time scales of seconds to minutes. Inspired by these observations, more and more researchers are motivated to examine the temporal dynamics of functional brain activities.

Currently, a dominant analysis technique used for describing the temporal dynamics of functional brain activities is the use of sliding windows. Sliding window-based approaches pre-specify the temporal resolution of the changing pattern (window size), map the spatial distribution of the networks and provide measures of dependence, e.g., linear correlation between the time course for an interested pair of voxels, regions or networks. These methods range from windowed versions of standard seed-based correlation or independent component analysis (ICA) techniques to new methods that consider information from individual time points. In addition to sliding window approaches, researchers also tried some alternative methods over the past few years. For instance, change point detection methods have been proposed to determine "brain state" changes based on the properties of data-driven partitioned resting state fMRI (rs-fMRI) data, such as amplitude and covariance of time series. In contrast to methods based on relationships between brain regions, event-based approaches assume that brain activity is primarily composed of distinct events, and these events can be deciphered from the BOLD fluctuations or through deconvolution of a given hemodynamic model from the time series. In general, these approaches have enriched the description of functional brain activities and contributed to a better understanding of the temporal dynamics underlying brain activities.

In this section, we introduce the earliest recurrent neural network that applied to fMRI: deep sparse recurrent neural network (DSRNN) [23]. Inspired by the great ability in modeling the temporal dependence of sequential data using RNN models, the deep sparse recurrent neural network (DSRNN) was designed to recognize the dynamical brain states at fast time-scales in tfMRI data. Briefly, the DSRNN model includes an input layer, one fully-connected layer, two recurrent layers and a softmax output layer.

Fig. 14.2 shows the overview of the DSRNN model. Adjacent layers are fully connected, and the connections between layers are forward. The fully connected layer plays a role as a filter of activated brain regions, which aims to winnow and combine significant fMRI volumes with proper weight values. Then two recurrent layers are employed following the same structure, as shown in Fig. 14.2, so that various scales of temporal dependences can be captured. The hidden state of the second recurrent layer is defined similar to that of the first recurrent layer, except for replacing the input with the hidden state of the first layer. Finally, a softmax layer is applied to obtain a vector of class probabilities. The DSRNN model can accurately identify the brain's state in different task fMRI data sets and significantly outperforms other auto-correlation methods or nontemporal approaches in dynamic brain state recognition accuracy. With the outstanding capability of capturing sequence temporal dependence, the DSRNN can recognize brain states accurately. In addition, the associated brain-activated regions also demonstrate meaningful correspondence with

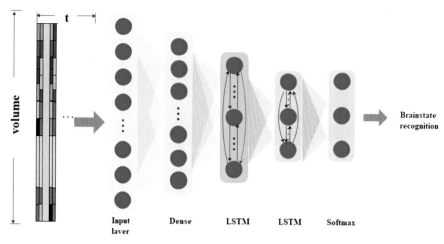

FIGURE 14.2

DSRNN model for brain state recognition.

traditional GLM activation results, which provide us novel insight on functional brain activities. Compared with the common auto-correlation modeling method and traditional nontemporal modeling approaches (Softmax and SVM), the DSRNN achieved obviously outstanding recognition accuracy. Though the current DSRNN model has achieved excellent performances in brain state recognition accuracy, it still can be developed in a few aspects. First, although the fully connected layer applied in DSRNN extracted distinctive activated brain regions successfully, there are many other neural network structures, such as CNN, DBN, etc., to be further revisited. These models are also widely used in computer vision and feature extraction and have more complicated structures than fully connected layers. Better performance might be achieved if these models are employed. Second, we recognize the brain states of every single task and obtained seven different state recognition models. Each model can identify subtasks or brain states of only one category of task. In the future, we can train one DSRNN model with all seven tasks. In this way, more distinctive activation maps and more differences can be obtained among tasks. Third, as a proposal, the DSRNN model might be applied online in the future. Because once the DSRNN model is trained successfully, real-time tfMRI data time series can be fed online and the brain behaviors can be detected in quite a short time. This application can be used widely as a brain states identifier. Finally, there are several potential applications in basic neuroscience and clinical research with the proposed DSRNN model. For instance, it has been observed that dynamic performance can be sensitive to psychiatric or neurologic disorders, and the associated brain areas in brain state recognition may provide novel insight for clinical diagnosis. Besides, many works of literature suggest that brain activities and states are under dynamic changes and the proposed model provides a useful tool to recognize the brain states at a fast time scale in task fMRI data. In general, the DSRNN model offers a new methodology for basic and clinical neuroscience research.

The DSRNN is an early recurrent neural network applied to the brain imaging field, which inspired some later works using modified RNNs, such as deep sparse recurrent auto-encoder (DSRAE), and deep recurrent variational auto-encoder (DR-VAE).

14.2.3 Deep belief network (DBN)

Prior studies of using deep learning models for fMRI data analysis, such as CNN/RBM/RNN [16–18,28–34], have exhibited great promises; however, it has rarely examined whether/how to infer and reconstruct hierarchical brain networks from volumetric fMRI data directly using deep learning models such as deep belief networks (DBN). A major advantage of using DBN for fMRI data modeling is that DBN can naturally represent the hierarchical patterns of FBNs in an unsupervised manner. Theoretically, unsupervised learning via DBN has solid interpretability based on maximizing likelihood estimation rather than minimizing the reconstruction error, which makes DBN attractive. However, the perceived difficulties of developing DBN models for fMRI data include a very large number of input variables (e.g., the hundreds of thousands of volumetric image intensities), a very large number of training parameters (e.g., millions of DBN weights), the lack of effective software tools (e.g., there is no TensorFlow implementation of DBN), the challenge of results interpretation (e.g., many volumetric brain network maps in multiple layers), etc. To bridge these technical and knowledge gaps, a novel volumetric sparse deep belief network (VS-DBN) model [15] was proposed and implemented based on the popular TensorFlow open-source platform and applied it on the Human Connectome Project (HCP) 900 subjects release. Our extensive experimental results have shown that a large number of meaningful FBNs can be robustly reconstructed from HCP 900 subjects in a hierarchical fashion, and importantly, these reconstructed networks can be well interpreted based on current neuroscience knowledge. Interestingly, these reconstructed brain networks by DBN exhibit reasonably good consistency and correspondence across multiple HCP task-based fMRI (tfMRI) data sets, suggesting a possible common functional organization architecture of the brain. In general, our works contributed a general DBN deep learning framework for inferring volumetric brain networks and offered new insights into the hierarchical functional organization architecture of the brain. The source codes and models of VS-DBN are available and released at: https://github.com/QinglinDong/vsDBN.

Fig. 14.3 illustrates the representing hierarchical structures of brain networks in tfMRI data by VS-DBN. First, preprocessed fMRI data were temporally concatenated in a spatial fashion for input. Each fMRI volume data was treated as a single training sample for VS-DBN. Second, the VS-DBN with 3 layers was trained with volumes, and each layer has 100 hidden nodes. Third, the weights of each layer in the trained VS-DBN were considered brain networks and visualized in the standard brain space.

Restricted Boltzmann Machines (RBMs) are generative models that approximate a closed-form representation of the underlying probability distribution of the training

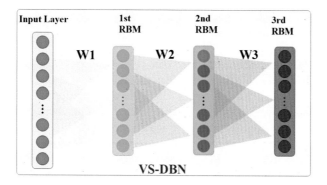

FIGURE 14.3

Illustration of representing hierarchical structures of brain networks in tfMRI data by VS-DBN.

data. RBMs can also be interpreted as deterministic feed-forward neural networks, and they are widely used as the building blocks of Deep Belief Nets (DBNs). RBMs consist of an input layer of visible variables $v_i \in R$ and a hidden layer of latent variables $h_i \in R$. Given the observed data, RBMs can model the dependencies of a set of visible variables v_i and a set of hidden variables h_i over the set of observed data. The sparse weight regularization works by causing most of the weights to become zero while allowing a few of the weights to grow large. As shown in Fig. 14.3, a DBN model consisting of 3 RBM with weight regularization was built in a spatial fashion, by taking tfMRI volumes as input. In the context of fMRI data, L1 regularization can denoise the FBNs and improve interpretability by suppressing useless weights and allowing important model parameters to become larger, which is considered an important methodology contribution of this work.

With respect to interpreting a trained VS-DBN in an fMRI context, each row of weight vector was mapped back into the original 3D brain image space, which was the inverse operation of masking in preprocessing steps and was interpreted as an FBN. After the DBN was trained layerwisely on a large-scale tfMRI data set, the trained weights modeled a feature representation with the latent variables in the hidden nodes, thus yielding interpretable FBNs. Each weight showed the dependency of each voxel with a latent variable. For deeper layers, the linear combination approach was used to interpret the connection. With this approach, W_1 was visualized for the first hidden layer as FBNs, $W_2 \times W_1$ for the second layer and $W_3 \times W_2 \times W_1$ for the third layer, respectively. Here, a groupwise scheme of VS-DBN was proposed to model fMRI data. Considering the large inter-subject variability among human brains, arbitrary selection of a single individual may not effectively represent the population, thus a groupwise learning scheme was needed to reduce inter-subject variability by jointly registering the volumes to a common reference template corresponding to the group average. Due to the wide individual variation of the human brain, the arbitrary selection of a single individual may not truly represent the population. In this work, a groupwise learning scheme was used to reduce biases by jointly registering the volumes to a common reference corresponding to the group average.

We designed and implemented the VS-DBN model and exploited its capability of a hierarchical representation of tfMRI data. With a groupwise experiment on massive HCP tfMRI data, the VS-DBN model quantitatively and qualitatively showed its promising capability of learning functional networks under a hierarchical structure. A comparison study using GLM validated that the functional networks learned by VS-DBN are meaningful and can be well interpreted. With networks at higher levels in the VS-DBN structure, the activated brain regions in a functional network tend to be larger and the patterns are more global involving both task-common and task-specific regions. It is inspiring that we observed some low-level task-related networks merging into one global task-related network layer, which indeed suggested the hierarchical architecture of FBNs. Also, the results on all 7 HCP task fMRI data sets show that different tasks exhibit a variety of common low-level FBNs to perform some basic core task-common functions, while high-level FBNs perform higher-level task-specific functions.

The VS-DBN is among the earliest attempts that uses deep learning to model fMRI volumes. It used network weights as hierarchical functional brain networks.

14.2.4 Variational auto-encoder (VAE)

Despite the fact that spatial deep learning models can effectively mapping functional brain networks from fMRI, there still exist at least two challenges. The first challenge is overfitting caused by data paucity. The application of deep learning (DL) models to the modeling of fMRI data are often hindered by the small sample size and high dimensionality of these data sets. The number of data dimensions far exceeding the number of data samples often yields serious overfitting issues in both deep learning models and traditional machine learning models. Especially, in clinical settings, the patient data often have hundreds of samples or volumes and several hundred thousand voxels in each volume. The second challenge is the lack of high-quality labels. Training supervised deep learning models requires large-scale labeled data sets. However, labels are often unavailable in fMRI blind source separation, due to the psychological label is usually coarse-grained and it is impossible to label the fMRI frames in a biologically meaningful way, in addition to the complex co-activities of multiple FBNs. Therefore, unsupervised deep learning models are naturally desirable. To deal with these challenges, deep generative learning models, such as the variational auto encoder (VAE) and generative adversarial network (GAN) have been applied to generate synthetic biomedical images. However, their powerful ability to learn representation from small data sets is still overlooked.

To bridge this gap to some extent, a deep recurrent variational auto-encoder (DR-VAE) [22] pipeline was proposed and designed to model FBNs from rfMRI data, as shown in Fig. 14.4. The DRVAE model can effectively overcome overfitting and capture more generative features of high-dimension fMRI data, which may solve the challenge of data paucity. The encoder-to-decoder framework makes the DRVAE a complete unsupervised model, without the need for any labels. As a typical generative model, DRVAE has the intrinsic capability of overcoming overfitting on small sites and is computationally tractable and scalable to high-dimensional data. The central computational challenge in fitting the models is approximating the posterior distribution $q(Z|X)$ over the latent variables z that are generated by input data x. The exact posterior inference is intractable, so the model is fitted with variational inference, which approximates the intractable posterior with a distribution q from some tractable family. In the context of rfMRI, an approximate posterior over the latent variables (encoder of DRVAE) is a physiological representation of fMRI volumes, which can be interpreted as a set of FBNs. The latent variables z extracted by DRVAE can be regarded as high-level features, which correspond to dictionaries of SDL. We applied Lasso regression on high-level features and input fMRI data to estimate a sparse coefficient matrix, which can be mapped back to the 3D brain space, forming a set of functional brain networks. The recurrent layers (LSTM) were introduced to the VAE to better model the temporal dynamics of fMRI. The DRVAE contains eight layers, which the first four layers are encoding layers, that model the probability distribution $q(z|x)$, and the last four layers are decoding layers that model the probability distribution $p(x|z)$. The latent variables are yielded by sampling from $q(x)$. The values μ and σ represent the mean and variance of input data, which are learned by the encoder. The six hidden layers include two fully connected layers (Dense) and four LSTM layers. The numbers of neurons are shown at the bottom of the layers.

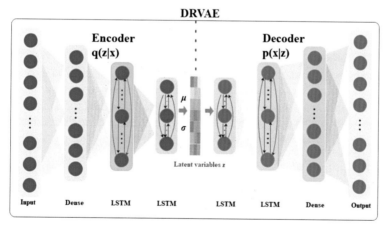

FIGURE 14.4

Illustration of DRVAE architecture.

We constructed a DRVAE and LASSO framework for learning meaningful temporal features and spatial networks from volumetric fMRI. Moreover, the DRVAE can generate high-quality fake data and potentially improve the classification accuracy on rfMRI data sets of brain disorders. The DRVAE model was trained on reorganized 2D fMRI data with the goal of generating similar outputs as the same distribution of inputs. After training, the encoder of DRVAE can be regarded as a high-level feature extractor, which can extract temporal features from a single subject or groupwise data. Then we applied LASSO regression on test fMRI data and temporal features to estimate a sparse coefficient matrix, which can be mapped back to the original brain space and visualized as FBNs. The experimental results showed the effectiveness and superiority of the DRVAE in deriving meaningful and interpretable temporal features and FBNs, by taking GLM-activated networks and task designs as benchmarks. We also found that the temporal features and FBNs from groupwise data are more stable and meaningful compared to those from a single subject, which may be due to that the brain activities obey a certain distribution. For fMRI data augmentation, the results on tfMRI data sets showed that the fake data generated by DRVAE can also be used to learn meaningful temporal features and spatial networks. Moreover, it is shown that the classification performance has been considerably improved on four rfMRI data sets from ADHD-200 after data augmentation, further demonstrating the effectiveness of the proposed DRVAE in fMRI modeling and augmenting.

The variational auto-encoder (VAE) has been proven to be effective in modeling fMRI, especially on small data sets. However, the VAE makes a presumption of the Gaussian distribution of fMRI data, which may not be consistent with the real distribution of fMRI.

14.2.5 Generative adversarial net (GAN)

To cope with the challenge of insufficient data, generative models such as variational autoencoder (VAE) and generative adversarial net (GAN) are proposed to generate synthetic data in the field of natural images. In this section, we introduce a novel Recurrent Wasserstein Generative Adversarial Net (RWGAN) [29] for learning brain representation. A standard GAN is usually hard to train. Thus the Wasserstein distance was used to measure the reconstruction error, aiming to improve the training efficiency. The RWGAN consists of two parts: a generator and a discriminator. The generator generates fake fMRI data using random noise, and the discriminator identifies differences between real data and fake data. Both generator and discriminator are stacked by fully-connected layers and recurrent layers. The introduction of the recurrent layer is for better capturing the local features on the fMRI time series. If the model is trained well, the generator can generate high-quality fake data with the same distribution as real data. Thus the discriminator cannot distinguish the input real and fake data, since it extracts similar generalized features from real and fake data. Then the discriminator can be regarded as a deep feature extractor, and high-level temporal features can be yielded from the discriminator. With LASSO (least absolute shrinkage and selection operator) regression, the input data can be decomposed into temporal features and sparse coefficient matrix, which can be mapped back to 3D brain space and visualized as FBNs, or called spatial features. The RWGAN can address the above-mentioned two challenges of deep learning models in fMRI analysis. First, as a generative model, the RWGAN can learn the distribution of the input data, which enables the extraction of generalized features from fMRI, and thus relieves the overfitting problem, and makes it easy to apply the model on other fMRI data sets without complete retraining. Second, the RWGAN is a data-driven model, and its training process is in an unsupervised manner without the need for any labels.

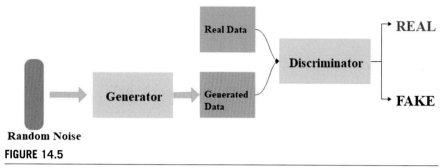

FIGURE 14.5

Illustration of the RWGAN.

Fig. 14.5 summarizes the proposed RWGAN. The RWGAN consists of two parts: a generator and a discriminator. After pre-processing and masking, the 4D fMRI data is converted to a 2D groupwise matrix. Then the RWGAN model is trained in an unsupervised manner, aiming to generate high-quality fake fMRI data compared to real fMRI data, and the discriminator cannot distinguish them. After training, the generator can generate fake data for fMRI data augmentation, and the discriminator can be regarded as a high-level feature extractor. As a deep learning model, the discriminator of RWGAN has three hidden layers. Thus the trained discriminator can extract hierarchical temporal features from each layer. In our previous works, we have studied hierarchical brain representation learned by deep learning models. But in this work, we focus on learning brain representation and generating new fMRI by the RWGAN. Thus we only studied the temporal features from the last hidden layer. To decompose the input data into temporal patterns and spatial patterns, then LASSO regression was applied on input data and temporal patterns to achieve a sparse coefficient matrix, which can be mapped back to 3D brain space (inverse operation of masking) and visualized as functional brain networks (FBNs).

This work proposed a novel recurrent Wasserstein generative adversarial net (RWGAN) framework to map functional brain networks from volumetric fMRI. After training, the discriminator of RWGAN can be regarded as a feature extractor that can extract temporal features from new inputs without the need for retraining. Then LASSO regression was applied to inputs and temporal features to estimate functional brain networks. As a generative model, the RWGAN can extract more generalized features than discriminative models, which may help relieve the overfitting problem. The introduction of recurrent layers in RWGAN is for better modeling the local features on time series. The experimental results demonstrated the effectiveness of the proposed RWGAN in deriving meaningful temporal and spatial features from fMRI, compared with traditional models and recent deep learning models. Furthermore, it is shown that the RWGAN performed better on small training data sets than other deep-learning models. Besides, the generator of RWGAN can generate high-quality fake fMRI data that can also be used to learn meaningful brain representation.

The RWGAN model is another generative model without the presumption of the specific distribution of data. It cannot only derive meaningful functional brain networks from fMRI but also generate fake fMRI data.

14.3 Spatio-temporal models of fMRI

14.3.1 Deep sparse recurrent auto-encoder (DSRAE)

Exploring the spatial patterns and temporal dynamics of human brain activity has been of great interest, in the quest to better understand connectome-scale brain networks. Though modeling spatial and temporal patterns of functional brain networks have been researched for a long time, the development of a unified and simultaneous spatial-temporal model has yet to be realized. For instance, although some deep learning methods have been proposed recently in order to model functional brain networks, most of them can only represent either spatial or temporal perspective of functional Magnetic Resonance Imaging (fMRI) data and rarely model both domains simultaneously.

Recently, sequential auto-encoders for brain decoding are successfully applied to connectome-scale spatial-temporal brain network decomposition from 4D fMRI data simultaneously. Here, we take the deep sparse recurrent auto-encoder (DSRAE) [21], which is used as an unsupervised way to learn spatial patterns and temporal fluctuations of brain networks at the same time, as a specific example. The DSRAE model makes use of both spatial and temporal information that is a deep unsupervised sequential neural network framework with two parts: encoder and decoder. Based on the architecture of DSRAE, the spatial-temporal brain network would derive from the latent layer of DSRAE. We assumed that the different participants would have different cognitive levels that would prove the model's effectiveness and robustness and assumed that the same participant would pay the same attention during different tasks, which would be a special criterion for the generalization capability. The results with DSRAE have shown consistently good performance in terms of inferring and characterizing both task-evoked and spontaneous brain networks at the connectome scale, demonstrating that the DSRAE model is effective and robust.

To examine what functional state the brain is in during the task period more specifically, it is a common way to investigate the correlation of the input fMRI volumetric data and the learned feature networks via Pearson correlation. It is a kind of representational similarity analysis method to measure how well the learned network map represents the original fMRI volume image. Via the brain state decoding tool based on DSRAE, some volumes have high positive correlations or negative correlations with some networks, which suggests that the brain would be in such certain states at those time points. However, some volumes have low correlations with all networks, mainly during the task transition periods, which might indicate that the brain stays in multiple states at the same time. For example, from the correlation matrix, some networks have a negative or positive correlation with the cue stimulations, respectively. Especially, the default mode network (DMN) has high positive relevance with the cue period, which is evidence that DMN could be suppressed during task stimuli. In general, the DSRAE model has revealed interesting patterns of spatial-temporal brain network dynamics that warrant future interpretation studies.

14.3.2 Spatio-temporal attention auto-encoder (STAAE)

It has been of great interest in the neuroimaging community to model spatio-temporal brain function and related disorders based on functional magnetic resonance imaging (fMRI). Although a variety of deep learning models have been proposed for modeling fMRI, the dominant models are limited in capturing the long-distance dependency (LDD) due to their sequential nature. In this section, we introduce a spatio-temporal attention auto-encoder (STAAE) [28] to discover global features that address LDDs in volumetric rfMRI. The unsupervised STAAE framework can spatio-temporally model the rfMRI sequence and decompose the rfMRI into spatial and temporal patterns. In respect of sequence modeling, especially high-dimension spatio-temporal sequence data like fMRI, both CNNs and RNNs have been used in the field. To utilize the CNN's hierarchical feature abstraction ability, a 1-D temporal convolution architecture was applied to the fMRI time series. This approach can extract local temporal features; however, it cannot deal with the LDDs due to the distance limit. In addition, it did not make use of the rich spatial information from fMRI. To incorporate the spatial and temporal information at the same time, a recurrent network was applied to the fMRI volumes and preserving temporal features with long short-term memory (LSTM), which is a typical recurrent module. This approach established a unified spatio-temporal framework. However, the inherently sequential nature of RNN/LSTM precludes parallelization, which causes notable time costs, especially for high-dimension data like fMRI. In addition, the long scan time of fMRI imposes a great burden on computing and memory resources, and a long memory unit of LSTM may cause a gradient vanishing problem.

In this section, we introduce an auto-encoder framework with an attention mechanism, named spatio-temporal attention auto-encoder (STAAE) to model global features in rfMRI sequence. Most sequence models follow an encoder $= -$decoder paradigm, and we also adopted this structure to our proposed STAAE, considering the intrinsic unsupervised nature of rfMRI since no external stimulus or task is performed. The STAAE model consists of an encoder and a decoder. The encoder aims to extract high-level features, while the decoder aims to reconstruct the exact inputs. As shown in Fig. 14.6(a), the encoder maps an input volume sequence of symbol representations $X = (x_1, \ldots, x_t)$ to a sequence of latent vectors $Z = (z_1, \ldots, z_t)$. Specifically, each x_i represents a volume of rfMRI and is embedded with a fully connected network. Given Z, the decoder tries to generate a reconstructed sequence of $X' = (x'_1, \ldots, x'_t)$. There are two fully-connected hidden layers in both the encoder and the decoder. The number of nodes in each layer is shown on the right of the corresponding layer.

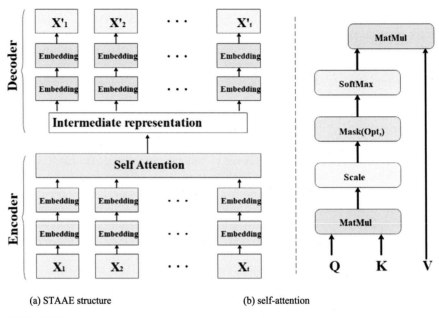

(a) STAAE structure   (b) self-attention

FIGURE 14.6

Structure of STAAE and illustration of self-attention mechanism. (a) STAAE structure. (b) Illustration of self-attention mechanism.

We applied the self-attention mechanism in STAAE to draw global dependencies in rfMRI by capturing the relation of two volumes in the sequence with an attention score measuring the distance of their embeddings. The self-attention mechanism consists of three matrices: queries Q, keys K, and values V, and they come from the same input. In the context of rfMRI, a key vector and a query vector are learned for each frame of volume, and the pairs of query-key are matched across all frames simultaneously. The output is computed as a weighted sum of the values, where the weight assigned to each value is computed by a compatibility function of the query with the corresponding key. If a pair of query-key matches, it generates a high value as output. As shown in Fig. 14.6(b), we compute each latent vector as

$$Z = Attention\,(Q, K, V)$$

$$= softmax\left(\frac{QK^T}{\sqrt{d}}\right) \cdot V \tag{14.1}$$

where d is a scale factor used to limit the attention matrix QK^T. The 3 matrices Q, K and V are calculated as follows:

$$Q = X \times W_Q \tag{14.2}$$

$$K = X \times W_K \tag{14.3}$$

$$V = X \times W_V \tag{14.4}$$

The three weight matrices W_Q, W_K and W_V are randomly initialized and updated in the training process. In one word, the STAAE model can attention to previous inputs by the attention score, thus the STAAE can model the fMRI data with sequence information.

With the attention mechanism, the STAAE becomes a spatio-temporal model that can simultaneously model the spatial and temporal features from volumetric rfMRI. As an unsupervised data-driven model, the STAAE can automatically capture meaningful temporal features that possibly represent cognitive or physiological variables under the resting state, and the corresponding spatial features (RSNs) may reflect related brain activities. If the model is trained well, that means the input rfMRI data is well reconstructed from the encoder to the decoder of STAAE. Thus the trained encoder can be regarded as a high-level feature extractor that can extract temporal features from rfMRI with sequence information.

Compared with other deep learning models that applied LSTM to model temporal dynamics of fMRI, the STAAE can capture global features in the fMRI series rather than local features, and there was no significant increase in the computing cost of the STAAE model. In recent years, attention network has become a popular model in spatio-temporal feature extraction of many applications.

14.3.3 Multi-head guided attention graph neural networks (multi-head GAGNNs)

Complex brain functional processes are realized by the interaction of multiple brain functional networks, all of which are spatially distributed in specific brain regions in a temporally dynamic manner. Therefore, modeling the spatio-temporal patterns of brain functional networks can help understand their functional mechanisms. However, the existing modeling methods have two limitations: (1) ignoring the overall networks in the whole brain and merely modeling a small number of ones; (2) the spatial and temporal characteristics of fMRI are not fully utilized in the network modeling process, and the model accuracy is therefore not guaranteed.

The proposed model [27] consists of two main parts: the "spatial part" (Multi-Head Attention Graph U-Net) and the "temporal part" (Multi-Head Guided Attention Network). Specifically, the "spatial part" adopted fMRI data as input and output spatial patterns of multiple targeted RSNs. This part is mainly based on the classical 3D U-Net with a down-sampling part and an up-sampling part. To better extract both spatial and temporal characteristics of fMRI, there is a novel operation called the Attention Graph (AG) block, which combines the attention mechanism with graph convolution. The "temporal part" adopted all n modeled spatial patterns from the "spatial part" together with fMRI data as input and output corresponding temporal patterns of the n-targeted RSNs. Different from the basic attention mechanism, this part multiplied the modeled spatial pattern with the 3D spatial block of each time point of the fMRI to extract the corresponding temporal features within the fMRI data for guidance and then performed the operations of fast down-sampling (Fast DS).

Based on the t-fMRI/rs-fMRI in the public HCP and ABIDE I data sets, the Multi-Head GAGNN model achieved better modeling performances in simultaneously modeling both spatial and temporal patterns of multiple functional brain networks compared to other SOTA methods, and had satisfying generalizability on other independent testing data sets. Moreover, the proposed Multi-Head GAGNN used to model spatio-temporal patterns of brain functional networks provided more accurate brain-cognitive behavior associations than other SOTA, suggesting better prediction ability for the cognitive behavioral measures. All in all, this study provided a novel and powerful tool for modeling brain function as well as for understanding brain-cognitive behavior associations.

Compared with the Multi-Head GAGNN model, the Multi-head Attention-Based Masked Sequence Model (MAMSM) [30] also uses the multi-head attention mechanism, but MAMSM pays more attention to two other limitations of the existing modeling methods: (1) These models are not designed to fully explore the characteristics of the fMRI data. Specifically, the same signal values at different time points in a fMRI time series may be in various states such as rising, falling and so on, hence they may represent different states/tasks or meanings; (2) Some prior knowledge was overlooked in the research process, such as the task design curve. The MAMSM uses Multi-head Attention mechanism and MSM to calculate different meanings corresponding to the same signal value in fMRI sequence. And this work uses a combination of random mask and continuous mask methods to improve the learning ability of the model. In order to make full use of the prior knowledge to obtain better features, this work uses a combination of cosine similarity error calculation and mean square error to design a new loss function, which is more conducive to tfMRI data. The model consists of two main parts: the Pre-training and the Further training. First, the MAMSM masks and encodes tfMRI time series, and obtains context information through Masked Sequence Model (MSM) pre-training. Next, the latent features obtained by pre-training are input into an asymmetric auto-encoder and incorporate the new loss function for further training. After training, the model performs lasso regression on the final feature matrix to obtain a sparse coefficient matrix and maps the sparse coefficient matrix to the 3D brain space, and thus obtained FBNs. The experiment on Motor tfMRI data set shows that the model can learn the meaningful temporal dynamics features of tfMRI and has reached the current advanced level. Moreover, some of the RSNs were found while extracting the task FBNs, suggesting that the MAMSM model is very helpful for understanding how the brain works.

14.3.4 SCAAE and STCA

In recent studies, spatial and channel-wise Attention Autoencoder (SCAAE) and spatial-temporal convolutional attention (STCA) are two novel spatial-wise attention based methods for mapping functional brain networks [31,32]. Different from the previous models, the SCAAE and STCA are used to discover dynamic functional brain networks and use the spatial-wise attention modules to directly generate the spatial pattern of the brain function. This is a novel paradigm for mapping functional brain networks. The previous models generating the functional brain networks by extracting the sources from the fMRI signals and use the generative linear model such as LASSO to reconstruct the raw fMRI signals; each row of the coefficient matrix of the LASSO is as the functional brain networks. In fact, the spatial pattern of the brain function can be represented at the feature extraction stage. Due to the widespread local correlations in the volumes, FBNs can be generated directly in the spatial domain in a self-supervised manner by using spatial-wise attention (SA), and the resulting FBNs has a higher spatial similarity with templates compared to the classical method, such as ICA, SDL and GLM. The results confirm its exceptional ability in capturing dynamic functional networks with high accuracy and reliability. The results also demonstrate that FBNs can be constructed solely using spatial information. Compared to traditional methods for mapping functional brain networks, these two approaches offer two significant advantages. Firstly, they overcome the limitations of linearity and independence assumptions. Secondly, they achieve more accurate capture of dynamic functional networks with the ability to use smaller sliding windows and higher confidence levels. Thirdly, they demonstrate faster processing speed compared to traditional methods.

14.4 Neural architecture search (NAS) of deep learning models on fMRI

In recent years, aiming to automatically search for optimal network architecture of deep learning models, many novel Neural Architecture Search (NAS) methods, e.g., based on reinforcement learning (RL) or evolutionary algorithms (EA), have been developed and applied in a variety of deep learning tasks. In RL-based methods, each choice of the architecture component is considered as an action. A sequence of actions determines the architecture of a neural network with a reward defined by training loss. In EA based method, architecture searching is based on swarm intelligence. Each individual in the swarm can learn from others with better performance, and the whole swarm can converge to a feasible optimal solution after iterations. Among other more recent NAS methods, an EA-based method, showed superb performances on image classification over RL-based methods, suggesting EA or RL-enhanced EA might be good choices in many cases. Although many existing NAS methods can learn network architectures that outperform manual designs, most of them were designed for image classification problems, which usually have high-quality labels. However, due to the lack of labels and high complexity of volumetric fMRI data, there are still few NAS applications in the field of brain imaging using fMRI. Different from applications in image classification, deep learning models of fMRI data have to be trained in an unsupervised fashion, aiming to extract latent sources of fMRI data and reconstruct spatial and temporal features.

14.4.1 Hybrid spatio-temporal neural architecture search net (HS-NASNet)

In 2019, given the evolutionary optimizer's efficiency, an evolutionary strategy and applied it to Deep Belief Network (DBN) was proposed to reveal the task-evoked functional connectivity networks (FCNs) [33] in the human brain using blood-oxygen-level-dependent (BOLD) functional magnetic resonance imaging (fMRI). Briefly, this evolutionary neural architecture search (NAS) framework is inspired by evolutionary computation (EC) jointly using Evolutionary Optimizer, Deep Belief Networks (DBN) and Deep LASSO to reasonably determine the neural architecture (NA), thus revealing the latent hierarchical spatio-temporal features based on the Human Connectome Project (HCP) 900 fMRI data sets. In detail, at first, the evolutionary strategy randomly initializes a series of deep neural networks with multiple hyper-parameters in order to expand the search space; meanwhile, the investigators employ the idea of aging evolution (AE) to generate dozens of random NAs of DBN, e.g., sub-nets. Furthermore, to increase the efficiency of AE, some potential sub-nets will be selected, treated as the particles and mutated. By using the efficient principle of PSO, the proposed evolutionary NAS generates the new generations of sub-nets for the next iteration and evaluates the signal reconstruction error using each sub-net. Finally, a single subnet, e.g., gBest, which owns the most accurate reconstruction, will be selected and replaced with the original one. Moreover, to avoid being rapidly trapped in the local optima, some other sub-nets will be selected simultaneously to perform the mutation. After replacing the previous global optimal NA, all sub-nets will be searched iteratively. In this work, 30 sub-nets are utilized as sub-nets to search the globally optimal NA. Besides, since the most vital hyper-parameters to determine the NA of DBN are the number of layers and units to avoid heterogeneous architectures, the number of units is set as the same through all hidden layers of DBN. After completion of NAS, with a large number of iterations, the original space of hyper-parameters is gradually decreased. The hyper-parameters in the final iteration determine the best architecture. The proposed evolutionary NAS can automatically search the optimal global NA of DBN given the search space, and then the optimized DBN can extract the weights between two adjacent layers of the optimal NA, which are then treated as the hierarchical temporal dictionaries for Deep LASSO to identify the corresponding hierarchical spatial maps. Importantly, the results demonstrate that the optimized deep model can achieve accurate fMRI signal reconstruction and identify spatio-temporal functional networks exhibiting multiscale properties that can be well characterized and interpreted based on current neuroscience knowledge. In summary, their evolutionary NAS contributes an effective, unsupervised evolutionary NAS method for modeling volumetric task-based fMRI data. Also, this work contributed a novel evolutionary framework to investigate the hierarchical organization of functional networks in fMRI data. As predicted, this evolutionary NAS framework will be further applied in various cognitive and clinical neuroscience applications, and thus potentially reveal altered hierarchical organization of functional networks in brain disorders.

14.4.2 Deep belief network with neural architecture search (NAS-DBN)

Inspired by the HS-NASNet, an unsupervised neural architecture search (NAS) framework on a deep belief network (DBN) that models volumetric fMRI data was proposed in 2020 [17], named NAS-DBN. The NAS-DBN framework is based on Particle Swarm Optimization (PSO) where the swarms of neural architectures can evolve and converge to a feasible optimal solution. The particle swarm consists of 30 particles, each of which represents a subnet with different initial architectures. The particle swarm can evolve and converge to an optimal solution, i.e., a DBN model with optimal architecture. The NAS process has two steps. In the first step of NAS, we investigate two main hyper-parameters including the number of layers and the number of neurons in each layer that are equal in this step. These two parameters are used to construct a mapping between a particle position and a solution of network architecture design. After training, we use the trained model to predict the testing data set, and the testing loss of DBN is regarded as the fitness function of PSO, which will be minimized in the searching process. In the second step of NAS, based on the results of the first step, we construct a new mapping to further investigate the number of neurons in each layer that are different in this step. After NAS, we applied this optimal architecture of DBN to model FBNs from task-based fMRI data. The k-dimensional temporal responses (k is the number of neurons in the hidden layer) are generated by each hidden layer, and the weights ($W1$, $W2$, $W3$) of the network are visualized and quantified as FBNs, which will be further compared with GLM-derived networks.

The NAS framework consists of two steps. In the first step, we designed a two-dimensional encoding to map the network architecture of DBN to a particle position. The dimensions of the particle represent the number of layers and the number of neurons in each layer with appropriate ranges, respectively. In this step, we assume the number of neurons in each layer is equal. In the second step, aiming to search for the number of neurons for each layer independently, the dimensions of the particle represent the number of neurons of each layer, respectively, while the number of neurons determined in the first step will give a suggestive range to each layer, and the number of layers is already determined in the first step.

This work contributes an effective unsupervised NAS method on DBN for modeling volumetric task fMRI data. The proposed NAS-DBN can find a feasible optimal solution for DBN structure within acceptable time under limited computing resources, yielding a hierarchy organization of meaningful FBNs and temporal responses.

14.4.3 eNAS-DSRAE

The existing spatio-temporal deep learning models for fMRI data including the abovementioned DSRAE, are limited as their neural network architectures are hand-crafted, and thus heavily rely on human expertise and prior knowledge, which would not be optimal in various senses, e.g., for different fMRI tasks and human subject populations. For instance, despite that these methods can achieve meaningful results, they are still limited to suboptimal models with ad hoc architectures and hyper-parameters. Essentially, the lack of optimal neural network architectures will fundamentally limit the great potential of using deep learning methods for fMRI data representation, e.g., mapping spatio-temporal brain networks, given that the characteristics of those meaningful spatio-temporal network patterns are unknown in advance across different fMRI tasks and human subject populations. Moreover, it should be pointed out that the learning and representation power of the above artificial neural networks is much less generalizable, compared with the human brain. Therefore, it is desirable to optimize and boost the artificial neural network architectures with hyper-parameter optimization so that they can potentially match the true spatio-temporal structures embedded in 4D fMRI data with more generalization capability. Along this direction, neural architecture search (NAS), the process of automating neural network architecture engineering, offers a promising framework for deep learning architecture optimization over hand-crafted ones. In this way, here, we would introduce a NAS approach, which is the evolutionary NAS, to optimize the width and depth of DSRAE models for optimal spatio-temporal decomposition of functional brain networks from 4D fMRI data [34]. Such neural networks derived by searching for the optimized width and depth will exhibit better generalization capabilities across different fMRI tasks and human subject populations.

In each iteration of the evolutionary process, the local best-optimized neural model is achieved. After mutation, a global best-optimized model is achieved. With eNAS framework, the architecture of optimized DSRAE would be different across different participants and cognitive tasks. That is, the width and depth of DSRAE would be optimized in different scenes. And the results showed the effectiveness of eNAS-DSRAE framework, i.e., the eNAS framework can truly optimize the corresponding deep learning model and derive meaningful brain networks compared with the original model and traditional linear models.

14.4.4 ST-DARTS

Inspired by the success of NAS frameworks in the machine learning areas, there have already been multiple promising applications of NAS on fMRI data for brain network modeling. For example, Dai et al. optimized the CNN model with AdaNet for the gyri and sulci fMRI signal classification; Qiang et al. optimized DBN with particle swarm optimization (PSO) for the functional brain network modeling. Li et al. optimized the overall structure of depth and width of DSRAE with PSO, and promising results have been obtained compared with the original DSRAE model. However, despite that those NAS approaches could achieve reasonably good performance by imposing a particular structure of the network structure search, the search space is still treated over a discrete domain and the optimal structures are still constrained by the original deep learning models. This challenge of scalability significantly constrains the architecture search and its optimization. Thus, searching the neural network architectures based on continuous space, instead of a discrete set of candidate architectures, is substantially more advantageous. Recently, an efficient NAS approach based on continuous space has been proposed by gradient descent and achieved competitive performance but with fewer computation resources, and is called Differentiable ARchiTecture Search (DARTS). The very important advantage is that DARTS could discover high-performance structures with complex graph topologies, which have been proven to be efficient on image classification and language modeling tasks, compared with other state-of-the-art NAS approaches. Instead of searching the depth and width of the overall structure, DARTS pays more attention to the RNN's inside cell structure that may help optimize such model without the dependence on the previous model structure, in order to relax the model from the constraint of the original model structure.

Here, we take the DARTS-based optimization framework, that is spatial/temporal —DARTS (ST-DARTS) [35], as an example. The same as the vanilla DARTS, the set of candidate choices of the particular operation as a softmax over all possible operations to make the search space continuous. But the bi-level optimization process would cause cooperation and competition between the architecture weight and the cell weight; the information prefers to flow through identity operation instead of nonlinear operations, which could cause the collapse problem in some cases. In this way, it is a good idea to early stop the optimization process. Li et al. further take the backward reasoning approach with two criteria as the early-stopping mechanism, which could improve the brain network decomposition capability.

And another way to solve the collapse issue in DARTS-based algorithms is to search the vanilla cell structure from the embedding features. Besides, in order to consider the topological information among the inner nodes with RNN cells, which might be trapped on a local optimum, and thus degenerates the performance further when not combined. In this way, a novel graph representation NAS (GR-NAS) method to optimize the RNN cell architecture for decomposing the spatial/temporal brain networks has been proposed very recently. With the graph-structured architectures, taking the Graph Isomorphism Network (GIN) as an auto-encoder to learn a continuous representation, a more stable cell structure could be derived.

14.5 Representing brain function as embedding

Despite the success and wide adoption of representing brain function as functional brain networks, a fundamental challenge is mapping the corresponding brain networks across individuals and populations. In this process, different functional brain networks are viewed as one-hot vectors and the mapping is performed based on similarity measurements such as spatial overlap. However, the one-hot vector representations do not encode the regularity and/or variability of different brains, and do not offer a general, comparable and stereotyped space for brain function, which limits the application for follow-up multi-modality studies, e.g., the homogeneity of visual representation in human brain function and artificial neural networks. To address this intrinsic limitation, an intuitive way is to represent the human brain function as embedding in a general, comparable and stereotyped space.

14.5.1 Hierarchical interpretable autoencoder (HIAE)

Deep learning models are capable of extracting hierarchical spatial/temporal features compared with traditional shallow models. However, the extracted features are usually abstract and complex, and of high dimensionality, making it difficult to analyze the spatio-temporal characteristics of those features. This work proposed a Hierarchical Interpretable Autoencoder (HIAE) [36] to embed the learned features from different layers into an embedding vector for the convenience of analysis. Specifically, the HIAE model relies on CAE model to extract the hierarchical features from fMRI time series. For each layer, the learned features are abstracted and embedded into a one-dimensional vector via a carefully designed Feature Interpreter (FI), which is jointly optimized with the CAE model. The Feature Interpreter is composed of two fully-connected layers: one for embedding the feature maps into an one-dimensional vector, i.e., representing the features maps $f \in R^{c \times t}$ as an embedding vector $v \in R^d$, where c is the number of channels, t is the number of time points and d is the dimensionality of embedding vector; another for mapping the embedding vector back to reconstruct the original feature maps. Meanwhile, the embedding vector from a different time series can be concatenated and then interpreted as the spatial patterns of the learned features, which can be further regressed with the fMRI time series to obtain the temporal patterns. In this way, the Feature Interpreter actually provides a comparable and compact space for representing the fMRI time series. Notably, the aim of this work is to explore the hierarchical functional differences of cortical gyri and sulci from fMRI time series. A potential limitation of HIAE model is that the spatial correlations of those fMRI time series are not fully explored during the embedding process.

14.5.2 Temporally correlated autoencoder (TCAE)

This work [37] formulated the representation learning of human brain function as an embedding problem for the first time. Based on the transformer model and self-attention mechanism, a novel unsupervised Temporally Correlated Auto-encoder (TCAE) model was proposed to represent the 3D volumes of fMRI data as dense embedding vectors, which record functional brain activities at different time points. Specifically, the TCAE model employed an encoder–decoder architecture. The encoder and decoder are composed of an embedding layer and a multi-head self-attention module. In the encoder, the embedding layer represents the 3D fMRI volumes as 1D embedding vectors through a linear transformation to compress the spatial dimensionality. Then the multi-head self-attention module take the embedding vectors of all time points as input to model the temporal correlations of different time points and generate the final embeddings, which profile both spatial and temporal information. Compared with the HIAE model, the TCAE model explicitly model both spatial and temporal correlations. The experiments on downstream tasks demonstrate that it effectively provides a general, comparable and stereotyped embedding space to encode the regularity and variability of brain function across individual brains and at different time points.

14.5.3 Potential applications

Representing the brain function in a general, comparable and stereotyped embedding space can greatly facilitate the multi-modality studies to bridge the gaps of semantic spaces between the brain function and artificial neural networks. For example, Huang et al. [38] proposed a brain inspired adversarial visual attention network (BI-AVAN) to decode the human visual attention from fMRI. Similar to the TCAE model, the 3D fMRI volumes are embedded as 1D vectors to represent the brain activities through an autoencoder model. Zhao et al. [39] coupled the visual semantics of artificial neural networks and human brain function, where the brain activities are embedded in a semantic space and the similarity of two semantic spaces are explored. In the future, similar approaches can be also applied to other domains such as language models in Natural Language Processing (NLP).

14.6 Deep fusion of brain structure-function in brain disorders

With the availability of large-scale multiple types of brain image data, integration of data acquired from different imaging techniques, termed as multimodal data fusion [40], has gained considerable attention in the neuroimaging field. Multimodal fusion provides an irreplaceable opportunity to take advantages of complementary cross-modal information that may only partially be contained in single modality data. Essentially, each imaging modality provides a different but unique view to represent brain structure and/or function. For example, diffusion tensor imaging (DTI) can provide information of brain structural connectivity (e.g., via tractography), and blood oxygen level-dependent (BOLD) signals derived from functional magnetic resonance imaging (fMRI) can be used to infer neural activity in vivo through measuring hemodynamic response. By jointly analyzing DTI and fMRI data, we can investigate organizational architecture of human brain in both structural and functional domains. Besides studying general relationships between brain structure and function, multimodal data fusion can provide complementary knowledge when exploring potential abnormalities occurred in brain disorders. For example, mild cognitive impairment (MCI), the precursor of Alzheimer's disease, is a progressive and irreversible neurodegenerative disorder characterized by severe cognitive decline and memory loss. Though the neuropathological mechanism is not fully understood, increasing evidence has shown that both structural and functional brain alterations are found in MCI patients. As a result, using a single modality, e.g., either structural or functional data, for brain disease studies including classification or prediction, can be sub-optimal.

14.6.1 Deep cross-model attention network (DCMAT)

Recent advances in deep learning have triggered a new era in AD/MCI classification and a variety of deep models and algorithms have been developed to classify multiple clinical groups (e.g., aged normal control—CN vs. MCI) and AD conversion. Unfortunately, it is still largely unknown what is the relationship between the altered functional connectivity and structural connectivity at individual level. To this end, this work [41] introduced a deep cross-model attention network (DCMAT) to jointly model brain structure and function. The DCMAT is composed of one RNN (Recurrent Neural Network) layer and multiple graph attention (GAT) blocks containing a GCN layer and an attention layer, which can effectively represent MCI-specific functional dynamics on an individual structural network. During the training process, the fMRI signals extracted from different brain regions are used as inputs for the RNN layer to capture the dynamic temporal features; then the output of RNN layer together with structural connectivity are fed into multiple GAT blocks to 1) calculate disease-based functional correlations and reorganize dynamic temporal features at each attention layer; and 2) model the brain structural and functional information simultaneously using structural connectivity matrix and reorganized dynamic temporal features at GCN layer (graph layer). The proposed DCMAT shows promising classification performance compared to recent studies. More importantly, the results suggest that the MCI related functional interactions might go beyond the directly connected brain regions.

14.6.2 Deep connectome

Motivated by the merits of multimodal fusion in neuroimage studies and the recent advancement of graph convolutional network (GCN), this work [42] attempts to develop a graph-based deep model (GBDM) to effectively incorporate neuroscience knowledge into multimodal data fusion with a single deep framework. Specifically, this work constructs a multi-layer GCN with trainable graph topology. The graph is parameterized by both DTI-derived brain structural network and functional activities so that the learned graph becomes a deeply hybrid connectome by retaining brain structural substrate and simultaneously considering the functional influences as a complementary cross-modal information. During the training process, the structural network was used as the initialization of graph topology, and the functional information was used by GBDM to iteratively update the topology of the graph—deep brain connectome, to maximize its classification power for MCI patients. In the prediction phase, given individual structural network and functional data, GBDM outputs the graph topology as well as the predicted clinical conditions. The major advantage of the Deep Connectome is that existing approaches exclusively rely on unimodal network (either structural or functional), or separately analyze multimodal connectome at population level, while this method can integrate multiple types of network connectome and characterize their deep relationship as an "individual connectome signature."

14.7 Conclusion

In the past few years, a variety of deep learning models have been successfully applied to fMRI data for mapping functional brain networks and associated applications. It has been shown that deep learning models have superior performances compared with traditional methods. Moreover, with a hierarchical structure, deep learning can provide much more information implied in the hierarchical temporal features and functional brain networks, which may be useful for brain cognitive and disorder analysis. In the future, new deep learning models should be studied and introduced to fMRI, such as transformer, ResNet and graph neural networks, to better model the dynamic functional activities from fMRI.

References

[1] M.A. Lindquist, J.M. Loh, L.Y. Atlas, T.D. Wager, Modeling the hemodynamic response function in fMRI: efficiency, bias and mis-modeling, NeuroImage 45 (1) (2009) S187–S198.

[2] N.K. Logothetis, What we can do and what we cannot do with fMRI, Nature 453 (7197) (2008) 869.

[3] D.M. Barch, G.C. Burgess, M.P. Harms, S.E. Petersen, B.L. Schlaggar, M. Corbetta, M.F. Glasser, S. Curtiss, S. Dixit, C. Feldt, Function in the human connectome: task-fMRI and individual differences in behavior, NeuroImage 80 (2013) 169–189.

[4] C.F. Beckmann, M. Jenkinson, S.M. Smith, General multilevel linear modeling for group analysis in FMRI, NeuroImage 20 (2) (2003) 1052–1063.

[5] C.F. Beckmann, M. DeLuca, J.T. Devlin, S.M. Smith, Investigations into resting-state connectivity using independent component analysis, Philosophical Transactions of the Royal Society of London. Series B, Biological Sciences 360 (1457) (2005) 1001–1013.

[6] V.D. Calhoun, T. Adali, G.D. Pearlson, J. Pekar, A method for making group inferences from functional MRI data using independent component analysis, Human Brain Mapping 14 (3) (2001) 140–151.

[7] V.D. Calhoun, J. Liu, T. Adalı, A review of group ICA for fMRI data and ICA for joint inference of imaging, genetic, and ERP data, NeuroImage 45 (1) (2009) S163–S172.

[8] M.J. McKeown, Detection of consistently task-related activations in fMRI data with hybrid independent component analysis, NeuroImage 11 (1) (2000) 24–35.

[9] Y. Lee, J. Lee, S. Tak, K. Lee, D.L. Na, S.W. Seo, Y. Jeong, J.C. Ye, Sparse SPM: group sparse-dictionary learning in SPM framework for resting-state functional connectivity MRI analysis, NeuroImage 125 (125) (2016) 1032–1045.

[10] J. Lv, X. Jiang, X. Li, D. Zhu, H. Chen, T. Zhang, S. Zhang, X. Hu, J. Han, H. Huang, Sparse representation of whole-brain fMRI signals for identification of functional networks, Medical Image Analysis 20 (1) (2015) 112–134.

[11] S. Zhao, J. Han, J. Lv, X. Jiang, X. Hu, Y. Zhao, B. Ge, L. Guo, T. Liu, Supervised dictionary learning for inferring concurrent brain networks, IEEE Transactions on Medical Imaging 34 (10) (2015) 2036–2045.

[12] A. McIntosh, W. Chau, A. Protzner, Spatiotemporal analysis of event-related fMRI data using partial least squares, NeuroImage 23 (2) (2004) 764–775.

[13] S. LaConte, S. Strother, V. Cherkassky, J. Anderson, X. Hu, Support vector machines for temporal classification of block design fMRI data, NeuroImage 26 (2) (2005) 317–329.

[14] S.M. Smith, A. Hyvärinen, G. Varoquaux, K.L. Miller, C.F. Beckmann, Group-PCA for very large fMRI datasets, NeuroImage 101 (2014) 738–749.

[15] Q. Dong, F. Ge, N. Qiang, Y. Zhao, J. Lv, H. Huang, J. Yuan, X. Jiang, D. Shen, T. Liu, Modeling hierarchical brain networks via volumetric sparse deep belief network (VS-DBN), IEEE Transactions on Biomedical Engineering (2019).

[16] G.E. Hinton, S. Osindero, Y.-W. Teh, A fast learning algorithm for deep belief nets, Neural Computation 18 (7) (2006) 1527–1554.

[17] N. Qiang, Q. Dong, W. Zhang, B. Ge, F. Ge, H. Liang, Y. Sun, J. Gao, T. Liu, Modeling task-based fMRI data via deep belief network with neural architecture search, Computerized Medical Imaging and Graphics (2020) 101747.

[18] H. Huang, X. Hu, Y. Zhao, M. Makkie, Q. Dong, S. Zhao, L. Guo, T. Liu, Modeling task fMRI data via deep convolutional autoencoder, IEEE Transactions on Medical Imaging 37 (7) (2018) 1551–1561.

[19] Y. Zhao, F. Ge, S. Zhang, T. Liu, 3D Deep Convolutional Neural Network Revealed the Value of Brain Network Overlap in Differentiating Autism Spectrum Disorder from Healthy Controls, 2018, pp. 172–180.

[20] Y. Cui, S. Zhao, H. Wang, L. Xie, Y. Chen, J. Han, L. Guo, F. Zhou, T. Liu, Identifying Brain Networks of Multiple Time Scales via Deep Recurrent Neural Network, 2018, pp. 284–292.

[21] Q. Li, Q. Dong, F. Ge, N. Qiang, Y. Zhao, H. Wang, H. Huang, X. Wu, T. Liu, Simultaneous Spatial-Temporal Decomposition of Connectome-Scale Brain Networks by Deep Sparse Recurrent Auto-Encoders, 2019, pp. 579–591.

[22] N. Qiang, Q. Dong, H. Liang, B. Ge, S. Zhang, Y. Sun, C. Zhang, W. Zhang, J. Gao, T. Liu, Modeling and augmenting of fMRI data using deep recurrent variational auto-encoder, Journal of Neural Engineering 18 (4) (2021) 0460b6.

[23] H. Wang, S. Zhao, Q. Dong, Y. Cui, Y. Chen, J. Han, L. Xie, T. Liu, Recognizing brain states using deep sparse recurrent neural network, in: IEEE Transactions on Medical Imaging, 2018.

[24] N. Qiang, Q. Dong, F. Ge, H. Liang, B. Ge, S. Zhang, Y. Sun, J. Gao, T. Liu, Deep variational autoencoder for mapping functional brain networks, IEEE Transactions on Cognitive and Developmental Systems (2020).

[25] K. Han, H. Wen, J. Shi, K.-H. Lu, Y. Zhang, D. Fu, Z. Liu, Variational autoencoder: an unsupervised model for encoding and decoding fMRI activity in visual cortex, NeuroImage 198 (2019) 125–136.

[26] J.-H. Kim, Y. Zhang, K. Han, Z. Wen, M. Choi, Z. Liu, Representation learning of resting state fMRI with variational autoencoder, NeuroImage 241 (2021) 118423.

[27] J. Yan, Y. Chen, Z. Xiao, S. Zhang, M. Jiang, T. Wang, T. Zhang, J. Lv, B. Becker, R. Zhang, Modeling spatio-temporal patterns of holistic functional brain networks via multi-head guided attention graph neural networks (Multi-Head GAGNNs), Medical Image Analysis 80 (2022) 102518.

[28] N. Qiang, Q. Dong, H. Liang, B. Ge, S. Zhang, C. Zhang, J. Gao, Y. Sun, A novel ADHD classification method based on resting state temporal templates (RSTT) using spatiotemporal attention auto-encoder, Neural Computing & Applications (2022) 1–19.

[29] N. Qiang, Q. Dong, H. Liang, J. Li, S. Zhang, C. Zhang, B. Ge, Y. Sun, J. Gao, T. Liu, Learning brain representation using recurrent Wasserstein generative adversarial net, Computer Methods and Programs in Biomedicine 223 (2022) 106979.

[30] M. He, X. Hou, Z. Wang, Z. Kang, X. Zhang, N. Qiang, B. Ge, Multi-head Attention-Based Masked Sequence Model for Mapping Functional Brain Networks, 2022, pp. 295–304.

[31] Y. Liu, E. Ge, M. He, Z. Liu, S. Zhao, X. Hu, D. Zhu, T. Liu, B. Ge, Discovering dynamic functional brain networks via spatial and channel-wise attention, arXiv preprint, arXiv: 2205.09576, 2022.

[32] Y. Liu, E. Ge, N. Qiang, T. Liu, B. Ge, Spatial-temporal convolutional attention for mapping functional brain networks, arXiv preprint, arXiv:2211.02315, 2022.

[33] W. Zhang, L. Zhao, Q. Li, S. Zhao, Q. Dong, X. Jiang, T. Zhang, T. Liu, Identify Hierarchical Structures from Task-Based fMRI Data via Hybrid Spatiotemporal Neural Architecture Search Net, 2019, pp. 745–753.

[34] Q. Li, W. Zhang, L. Zhao, X. Wu, T. Liu, Evolutional neural architecture search for optimization of spatiotemporal brain network decomposition, IEEE Transactions on Biomedical Engineering 69 (2) (2021) 624–634.

[35] Q. Li, X. Wu, T. Liu, Differentiable neural architecture search for optimal spatial/temporal brain function network decomposition, Medical Image Analysis 69 (2021) 101974.

[36] L. Zhao, H. Dai, X. Jiang, T. Zhang, D. Zhu, T. Liu, Exploring the functional difference of gyri/sulci via hierarchical interpretable autoencoder, 2021, pp. 701–709.

[37] L. Zhao, Z. Wu, H. Dai, Z. Liu, T. Zhang, D. Zhu, T. Liu, Embedding Human Brain Function via Transformer, 2022, pp. 366–375.

[38] H. Huang, L. Zhao, X. Hu, H. Dai, L. Zhang, D. Zhu, T. Liu, BI AVAN: brain inspired adversarial visual attention network, arXiv preprint, arXiv:2210.15790, 2022.

[39] L. Zhao, H. Dai, Z. Wu, Z. Xiao, L. Zhang, D.W. Liu, X. Hu, X. Jiang, S. Li, D. Zhu, Coupling visual semantics of artificial neural networks and human brain function via synchronized activations, arXiv preprint, arXiv:2206.10821, 2022.

[40] J.S. Damoiseaux, M.D. Greicius, Greater than the sum of its parts: a review of studies combining structural connectivity and resting-state functional connectivity, Brain Structure and Function 213 (6) (2009) 525–533.

[41] L. Zhang, L. Wang, D. Zhu, Jointly Analyzing Alzheimer's Disease Related Structure-Function Using Deep Cross-Model Attention Network, 2020, pp. 563–567.

[42] L. Zhang, L. Wang, J. Gao, S.L. Risacher, J. Yan, G. Li, T. Liu, D. Zhu, A.s.D.N. Initiative, Deep fusion of brain structure-function in mild cognitive impairment, Medical Image Analysis 72 (2021) 102082.

Detecting, localizing and classifying polyps from colonoscopy videos using deep learning

15

Yu Tian[a,b,c], **Leonardo Zorron Cheng Tao Pu**[d], **Yuyuan Liu**[a], **Gabriel Maicas**[a], **Johan W. Verjans**[c], **Alastair D. Burt**[e,f], **Seon Ho Shin**[g], **Rajvinder Singh**[g], and **Gustavo Carneiro**[a,h]

[a]*Australian Institute for Machine Learning, University of Adelaide, Adelaide, SA, Australia*
[b]*Harvard Medical School, Harvard University, Cambridge, MA, United States*
[c]*South Australian Health and Medical Research Institute, Adelaide, SA, Australia*
[d]*Department of Gastroenterology at Austin Health, Heidelberg, VIC, Australia*
[e]*Faculty of Health and Medical Sciences, University of Adelaide, Adelaide, SA, Australia*
[f]*Translational and Clinical Research Institute, Newcastle University, Newcastle upon Tyne, United Kingdom*
[g]*Lyell McEwin Hospital, University of Adelaide, Adelaide, SA, Australia*
[h]*Centre for Vision, Speech and Signal Processing, University of Surrey, Guildford, United Kingdom*

15.1 Introduction

Colorectal cancer (CRC) is the third most commonly diagnosed cancer in the world and recent studies show that CRC will increase by 60% by 2030 to more than 2.2 million new cases and 1.1 million cancer deaths [1]. These numbers were used as an incentive for the introduction of CRC screening programs in several countries, such as in Australia.[1] An important step in all CRC screening programs is the colonoscopy, where the goal is to detect and classify malignant or pre-malignant polyps using a camera that is inserted into the large bowel. Accurate early polyp detection and classification may improve survival rates [59], but such accuracy is affected by several human factors, such as expertise and fatigue [69,65,50]. Hence, a system that can accurately detect and classify polyps during a colonoscopy exam has the potential to improve colonoscopists' efficacy [61,39,69]. According to the American Society for Gastrointestinal Endoscopy, an accurate classification represents an agreement of over 90% with pathologic assessment [54]. Furthermore, polyp classification during a

---

[1] Bowel Cancer Australia. A Colonoscopy Wait-time and Performance Guarantee. Available at: https://www.bowelcanceraustralia.org/earlydetection/a-colonoscopy-wait-time-and-performance-guarantee.

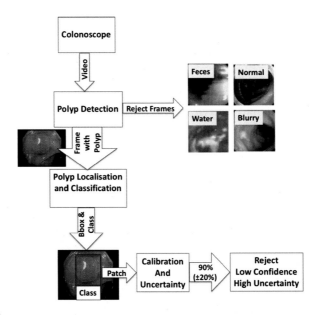

FIGURE 15.1

Detection, localization and classification (with confidence calibration and uncertainty estimation) of polyps from colonoscopy videos. In the polyp detection phase, frames that show normal tissue, blurry images, feces and water jet sprays are rejected. Then we localize and classify the polyps using classification uncertainty and calibration. The last step consists of rejecting classifications with low confidence and high uncertainty to improve classification accuracy and model interpretability.

colonoscopy can be advantageous since it can [69]: 1) reduce the need for histopathologic assessment after resecting pre-malignant polyps with a small risk of an invasive component, 2) avoid resection of benign polyps, 3) determine the most appropriate resection method, 4) enable the estimation of a follow-up period by the end of the procedure and 5) reduce complications associated with unnecessary polypectomies.

As shown in Fig. 15.1, automated polyp classification depends on polyp detection, localization and classification. Polyp detection consists of the identification of colonoscopy video frames containing polyps, and the rejection of frames containing normal tissue, blurry frames and frames showing feces or water jet sprays to clean the colon. The rejection of blurry frames is reached with image processing tools and the rejection of frames showing feces or water jet sprays is achieved with a binary classifier. The classification of frames containing normal tissue or polyps is formulated as a few-shot anomaly detection [39,61] using a training set that contains a large percentage of normal (i.e., healthy) and a very small proportion abnormal (i.e., unhealthy with polyps) samples. Our formulation is designed to detect unforeseen types of polyps not present in the training. For instance, if the training images contain only a sub-set of all possible polyp types, the detection should be able to identify all types of polyps, even though they were not included in the training set. Next, given a frame containing a polyp, the localization and classification of the polyp in the image is performed simultaneously [64] using state-of-the-art deep learning models [38], which are typically accurate, but poorly calibrated [19] and without an uncertainty estimation [12,13,29]. These two issues must be addressed to increase the reliability of the system [6].

In this chapter, we integrate recently proposed few-shot anomaly detection methods designed to perform the detection of frames containing polyps from colonoscopy videos [61,39] with a method that rejects frames containing blurry images, feces and water jet sprays. Taking images containing polyps, we analyze the results of our recently proposed method that simultaneously localizes and classifies polyps into five classes [64]. Finally, we analyze the results of our recently proposed polyp classifier [6] that outputs classification uncertainty [58,12,13,29] and calibrated confidence [19]. We also demonstrate that classification accuracy increases by rejecting low-confidence and uncertain classifications. For each of the proposed methods, we present thorough experiments in multiple data sets to provide evidence of their functionality.

15.2 Literature review
15.2.1 Polyp detection

The detection of polyps is typically addressed using binary classifiers [32] trained with a large training set containing images without polyps (i.e., normal) and with polyps (i.e., abnormal). In this context, it is natural to explore imbalanced learning algorithms [35,37,51] because the number of normal images tends to overwhelm that of the abnormal ones, but the extreme imbalanced proportion of normal and abnormal images tend to harm the ability of these algorithms to handle imbalanced learning (e.g., colonoscopy data sets can have 3 to 4 orders of magnitude more normal than abnormal images [61]). Furthermore, colonoscopy frames may contain many distractors, such as blurry images, water jet sprays and feces [39]. If not present in the training set of the normal class, such images can be mistakenly classified as abnormal.

An alternative approach to binary classification is based on zero-shot anomaly detection trained using normal images, exclusively [17,40,67,57,56,49,39,63,7], where the idea is to learn the distribution of normal images, and abnormal images are detected based on how they fail to fit in this distribution. Zero-shot anomaly detection works well when what characterizes an anomaly covers a relatively large area of the image, which is not always the case for polyps. Therefore, using a few abnormal images (less than 100) to train anomaly detection methods enables the implementation of better polyp detectors [61], referred to as few-shot anomaly detection [45,62].

Few-shot anomaly detection has been proposed for nonmedical image analysis problems [44], where their main challenge is on how to deal with the high-dimensionality of the image space. Our method [61] solves this high-dimensional issue by relying on deep infomax (DIM) [24] to reduce the dimensionality of the feature space.

15.2.2 Polyp localization and classification

Once frames containing polyps have been identified, the next stage is to localize and classify the polyp. The most straightforward approach consists of a two-stage process that first localizes the polyp with a bounding box, and then classifies the image patch within this bounding box [16,52]. Nevertheless, this process can be streamlined with a one-stage localization and classification approach [37]. We explore this one-stage method in [64].

The classification of polyps typically focuses on solving problems containing two classes [23,31], three classes [20,55] or four classes [26], while our approach is one of the first to study the five-class polyp classification problem [60,68,64]. This five-class classification is claimed to be more effective than the other alternatives since it can enable colonoscopists to assess if a detected polyp is endoscopically resectable (i.e., pre-cancerous or early cancerous lesions—classes IIo, II and $IIIa$) or not endoscopically resectable (i.e., benign or invasive cancer—classes I or $IIIb$, where for the latter class, the case is referred to surgery). Furthermore, other less-than-5 classifications mix the benign hyperplastic polyp with the pre-cancerous sessile serrated lesion in the same class (usually classifying both within the first class of such classifications). In the 5-class Modified Sano's classification [60], hyperplastic polyps are classified as class I while sessile serrated lesions are classified as class IIo. Also, this classification can reduce costs and complications associated with polypectomy since the follow-up interval and method for endoscopic resection can differ depending on the number, size and type of the lesions found during the exam [33,53]. These advantages come with the drawback that this 5-class classification tends to be more challenging for the classification model.

15.2.3 Uncertainty and calibration

Deep learning models are generally trained with maximum likelihood estimation (MLE) that tends to produce over-confident classifiers that represent poorly its expected accuracy [19]. Apart from a few papers [28,5,11], this issue has been overlooked by the medical image analysis community, even though it is an important feature in the deployment of systems in clinical settings. Furthermore, MLE training cannot provide an estimation of uncertainty, unless through classification entropy [58] or some specific types of loss functions [66]. The use of Bayesian learning can provide a more reliable uncertainty estimation [12,13,29] by considering that the model and observations are affected by noise processes. Such a learning process tends to have high training and testing computational costs [14,27], but recent work by Gal and Ghahramani [12], Gal et al. [13], Kendall and Gal [29] addressed this issue with the proposal of efficient methods. In fact, this method has been recently explored by medical image analysis methods [11,42]. We argue that classification calibration and uncertainty estimation are two independent ideas and show that their combination can lead to effective classification strategies [6].

15.2.4 Commercial systems

Recently, several companies have deployed commercially viable systems that integrate computer-aided detection and/or classification directly to the colonoscope output in real-time. For instance, polyp detection and classification systems have been developed by Olympus© in collaboration with ai4gi©, by Fujifilm© with the CAD EYE technology and by Medtronic© through GI GENIUS. These systems tend to produce reliable polyp detection results, but the classification module does not seem to be integrated well with the detection module and appears to only separate the lesions into neoplastic (i.e., cancerous or precancerous) or nonneoplastic. Moreover, it is unclear if any of these systems can classify serrated lesions. The classification of serrated lesions into neoplastic (i.e., traditional serrated adenomas and sessile serrated lesions/adenomas/polyps) and nonneoplastic (i.e., hyperplastic polyp) is clinically relevant and often difficult even for experienced endoscopists.

15.3 Materials and methods

15.3.1 Data sets

We use four data sets for testing the proposed methods. One is for the detection of colonoscopy frames containing polyps, and the other two are for the localization and classification of polyps within an image that contains a polyp, where uncertainty and calibration are tested in one of these two data sets. These three data sets contain images and clinical information approved by the Human Research Ethics Committee (TQEH/LMH/MH/2008128 and HREC/16/TQEH/283) in Australia and by the Nagoya University Hospital Ethics Review Committee (2015-0485) in Japan. The fourth data set is the publicly available data set MICCAI 2015 Endoscopic Vision Challenge [3] to test the localization of polyps.

15.3.1.1 Polyp detection

For the detection of frames containing polyps, we used colonoscopy videos captured with the Olympus 190 dual focus endoscope from 17 patients. We automatically remove frames with blurred visual information using the variance of the Laplacian method [22]. Next, we take one of every five consecutive frames to prevent the modeling of correlation between frames that are too close in time domain. Table 15.1 shows details of the training and testing sets. This data set is represented by $\mathcal{D}^{(d)} = \{\mathbf{x}_i, t_i, y_i\}_{i=1}^{|\mathcal{D}^{(d)}|}$, where $\mathbf{x} : \Omega \to \mathbb{R}^3$ denotes an RGB colonoscopy frame (Ω represents the frame lattice), $t_i \in \mathbb{N}$ represents patient identification,[2] and

---

[2] Note that the data set has been de-identified, so t_i is useful only for splitting $\mathcal{D}^{(d)}$ into training, testing and validation sets in a patientwise manner.

Table 15.1 The training and testing sets used for polyp detection.

	Patients	Normal	Abnormal	Water&Feces	Total Images
Training set	13	13,250	100	3302	16,652
Testing set	4	700	212	500	1612

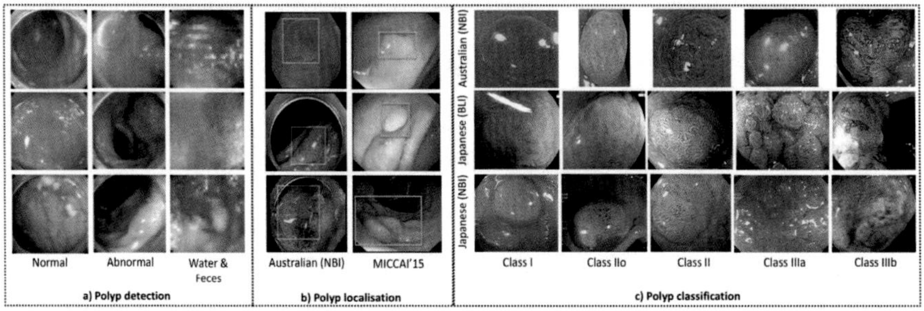

FIGURE 15.2

Data sets used in this chapter: a) polyp detection uses frames, labeled as Normal (showing healthy tissue), Abnormal (containing polyp), and Water&Feces; b) polyp localization from an image containing a polyp (the annotation is represented by a bounding box around the polyp) and c) polyp classification using the image patch inside the polyp bounding box.

$y \in \mathcal{Y}^{(d)} = \{\text{Normal, Polyp, Water\&Feces}\}$ denotes the label. In particular, the class Normal represents frames in the set $\mathcal{D}_N^{(d)} \subset \mathcal{D}^{(d)}$, displaying healthy colon tissue; Abnormal denotes frames in $\mathcal{D}_A^{(d)} \subset \mathcal{D}^{(d)}$, showing polyps; and Water&Feces in $\mathcal{D}_W^{(d)} \subset \mathcal{D}^{(d)}$, are frames containing water jet sprays and feces. The patients in the testing, training and validations sets are mutually exclusive and the proportion of abnormal samples in the testing set is the typical proportion defined for other anomaly detection papers [49,57]. Samples of this data set are shown in Fig. 15.2(a).

15.3.1.2 Polyp localization and classification (with uncertainty and calibration)

For the localization and classification of polyps, we rely on the data set defined by $\mathcal{D}^{(c)} = \{\mathbf{x}_i, t_i, \mathbf{b}_i, y_i\}_{i=1}^{|\mathcal{D}^{(c)}|}$, where $\mathbf{x}$ and t_i are as defined in Section 15.3.1.1, $\mathbf{b}_i \in \mathbb{R}^4$ denotes the two 2-D coordinates of the bounding box containing the polyp, and $y_i \in \mathcal{Y}^{(c)} = \{I, II, IIo, IIIa, IIIb\}$ denotes the five-polyp classification [60,68,64], divided into: 1) hyperplastic polyp (I), 2) sessile serrated lesion (IIo), 3) low-grade tubular adenoma (II), 4) high-grade adenoma/ tubulovillous adenoma /superficial cancer ($IIIa$) and 5) invasive cancer ($IIIb$); see Fig. 15.2(b),(c). Fig. 15.2(b) also shows samples of the MICCAI 2015 Endoscopic Vision Challenge data set [3].

The data set $\mathcal{D}^{(c)}$ contains images collected from two different sites, referred to as Australian and Japanese sites, which allow us to test our classification method in a more realistic experimental set-up, where the training and testing are from different domains; see Fig. 15.2-(c). The Australian data set contains images of colorectal polyps collected from a tertiary hospital in South Australia with the Olympus 190 dual focus colonoscope using Narrow Band Imaging (NBI), and is represented by $\mathcal{D}_A^{(c)} \subset \mathcal{D}^{(c)}$. The number of images of $\mathcal{D}_A^{(c)}$ is 871, which were scanned from 218 patients, where 102 images from 39 patients are of class I, 346 images from 93 patients are of class II, 281 images from 48 patients are of class IIo, 79 images from 25 patients are of class $IIIa$ and 63 images from 14 patients are of class $IIIb$. The Japanese data set, denoted by $\mathcal{D}_J^{(c)} \subset \mathcal{D}^{(c)}$, contains two subsets of colorectal polyp images acquired from a tertiary hospital image database in Japan: magnified NBI images obtained from the Olympus 290 series, and magnified Blue Laser Imaging (BLI) images from the Fujifilm 700 series. The Japanese data set has 20 NBI images from 20 patients and 49 BLI images from 49 patients, where the NBI set has 3 images of class I, 5 images of class II, 2 images of class IIo, 7 images of class $IIIa$ and 3 images of class $IIIb$. The BLI data set contains 9 images of class I, 10 images of class II, 10 images of class IIo, 11 images of class $IIIa$ and 9 images of class $IIIb$. All images from the Australian and Japanese data sets were correlated with histology and de-identified into folders according to the five classes defined above [60,68,64].

The MICCAI 2015 Endoscopic Vision Challenge data set [3], represented by $\mathcal{D}_M^{(l)}$, used for the polyp localization experiment, comprises the CVC-CLINIC and ETIS-LARIB data sets. CVC-CLINIC has 612 images (size 388 × 284 pixels) from 31 different polyps and 31 sequences (captured with Olympus Q160AL and Q165L, Exera II video-processor). ETIS-LARIB has 196 frames (size 1225 × 966) from 44 different polyps and 34 sequences (captured with Pentax 90i series, EPKi 7000 video-processor). All images in this MICCAI 2015 data set have at least one polyp annotated by expert endoscopists.

We consider three experiments: 1) training and testing from the MICCAI 2015 data set, 2) training and testing images are from the Australian data set and 3) training from the Australian data set and testing from Japanese data set. For the MICCAI 2015 data set, we follow the experimental setup described in [3]. For the experiment based on training and testing sets from the Australian data set, the training set $\mathcal{T}^{(c)}$ has images from 60% of the patients, the validation set $\mathcal{V}^{(c)}$ has images from 20% of the patients and the testing set has images from the remaining 20% of the patients, where the patients in the testing, training and validations sets are mutually exclusive and each one of these subsets are randomly formed to have a similar proportion of the five classes. For the experiment based on training on the Australian data set and testing on the Japanese data set, the testing set contains only images from the Japanese site. The Australian data set is used for training and testing the proposed method using a cross-validation experiment, while the Japanese data set is used exclusively for testing the system, enabling us to test the performance of the method with images collected from different colonoscopes (Olympus 190 and 290 series) and different technologies (i.e., NBI and BLI).

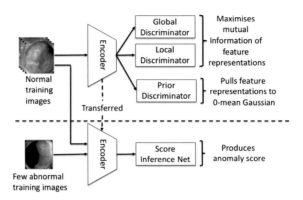

FIGURE 15.3

Diagram of the few-shot anomaly detector FSAD-NET with the representation learning (top) and SIN learning (bottom).

15.3.2 Methods

In this section, we present the binary classifier that rejects frames with water jet sprays and feces, then we describe the few-shot anomaly detection method for identifying frames with polyps. Next, we explain the method for localizing and classifying polyps, followed by the approach to calibrate confidence and estimate classification uncertainty.

15.3.2.1 Detection of frames with water jet sprays and feces

This first stage consists of a model, trained with binary cross-entropy (BCE) loss [4], which classifies images belonging to the Water&Feces class versus images belonging to the Normal and Abnormal classes, using the data set in Table 15.1. This model is represented by

$$D(y|\mathbf{x}, \theta_D), \tag{15.1}$$

where $y \in \{$Normal OR Abnormal, Water&Feces$\}$, and θ_D represents the model parameters.

15.3.2.2 Few-shot polyp detection

Anomaly detection approaches are usually designed as a one-class classifier or a few-shot learning method [46]. Results from approaches exploring these two ideas [39,61] suggest that the latter is more effective, so we focus on it and propose FSAD-NET [61], which consists of a feature encoder and a score inference network (SIN), as displayed in Fig. 15.3. The training process is divided into two stages: 1) training of the feature encoder $\mathbf{e} = E(\mathbf{x}; \theta_E)$ (θ_E represents the encoder parameter and $\mathbf{e} \in \mathbb{R}^E$ denotes the embedding) to maximize the mutual information (MI) between normal images $\mathbf{x} \in \mathcal{D}_N^{(d)}$ and their embeddings $\mathbf{e}$ [24]; and 2) training of the SIN $S(E(\mathbf{x}; \theta_E); \theta_S)$ [47] (θ_S represents the SIN parameter), with a contrastive-like loss that relies on $\mathcal{D}_N^{(d)}$ and $\mathcal{D}_A^{(d)}$ to reach the following condition: $S(E(\mathbf{x} \in \mathcal{D}_A^{(d)}; \theta_E); \theta_S) > S(E(\mathbf{x} \in \mathcal{D}_N^{(d)}; \theta_E); \theta_S)$.

The MI maximization in step one is achieved with [24]:

$$
\begin{aligned}
\theta_E^*, \theta_D^*, \theta_L^* = \arg \max_{\theta_E, \theta_D, \theta_L} & \left(\alpha \hat{I}_{\theta_D}(\mathbf{x}; E(\mathbf{x}; \theta_E)) \right. \\
& + \frac{\beta}{|\mathcal{M}|} \sum_{\omega \in \mathcal{M}} \hat{I}_{\theta_L}(\mathbf{x}(\omega); E(\mathbf{x}(\omega); \theta_E)) \Big) \\
& + \gamma \arg \min_{\theta_E} \arg \max_{\phi} \hat{F}_\phi(\mathbb{V} \| \mathbb{U}_{\mathbb{P}, \theta_E}),
\end{aligned}
\tag{15.2}
$$

where α, β, γ denote model hyper-parameters, $\hat{I}_{\theta_D}(.)$ and $\hat{I}_{\theta_L}(.)$ represent an MI lower bound based on the Donsker–Varadhan representation of the Kullback–Leibler (KL)-divergence [24], defined by

$$
\begin{aligned}
\hat{I}_{\theta_D}(\mathbf{x}; E(\mathbf{x}; \theta_E)) = & \\
& \mathbb{E}_{\mathbb{J}}[D(\mathbf{x}, E(\mathbf{x}; \theta_E); \theta_D)] - \log \mathbb{E}_{\mathbb{M}}[e^{D(\mathbf{x}, E(\mathbf{x}; \theta_E); \theta_D)}],
\end{aligned}
\tag{15.3}
$$

with $\mathbb{J}$ denoting the joint distribution between images and their embeddings, $\mathbb{M}$ representing the product of the marginals of the images and embeddings and $D(\mathbf{x}, E(\mathbf{x}; \theta_E); \theta_D)$ being a discriminator with parameter θ_D. The function $\hat{I}_{\theta_L}(\mathbf{x}(\omega); E(\mathbf{x}(\omega); \theta_E))$ in (15.2) has a similar definition as (15.3) for the discriminator $L(\mathbf{x}(\omega), E(\mathbf{x}(\omega); \theta_E); \theta_L)$, and represents the local MI between image regions $\mathbf{x}(\omega)$ ($\omega \in \mathcal{M} \subset \Omega$, with $\mathcal{M}$ denoting a sub-set of the image lattice) and respective local embeddings $E(\mathbf{x}(\omega), \theta_E)$. Also in (15.2),

$$
\begin{aligned}
\arg \min_{\theta_E} \arg \max_{\theta_F} \hat{F}_\phi(\mathbb{V} \| \mathbb{U}_{\mathbb{P}, \theta_E}) = & \\
& \mathbb{E}_{\mathbb{V}}[\log F(\mathbf{e}; \theta_F)] + \mathbb{E}_{\mathbb{P}}[\log(1 - F(E(\mathbf{x}; \theta_E)); \theta_F))],
\end{aligned}
\tag{15.4}
$$

where $\mathbb{V}$ represents a prior distribution for the embeddings $\mathbf{e}$ (we assume $\mathbb{V}$ to be a normal distribution $\mathcal{N}(.; \mu_{\mathbb{V}}, \Sigma_{\mathbb{V}})$, with mean $\mu_{\mathbb{V}}$ and covariance $\Sigma_{\mathbb{V}}$), $\mathbb{P}$ is the distribution of the embeddings $\mathbf{e} = E(\mathbf{x} \in \mathcal{D}_N^{(d)}; \theta_E)$ and $F(.; \theta_F)$ represents a discriminator learned with adversarial training to estimate the probability that the input is sampled from either $\mathbb{V}$ or $\mathbb{P}$. This objective function attracts the normal image embeddings toward $\mathcal{N}(.; \mu_{\mathbb{V}}, \Sigma_{\mathbb{V}})$.

The SIN training takes the embeddings of normal and abnormal images with $\mathbf{e} = E(\mathbf{x} \in \mathcal{D}_A^{(d)} \bigcup \mathcal{D}_N^{(d)}; \theta_E^*)$ to learn θ_S^* for $S(.)$ using the contrastive-like loss [47]

$$
\begin{aligned}
\ell_S = & \mathbb{I}(y \text{ is } Normal) |T(S(\mathbf{z}; \theta_S); \mu_T, \sigma_T)| + \\
& \mathbb{I}(y \text{ is } Abnormal) \max(0, a - T(S(\mathbf{e}; \theta_S); \mu_T, \sigma_T)),
\end{aligned}
\tag{15.5}
$$

where $\mathbb{I}(.)$ denotes the indicator function, $T(x; \mu_T, \sigma_T) = \frac{x - \mu_T}{\sigma_T}$ with $\mu_T = 0$ and $\sigma_T = 1$ representing the mean and standard deviation of the prior distribution for

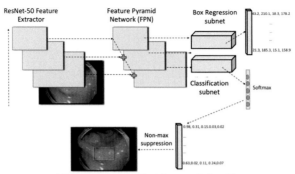

a) One-stage polyp localiser and classifier

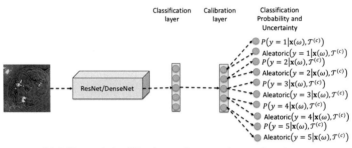

b) Calibrated classification and uncertainty estimation

FIGURE 15.4

Diagrams of the one-stage polyp localizer and classifier (a) and the calibrated classification and uncertainty estimation model (b).

the anomaly scores for normal images, and a is the margin between μ_T and the anomaly scores of abnormal images [47]. The loss in (15.5) pulls the scores from normal images to μ_T and pushes the scores of abnormal images away from μ_T with a minimum margin of a.

The inference consists of taking a test image $\mathbf{x}$, estimating the embedding with $\mathbf{e} = E(\mathbf{x}; \theta_E^*)$ and computing the score with $s = S(\mathbf{e}; \theta_S^*)$. We then compare this score s to a threshold τ to estimate if the test image is normal or abnormal.

15.3.2.3 Localization and classification of polyps

Our approach explores the efficient method that can detect and classify polyps simultaneously [37,64]. This one-stage model, depicted in Fig. 15.4(a), consists of a feature pyramid network (FPN) [36], followed by a regressor that outputs a fixed list of bounding boxes and a classifier that returns a 5-class classification probability vector for each bounding box. This model is represented by [37]:

$$\mathbf{b}, \mathbf{p} = C(\mathbf{x}, \theta_C), \tag{15.6}$$

where $\mathbf{b} \in \mathbb{R}^4$ represents the detected bounding box and $\mathbf{p} \in [0, 1]^{|\mathcal{Y}^{(c)}|}$ denotes the 5-class classification probability vector of the image patch.

The training for the polyp localization in (15.6) assumes only two classes for a bounding box: normal (background) or polyp of any class (foreground), and we rely on the focal loss to train the polyp localization [37]:

$$\ell_F(p) = -\alpha(1 - p)^\gamma log(p), \tag{15.7}$$

where $p = P(y = \text{foreground}|\mathbf{x}(\mathcal{M}), \theta_C)$ if the image patch $\mathbf{x}(\mathcal{M})$ ($\mathcal{M} \subset \Omega$) contains a polyp, $p = 1 - P(y = \text{foreground}|\mathbf{x}(\mathcal{M}), \theta_C)$; otherwise, with $P(y = \text{foreground}|\mathbf{x}(\mathcal{M}), \theta_C) \in [0, 1]$ denoting the model's probability that the image patch $\mathbf{x}(\mathcal{M})$ shows a polyp, $\gamma \in [0, 5]$ modulates the loss for well-classified image patches, and $\alpha \in [0, 1]$ denotes a hyper-parameter for the class weight (foreground or background) of the image patch $\mathbf{x}(\mathcal{M})$. The decision of whether an image patch contains a polyp is based on an intersection over union (IoU) larger than a threshold τ between $\mathbf{x}(\mathcal{M})$ and the patch formed by the manual annotation for the bounding box $\mathbf{b} \in \mathbb{R}^4$ present in $\mathcal{D}^{(c)}$, defined in Section 15.3.1.2. The training for the polyp classification part of the model in (15.6) is based on the bounding boxes that have an IoU larger than a threshold τ and a confidence score for each class. To reduce the number of the bounding boxes, we merge the ones with same classes and IoU larger than 0.5 and assigned with the maximum confidence score. To represent each image with only one class, we first select the bounding box with the maximum confidence score as the location of the polyp but omit the class label. For each class, we compute the sum of the scores on all bounding boxes as the final confidence score of that class. Then the class is determined by the maximum confidence score. The classification model is trained with multi-class cross-entropy loss.

During inference, the bounding boxes with confidence scores larger than a threshold $\tau = 0.05$ and IoU > 0.5 are merged with nonmaximum suppression, where the confidence of the merged bounding boxes is represented by the sum of the confidences of the merged bounding boxes. The final classification is obtained from the maximum confidence.

15.3.2.4 Polyp classification uncertainty and calibration

For the model in Fig. 15.4(b) that produces a calibrated confidence and uncertainty estimation, we assume that the input is an image patch $\mathbf{x}(\mathcal{M})$ (sampled to have a fixed size) inside the bounding box $\mathbf{b}$ that contains the polyp. This model estimates the probability of each class $y \in \mathcal{Y}^{(c)}$ with

$$P(y|\mathbf{x}(\mathcal{M}), \theta_P), \tag{15.8}$$

where θ_P parameterizes the model. To allow the estimation of classification uncertainty, we rely on a Bayesian approach, where the goal is to estimate a distribution for θ_P (with prior $P(\theta_P)$ and posterior $P(\theta_P|\mathcal{T}^{(c)})$), and inference is processed with [6,12]:

$$P(y|\mathbf{x}(\mathcal{M}), \mathcal{T}^{(c)}) = \int_{\theta_P} P(y|\mathbf{x}(\mathcal{M}), \theta_P) P(\theta_P|\mathcal{T}^{(c)}) d\theta_P. \tag{15.9}$$

The inference in (15.9) is generally intractable, an issue that can be mitigated with the use of a variational distribution $Q(\theta_P|\psi_Q)$ to approximate $P(\theta_P|\mathcal{T}^{(c)})$, where $\psi_Q = \{\mathbf{M}_l, p_l\}_{l=1}^{L}$, with L denoting the number of layers in the model, $\mathbf{M}_l$ representing the layerwise mean weight matrices and p_l the dropout probabilities. This means that $Q(\theta_P|\psi_Q) = \prod_l \mathbf{M}_l \times \text{diag}(\text{Bernoulli}(1 - p_l)^{K_l})$, with the weight matrix in layer l having dimensions $K_{l+1} \times K_l$ [12,13]. Then Eq. (15.9) can be solved with Monte Carlo (MC) integration:

$$\begin{aligned} Q(y|\mathbf{x}(\mathcal{M}), \psi_Q) &= \frac{1}{N} \sum_{j=1}^{N} P(y|\mathbf{x}(\mathcal{M}), \hat{\theta}_{P_j}) \\ &= \frac{1}{N} \sum_{j=1}^{N} \sigma(f^{\hat{\theta}_{P_j}}(\mathbf{x}(\mathcal{M}))), \end{aligned} \tag{15.10}$$

where $\hat{\theta}_{P_j} \sim Q(\theta_P|\psi_Q)$, $\sigma(.)$ represents the softmax function, and $f^{\hat{\theta}_{P_j}}(\mathbf{x}(\mathcal{M})) \in \mathbb{R}^{|\mathcal{Y}^{(c)}|}$ is the logit vector for the final softmax function applied by the classifier. The learning of the variational distribution parameter ψ_Q^* is based on the minimization of the following loss [12,13]:

$$\begin{aligned} \ell(\psi_Q) = &- \int Q(\theta_P|\psi_Q) \log \prod_{i=1}^{|\mathcal{T}^{(c)}|} P(y_i|\mathbf{x}_i(\omega), \theta_P) d\theta_P + \\ &KL(Q(\theta_P|\psi_Q)||P(\theta_P)), \end{aligned} \tag{15.11}$$

where $KL(.)$ represents the Kullback–Leibler divergence. The integral in (15.11) is approximated with MC integration,

$$\begin{aligned} \ell(\psi_Q) \approx &- \frac{1}{N} \sum_{j=1}^{N} \log \prod_{i=1}^{|\mathcal{T}^{(c)}|} P(y_i|\mathbf{x}_i(\omega), \hat{\theta}_{P_j}) + \\ &KL(Q(\theta_P|\psi_Q)||P(\theta_P)), \end{aligned} \tag{15.12}$$

with $\hat{\theta}_{P_j} \sim Q(\theta_P|\psi_Q)$. As explained in [13], we assume that $P(\theta_P)$ has a prior distribution represented by a discrete quantized Gaussian prior that enables an analytically derivation of $KL(Q(\theta_P|\psi_Q)||P(\theta_P))$ in (15.11). As depicted in Fig. 15.4(b), the training process, based on concrete dropout [13], produces a model that outputs the classification probability and the aleatoric uncertainty for each class [29]. The estimation of classification uncertainty can then be performed in many ways, such as based on the entropy of the probability vector [58,29], computed with [6]:

$$H(P(y|\mathbf{x}(\mathcal{M}), \mathcal{T}^{(c)})) =$$
$$- \sum_{c \in \mathcal{Y}^{(c)}} P(y = c|\mathbf{x}(\mathcal{M}), \mathcal{T}^{(c)}) \log(P(y = c|\mathbf{x}(\mathcal{M}), \mathcal{T}^{(c)})), \qquad (15.13)$$

where $P(y|\mathbf{x}(\mathcal{M}), \mathcal{T}^{(c)})$ can be replaced by $P(y|\mathbf{x}(\mathcal{M}), \theta_P^*)$ from (15.8), $Q(y|\mathbf{x}(\mathcal{M}), \psi_Q^*)$ from (15.10) or the calibrated classifiers from (15.14).

Another issue with the training above is that the classification result is likely to be over-confident [19]. This is certainly undesirable in a clinical setting, but it can be fixed with confidence calibration [19] using a post-processing method that modifies the output classification probability computation as follows [6]:

$$\tilde{Q}(y|\mathbf{x}(\mathcal{M}), s, \psi_Q^*) = \frac{1}{N} \sum_{j=1}^{N} \sigma(\mathbf{f}^{\hat{\theta}_{P_j}}(\mathbf{x}(\mathcal{M}))/s), \qquad (15.14)$$

where $\hat{\theta}_{P_j} \sim Q(\theta_P|\psi_Q^*)$, $\mathbf{f}^{\hat{\theta}_P}(\mathbf{x}(\mathcal{M}))$ denotes the logit from (15.10), and $s \in \mathbb{R}^+$ is a temperature parameter that smooths the softmax function $\sigma(.)$ by increasing its entropy and is learned with stochastic gradient descent using the validation set $\mathcal{V}^{(c)}$ [19].

Using uncertainty estimation and confidence calibration, we formulate a method that uses that information to improve classification accuracy. In particular, we define two hyper-parameters $\tau_1^*(Z)$ and $\tau_2^*(Z)$, learned from the validation set $\mathcal{V}^{(c)}$ to enable the rejection of a percentage Z of samples that have low confidence and high uncertainty, respectively, as follows:

$$\begin{aligned}
&1) \quad P(y|\mathbf{x}(\mathcal{M}), \mathcal{T}^{(c)}) < \tau_1^*(Z), \text{ and} \\
&2) \quad H(Q(y|\mathbf{x}(\mathcal{M}), \psi_Q^*)) > \tau_2^*(Z),
\end{aligned} \qquad (15.15)$$

where the thresholds are learned with $\tau_1^*(Z) = P_{sorted}(Z \times |\mathcal{V}^{(c)}|)$ and $\tau_2^*(Z) = H_{sorted}(Z \times |\mathcal{V}^{(c)}|)$. P_{sorted} has the values of $\max_{y \in \mathcal{Y}^{(c)}} P(y|\mathbf{x}(\mathcal{M}), \mathcal{T}^{(c)})$ sorted in ascending order for the samples in the validation set $\mathcal{V}^{(c)}$, and H_{sorted} has the values of $H(Q(y|\mathbf{x}(\mathcal{M}), \psi_Q^*))$, defined in (15.13), sorted in descending order for the samples in $\mathcal{V}^{(c)}$.

15.4 Results and discussion

In this section, we first present the experiments that test the polyp detection methods, followed by another set of experiments on polyp localization and classification, and final experiments on confidence calibration and uncertainty estimation.

15.4.1 Polyp detection experiments

We test the polyp detection method under two assumptions. We first present the results of FSAD-NET from Section 15.3.2.2 working under the assumption that there are no frames containing water and feces—this means that we use the training and testing set from Table 15.1 without the Water&Feces frames. We then show FSAD-NET results using all sets in Table 15.1, where the Water&Feces frames are rejected by the binary classifier in (15.1).

For these two experiments, the original colonoscopy image had the original resolution of $1072 \times 1072 \times 3$ reduced to $64 \times 64 \times 3$ to reach a good trade-off between computational cost (for training and testing) and detection accuracy. For the proposed FSAD-NET, we use Adam [9] optimizer during training with a learning rate of 0.0001, where model selection (to estimate architecture, learning rate, mini-batch size and number of epochs) is done with the validation set $\mathcal{V}^{(d)}$. The binary classifier to detect Water&Feces frames is represented by a DenseNet [25] trained from scratch with Adam optimizer [9] with a learning rate of 0.001 and mini-batch of 128 for 200 epochs.

For the few-shot anomaly detector FSAD-NET [61], we use a similar backbone architecture as other competing approaches in Table 15.2, where the encoder $E(.; \theta_E)$ uses four convolution layers (with 64, 128, 256, 512 filters of size 4×4), the global discriminator (used in $\hat{I}_{\theta_D}$ from Eq. (15.2)) has three convolutional layers (with 128, 64, 32 filters of size 3×3), and the local discriminator (used in $\hat{I}_{\theta_L}$ from Eq. (15.2)) has three convolutional layers (with 192, 512, 512 filters of size 1×1). The prior discriminator $F(.; \theta_F)$ in (15.4) has three linear layers with 1000, 200 and 1 node per layer. We also use the validation set to estimate $a = 6$ in (15.5). In (15.2), we follow the DIM paper for setting the hyper-parameters with [24]: $\alpha = 0.5$, $\gamma = 1$, $\beta = 0.1$. For the prior distribution for the embeddings in (15.4), we set $\mu_{\mathbb{V}} = \mathbf{0}$ (i.e., a Z-dimensional vector of zeros), and $\Sigma_{\mathbb{V}}$ is a $Z \times Z$ identity matrix. To train the model, we first train the encoder, local, global and prior discriminator (they denote the representation learning stage) for 6000 epochs with a mini-batch of 64 samples. We then train SIN for 1000 epochs, with a batch size of 64, while fixing the parameters of encoder, local, global and prior discriminator. We implement all methods above using Pytorch [48].

The detection results are measured with the area under the receiver operating characteristic curve (AUC) on the test set [57,49], computed by varying a threshold τ for the SIN score $S(\mathbf{e}; \theta_S)$ in (15.5) for FSAD-NET.

Table 15.2 shows the results of several methods working under the assumption that there are no frames containing water and feces. In this table, the results of the proposed FSAD-NET [61] are compared with[3] other zero-shot and few-shot anomaly detectors. The zero-shot detectors considered are: DAE [41] and VAE [10], OC-GAN [49], f-anoGAN and its variants [57] represented by image-to-image mean

---

[3] Codes for the other methods were downloaded from the authors' Github pages and tuned for our problem.

Table 15.2 Results on the data set that does not include Water&Feces frames, where we compare our proposed FSAD-NET with several zero-shot anomaly detection methods and state-of-the-art and few-shot anomaly detection methods.

	Methods	AUC
Zero-Shot	DAE [41]	0.6384
	VAE [10]	0.6528
	OC-GAN [49]	0.6137
	f-AnoGAN(ziz) [57]	0.6629
	f-AnoGAN(izi) [57]	0.6831
	f-AnoGAN(izif) [57]	0.6997
	ADGAN [39]	**0.7391**
Few-Shot	Densenet121 [25]	0.8231
	cross-entropy	0.7115
	Focal loss [37]	0.7235
	without RL	0.6011
	Learning to Reweight [51]	0.7862
	AE network	0.835
	FSAD-NET [61]	**0.9033**

square error (MSE) loss (izi), Z-to-Z MSE loss (ziz) and its hybrid version (izif) and ADGAN [39]. For the few-shot approaches, we considered several methods trained with 40 polyp images and all normal images from Table 15.1 (40 polyp images is the number of training images needed to get stable results before reaching a diminishing return behavior [61]), such as Densenet121 [25] trained with a large amount of data augmentation to deal with the extreme training imbalance, and several variants of the FSAD-NET [61]. The variants "cross-entropy" and "focal loss" replace the contrastive loss in (15.5) by the cross-entropy loss (commonly used in classification problems) [18] and the focal loss (robust to imbalanced learning problems) [37], respectively. The method "without RL" tests the representation learning (RL) role by removing it from the FSAD-NET formulation. The few-shot training algorithm "Learning to Reweight" [51] represents an example of a method designed to handle imbalanced learning and we use it for training FSAD-NET. The importance of DIM to train the encoder is tested by replacing it with a deep auto-encoder [41]—this is labeled as the "AE network."

The results in Table 15.2 show that few-shot anomaly detection is generally more accurate than zero-shot. When comparing FSAD-NET with Densenet121 [25], we notice that FSAD-NET is more accurate by a large margin. Results also demonstrate that the contrastive loss used in FSAD-NET is more appropriate for few-shot anomaly detection, compared with cross-entropy. The removal of the representation learning reduces substantially the AUC result. The use of Learning to Reweight [51] for FSAD-NET shows relatively good results, with an AUC of 78.62%, but they are not competitive with the final FSAD-NET results. The results from the AE network

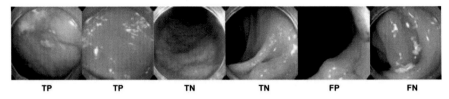

| TP | TP | TN | TN | FP | FN |

FIGURE 15.5

Example of the FSAD-NET detection results, where TN denotes a successful detection of a normal frame, TP is a successful detection of an abnormal frame, FN denotes an unsuccessful detection of a normal frame and FP, an unsuccessful detection of an abnormal frame.

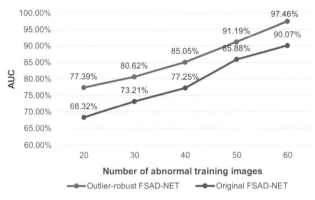

FIGURE 15.6

Results on the data set that includes Water&Feces frames. Mean AUC results from our outlier-robust FSAD-NET as a function of the number of abnormal training images present in the training set, comparing with the original FSAD-NET model.

show that FSAD-NET is more accurate, suggesting the effectiveness of using MI and prior distribution for learning the feature embeddings. Fig. 15.5 shows examples of the FSAD-NET detection results.

By rejecting Water&Feces frames by the binary classifier in (15.1), we build the "outlier-robust FSAD-NET." During the first training stage of the "outlier-robust FSAD-NET," we train the DenseNet using the whole training data from Table 15.1, and then we train the FSAD-NET using the training data not rejected from the first stage. Fig. 15.6 shows the mean AUC results using the whole testing set from Table 15.1 (that contains the Water&Feces frames) as a function of the number of abnormal (i.e., containing polyp) training images. This figure compares the outlier-robust FSAD-NET with the original FSAD-NET trained with the whole training set in Table 15.1. The results indicate that the outlier-robust FSAD-NET achieves better performance for all cases, suggesting that the detector of feces and water jet sprays can effectively exclude these frames. With 60 abnormal images in the training set, the outlier-robust FSAD-NET achieves an AUC of 97.46%, which is close to human-level performance from medical practitioners.

15.4.2 Polyp localization and classification experiments

The polyp localization and classification experiment using the Australian and Japanese data sets described in Section 15.3.1.2 relied on a 5-fold cross-validation experiment, where in each fold, the training set contains images from 60% of the patients, the validation set has images of 20% of patients and the test set contains images of the remaining 20% of the patients. The experiment based on training on the Australian data set and testing on the Japanese data set uses the five models learned from the 5-fold cross-validation procedure to classify all images from the Japanese data set. Results are shown in terms of the mean and standard deviation of accuracy and AUC for classification, using the 5-fold cross-validation experiment. For polyp localization, we present our results on the MICCAI 2015 polyp detection challenge [3] (also described in Section 15.3.1.2), using the following measures: number of true positives and false positives, mean precision and recall and F1 and F2 scores.

For the polyp localization and classification approach in (15.6) presented in Section 15.3.2.3, we use Resnet50 [21] as the base model for Retinanet [37], trained with the focal loss function (15.7) [37]. This base model is pre-trained using ImageNet [8] because it shows more accurate results than if we train from scratch [2]. We also rely on data augmentation to improve generalization, where we increase six-fold the training set size using random transformations (rotation, scaling, shearing and horizontal flipping). The validation set is used to tune the hyper-parameters, where the selected values are: 800 epochs, batch size of 32, Adam optimizer, learning rate of 10^{-4}, dropout rate of 0.3, $\alpha = 0.25$ and $\gamma = 2$ in Section 15.3.2.3.

The results in Fig. 15.7(a) shows the classification performance of our proposed model, using as baseline a classifier that relies on manually detected polyps [68]. This baseline is based on a Resnet-50 classifier trained and tested on manually localized polyps, which means that it can only handle correct localizations, so it can be considered as an upper bound to the performance of our approach. If we restrict our method to produce classification results only for true positive localizations (e.g., the bounding boxes have an IoU greater than 0.5 with polyps), then the result in Fig. 15.7(a) shows that the performance of our method and the baseline are comparable. On the other hand, when we do not make such restriction, allowing potential false–positive localizations to contaminate the classification process of our approach, then Fig. 15.7(a) shows that the baseline is superior. These results suggest that the classification mistakes made by our approach are mainly due to incorrect localizations. The polyp localization results in Fig. 15.7(b) suggest that although our method is implemented for localizing and classifying polyps, it is competitive with the state of the art designed specifically for localizing polyps.

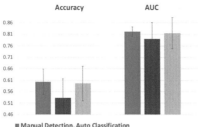

	TP	FP	Prec	Rec	F1	F2
CUMED	144	55	72.3	69.2	70.7	69.8
CVC-CLINIC	102	920	10	49	16.5	27.5
ETIS-LARIB	103	1373	6.9	49.5	12.2	22.3
OUS	131	57	69.7	63	66.1	64.2
PLS	119	630	15.8	57.2	24.9	37.6
SNU	20	176	10.2	9.6	9.9	9.7
UNS-UCLAN	110	226	32.73	52.8	40.4	47.1
1-stage Detector	134	48	**73.6**	64.42	68.72	66.07

a) **Classification Results**   b) **Localisation Results**

FIGURE 15.7

The classification results in (a) shows a comparison between our proposed one-stage localization and classification method and a classification method that uses manual localization and automated classification of polyps [68] using the mean and standard deviation of the classification accuracy and AUC over the 5-fold cross-validation experiment. In this bar plot, we also compute the results from our method considering only the true positive (TP only) polyp localizations to isolate the performance of the classifier. The localization results in (b) displays a comparison between our one-stage detector and the state of the art from the MICCAI 2015 Polyp detection Challenge [3].

15.4.3 Uncertainty estimation and calibration experiments

The polyp classification uncertainty and calibration from Section 15.3.2.4 uses an ImageNet pre-trained DenseNet-121 [25] as the backbone. For the non-Bayesian learning models, the training consists of removing the last 1000-node layer from the pre-trained model and replacing it by a softmax activated five-node layer, representing the five classes of the polyp classification problem. For the Bayesian learning models, we use concrete dropout [13], where the 1000-node layer from the original model is replaced by two fully connected layers: one layer with five nodes activated by a rectified linear unit (ReLU) [43] and a second layer with ten nodes (first five nodes activated by softmax, representing the classification probability vector, and the next five nodes denoting the aleatoric uncertainty [29]); see Fig. 15.4(b). The parameters of the variational distribution $Q(\theta_P | \psi_Q)$, represented by the mean values of the weights and the dropout probabilities (15.9) are learned only for these two last layers.

For all training procedures, we use mini-batches of size 32, 800 training epochs, initial learning rate of 10^{-3}, which decays by 0.9 after every 50 training epochs, and $10\times$ data augmentation using random translations and scalings. The input image size is $224 \times 224 \times 3$ (the original polyp images acquired from colonoscopy videos are transformed to this size by bicubic interpolation). For the optimization, we use Adam [30] with $\beta_1 = 0.9$, $\beta_2 = 0.999$ and $\epsilon = 10^{-8}$. For Bayesian inference, the number of samples drawn from $Q(\theta_P | \psi_Q)$ in (15.10) is $N = 10$. For training the confidence calibration, we retrain the last layer of the model for 100 epochs, using the validation set $\mathcal{V}^{(c)}$ to estimate s in (15.14). The models tested in this section are labeled as follows: 1) Bayesian learning and inference models in (15.9) are labeled with **-Bayes** and non-Bayesian models have no label, and 2) models trained with confidence calibration are labeled as **+Temp. Scl.** and without calibration as **+No Scl.**. The combination of these models form a total of four models.

Our classifier that rejects samples using the condition in (15.15) is trained by estimating the hyper-parameters $\tau_1^*(Z)$ and $\tau_2^*(Z)$ using the validation set $\mathcal{V}^{(c)}$, where Z in (15.15) is set as $Z \in \{0.5, 0.6, ..., 0.9, 1.0\}$ (for the training and testing on the Australian data set) and $Z \in \{0.7, 0.8, 0.9, 1.0\}$ (for the training on the Australian and testing on the Japanese data set—the range for this Japanese data set is smaller because of the smaller size of the data set). For this classifier, the uncertainty is computed from the classification entropy (15.13) and confidence is calculated by $P(y|\mathbf{x}, \theta_P^*)$ from (15.8), $Q(y|\mathbf{x}, \psi_Q^*)$ from (15.10) or the calibrated classifiers from (15.14). The experiments show results where both conditions are applied jointly.

The proposed classifiers in this section are assessed with accuracy and average precision (AP), where accuracy is represented by the proportion of correctly classified samples, and AP is computed by averaging the precision across all recall values between zero and one, and then calculating the mean AP over the five classes. The calibration results are calculated with the expected calibration error (ECE) and maximum calibration error (MCE), where both measures are computed from the reliability diagram, which plots sample classification accuracy as a function of expected accuracy [19]. These measures are based on the mean (for ECE) or maximum (for MCE) difference between the classification and expected accuracies.

Fig. 15.8(a) displays the accuracy and AP using the training and testing sets from the Australian data set, and Fig. 15.8(b) shows results from the training on Australian and testing on the Japanese data set—all bar plots are grouped as a function of the rejection percentage Z from (15.15). We also compare with our polyp localization and classifier from (15.6), labeled as "1-stage Loc. Clas.," where the polyp localization is manually provided and samples are rejected based solely on the first condition in Eq. (15.15) (i.e., classification probability).

The results in Fig. 15.8 show that the Bayesian DenseNet (with and without calibration) produces the most accurate results. It is worth noticing the discrepancy in accuracy improvement (as a function of Z), compared with AP improvement. This can be explained from the imbalanced training set introduced in Section 15.3.1.2, with around 40% of the training samples belonging to class II and 20% to class IIo. This biases the classification probability toward these two classes, which explains the better improvement for accuracy, in particular for the Australian set experiment. Also from Fig. 15.8, it is clear that accuracy and AP results reduce significantly for the experiment based on training on Australian and testing on Japanese data set, indicating that further studies are necessary to improve the generalization of the proposed method to new data domains. The Bayesian models that reject high-uncertainty and low-confidence samples, trained and tested on the Australian data set, show the best results, with DenseNet-Bayes+Temp.Scl. showing the best overall improvement. The comparison with "1-stage Loc. Clas." shows that the DenseNet-Bayes methods with-

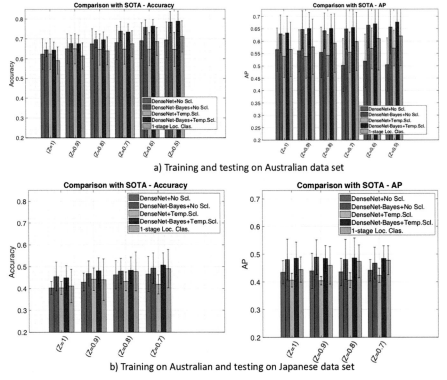

a) Training and testing on Australian data set

b) Training on Australian and testing on Japanese data set

FIGURE 15.8

Relying on training and testing from the Australian data set, we show in (a) the mean and standard deviation of the accuracy and mean average precision (AP) results over the 5-fold cross-validation experiment for several versions of our proposed method (with different models, calibration and learning algorithm). This graph also displays a comparison (in terms of accuracy and AP) between the method to reject high-uncertainty and low-confidence samples in (15.15) for all models and also for the "1-stage Loc. Clas." using manually detected polyps. The same results for the training on the Australian set and testing on the Japanese set are displayed in (b).

out rejecting samples have superior classification accuracy and AP. After rejecting samples based on uncertainty and calibrated confidence, DenseNet-Bayes methods reaches around 70% when rejecting around 20% of the testing samples and close to 80% when rejecting 50% of the testing samples. The AP also improves, reaching around 64% when rejecting 20% of the testing samples and around 68% when rejecting 50% of the testing samples. The rejection process for "1-stage Loc. Clas.," based on uncalibrated confidence, also shows improvements, reaching 71% accuracy and 62% AP when rejecting 50% of the testing samples, but this result is not competitive to the results produced by the DenseNet-Bayes methods. For the experiment with the training on Australian and testing on Japanese data sets, the classification accuracy

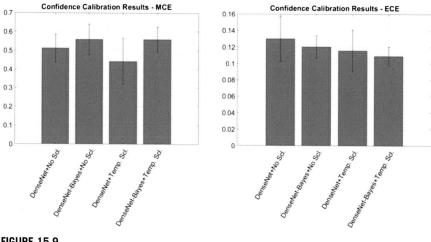

FIGURE 15.9

Mean and standard deviation of the MCE (left), and ECE (right) of the methods over the 5-fold cross-validation experiment for the training and testing on the Australian data set.

Table 15.3 The inference time of our proposed methods.

Method	Inference Time
FSAD-Net	0.016 s per image
Outlier-robust FSAD-Net	0.032 s per image
1-stage localization and detection	0.067 s per image
Calibration and Uncertainty	2.170 s per image

of the DenseNet-Bayes methods starts at around 45% and reaches 51% when rejecting around 30% of the testing samples. This compares favorably with "1-stage Loc. Clas." that has accuracy of 41% with all samples, and reaches 49% when rejecting 30% of the testing samples. Regarding AP, results of the DenseNet-Bayes methods are stable at around 48% with the rejection of testing samples, while "1-stage Loc. Clas." improves from 44% to around 48% when rejecting around 30% of the testing samples, suggesting that this experiment is more challenging for the DenseNet-Bayes methods, particularly at small values for Z.

The ECE and MCE results are displayed in Fig. 15.9. The calibrated methods tend to show smaller ECE and MCE, but the differences are more noticeable for the non-Bayesian methods. This can be explained by the fact that Bayesian methods tend to produce relatively calibrated results even without an explicit confidence calibration training.

15.4.4 System running time

We measure the run time of all steps of the system for inference in one image. Table 15.3 shows the running time of the FSAD-Net, Outlier-robust FSAD-Net, 1-stage localization and detection and Calibration and Uncertainty. The results indicate that our system is applicable in real-time colonoscopy procedure, except for the calibration and uncertainty estimator.

15.5 Conclusion

In this chapter, we showed the results of several stages of a system that can detect and classify polyps from a colonoscopy video. The system first rejects frames containing water and feces that can be considered as distractors. Then the detection of frames containing polyps is based on the few-shot anomaly detector FSAD-NET. The FSAD-NET comprises an encoder trained to maximize the mutual information between normal images and respective embeddings and a score inference network that classifies between normal and abnormal colonoscopy frames. Results showed that FSAD-NET achieved state-of-the-art few-shot anomaly detection performance on our colonoscopy data set, compared to previously proposed anomaly detection methods and imbalanced learning methods. Next, the one-stage polyp localization and classification method proposed is shown to be an effective approach, and when it is compared with a classification method based on manually detected polyps [68], we noted that the small accuracy gap was due to the mis-detected polyps. The results for the polyp classification method that relies on confidence calibration and uncertainty estimation showed that: 1) confidence calibration reduced calibration errors; and 2) rejecting test samples based on high classification uncertainty and low classification confidence improved classification accuracy and average precision for Bayesian methods. These results can motivate the development of better interpretable polyp classification methods that outputs not only a classification, but also confidence and uncertainty results.

In the future, we plan to improve polyp localization accuracy since it is shown to be the major factor causing a gap in classification accuracy with respect to the method that relies on manual polyp detection. Moreover, the polyp classification accuracy also needs to be improved particularly regarding the classes that are underrepresented in the training set. These issues can be solved with larger annotated data sets. Another solution for these problems is based on the use of temporal information from the colonoscopy video, where we seek stable polyp detection, localization and classification over time. Another issue that we plan to address is the slow running time of the confidence calibration and uncertainty estimator. Finally, the generalization of the methods to new domains also needs to be explored further, and we plan to address that with domain adaptation [15] and generalization methods [34].

References

[1] M. Arnold, M.S. Sierra, M. Laversanne, I. Soerjomataram, A. Jemal, F. Bray, Global patterns and trends in colorectal cancer incidence and mortality, Gut 66 (2017) 683–691.

[2] Y. Bar, I. Diamant, L. Wolf, S. Lieberman, E. Konen, H. Greenspan, Chest pathology detection using deep learning with non-medical training, in: 2015 IEEE 12th International Symposium on Biomedical Imaging (ISBI), IEEE, 2015, pp. 294–297.

[3] J. Bernal, N. Tajkbaksh, F.J. Sánchez, B.J. Matuszewski, H. Chen, L. Yu, Q. Angermann, O. Romain, B. Rustad, I. Balasingham, et al., Comparative validation of polyp detection methods in video colonoscopy: results from the miccai 2015 endoscopic vision challenge, IEEE Transactions on Medical Imaging 36 (2017) 1231–1249.

[4] C.M. Bishop, Pattern Recognition, Machine Learning, 2006.

[5] J. Bullock, C. Cuesta-Lazaro, A. Quera-Bofarull, Xnet: a convolutional neural network (cnn) implementation for medical x-ray image segmentation suitable for small datasets, arXiv preprint, arXiv:1812.00548, 2018.

[6] G. Carneiro, L. Zorron Cheng Tao Pu, R. Singh, A. Burt, Deep learning uncertainty and confidence calibration for the five-class polyp classification from colonoscopy, Medical Image Analysis 101653 (2020).

[7] Y. Chen, Y. Tian, G. Pang, G. Carneiro, Unsupervised anomaly detection with multi-scale interpolated Gaussian descriptors, arXiv preprint, arXiv:2101.10043, 2021.

[8] J. Deng, W. Dong, R. Socher, L.J. Li, K. Li, L. Fei-Fei, Imagenet: a large-scale hierarchical image database, in: Computer Vision and Pattern Recognition, 2009, in: CVPR 2009. IEEE Conference on, IEEE, 2009, pp. 248–255.

[9] D.P. Kingma, J. Ba, Adam: A Method for Stochastic Optimization, ICLR, 2015.

[10] C. Doersch, Tutorial on variational autoencoders, arXiv preprint, arXiv:1606.05908, 2016.

[11] Z. Eaton-Rosen, F. Bragman, S. Bisdas, S. Ourselin, M.J. Cardoso, Towards safe deep learning: accurately quantifying biomarker uncertainty in neural network predictions, arXiv preprint, arXiv:1806.08640, 2018.

[12] Y. Gal, Z. Ghahramani, Dropout as a Bayesian approximation: representing model uncertainty in deep learning, in: International Conference on Machine Learning, 2016, pp. 1050–1059.

[13] Y. Gal, J. Hron, A. Kendall, Concrete dropout, in: Advances in Neural Information Processing Systems, 2017, pp. 3581–3590.

[14] D. Gamerman, H.F. Lopes, Markov Chain Monte Carlo: Stochastic Simulation for Bayesian Inference, Chapman and Hall/CRC, 2006.

[15] Y. Ganin, V. Lempitsky, Unsupervised domain adaptation by backpropagation, in: International Conference on Machine Learning, PMLR, 2015, pp. 1180–1189.

[16] R. Girshick, Fast r-cnn, in: Proceedings of the IEEE International Conference on Computer Vision, 2015, pp. 1440–1448.

[17] D. Gong, L. Liu, V. Le, B. Saha, M.R. Mansour, S. Venkatesh, A.v.d. Hengel, Memorizing normality to detect anomaly: memory-augmented deep autoencoder for unsupervised anomaly detection, in: Proceedings of the IEEE International Conference on Computer Vision, 2019, pp. 1705–1714.

[18] I. Goodfellow, Y. Bengio, A. Courville, Deep Learning, MIT Press, 2016.

[19] C. Guo, G. Pleiss, Y. Sun, K.Q. Weinberger, On calibration of modern neural networks, arXiv preprint, arXiv:1706.04599, 2017.

[20] N. Hayashi, S. Tanaka, D.G. Hewett, T.R. Kaltenbach, Y. Sano, T. Ponchon, B.P. Saunders, D.K. Rex, R.M. Soetikno, Endoscopic prediction of deep submucosal invasive carcinoma: validation of the narrow-band imaging international colorectal endoscopic (nice) classification, Gastrointestinal Endoscopy 78 (2013) 625–632.

[21] K. He, X. Zhang, S. Ren, J. Sun, Deep residual learning for image recognition, in: Proceedings of the IEEE Conference on Computer Vision and Pattern Recognition, 2016, pp. 770–778.

[22] X. He, D. Cai, P. Niyogi, Laplacian score for feature selection, in: Advances in Neural Information Processing Systems, 2006, pp. 507–514.

[23] D.G. Hewett, T. Kaltenbach, Y. Sano, S. Tanaka, B.P. Saunders, T. Ponchon, R. Soetikno, D.K. Rex, Validation of a simple classification system for endoscopic diagnosis of small colorectal polyps using narrow-band imaging, Gastroenterology 143 (2012) 599–607.

[24] R.D. Hjelm, A. Fedorov, S. Lavoie-Marchildon, K. Grewal, P. Bachman, A. Trischler, Y. Bengio, Learning deep representations by mutual information estimation and maximization, arXiv preprint, arXiv:1808.06670, 2018.

[25] G. Huang, Z. Liu, L. Van Der Maaten, K.Q. Weinberger, Densely connected convolutional networks, in: Proceedings of the IEEE Conference on Computer Vision and Pattern Recognition, 2017.

[26] M. Iwatate, Y. Sano, S. Tanaka, S.e. Kudo, S. Saito, T. Matsuda, Y. Wada, T. Fujii, H. Ikematsu, T. Uraoka, et al., Validation study for development of the Japan nbi expert team classification of colorectal lesions, Digestive Endoscopy 30 (2018) 642–651.

[27] T.S. Jaakkola, M.I. Jordan, Bayesian parameter estimation via variational methods, Statistics and Computing 10 (2000) 25–37.

[28] X. Jiang, M. Osl, J. Kim, L. Ohno-Machado, Calibrating predictive model estimates to support personalized medicine, Journal of the American Medical Informatics Association 19 (2011) 263–274.

[29] A. Kendall, Y. Gal, What uncertainties do we need in Bayesian deep learning for computer vision?, in: Advances in Neural Information Processing Systems, 2017, pp. 5574–5584.

[30] D.P. Kingma, J. Ba, Adam: a method for stochastic optimization, arXiv preprint, arXiv:1412.6980, 2014.

[31] Y. Komeda, H. Handa, T. Watanabe, et al., Computer-aided diagnosis based on convolutional neural network system for colorectal polyp classification: preliminary experience, Oncology 93 (2017) 30–34.

[32] B. Korbar, A.M. Olofson, A.P. Miraflor, C.M. Nicka, M.A. Suriawinata, L. Torresani, A.A. Suriawinata, S. Hassanpour, Deep learning for classification of colorectal polyps on whole-slide images, Journal of Pathology Informatics 8 (2017).

[33] B. Levin, D.A. Lieberman, B. McFarland, R.A. Smith, D. Brooks, K.S. Andrews, C. Dash, F.M. Giardiello, S. Glick, T.R. Levin, et al., Screening and surveillance for the early detection of colorectal cancer and adenomatous polyps, 2008: a joint guideline from the American cancer society, the us multi-society task force on colorectal cancer, and the American college of radiology, CA: A Cancer Journal for Clinicians 58 (2008) 130–160.

[34] D. Li, Y. Yang, Y.Z. Song, T.M. Hospedales, Learning to generalize: meta-learning for domain generalization, arXiv preprint, arXiv:1710.03463, 2017.

[35] Z. Li, K. Kamnitsas, B. Glocker, Overfitting of neural nets under class imbalance: analysis and improvements for segmentation, in: International Conference on Medical Image Computing and Computer-Assisted Intervention, Springer, 2019, pp. 402–410.

[36] T.Y. Lin, P. Dollár, R. Girshick, K. He, B. Hariharan, S. Belongie, Feature pyramid networks for object detection, in: Proceedings of the IEEE Conference on Computer Vision and Pattern Recognition, 2017, pp. 2117–2125.

[37] T.Y. Lin, P. Goyal, R. Girshick, K. He, P. Dollár, Focal loss for dense object detection, in: IEEE Transactions on Pattern Analysis and Machine Intelligence, 2018.

[38] G. Litjens, T. Kooi, B.E. Bejnordi, A.A.A. Setio, F. Ciompi, M. Ghafoorian, J.A. van der Laak, B. Van Ginneken, C.I. Sánchez, A survey on deep learning in medical image analysis, Medical Image Analysis 42 (2017) 60–88.

[39] Y. Liu, Y. Tian, G. Maicas, L. Zorron Cheng Tao Pu, R. Singh, J.W. Verjans, G. Carneiro, Photoshopping colonoscopy video frames, in: 2020 IEEE 17th International Symposium on Biomedical Imaging (ISBI), IEEE, 2020, pp. 1–5.

[40] A. Makhzani, J. Shlens, N. Jaitly, I. Goodfellow, B. Frey, Adversarial autoencoders, arXiv preprint, arXiv:1511.05644, 2015.

[41] J. Masci, U. Meier, D. Cireşan, J. Schmidhuber, Stacked convolutional auto-encoders for hierarchical feature extraction, in: International Conference on Artificial Neural Networks, Springer, 2011, pp. 52–59.

[42] T. Nair, D. Precup, D.L. Arnold, T. Arbel, Exploring uncertainty measures in deep networks for multiple sclerosis lesion detection and segmentation, Medical Image Analysis 59 (2020) 101557.

[43] V. Nair, G.E. Hinton, Rectified linear units improve restricted Boltzmann machines, in: Proceedings of the 27th International Conference on Machine Learning (ICML-10), 2010, pp. 807–814.

[44] G. Pang, L. Cao, L. Chen, H. Liu, Learning representations of ultrahigh-dimensional data for random distance-based outlier detection, in: Proceedings of the 24th ACM SIGKDD International Conference on Knowledge Discovery & Data Mining, 2018, pp. 2041–2050.

[45] G. Pang, C. Ding, C. Shen, A.v.d. Hengel, Explainable deep few-shot anomaly detection with deviation networks, arXiv preprint, arXiv:2108.00462, 2021.

[46] G. Pang, C. Shen, L. Cao, A.v.d. Hengel, Deep learning for anomaly detection: a review, arXiv preprint, arXiv:2007.02500, 2020.

[47] G. Pang, C. Shen, A. van den Hengel, Deep anomaly detection with deviation networks, in: Proceedings of the 25th ACM SIGKDD International Conference on Knowledge Discovery & Data Mining, 2019, pp. 353–362.

[48] A. Paszke, S. Gross, S. Chintala, G. Chanan, E. Yang, Z. DeVito, Z. Lin, A. Desmaison, L. Antiga, A. Lerer, Automatic differentiation in pytorch, 2017.

[49] P. Perera, R. Nallapati, B. Xiang, Ocgan: one-class novelty detection using gans with constrained latent representations, in: Proceedings of the IEEE Conference on Computer Vision and Pattern Recognition, 2019, pp. 2898–2906.

[50] L. Pu, Z.C. Tao, G. Maicas, Y. Tian, T. Yamamura, G. Singh, K. Rana, H. Suzuki, M. Nakamura, Y. Hirooka, et al., Prospective study assessing a comprehensive computer-aided diagnosis for characterization of colorectal lesions: results from different centers and imaging technologies, Journal of Gastroenterology and Hepatology (2019) 25–26.

[51] M. Ren, W. Zeng, B. Yang, R. Urtasun, Learning to reweight examples for robust deep learning, arXiv preprint, arXiv:1803.09050, 2018.

[52] S. Ren, K. He, R. Girshick, J. Sun, Faster r-cnn: towards real-time object detection with region proposal networks, in: Advances in Neural Information Processing Systems, 2015, pp. 91–99.

[53] D.K. Rex, C.R. Boland, J.A. Dominitz, F.M. Giardiello, D.A. Johnson, T. Kaltenbach, T.R. Levin, D. Lieberman, D.J. Robertson, Colorectal cancer screening: recommendations for physicians and patients from the us multi-society task force on colorectal cancer, The American Journal of Gastroenterology 112 (2017) 1016.

[54] D.K. Rex, C. Kahi, M. O'Brien, T. Levin, H. Pohl, A. Rastogi, L. Burgart, T. Imperiale, U. Ladabaum, J. Cohen, et al., The American society for gastrointestinal endoscopy

pivi (preservation and incorporation of valuable endoscopic innovations) on real-time endoscopic assessment of the histology of diminutive colorectal polyps, Gastrointestinal Endoscopy 73 (2011) 419–422.

[55] E. Ribeiro, M. Häfner, G. Wimmer, et al., Exploring texture transfer learning for colonic polyp classification via convolutional neural networks, in: Biomedical Imaging (ISBI 2017), 2017 IEEE 14th International Symposium on, IEEE, 2017, pp. 1044–1048.

[56] T. Schlegl, Unsupervised anomaly detection with generative adversarial networks to guide marker discovery, in: International Conference on Information Processing in Medical Imaging, Springer, 2017, pp. 146–157.

[57] T. Schlegl, P. Seeböck, S.M. Waldstein, G. Langs, U. Schmidt-Erfurth, f-anogan: fast unsupervised anomaly detection with generative adversarial networks, Medical Image Analysis 54 (2019) 30–44.

[58] B. Settles, Active Learning, Synthesis Lectures on Artificial Intelligence and Machine Learning, vol. 6, 2012, pp. 1–114.

[59] R. Siegel, C. DeSantis, A. Jemal, Colorectal cancer statistics, 2014, CA: A Cancer Journal for Clinicians 64 (2014) 104–117.

[60] R. Singh, M. Jayanna, S. Navadgi, A. Ruszkiewicz, Y. Saito, N. Uedo, Narrow-band imaging with dual focus magnification in differentiating colorectal neoplasia, Digestive Endoscopy 25 (2013) 16–20.

[61] Y. Tian, G. Maicas, L. Zorron Cheng Tao Pu, R. Singh, J.W. Verjans, G. Carneiro, Few-shot anomaly detection for polyp frames from colonoscopy, in: International Conference on Medical Image Computing and Computer-Assisted Intervention, Springer, 2020, pp. 274–284.

[62] Y. Tian, G. Pang, Y. Chen, R. Singh, J.W. Verjans, G. Carneiro, Weakly-supervised video anomaly detection with robust temporal feature magnitude learning, arXiv preprint, arXiv:2101.10030, 2021.

[63] Y. Tian, G. Pang, F. Liu, S.H. Shin, J.W. Verjans, R. Singh, G. Carneiro, et al., Constrained contrastive distribution learning for unsupervised anomaly detection and localisation in medical images, arXiv preprint, arXiv:2103.03423, 2021.

[64] Y. Tian, L. Zorron Cheng Tao Pu, R. Singh, A. Burt, G. Carneiro, One-stage five-class polyp detection and classification, in: Biomedical Imaging (ISBI 2019), 2017 IEEE 16th International Symposium on, IEEE, 2019.

[65] J.C. Van Rijn, J.B. Reitsma, J. Stoker, P.M. Bossuyt, S.J. Van Deventer, E. Dekker, Polyp miss rate determined by tandem colonoscopy: a systematic review, The American Journal of Gastroenterology 101 (2006) 343–350.

[66] L. Ziyin, R. Wang, P.P. Liang, R. Salakhutdinov, L.P. Morency, M. Ueda, A simple approach to the noisy label problem through the gambler's loss, 2019.

[67] B. Zong, Q. Song, M.R. Min, W. Cheng, C. Lumezanu, D. Cho, H. Chen, Deep autoencoding Gaussian mixture model for unsupervised anomaly detection, in: International Conference on Learning Representations, 2018.

[68] L. Zorron Cheng Tao Pu, B. Campbell, A.D. Burt, G. Carneiro, R. Singh, Computer-aided diagnosis for charaterising colorectal lesions: interim results of a newly developed software, Gastrointestinal Endoscopy 87 (2018) AB245.

[69] L. Zorron Cheng Tao Pu, G. Maicas, Y. Tian, T. Yamamura, M. Nakamura, H. Suzuki, G. Singh, K. Rana, Y. Hirooka, A.D. Burt, et al., Computer-aided diagnosis for characterisation of colorectal lesions: a comprehensive software including serrated lesions, Gastrointestinal Endoscopy (2020).

OCTA segmentation with limited training data using disentangled representation learning

16

Yihao Liu[a], Lianrui Zuo[a,b], Yufan He[a], Shuo Han[c], Jianqin Lei[d], Jerry L. Prince[a], and Aaron Carass[a]

[a]*Department of Electrical and Computer Engineering, Johns Hopkins University, Baltimore, MD, United States*

[b]*Laboratory of Behavioral Neuroscience, National Institute on Aging, National Institutes of Health, Baltimore, MD, United States*

[c]*Department of Biomedical Engineering, The Johns Hopkins School of Medicine, Baltimore, MD, United States*

[d]*Department of Ophthalmology, First Affiliated Hospital of Xi'an Jiaotong University, Xi'an, PR China*

16.1 Introduction

Optical coherence tomography (OCT) angiography (OCTA) is a noninvasive imaging technique based on OCT that was developed to visualize the vascular network structure [14,19,23,36–39] and the foveal avascular zone (FAZ) [6,27] in the human retina [33] and choroid [16]. OCTA is acquired volumetrically and for a variety of reasons, including the presence of projection artifacts [28,49], it is common to project selected slabs into *en face* images for analyzing macular OCTA images [19,37,38]. Typically two *en face* OCTA images are generated capturing the superficial vascular plexus (SVP) and the deep vascular plexus (DVP), representing the inner retina within the macula.

Current analyses methods for these *en face* OCTA images are focused on the segmentation [29] of the retinal vasculature and parcellation into arterial and venous labels [18]. Several segmentation methods for OCTA images have been proposed [15,22,24,25,29,35]. Supervised deep learning (DL) methods have gotten a lot of attention because of their success in other medical imaging applications like segmentation [3,48] and registration [7,9,47] tasks. Unfortunately, the drawback of such approaches is the required pixel-level manual delineations for training. In particular for OCTA images, it is extremely time-consuming to generate fine detailed delineations that are consistent across scanners and sites. Further compounding this issue is the large number of such data sets that would be required to train a deep network.

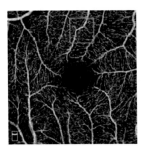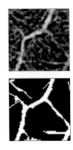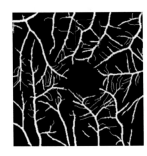

FIGURE 16.1

On the left is an Optovue *en face* SVP image from the ROSE data set [32]. On the right is the corresponding manual delineation, and in the center are the zoomed up regions corresponding to the SVP image (green box) and the manual delineation (red box). We use a ×2.5 magnification factor.

Building a deep network approach that can handle different scanners could add to this burden, although domain adaptors like He et al. [17] might alleviate this to some extent. In our experience, to accurately delineate a 3 mm × 3 mm *en face* SVP image requires in excess of 40 hours. Moreover, for many scans identifying the capillaries is impossible because of the limited image resolution and the presence of noise and artifacts. Because of this, publicly available images with manual delineations have focused on large vessels [25] with limited (or no) capillary delineations [32]. An example image and its corresponding manual delineation are shown in Fig. 16.1. We can identify capillaries in the zoomed inset images of Fig. 16.1, but the creators of these manual delineations have chosen to not include many capillaries in their released data.

Creating detailed vasculature delineations is, as noted above, very time-consuming. An alternative that is more viable is the use of multiple OCTA acquisitions of a subject's eye from the same or different scanners [10,22,24,27,29]. These scans are considered to be paired data, and although there are scanner differences, these repeated scans from the same eye capture similar regions within the retina and necessarily have the same anatomy. The differences between the scans predominately reflect the different artifacts and noise patterns coming from the scanning platforms. From such paired scans, we can readily identify the vasculature from the shared intensity patterns, while inconsistent patterns can usually be attributed to noise and other imaging artifacts. We show an example of this in Fig. 16.2, which shows the same anatomy captured on three different scanning platforms together with the corresponding delineations. These images are depicted prior to our registration step, which we outline later. We have created these manual delineations to identify as detailed a picture of the anatomy as possible, thus they include all identifiable components of the vasculature (arteries, veins and capillaries). It is clear that we can see different noise and artifact patterns, and we can also see quite clearly the similarities in their appearances of anatomical structures. In practice, we do not require such multiple

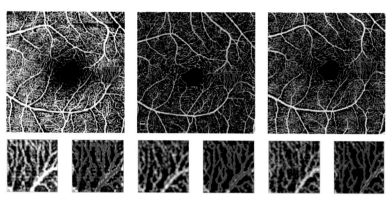

FIGURE 16.2

The top row from left to right shows OCTA images acquired on a Spectralis OCT2 device (Heidelberg Engineering, Germany), an Angiovue (RTVue XR Avanti, Optovue Inc., Fremont, CA) and a Triton (Topcon DRI OCT Triton, Topcon, Japan) of the same eye. Beneath each figure, we show zoomed up images of the original scan and manual delineation (magenta) for the same anatomical region (green box in the main figure). We use a ×3 magnification factor for the zoomed images.

scans to be available for us to process an image. Instead, we use the existence of such images during the training of our approach to disentangle image acquisition factors including artifacts, contrast and noise from the anatomy, from which a segmentation can be acquired. Ultimately, our trained network segments images while being able to overcome artifacts, contrast variations and noise.

The method described in this chapter, named <u>A</u>rtifacts and <u>C</u>ontrast <u>R</u>obust <u>Rep</u>resentation for <u>OCTA</u> <u>S</u>emi-supervised <u>S</u>egmentation (ACRROSS), disentangles the anatomy and contrast in OCTA images for accurate segmentation of retinal vasculature. Our approach is trained using two data sets in concert: the first contains unlabeled registered paired OCTA images and the second contains OCTA images with delineations that cover a small proportion of the corresponding entire OCTA image. ACRROSS is designed to disentangle the OCTA images into contrast and anatomy components by identifying shared structures in the paired images. In doing this, our approach also learns to segment the vasculature from the anatomy component of the disentanglement using a limited amount of manual training examples. In this chapter, we outline how ACRROSS improves OCTA vessel segmentation in comparison to existing supervised methods. As the FAZ is an important structure that is also identified from an OCTA image, we demonstrate how ACRROSS can also identify the FAZ as a simple post-processing of our binary vasculature map. We also compare our FAZ segmentation, showing that it matches the performance of the state-of-the-art methods.

16.2 **Related work**

U-Net [43] like networks have been previously proposed to perform vasculature segmentation of OCTA images. Prentašić et al. [41] used such a network for both vessel and FAZ segmentation for SVP images on two different scanners. Mou et al. [34,35] used an attention module to improve results for OCTA vessel segmentation. Pissas et al. [40] used convolutional neural networks that iteratively refine the quality of the produced vessel segmentations. Li et al. [25] proposed a network with a built-in projection learning module (PLM), which uses a unidirectional pooling layer to conduct effective feature selection and dimension reduction concurrently. Their proposed network can take 3D OCTA data as input and produce 2D vessel segmentations. All of these supervised network based approaches require tens (if not hundreds) of training data scans and corresponding manual delineations. Our approach, ACRROSS, however needs less than a single scan to achieve similar performance. This can happen if the input data has anatomy and contrast properly disentangled, and thus identifying anatomy becomes a trivial task. In contrast to our previous work, Liu et al. [29], which had involved an encoder–decoder structure for each scanner, the majority of the network weights in ACRROSS are shared by all scanners. As a result, the presented network requires less computational resources and is readily extended to multiple scanners without any additional computational overhead.

Semi-supervised methods have typically employed weak labels in their training. Examples of this include unsupervised image-to-image translation between disease and healthy subjects with the difference serving as a means to segment brain lesions [2,46]. While others have used the disease severity grading to learn lesion focused attention maps [51]. The idea of semi-supervised learning for disentanglement is not novel, and has been used previously for classification and segmentation. Robert et al. [42] introduced a two-branch auto-encoder structure; the first branch is supervised and identifies class invariant representations, while the second is fully unsupervised and dedicated to model information discarded by the first branch to reconstruct input data. Chartsias et al. [8] used a similar structure for segmenting cardiac cine magnetic resonance (MR) images, with the branches representing spatially and nonspatially dependent components. Both of these methods share the feature of using the self-reconstruction loss to learn the disentanglement. This is problematic as these two goals—self-reconstruction and segmentation—are contradictory for optimal feature extraction [42]. The self-reconstruction portion of the loss reinforces the noise and artifacts within the image and can cause them to be encoded in the anatomy representation. As our method also has an autoencoding portion, we could also have been susceptible to this problem. However, we avoid this issue by learning the disentanglement from paired images, which necessarily have different anomalies and uncorrelated noise, while also having the same anatomy.

There have been several previous works that have used an auto-encoding element to learn a disentangled representation [8,11,44,50,52,53]. Zhang et al. [50] disentangle the spatial structure and style code for synthesis. MR image disentanglement was handled by Dewey et al. [11] with an encoder–decoder structure that separates

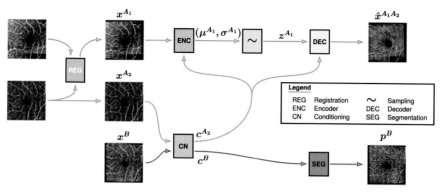

FIGURE 16.3

A schematic overview of our method. We first register (REG) the input training OCTA images together. We use pairs to train the encoder (ENC) network and the conditioning network (CN). We then sample ($\sim$) the contrast representation and pass this sample into our decoder (DEC) network. Simultaneously with training the encoder–decoder pathway, we train a segmentation network (SEG) that uses the input from the CN and example OCTA-delineation pairs. The mathematical notation corresponds to our explanation in Section 16.3.2.

contrast from anatomy. The method was not presented as a conditional variational auto-encoder (CVAE), however, the modality vector learned from the encoder is fed into their decoder as a condition. Similarly, although the work of Chartsias et al. [8] was not presented as a CVAE, it is in fact a CVAE since the spatial component serves as the conditioning.

Our approach, ACRROSS, differs from previous work in two ways. First, [8,11, 50] all seek to disentangle spatial and non-spatial dependent components. We also have a spatially dependent anatomy component, however, the nature of contrast in OCTA means that it is also spatially dependent. This allows for localized modeling of the contrast component. Second, we treat the anatomical component as our conditioning. In contrast, Zhang et al. [50] and Dewey et al. [11] treat the spatially-dependent component as the latent representation of the CVAE. Our network design decision avoids having to independently sample the anatomy representation at each pixel, giving rise to a less noisy anatomical representation, which benefits our segmentation task.

16.3 Method

16.3.1 Overview

Fig. 16.3 shows a schematic of our proposed method. It is composed of four networks: an encoder (ENC), a decoder (DEC), a conditioning network (CN) and a segmentation network (SEG). The figure also includes the preprocessing step of registration (REG) of the OCTA *en face* image pairs for training. We use the symmetric image normalization method [4] implemented in the Advanced Normalization Tools (ANTs) [5] to do the registration. This is done with deformable registration using mutual information (MI) based optimization. Despite the paired images being of the same anatomy, we have to use deformable registration since the 2D OCTA image are generated from a projection, which can be along a different projection path based on the subjects head position in the OCT device. We use MI as the cost function to account for the contrast variability in the OCT devices. Given that a cross-entropy loss computed between the output of SEG and the manual delination can be back-propagated to both the CN and the SEG, we can thus train both the CN and SEG in an end-to-end manner with manual delineations to perform segmentation, as in most existing supervised segmentation methods. However, such a network would have been sensitive to the amount of training data available, which is particularly an issue for OCTA as there is only a small amount of high-quality training data available in the OCTA domain. This issue is compounded by the variety of artifacts and contrast variations in current OCTA images. We avoid this issue by having the additional ENC and DEC networks. Once the four networks (ENC, DEC, CN and SEG) are trained, the CN and SEG networks can be used together to provide segmentation of any input image. The ENC, DEC and CN form a CVAE that uses a second data set of unlabeled, registered, paired OCTA scans during training. The addition of the ENC and DEC allows the CN to learn how to disentangle contrast and anatomy. It can thus provide a contrast-disentangled anatomy representation for the SEG. Complete details of the training and test-time execution are provided in subsequent sections.

16.3.2 Conditional variational auto-encoder

We input two OCTA images (see Fig. 16.3) of the same eye (acquired contemporaneously) and register one to the other. The registered images are denoted as x^{A_1} and x^{A_2}. We note that we impose no restrictions on the two OCTA images except that they are from the same eye and were scanned relatively close in time; thus they could be acquired on different scanners or the same scanner within a time-frame that would not see any anatomical changes. The CVAE framework assumes that ENC's input (x^{A_1}) can be reconstructed by DEC from the latent representation z^{A_1} given the conditioning c^{A_2}. We note that the superscript indicates the source of the conditioning or latent representation. That is, z^{A_1} is generated from x^{A_1}, while c^{A_2} is the conditioning from the paired scan x^{A_2}. Training ENC is actually approximating the posterior $q(z^{A_1}|x^{A_1}; c^{A_2})$ for the parametric encoder q_ϕ; we note that q_ϕ is a Gaussian distribution with data-dependent mean and standard deviation. In contrast, DEC is approximating the likelihood $p(x^{A_1}|z^{A_1}; c^{A_2})$ with a parametric decoder p_θ.

A CVAE is trained similarly to a variational auto-encoder (VAE) [21] by using the negative variational lower bound given by the loss

$$\mathcal{L}_{\text{CVAE}} = -E_{q_\phi}[\log p_\theta] + D_{\text{KL}}(q_\phi||p(z')), \tag{16.1}$$

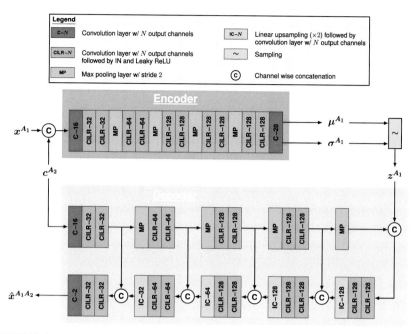

FIGURE 16.4

Detailed architecture of the encoder and decoder, and the integration between these two networks. All convolutional layers used in this work have a kernel size of 3 × 3 and a padding of 1. IN in the legend refers to instance normalization.

where $p(z')$ is assumed to be a multivariate Gaussian. The first term in Eq. (16.1) encourages the reconstruction of x^{A_1} from conditioning c^{A_2}, which we denote as $\hat{x}^{A_1 A_2}$. The second term in Eq. (16.1) is the Kullback–Leibler divergence between the two distributions, which acts as a regularization term on the latent representations.

The network architectures for ENC and DEC are shown in Fig. 16.4. To ensure q_ϕ has a Gaussian distribution, the output of ENC is a map of means, μ^{A_1}, and standard deviations, σ^{A_1}. We sample from the distribution $\mathcal{N}(\mu^{A_1}, \sigma^{A_1})$ to give us the latent representation, z^{A_1}. The number of channels in μ^{A_1} and σ^{A_1} is a tunable parameter that determines the compression rate of the ENC-DEC branch. In our work, we have found this parameter to be stable in the range $4-32$ and have used 10 channels for this work. For reference in Table 16.1, we denote the sizes of the various arrays in this work.

16.3.3 Anatomy-contrast disentanglement

A CVAE can be thought of as a generative model, which can produce diverse samples of a particular class. This is done by a decoder based on the provided latent representation, with the class label serving as the conditioning. In contrast, our CVAE

Table 16.1 For input images (x^{A_1} and x^{A_2}) with height H and width W, we denote the dimensions of the conditioning (c^{A_2}), segmentation (p^{A_2}), latent representation (z^{A_1}) and the mean (μ^{A_1}) and standard deviation (σ^{A_1}).

Variable	Dim.	Variable	Dim.
x^{A_1} and x^{A_2}	$H \times W$	μ^{A_1}	$\frac{H}{16} \times \frac{W}{16} \times 10$
c^{A_2}	$H \times W$	σ^{A_1}	$\frac{H}{16} \times \frac{W}{16} \times 10$
p^{A_2}	$H \times W$	z^{A_1}	$\frac{H}{16} \times \frac{W}{16} \times 10$

disentangles the anatomy and contrast components based on paired scans. To assign the conditioning, which is traditionally done manually, we use a forward pass through CN to learn the conditioning c^{A_2} from x^{A_2}. The reconstruction of x^{A_1} thus requires the latent representation z^{A_1} from ENC and c^{A_2} being fed into DEC; we denote the reconstruction as $\hat{x}^{A_1 A_2}$. Like traditional auto-encoder structures, z^{A_1} produced by ENC is a low-dimensional representation of x^{A_1}. Due to this, z^{A_1} can only encodes a limited amount of information. Thus, the more information for reconstructing x^{A_1} can be extracted from x^{A_2}, the more capacity of z^{A_1} can be used for encoding information specific to x^{A_1}. As x^{A_1} and x^{A_2} share anatomy information, the conditioning c^{A_2} will guide ENC to focus on compressing the local contrast information that is specific to x^{A_1}.

To achieve the anatomy-contrast disentanglement, we designed CN so that the conditioning c^{A_2} would have the same spatial extents as the input images x^{A_1} and x^{A_2} (see Table 16.1 for all array sizes). The registered OCTA pairs used as input to ENC and CN, respectively, share the same vasculature whereas the contrast and artifacts are specific to x^{A_1}. Thus ENC can focus on contrast and artifacts and ignore the vasculature since the DEC can anticipate that information coming from the conditioning c^{A_2}, which has 25 times the capacity of z^{A_1}. As a result of this, ENC and CN learn to cooperate for a better reconstruction. Specifically, CN learns to extract the vasculature that x^{A_1} and x^{A_2} have in common, leaving ENC to focus on the information that is specific to x^{A_1}, namely, local contrast and artifacts.

Several frameworks have explored using the image itself to learn the conditioning. We note that this design is prone to learning an identity mapping, which would easily produce a perfect reconstruction for the CVAE but would not have the capability of disentangling. To alleviate this issue, Dewey et al. [11] used a forced binarization to limit the capacity of the conditioning and Chartsias et al. [8] added a cycle-consistency loss. In contrast, we avoid this trivial solution by learning the conditioning from x^{A_2}. Once fully trained, CN identifies the patterns from x^{A_2} that are useful in reconstructing x^{A_1}, without observing x^{A_1}. This means that at test-time, CN can remove contrast and artifacts from x^{A_2} that are irrelevant for reconstructing x^{A_1} without the need for the corresponding paired scan.

16.3.4 Semi-supervised segmentation

The CN learns a representation which reduces the contrast variations seen in OCTA images. This representation allows the use of a straightforward segmenter (SEG) network with just two convolution layers that we train based on the output from CN. We train SEG with manual delineations that we have curated and which have undergone multiple internal reviews. At test-time to segment an image x^B, we pass the image through CN and SEG to produce the segmentation p^B. During training, p^B is compared to the manual delineations using a cross-entropy loss $\mathcal{L}_{CE}$; see Fig. 16.3 for the network overview. In Fig. 16.5, we show an example of an input image and the corresponding segmentation. A core advantage of our approach is the ability of supervised training to inject our preferences into the segmentation model. This can manifest itself in the thickness of the vessels we segment or if we assign different labels for arteries, veins, and capillaries.

During each forward pass of training, both $\mathcal{L}_{CVAE}$ and $\mathcal{L}_{CE}$ are calculated. $\mathcal{L}_{CVAE}$ is computed on paired OCTA image data and $\mathcal{L}_{CE}$ is computed against the available manual delineations. We note that our manual delineations are highly detailed, but they only cover a portion of an image. Thus, the $\mathcal{L}_{CE}$ loss is only computed over the available portion of the image. The combination of the two losses is back-propagated to update the parameters in all sub-networks. $\mathcal{L}_{CVAE}$ affects ENC, DEC and CN, whereas $\mathcal{L}_{CE}$ affects SEG and CN. When training is complete, only CN and SEG— i.e., no paired images—are needed for the vasculature segmentation of an OCTA image.

16.3.5 Data sets and manual delineations

We created manual delineations on a proprietary data set, XJU [22]. XJU consists of scans from four different OCT devices: Angiovue (RTVue XR Avanti, Optovue, Inc. Fremont, CA), Angioplex (Cirrus HD-5000, Zeiss Meditec. Dublin, CA), Triton (Topcon DRI OCT Triton, Topcon, Japan) and Spectralis OCT2 module (Heidelberg Engineering, Germany). Each eye in the data set was scanned twice on the Topcon, Zeiss and Optovue scanners and once on the Heidelberg scanner. For each eye, all seven scans were registered to one of the Optovue scans, as described in Section 16.3.1. These registered scans underwent manual review to confirm the quality of the registration process; of the 146 eyes scanned, 138 were found to have successfully registered the six images to the seventh. The eight failure cases resulted from major artifacts in the scans or large discrepancies in the fields-of-view. These failed eyes were excluded from further use. Fig. 16.6 shows a zoomed portion of a scan from an Optovue Angiovue device as well as the manual delineation and segmentation from ACRROSS. We note that from the 138 successful intra-subject registrations in the XJU data set, we randomly selected 110 retinas to train the CVAE in ACRROSS. Each training sample consisted of a pair of different OCTA images randomly selected from the seven available images for each retina. Of the remaining 28 successful intra-subject registrations in the XJU data set, we randomly selected three retinas (21 scans) for manual delineation. The scans were divided into patches consisting of $1/64^{th}$ of the

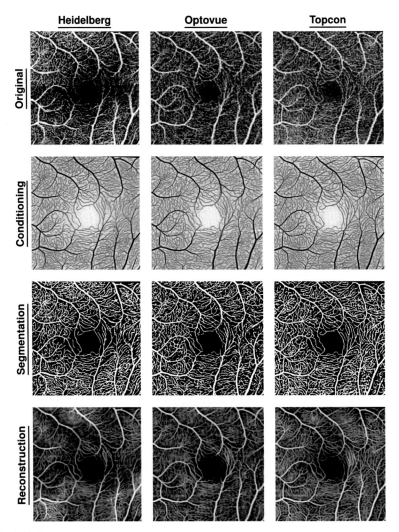

FIGURE 16.5

An example of the inputs and outputs from ACRROSS. The three columns represent the processing of three different scanner manufacturers; from left to right they are: Heidelberg, Optovue and Topcon. From top to bottom, the rows are the original input OCTA images, the conditioning output from CN, the corresponding segmentation from SEG and the reconstruction of the input.

image area and a set of such patches were selected for delineation. To guarantee the quality of delineations, potential capillaries were verified by examining the same location in multiple scans. This verification of capillaries across the seven scans is what contributes to the time complexity of our manual delineation task. All of our manual

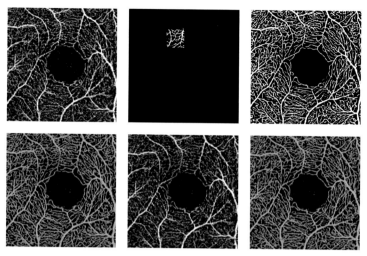

FIGURE 16.6

Shown in the top row from left to right are a zoomed portion of a scan from an Optovue Angiovue device, our manual delineation and the generated segmentation as output by ACRROSS. On the bottom row from left to right are both the manual delineation (in red) and segmentation from ACRROSS (in green) overlaid on the original scan, the manual delineation (in red) overlaid on the original scan and the segmentation from ACRROSS (in green) overlaid on the scan. The first image in the bottom row allows for comparison between the manual delineation and result from ACRROSS.

delineations were reviewed by a second delineator and corrected as necessary. We completed 47 manual delineation patches including 14 from the Heidelberg device, 13 from the Optovue device, 11 from the Topcon device and 11 from the Zeiss device. The total area that these patches cover is equivalent to just 73.5% of the area of a single scan. Examples of our manual delineations can be seen in Figs. 16.1 and 16.6. Despite the fact that our total manual delineations only cover such a small overall area, the task is quite burdensome; it includes initial delineations, verification on repeat scans and review by a second delineator. It was extraordinarily time consuming, taking eight weeks to complete.

We also used the publicly available OCTA-500 [26] data set to evaluate our vessel segmentation. All two hundred subjects (IDs. 10,301—10,500) with 3 mm × 3 mm SVP scans collected using an RTVue-XR (Optovue, Fremont, CA) are included in our experiments. We used the maximum intensity projection from the internal limiting membrane (ILM) to the outer plexiform layer (OPL), as these are the bounds used for the manual delineation of the vessels. We used the recommended training, validation and test split as in Li et al. [26]. We compare our vasculature segmentation with other methods in Table 16.2, reporting the accuracy and Dice coefficient [13]. Included in Table 16.2 are two variations of ACRROSS with two different backbone networks for the CN, one U-Net [43] based and the other based on CS-Net [34]. In addition,

Table 16.2 Vessel segmentation results for 50 SVP *en face* test scans from the OCTA-500 data set. We report the accuracy (ACC) and Dice Coefficient [13] (DICE) in the format of mean ± standard deviation. The reported methods are U-Net [43], the R2U-Net of Alom et al. [1] and CS-Net by Mou et al. [34]. We include two varieties of ACRROSS, using a U-Net or CS-Net backbone for the CN, ACRROSS (U-Net) and ACRROSS (CS-Net), respectively. We also report a version of ACRROSS (U-Net) trained with only 64 or 128 patches, instead of the 140 scans used by the other networks. See the text for complete details. Bold numbers indicate the best mean value in that column. Portions of this table have previously appeared in Liu et al. [30].

Method	ACC	DICE
U-Net [43]	0.988 ± 0.002	0.909 ± 0.020
R2U-Net [1]	0.985 ± 0.003	0.884 ± 0.026
CS-Net [34]	0.987 ± 0.002	0.900 ± 0.020
ACRROSS (CS-Net)	0.986 ± 0.003	0.895 ± 0.021
ACRROSS (U-Net)	**0.988 ± 0.003**	**0.912 ± 0.021**
ACRROSS (U-Net) 64 patches	0.986 ± 0.003	0.889 ± 0.024
ACRROSS (U-Net) 128 patches	0.986 ± 0.003	0.895 ± 0.022

we included two extra experiments using ACRROSS but trained with only 64 and 128 patches of manual delineation randomly selected from 4 scans from the original OCTA-500 training data set. The size of each patch is $1/64^{th}$ of an OCTA-500 scan. We use the U-Net backbone for these experiments since that provided for the best performing CN. These additional experiments demonstrate that our method can be trained on a small fraction of the data that other networks required and yet achieve comparable results. Recall that the other presented results are trained networks which were trained with 140 scans. The OCTA-500 data set also includes a manually delineated FAZ, which we use in Section 16.3.6 to validate our automatic FAZ detection.

16.3.6 Foveal avascular zone segmentation

The foveal avascular zone (FAZ) is a region around the fovea at the center of human retina that lacks vasculature. If we are not identifying noise (or artifacts) as vasculature and correctly identifying the capillaries in the OCTA image, then a straightforward post-processing step can be applied to our vessel segmentation to provide an accurate segmentation of the FAZ. We use a morphological closing operation to our vessel segmentation and then find the largest connected component of the background, which we label as the FAZ; we refer to this method as ACCROSS-FAZ. We have compared our FAZ segmentation with two previously reported FAZ segmentation methods [12,31] using the OCTAGON [12] data set. OCTAGON is a publicly available data set for FAZ segmentation evaluation; it includes 55 SVP 3 mm × 3 mm scans ac-

Table 16.3 We report the mean Jaccard Indexes [20] for the 3 mm × 3 mm SVP scans; for ACRROSS-FAZ, we also report standard deviations in parentheses. The previous methods have not reported their standard deviations. Bold numbers indicate the best mean value in that row. Portions of this table have previously appeared in Liu et al. [30].

Cohort	Díaz et al. [12]	Lu et al. [31]	ACRROSS-FAZ
Healthy	0.82	**0.87**	0.83(±0.07)
Diabetic	0.83	0.82	**0.85(± 0.08)**

quired from a Topcon device (DRI OCT Triton) and their manual FAZ segmentations. Our FAZ segmentation is a simple post-processing of our vessel segmentation and yet achieves comparable results to these state-of-the-art methods; see the reported Jaccard Index [20] in Table 16.3 for comparisons. The publicly available OCTA-500 [26] data set also contains manual delineations of the FAZ that we have used for comparison. ACRROSS-FAZ achieves a mean Dice coefficient [13] of 0.954 ± 0.025 and a Jaccard index of 0.912 ± 0.044 on the OCTA-500 data set. Our performance is on par with several of the fully supervised deep learning based methods reported in Li et al. [26]. Example segmentations can be seen in Fig. 16.7.

There are two critical points to understand when comparing our results to the state-of-the-art methods in Li et al. [26]: 1) the model we used for this experiment was trained using patches of the manual delineations of the vasculature from the XJU data, with the patches only covering the equivalent of one-half of a subject's retina and 2) the state-of-the-art methods are actually trained with FAZ masks from the same OCTA-500 cohort, which offers a significant advantage to these other methods.

16.4 Discussion and conclusion

We presented the framework ACRROSS, which is a deep network architecture for disentangling local contrast and vascular structures from *en face* OCTA images. ACRROSS allows for retinal vasculature to be learned with a limited number of manual delineations. ACRROSS is closely related to VICCE [29], our previously reported method for disentangling contrast and anatomy in OCTA. The CVAE component of ACRROSS is equivalent to the cross-scanner synthesis in VICCE but is applied to the CN and DEC. Both methods can also be considered as special cases of unsupervised representation learning [45], in which similar anatomy depictions are learned from the paired images. Typically, unsupervised representation learning methods use negative samples to help the process; in contrast, VICCE forcing the learned representation to be able to synthesize its corresponding pair, to avoid model collapse. The VICCE approach has the inherent assumption that the anatomical information in both scans is the same; unfortunately, this is not true in general as the hardware and software differences between devices do lead to subtle pseudo-anatomical changes between scanners. In contrast to VICCE, ACRROSS uses the additional input to its DEC, in the form of z^{A_1}, to encapsulate scan-specific information including scan-specific anatomy. This approach can handle many different issues that can induce pseudo-anatomical changes; if the ILM and/or OPL layer segmentations are inaccurate, this can change the number of vessels in the SVP projection map. This would negatively affect VICCE, however, ACRROSS can simply encode this information in the scan-specific z^{A_1}. To capture *true* anatomy, we turn to the scanner-specific anatomical encoding, which is captured in c^{A_2}, as it is anatomical information that is shared between the repeat scans on the scanning device.

Supervised training is typically done with a diverse data pool that allows a method to learn the true variability seen in real data distributions. A unique advantage of ACRROSS is that it learns the disentanglement from unlabeled data, which reduces the requirements for training. In particular, it allows for a greater range of truly diverse data to be used as we no longer require labeled images. Our learned disentanglement also shows us that we can apply manual delineations created in one domain to segment vessels in another domain. ACRROSS trained using the OCTA-500 [26] data set and the XJU [22] data set is able to segment Topcon scans—which are not in either training pool—from the OCTAGON [12] data set. See an example of these segmentations on the OCTAGON data set in Fig. 16.7. We note that this is different from what is done by domain shift based methods [17], because our CN uses unlabeled scans to learn disentangled representations.

Even with these advantages, ACRROSS and other unsupervised disentangled representation learning methods are restricted to only label structures for which there are available labels. This can only be circumvented with additional manual delineations. We can think of this as the labeled and unlabeled structures, from the manual delineation, being entangled components within the anatomy representation. These can cause an issue with tasks similar to those of Chartsias et al. [8], as the segmentation is unable to take full advantage of the disentanglement. Other limitations include over-segmentation, by which we mean noisy pixels in the image being labeled as some part of the vasculature. We are able to observe this in application of the trained ACRROSS model to healthy controls and patients. This over-segmentation comes about from artifacts in our XJU training data. Our paired scans are extremely unlikely to have the same imaging artifact, thus the CN training allows artifacts to be disentangled from the anatomical representation and recover capillaries in the areas of such artifacts. This has an unfortunate consequence when a subject has a true loss of capillaries. As the XJU training data set only consists of healthy controls, any loss of capillaries associated with disease can be interpreted by ACRROSS as an imaging artifact. This is readily addressable by the inclusion of images during CN training that contain some level of pathology. More detailed analysis is required to completely understand this, and it is a fruitful avenue for further research.

We limited ourselves in the presented results to 3 mm × 3 mm SVP scans. We have done this as we have found it difficult to acquire and consistently delineate vasculature in deep vascular plexus (DVP) images. In our experience, acquiring repeated scans from one or more scanners in not an onerous burden, though it is more common

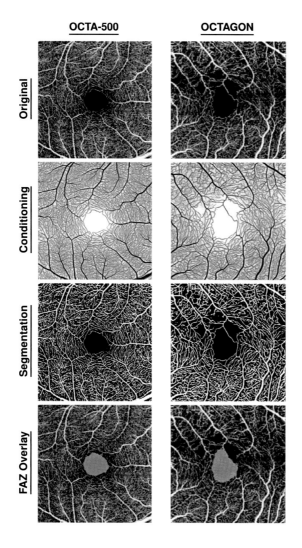

FIGURE 16.7

In the left column is an example of an OCTA scan from the public OCTA-500 [26] data set and the right column has an image from the OCTAGON [12] data set. From top to bottom, we have the original OCTA image (Original), the conditioning output from CN, the segmentation from SEG and the output of our foveal avascular zone (FAZ) segmentation, ACRROSS-FAZ. The FAZ segmentations are overlaid in yellow on the original OCTA image.

to see repeated scans on the same device. As such, we explored training ACRROSS using only Optovue scans; we then repeated our experiments and found ACRROSS to still outperform the comparison methods. However, including scans from another scanner does improve the results. It is still unclear to us if the inclusion of multiple scanners improves the disentangled representation learning or it simply prevents the deep networks from over-fitting.

References

[1] M.Z. Alom, C. Yakopcic, M. Hasan, T.M. Taha, V.K. Asari, Recurrent residual U-Net for medical image segmentation, Journal of Medical Imaging 6 (1) (2019) 014006.

[2] S. Andermatt, A. Horváth, S. Pezold, P. Cattin, Pathology segmentation using distributional differences to images of healthy origin, in: International MICCAI Brainlesion Workshop, Springer, 2018, pp. 228–238.

[3] H.E. Atlason, A. Love, S. Sigurdsson, V. Gudnason, L.M. Ellingsen, SegAE: unsupervised white matter lesion segmentation from brain MRIs using a CNN autoencoder, NeuroImage: Clinical 24 (2019) 102085.

[4] B.B. Avants, C.L. Epstein, M. Grossman, J.C. Gee, Symmetric diffeomorphic image registration with cross-correlation: evaluating automated labeling of elderly and neurodegenerative brain, Medical Image Analysis 12 (1) (2008) 26–41.

[5] B.B. Avants, N. Tustison, G. Song, Advanced normalization tools (ANTS), Insight 2 (365) (2009) 1–35.

[6] C. Balaratnasingam, M. Inoue, S. Ahn, J. McCann, E. Dhrami-Gavazi, L.A. Yannuzzi, K.B. Freund, Visual acuity is correlated with the area of the foveal avascular zone in diabetic retinopathy and retinal vein occlusion, Ophthalmology 123 (11) (2016) 2352–2367.

[7] M. Blendowski, N. Bouteldja, M.P. Heinrich, Multimodal 3D medical image registration guided by shape encoder–decoder networks, International Journal of Computer Assisted Radiology and Surgery 15 (2020) 269–276.

[8] A. Chartsias, T. Joyce, G. Papanastasiou, S. Semple, M. Williams, D.E. Newby, R. Dharmakumar, S.A. Tsaftaris, Disentangled representation learning in cardiac image analysis, Medical Image Analysis 58 (2019) 101535.

[9] J. Chen, Y. He, E.C. Frey, Y. Li, Y. Du, ViT-V-Net: vision transformer for unsupervised volumetric medical image registration, in: Medical Imaging Deep Learning (MIDL 2021), Lübeck, Germany, July 7–9, 2021.

[10] P.A. Dave, K.K. Dansingani, A. Jabeen, A. Jabeen, M. Hasnat Ali, K.K. Vupparaboina, H.H. Peguda, R.R. Pappurru, R. Agrawal, J. Chhablani, Comparative evaluation of foveal avascular zone on two optical coherence tomography angiography devices, Optometry and Vision Science 95 (7) (2018) 602–607.

[11] B.E. Dewey, L. Zuo, A. Carass, Y. He, Y. Liu, E.M. Mowry, S. Newsome, J. Oh, P.A. Calabresi, J.L. Prince, A disentangled latent space for cross-site mri harmonization, in: International Conference on Medical Image Computing and Computer-Assisted Intervention, Springer, 2020, pp. 720–729.

[12] M. Díaz, J. Novo, P. Cutrín, F. Gómez-Ulla, M.G. Penedo, M. Ortega, Automatic segmentation of the foveal avascular zone in ophthalmological oct-a images, PLoS ONE 14 (2) (2019) e0212364.

[13] L.R. Dice, Measures of the amount of ecologic association between species, Ecology 26 (3) (1945) 297–302.

[14] M. Díez-Sotelo, M. Díaz, M. Abraldes, F. Gómez-Ulla, M.G. Penedo, M. Ortega, A novel automatic method to estimate visual acuity and analyze the retinal vasculature in retinal vein occlusion using swept source optical coherence tomography angiography, Journal of Clinical Medicine 8 (10) (2019) 1515.

[15] N. Eladawi, M. Elmogy, O. Helmy, A. Aboelfetouh, A. Riad, H. Sandhu, S. Schaal, A. El-Baz, Automatic blood vessels segmentation based on different retinal maps from OCTA scans, Computers in Biology and Medicine 89 (2017) 150–161.

[16] A. Giani, A. Thanos, M.I. Roh, E. Connolly, G. Trichonas, I. Kim, E. Gragoudas, D. Vavvas, J.W. Miller, In vivo evaluation of laser-induced choroidal neovascularization using spectral-domain optical coherence tomography, Investigative Ophthalmology & Visual Science 52 (6) (2011) 3880–3887.

[17] Y. He, A. Carass, L. Zuo, B.E. Dewey, J.L. Prince, Autoencoder based self-supervised test-time adaptation for medical image analysis, Medical Image Analysis 72 (2021) 102136.

[18] D. Hu, C. Cui, H. Li, K.E. Larson, Y.K. Tao, I. Oguz, LIFE: a generalizable autodidactic pipeline for 3D OCT-a vessel segmentation, in: 24th International Conference on Medical Image Computing and Computer Assisted Intervention (MICCAI 2021), in: Lecture Notes in Computer Science, vol. 12901, 2021, pp. 514–524.

[19] T.S. Hwang, S.S. Gao, L. Liu, J.K. Lauer, S.T. Bailey, C.J. Flaxel, D.J. Wilson, D. Huang, Y. Jia, Automated quantification of capillary nonperfusion using optical coherence tomography angiography in diabetic retinopathy, JAMA Ophthalmology 134 (4) (2016) 367–373.

[20] P. Jaccard, The distribution of the flora in the Alpine zone, New Phytologist 11 (2) (1912) 37–50.

[21] D.P. Kingma, M. Welling, Auto-encoding variational Bayes, arXiv preprint, arXiv:1312.6114, 2013.

[22] J. Lei, C. Pei, C. Wen, N.S. Abdelfattah, Repeatability and reproducibility of quantification of superficial peri-papillary capillaries by four different optical coherence tomography angiography devices, Scientific Reports 8 (1) (2018) 1–7.

[23] J. Lei, E. Yi, Y. Suo, C. Chen, X. Xu, W. Ding, N.S. Abdelfattah, X. Fan, H. Lu, Distinctive analysis of macular superficial capillaries and large vessels using optical coherence tomographic angiography in healthy and diabetic eyes, Investigative Ophthalmology & Visual Science 59 (5) (2018) 1937–1943.

[24] E.S. Levine, M. Arya, J. Chaudhari, E.C. Greig, A.Y. Alibhai, C.R. Baumal, A.J. Witkin, J.S. Duker, N.K. Waheed, Repeatability and reproducibility of vessel density measurements on optical coherence tomography angiography in diabetic retinopathy, Graefe's Archive for Clinical and Experimental Ophthalmology (2020) 1–9.

[25] M. Li, Y. Chen, Z. Ji, K. Xie, S. Yuan, Q. Chen, S. Li, Image projection network: 3D to 2D image segmentation in OCTA images, IEEE Transactions on Medical Imaging (2020).

[26] M. Li, Y. Zhang, Z. Ji, K. Xie, S. Yuan, Q. Liu, Q. Chen, IPN-V2 and OCTA-500: methodology and dataset for retinal image segmentation, arXiv preprint, arXiv:2012.07261, 2020.

[27] A. Lin, D. Fang, C. Li, C.Y. Cheung, H. Chen, Reliability of foveal avascular zone metrics automatically measured by cirrus optical coherence tomography angiography in healthy subjects, International Ophthalmology 40 (3) (2020) 763–773.

[28] Y. Liu, A. Carass, A. Filippatou, Y. He, S.D. Solomon, S. Saidha, P.A. Calabresi, J.L. Prince, Projection artifact suppression for inner retina in OCT angiography, in: 2019 IEEE 16th International Symposium on Biomedical Imaging (ISBI 2019), IEEE, 2019, pp. 592–596.

[29] Y. Liu, L. Zuo, A. Carass, Y. He, A. Filippatou, S.D. Solomon, S. Saidha, P.A. Calabresi, J.L. Prince, Variational intensity cross channel encoder for unsupervised vessel segmen-

tation on OCT angiography, in: Medical Imaging 2020: Image Processing, vol. 11313, International Society for Optics and Photonics, 2020, p. 113130Y.

[30] Y. Liu, A. Carass, L. Zuo, et al., Disentangled representation learning for OCTA vessel segmentation with limited training data, IEEE Transactions on Medical Imaging 41 (12) (2022) 3686–3698.

[31] Y. Lu, J.M. Simonett, J. Wang, M. Zhang, T. Hwang, A.M. Hagag, D. Huang, D. Li, Y. Jia, Evaluation of automatically quantified foveal avascular zone metrics for diagnosis of diabetic retinopathy using optical coherence tomography angiography, Investigative Ophthalmology & Visual Science 59 (6) (2018) 2212–2221.

[32] Y. Ma, H. Hao, J. Xie, H. Fu, J. Zhang, J. Yang, Z. Wang, J. Liu, Y. Zheng, Y. Zhao, ROSE: a retinal OCT-angiography vessel segmentation dataset and new model, IEEE Transactions on Medical Imaging 40 (3) (2021) 928–939.

[33] D. Matsunaga, J. Yi, C.A. Puliafito, A.H. Kashani, OCT angiography in healthy human subjects, Ophthalmic Surgery, Lasers and Imaging Retina 45 (6) (2014) 510–515.

[34] L. Mou, Y. Zhao, L. Chen, J. Cheng, Z. Gu, H. Hao, H. Qi, Y. Zheng, A. Frangi, J. Liu, CS-Net: channel and spatial attention network for curvilinear structure segmentation, in: International Conference on Medical Image Computing and Computer-Assisted Intervention, 2019, pp. 721–730.

[35] L. Mou, Y. Zhao, H. Fu, Y. Liux, J. Cheng, Y. Zheng, P. Su, J. Yang, L. Chen, A.F. Frangi, M. Akiba, J. Liu, CS2-Net: deep learning segmentation of curvilinear structures in medical imaging, Medical Image Analysis (2020) 101874.

[36] O.C. Murphy, O. Kwakyi, M. Iftikhar, S. Zafar, J. Lambe, N. Pellegrini, E.S. Sotirchos, N. Gonzalez-Caldito, E. Ogbuokiri, A. Filippatou, H. Risher, N. Cowley, S. Feldman, N. Fioravante, E.M. Frohman, T.C. Frohman, L.J. Balcer, J.L. Prince, R. Channa, P.A. Calabresi, S. Saidha, Alterations in the retinal vasculature occur in multiple sclerosis and exhibit novel correlations with disability and visual function measures, Multiple Sclerosis Journal 26 (7) (2020) 815–828.

[37] P.L. Nesper, P.K. Roberts, A.C. Onishi, H. Chai, L. Liu, L.M. Jampol, A.A. Fawzi, Quantifying microvascular abnormalities with increasing severity of diabetic retinopathy using optical coherence tomography angiography, Investigative Ophthalmology & Visual Science 58 (6) (2017) BIO307–BIO315.

[38] A.C. Onishi, P.L. Nesper, P.K. Roberts, G.A. Moharram, H. Chai, L. Liu, L.M. Jampol, A.A. Fawzi, Importance of considering the middle capillary plexus on oct angiography in diabetic retinopathy, Investigative Ophthalmology & Visual Science 59 (5) (2018) 2167–2176.

[39] M. Parravano, E. Costanzo, R. Borrelli, R. Sacconi, G. Virgili, S.R. Sadda, F. Scarinci, M. Varano, F. Bandello, G. Querques, Appearance of cysts and capillary non perfusion areas in diabetic macular edema using two different OCTA devices, Scientific Reports 10 (1) (2020) 1–9.

[40] T. Pissas, E. Bloch, M.J. Cardoso, B. Flores, O. Georgiadis, S. Jalali, C. Ravasio, D. Stoyanov, L. Da Cruz, C. Bergeles, Deep iterative vessel segmentation in OCT angiography, Biomedical Optics Express 11 (5) (2020) 2490–2510.

[41] P. Prentašić, M. Heisler, Z. Mammo, S. Lee, A. Merkur, E. Navajas, M.F. Beg, M. Šarunic, S. Lončarić, Segmentation of the foveal microvasculature using deep learning networks, Journal of Biomedical Optics 21 (7) (2016) 075008.

[42] T. Robert, N. Thome, M. Cord, HybridNet: classification and reconstruction cooperation for semi-supervised learning, in: Proceedings of the European Conference on Computer Vision (ECCV), 2018, pp. 153–169.

[43] O. Ronneberger, P. Fischer, T. Brox, U-net: convolutional networks for biomedical image segmentation, in: International Conference on Medical Image Computing and Computer-Assisted Intervention, Springer, 2015, pp. 234–241.

[44] K. Sohn, H. Lee, X. Yan, Learning structured output representation using deep conditional generative models, in: Advances in Neural Information Processing Systems, 2015, pp. 3483–3491.

[45] Y. Taigman, M. Yang, M.A. Ranzato, L. Wolf, Deepface: closing the gap to human-level performance in face verification, in: Proceedings of the IEEE Conference on Computer Vision and Pattern Recognition (CVPR 2014), 2014, pp. 1701–1708.

[46] E. Vorontsov, P. Molchanov, W. Byeon, S. De Mello, V. Jampani, M.-Y. Liu, S. Kadoury, J. Kautz, Boosting segmentation with weak supervision from image-to-image translation, arXiv preprint, arXiv:1904.01636, 6, 2019.

[47] X. Yang, R. Kwitt, M. Styner, M. Niethammer, Quicksilver: fast predictive image registration–a deep learning approach, NeuroImage 158 (2017) 378–396.

[48] H. Zhang, A.M. Valcarcel, R. Bakshi, R. Chu, F. Bagnato, R.T. Shinohara, K. Hett, I. Oguz, Multiple sclerosis lesion segmentation with tiramisu and 2.5 D stacked slices, in: 22nd International Conference on Medical Image Computing and Computer Assisted Intervention (MICCAI 2019), in: Lecture Notes in Computer Science, vol. 11766, 2019, pp. 338–346.

[49] M. Zhang, T.S. Hwang, J.P. Campbell, S.T. Bailey, D.J. Wilson, D. Huang, Y. Jia, Projection-resolved optical coherence tomographic angiography, Biomedical Optics Express 7 (3) (2016) 816–828.

[50] Z. Zhang, L. Sun, Z. Zheng, Q. Li, Disentangling the spatial structure and style in conditional VAE, in: 2020 IEEE International Conference on Image Processing (ICIP), IEEE, 2020, pp. 1626–1630.

[51] Y. Zhou, X. He, L. Huang, L. Liu, F. Zhu, S. Cui, L. Shao, Collaborative learning of semi-supervised segmentation and classification for medical images, in: Proceedings of the IEEE Conference on Computer Vision and Pattern Recognition, 2019, pp. 2079–2088.

[52] L. Zuo, B.E. Dewey, A. Carass, Y. Liu, Y. He, P.A. Calabresi, J.L. Prince, Information-based disentangled representation learning for unsupervised MR harmonization, in: 27th Inf. Proc. in Med. Imaging (IPMI 2021), in: Lecture Notes in Computer Science, vol. 12729, 2021, pp. 346–359.

[53] L. Zuo, B.E. Dewey, Y. Liu, Y. He, S.D. Newsome, E.M. Mowry, S.M. Resnick, J.L. Prince, A. Carass, Unsupervised MR harmonization by learning disentangled representations using information bottleneck theory, NeuroImage 243 (2021) 118569.

Others

Considerations in the assessment of machine learning algorithm performance for medical imaging

17

Alexej Gossmann, Berkman Sahiner, Ravi K. Samala, Si Wen, Kenny H. Cha, and Nicholas Petrick

Division of Imaging, Diagnostics, and Software Reliability, CDRH, U.S Food and Drug Administration, Silver Spring, MD, United States

17.1 Introduction

Performance assessment of machine learning (ML), deep learning (DL) and artificial intelligence (AI) algorithms is a very important topic that plays a significant role in AI/ML/DL algorithm development, design and deployment.[1] Performance testing is relevant across the entire lifecycle of an ML algorithm, from pure research settings to large-scale real-world deployments. However, the goals and requirements are different in different settings. In a research setting, the goal is often to find ML algorithms, architectures, training processes, data pre- or post-processing techniques, etc. that yield the best possible performance for a given task on a given population while overcoming theoretical and technical challenges. In order to reduce the chances of arriving at a false conclusion to one's research question, this requires carefully designed and executed performance evaluation studies. An ML algorithm that is intended for real-world deployment requires a substantially higher level of rigor and extent of performance evaluation activities before deployment, and the assessment can halt algorithm deployment if predetermined success criteria are not met. Inaccurate or otherwise flawed ML algorithms that have not been sufficiently tested before deployment can cause serious harm. In medicine and healthcare, faulty ML algorithms could pose threats to health, well-being or even life of patients. Thus it is of utmost importance to avoid subjecting patients to ML systems without understanding their performance characteristics at an appropriate level (which should be sufficiently

---

[1] To improve the readability of this chapter, we predominantly use the term "ML," but the chapter contents apply to DL and other types of AI algorithms as well.

Deep Learning for Medical Image Analysis. https://doi.org/10.1016/B978-0-32-385124-4.00029-5
2024 Published by Elsevier Inc.

thorough to be able to weigh the benefits against the risks for a given patient). More-over, from a regulatory point of view, before an ML algorithm can be marketed and eventually deployed in the clinic, the developer needs to demonstrate the safety and effectiveness of their algorithm as well as the veracity of their performance claims be-fore marketing an ML system. As discussed below, the vast diversity of tasks, types of algorithms, patient and user populations, usage scenarios, potential performance claims and risk-benefit profiles entail the need for careful consideration of appropri-ate performance evaluation approaches and data for any ML algorithm in the medical imaging field.

In this chapter, we focus primarily on applications of ML in the broad medical imaging domain, which represents one of the most common commercial applica-tion areas of ML in medicine, if not the most common, especially for deep con-volutional neural network (DCNN) algorithms, which have proven themselves to be very useful in medical imaging [1]. Nowadays, ML can be used at every stage of the medical imaging pipeline, starting with image acquisition [2]. The acquired raw image data can be fed into ML-based reconstruction, denoising, filtering or en-hancement algorithms, to produce a medical image that is used for interpretation [3]. Image interpretation can rely heavily on different types of ML algorithms, includ-ing computer-aided diagnosis, detection or triage algorithms along with many other possibilities [3]. When a patient report (such as a radiologist report) is produced, it could be written jointly by a human-AI team or go as input into another AI system, for example, for quality control purposes. Moreover, different usage scenarios of ML are possible even within the same general clinical purpose. For example, ML algo-rithms targeted to aid in the diagnosis of the same disease using the same type of input data can still produce different output, such as a binary indication for presence or absence of disease, a continuous score of disease severity or stage, the prognosis of a future state of disease or response to therapy or additional information about the lo-cation, extent and spread of disease, as well as many other possibilities. In addition, different ML algorithms could be designed to aid different types of clinical users, such as a subspecialty expert as opposed to a general radiologist, nurse or patient. ML algorithms differ also with respect to the level of autonomy ranging from minor semi-automatic procedures with editable output to fully autonomous ML systems.

Since applications of ML in medical imaging are very diverse, the performance evaluation procedures and objectives are diverse as well. There are many different types of performance testing activities that are commonly used in the broader ML field [4]. In the medical imaging application domain, ML performance considera-tions can include the overall accuracy of predictions on the population, the precision, variability or reproducibility of ML algorithm output, uncertainty analysis, algorithm robustness to confounders and noise patterns, time savings for the user, interoperabil-ity and robustness with respect to different data acquisition equipment and parameters as well as deployment platforms, performance on important subgroups of the pa-tient or user population, human-AI team interaction and performance and other topics [5–8].

In this chapter, we provide an overview of key topics in performance evaluation of medical ML algorithms before deployment. Our primary focus is in medical imaging ML, but much of the material covered applies to medical ML in general. We note that the authors' perspective is colored by their regulatory experience in this space. To limit the scope and keep the length of the chapter manageable we focus on pre-market performance assessment, i.e., the performance testing before the marketing and final deployment of the ML algorithm in the clinic but recognize that post-market performance assessment and real-world surveillance of ML systems in medical imaging are also topics of immense importance [9,10].

In the following, we start with a brief discussion of medical devices in general, and how ML algorithms fit in this context, leading up to a discussion of the very important topic of intended use of a medical device, which has crucial implications for performance testing. We continue with considerations and issues pertaining to training and test data sets for ML algorithms, including general principles for data collection, data independence, reference standard determination, fairness and data quality considerations. Next, we introduce a range of performance evaluation study endpoints and metrics, tailored to the different types of ML-based medical devices, tasks and usage scenarios. We follow with an introduction to study design for ML performance assessment in medical imaging, covering standalone as well as clinical performance assessment, prospective as well as retrospective study designs and the topic of transportability. We also discuss the topics of bias and generalizability, characterizing many common types of bias pertaining to performance evaluation studies of ML algorithms in medical imaging and beyond. We end the chapter by considering emerging applications and new areas that we foresee as being significant in the future and where more research is needed. Fig. 17.1 presents a visual overview of the topics and issues that are vital to the performance evaluation of ML algorithms in medical imaging. These various aspects are covered in the different sections of this chapter.

17.1.1 Medical devices, software as a medical device and intended use

ML algorithms used for medical purposes are generally considered medical devices. While the exact definition of the term *medical device* differs by region and the respective regulatory bodies worldwide, a simple and inexact definition is that a medical device is something used for medical purposes that is not a drug or a biologic product. This includes software. The term *Software as a Medical Device (SaMD)* is defined by the International Medical Device Regulators Forum (IMDRF) as "software intended to be used for one or more medical purposes that perform these purposes without being part of a hardware medical device" [11]. Many medical ML algorithms fall under this definition.

Any medical device has an *intended use* (sometimes also called *intended purpose*), which must be clearly defined and communicated to the user. The intended use statement includes the general purpose of the medical device or its function, including a description of the disease or condition the device will diagnose, treat, prevent,

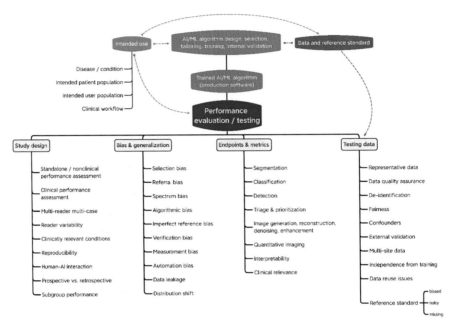

FIGURE 17.1

An overview of topics and relationships that are important for the performance evaluation of ML algorithms in medical imaging. The individual components are covered in different sections of this chapter.

cure or mitigate, and a description of the patient population for which the device is intended [11,12], to which we refer as the *intended patient population* or simply *intended population*. An ML-based device that is intended to aid a clinical user must also specify the *intended user population*, including user qualifications. Depending on context we may also refer to the intended patient population or the intended user population as the *target population* of the ML-enabled medical device. A clearly defined intended use will help answer questions such as: What is the proposed clinical workflow, and how does it compare to the current clinical practice for the disease or condition of interest? How is the device supposed to help users and patients? What are the claims associated with the device and how is it labeled?

Performance testing activities must be consistent with the intended use of the ML-enabled medical device and should match the claims and the proposed clinical workflow. If the intended use of a medical device is not well understood, then there is substantial risk that the performance evaluation studies will not ask and answer the right questions. All aspects of performance evaluation of a medical device crucially depend on its intended use. This is evident in the following sections of this chapter, which describe the various performance evaluation components. This is also represented in Fig. 17.1 where the intended use is identified as an overarching concept that is vital to all other components.

17.2 **Data sets**

With the proliferation of platforms for the design of ML systems in medical imaging, the main factor that distinguishes one system from another is the data used for training and testing it. The design of most modern imaging ML systems is data-driven (rather than physics- or biology-inspired), which makes data collection one of the most important factors in system design and evaluation. In this section, we discuss issues related to data set collection for medical imaging ML performance assessment. Some of these issues are closely related to bias and study design and will be expanded upon in the relevant sections below.

17.2.1 **General principles**

We refer to all the information (including, but not limited to medical images) from a patient that may be utilized for training or testing an ML system as a *case* [13]. Case collection for performance assessment of an ML system should be consistent with the purpose of the assessment study. Often, the purpose of the study is to characterize the performance of the ML system in clinical deployment, using a pre-defined performance metric, which in binary classification tasks, can be sensitivity-specificity pair or other measures related to the receiver operating characteristic curve. In this situation, the cases in the performance assessment study should be representative of the population that the ML system is targeted for, including the distribution of key variables that can affect the performance metric, such as the distribution of patients, disease severity and image acquisition parameters. This can be achieved by first establishing case eligibility criteria (typically, inclusion and exclusion criteria) consistent with the intended use of the ML system, and then prospectively collecting images and other patient or image-related data, including the reference standard. As discussed in the literature [14], such a prospective data collection approach may enhance the chances of identifying all eligible case samples and improve data quality. However, an ML study, for instance one mainly aimed at developing new techniques (e.g., a development study as opposed to a validation study), may also rely on retrospective data collection, where image acquisition happens first, and the study design and patient allocation for the study come second. Retrospective collection may significantly reduce the burden for acquiring a large enough sample size, enable the use of existing registries and public data sets, and facilitate cross-institution collaboration. Whenever retrospective data collection is used, any potential limitations or resulting biases should be clarified. Prospective vs. retrospective studies are discussed further in Section 17.4.2.3, and the potential biases are discussed in more detail in Section 17.5.

Case sampling is another important factor in data collection. Many ML devices are targeted for binary tasks (e.g., the reference standard is "disease present" or "disease absent") with low prevalence, and one may collect disease-positive and negative cases separately but consecutively from the same site with a longer period for disease-positive cases to obtain a large enough disease-positive data set.

State-of-the-art ML systems such as DCNNs have a high learning capacity. Although high learning capacity has proven to be useful in many applications, a potential disadvantage is that the system may learn particular, nongeneralizable associations that are confined to one site or one specific image acquisition condition. Several recent studies have indicated that systems developed and tested with data from one collection site failed to achieve similar test results when applied to data from a different site [15,16]. For this reason, especially for validation studies, it is essential to have multi-site data collection and to perform external validation [17], as discussed below.

17.2.2 Independence of training and test data sets

In addition to data set representativeness, an important issue in ML data collection is ensuring the independence of training and test data sets. For representative training and test data sets, independence means that the data or features for test cases do not depend on the features or data for training cases beyond the fact that both data sets are sampled from the same target population. The opposite of independence, data leakage between training and test cases, refers to the existence of information between the training and test data sets beyond the fact that they were sampled from the same target population. Data leakage allows an ML model to be trained to make unrealistically good (biased) predictions for the cases in the test data set. A simple mechanism that results in data leakage is the presence of different images or regions of interest of the same patient in both training and test data sets. It is expected that images of a patient that were acquired at different times, or regions of interest that were extracted from the same imaging study will exhibit a high correlation and will result in leakage between training and test data. For example, in digital pathology, it has been documented that predictive scores can be widely inflated when tiles from the same subject are used both in training and test sets [18]. When constructing training and test data sets, it is therefore necessary to ensure that a patient's imaging and data does not span both data sets.

A more subtle form of data leakage may occur when previously-collected data is partitioned into training and test data sets randomly or in a balanced way across a given attribute. A previously-collected sample, even if it was designed to be collected in a random manner, may not perfectly follow the true distribution of the target population [19]. For example, there may be a systematic deviation in a particular sample from the true distribution if the sample was collected only at a particular site or using only (or predominantly) a particular image acquisition system that does not represent the true distribution. When such a data set is partitioned into training and test data sets, knowledge about the distribution of the training data may provide unfair information about the distribution of the test data set that would have been impossible to know had the training and test data sets been sampled independently from the true population. A practical approach to reduce this type of dependence is to sample the training and test data sets from a number of different, independent sites, a practice known as external testing [19–22].

17.2.3 **Reference standard**

Evaluation of a medical imaging ML system is typically performed by comparing the system output to a desired output. We refer to this desired output as the *reference standard* in this chapter. For diagnostic accuracy studies, the *reference standard* is defined as the best available method for establishing the presence or absence of the target condition [14]. Ideally, the reference standard is a *ground truth* or *gold standard* that is established independently and with negligible error and variability. For some tasks, a gold standard for the presence or absence of the target condition may indeed exist. For example, results of pathology specimen analysis can be considered as the gold standard to establish the presence or absence of many diseases. Likewise, patient follow-up for a specific duration may establish with reasonable confidence if the patient was diseased or disease-free at the beginning of the follow-up period. If such a gold standard exists and it can be accessed with reasonable effort, the assessment study is expected to compare the output of the ML system to the gold standard. If a gold standard method exists but is missing for some cases in the test set (e.g., a subject that was not followed-up for establishing a disease-free label), statistical analysis plans for handling these cases must be established at the beginning of a study. Possible approaches include sensitivity analysis [23] and multiple imputation [24].

For other tasks, especially those that involve human interpretation, there may not exist a definitive gold standard. One such example is lesion segmentation. Multiple radiologists may disagree on the extent of the lesion, and an independent, high-resolution, definitive source to determine lesion extent is typically unavailable. In the absence of a gold standard, a common approach is to employ a panel of experts for the interpretation of any available clinical data and to assess the ML system based on the panel review results. One can combine expert interpretations into a reference standard by using an adjudication method [25]. Alternatively, one can assess the ML system with the reference standard provided by each expert in the panel, and then combine these different assessments. Either way, the lack of a gold standard introduces additional variability into the estimates for the evaluation metric, and this variability needs to be considered when the total variability is assessed [26].

As discussed in Section 17.3, there can be a variety of tasks that the ML system is designed for, including binary and non-binary tasks, and tasks that involve estimation and lesion localization. It is expected that the content of the reference standard will reflect the clinical task. For example, in mammography, the reference standard for a ML system designed for classifying regions of interest as malignant versus benign may be patient biopsy results combined with patient follow-up, whereas the reference standard for cancer detection and localization may be a bounding box defined by experts containing a biopsy-proven cancer, extracted using all the clinical information (e.g., images acquired during biopsy, images from other modalities, etc.).

17.2.4 **Image collection and fairness**

As discussed above, collection of training data is a major component in ML algorithm design, and non-representative training data may result in an algorithm with poor overall performance. In addition to this well-known effect, a more subtle result of unsatisfactory data collection is a trained algorithm with poor performance for certain subgroups or sub-populations of the intended population, which can be a result of under-representation of those subgroups in the training data set. If the overall performance of the algorithm is satisfactory, then it may sometimes be difficult to discern differences in sub-populations unless one pays special attention and collects enough data from important sub-groups to characterize the algorithm performance for these sub-groups with sufficient precision. Under-representation of specific sub-populations can have many causes and can often take place inadvertently. For example, if the algorithm designer is collecting data from multiple sources (imaging from multiple years, electronic health records, conclusive reference tests), and decides to include in the data set only those patients whose data do not have any missing elements, then data from socio-economically disadvantaged groups or racial or ethnic minorities may be excluded more often because these groups tend to have more missing data.

ML algorithms for processing of natural images, such as photographs containing human faces, have been shown to have biases for racial or ethnic sub-populations. For example, it was found that darker-skinned females had a much higher misclassification rate than lighter-skinned males in three commercial gender classification systems [27]. More recently, researchers have started investigating the effect of race and gender in medical imaging AI applications. Banerjee et al. [28] showed that it is possible to train ML models that can predict race from medical images of different organs and acquired with different imaging modalities with high accuracy. Puyol-Anton et al. [29] investigated bias due to data imbalance in segmentation of cardiac MR images from the UK Biobank data set. They found statistically significant differences in algorithm performance measured using the Dice coefficient between different racial groups when the models were trained without any safeguards for racial bias, and investigated a number of strategies to reduce bias. Larrazabal et al. [30] studied the effect of training data set gender imbalance for computer-aided diagnosis systems for chest X-ray imaging and found a consistent decrease in performance for under-represented genders when a minimum balance is not fulfilled. It is therefore important to be vigilant in ML applications in medical imaging and incorporate safeguards in the data collection process so that "invisible" distortions for minority and/or vulnerable populations are minimized, and so that already-existing healthcare inequities are not perpetuated or exacerbated.

17.2.5 Image and data quality

In the chain for data collection for ML, there are multiple points where data quality assurance is needed, including the search for images, the metadata, the quality of the images themselves and the reference standard.

As discussed above, training data sets may be collected in a retrospective fashion, with a search for images matching certain criteria, using all available sources such as radiology reports, radiology information systems (RIS), picture archiving and communication systems (PACS) and electronic health records (EHR). For unbiased and comprehensive data collection, data in these systems and search tools need to have high quality, which may not always be the case. For example, a study in 2002 found that more than 15% of DICOM tags for the "body part examined" in a series of over 1000 images were incorrect [31]. This was attributed to clinical personnel choosing a protocol different from the body part being imaged to optimize image quality for certain patients. A study comparing RIS and PACS data found that the two did not match for the date of the exam in 5% of studies, and for patient age in 20% of studies for a set of 430 two-view chest images [32]. Differences between patient-reported symptoms and the data in the EHR have been reported by many publications [33,34]. Researchers are therefore cautioned against a blind reliance on data from a single source [35].

Image quality may have a strong impact on the reported ML system performance. Fortunately, many centers have an image quality assurance program already in place, and technologists and radiologists typically require re-acquisition if the image quality is sub-standard. However, it is still a good practice to visualize key images used in ML training to ensure image quality is acceptable and to inspect their associated metadata before entering a case into a database, if it is practically feasible. It may also be possible to use automated tools for this purpose (e.g., automated check for patient motion, image artifact, noise, etc.) [36,37].

An additional consideration for a high-quality image data set is whether the image acquisition reflects currently-relevant equipment and current standard-of-care. This ensures that the ML system trained or tested with the data set answers currently-relevant questions.

17.2.6 Discussion

Data collection is a step in ML algorithm design and evaluation where good collaboration among developers, clinicians and statisticians is essential. This section discussed the general principles for data collection for ML-enabled medical devices, with particular emphasis on representativeness, independence of training and test data sets, the reference standard and issues about image and data quality and fairness. Data sets collected with attention to these principles and key points not only allow the design of well-performing ML algorithms but also lead to successful evaluation studies, where the performance of the device is characterized with sufficient accuracy and precision for its intended use.

17.3 Endpoints

To measure the accuracy of an algorithm and understand its performance, a properly designed study should be conducted. The National Cancer Institute defines an endpoint as "an event or outcome that can be measured objectively to determine whether the intervention being studied is beneficial" [38]. The study endpoints should be selected to establish meaningful and statistically relevant performance for the algorithm. The endpoints should involve metrics that are useful, justified, suitable to support the intended use of the ML tool and interpretable to the intended users of the device and the device regulators.

17.3.1 Metrics

A medical image is always produced for some specific purpose or task. As such, measuring the performance of ML algorithms in medical imaging should start with a specification of the task, then determine quantitatively how well the task is performed [39]. Different tasks require different metrics to measure the performance. For a given task performed by the medical imaging ML algorithm, the metric used should have clinical significance, while also allowing for the evaluation of the device performance.

The following covers some of the metrics for given tasks, and when they are good choices for a given study.

17.3.1.1 Segmentation

Segmentation is the task of outlining, delineating or defining a region or object in an image. In medical imaging, segmented objects typically include organs, tumors or the extent of disease. Evaluations of segmentation metrics have been summarized in literature [40–42]. Briefly, metrics to evaluate segmentation performance can be divided into two types: a measure of overlap and a measure of boundary accuracy, both comparing the algorithm output to the reference standard. Measures such as the Dice Similarity Coefficient [43], and the Jaccard Index [44] are used to measure how well two segmentations overlap. These metrics measure how well the two contours overlap relative to the total area given by the two segmentations and are generally used to show how close the ML output matches the reference standard. The measures of boundary accuracy are used when the extent of a segmentation is important to the clinical task, such as the extent of a tumor for a radiotherapy application. Measures such as the Hausdorff distance [45] can be used when such a metric is warranted.

17.3.1.2 Classification (e.g., computer-aided diagnosis, or CADx, algorithms)

Classification tasks involve identification of a given object as belonging to a predetermined class. While classification can involve designating an object as one of multiple different possibilities (multi-class classification), additional research is needed in this area to identify metrics that are appropriate for such tasks. As such, this section will be limited to binary classification, which involves only two classes (e.g., cancer vs. noncancer). In medical imaging, the most widely accepted performance assessments include the receiver operating characteristic (ROC) analysis [46]. ROC analyzes an observer's (e.g., the user of the device) confidence that an abnormality is present or not. Some widely-used additional metrics include sensitivity, specificity, area under the ROC curve (AUC) and the positive and negative likelihood ratios [25,47,48]. Metrics such as sensitivity and specificity measure the performance at a specific operating point, or decision threshold. ROC analysis and AUC measure the performance across all operating points of the user or the device output, providing a summary metric that is useful for comparing performance independent of the operating point. Note that these metrics are not dependent on the class prevalence. Because in many medical imaging applications, the number of cases without a disease or condition of interest greatly exceed the number of cases with the disease or condition, metrics that are dependent on the prevalence, such as the overall accuracy, should be avoided in many settings as such metrics can falsely show high performance even when the performance on the class with low prevalence is low.

A metric that is commonly used in the pattern recognition field is the precision-recall curve. The definition of the terms precision and recall used in this curve are different than what is used in other disciplines. The term "precision," as used in the precision-recall curve, is also known as the positive predictive value (PPV) in statistics. In statistics, "precision" often refers to the variability of an estimator. The "recall" portion of the precision-recall curve uses the mathematical equation for sensitivity as defined in statistics, whereas "recall" in the medical imaging field, measures the number of patients brought back to the clinic for additional imaging or clinical evaluations.

The precision-recall curve does not reflect the true negative rate, which is the ratio of the number of correctly identified negative cases in the algorithm output relative to the total number of negative cases. While this leads to an uncertainty in an algorithm's ability to perform on nonabnormal cases (i.e., specificity), precision-recall analysis can be useful for tasks where the true negative rate cannot be measured easily.

17.3.1.3 Detection (e.g., computer-aided detection, or CADe, algorithms)

Detection tasks are those that involve localization of an object of interest within an image. An example would be to find the location of lung nodules within a chest CT scan. As these tasks require localization, methods following the principles of ROC analysis have been developed, such as the free-response receiver operating characteristic (FROC) analysis and the localization receiver operating characteristic (LROC) analysis [6,49–51].

17.3.1.4 Triage, prioritization and notification (e.g., computer-aided triage, or CADt, algorithms)

Algorithms that perform triage, prioritization and notification are those that provide time savings in the reading of patient images via, for example, notifications to specialists or re-ordering of the patient queue. The purpose of these devices is usually to assist the clinicians in bringing treatment more quickly to those who have a time-sensitive condition, such as a stroke. These devices are not intended to identify, detect or classify a case. As such, a casewise evaluation metrics such as sensitivity, specificity and ROC analysis and AUC are used to evaluate such algorithms, along with a measure of time savings.

17.3.1.5 Image generation, noise reduction, reconstruction

The most appropriate endpoints for evaluating algorithms that generate an image, such as those used for denoising and image reconstruction, are still being studied. The end goal to consider when evaluating such algorithms is to determine if the image output can provide diagnostic information. Several quantitative measures are commonly used to estimate the performance of these algorithms, such as an improvement in the signal-to-noise ratio (SNR), the AUC of detectability of signals in the image, low contrast detectability (LCD) studies and a Likert scale measure to determine image quality by qualified intended users, but these metrics do not represent real task-based performance [52,53]. They do not answer the questions regarding how these outputs affect clinical decisions and fail to identify many of the risks associated with the generated images.

17.3.1.6 Quantitative imaging tools

For algorithms that provide quantitative imaging measurements, there are three factors to consider: 1) ability to provide measurements that reliably represent the actual value of the targeted quantity, 2) repeatability of the measurement when the measurement is acquired by the algorithm under identical or nearly identical conditions and 3) reproducibility of the measurement when the measurement is subjected to external factors that cannot be tightly controlled in real world clinical settings [54]. Endpoints used for quantitative imaging measurement are generally those of agreement. The estimates provided by the ML algorithm are compared against the reference standard to understand how accurate and precise the output values are, as well as to understand if there are systemic biases associated with the ML algorithm. Common agreement-based endpoints that are used are the Bland–Altman analysis, regression-based metrics, such as Deming regression and other agreement-based metrics that measure the accuracy of the algorithm output. Measures for repeatability include the repeatability coefficient and limits of agreement and the intraclass correlation coefficient [54]. For reproducibility, measures include the reproducibility coefficient and the concordance correlation coefficient [54].

17.3.1.7 Discussion

Study endpoints using appropriate metrics is essential to understand how a ML algorithm performs. Algorithm developers may use a set of metrics to benchmark their performance while trying to improve the algorithm, while clinicians use a different set to understand how such device could aid their practice of medicine. Clinical experts with specific related clinical experience should provide information on the clinical significance and interpretability of the metric to help determine if the endpoints and metrics coincide with the intended use. Regulators may rely on additional metrics to show that the algorithm is safe and effective. Metrics that are most meaningful to device developers and the intended users may not be the same for regulators. These differing perspectives require that different stakeholders collaborate on determining the appropriate endpoints and metrics to understand how the ML algorithm performs when used as intended.

17.4 **Study design**

ML-enabled medical devices require confirmation of the device's clinical performance and utility before wide adoption into the clinical setting. In particular, the assessment of the ML algorithm requires applying epidemiologic and statistical principles to produce high-level evidence of device efficacy [55]. In this section, we discuss various types and aspects of evaluation studies for ML algorithms in medical imaging that are used to support clinical and nonclinical performance assessment ranging from early technical assessments to approaches for verifying algorithm performance in the real-world clinical setting.

17.4.1 **Transportability**

Cross-validation is one type of internal validation [19,22] commonly used as a preliminary assessment of ML algorithm performance, or as part of the assessment process used to tweak model parameters or ML architectures in the course of algorithm development. The concept of *transportability* in assessing prognostic models is defined as the model showing an acceptable performance in patients from a different but related population or in data collected using methods or techniques that differ from those used in development [56]. The concept of transportability can be applied to ML model assessment as well [55]. In order to assess the transportability of an ML tool's clinical performance, the assessment should be conducted using independent data (see also Sections 17.2.2 and 17.5.3). Justice, Covinsky and Berlin discuss five different types of transportability [56]:

- *Historical*: maintaining performance on patient data from a different period of time from that of the development data set.
- *Geographic*: maintaining performance on patient data acquired at different locations from that of the development data set.
- *Methodologic*: maintaining performance on patient data collected using alternative methods/acquisition techniques from that of the development data set.
- *Spectrum*: maintaining performance on patient data who are, on average, more (or less) advanced in their disease process or who have a somewhat different disease from that of the development data set.
- *Interval*: maintaining performance on patient data tested over a longer or shorter follow-up period from that of the development data set.

Justice, Covinsky and Berlin [56] also describe a hierarchy of external validation for predictive systems, which are also applicable to ML-enabled medical device assessment. While a tool can never be fully validated such that there is certainty in how it will apply to a new patient, there is a hierarchy of confidence based on progressively establishing performance across increasingly diverse settings and ranges of validation levels [57]:

0) Internal validation

- establishing reproducibility

1) Prospective validation

- establishing reproducibility, historic transportability

2) Independent validation

- establishing reproducibility, historic transportability, geographic transportability, methodologic transportability, spectrum transportability

3) Multi-site validation

- establishing reproducibility, historic transportability, geographic transportability, methodologic transportability, spectrum transportability

4) Multiple independent validations

- establishing reproducibility, historic transportability, geographic transportability, methodologic transportability, spectrum transportability

5) Multiple independent validations with life-table analyses

- establishing reproducibility, historic transportability, geographic transportability, methodologic transportability, spectrum transportability, interval transportability

While validation for all the levels of the hierarchy may not be conducted for every ML tool, the hierarchy serves as a useful model for understanding the extent of confidence in an ML algorithm at a given point in time based on the level of validation achieved. In general, one should evaluate an algorithm's performance to the level of geographic and temporal transportability to establish a minimum level of confidence before wider clinical introduction [55] (see also Sections 17.2.2, 17.5.2 and 17.5.3).

17.4.2 Assessment studies for ML algorithms in medical imaging

17.4.2.1 Standalone performance assessment

The standalone performance of an ML algorithm is simply a direct measure of performance of the ML algorithm alone, independent of any human or clinical interaction with this ML tool [25]. Standalone performance assessment is the primary assessment for autonomous ML decision making tools. An example of an autonomous ML-enabled medical device is a tool for use by the general public to assess skin lesions via a mobile phone acquired photograph to determine if it requires further clinical assessment. In this case, the ML algorithm impacts patient care because it autonomously makes a specific clinical recommendation on follow-up care. Other types of ML-enabled medical devices only support clinical decision-making. An example of this is a tool that identifies potential colon polyps during optical colonoscopy. Such an ML algorithm aids the endoscopist in identifying colon polyps but the endoscopist is still responsible for identifying polyps not marked by the ML algorithm and for making the final clinical determination of how best to handle each mark provided by the algorithm. In this case, the standalone testing is important but not the primary determination of clinical efficacy. Instead, the clinical performance assessment study, discussed next, is typically the primary method for establishing clinical benefit.

Standalone testing can span the hierarchy of validation from initial validation during the development phase to multiple independent validations with life-table analyses as part of assessing the true clinical value associated with an ML tool. Higher levels of validation and effectiveness are required for ML algorithms that automate clinical decision making or ML systems designed for a direct-to-consumer user.

The importance of standalone testing even when an additional clinical assessment study is being conducted should not be under-estimated. Standalone testing is critical to benchmark overall performance in the clinical population of interest, which is crucial to understanding and comparing performance among and across similar ML algorithms. In addition, standalone testing is a critically important tool for understanding ML performance by usually allowing for a more thorough assessment of subgroups or cohorts within the larger patient population (see also Sections 17.2.4 and 17.5.3). This can often allow for a more robust assessment of historic, geographic, methodologic and spectrum transportability. Therefore well-defined standalone testing provides an assessment approach that includes more refined and tailored additional information of the ML algorithm performance, which typically cannot be gleaned from the types of clinical performance assessment studies commonly conducted for ML algorithms in medical imaging.

As discussed in Section 17.3 above, there are different performance metrics that are appropriate for assessing standalone performance depending on the clinical task, ML algorithm output and the assessment study design. Please refer to Section 17.3 for more information on how to determine appropriate standalone performance metrics for various types of ML tools.

17.4.2.2 Clinical performance assessment

For many ML-enabled assist devices, such as computer-aided detection (CADe) and computer-aided diagnosis (CADx) systems, the utility is in providing supporting information or aid to the clinician such that the clinicians' clinical decision making is improved [5]. The relationship between the ML device output and the clinician is complex and affected by many factors. Therefore a clinical performance assessment is essential to evaluate the clinical utility of the device [5]. Typically, a clinical performance assessment is a two-arm study. In one arm, the clinicians interpret a set of medical images with the assistance of the ML-enabled medical device, while the other is a control arm following conventional clinical interpretation. The conventional clinical interpretation is typically an interpretation by the clinician without any aid by an ML algorithm. Another possible control is double reading by two clinicians [58]. Another option for the control arm could be clinical interpretation aided by another ML tool if the other ML tool was shown to improve the clinicians' performance for the same clinical task. In this section, we focus on the comparison of clinician performance with and without the assistance of an ML-enabled medical device and the two different arms are referred to as the different reading modalities (i.e., aided vs. unaided reading).

As discussed in Section 17.3, there are a range of performance metrics that may be used in assessing clinician performance depending on the clinical task and the study design. We refer to Section 17.3 for more details on how to pick appropriate clinical performance endpoints for various types of ML-enabled assist devices. Besides estimating performance, it is critical to estimate the uncertainty in the performance estimate. Unlike standalone performance assessment, where the uncertainty comes mainly from the cases utilized in the assessment study, the variation of the performance estimate in a clinical performance study also includes contributions from the readers. Given differences in training, experience and expertise, there is variability between different readers in the interpretation of the same image. Both standalone and clinical performance studies may have other important sources of uncertainty (e.g., uncertainly in the reference standard) that also need to be accounted for in an analysis, but these usually are not as substantial as the case and reader variability.

There are two main types of reader variability: *intra-* and *inter-reader variability*. The inter-reader variability stems from different readers having different diagnostic ability and different levels of aggressiveness [47]. Intra-reader variability is due to a reader's inability to provide exactly the same interpretation for the same image at different times (i.e., a reader's self-consistency). To account for reader variability in a clinical performance study, multiple readers, with different levels of experience, read multiple cases in either one or both modalities. This study design is often called a *multiple reader multiple case* (MRMC) reader study.

There are different types of MRMC study designs depending on whether different readers read the same set of images, or whether readers or cases are repeated in both arms of the study. A *fully crossed* MRMC study is a study where all readers read all cases under both modalities. This design offers the greatest statistical power for a given number of cases and readers [59]. However, it is not the most efficient design in optimizing the total number of image interpretations performed by the set of readers and may not be practical in all clinical scenarios. Image interpretation for some clinical tasks is labor-intensive and time-consuming. To reduce the number of interpretations required from each reader, Obuchowski proposed the *split-plot* MRMC study design as an approach to optimize the total number of reads and to provide another option for conducting MRMC studies [60]. It is a balanced design in which all the readers and cases are randomized to one of G blocks. All the readers read all the cases under the two modalities within each block, so that the pairing across modalities is retained. Some of the positive between-readers correlations are eliminated since there are no readings across the block [61]. A split-plot study design can achieve the same statistical power as the fully crossed design with a reduced number of readings. However, a larger number of labeled cases is the trade-off for the increased precision in the split-plot design [59]. Fig. 17.2 shows a simple visual representation of the two study designs discussed in this paragraph.

When the readers need to read the cases in both aided and unaided reading modalities, the reading order matters and should be consistent with the intended use of the

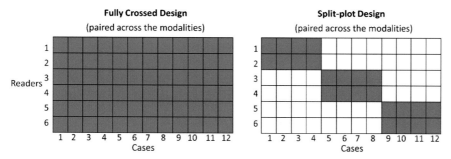

FIGURE 17.2

Illustration of the fully crossed study design and the split-plot study design.

ML-enabled medical device [5]. If the ML device is for second reader use only, which means the device output is displayed immediately after the readers have conducted a full conventional interpretation, then the performance assessment of the two modalities, with and without the ML device, could be done within the same reading session using a sequential reading order design [47]. This study design collects the clinical interpretation and any ratings both before the output is displayed, and again after it is provided to the reader. If the device is for concurrent use, which means the device output is available to the reader throughout the interpretation process, then the sequential design is not appropriate because it does not match the clinical use for the ML aid tool. In this case, an *independent or crossover study design*, which includes two distinct reading sessions separated by a time period called the washout period, is required. Each case is interpreted by the reader in both sessions with one reading session for unaided reading and the other for aided reading. To reduce potential reading order bias, half of the readers are randomly selected to read cases unaided, and the other half-read cases aided by the ML tool in a session. Reading order for the cases are randomized or shuffled across readers within the session. After a washout period, which must be of a sufficient duration to reduce potential memory bias, the readers that read aided in the first session now read the same cases unaided (after a re-shuffling) in the second session, and the readers that read unaided in the first session now read these cases with the ML aid in the second session.

In both fully crossed and split-plot study design, readers and cases are paired across modalities. This controls the case difficulty and other confounding factors between the two reading modalities. The positive correlation between the modalities also reduces the variability in estimating a difference in aided and unaided performance, which increases the statistical power to detect the significant difference between the two modalities. That being said, MRMC studies can be conducted within the normal clinical workflow, but this generally adds more complexity to the analysis because it may not be possible for the same reader to read a case in both modalities.

17.4.2.3 Prospective vs. retrospective studies

As discussed in Section 17.2.1, when validating the standalone performance of ML algorithms for medical imaging analysis, researchers focus on whether the data are prospectively or retrospectively collected [62]. A data set that is prospectively collected may be best suited in representing the current target population and can provide greater transparency from a regulatory approval viewpoint. Retrospective collection of data has substantial advantages with respect to the efficiency in the acquisition of cases and the ability to target rare diseases or conditions, but also runs the risk of biases, including selection bias and referral bias among others [55] discussed in more detail in Section 17.5.

The concept of prospective/retrospective MRMC study is somewhat different from prospective/retrospective data collection. A retrospective MRMC study has readers review previously collected cases, using either retrospective or prospective data collection techniques, offline and outside the normal clinical workflow, typically well after any patient management decisions have been made [63]. There are several advantages of retrospective studies. First, the context of the study can be more tailored to the assessment task. This includes the ability to tailor the data set to allow a more efficient or focused assessment. For example, the most common modification in retrospective CADx or CADe reader studies is to enrich diseased cases in low-prevalence applications. This substantially reduces the number of cases required for achieving statistically significant results but can also have some impact on how readers interpret a case since the rate of diseased patients in the study data set is larger than in the clinical setting. Care needs to be taken to minimize this impact while also allowing for reasonably sized MRMC studies. Another area that is often tweaked in a retrospective MRMC study is the information provided to the clinician during the case interpretation within the study. In imaging MRMC studies the reader often only assesses the medical image without any additional patient or ancillary medical information. This has the advantage of focusing the MRMC study on the medical image interpretation in which the ML tool is claiming to aid. However, it has the disadvantage of moving the MRMC study further from clinical reality. Care needs to be taken in developing which design efficiencies are acceptable and which move the study too far from the clinical scenario to be appropriate for inclusion in a retrospective MRMC study.

A prospective MRMC study has readers review patients with and without the ML aid tool within the normal clinical workflow, obviously based on prospective data collection. Prospective studies allow the ML tool to be assessed under actual clinical conditions, which can provide a more reliable assessment of clinical utility and impact. This is a major advantage and a strong rationale for pursuing prospective assessment of ML-enabled medical devices before widespread clinical implementation, but prospective studies are complicated to implement and assess because of the clinical reality. As mentioned above, a low prevalence of disease will drive the case numbers substantially higher than a retrospective study. In addition, it can be difficult to have multiple readers review a patient prospectively and, therefore, prospective studies often follow a doctor-patient MRMC study design where each reader reads only their own cases.

For second reader type aids a sequential reader study design may be appropriate [47]. Again, the sequential design has a reader assess the patient without the ML aid tool, record a specific unaided interpretation, then reassess the patient with the ML aid tool and record a specific aided interpretation. As a prospective reading design, this is effective because it allows the patient to serve as a self-control by being assessed with and without ML algorithm aid by the reader, but it also may not fully replicate the clinical interpretation process because the unaided read is not the final interpretation used to determine patient management. The management decision would only be made after the second aid review.

For concurrent ML aids, the only option for a prospective assessment is to implement a two-arm study comparing reader performance with vs. without ML aid. One option is to have a reader prospectively assess the patient without the ML algorithm aid and another reader to do the same using the ML algorithm [58]. This has the advantage that each patient is read with and without AI, but it also requires substantial resources if double reading is not standard practice. Likewise, the two readers will need to reconcile the final clinical interpretation, which again may push this process somewhat outside true clinical reality. Another approach for a prospective assessment of a concurrent ML aid is to have each reader read an individual patient only once, either with or without the ML aid. In this two-arm study design, each patient is randomized to either the ML aid or the standard unaided reading arm, and only a single reader interprets each patient. An example of this is the prospective study conducted for the evaluation of an optical colonoscopy CADe device [64]. This was a three-center prospective study of 685 subjects undergoing screening colonoscopies, post-polypectomy surveillance or workup due to positive fecal immunochemical test or signs or symptoms of Colorectal Cancer (CRC). Patients were randomly assigned to groups who underwent high-definition colonoscopies with the CADe system or without [64]. This type of prospective study follows clinical practice closely, but a great deal of care is needed in selecting and randomizing the patients to ensure that even small differences in the patient population across study arms do not overwhelm any CADe effect.

The above discussion of prospective studies focuses on obtaining performance data before an ML tool is widely available to establish the potential clinical value. Once an ML tool is widely available in the clinical setting, other prospective approaches for assessing clinical value have been used including cross-section comparison studies, similar to the prospective sequential reader study described above but applied after wider adoption, and historical control studies. Historical control studies compare the performance for the same or similar set of readers with and without an ML aid tool from two different time intervals [65]. These types of studies should be performed only after the readers had time to develop a comfort level with the ML tool. This is because the initial use and performance of an ML-enabled medical device is not always the same as the use and performance after a clinician has spent sufficient time with the device to identify how best to utilize it. Often, the performance of early or new adopters is different from users who have a great deal of experience with the technology. Dean et al. [66] found that the recall rate initial increased from 6.2% to 13.4% in the first 2 months after the introduction of a mammography CADe device, fell back to 7.8% in months 4–21 - and then fell further to 6.75% in months 22–25.

Both retrospective and prospective studies are crucial tools for assessing and benchmarking the ML algorithm performance, with retrospective studies typically having an efficiency/control advantage, while prospective studies may provide a less biased estimate of absolute performance within the clinical setting. Retrospective studies can be highly effective in ranking (or comparing) two technologies even though they may be prone to bias in estimating absolute performance (e.g., due to enrichment, limited information). The use of retrospective comparison studies between new and established ML algorithms are typical in the premarket setting.

17.4.3 Discussion

In this section, we discuss the details around design and conduct of assessment studies for ML-enabled medical devices in medical imaging. The main takeaway points are that there is a range of validation levels for an ML tool, and that the transportability of the ML algorithm is an important consideration in the design of assessment studies. We also discussed how standalone testing is the main assessment technique benchmarking ML algorithm performance for both the wider clinical patient population and for important subgroups or cohorts within it. Standalone testing is a critical tool because it is typically conducted for much larger data sets than clinical performance testing, and it may even serve as the primary arbiter of performance for some types of autonomous ML tools. Finally, we discussed clinical performance testing for ML assist devices, such as CADe and CADx systems. In these studies, the goal is to assess the clinician performance with and without the ML aid tool (or compared to another established ML aid tool) in order to establish the clinical value of the tool. The main clinical performance assessment approach of clinical studies for ML algorithms in the medical imaging domain is through MRMC studies which generalize to both the intended population of readers and cases. MRMC is a very powerful and flexible study design that allows for both prospective or retrospective assessment of the added value provided by an ML-enabled medical device to clinical interpretation.

17.5 Bias

ML tools in medical imaging have the potential to improve quality of life through improving screening, diagnostic and prognostic capabilities of the healthcare system. However, development and evaluation procedures used for these tools are not immune to sources that lead to unwanted biases, which can have detrimental effects on the patients. In statistics, the *bias* or *systematic error* of an estimator $f(X)$, which estimates the unknown value of a population parameter θ based on a data set X, is defined as the difference between the expected value of the estimator and the true value of the estimand, i.e., $\mathrm{E}(f(X)) - \theta$. In the context of performance evaluation studies for ML systems the estimation target θ is the true value of the ML algorithm performance, and *bias* refers to how the measured performance estimate systematically deviates from the true performance on the intended population [67]. That is, a performance evaluation study that is affected by bias would consistently over-estimate or under-estimate the true population level performance if the same study were repeated. Bias arises from deficiencies in study design, conduct or analysis, including the data collection and annotation procedures, performance assessment methodologies, metrics and other study design considerations, as discussed in Sections 17.2, 17.3 and 17.4 above.

Moreover, an ML algorithm itself can be called *biased* if the algorithm output systematically deviates from what the algorithm is intended for. The bias of an ML algorithm is a function of the training, data collection, annotation and algorithm development processes. Thus the bias of an ML algorithm when used as a medical device is a complex culmination of deficiencies in all aspects of ML software development, testing and use.

In this section, we introduce various types of biases that can affect performance evaluation studies of ML algorithms in medical imaging, and how the different types of bias relate to study design considerations, including data collection, assessment methodology, metrics and other aspects. To limit the scope, we do not discuss specific bias mitigation techniques here. We further limit the scope of this section by considering only those types of bias that may affect the ML algorithm development processes and validation studies prior to the final deployment of the validated algorithm. Thus we do not discuss biases resulting from the use of an ML system outside of its training and validation data domains (e.g., distribution shift, concept drift, emergent bias) [68,69], inappropriate operation of the AI system by the user (e.g., automation bias, confirmation bias, alarm fatigue) [70,71] or the category of biases related to the socio-technical factors of algorithm deployment (e.g., resulting from complex interactions between institutional structures and human decision makers) [72]. Even though these types of bias are out-of-scope of this section, which covers biases in pre-deployment performance evaluation studies of ML algorithm, we acknowledge their immense importance for real-world application of ML and the need for much additional research.

17.5.1 Bias and precision

While in the performance evaluation context bias describes the study flaws that lead to a systematic deviation in the performance estimates, *precision* (or *imprecision*) describes the variability arising from sources of randomness that do not lead to systematically distorted performance estimates (e.g., variability of results due to a small sample size) [67,73]. That is, if we were to repeat the same study many times, deviations due to insufficient precision would not consistently go in the same direction but would balance each other out if aggregated. There are clear connections between bias and precision of an estimator, such as the bias-variance tradeoff that in its simplest form can be expressed as

$$\text{Mean Squared Error}\,(f) = [\text{Bias}\,(f)]^2 + \text{Variance}\,(f) + \text{Irreducible Error}.$$

However, in this section we focus only on the different sources and types of bias, while some considerations regarding precision and variance are included in Section 17.4.

17.5.2 Bias and generalizability

Generalizability or *generalization* is a concept related to bias. Broadly speaking, it refers to the performance of an ML algorithm on unseen samples from the intended population, including similar patients at another time or location [19,20]. As such, it is also closely related to the concept of transportability discussed in Section 17.4.1. In statistics and ML the term *generalization error* often refers to the expected value of the prediction or classification error on a random data point from the population [74,75]. The difference between the ML algorithm performance on its development data set and the intended population is often termed *generalization gap*. Many theoretical bounds on the generalization error and the generalization gap have been derived in the literature for different types of ML algorithms and under a variety of theoretical conditions [75,76]. Such theoretical results can play a role in the study design considerations. However, biases in the performance evaluation study, such as the ones discussed below, will prevent a sufficient assessment of an ML algorithm with respect to its generalizability capabilities and the types of transportability (see Section 17.4.1) relevant to its intended use. Thus addressing potential biases in the performance evaluation study is crucial for understanding how the study results or findings can be transferred to situations or people other than those originally studied and within the intended population.

17.5.3 Types and sources of bias in pre-deployment performance evaluation studies of ML algorithms in medical imaging

The holy grail of biomedical research is bringing technological advancements from bench to bedside [77–80]. For this transition to occur, one needs to ensure that neither the device development processes nor the performance evaluation studies are affected by substantial bias. Common types of bias for performance evaluation studies of ML algorithms in medical imaging, which are carried out before the algorithm deployment to demonstrate its safety and effectiveness, can occur during data collection and reference standard determination, algorithm development or training, and the conduct of studies (see Fig. 17.3).

17.5.3.1 Case collection

Data collection in medical imaging is a tedious and expensive process. The data collected for the algorithmic development, which may be related to patients, device users or both, should be representative of the device target population. *Selection bias* can arise when the sample of patients or readers is not representative of the target population leading to bias in the results. For example, breast cancer screening programs using mammography are affected by *self-selection bias* because of the voluntary nature of the program. Women who participate in these programs have been shown to

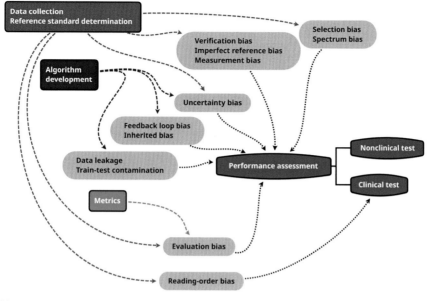

FIGURE 17.3

Common sources and types of bias that affect performance evaluation studies of ML algorithms in medical imaging.

have a different risk profile compared to the general population [81]. The difference in the risk profile may wrongly estimate the ML performance and could have varying performance in the real-world setting [81]. *Referral bias* describes a type of selection bias, which applies when the study patients are sampled from a referral population (e.g., patients that were referred to a specialist), which represents only a subset of the intended patient population. The referral population has often a higher prevalence or more severe disease than the general intended population [82], which can lead to overly optimistic estimates of an algorithm's classification performance. The referral population can also systematically have less severe disease than comparable patients from the general population [83]. Another possibility is that the referral patients incorporate only cases that are far from either extreme on the disease severity spectrum, thus including the subset of cases that may be "hard" to diagnose.

The described scenarios of referral bias can also be regarded as special cases of *spectrum bias*. Spectrum bias describes a systematic error in performance assessment that occurs when the sample of patients (or users) studied does not include a complete spectrum of the target population, and it can be viewed as a consequence of selection bias [84]. For example, consider an algorithm that is intended for patients with suspected severe, mild or moderate disease, but in the performance evaluation study the proportion of suspected mild and moderate disease is different from the proportion in the intended patient population. Accuracy of a diagnostic algorithm may, for instance, be over-estimated if the disease is easier to diagnose for severe cases, which are over-represented in the study population. This can happen, for instance, if validation study data come from (specialized) tertiary institutions, where disease severity is higher than in the intended patient population.

Issues of algorithmic fairness are also often a consequence of selection bias that goes unnoticed. Under-representation of patients from specific sub-groups or sub-populations, such as socio-economically disadvantaged groups or racial or ethnic minorities, can occur inadvertently and, therefore, has to be given special attention in the data collection process, as discussed in Section 17.2.4.

Another widely reported form of selection bias that has major effects on ML applications in medical imaging is the lack of sufficient variability in data collection sources or image acquisition equipment or parameters [15,16,85–89]. A simple example is the over-estimation of ML algorithm performance, when it is assessed based on testing data from the same institution where training data were collected. Such performance results will often over-estimate the true population performance, because such an assessment does not account for the potentially very wide variability in case-mix [19], data acquisition, processing and analysis practices at different institutions, and the ML algorithm may be over-fit to these characteristics associated with the specific institutions where the training data were collected. Thus it is not possible to judge the generalization capabilities of an ML system without a sufficient diversity in data sources, acquisition equipment and processes. As also discussed in Sections 17.2.1, 17.2.2 and 17.4.1, appropriate external testing approaches and rigorous study criteria are needed to mitigate this issue [19–22].

The above considerations show that patient sources and sub-groups have to be considered when assessing the prevalence and severity levels of a disease or condition, and when measuring the performance of an ML-based medical device. Appropriate randomization of data or readers and broad inclusion criteria have shown to mitigate some of the issues arising due to selection bias [90].

17.5.3.2 Over-fitting, train-test contamination and data leakage

When assessing the performance of ML algorithms that were trained or fit on some data, it is very important that cases included in the validation study data (i.e., testing) should be independent of cases used during the algorithm development (e.g., training, tuning). Testing an ML algorithm on data that are not entirely independent of the training or tuning data results in substantial over-estimates of algorithm performance [74]. This phenomenon is a bias due to over-fitting, as the ML algorithm over-fits to the specific noise structures or idiosyncrasies present in data used for algorithm development, training or tuning. Likewise, re-using the same testing data set repeatedly can result in optimistically biased performance estimates, because the ML algorithm design and development may be informed by the previously reported performance estimates measured on the test data set [91,92]. This is a form of bias due to train-test contamination or data leakage, where information about the testing data leaks into the algorithm development and training processes. Especially if the performance study data set is not very large, then the repeated use of that data without precaution will make it largely impossible to reliably estimate the generalizability and performance of the assessed algorithm on cases outside of the validation study data.

17.5.3.3 Reference standard

If different patient sub-sets in a given data set undergo different reference standard determination or verification methods, this practice may result in a systematic over- or under-estimation of the performance, called *verification bias*. Another type of verification bias occurs when a specific subset of the data lacks the reference standard entirely. An example in the context of medical imaging AI would be when the study only uses biopsy data (or a similarly invasive procedure) for verification when many patients do not undergo biopsy for a variety of reasons (e.g., health concerns, patient opt out, etc.). In addition, biopsy procedures have several considerations that limit the selection of nodules to be excised for pathological analysis. To avoid this type of verification bias, it is common to use image interpretation by human expert readers as the reference standard instead of the biopsy results. This in turn when used as reference standard for ML development in the individual studies can lead to a wide variability of performance estimates due to issues of inter-reader and intra-reader variability. Moreover, this type of reference standard can exhibit a systematic bias due to the subjectivity in the interpretations of individual clinicians, whereby the subjectivity may for instance result in a systematic deviation of the reference standard for certain socio-economically disadvantaged groups relative to the rest of the population in certain medical applications [93,94]. Thus it is possible that the reference standard itself is far from perfect—a phenomenon referred to as *imperfect reference bias*. For example, CADe for lung nodules in CT uses radiologist's subjective assessment as reference standard. However, these reader observer studies have been shown to suffer from both inter- and intra-observer variability [95]. Using radiologists' subjective assessment as a proxy for assessing malignant or benign classification of lung nodules is also referred to as a type of *measurement bias* [96]. This type of measurement can be problematic when used as reference standard because it can vary across radiologists who may come from different types of clinical establishments with varying levels of experience [95,97]. Similar issues also appear in clinical evaluation studies of medical ML-based devices outside of the reference standard determination process. For instance, a related and important component of MRMC studies is the use of appropriate randomization procedures to remove *reading-order bias*. A typical scenario is an observer reader study comparing the performance improvement of using a CADx or CADe device as a second reader, which is discussed in more detail in Section 17.4.2.2.

17.5.3.4 Study endpoints and metrics

A type of bias that arises due to usage of performance metrics that do not succinctly capture the improvement offered by the device is a form of *evaluation bias* [98]. For instance, common pixel-based metrics for image denoising such as signal-to-noise ratio (see Section 17.3.1.5), and commonly used segmentation metrics such as the Dice similarity coefficient (see Section 17.3.1.1) often do not measure the performance that directly translates to the intended use of the device [41,42,52,97]. Moreover, reporting of only aggregate metrics can hide poor performance on important sub-groups.

Importantly, in order to evaluate the benefits and risks of a medical ML-based device, one must make sure that the chosen endpoints and reference standard adequately reflect the relevant clinical task or question. Several cases of medical ML applications have been documented in the research literature, where the reported performance results do not adequately represent the real-world performance or utility of the AI algorithm, because of a reference standard that does not reflect the targeted real-world clinical task sufficiently well [71,99]. This type of bias is sometimes referred to as *measurement bias* [98]. In particular, such performance discrepancies may disproportionately affect socio-economically disadvantaged groups or racial or ethnic minorities. Differences between the reference standards or metrics used in the performance evaluation study and the real-world implementation of a deployed AI system may lead to questioning the trustworthiness of medical ML devices, which in turn can significantly hamper the progress toward development and deployment of all types of computer-assisted decision support systems.

17.5.4 Discussion

Sufficient information about the data and reference standard, study design, the algorithm and its intended use is needed in order to be able to assess the types and extent of biases affecting a given performance evaluation study. However, certain types of bias may be more or less relevant than others for a given ML algorithm assessment. For certain device types, target conditions, or diseases (e.g., rare diseases) it may be challenging, costly or impossible to collect sufficient data for a study that is free of bias. For example, to account for selection bias in the study population or bias in reader behavior it may be desirable to perform a prospective data collection or a prospective clinical study, but such study designs may often be too inefficient or even entirely infeasible for certain types of ML-based medical devices and tasks, as discussed in Section 17.4.2.3. Such constraints can necessitate making compromises, whereby one must carefully weigh the probable benefits of a new ML-based medical device against its risks, to determine whether a study is acceptable despite the remaining potential for bias that cannot be feasibly mitigated under the given circumstances. Nevertheless, a thorough assessment of potential for bias in such cases will allow to anticipate the degree of deviation of the (possibly biased) reported performance from the true performance on the intended population. It is also worth noting that different levels of safety and efficacy are required at different stages of development and deployment of the ML-based medical device (see Section 17.4.1).

17.6 Limitations and future considerations

This chapter mainly focused on pre-market assessment of ML algorithms in medical imaging. Assessment of the algorithm as it is used in clinical practice or *post-market*, was generally not discussed in detail but is equally important. The reality of how an ML algorithm fits into the clinical workflow and how clinicians interact with the algorithm may not be entirely consistent with pre-market evaluation since the use of ML can evolve in the post-market arena. Data set characteristics in post-market may be different from those used in pre-market, either because of the special design considerations in pre-market, or because patient populations and disease characteristics evolve over time. In addition, as discussed later in this section, the class of "learning" algorithms will also evolve in time, ideally within bounds that are established at the time the algorithm reaches the market. For all these reasons, post-market assessment of algorithm performance is essential to confirm and expand upon the findings of pre-market assessment, to monitor device performance as the environment and the algorithm evolve, and to provide feedback for design improvement in future pre-market assessment studies [9,10].

Unanticipated socio-technical factors that can be harmful to ML performance may often emerge in the post-market deployment phase of an ML algorithm. These socio-technical factors may include issues associated with institutional structures, policies, real-world use patterns of the ML system, human decision makers and their corresponding complex interaction effects. The extent to which we discussed AI ethics and fairness in Sections 17.2.4 and 17.5 is limited to how they most directly apply to pre-market performance evaluation studies (e.g., data collection criteria or study endpoints), and quite possibly, only touches the tip of the iceberg with respect to possible issues of AI ethics, trustworthiness, privacy and fairness. To identify the flaws of a deployed ML algorithm in this area, and to address them appropriately would likely require continuous or periodic post-market surveillance of the algorithm and well-designed post-market assessment studies, which is an area for much needed research.

In this chapter, we predominantly focused on the performance evaluation of individual ML algorithms in medical imaging. However, there is a growing number of ML algorithms along the entire medical imaging pipeline, starting from ML algorithms used in image acquisition up to AI systems informing or producing the final patient report, and there is a multitude of ways in which different ML-based medical devices can potentially be combined in sequence or in parallel. It is not clear what the performance and behavior of such a chain or combination of ML algorithms would be when only the performance results of individual ML components within the chain are known. Therefore understanding the expected performance and failure modes of combinations of ML-based medical devices and the limits of their interoperability and interaction is an important topic for future research.

In addition, a substantial increase in the use of ML-based medical devices can lead to certain biases in the collection of new data for the development and performance evaluation of new algorithms (or modifications to algorithms currently in use). In the most extreme case, one can imagine a feedback loop that leads to an ML algorithm being inadvertently trained to replicate another algorithm's behavior rather than the underlying truth state. Similar feedback loops would also complicate and bias the performance evaluation process. Further research is needed to understand how to address the potential feedback loop problem resulting from the growing use of AI systems in the clinic.

Because medical ML algorithms are potentially exposed to new data throughout their product lifecycle, letting ML algorithms "learn" from new data or real-world experience appears to be a natural extension of the traditional medical device development and deployment paradigm. Such continuous or periodic algorithmic modifications to ML-based tools, if possible, carry many potential benefits to continuously improve healthcare for patients. They could improve the ML performance over time, including important sub-types of disease or sub-groups of the population leading to more personalized medicine. Likewise, the ML model could adapt to changes in the patient populations or disease over time, or to its specific deployment setting. It could even extend its capabilities to new populations or tasks without the need to re-train from scratch. However, there are many open challenges in evaluating the performance of continually learning or adaptive medical ML algorithms. This new algorithm development paradigm would introduce severe complications to many of the issues discussed in this chapter that are not addressed by the conventional paradigm of performance evaluation, including from a regulatory perspective [100].

The accelerated rate of innovation in and adoption of medical ML carries a strong potential to improve public health. However, the above-mentioned limitations in ML development and assessment are significant concerns, especially in light of fully autonomous ML systems, which are intended to perform a clinical task without oversight by a human expert or independently from a physician review. There remain many open questions about how to best perform rigorous performance evaluation and post-market monitoring of autonomous medical ML algorithms [9,10].

17.7 Conclusion

In this chapter, we presented a broad overview of performance evaluation of ML algorithms in medical imaging. We aimed to cover the most important aspects of pre-market (or pre-deployment) clinical and nonclinical studies of such ML-enabled medical devices. The diversity of ML algorithms, patient and user populations, usage scenarios, potential performance claims and risk-benefit profiles makes it difficult to provide specific recommendations, so we attempted to provide a survey of options and important considerations instead of recommendations. To set the stage, we introduced the terminology of medical devices, SaMD and intended use. We discussed important issues in data collection for the performance evaluation of medical imaging ML algorithms, covering topics of external and multi-site testing, the importance of the reference standard, data quality limitations, as well as the role of data collection with respect to AI fairness and ethics. We discussed study endpoints and metrics for the wide range of possibilities regarding clinical tasks, ML algorithm output and other aspects of the intended use of an ML tool in medical imaging, as well as study design. The study design topics covered in this chapter include standalone performance assessment of ML algorithms, clinical performance assessment of ML assist tools such as CADx and CADe medical devices, as well as a discussion of prospective vs. retrospective study designs. We also discussed the different validation levels required and transportability considerations that may apply depending on the type of an ML-enabled medical device, its intended use and the different stages of ML development and deployment. We considered a variety of bias and generalizability issues that are particularly relevant for performance evaluation of ML algorithms in medical imaging, including the different types of bias that can arise during case collection and reference standard determination, in the course of algorithm development and training, or due to issues of study design and endpoints. We saw the importance of external or multi-site validation, rigorous study criteria and reporting standards [22,101–104].

We would like to emphasize that all of these topics must be considered as a whole, whereby a decision in any given area will influence how other issues should be resolved. Importantly, the intended use of a medical device has major implications on all areas of ML algorithm development, testing and deployment. Likewise, the performance evaluation study needed to support a given intended use may not always be feasible, prompting adjustments to the intended use, such as modifications to the ML functionality or narrowing the intended population of patients or users, which in turn would prompt modifications to the performance evaluation study design and data, and so on.

We live during an exciting time period when technological challenges in the theory and application of ML are being addressed at an accelerated pace, leading to innovations and performance improvements in medical devices. This chapter ends by considering some of the limitations of the predominant performance evaluation paradigm and some areas of future importance in light of recent developments in the fast-paced ML field. Many open questions regarding performance testing of ML algorithms are raised, and the need for additional attention from the research community is apparent, almost as if the performance evaluation research field has to play catch-up with cutting-edge ML research and practice. However, it is clear that new developments, accelerated adoption and accelerated efforts in the ML field are geared toward improving public health, if supplemented by an appropriate performance evaluation methodology to ensure their safety and effectiveness. Thus, especially in light of these new challenges, the performance assessment of ML algorithms will be more important than ever, and development of appropriate performance testing methodologies clearly remains a necessary and worthwhile undertaking.

References

[1] S. Benjamens, P. Dhunnoo, B. Meskó, The state of artificial intelligence-based FDA-approved medical devices and algorithms: an online database, npj Digital Medicine 3 (1) (2020) 118.

[2] A. Narang, et al., Utility of a deep-learning algorithm to guide novices to acquire echocardiograms for limited diagnostic use, JAMA Cardiology 6 (6) (2021) 624.

[3] B. Sahiner, et al., Deep learning in medical imaging and radiation therapy, Medical Physics 46 (1) (2019) e1–e36.

[4] J.M. Zhang, et al., Machine learning testing: survey, landscapes and horizons, IEEE Transactions on Software Engineering (2020) 1.

[5] U.S. Food and Drug Administration, Clinical performance assessment: considerations for computer-assisted detection devices applied to radiology images and radiology device data in premarket notification [510(k)] submissions - guidance for industry and food and drug administration staff, in: FDA Guidance Document, U.S. Food and Drug Administration, 2020.

[6] U.S. Food and Drug Administration, Computer-Assisted Detection Devices Applied to Radiology Images and Radiology Device Data – Premarket Notification [510(k)] Submissions, 2012.

[7] U.S. Food and Drug Administration, Technical Performance Assessment of Quantitative Imaging in Device Premarket Submissions. Draft Guidance for Industry and Food and Drug Administration Staff, 2019.

[8] U.S. Food and Drug Administration, Software as a medical device (SAMD): clinical evaluation. Guidance for industry and food and drug administration staff, in: FDA Guidance Document, 2020.

[9] ACR/RSNA, Subject: (Docket No. FDA-2019-N-5592) "Public Workshop—Evolving Role of Artificial Intelligence in Radiological Imaging;" Comments of the American College of Radiology, 2020.

[10] H.B. Fleishon, C. Wald, Patient safety: considerations for artificial intelligence implementation in radiology, Journal of the American College of Radiology 17 (10) (2020) 1192–1193.

[11] IMDRF SaMD Working Group, Software as a Medical Device (SaMD): Key definitions, 2013.

[12] U.S. Food and Drug Administration, The 510(k) Program: Evaluating Substantial Equivalence in Premarket Notifications [510(k)], 2014.

[13] B. Sahiner, N. Petrick, Evaluation of CAD and radiomic tools, in: E. Samei, E.A. Krupinski (Eds.), The Handbook of Medical Image Perception and Techniques, Cambridge University Press, Cambridge, UK, 2018, pp. 389–406.

[14] J.F. Cohen, et al., STARD 2015 guidelines for reporting diagnostic accuracy studies: explanation and elaboration, BMJ Open 6 (11) (2016).

[15] I. Pan, S. Agarwal, D. Merck, Generalizable inter-institutional classification of abnormal chest radiographs using efficient convolutional neural networks, Journal of Digital Imaging 32 (5) (2019) 888–896.

[16] J.R. Zech, et al., Variable generalization performance of a deep learning model to detect pneumonia in chest radiographs: a cross-sectional study, PLoS Medicine 15 (11) (2018).

[17] K.G.M. Moons, et al., Transparent reporting of a multivariable prediction model for individual prognosis or diagnosis (TRIPOD): explanation and elaboration, Annals of Internal Medicine 162 (1) (2015) W1–W73.

[18] N. Bussola, et al., AI Slipping on Tiles: Data Leakage in Digital Pathology, in: D.B. A (Ed.), Lecture Notes in Computer Science, vol. 12661, Springer, 2021.

[19] D.G. Altman, P. Royston, What do we mean by validating a prognostic model?, Statistics in Medicine 19 (4) (2000) 453–473.

[20] U.S. Food and Drug Administration, Executive Summary for the Patient Engagement Advisory Committee Meeting. Artificial Intelligence (AI) and Machine Learning (ML) in Medical Devices, 2020.

[21] D.W. Kim, et al., Design characteristics of studies reporting the performance of artificial intelligence algorithms for diagnostic analysis of medical images: results from recently published papers, Korean Journal of Radiology 20 (3) (2019) 405–410.

[22] R.F. Wolff, et al., PROBAST: a tool to assess the risk of bias and applicability of prediction model studies, Annals of Internal Medicine 170 (1) (2019) 51–58.

[23] A.S. Kosinski, H.X. Barnhart, A global sensitivity analysis of performance of a medical diagnostic test when verification bias is present, Statistics in Medicine 22 (17) (2003) 2711–2721.

[24] J.A.H. de Groot, et al., Multiple imputation to correct for partial verification bias revisited, Statistics in Medicine 27 (28) (2008) 5880–5889.

[25] N. Petrick, et al., Evaluation of computer-aided detection and diagnosis systems, Medical Physics 40 (2013) 087001.

[26] D.P. Miller, et al., Gold standards and expert panels: a pulmonary nodule case study with challenges and solutions, Proceedings of the SPIE - Medical Imaging 5372 (2004) 173–184.

[27] J. Buolamwini, T. Gebru, Gender shades: intersectional accuracy disparities in commercial gender classification, Proceedings of Machine Learning Research 81 (2018) 1–15.

[28] I. Banerjee, et al., Reading race: AI recognises patient's racial identity in medical images, arXiv:2107.10356, 2021.

[29] E. Puyol-Anton, et al., Fairness in cardiac MR image analysis: an investigation of bias due to data imbalance in deep learning based segmentation, in: International Conference on Medical Image Computing and Computer-Assisted Intervention, Springer, 2021, pp. 413–423.

[30] A.J. Larrazabal, et al., Gender imbalance in medical imaging datasets produces biased classifiers for computer-aided diagnosis, Proceedings of the National Academy of Sciences of the United States of America 117 (23) (2020) 12592–12594.

[31] M.O. Guld, et al., Quality of DICOM header information for image categorization, in: E.L. Siegel, H.K. Huang (Eds.), Medical Imaging 2002: Pacs and Integrated Medical Information Systems: Design and Evaluation, 2002, pp. 280–287.

[32] J. Almeida, et al., Analysis of the data consistency of medical imaging information systems: an exploratory study, Procedia Computer Science 164 (2019) 508–515.

[33] N.G. Valikodath, et al., Agreement of ocular symptom reporting between patient-reported outcomes and medical records, JAMA Ophthalmology 135 (3) (2017) 225–231.

[34] J.F. Echaiz, et al., Low correlation between self-report and medical record documentation of urinary tract infection symptoms, American Journal of Infection Control 43 (9) (2015) 983–986.

[35] K.B. Bayley, et al., Challenges in using electronic health record data for CER experience of 4 learning organizations and solutions applied, Medical Care 51 (8) (2013) S80–S86.

[36] A.R. Sadri, et al., Technical note: MRQy - an open-source tool for quality control of MR imaging data, Medical Physics 47 (12) (2020) 6029–6038.

[37] W. Fu, et al., Automated patient-specific and organ-based image quality metrics on dual-energy CT datasets for large scale studies, in: SPIE Medical Imaging, SPIE, 2021.

[38] Definition of endpoint - NCI Dictionary of Cancer Terms - National Cancer Institute; cited 2021; available from: https://www.cancer.gov/publications/dictionaries/cancer-terms/def/endpoint.

[39] H.H. Barrett, Objective assessment of image quality: effects of quantum noise and object variability, Journal of the Optical Society of America. A, Online 7 (7) (1990) 1266–1278.

[40] A.A. Taha, A. Hanbury, Metrics for evaluating 3D medical image segmentation: analysis, selection, and tool, BMC Medical Imaging 15 (1) (2015) 29.

[41] H. Kim, et al., Quantitative evaluation of image segmentation incorporating medical consideration functions, Medical Physics 42 (6) (2015) 3013–3023.

[42] M. Hatt, et al., Classification and evaluation strategies of auto-segmentation approaches for PET: report of AAPM task group No. 211, Medical Physics 44 (6) (2017) e1–e42.

[43] L.R. Dice, Measures of the amount of ecologic association between species, Ecology 26 (3) (1945) 297–302.

[44] P. Jaccard, The distribution of the flora in the Alpine zone, New Phytologist 11 (2) (1912) 37–50.

[45] D.P. Huttenlocher, G.A. Klanderman, W.J. Rucklidge, Comparing images using the Hausdorff distance, IEEE Transactions on Pattern Analysis and Machine Intelligence 15 (9) (1993) 850–863.

[46] C.E. Metz, ROC methodology in radiologic imaging, Investigative Radiology 21 (1986) 720–733.

[47] B.D. Gallas, et al., Evaluating imaging and computer-aided detection and diagnosis devices at the FDA, Academic Radiology 19 (4) (2012) 463–477.

[48] K. Doi, et al., Computer-aided diagnosis in radiology: potential and pitfalls, European Journal of Radiology 31 (2) (1999) 97–109.

[49] D.P. Chakraborty, Analysis of location specific observer performance data: validated extensions of the jackknife free-response (JAFROC) method, Academic Radiology 13 (10) (2006) 1187–1193.

[50] D.P. Chakraborty, L.H.L. Winter, Free-response methodology: alternate analysis and a new observer-performance experiment, Radiology 174 (3 Pt 1) (1990) 873–881.

[51] X. He, E. Frey, ROC, LROC, FROC, AFROC: an alphabet soup, Journal of the American College of Radiology 6 (9) (2009) 652–655.

[52] A. Badal, et al., Virtual clinical trial for task-based evaluation of a deep learning synthetic mammography algorithm, in: Physics of Medical Imaging, SPIE, 2019.

[53] V. Antun, et al., On instabilities of deep learning in image reconstruction and the potential costs of AI, Proceedings of the National Academy of Sciences 117 (48) (2020) 30088–30095.

[54] D.L. Raunig, et al., Quantitative imaging biomarkers: a review of statistical methods for technical performance assessment, Statistical Methods in Medical Research (2014).

[55] S.H. Park, K. Han, Methodologic guide for evaluating clinical performance and effect of artificial intelligence technology for medical diagnosis and prediction, Radiology 286 (3) (2018) 800–809.

[56] A.C. Justice, K.E. Covinsky, J.A. Berlin, Assessing the generalizability of prognostic information, Annals of Internal Medicine 130 (6) (1999) 515–524.

[57] E.W. Steyerberg, Overfitting and optimism in prediction models, in: Clinical Prediction Models, Springer, 2019, pp. 95–112.

[58] M. Gromet, M. Gromet, Comparison of computer-aided detection to double reading of screening mammograms: review of 231, 221 mammograms. [see comment], American Journal of Roentgenology 190 (4) (2008) 854–859.

[59] W. Chen, Q. Gong, B.D. Gallas, Paired split-plot designs of multireader multicase studies, Journal of Medical Imaging (Bellingham) 5 (3) (2018) 031410.

[60] N.A. Obuchowski, Reducing the number of reader interpretations in MRMC studies, Academic Radiology 16 (2) (2009) 209–217.

[61] N.A. Obuchowski, B.D. Gallas, S.L. Hillis, Multi-reader ROC studies with split-plot designs: a comparison of statistical methods, Academic Radiology 19 (12) (2012) 1508–1517.

[62] R. Aggarwal, et al., Diagnostic accuracy of deep learning in medical imaging: a systematic review and meta-analysis, npj Digital Medicine 4 (1) (2021) 65.

[63] N. Petrick, Methodologies for evaluation of effects of CAD on users, Medical Physics 39 (6) (2012) 3962.

[64] A. Repici, et al., Efficacy of real-time computer-aided detection of colorectal neoplasia in a randomized trial, Gastroenterology (2020).

[65] R.M. Nishikawa, L.L. Pesce, Computer-aided detection evaluation methods are not created equal, Radiology 251 (3) (2009) 634–636.

[66] J.C. Dean, C.C. Ilvento, Improved cancer detection using computer-aided detection with diagnostic and screening mammography: prospective study of 104 cancers, American Journal of Roentgenology 187 (1) (2006) 20–28.

[67] R.L. Schmidt, R.E. Factor, Understanding sources of bias in diagnostic accuracy studies, Archives of Pathology & Laboratory Medicine 137 (4) (2013) 558–565.

[68] A. Torralba, A.A. Efros, Unbiased look at dataset bias, in: CVPR 2011, 2011.

[69] B. Nestor, et al., Feature robustness in non-stationary health records: caveats to deployable model performance in common clinical machine learning tasks, in: Machine Learning for Healthcare Conference, PMLR, 2019.

[70] D. Lyell, E. Coiera, Automation bias and verification complexity: a systematic review, Journal of the American Medical Informatics Association 24 (2) (2017) 423–431.

[71] A. Wong, et al., External validation of a widely implemented proprietary sepsis prediction model in hospitalized patients, JAMA Internal Medicine 181 (8) (2021) 1065.

[72] B. Eshete, Making machine learning trustworthy, Science 373 (6556) (2021) 743–744.

[73] R.K. Samala, et al., Breast cancer diagnosis in digital breast tomosynthesis: effects of training sample size on multi-stage transfer learning using deep neural nets, IEEE Transactions on Medical Imaging 38 (3) (2019) 686–696.

[74] T. Hastie, R. Tibshirani, J. Friedman, The Elements of Statistical Learning, 2nd (corrected 12th printing) ed., Series in Statistics, Springer, New York, 2017.

[75] S. Shalev-Shwartz, S. Ben-David, Understanding Machine Learning: From Theory to Algorithms, Cambridge University Press, 2014, p. 415.

[76] M. Hardt, B. Recht, Patterns, predictions, and actions: a story about machine learning, arXiv:2102.05242 [cs, stat], 2021.

[77] M. Nagendran, et al., Artificial intelligence versus clinicians: systematic review of design, reporting standards, and claims of deep learning studies, BMJ 368 (2020) m689.

[78] M. Roberts, et al., Common pitfalls and recommendations for using machine learning to detect and prognosticate for COVID-19 using chest radiographs and CT scans, Nature Machine Intelligence 3 (3) (2021) 199–217.

[79] L. Wynants, et al., Prediction models for diagnosis and prognosis of Covid-19: systematic review and critical appraisal, BMJ 369 (2020) m1328.

[80] P. Omoumi, et al., To buy or not to buy—evaluating commercial AI solutions in radiology (the ECLAIR guidelines), European Radiology 31 (6) (2021) 3786–3796.

[81] L. Tabar, et al., Mammography service screening and mortality in breast cancer patients: 20-year follow-up before and after introduction of screening, The Lancet 361 (9367) (2003) 1405–1410.

[82] J.A. Ladapo, et al., Clinical implications of referral bias in the diagnostic performance of exercise testing for coronary artery disease, Journal of the American Heart Association 2 (6) (2013) e000505.

[83] M.E. Salive, Referral bias in tertiary care: the utility of clinical epidemiology, Mayo Clinic Proceedings 69 (8) (1994) 808–809.

[84] X.H. Zhou, N.A. Obuchowski, D.K. McClish, Statistical Methods in Diagnostic Medicine, Wiley, 2002.

[85] B. Glocker, et al., Machine Learning with Multi-Site Imaging Data: an Empirical Study on the Impact of Scanner Effects, 2019.

[86] G. Campanella, et al., Clinical-grade computational pathology using weakly supervised deep learning on whole slide images, Nature Medicine 25 (8) (2019) 1301–1309.

[87] J. Couzin-Frankel, Medicine contends with how to use artificial intelligence, Science 364 (6446) (2019) 1119–1120.

[88] G. Mårtensson, et al., The reliability of a deep learning model in clinical out-of-distribution MRI data: a multicohort study, Medical Image Analysis 66 (2020) 101714.

[89] M.A. Badgeley, et al., Deep learning predicts hip fracture using confounding patient and healthcare variables, npj Digital Medicine 2 (1) (2019) 31.

[90] V.W. Berger, C.A. Christophi, Randomization technique, allocation concealment, masking, and susceptibility of trials to selection bias, Journal of Modern Applied Statistical Methods 2 (1) (2003) 8.

[91] C. Dwork, et al., STATISTICS. The reusable holdout: preserving validity in adaptive data analysis, Science 349 (6248) (2015) 636–638.

[92] A. Gossmann, et al., Test data reuse for the evaluation of continuously evolving classification algorithms using the area under the receiver operating characteristic curve, SIAM Journal on Mathematics of Data Science (2021) 692–714.

[93] K.L. Calderone, The influence of gender on the frequency of pain and sedative medication administered to postoperative patients, Sex Roles 23 (11) (1990) 713–725.

[94] K.M. Hoffman, et al., Racial bias in pain assessment and treatment recommendations, and false beliefs about biological differences between blacks and whites, Proceedings of the National Academy of Sciences 113 (16) (2016) 4296–4301.

[95] S.J. van Riel, et al., Observer variability for classification of pulmonary nodules on low-dose CT images and its effect on nodule management, Radiology 277 (3) (2015) 863–871.

[96] F.J. Oort, M.R. Visser, M.A. Sprangers, Formal definitions of measurement bias and explanation bias clarify measurement and conceptual perspectives on response shift, Journal of Clinical Epidemiology 62 (11) (2009) 1126–1137.

[97] A. Penn, et al., Inter-reader variability when applying the 2013 Fleischner guidelines for potential solitary subsolid lung nodules, Acta Radiologica 56 (10) (2015) 1180–1186.

[98] H. Suresh, J.V. Guttag, A framework for understanding sources of harm throughout the machine learning life cycle, arXiv:1901.10002 [cs, stat], 2021.

[99] Z. Obermeyer, et al., Dissecting racial bias in an algorithm used to manage the health of populations, 2019, p. 8.

[100] U.S. Food and Drug Administration, Proposed Regulatory Framework for Modifications to Artificial Intelligence/Machine Learning (AI/ML)-Based Software as a Medical Device (SaMD) - Discussion Paper and Request for Feedback, 2019.

[101] G.S. Collins, et al., Transparent reporting of a multivariable prediction model for individual prognosis or diagnosis (TRIPOD): the TRIPOD Statement, BMC Medicine 13 (1) (2015) 1.

[102] S. Cruz Rivera, et al., Guidelines for clinical trial protocols for interventions involving artificial intelligence: the SPIRIT-AI extension, Nature Medicine 26 (9) (2020) 1351–1363.

[103] X. Liu, et al., Reporting guidelines for clinical trial reports for interventions involving artificial intelligence: the CONSORT-AI extension, Nature Medicine 26 (9) (2020) 1364–1374.

[104] V. Sounderajah, et al., Developing specific reporting guidelines for diagnostic accuracy studies assessing AI interventions: the STARD-AI Steering Group, Nature Medicine 26 (6) (2020) 807–808.

Index

Printed in the United States
by Baker & Taylor Publisher Services